A Spaceman's view of the Earth *by courtesy of National Aeronautics and Space Administration, Washington D.C.*

Encyclopedia of the World in colour

Picture maps and illustrations by
Wilhelm Eigener and August Eigener

HAMLYN

London · New York · Sydney · Toronto

ACKNOWLEDGEMENTS

The publishers wish to acknowledge the use of colour photographs
provided by the following persons, organisations and agencies:—

Aer Lingus
American Airlines
Austin Motor Company
Australian News and Information
 Bureau
Ruth V. Bair
Joe Barnell — Shostal
Frenec Berko — Black Star
Bips from Photo-Representatives
Fred Bond — F.P.G.
Horace Bristol—Photo-Representatives
British Aircraft Corporation
British European Airways
British Information Service
British Travel Association
Dana Brown — F.P.G.
Julien Bryan — Photo-
 Representatives
Brian Bunting
J.C. Burke — Photo Library, Inc.
Canadian Government Travel Bureau
Canadian Pacific Railway Company
J. Allen Cash
Central Office of Information
Commonwealth of Puerto Rico
Beatrice H. Criner
André De Lavarre — Gendreau

Homer L. Dodge — F.P.G.
Eastfoto
Duncan Edwards — F.P.G.
Bob Ellis — F.P.G.
Esso
Florida State News Bureau
French Government Tourist Office
Ewing Galloway
Sheridan H. Garth
Robert E. Gerlach — Shostal
W.R. Grace and Company
Edward Gray — F.P.G.
Arthur Griffin — F.P.G.
Jørgen Grønlund
Elvajean Hall
Paul Hamlyn Library
Fritz Henle — Monkmeyer
Eric Hess — Triangle
High Commissioner for New Zealand
Wendy Hilty — Monkmeyer
C.M. Hjelmervick — F.P.G.
Artha Hornbostel
Max Hunn — F.P.G.
Indian Tourist Office
Ionesco
Japan Air Lines
Kåre Per Johannesen

Bern Keating — Black Star
Ewing Krainin — Monkmeyer
Herbert Lanks — Black Star
Herbert Lanks — F.P.G.
Herbert Lanks — Shostal
Paulus Leeser — Camera Clix
R.G. Lock
Royal Lowy — American Indian
 Archives
Richard Magruder — F.P.G.
Pierre M. Martinot
Steve McCutcheon
Alfred and Elma Milotte
Josef Muench — Photo Library, Inc.
National Academy of Sciences
 (USA) — I.G.Y. photograph
Frank Newton — F.P.G.
Northern Ireland Tourist Board
Odhams Press Syndication
Alfred T. Palmer
Panagra
Pan American World Airways
K. Pazovski — F.P.G.
James R. Perkins — F.P.G.
Pictorial Press Limited
Rutherford Platt
Alfons Preindl — Shostal

Fred Ragsdale — F.P.G.
Réalités — Photo-Representatives
Richard Thomas and Baldwins Ltd.
Riggs — Photo-Representatives
Mavis Ronson — Picturepoint Ltd.
Scotsman Publications
Scottish Tourist Board
Bill Sears — Black Star
Marilyn Silverstone — Gamma
Bradley Smith — F.P.G.
Bradley Smith — Photo Library, Inc.
South African Tourist Corporation
Southern Pacific Lines
Charlotte Stine — Photo Library, Inc.
Harry Tabor — Black Star
Louis Tager — Black Star
Bob Taylor — F.P.G.
Trans World Airlines
U.S.I.S. Photo Library
U.S.S.R. Magazine from Sovfoto
United Arab Republic Tourist Office
United Kingdom Atomic Energy
 Authority
United Nations Organisation
Werner Wolff — Black Star
West Australian Government
Jack Zehrt — F.P.G.

Front Jacket:
Left to right:
Hamlyn Group Picture Library
Hamlyn Group Picture Library
Italian State Tourist Office
Vanessa Hamilton

Back Jacket:
Left to right top:
Hamlyn Group Picture Library
Sound Stills (Photographers) Ltd.
Shell International Petroleum Co., Ltd.
Massey Ferguson Ltd., Canada

Left to right bottom:
Australian News & Information Bureau,
 London
Donald Porter
British Broadcasting Corporation
Serena Fass

The publishers also wish to acknowledge the use of the cross-sectional diagram,
continent of North America, on page 4, drawn by Raymond Perlman and
taken from The Golden Nature Guide: *Rocks and Minerals*, © 1957.

The encyclopedia upon which this book is based was originally adapted from
the *Westermann Bildkarten Lexicon*, by arrangement with Georg Westermann Verlag.

Revised edition, entitled *Geographic Encyclopedia for Children*, first published 1967,
Second revised edition 1972,
Published by The Hamlyn Publishing Group Limited
London . New York . Sydney . Toronto
Hamlyn House, Feltham, Middlesex, England
by arrangement with Western Publishing Company Inc.,
© 1958 by Western Publishing Company Inc., All rights reserved
SBN 600 33914 9
Printed in Czechoslovakia

CONTENTS

The Earth

Recent scientific determinations have established the age of the earth at about 6 thousand million years. Its history is a story of successive advances and retreats of the sea, and periods of uplift and denudation of the land. Where today the great Alpine, Himalayan and other mountain chains rise, there were once extensive seas. Fossil remains of animals and plants found in rock provide a clue to the relative ages of their various strata, as well as there being several methods of determining the absolute ages of rocks.

Fossils are not the only indicators of the age of rocks. The stratigraphical positions of rock layers tell part of the story. Since sedimentary rocks originate as loose material, deposited layer upon layer, the oldest bed is normally at the bottom of the sequence and each bed in turn is usually younger than the one on which it rests. Very often this normal succession is inverted, interrupted, or duplicated, by disturbances of the earth's crust. The Tertiary period, or Early Cenozoic, was a period of great crustal upheaval. Enormously thick layers of rock, accumulated for millions of years within the seas, were then compressed and pushed up to form the world's present great mountain chains: the mountain ranges of western North America, the Andes, the Alps, Caucasus, Himalayas, and others. But the enormous force necessary to 'build' mountains is still largely beyond man's power to explain.

Granites and basalts, and the sedimentary rocks derived from them, make up the crust of the earth, and although man has drilled very deep holes, he has not even approached the lower limit of this crust. Yet, when one considers the diameter of the earth, the crust appears to be very thin indeed — its relative thickness is comparable to the skin of an apple. The most reliable information about the earth's interior can be obtained by studying earthquake waves. From their behaviour it has been concluded that basalt-type rock predominates under the deep seas, whereas lighter granite makes up the continental masses. Earthquake studies have established a crust varying in thickness from 10 to 40 miles, an intermediate zone about 1,800 miles thick, and a core with a radius of about 2,100 miles. Temperatures and pressures at these depths are known to be very great and mineral matter of high density may exist in states other than solid.

Even today the face of the earth is being constantly changed by the same forces that have been operative for millions of years. Volcanic eruptions and earthquake shocks give evidence of inner forces at work. Weathering and erosion (heat and cold, wind and ice, rivers and rainfall) carry on their work constantly, but almost imperceptibly, on the surface.

Yet man is quite aware of the internal forces of the earth when they manifest themselves in the form of sudden crustal upheavals of tremendously destructive power. In the Japanese earthquake of 1923 almost 100,000 people lost their lives. Fortunately, of the 10,000 earthquakes that occur every year, only 2 or 3 per cent are classified as very severe. There are about 500 earthquake or seismic stations to record earth tremors all around the world, but even the severest of quakes cannot be foretold. An earthquake belt runs from the Mediterranean through south Asia into China. Another — a very active one — circles the Pacific, running along the west coast of North and South America, through the Aleutian and Kurile Islands, Japan, the Philippines, and as far south as Australia. Twenty earthquakes were recorded along this belt during a recent four-month period.

The Pacific earthquake zone is sometimes called the 'ring of fire' because of the number of volcanoes that occur along it. About 500 active volcanoes are known today. Many have built their cones on older eroded mountains and plateaux as, for example, Cotopaxi in the Andes of Ecuador. On the other hand, Paricutín, in Mexico, suddenly burst out of a level field, and Surtsoy, in Iceland, from the sea, and proceeded to build cones out of lava and cinder accumulations. In 1952, an underwater volcano south of Tokyo shot up a column of water 600 feet in diameter. Island volcanoes cause greater destruction with the tidal waves they generate than with the molten lava they emit. Such a wave killed 36,000 people when Krakatoa erupted in Indonesia in 1883.

Anyone who looks at a map or a globe will readily see that areas of land and sea are not evenly distributed. Water covers by far the greater part of the globe. Of the total area of the earth (197 million square miles), less than a third is land. By tilting the globe so that Polynesia is on top, one sees a half sphere covered almost entirely with water. Only about one-fifth of the Southern Hemisphere is land. In the Northern Hemisphere, land takes up two-fifths of the area.

The earth's water area consists of three great oceans: the Pacific (70 million square miles), the Atlantic (40 million square miles including the Arctic Ocean) and the Indian (30 million square miles). Islands and peninsulas cut off portions of these oceans, forming marginal seas. Some of the most familiar seas, such as the Caribbean, the Gulf of Mexico and the Mediterranean, are almost completely surrounded by land.

The earth today seems abundantly full of life, yet it has not always been so. The land was once dead and empty, and even after three-quarters of recorded geological time the sea still contained only the most primitive forms of life, such as algae and very simple sponges. The beginning of the Paleozoic Era (500 million years ago) marked the beginning of more complex life, but even this was confined to the water for 175 million years. At the beginning of the Devonian Period, primitive trees and ferns became established on dry land. Animals, too, originated in the seas and remained there until they had developed lungs to enable them to breathe on land. The lungfish (which still lives today) was one of the first animals to make this transition because it had developed an organ that could function as a lung out of water. The early land animals are related to our present-day amphibians and reptiles. A great diversity of land animals gradually evolved, adapting themselves in varying degrees to their environment. They died out as changing conditions rendered their specific adaptations inadequate. The best-known of the prehistoric animals are the dinosaurs, which roamed the earth for 75 million years. The forerunners of today's mammals appeared in the Tertiary, though it was not until the

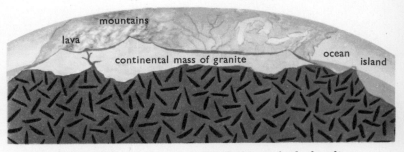

Cross-section of North America. The dark area is the basalt crust of the earth, underlying the continents and the oceans.

beginning of recorded history that they assumed their present appearance.

The last major phenomenon to shape the crust of the earth and influence life upon it was the extensive glaciations of the Pleistocene Period. Starting about one million years ago, ice covered approximately one-third of the earth several times over. During this period the ice sheets in the British Isles reached as far south as the valley of the Thames. Each glacial age was followed by an inter-glacial period when the ice retreated. The glacial and inter-glacial periods were marked by extensive migrations of both man and animals. Life was abundant — elephants, mammoths, mastodons, buffaloes, horses and even camels roamed the northern lands — and those forms that could adapt themselves to the colder temperatures, or migrate, managed to survive. There is evidence that the giant mastodons survived the last ice age and lived on in Europe until a few thousand years ago, for the last glacier retreated from the British Isles just over 10,000 years ago.

Prehistoric human remains are among the rarest of fossils. Prehistoric man kept out of swamps where his body would have been preserved. Futhermore, funeral rites often destroyed his remains, or left them where weathering or predators were able to finish the job. A few caves in Europe, Asia and Africa have yielded the best preserved remnants of ancient man. His artifacts, or tools, are better preserved and give the best indication of how he lived. Ancient man, having little but his bare hands to work with, established his home in the temperate lowlands where he could support himself most easily. It is generally believed that man evolved in the Eastern Hemisphere, for remains of higher primates have not been found in the West. There is evidence that he arrived in the west of Europe before the extinction of some of the large Pleistocene animals, and it is possible that he may have contributed to their extinction.

It took men hundreds of years to venture away from their immediate homelands. Merchants and bold seafarers were the early roamers, but in 400 B.C. only about 3 per cent of the earth was known. The Romans knew of the existence of the people of central Asia and China. Later, permanent contacts were established with the East, and by 1600, one-half of the world was known. Columbus had rediscovered America (1492) and Vasco da Gama had sailed around Africa (1498). In 1522, one of Ferdinand Magellan's ships had succeeded in sailing round the world. Not until the 19th century, however, were the interiors of the newly-discovered lands penetrated.

Since his arrival on the face of the earth, man has increased astonishingly in numbers. Since the birth of Christ, the world's population has grown from 200 million to more than 3.2 thousand million, with the rate of growth considerably speeded up in the last 300 years. Every day there are 100,000 new mouths to feed. Every possible corner of the earth must therefore contribute its share to their support.

Throughout history men have formed national groupings and have recognised and prized the privileges and duties of national sovereignty. The political groupings they have created vary in size and importance from such small communities as Monaco, Andorra, or the sheikhdoms of Arabia, to the great super-states whose influence is felt throughout the world. The five most populous countries, taken together, encompass one-third of the earth's land area and more than half its total population; they are mainland China (population 700 million), India (547 million), the Union of Soviet Socialist Republics (241 million), the United States (204 million) and Japan (104 million). Although nationalism tends to pit one nation against another, 132 countries have joined the United Nations, an organisation established at the end of World War II to maintain peace and improve living conditions throughout the world.

GEOLOGIC TIME SCALE

Paleozoic Era	Mesozoic Era
C — Cambrian	I — Triassic
D — Ordovician	J — Jurassic
E — Silurian	K — Cretaceous
F — Devonian	**Cenozoic Era**
G — Carboniferous	L — Tertiary
H — Permian	M — Quaternary

This geologic time table shows large units of geologic time, called Eras, which are, in turn, subdivided into Periods. These divisions are made on the basis of sequences in crustal disturbances and mark stages in the development of life on Earth.

For the first half of its existence, Earth probably had no life, and for the next quarter, only the lowliest forms of plant life. This enormously long Era, called the Pre-Cambrian, came to an end perhaps 6—800 million years ago. We know very little about it. Thereafter, the record of the evolution of life is fairly clear. The end of the Pre-Cambrian marked the beginning of the Paleozoic Era, which lasted 3—500 million years. This was followed by the Mesozoic Era, lasting 200 million years, and the Cenozoic Era, lasting 70 million years into the present. For the last 2½ million years we have been in the Quaternary Period of the Cenozoic Era. This is often called the Pleistocene Epoch, or Ice Age. It was in this period that man first made his appearance. Thus the geologic time scale and the evolution of life on Earth are shown here, compressed into one 24-hour period. According to this scale (based on the assumption that Earth is 2 billion years old) man has lived on Earth for only a matter of seconds. However, if more recent theories (assuming the age of Earth to be 4—5 billion years) are correct, the rainbow coloured quadrant at right should be less than ½ as large as shown.

The British Isles

Though regarded as a remote territory by the earliest Mediterranean civilisations, the British Isles have abundant Palaeolithic remains dating back to the middle parts of the Pleistocene period, over 250,000 years ago. Later, Neolithic cultivators came from the south and east, while extensive settlement occurred in the Bronze Age about 1500 B.C., leaving behind Stonehenge, Avebury and other megalithic monuments as witness to the rich cultures of those times. Celtic peoples invaded Britain in the 6th century B.C., providing us with an abundance of hill and river names. They were the precursors of many of the peoples now living in the mountain areas of the west.

The Roman Conquest of Britain was first attempted by Julius Caesar in 55 B.C., and finally accomplished in A.D. 42 by Aulus Plautius, and there followed four centuries of occupation until A.D. 442, during which time an impressive network of towns, fortified points, roads and mining centres had been established.

Later, Saxon invasions extinguished Latin speech and the Christian religion, though these survived in Ireland. Jutes invaded Kent, and Angles and Norsemen moved into east and north, giving rise, later, with the coming of the Normans, to a diverse cultural background, and a kingdom united from a collection of smaller kingdoms.

After the passing of medieval times, when British trade in wool, grain and other agricultural commodities led to prosperity and to strong links with Flanders and France, the discovery of America in 1492, and voyages of exploration by English navigators to North America and the Arctic Ocean, caused Britain to become better known, and the islanders started looking outwards to trade and conquest, instead of inwards to defence against invasion. The British Isles became a stepping-off point, with considerable advantages to be gained from their insularity and situation, contained between 50° and 60° North latitudes and 1½° East and 10° West latitudes. The total area of the British Isles — over 120,000 square miles — is only one-thirtieth part of the European land area, though the population amounts to one-tenth of the population of Europe. Separated from the European mainland by the shallow North Sea, the English Channel and the Strait of Dover — the latter a land bridge until 6,000 years ago — Britain has remained free of invasion since A.D. 1066.

Though highly populated and industrialised, Britain is nevertheless famed for her highly productive, well-developed agriculture, obtaining high yields from well-bred livestock and fertile soils, based largely on alluvium, or boulder clay, or other recent geological deposits. Yet Britain's former industrial pre-eminence was based on native supplies of coal, iron ore and other minerals, which she was later able to obtain from her colonies or from friendly European neighbours, especially Scandinavia and Iberia. Similarly, large quantities of foodstuffs for Britain's urbanised population are derived from overseas sources. Resources of hydro-electric power, oil and base metals are limited with the exception of the natural gas being drilled in the North Sea. Today Britain must concentrate on products for export in order to pay her heavy imports bill.

The houses of Britain are many and varied, for she has never lacked building materials from rocks, nor clays for brickmaking. Even today Britain is an important producer of cement from her supplies of chalk and limestone, which adjoin clays or shales. Indeed the geological structure and stratigraphy of the British Isles is extremely varied. Sedimentary rocks, igneous rocks and much-altered metamorphic rocks are well-represented, and strata from all ages are present in Britain. Ancient Archaean rocks are to be found in north-west Scotland, much disturbed by Caledonian earth movements. The Hercynian mountain building of Palaeozoic times created the Pennines, Exmoor and Dartmoor, and their denudation under a tropical climate covered and compressed the rich forest swamps on their flanks into coal-seams. The English lowlands are composed of sedimentary rocks, limestones, clays and sandstones, laid down in Mesozoic or Tertiary seas, and largely remain unfolded, for the Palaeozoic substrata are at shallow depth and resisted the elevation of the Alps and the lateral pressures thereby created.

During Pleistocene times, much of Britain was covered by ice sheets, which eroded and etched the uplands and deposited thick layers of boulder clay in Cheshire, East Anglia and other areas, or else, with their melt water, created great but now vanished lakes, such as Lake Harrison in the Midlands, whose sediments are highly productive.

The climate of today is a mild and equable one, with no great extremes, but highly stimulating in its day-to-day, or hour-by-hour, changes brought by passing depressions, importing, so to speak, the mild warm air from the North Atlantic and Gulf Stream, but occasionally permitting the invasion of cold Arctic air. The mean temperature of the south-west peninsula of Cornwall is 44°F, which permits all-the-year-round growth of grass, while parts of eastern Britain, notably Cambridge and certain valleys in Scotland, can experience considerable frost. The London area is warmest in summer (64°F), though the South Coast experiences most hours of sunshine per annum. The amount of rainfall is extremely variable, both in time and space: from about 20 inches in the lowlands of the Thames estuary, to nearly 200 inches in the high mountains of the north-west. Thus the areas of intensive agriculture and industry are those most deficient in rain, and problems of water supply and transfer from the moist uplands to the drier lowlands are among the most pressing of our time.

Very little of the present vegetation, which makes the British scene so green and attractive, is natural; it has been modified, if not promoted, by the activity of man. Even before medieval times, forest clearance had spread to the damp oak woods on the intractable clays of southern England, large areas were felled by the Romans to smelt lead and other ores, and much forest clearance was carried on for naval purposes four centuries ago.

The lowlands have many varied uses in agriculture, often with their own distinctive breeds of livestock and with greater or lesser intensity of crop production according to varying climate, soil, proximity to market, or to techniques developed over the ages. Mining, industry, trade and transportation have produced an even greater variety of regional activities, and everywhere have been accompanied by the emergence of urban life, sometimes with a long-continued cultural tradition, but mainly by a virtually characterless spread of housing which often tends to occupy far more valuable land than it needs.

Migration of industry to the coalfields in the 19th century caused the decline of certain areas — Suffolk, Gloucestershire and the Forest of Dean. Yet, today, the areas which grew up out of the industrial revolution — such as Lancashire, the West Riding, the Black Country and Central Scotland — are themselves on the point of decline or reorganisation, as a result of the movement of industry, people and wealth to the South-East and the London area, the Bristol area, and the East Midlands.

THE BRITISH ISLES

Scale 1:4,000,000

0   25   50   75   Miles

0 20 40 60 80 100 120   Kilometres

SHETLAND ISLES

Lerwick

ORKNEY ISLES

Kirkwall

Pentland Firth

Cape Wrath

Thurso
Wick
CAITHNESS

Stornoway
Lewis

SUTHERLAND

Helmsdale

Harris

Outer Hebrides

North Uist

Ullapool
Dornoch
Dornoch Firth

ROSS AND CROMARTY

Invergordon
Cromarty

Moray Firth
Lossiemouth
Elgin
Nairn
MORAY
Banff
Fraserburgh
BANFF
Peterhead

South Uist

Skye

Inner Hebrides

Loch Ness
Caledonian Canal
Aviemore
Inverness

INVERNESS
River Spey
CAIRNGORMS
ABERDEEN
River Don
ABERDEEN
River Dee
KINCARDINE
Stonehaven

Port William

GRAMPIAN MOUNTAINS
Blair Atholl

SCOTLAND
ANGUS
Forfar
Montrose
Arbroath

PERTH
DUNDEE
Firth of Tay

Mull

Oban

ARGYLL

L. Lomond
Crieff
Perth

KIN.
FIFE
St Andrews

Jura

Kinross
Kirkcaldy
Dunfermline

STIRLING
Stirling
Alloa
Firth of Forth
Dunbar

Dumbarton
Falkirk
Linlithgow
EDINBURGH
Leith
Haddington
LOTHIAN

Islay

Greenock
Paisley
GLASGOW
Airdrie
MIDLOTHIAN
Duns
BERWICK
Berwick

Rothesay
RENFREW
Hamilton
Peebles
Galashiels
Kelso

Kintyre

Irvine
Lanark
LANARK
PEEBLES
SELKIRK
Selkirk
Jedburgh

Arran I.

Kilmarnock
AYRSHIRE
Hawick
Roxburgh

Brodick

Ayr
R. Nith
CHEVIOT HILLS

Firth of Clyde

DUMFRIES
Dumfries
NORTHUMBERLAND
R. Tyne
North Shields
South Shields

KIRKCUDBRIGHT
Castle Douglas
Carlisle
NEWCASTLE
Hexham
Gateshead
Sunderland

WIGTOWN
Stranraer
Portpatrick
CUMBERLAND
DURHAM
Durham
Hartlepools

Wigtown
Kirkcudbright
Solway Firth
Penrith
Appleby
DURHAM
Darlington
Teesside

Workington
Whitehaven
WESTMORLAND
Lake District
Richmond
R. Tees
NORTH YORK MOORS
Scarborough

ISLE OF MAN
Kendal
Windermere
R. Swale

L. Foyle
Coleraine
Portrush

Douglas

Morecambe Bay
YORKSHIRE
R. Wharfe
York
YORKSHIRE WOLDS
HULL

Londonderry
ANTRIM
Larne
L. Neagh
R. Bann
Carrickfergus

DONEGAL
SPERRIN MTNS
Strabane
Lifford
Donegal

Donegal Bay
Ballyshannon
TYRONE
Omagh
Cookstown
NORTHERN IRELAND
BELFAST
Newtownards

R. Ribble
R. Aire
LEEDS

IRISH
Lancaster
Blackpool
Burnley
BRADFORD
R. Ouse
LANCASHIRE
Preston
Blackburn
Halifax
Huddersfield
SEA
Bolton
Oldham
Doncaster
Scunthorpe
Grimsby

Sligo
SLIGO
LEITRIM
R. Erne
Upper L. Erne
Enniskillen
FERMANAGH
DUNGANNON
Armagh
ARMAGH
DOWN
Portadown
Downpatrick
Newry
Strangford
MOURNE MTNS

Southport
Wigan
Sheffield
R. Don

Castlebar

Carrick
Lower L. Erne
Clones
Monaghan
MONAGHAN
Cootehill
Dundalk
LOUTH

Southport
Liverpool
Birkenhead
Bootle
MANCHESTER
R. Mersey
Stockport
SHEFFIELD

MAYO
CONNACHT
ROSCOMMON
L. Mask
Roscommon
Longford
LONGFORD
CAVAN
Kells
Navan
MEATH

Holyhead
ANGLESEY
Rhyl
Llandudno
FLINT
Macclesfield
NOTTINGHAM
Lincoln
Skegness

L. Conn
L. Corrib
WESTMEATH
Mullingar
R. Boyne

Bangor
Caernarvon
Denbigh
Flint
CHESHIRE
Chester
Crewe
DERBY
Chesterfield
Mansfield
NOTTINGHAM
LINCOLN

GALWAY
Galway
Galway Bay
EIRE
OFFALY
Tullamore
KILDARE
Kildare
R. Liffey
DUBLIN

Menai St.
DENBIGH
Wrexham
STOKE-ON-TRENT
Derby
Nottingham
Grantham
The Wash

Port Laoise
(Republic of Ireland)
LEINSTER

CAERNARVON
R. Dee
FLINT
Stafford
Loughborough
Spalding
Kings Lynn
NORWICH
Gt. Yarmouth

CLARE
Ennis
LEIX
Carlow
CARLOW
WICKLOW
Wicklow

Aberystwyth
MERIONETH
Welshpool
Shrewsbury
Wellington
STAFFORD
Burton
LEICESTER
Leicester
RUT.
PETERBORO
HUNTS
CAMBRIDGE
NORFOLK
Lowestoft

Nenagh
KILKENNY
Kilkenny
R. Barrow
R. Slaney
Wexford

Dolgelley
MONT-GOMERY
Montgomery
R. Severn
Oswestry
Walsall
Lichfield
COVENTRY
Corby
Kettering
NORTHAMPTON
Peterborough
Huntingdon
CAMBRIDGE
Little Ouse
R. Stour
SUFFOLK
Newmarket
Bury St. Edmunds

Kilrush
Limerick
TIPPERARY
Thurles
Tipperary
Clonmel
New Ross
WEXFORD

Cardigan Bay
CARDIGAN
CAMBRIAN
RADNOR
New Radnor
SHROPSHIRE
Ludlow
WORCESTER
Kidderminster
Birmingham
WARWICK
Rugby
Warwick
NORTHAMPTON
Northampton
Bedford
BEDFORD
Cambridge
R. Stour
Ipswich
Harwich

River Shannon
LIMERICK
Rathkeale
MUNSTER
WATERFORD
Waterford
Dungarvan

Tralee
Dingle
KERRY
Killarney
R. Blackwater
CORK
Cork
Cobh
Kinsale

Fishguard
PEMBROKE
Carmarthen
CARMARTHEN
BRECON
Brecon
BRECKNOCK
HEREFORD
Hereford
Gt. Malvern
Gloucester
Stratford-on-Avon
Banbury
OXFORD
Luton
Hertford
St. Albans
HERTFORD
Enfield
Chelmsford
Colchester
ESSEX

Dingle Bay
Milford Haven
Pembroke
Llanelly
GLAMORGAN
Neath
Rhondda
MONMOUTH
Pontypool
Chepstow
Monmouth
COTSWOLD HILLS
Cheltenham
GLOUCESTER
Swindon
OXFORD
CHILTERNS
Aylesbury
BUCKINGHAM
Watford
Slough
Jarrow
GREATER LONDON
Romford
Southend
Margate

Bantry Bay
SWANSEA
NEWPORT
CARDIFF
BRISTOL
Chippenham
Bath
R. Thames
R. Kennet
BERKSHIRE
Reading
Kingston
LONDON
Croydon
Rochester
Chatham
Gravesend
N. DOWNS
CANTERBURY
Ramsgate

Bristol Channel
WILTSHIRE
Trowbridge
Marlborough
Basingstoke
Guildford
SURREY
Dorking
Maidstone
KENT
Ashford
Dover
STRAIT OF DOVER

EXMOOR
MENDIP HILLS
Wells
R. Avon
Salisbury
HAMPSHIRE
Winchester
S. DOWNS
Tunbridge Wells
Rye

Barnstaple
SOMERSET
Taunton
Yeovil
R. Exe
SUSSEX
Lewes
Newhaven
Hastings
Brighton
Eastbourne

DEVON
Exeter
DORSET
Dorchester
Weymouth
Poole
Bournemouth
Southampton
PORTSMOUTH
Chichester
Solent
Newport
Isle of Wight

DARTMOOR
Torbay
Portland Bill

Bodmin
CORNWALL
Truro
PLYMOUTH

Falmouth

Scilly Isles
Lands End

ATLANTIC OCEAN

NORTH SEA

IRISH SEA

ST. GEORGE'S CHANNEL

Bristol Channel

ENGLISH CHANNEL

CL. CLACKMANNAN
KIN. KINROSS
RUT. RUTLAND
W. LOTH. WEST LOTHIAN

FRANCE

A scene from the highlands of Scotland, looking towards the Cairn-na-Glasha (3,484 ft.) from the Allt Bhruididh

● **Aberdeen** Largest burgh (population 182,117) in the north of Scotland, the city of Aberdeen is situated at the head of the estuary of the Dee, a river which rises in the central Grampians and flows eastwards to the North Sea. The Don valley, leading into the mountains, lies just north of the town. Aberdeen is, therefore, a market and retail centre for the farming country inland, which is noted for a breed of beef cattle, the famous Aberdeen-Angus. Much of the town is built of the local silver-grey granite, a stone much prized in other parts of Britain for special buildings. Aberdeen is the most important fishing port in Scotland, with wet docks to accommodate all kinds of boats engaged in fishing. Fresh fish is sent by express freight trains to towns in the Central Lowlands, while great quantities of herring and cod are smoked and salted. The burgh is the cultural and educational headquarters of the north of Scotland, with its university founded in 1494. In 1972 a very large oil-field was discovered off the coast here, which will boost Aberdeen's economy.

● **Aberdeenshire** A large county (1,971 square miles) in north-east Scotland, extending from the high Cairngorms to the lowlands near Rattray Head and the mouths of the rivers Dee and Don. It has a drier, warmer climate than most other parts of Scotland, aiding agriculture. A fifth of the area supports seeded grasslands (e.g., rye grass and clover) and 15 per cent produces oats, crops directly related to stock-rearing, for Aberdeen has the greatest number of cattle in Scotland (14 per cent of the total). Seventeen per cent of Scotland's pigs are in Aberdeenshire and it is also the premier poultry-producing county. Its population of 319,731 is distributed on the coastal lowlands and in the main valleys, but the large towns, Aberdeen, Peterhead (14,164) and Fraserburgh (10,605), account for more than three quarters.

● **aircraft industry** The construction of aeroplanes is a modern industry, for it was only in 1903 that the Wright brothers made their first successful flight in a power-driven machine. Aircraft were first made of wood; then steel was used; and now very light but strong non-ferrous alloys are the most favoured materials. The production of aircraft resembles that of motor-cars in that many of the components are prefabricated in specialised factories before being brought together in assembly plants where the machines are completed. In 1955 much of the industry was concentrated in the Home Counties, with smaller centres in the West at Bristol and Yeovil, and in the Midlands at Coventry and Wolverhampton, which have expanded greatly since the war. Highly skilled labour is needed in all branches of the industry, and the assembly shops have adjacent aerodromes for testing. Aircraft and parts constitute a valuable proportion of the country's exports.

● **Anglesey** An island off the north coast of Wales. Together with Holy Island, Anglesey forms an administrative county (276 square miles) of Wales. It is predominantly lowland, for nowhere does the height exceed 500 feet. Over half (53 per cent) of the area is under permanent grass and 23 per cent is arable land. The island is connected with the mainland by road and rail bridges across the Menai Straits. Holyhead (10,563) on Holy Island is the terminus of a boat train from London, passengers embarking for the passage to Dublin. Beaumaris (2,134), on the north shore of the straits, is a seaside resort — otherwise the 59,705 total population has rural occupations, chiefly dairy farming. The county town is Llangefni (3,949).

● **Angus** A county (873 square miles) in eastern Scotland, containing a stretch of coast north of the Firth of Tay and reaching inland to mountains over 3,000 feet high in the Braes of Angus. The county also includes the northern end of the Vale of Strathmore, between the Sidlaw Hills and the main Grampians. These lowlands are extremely fertile and suited to arable crops — wheat, oats, potatoes and rotation grassland. It is the third most important pig-rearing county in Scotland. Dundee is the largest town, with Arbroath (22,585) and Montrose (9,963) smaller ports on the North Sea coast. Forfar (10,500), the inland market town, also contributes to the total population of 279,396.

● **Antrim** A county of Northern Ireland, extending from Belfast Lough and the River Lagan to the north coast. Its western boundary is Lough Neagh and the River Bann. The Antrim Mountains occupy the eastern half of the county and the high land reaches the coast in many places, forming a rocky cliff shoreline. On the north coast is the famous Giant's Causeway, formed of massive columnar basalt. The total population of 712,396 includes that of Northern Ireland's capital city, Belfast, but other centres of importance are Carrickfergus (11,990) and Larne (17,670). Tiny Antrim town (1,448) produces linen.

● **Argyllshire** A large county (3,124 square miles) of western Scotland, extending for over 100 miles from Loch Shiel in the north to the southern tip of the Mull of Kintyre. It is much dissected by sea lochs — Loch Linnhe and Loch Lyne — and contains many noted islands — Mull, Jura and Islay. Much of it is wild, inaccessible, beautiful country with high mountains and sheltered glens. The county contains a tenth of the sheep of Scotland, sheep farming being the greatest source of revenue for the scattered population of 59,909. The chief town is Oban (6,910), a fishing port, terminus of the inter-island steamers and a flourishing holiday resort.

● **Armagh** The smallest county (489 square miles) of Northern Ireland. It extends southwards from Lough Neagh and contains a large part of the broad alluvial plains surrounding the lake. It is this area that supports most of the 125,164 population, both in agriculture and in the industries of the towns of Armagh (11,800), Portadown (21,010) and Lurgan (21,900).

● **atomic energy** When uranium, thorium or certain other elements are bombarded with neutrons in atomic reactors, the nuclei of these elements 'split' with the release of enormous energy. A chain reaction involving the entire mass of fissionable matter results. When slowed down and controlled, atomic energy can be converted into industrial power. The countries that have made the greatest progress in applying atomic energy for peaceful purposes are the ones that have advanced farthest with its military applications. These are Great Britain, the Soviet Union and the United States. The principal achievements are the development of atomic power stations and of atomic propulsion for submarines and surface ships. The world's first large-scale atomic energy station, Calder Hall, Cumberland, was officially opened in October, 1956. Many smaller nations are producing radioactive isotopes in small experimental atomic reactors. These isotopes have largely replaced radium in the treatment of malignant diseases, in X-ray photography and as tracer elements in the study of biological processes.

● **Ayrshire** A county (1,132 square miles) of south-west Scotland, with a long coastline bordering the Firth of Clyde, fringed inland by the Southern Uplands. These in turn enclose a broad fertile coastal plain crossed by the rivers Ayr and Irvine. A fifth of the county is under permanent pasture, indicating a specialisation in animal husbandry. Ayrshire, with its distinctive dairy breed, contains 9 per cent of the cattle in Scotland and is important for pig and poultry production. Many of the 361,074 population are concentrated in the industrial towns on the coalfield, such as Irvine (23,011) and Kilmarnock (48,884), while Troon (9,932), a holiday resort, and Ayr (48,785), the county town, are on the coast. Robert Burns, the famous poet, was born in the county at Alloway, near Ayr.

● **badger** About 30 inches long, grey above and black below, with a black and white striped head, the badger is an attractive animal. Common locally, it is rarely seen since it hunts at night, Its food includes rats, mice, insects, berries and fungi. A prodigious digger, the badger's many-galleried earth (or 'sett') is kept scrupulously clean, and a dung-pit away from the sett is always used. Usually harmless, the badger fights courageously if cornered.

- **Banffshire** An elongated county of 630 square miles, extending from the Cairngorms north-eastwards to the North Sea. Part of its western boundary is formed by the River Spey. Most of the area is over 600 feet above sea level, moorland and mountain, but a tenth of the county grows oats. The arable land is restricted to the coastal lowlands which are part of the relatively dry and sunny area of eastern lowland Scotland. The population of 43,501 are found mainly in the little towns and ports along the coast, such as Banff (3,723) and Macduff (3,708).

- **Bedfordshire** A small county (473 square miles) north of London. The southern part of the county includes some of the uplands of the Chilterns, while the flat plains of the north resemble the peaty fens. Fifty-eight per cent of the land is used for arable crops, and farming occupies 2 per cent of the 463,493 population. Bedford (73,064), the county town on the Great Ouse, once a Roman station, manufactures farm machinery, and Luton (161,178), in the south, is a growing industrial centre, concerned with vehicle production and the older-established hat-making industry.

- **beech** The beech, *Fagus sylvaticus*, is a tall, graceful tree of southern England, where it forms shady 'hangers' on the clay soils which cap some of the chalk hills. The oval leaves cast such dense shade that little will grow beneath them. The smooth silver-grey boles stand clear of undergrowth. The fruits, or masts, are edible nuts; the wood is strong and used in furniture-making.

- **Belfast** The capital and chief industrial centre (population 390,700) of Northern Ireland. Belfast stands on the banks of the River Lagan, where it flows into the head of a long sea lough. The city was noted originally for its manufacture of linen, based on the local cultivation of flax. Much of the raw material is imported now, but the products continue to be of good quality and are exported widely. The rise of the linen industry led to the growth of many factory towns round Belfast — e.g., Lisburn (23,500), Lurgan (21,960) and Newtownards (13,339) — but the city remains the headquarters. Ship-building is the second great industry of Belfast. Coal is brought from Scotland and iron from Canada, for Ireland cannot supply these although a suitable large labour force is available. The River Lagan was improved for navigation last century and extensive docks were constructed. These handle various commodities, most of the trade being with the ports of Glasgow and Liverpool.

- **Ben Nevis** The highest mountain (4,406 feet) in the British Isles. Ben Nevis is in the western Grampians and dominates the southern end of Glen More at the head of Loch Linnhe. It is formed of granite, an intrusive igneous rock. Although the top is smoothly rounded, its northern slopes have been eroded by glaciers into corries with frost-shattered cliffs and mounds of screes. It is a favourite mountain with rock-climbers.

- **Berkshire** A county of 725 square miles, west of London. The River Thames forms the long northern boundary, and the area includes part of the Marlborough Downs and much of the Kennet

Calder Hall was Britain's – and the world's – first large-scale reactor power plant when it started to operate in May, 1956

valley. Nearly half the county is arable land, but many of the 633,457 population live in towns such as Reading 132,023), Windsor (30,065), Maidenhead (45,306) and Abingdon (18,596). Reading, a county borough and the administrative centre, benefits from its proximity to London.

- **Berwickshire** A Scottish border county (457 square miles). Its northern boundary is the crest of the Lammermuir Hills, from which the land slopes down with a southerly aspect to the River Tweed. The coastal stretch round St Abbs Head is rocky and picturesque. In the hills, sheep-raising is the

chief occupation, but the Tweed valley is rich farming land, growing crops of cereals and roots. The principal centres are small market towns such as Lauder (602), Greenlaw and Coldstream (1,270) and the total population numbers only 20,750.

- **Birkenhead** An industrial port (population 137,738) on the Mersey estuary. Birkenhead is on the Wirral Peninsula of Cheshire, across the river from Liverpool. It shares in many of the important activities of its larger neighbour, and they are

A general view of the docks at Belfast, the capital and principal commercial city of Northern Ireland, an internally selfgoverning region consisting of six counties

B.A.C. short-haul jet airliner being built at the B.A.C. factory at Hurn, Bournemouth for T.A.C.A. International of El Salvador, Central America

connected by an electric railway and the famous Mersey road tunnel under the river. Each day these routes and many ferries carry large numbers of office workers into Liverpool from the residential areas of Wallasey (97,061), Seacombe and New Brighton. There are also ferry-boats, plying between the two river-banks, carrying many of the dockers to and from work. Birkenhead has large ship-building yards and facilities for ship repairing, in addition to extensive docks. Its other industries include engineering, clothing, wood and glass.

● **Birmingham** The second largest city in the British Isles (population 1,013,366) and covering almost 90 square miles. Situated in the English Midlands, it is the main centre of the important industrial district known as 'The Black Country' and of the hardware trade. The 16th century marked the beginning of Birmingham's famous iron industry, founded on local iron ore and wood from the Forest of Arden. With the coming of the Industrial Revolution and the growing use of coal, the importance of the industry increased, particularly when further supplies of iron ore were found within the South Staffordshire coal seams. A wide range of iron products — nails, bars, weapons, locks, etc. — were the first manufactured goods to be made and sold in large quantities. Then other metals were introduced: steel, silver, bronze, brass and gold for articles of jewellery, buckles, buttons and coins, while the original iron products continued to multiply, and included new inventions such as steam-engines and railway rolling-stock. Recent developments have shown a decline in the production of heavy goods, and a greater specialisation in the making of articles requiring a high standard of skill and workmanship or those requiring female labour, such as confectionery and toys. There is a rapid growth of new industries, the manufacture of motor-cycles and cars, electrical apparatus, machine tools, and wireless and television sets, as well as the industries linked to car manufacture, such as glass and rubber. The annual British Industries Fair was held in Birmingham. The city had only 15,000 inhabitants in 1700, growing to 70,000 in 1800. It receives its water supply from reservoirs in central Wales. In recent

years the town centre and housing areas have undergone great redevelopment.

● **blackbird** The male has a glossy black coat and a brilliant yellow beak; the female is a drab brown. Popular in our gardens because of its beautiful song, it can do much damage to fruit crops. Its nest has a mud lining covered with grass, and its eggs are pale green speckled with brown.

● **Bolton** One of the largest Lancashire cotton towns (population 153,977). It is situated on a tributary of the River Mersey on the southern side of Rossendale Forest, a western spur of the Pennines. Bolton and its neighbouring towns owe their growth and importance to the specialised cotton industry established originally in the Manchester district in the 17th century. The mills of Bolton are concerned primarily with the spinning of finer yarns from high-quality American and Egyptian cottons, but there is also weaving, dyeing, bleaching and finishing carried on in many factories. The town lies on the Lancashire coalfield, so that power is readily available, an asset which has encouraged the establishment of allied industries — e.g., textile engineering (the oldest firm in the world was founded in Bolton in 1790), and the manufacturing of spinning machines and looms, which are exported to many countries.

● **Bradford** The chief manufacturing and commercial centre of the Yorkshire woollen and worsted industry. In a small valley, tributary to Airedale, Bradford grew from an 18th-century village into a small town of 13,000 in 1810; then, in the middle of last century, it began to develop rapidly, a trend which has continued until the present (population 293,756). Many branches of the woollen industry are to be found in the city, wool-combing, dyeing and the manufacture of high-grade worsteds and suitings, velvets and plushes. There are also factories producing cloths of mixed fibres — e.g., wool with cotton, silk or mohair. Bradford owes much of its supremacy to a keen sense of business, hence the establishment of the office headquarters

of the wool brokers and dealers in the city and the foundation of the Bradford Chamber of Commerce.

● **Brecknockshire** A mountainous inland county of South Wales, 733 square miles in area. Its northern boundary is the River Wye, and the River Usk, flowing across the county, provides the only lowland in the east. Most of the 53,234 population live in the sheltered valleys. Brecknock (Brecon) (6,283), on the Usk, is the chief town.

● **Brighton** A seaside resort on the Sussex coast, due south of London (population 166,081). Brighton is one of several residential towns along the south coast which enjoy a greater number of hours of sunshine than any other area of the British Isles. It is sheltered by the South Downs from cold north winds in the winter, and has a mild, clear atmosphere. Brighton owes its pre-eminence to the patronage of the Prince Regent (later George IV) at the beginning of the last century. He built the famous 'Pavilion', now a museum, and many beautiful terraces and squares also date from this period. The town is a shopping centre for the surrounding countryside; and of recent years, with the electrification of the railway, has the added function of a dormitory for London.

● **Bristol** A major seaport (population 425,203) of western England, situated at the lowest bridging point of the River Avon, eight miles from the Severn estuary. Bristol was a Royal Borough before the Norman conquest. Its position encouraged trade with America after the 15th century, for it was from Bristol that John and Sebastian Cabot sailed for the New World in 1496. The port acquired the monopoly of the West Indian trade; the merchant ships took manufactured goods to West Africa, exchanged them for negro slaves, who were sold to the West Indian planters, and then completed their triangular voyage to Bristol laden with sugar, rum, tobacco and rice. These imports gave rise to the local industries — sugar refining, and cocoa and tobacco manufacturing. At the end of the last century the increasing size of ships necessitated the building of an outport at Avonmouth, with large modern docks. Imports are sent to the Midlands and London, and consist mainly of raw materials such as cereals, meat, petrol, sugar, tobacco, timber, West Indian fruit (especially bananas) and Irish dairy produce. Additional industries are also concerned with the processing of this wide range of goods and include sawmills, soap works, boot and shoe factories, copper works, aircraft factories and railway workshops. Bristol has a university and cathedral, and is famous for the beautiful Avon Gorge, spanned by Brunel's suspension bridge.

● **Buckinghamshire** A long, narrow county extending over 50 miles from north to south. Its 749 square miles contain a cross-section of the countryside from the fertile lowlands around Buckingham, through the Chiltern Hills, to the flood plain of the Thames at Marlow and Eton. The county is well named 'Leafy Bucks', for the abundance of trees in the hedgerows gives it a wooded appearance. Aylesbury (41,288), centrally placed at the foot of the chalk scarp of the Chilterns, is the county town, and is noted for poultry and dairy products. The county population is 586,211.

● **Bute** A small Scottish county (218 square miles) comprising the islands of Arran and Bute, together with several small neighbouring islands in the Firth of Clyde. The whole area is noted for its beautiful scenery. Arran, of great geological interest, is mountainous, with Goat Fell rising to

2,866 feet, and is frequented by tourists. The small population of 13,237 is scattered, but Brodick on Arran and Rothesay (6,524) on Bute are important centres in the region.

Caernarvonshire The north-western county (569 square miles) of Wales. Fifty-three per cent of the land area is rough grazing and 10 per cent provides agricultural crops, including hay. Many of the 122,852 population are to be found in the coastal settlements: Caernarvon (9,253), the historic capital; Bangor (14,526), a university town; and the holiday resorts of Llandudno (19,009), Pwllheli (3,832) and Criccieth (1,509). Snowdon is the highest point in the county and in Wales, reaching a height of 3,560 feet.

Caithness The most northerly county (686 square miles) of the Scottish mainland. The south-west half of the county is mountainous, and partly drained by the River Thurso flowing northwards to the Pentland Firth, while broad lowlands occupy the north-east corner. Offshore from the famous remote village of John o' Groats is the island of Stroma, also part of Caithness. The two main towns are Thurso (9,074), rejuvenated by the establishment of an atomic power station, and Wick (7,613), on the North Sea coast, an important fishing port. Numerous small settlements are found round the coast, but the total population numbered only 27,754 in 1971.

Cambrian Mountains or **Welsh Mountains** The highland retreat of the Ancient Britons, who were displaced from the lowlands by successive invaders from the Continent. The Cambrian mountains are composed of hard, slatey rocks of the Cambrian, Silurian and Devonian times. The Snowdon Range to the north-west, owes much of its spectacular scenery to intrusive igneous rocks, which, being more resistant to erosion, form some of the highest peaks. The Old Red Sandstone of the Brecon Beacons dips southwards under the extensive coalfield of South Wales, where busy mining districts penetrate up the deep valleys into the upland region. The Cambrian Mountains are a valuable source of water for the densely populated districts of Birmingham and Liverpool, yet are poorly populated and used for sheep-rearing and forestry.

Cambridge The university town (population 98,519). Built on the banks of the River Cam (or Granta) at the southern edge of the Fenlands, Cambridge was once a port for small seagoing boats, and had considerable trade in wool and cloth. It served as a local market and route centre for the rich, fertile, agricultural district surrounding the city. The university was founded in the 13th century, and many of the old college buildings, often of great architectural interest, are sited in beautiful park-like settings along the banks of the river. Much of the business of the town is concerned with the university in meeting the requirements of academic life. The town still serves the local community and is very busy on market days. Light industries are to be found, some connected with agriculture, some with cement and others with a wider market, such as radio and television factories, and scientific instrument makers.

Cambridgeshire and Isle of Ely An agricultural county (population 302,507) of eastern England with 74 per cent of its 492 square miles used for arable crops, which includes 18 per cent of the land devoted to wheat production. The county is nearly all lowland; only along the south-eastern border is there a section of the chalky East Anglian Heights, with Newmarket (11,207), the most famous horse-racing centre in the British Isles. The administrative capital is Cambridge, on the River Cam, a tributary of the Great Ouse.

Canterbury The capital of the Anglican Communion, and founded in pre-Roman times as a fortified point. In A.D. 597 the conversion of England to Christianity was begun there by St Augustine. Huguenot refugees introduced weaving in later times, and the town has always had varied industries and some commercial importance. Its great Cathedral was commenced in the 11th century. Canterbury has a population of 33,157, and has recently become a university city.

Cardiff The largest city (population 278,221) in Wales. Cardiff is situated on the north shore of the Bristol Channel at the mouth of the River Taff. The city's importance dates from the 19th century, when iron and coal from the Merthyr Tydfil district was shipped from the port. At the beginning of this century, coal, forming four-fifths of Cardiff's exports, was sent to many countries, and the famous smokeless steamcoal had a wide market. Metallurgical industries, based on local iron and coal, developed in the area; then foreign ores were imported through Cardiff, which became the chief distributing centre for South Wales. In the economic depression of the 1930s, Cardiff suffered greatly and unemployment was widespread. The coal industry declined owing to the conversion of many ships to the burning of crude oil. Renewed prosperity has come to Cardiff with the establishment of many light industries, giving a broader base to the economy, including many food industries, some based on the horticultural produce of the Vale of Glamorgan.

Cardiganshire A Welsh county (692 square miles) bordering Cardigan Bay, a wide embayment of the west coast. Most of the county is mountainous and the coastal lowlands are very narrow. Cardigan is remote and has a total population of only 54,844. Aberystwyth 10,680 inhabitants), the largest town, has several functions — e.g., as a university town and seaside resort.

Carlisle The border city (population 71,497) of north-west England, Carlisle is on the south bank of the River Eden, which flows into the Solway Firth. The city has been a strategic settlement throughout historical times in Britain, having been a fortress before the coming of the Romans, who recognised its value when their territory was bounded on the north by Hadrian's Wall. From that time the city has always controlled the western routeway into Scotland, and many times its own defences were sorely tried during the troublesome periods of the Border feuds and the Jacobite Rebellions. On 8th November, 1745, Charles Edward, the Young Pretender, invaded England and captured Carlisle.

The relative importance of Carlisle has declined over the last 200 years, partly because industrial development needs coal and there are no workable deposits in the near vicinity, and partly because transport of heavy industrial commodities has not

Sheep graze on the rolling green pasturelands near Pwllheli, Wales. In the distance is Snowdon

The production of steel, pictured here at a large factory in South Wales, ranks as one of Britain's major industries

biscuits and machine manufacture — flourish.

● **Carmarthenshire** The largest county (919 square miles) of Wales, comprising the drainage basin of the River Towy, with stretches of the coastal plains bordering the Bristol Channel. The agricultural activities tend to be concerned with animal husbandry, 50 per cent of the county in permanent grassland supporting a seventh of the Welsh cattle and calves. Hence many of the county's 162,313 population are connected with farming, but a large proportion are also to be found in the industrial town of Llanelly (26,320) and in the western end of the South Wales coalfield which produces the much sought after anthracite. Other centres of note are Carmarthen (13,072) and Llandilo (1,794).

● **Carrantouhill** The highest peak (3,414 feet) in Ireland. Carrantouhill is one of the Kerry mountains in the south-west of Eire. It is formed of Devonian Old Red Sandstone and, with its glacially carved rocky features, is one of the main sights in the beautiful Killarney district.

● **Channel Islands** These are a group of islands (75 square miles; population 125,240) between 10 and 20 miles off the west coast of the Cotentin peninsula of Normandy, France. They are the last remnants of the Duchy of Normandy, which once belonged to the King of England, and since 1568 they have been included in the diocese of Winchester. They were under German occupation from 1940 to 1945. The four largest islands are Jersey, Guernsey, Alderney and Sark and there are numerous others. The islands are structurally a part of the nearby French mainland, being composed of granites and other crystalline rocks. They are greatly affected by the rough seas and fierce, complex currents that erode the rocks into steep cliffs and jagged promontories and wash their shores. The climate is mild, with few frosts and a low daily range of temperature. Ample rainfall and warmth promotes luxuriant growth of vegetation in the sheltered parts, and a long growing season allows double cropping on the arable land. Jersey and Guernsey are noted for their special breeds of cow, which yield a rich milk. Early vegetable crops, particularly potatoes, are produced for the English market, Guernsey producing flowers and grapes, and both producing tomatoes. The islands are densely populated, and the official language is English, though a Norman patois is widely used. Jersey and Guernsey are much favoured as places of retirement, and in spring and summer a large number of people visit the islands for holidays. Fuel, building materials and foodstuffs are the main imports.

● **Cheshire** One of the counties of northern England. Cheshire lies between the Welsh mountains and the southern Pennines and most of its area — 1,015 square miles — is below 300 feet. It is an extensive pastoral county (37 per cent permanent grass), noted for its cheese. A high proportion of the 1,542,642 population is concentrated in the industrial towns along the Mersey — e.g., Birkenhead, Runcorn (35,953) and Stockport (139,633), with other centres at Macclesfield (44,240), the silk and nylon town; Crewe (51,302), the railway junction and big cattle market; and Chester, the cathedral city.

● **Chester** This historic city (population 62,696) was founded on the banks of the River Dee by the Romans. The actual site of the city centre is a 100-foot-high red sandstone hill which stands out from the surrounding plain. The city has always been a focus of routes, and is the last major town on the way to North Wales and Anglesey. Until the 14th century, Chester was the chief port for trade with Ireland, but it then lost its maritime business to Liverpool, owing to the silting up of the Dee estuary. Most of this picturesque city is constructed from the local red sandstone. Its beautiful Gothic cathedral and the old city walls attract many visitors. Chester is a busy market town serving the fertile Cheshire Plain, and industrial development is left to other areas, notably Ellesmere Port on the Mersey estuary.

● **Cheviot Hills** These hills have formed the boundary between England and Scotland since the 13th century. The Cheviot (2,676 feet), the highest peak in the range, is of volcanic origin and much of the surrounding land is formed of igneous material. The Cheviots are noted for sheep, the predominant farming occupation of the widely scattered population. The hills are crossed by a main road (A.68), leading from N.E. England to Edinburgh, which reaches its highest point (1,371 feet) at Carter Bar. A large area of the moors in the North Tyne valley have been planted by the Forestry Commission at Kielder.

● **Clackmannan** The smallest Scottish county, 55 square miles in area. It is situated on the north shore of the inner Forth estuary, and, in addition to a portion of the Forth plains, it contains a small area of the Ochil Hills. It is noted specially for its productive coalfield, a continuation of the large Lanark field. Allqa (14,110) is its chief town and port. With a population of 45,553, this small area is densely populated.

● **Clyde River** The river rises in the Lowther Hills, part of the Southern Uplands of Scotland,

been possible by water, since the Solway Firth suffers from considerable silting. Nevertheless, Carlisle is a major railway centre, and certain industries which are able to bear high transport costs — such as cloth-printing, the making of

The coastline of south-west England is dotted with rocky offshore islets, the most famous of which is St. Michael's Mount, off the Cornish coast

A colourful ceremonial occasion outside Coventry's new Cathedral, showing the shell of the former building on the left

and flows in a general north-westerly direction for 106 miles across the Central Lowlands to reach the western seaboard in the Firth of Clyde. The Clyde valley provides an important routeway for the railway and roads leading from the populated area of Glasgow towards Carlisle and the rest of England. The middle course of the valley is rich agricultural land and its sheltered aspect encourages the production of specialised crops — e.g., soft fruits. The Clyde owes its fame, however, to the important industries flanking both sides of the river along its course. The natural advantages of the river have stimulated the growth of ship-building and repairing with all their associated activities — e.g., machine engineering — and the development of the major port of Glasgow. The beautiful scenery of the shores of the Firth and of the Kyles of Bute attract many visitors from all over the world.

coalmining Coal, a mineral of organic origin, has been the basis for the expansion of the major industries of the United Kingdom. It is found in three distinctive forms in this country: anthracite, hard and slow burning; bituminous steam coal, hot and making no soot; and bituminous household or coking coal, gassy and quick burning. The coal seams of Northumberland and Durham have been worked since the 12th century, and coal was shipped to London in the 14th century. It was not until the Industrial Revolution, in the 18th century, that coal became so important as a source of power for the many new machines in all branches of industry. With this development came the reliance of industry on cheap fuel and the resultant location of factories on the coalfields. The United Kingdom has many deposits of coal. In some coalfields the seams dip under younger strata, and these are worked in deep modern mines in the concealed fields.

Coniston Water A long, narrow lake to the west of Windermere in the Lake District. It is just over 5 miles long, and its straight course and sheltered

waters have made it an attractive haunt for speedboat enthusiasts.

Connacht (Connaught) The north-western province (6,611 square miles; population 401,950) of the Irish Republic. Connacht contains five administrative counties and no major towns. Over 80 per cent of the population are dependent on the land for their livelihood, and in Galway and Mayo particularly, where much of the land is of poor quality, there are instances of extreme poverty, sometimes relieved by emigration or seasonal labouring in England.

Cork (Corcaig'h) The second largest town of Ireland, Cork (population 122,146) has a transatlantic port at Cóbh (Queenstown) with a large natural harbour, the estuary of the River Lee.

Cornwall The most south-westerly county of England, 1,357 square miles in area. Cornwall has a very irregular coastline and is bounded by the sea, except to the east, where the county is separated from Devonshire by a border 36 miles in length. Forty-four per cent of the land is arable, for the county takes advantage of its equable climate to grow early vegetables for less-favoured industrial areas, especially the Midlands. Most of the 377,464 population are to be found in coastal settlements, where fishing and tourism are the chief sources of income. The administrative centre and county offices are at the beautiful cathedral city of Truro (14,830) and the county town is Bodmin (9,204).

Coventry A modern industrial city (population 334,839) in the Midlands at the head of the Avon Valley, Coventry was originally an old monastic settlement, and became a prosperous market town and weaving centre in the Middle Ages. Its interests in textiles were stimulated by the arrival of French Huguenot emigrants in the early 18th century, who introduced the manufacture of silk and ribbons. The latter are still produced in association with the making of rayon. A watch-

making industry, also introduced from abroad, declined with the competition of cheaper Swiss and American products, but the inherited skill of the craftsmen has been diverted into the manufacture of bicycles, motor-cars and, more recently, aircraft. Daimler made his first motor-car in Coventry in 1896. In the Second World War, Coventry was the first target for the German Air Force's new strategic bombing plan, using radar. On the night of 14th November, 1940, German bombing caused tremendous damage and destroyed the cathedral. A new cathedral was dedicated in 1962, built on a site next to the ruins of the old one, and an entirely new, modern civic centre has been built.

cuckoo The cuckoo is usually first heard in mid-April and stays in Britain until August, though the young ones may not leave until October or November. They do not built their own nests, but lay 12 to 25 eggs separately in nests of other species of bird. The young cuckoo grows rapidly and hoists the other bird's eggs on to its back, tipping them out of the nest so that the foster parent has no other mouths to feed.

Cumberland A large county (1,521 square miles) in north-west England, containing the greater part of the Lake District and a large area of lowland bordering Solway Firth. Many of the 292,000 population live in the coastal coalfield at Workington (28,414), Whitehaven (26,720) and Cockermouth (6,365). Other centres are Carlisle, Penrith (11,299) and Keswick (5,169).

Cumbrian Mountains The highlands of the English Lake District. Shaped like a dome, the Cumbrian Mountains are formed of a central core of intrusive volcanic and metamorphic rocks with bounding outcrops of hardened Silurian sedimentaries. The region was heavily glaciated during the Ice Age, and supported its own ice-cap. The peaks and valleys today show the characteristic features of a glaciated upland area with bare, steep rock-faces, corries and U-shaped valleys containing long narrow lakes, sometimes dammed by glacial moraines. All these natural assets make the Lake District an attractive tourist area, as well as a famous rock-climbing centre. It is now one of Britain's largest National Parks.

curlew The curlew is a speckled brown bird about 22 inches long. It has a long, curved beak. A bird of the moors and boglands, it is also common, in large flocks, on the coast during its migrations in spring and autumn.

Dartmoor A high moorland expanse in Devonshire, Dartmoor is an old granite boss about 25 miles in diameter. Its highest point is High Willhays (2,039 feet), in the north. On many of the hills, bare blocks of granite — called 'tors' — rise above the smooth surface. The moors are inhabited only by deer and wild ponies, but on the lower slopes and in sheltered valleys sheep-farming is possible. In some parts of Dartmoor, kaolin, a white clay formed by the decomposition of granite, is mined and shipped to the Potteries for making china. Dartmoor is also noted for its prison, containing hardened criminals, at Princetown.

Denbighshire A county (669 square miles) of North Wales. Mixed farming predominates, with dairying on the greater proportion of agricultural land, for 37 per cent of the county is under permanent grass. Of the 184,824 population, a great number live in urban settlements on the small coalfield in the east of the county, near Wrexham (38,955), the largest town. Llangollen (3,108), in the beautiful Dee valley, is a favourite holiday resort in the area. Denbigh (population 8,100) is the county town.

At the heart of wild Dartmoor, in south-western England, stands the typical Devonshire village of Widecombe-in-the-Moor

Derby An industrial county town at the southern end of the Pennine Chain (population 219,348), Derby is situated where the left-bank tributary of the Trent, the Derwent, flowing from the Peak district, reaches the plains. In early times the castle guarded the routes to the north, and the market handled the large quantities of lead mined in the Pennine valleys nearby. The chief industry of Derby was the manufacture of silk, begun in 1718, and now includes the production of hosiery and lace. Coal from the York, Derby and Nottingham coalfields, and the proximity of the iron and steel works in the Black Country and Yorkshire, together with the ease of communications, have encouraged engineering works for construction of railway locomotives, and there are also aero-engine works south of the town.

Derbyshire One of England's upland counties, although its 1,006 square miles extend from the Peak District in the southern Pennines southwards to the River Trent and to the northern borders of the Midland Plain. Only 23 per cent of the land is arable, since large parts of the county are bleak moorlands, and the deep valleys of the Wye and Derwent are used only for hay and grazing. In the east is a section of the York, Derby and Nottingham coalfields. The population of 884,339 for the whole county includes the large towns of Derby, Chesterfield (70,153), Buxton (20,316) and Matlock (19,575), the county headquarters.

Devonshire A large county (2,612 square miles, population 896,245) of south-west England. Devon has coasts along the shores of the Bristol Channel in the north and the English Channel in the south. The county also includes the mountainous areas of Dartmoor and part of Exmoor. It is a productive, agricultural county with 33 per cent of the land arable and 36 per cent permanent grass, and, after Yorkshire, has the largest number of sheep in any English county. Plymouth and Devonport (population together 239,314) and Exeter (95,598) contain a large proportion of the county's 896,245 inhabitants. Coastal towns like Barnstaple (17,342), Ilfracombe (9,846) and the new borough of Torbay (108,888), formed from the settlements round Torquay, attract many summer visitors. Salcombe is a favoured yachting and fishing centre.

Dorsetshire A small agricultural county (973 square miles) of southern England, containing an attractive stretch of the South Coast. In this farming area, 33 per cent of the land is in permanent grass and 39 per cent is arable, indicating a varied and well-balanced agricultural economy. The small population of 361,213 is concentrated in the coastal districts of Weymouth (42,332) and Poole (106,697) and, to a lesser extent, in the valleys of the Frome and Stour. Dorchester (13,737) is the county town.

Dover This small port and packet station is responsible, together with Folkestone, for vital passenger, car and train ferries to Ostend, Calais and Boulogne, in Belgium and France. Dover (34,322) has a castle which is the guardian of the Strait of Dover, thought to have been formed about 6,000 years ago. Near to Dover is the small Kent coalfield, and a Cross-Channel tunnel is planned to ease communications with the continent.

Down The most easterly county (952 square miles) of Ulster (Northern Ireland). In the extreme south of the county are the Mourne Mountains, the source of the River Bann. The lowlands round Strangford Lough are distinguished by their hummocky surface, formed by glacial drumlins. The population of 286,631 is concentrated along the shores of Belfast Lough, the peninsula of Ards and the northern lowlands. The main towns are Newtownards (13,339), Downpatrick (4,219) and Newry (12,450).

Dublin The capital (population 849,542) of the Irish Republic (Eire). Dublin is situated at the mouth of the River Liffey on the east coast of Ireland, facing across the Irish Sea. Regular passenger-boat services operate from Dun Laoghaire (52,992) the outport for Dublin to Liverpool (120 miles) and to Holyhead (60 miles). Originally a Norse settlement, throughout the major part of its history Dublin has belonged to the 'foreign invader'. The 18th century was the period of growth and prosperity, and Dublin became a great centre of commerce, especially with the improvement of the city's docks. The chief industries of Dublin are distilling and brewing, developed from the Irish agricultural products and consumed by the large British market. The Guinness brewery is the most famous example. Other industries are connected with agriculture — e.g., the chemical fertiliser factories, and biscuit and shoe factories; while other activities — printing, railway maintenance and the making of agricultural machinery — serve the needs of the country. Dublin is the

O'Connell Street, the busy main thoroughfare of Dublin, Eire's capital city. Nelson's column no longer exists

seat of the Irish Government, the Dail, and the administrative and cultural centre. It contains the university of Trinity and University College, and the well-known Abbey Theatre, the training ground of many famous actors. The Irish name for Dublin is Baile Atha Cliath.

● **Dumfriesshire** The first Scottish county (1,072 square miles) reached from Carlisle, on the western coast route from England. The northern boundary stretches irregularly along the Southern Upland crests to include three long, penetrating valleys — Nithsdale, Annandale and Eskdale. These join together to form broad lowlands bordering the Solway Firth. Dumfriesshire is an important agricultural county, producing oats, and containing 7 per cent of the total cattle in Scotland; it is also the fourth county for sheep. Many of the 88,215 population are occupied in farming, and the main centres are market towns — e.g., Dumfries (29,384) on the River Nith, Annan (6,053) and Moffat (2,034).

● **Dunbartonshire** A long, narrow county (246 square miles) partly in the west of the Central Lowlands of Scotland. It extends from the head of Loch Lomond southwards, including only the western shores, to the banks of the Firth of Clyde. Many of the 237,518 population are engaged in industry such as whisky making and engineering in Helensburgh (12,874) and Dumbarton (25,406), ship-building and sewing machines at Clydebank (48,296) and light industries in the towns of the Vale of Leven. All these towns are west of Glasgow, whilst 15 miles to the east of this city is a small enclave of the county where light industries are important at Kirkintilloch (25,185) and Cumbernauld (31,787) the town famous in Europe for its advanced road system. The northern parts of the county form a favoured tourist area and playground for the population of Glasgow.

● **Dundee** An industrial town (population 182,084) of eastern Scotland. Dundee is situated on the north shore of the Firth of Tay, with good port facilities and road and rail communications over the Tay Bridges. It is the chief linen, hemp and jute manufacturing towns of Great Britain; coarse cloths, sacking, carpets and linoleum are produced. Fruit-growing in the Carse of Gowrie nearby has led to a jam-making industry, which now includes the production of marmalade from imported oranges. Thus sugar is among the many imported raw materials handled in the docks. Engineering works, machine works for the jute industry, shipyards, sawmills and paper-mills are included among the town's varied activities.

● **Durham Co.** A county (1,015 square miles) of north-east England, between the rivers Tyne and Tees and on the eastern flanks of the Pennines. Durham was once part of the old province of Northumbria and then the centre of the powerful prince-bishopric. Most of the 1,408,103 population are engaged in coalmining and other industries. Nearly a third of the land is arable. Sunderland (population 216,892) and The Hartlepools (96,898) on the coast, are large industrial centres, while inland are the county boroughs of Darlington (85,889) and Gateshead (94,457). Durham City (24,744), the administrative centre, is noted for its cathedral and university, which is the third oldest in England.

● **East Lothian (Haddington)** A small county of 267 square miles in south-eastern Scotland. It contains the northern slopes of the Lammermuir Hills, which give way to hummocky lowlands limited by an alternatively rocky and sandy shoreline, mainly bordering the Firth of Forth. The lowlands form an area of prosperous mixed farming,

The heart of Edinburgh, imposing capital and festival city of Scotland

with cereals important on the arable land. There are several large market towns with small industries, usually flour mills and distilleries — e.g., Haddington (6,505 inhabitants) and Dunbar (4,586); while North Berwick (4,414) is a fashionable holiday resort for Edinburgh people. The total population is 55,891.

● **Edinburgh** The capital (population 453,422) of Scotland. Edinburgh is situated where the Central Lowlands narrow between the Pentland Hills and the Firth of Forth. The city was originally built on the old basaltic masses of Castle Rock and Carlton Hill, and extended narrowly from the castle eastwards to Holyrood Palace early in the 18th century. Gradually the settlement spread out on to the lowland in all directions and finally to the north, joining up with Leith, the port of Edinburgh, two miles away. Throughout its history Edinburgh has retained the function of Scotland's capital, and its activities are all connected with the duties of a chief city. It is the intellectual, scientific and legal centre of the country, and the associated industries include printing and publishing, paper manufacture and the marketing of foodstuffs. Leith imports cereals, butter, meat, etc., and processing is carried out in cloth mills, soap factories, distilleries and flour mills. Edinburgh is also a wealthy financial centre, with large banking and insurance houses. The city has a busy tourist trade, which has been stimulated in recent years by the annual International Festival of Music and Drama.

● **Eire (Republic of Ireland)** A sovereign independent state occupying the largest part (26,600 square miles) of Ireland, the smaller of the two main islands of the British Isles. The independence of Southern Ireland was declared in 1919 by the National Parliament (Dail Eireann), and in 1921 the new Irish Free State accepted dominion status within the British Empire. Since then Eire has gradually limited its connections with the United Kingdom, remaining neutral during the Second World War, although many Irishmen crossed to England to join the British Army. Finally, in 1948, by the Republic of Ireland Act, the country became completely separated, and Eire is now an independent state separated from the British

Commonwealth, with a constitution dating from December, 1937.

Although Ireland has been dominated by England for many centuries, in the 5th century the country was the centre of the Celtic civilisation, with a vigorous life and culture far in advance of that of the tribes of Britain. The early Christian monasteries, established while the English were still pagan, were important centres of learning from which missionaries spread out over much of Western Europe. The late 12th century saw the beginning of English colonisation, which continued until the present century. Most of the Anglo-Scottish settlers became landowners, often depriving the Irish of their inheritance without providing any material or economic improvements. English became the language of trade and commerce, but the Gaelic remained the tongue of the country people and peasants. Religious differences between the immigrants and the Irish became

Sheltered cottages at Bloody Foreland, County Donegal, Ireland

pronounced from the 17th century onwards, most of the settlers being protestant, while the Irish adhere to Roman Catholicism.

The Republic of Ireland is divided into 26 counties for administrative purposes, and a large proportion of the population of 2,971,230 is concentrated in the capital, Dublin, though several densely peopled areas are to be found round the southern towns of Cork (122,146), Wexford (11,542) and Waterford (29,842). Eire is primarily an agricultural country, relying on the export of her crops and animal products for the purchase of necessary manufactured commodities and industrial raw materials, particularly the fuel and machinery which she lacks.

● **elm** Elms are tall trees with rough, fissured bark. The English elm (*Ulmus procera*) is a typical tree of the English countryside, but is not a native of Ireland or Scotland. It is a massive tree, often clothed in leaves to the ground. It takes 150 years to reach maturity, but many of our older specimens are diseased. Dutch elm disease, in particular, has been responsible for recent widespread felling. The Wych elm (*Ulmus glabra*) is native throughout Britain, has larger leaves, thicker twigs, fewer suckers and more conspicuous fruits.

● **England** The largest political division (50,327 square miles) of the British Isles. The country's northern boundary extends from the Solway Firth to the North Sea, along the crest of the Cheviot Hills and the lower course of the River Tweed. The other land boundary, with Wales, follows an irregular course in a general southerly direction from the mouth of the River Dee to the Severn estuary, near to Cardiff. However, the greater proportion of England's limits is bounded by the sea, which has served the country well, throughout her history, as a means of communication with the world, and also as a protective barrier in times of trouble. After the departure of the Romans, three tribes from the continent — the Angles, Saxons and Jutes — invaded the country, and gradually their descendants became amalgamated. By the 10th century, the King of Wessex had conquered the other two kingdoms, Mercia and Northumbria, and assumed the title of King of England. For a short time England became a part of the Danish Empire, but the Norman conquest, in 1066, firmly established the unity of the country. Since that time there have been no further foreign invasions; the threats of Philip of Spain, Napoleon and Hitler were curbed by the sea barrier. The Anglo-Saxons were responsible for the sub-division of the country into the forty-six counties (or shires), which are the bases of local administration. Large towns gradually became independent, and now, as county boroughs, are responsible for their own affairs. London has always been a special case, developing metropolitan characteristics, and assuming powers and liberties comparable with its outstanding growth. The population of England in Roman times has been estimated at about one million; during the Middle Ages, and until the end of the 17th century, the total was about five million, except during times of famine and plague, but the Industrial Revolution caused a rapid increase. The census of 1971 recorded 45,870,062 people in England and, although the numbers are still rising, the rate of increase is declining.

A large proportion of the population is concentrated into three great conurbations centred on Manchester, Birmingham and London. The provincial areas of dense settlement are a result of intensive industrial activities, particularly textile production and engineering. England is unable to grow enough food for her requirements, even though 68 per cent of the total area is productive agricultural land. This has made the country rely on imported foodstuffs and, to pay for these, manufactured goods are exported. Thus foreign trade, vital to England's well-being, has developed with the United States, the Commonwealth countries,

With a total length of 6,156 ft. (over water) and a single span of 3,300 ft., Scotland's Forth Road Bridge was completed in 1964

many of the neighbouring States of Europe and elsewhere in the world.

● **English Channel** An arm of the Atlantic Ocean between England and France. It narrows gradually from west to east until it reaches the Strait of Dover, which links the Channel to the North Sea. The French name for the English Channel is *La Manche* (The Sleeve).

● **Essex** A large county (geographically, 1,528 square miles; administratively, 1,402 square miles) of south-east England, north of the Thames estuary. Essex is primarily an agricultural county with 56 per cent of the land arable and 15 per cent producing wheat. Large portions of the densely populated areas in the south are now administered by the Greater London Council, reducing the administrative population of Essex to 1,353,564, about half its former size. Towns of note include: Chelmsford (58,125), the county town; Colchester (76,145); Southend (162,326); and Harwich (14,892), an important port for continental traffic to Denmark, the Netherlands and Belgium.

● **Exeter** A cathedral city (population 95,598) in Devon. Exeter stands on the left bank of the River Exe at its lowest bridging point. It has been an important settlement since early times. The Romans, Saxons and Normans each added to the town, and with the building of the cathedral in the 12th century it became a noted medieval city. Throughout this period Exeter was a great market for the woollen industry and, by the 18th century, was rivalling Leeds in the 'serge' trade. As ships increased in size, however, Exeter declined in importance as a port, since the estuary of the Exe is too shallow to take large vessels; but it still remains the county town of Devonshire, and other industries have developed in the city, notably flour-milling, and the manufacture of farm machinery and paper — all activities connected with the products and needs of the district.

● **Exmoor** A bleak upland area of south-west England. Exmoor rises to 1,707 feet at Dunkery Beacon,

but there are no true mountain peaks, since the broad outcrop of the Devonian red sandstone makes for a plateau-like surface supporting only heather, gorse and bracken. The moors extend to the shores of the Bristol Channel, where numerous bays have been carved out of the high cliffs, giving a picturesque coast-line much favoured by summer visitors.

● **Fermanagh** A county (653 square miles) of Northern Ireland in its far western part. It is an inland county comprising the greater part of the Erne drainage basin and including two large lakes. It is a very sparsely populated district with a total population of only 51,000. The chief town is Enniskillen (7,438) on the only routeway across the county between the lakes.

● **Fifeshire** A county (504 square miles) of eastern Scotland lying between the Firths of Forth and Tay. Nine per cent of the county grows oats and 6 per cent potatoes. The large population (326,989) is due to the attraction of the small coalfield on the south coast and the growth of several large industrial towns encouraged by ease of communications. Of these, Dunfermline (49,882) and Kirkcaldy (50,338) are the largest, and Burntisland (5,694) is associated with aluminium smelting. The ancient university town of St Andrews (11,633), with its famous golf-course, lies on a bay on the east coast.

● **Flintshire** The smallest Welsh county (256 square miles), situated in the extreme north-east of Wales and divided into two parts. It lies between the lower valley of the River Clwyd and the estuary of the Dee. Much of the area is upland, and thus grazing land and permanent pastureland (47 per cent of the county) predominate in the agricultural scene. The small coalfield in the south-east, which it shares with Denbighshire, takes its name, however, from Flint and employs most of the 175,396 population. The main towns are: Mold (8,239), the county town; Rhyl (21,715), a seaside resort; Flint (14,660); and St Asaph (11,155), the historic diocesan centre.

Forth River The headstreams of the River Forth rise on the eastern slopes of Ben Lomond (3,192 feet). At Aberfoyle the river flows on to a broad, low plain, and most of its 66-mile course consists of a series of large meanders extending to the tidal estuary at Stirling. The gradient of the stream is very small, and hence natural drainage of the wide valley was restricted. The resultant peat mosses have been forested, but where peat has been cleared the 'carse' lands form fertile agricultural areas. Two miles south of Stirling is the site of the Battle of Bannockburn, where Robert Bruce defeated the English army of Edward II in 1314. Below Kincardine Bridge the estuary widens and becomes important for shipping — Grangemouth for commercial docks and Rosyth for Royal Naval yards. The Firth of Forth is bridged at Queensferry, 7 miles west of Edinburgh, by the famous railway bridge built in the 1880s, and by a road bridge opened in 1964.

frog The common frog is an amphibian, spending most of its life on land in damp places, but returning to water in order to breed. On land it moves by hopping, and sometimes by crawling, and in water it swims well with its webbed hind feet. It catches insects with its sticky tongue.

gannet The gannet is a large white bird resident in large colonies on the rocky part of our coastline. It is a spectacular diver.

Glamorganshire A county (818 square miles) in South Wales. It includes the southern extremities of the Cambrian Mountains and a broad coastal plain bordering the Bristol Channel. Agriculture is of secondary importance, but nearly a third of the county is permanent grassland, and animal husbandry predominates over the production of arable crops. Glamorganshire is an industrial county, with coalmining the major occupation in the deep valleys of the coalfield, such as the Tawe, Neath and Rhondda, which are densely populated. Swansea and Cardiff, the ports and metal manufacturing centres, also share a great number of the total population of 1,255,374.

Glasgow The largest city (population 896,958), a Royal burgh and the commercial capital of Scotland. Glasgow is situated on the lower reaches of the River Clyde and urban development has spread along both banks. The rapid growth of the city began after the union of England and Scotland in 1707, and trade was extended at once to include such commodities as tobacco, sugar, rum and cotton. During the 18th century, merchant ships docked 18 miles downstream at Port Glasgow, owing to the shallow nature of the river up to the city. Navigation has been improved by the construction of embankments and continuous dredging, until the waterway up to Glasgow has now a depth of 25 feet at low tide and 35 feet at high tide. Several docks were constructed at the end of last century to accommodate the world's largest merchant ships. In 1961, over 16 million tons of shipping used the harbour. Ship-building is an important industry along the waterfront, Clydebank being renowned for the construction of the liners *Queen Elizabeth*, *Queen Mary* and recently *Queen Elizabeth 2*. The supremacy of Glasgow as a commercial centre is also due to its central position in an industrial area based on the nearby coalfields. The region is unique in its development of a wide variety of industries and lack of specialisation. Iron and steel works, shipbuilding yards, cotton mills and chemical works can all be found within a few miles of the centre of Glasgow. The Cathedral dates from the 13th century.

Gloucester A cathedral city (population 90,134) of western England. Gloucester stands at the lowest bridging point of the River Severn. The winding nature of the river prevented the growth of the city as a port; even the construction of a canal, in 1827, came too late for Gloucester to compete with Bristol. The city was a Roman settlement (Glevum) on the southern route to Wales. Gloucester still remains the chief crossing place of the lower Severn Valley, despite the new road bridge to South Wales and the Severn tunnel — nearly 4½ miles in length and completed in 1886 — carrying the railway to South Wales about 30 miles downstream. Nevertheless, Gloucester, with its well-known cathedral and aircraft industry, shared with Cheltenham is a stately English city.

Gloucestershire A county (1,258 square miles) of western England. The boundaries include the lower plains of the Severn valley and the Jurassic limestone uplands of the Cotswolds. Three-quarters of the county is productive agricultural land, and this is divided equally between permanent pasture and arable land. The county (1,069,454 population) borders Somerset and the large port of Bristol on its south-western limits. Gloucester is the county town, and other centres are Cheltenham (69,734) and Cirencester (13,022).

Grampian Mountains The south-central part of the Scottish Highlands. The Grampians are bounded on the north-west by the tectonic trough of Glen More and on the south by the structural fault-line from Stonehaven to Greenock. The mountains are of old metamorphic rocks, crystalline schists, with many separate patches of granite, and their average height decreases from west to east. The highest peak is Ben Nevis (4,406 feet), and Ben Macdhui (4,296 feet) in the Cairngorms is second. Sheep- and cattle-rearing are the basic occupations, but recent hydro-electric installations have brought about badly needed localised industries. The area is becoming a popular skiing and tourist area, along the Spey Valley, especially at Aviemore.

grass snake Also called the Common Water Snake and Ringelnatter, the grass snake (often nearly three feet in length) is greyish-blue — sometimes greyish-yellow or greyish-brown — in colour with a greenish, and sometimes dark-greyish, hue. On both sides of its head, this snake has a light yellow, crescent-shaped patch, bordered with black at the back. The belly is usually covered with a black-and-white chequer pattern. The grass snake hunts by day and feeds on frogs, fish or insects, which it swallows alive. If captured it is not poisonous and never bites, but it will discharge an evil-smelling liquid.

Grimsby One of the major fishing ports (population 95,685) of the British Isles, on the south bank of the Humber estuary. It has grown to its present size in the short space of 100 years, the result of the spread of the railways in the 19th century and the connection of main lines to the port. Special express fish-trains now run to all parts of the country and ensure speedy delivery of fresh fish, a perishable commodity. The railways were responsible for the construction of the harbour works so that the landing, selling and despatching of the fish are carried out expeditiously, and facilities for servicing the trawlers are incorporated. Although Grimsby is pre-eminently a fishing port, there are other items of trade, notably the importing of timber and iron ore, and oil refineries and fertiliser factories are being established nearby.

gull There are many types of gull round our coasts. Many now come inland to feed on farms and in riverside towns. The *black-headed gull*, which is the most common in England, is well known on the Thames embankment in London.

Hampshire and the **Isle of Wight** A large county (1,650 square miles) of southern England, consisting of the Test and Itchen drainage basins, the lower Avon valley, part of the Thames basin between Aldershot and Basingstoke, and the Isle of Wight (area, 147 square miles; population 109,284), off the south coast. Arable crops occupy the largest area, 42 per cent of the county (barley 12 per cent), but a large area is forested (the New Forest). The 1,561,605 population is concentrated along the south coast, especially in the big ports of Portsmouth and Southampton. Winchester (31,041) on the River Itchen, is a cathedral city and the county town, and Newport (22,286) is capital of the Isle of Wight.

hare The hare is somewhat larger than the rabbit, and has longer legs and longer ears. It is a very fast, strong runner and can swim well. Two to five leverets, covered with hair and with their eyes open, are born in spring in a grassy hollow or 'form'. The jack hare, when courting the female, gives an amazing display, from which has come the phrase 'as mad as a March hare'. Too many can be a nuisance to the farmer, but they are not nearly such a pest as the rabbit.

hawks The *kestrel*, or *windhover*, is our most common hawk and can be recognised by its hovering flight. It has the ability to remain virtually stationary in one place in the air. It is a useful bird, feeding chiefly on mice and insects. The *sparrowhawk* hunts small birds and can be a great nuisance to the gamekeeper and poultry farmer. The *buzzard* is the largest of our hawks and is found in wilder country.

Hebrides, or **Western Isles** The group comprises over 500 islands, but only 102 of these are inhabited. They form a large area of 2,800 square miles, with a population of 80,000. Only a small proportion is farmed — about 300 square miles. The Inner Hebrides include Skye, a famed tourist and climbing area, with its capital Portree (2,120). The islands of Mull, Islay, Jura and others are relatively sheltered and close to the mainland of Argyll. The Outer Hebrides are separated from the Inner by the Little Minch channel, and from the mainland by the North Minch channel, and include Harris, Lewis and Uist. They support a number of scattered crofters, and are world-famous for their home-spun tweed-cloth.

hedgehog This is a small brown animal, about 10 inches long and covered with spines. When frightened, the creature rolls into a ball, and its spines protect it. Badgers, foxes and some dogs, however, know how to unroll it, and many are also killed on the roads. It is quite common in the countryside, and found frequently in gardens, where it may become quite tame. As the hedgehog is nocturnal by nature, it is rarely seen. Small animals, such as slugs and earthworms, are its chief food. Four to six young are born in the spring. In winter, hedgehogs hibernate, rolling up in holes or rabbit burrows.

Herefordshire A county of western England (842 square miles) and the Welsh marches, Hereford consists of the lowland plain of the Wye valley, sheltered on all sides by mountains and hills. It is a rich, agricultural region with over four-fifths of the land productive (40 per cent permanent grassland and 42 per cent arable). The county is famous for its distinctive breed of beef cattle, and hops are among the cultivated crops. The low population (138,425) reflects the absence of any major industrial towns. Hereford (46,503), the county town and a cathedral city, is on the Wye.

Boating is becoming an increasingly popular hobby in Britain, and coastal waters are often dotted with small craft. These sheltered waters near the Isle of Wight make an ideal mooring place

● **herring** The herring is found in large numbers off our North Sea coasts, feeding on a great variety of smaller marine animals, such as the larvae of crabs. During spawning the female swims on her side and extrudes a stream of eggs which stick to the rocks and weeds on which she rubs her body. The male follows her, extruding milt to fertilise the eggs. Herring are exceedingly prolific and great numbers are caught each year, for curing or salting, at Aberdeen and other east coast ports.

● **Hertfordshire** An English county (631 square miles) in the Lower Thames Basin, north of London. Hertfordshire includes the northern Chiltern Hills and the upper valleys of the Colne and Lea, tributaries of the Thames. Half of its area is devoted to arable crops, and many of these are vegetables grown in market gardens for the metropolis. The old towns — e.g., Watford (78,117), St Albans (52,057), Hertford (the county town, with 20,379) and Bishop's Stortford (22,084) — have their own individual characteristics and functions, but a great number of the 922,188 population live in the new dormitory towns, part of the urban spread beyond the new administrative area of Greater London.

● **holly** *Ilex aquifolium* is an evergreen shrub or small tree found almost throughout the British Isles. The leathery, dark-green leaves are prickly, except at the tops of mature trees. The male and female flowers are borne on separate trees and the scarlet berries are widely used as a Christmas tree decoration.

● **Hull (Kingston-upon-Hull)** A busy seaport on the east coast of England (population 285,472). Known as Hull, the city has grown round the confluence of the little River Hull with the Humber, where the ebb current flows near the river bank round a curve and so provide a permanent deep-water channel. These advantages of position have ensured continued development since the Middle Ages. The city was given its name, King's Town upon Hull, after the visit of Edward I in 1299, who granted its first charter. The port serves a wide hinterland, ranging from the industrial areas of the West Riding of Yorkshire to the populated areas in the Midlands, communications being maintained first by natural waterways, and then by canals and railways. With the increase in ship size in the 19th century, docks were constructed along the waterfront. Considerable trade is carried on with the countries across the North Sea. Wheat, timber, butter and bacon are imported, and a large fishing fleet is based on Hull. It is the third British port according to total value of trade.

● **Humber River** An important waterway of eastern England. The Humber is a large estuary, over a mile wide throughout its length, and the outlet for many long rivers which drain a large area, extending from the northern Pennines to Northampton Uplands. These natural waterways, supplemented where necessary by canals, serve mainly populated districts with varied industrial activities. Thus the Humber is a busy commercial highway for the import of raw materials and foodstuffs, and the export of manufactured products. Hull is the point of trans-shipment of goods to barges using inland waterways, but some small sea-going vessels reach upstream to Goole. On the south bank a large industrial complex based on chemicals is developing.

● **Huntingdonshire** and **Peterborough** A small county (366 square miles) of east-central England. It is part of the extensive plain which borders The Wash, and some of the land is low-lying fen with thick, black peaty soil which needs careful drainage. Two-thirds of the county is arable land. Of the 202,337 population, a large proportion live in rural settlements. The town of Huntingdon and Godmanchester (16,540) on the banks of the Great Ouse, is a market centre; its industries are connected with agriculture, machinery, manufacturing and flour milling. Peterborough has 70,021 inhabitants.

● **Inverness-shire** The largest county (4,211 square miles) in Scotland. It occupies the centre of the Highlands and is sundered by Glen More which, traversed by the Caledonian Canal, reaches the east coast in the Moray Firth and the west among the islands of the Inner Hebrides — Skye, Eigg and Rum. Harris, and the southern islands of the Outer Hebrides, are also included in Inverness-shire. The land is very mountainous, and the existing lowlands are to be found only in narrow strips along the coasts and in the deep valleys or glens. Many of the slopes are forested, and above there are remote summer pastures for sheep and stock. Long-horned Highland cattle are bred in the valleys. The population of 83,000 is scattered; but there are two main centres, Inverness (32,000), and Fort William (2,700), where pulp and paper making are becoming an important industry.

● **iron and steel industry** Iron was used for weapons and tools very early in history by the Iron Age peoples and then, later, by the Romans. It was not until medieval times that special centres of the iron industry became significant — e.g., in the Forest of Dean and in the Weald of Sussex and Kent, both areas depending on local ore and abundant timber for charcoal. In the 18th century coal was substituted for charcoal in the smelting processes, and yet greater expansion in the industry followed with the introduction of coke in blast furnaces and with the use of the steam engine. An increasing number of uses were found for iron in the manufacture of machinery of all kinds, and the industry came to be concentrated near to the coalfields. Further expansion in output was caused by the coming of the railways. The making of steel on a large scale in the second half of the 19th century resulted from the introduction of cheaper processes — e.g., Bessemer's 'converter' and Siemen's 'open hearth' furnace, and the production of wrought iron gradually declined. In 1913 the United Kingdom's output of 8 million tons represented a tenth of the total world output of steel, while 10 million tons of pig-iron was an eighth of the world production. With the exhaustion of many of the coal seams — claybank and blackband ores containing 30 per cent of iron — and the diminution in the mining of hematite, which had an iron content of 50 to 60 per cent, the iron and steel industry moved to new centres near the large Jurassic ore deposits, which are poorer, containing only 20 to 33 per cent of iron, or to the coast, where imported ores could be brought most economically. The chief iron and steel producing areas are the north-east coast of England, Teeside, South Wales, Sheffield, Scunthorpe, Corby, and Glasgow. Recently the nationalisation of steel companies into the British Steel Corporation has led to the modernisation of many plants and the running down of older, less profitable ones.

● **Isle of Man (Mona)** An island of 227 square miles in area, lying in the Irish Sea, midway between the coasts of Ulster and Cumberland. The major portion of the Isle of Man is composed of Cambrian schists comparable with those of the Lake District, while the plain at the northern end of the island is of younger Triassic rocks overlain by boulder clay. Although only 10 miles in breadth, the land rises to over 2,000 feet on Snaefell (2,034 feet) and the uplands are dissected by deep valleys; there are stretches of high rocky cliffs along the coast. Most of the population of 49,743 live in coastal settlements, from which a good deal of herring and mackerel fishing is carried on in the neighbouring seas. The capital, Douglas (20,000), is the centre of administration and government, for the Manx people — between 150-200 of whom can speak Manx — are independent of the Parliament of Westminster, unless specifically included in any legislation. The Queen is represented by a Governor, who acts in conjunction with the Executive Council. The Isle of Man is noted for its annual motor-cycle races, which draw large crowds in addition to ordinary holidaymakers from the mainland, who number about 500,000 each year.

● **Kent** A large county (1,400 square miles) of south-east England, occupying the peninsula between the Thames estuary and the English Channel. Much of the county is lowland, but it is crossed by the chalk ridge of the North Downs, cut by two major valleys — the Medway and the Stour. Forty-four per cent of the land supports arable crops, and a quarter of this area is divided equally between wheat and barley. Kent is often called the 'Garden of England', for it is the major fruit-growing county in the country. A third of the country's orchard fruits and a fifth of the small fruits are grown in Kent, which is also the premier hop-growing area, with over half the English total acreage. The population is 1,396,030 (including Canterbury). Many densely populated districts and towns, such as Bromley, have now been transferred from Kent to the region administered by the Greater London Council, but there remain heavy concentrations along the lower Thames, in the ports of Gravesend (54,044), Chatham (56,921) and Rochester (55,460). Other towns are: the ancient City of Canterbury, on the Stour; Maidstone (70,918), the county town, on the Medway; Ashford (35,960), on the Stour; and Dover and Folkestone (43,760), the Channel ports. Holiday centres are found on the north-east coast, on Thanet, at Margate (50,145), and Ramsgate (39,482), with the first Hoverport terminal for the continent; other resorts are Deal (25,415) and Herne Bay (25,117).

● **Kincardineshire** A small Scottish county of 382 square miles, situated on the east coast between Aberdeen and Montrose. There are extensive lowlands along the coast and up the two valleys in which the rivers (Dee and N. Esk) form the boundaries of the county. Most of the 26,156 population are found in the coastal districts — e.g., at Stonehaven (4,796) and Inverbervie (865).

● **Kinross** The second smallest county (82 square miles) in Scotland, Kinross borders Perthshire and Clackmannanshire to the west and adjoins Fifeshire in the east. Loch Leven, a lowland lake within the county, has an island castle in which Mary, Queen of Scots, was imprisoned. Near its shores lies the county burgh of Kinross, the largest town, containing 2,418 of the county's 6,422 inhabitants.

● **Kirkcudbright** A county of south-western Scotland (900 square miles) extending from some of the highest western parts of the Southern Uplands (Merrick, 2,764 feet) southwards to the Galloway lowlands and the Solway Firth. Primarily a farming county, sheep rearing on the uplands and cattle-fattening on the lowlands are the main occupations. The coastal lowlands have a remarkably mild climate for Scotland, promoting rich growth of pastures over a relatively much longer season. The small market towns, such as the county burgh of Kirkcudbright (2,506) and Castle Douglas (3,314), contain a large part of the 27,450 population, and farms are usually large and scattered.

● **Lanarkshire** One of the most densely peopled counties (879 square miles) of central Scotland. It comprises mainly the drainage basin of the River Clyde, and thus contains large areas of the moors of the Southern Uplands — the Lowther Hills. Eighteen per cent of the land area is under permanent pasture, hence its importance for cattle-grazing and supplying milk to the cities. The population of 1,524,175 lives principally in the north of the county, on the coalfield and in its associated industrial towns, such as Motherwell (74,184), Coatbridge (52,131) and Airdrie (37,736). The great city and port of Glasgow is also in Lanarkshire, as well as the new town of East Kilbride (63,505) and several trading estates.

● **Lancashire** This, the largest county (1,878 square miles) of north-west England, once formed part of the old province of Lancastria. It extends from the Furness Fells of the Lake District, southwards to the Mersey estuary. The eastern margins contain parts of the Pennine Chain, where sheep-farming, cattle-rearing and water supply, are important. Lancashire is the second county in England for poultry, chiefly in the Fylde, inland from Blackpool. However, it is essentially industrial, with the 5,106,123 population concentrated on the coalfield round Rossendale, and in the great conurbations of Manchester and Liverpool. Preston

(97,365), on the Ribble, is the administrative centre, and farther north is historic Lancaster (49,523), on the Lune, the site of a new university. Blackpool (151,311), the country's most famous playground and holiday resort, is on the west coast. In the south, around Widnes (56,709), there is a large-scale chemical and glass industry.

● **Leeds** The largest city (population 494,971) and the chief distributing and market centre of Yorkshire. Situated on the River Aire, the growth of Leeds is relatively recent since it was only a small village in the 14th century, becoming a prosperous woollen town by the 18th century. The construction of the Leeds-Liverpool canal across the Pennines, via the Aire Gap, provided a commercial routeway to the west coast. Leeds, having lost much of its trade in raw wool to Bradford, has become a centre of the large-scale manufacturing of ready-made clothing. The greater proportion of the textile factory workers are women, while the men are engaged in other activities, such as textile machinery manufacture, the engineering workshops, and leather and aeroplane component factories. As a market or shopping centre, Leeds extends its influence over most of the county, and it is an important railway centre.

● **Leicester** A specialised industrial city of the Midlands (population 283,549) on the River Soar, a tributary of the Trent, and a city founded by the Romans. A castle was built in Norman times and there are numerous medieval buildings, indicating prosperity in the Middle Ages. It was at Leicester that Richard III stayed before being defeated and killed at the Battle of Bosworth (1485). The present importance of Leicester dates from the Industrial Revolution and the growth of manufacturing industries. High-quality wool from local sheep encouraged the woollen industry, which has now reached a high degree of specialisation in the production of 'knitwear'. The second major industry is boot-and-shoe manufacturing and, as in other centres of localised industries, Leicester makes the special machinery needed for the highly skilled branches of engineering and manufacture carried on in the city's factories.

● **Leicestershire** A Midland county (832 square miles) of England. Thirty-seven per cent of the county is under high-quality permanent grass, and animal husbandry predominates among the agricultural activities. Leicestershire is noted for its special breed of sheep. Industries have developed on the coalfield in the west of the county round Ashby-de-la-Zouch and in the centre of the county at Leicester and Loughborough (45,863), employing many of the 721,213 population. The market towns of Melton Mowbray (19,932) and Market Harborough (14,527) serve the farming population.

● **Leinster** The eastern province (7,580 square miles; population 1,414,415) of the Irish Republic. It is now composed of 12 counties and the city of Dublin for administrative purposes. Before the Norman invasion of Ireland, in 1170, the Kingdom of Leinster contained the smaller area of the Leinster chain of mountains (Wicklow Mountains) and the neighbouring valleys and lowlands.

● **lime** *Tilia europea* is a deciduous tree reaching 60 feet in height. The leaves are fairly large, heart-shaped, rather thin and a conspicuous light green. The yellowish-green flowers are sweetly scented and much visited by bees. The wood is white and often used for wood-carving.

● **Lincoln** An historic cathedral city (population 74,207) of eastern England. Lincoln is situated in a gap in the Jurassic limestone ridge of Lincoln Edge. The River Witham flows through the gap on

its way to the Wash, and at one time Lincoln marked the head of navigation. The old Roman settlement Lindum stood at the junction of Fosse Way and Ermine Street, and traces of these remain on the Edge. During Norman times the city grew in importance; the castle and cathedral formed the nucleus on the dominating north slopes of the gap. Besides its cultural and ecclesiastical functions, Lincoln serves its surrounding countryside as a market, and in manufacturing farm machinery and preparing animal foodstuffs.

● **Lincolnshire** An extensive county of eastern England, occupying 2,663 square miles between the Humber and the Wash. It is divided into three administrative counties: Lindsey, the largest, in the north; Kesteven in the south-west; and Holland in the south-east. Lincolnshire is predominantly lowland, but is traversed from north to south by the limestone Lincoln Edge and the chalk hills of the Wolds to the east. Much of the land is highly fertile and 72 per cent is devoted to arable crops. One quarter of the county produces wheat, a seventh barley, and one-twelfth potatoes. It has the largest acreage in the country for potatoes and is the second for acreage of sugar-beet. In the low-lying fenland of Holland, vegetables, flowers and glasshouse crops form specialised activities. The fields of flowers resemble those of the Netherlands, and in this specialised type of agriculture Lincolnshire leads the country. Although Lincolnshire is a large county, the population, mostly rural, is only 808,384. The main urban centres are the city of Lincoln, Grimsby, Grantham (27,913), Boston (25,995), Spalding (16,950), and the industrial city of Scunthorpe (70,880).

● **Liverpool** The second port of the United Kingdom (population 606,834), situated on the right bank of the River Mersey at a point where the estuary narrows and the water flows swiftly and deeply before entering the Irish Sea. Although there is a tidal range of nearly 30 feet, the channel at the seaward side of the narrow river entrance has to be constantly dredged to remove silt, so that the largest ships can dock or sail at any time. The freedom from silting near the city has guaranteed the growth of the port, while its competitors in the Ribble and Dee estuaries have declined. The first wet dock was built here in 1715. Liverpool's first trade was with the West Indies and North America in the 17th century, and the countries in those parts of the world have remained prominent in the activities of the port. Tobacco, sugar and cotton were the first imports, while today Liverpool serves an extensive industrial hinterland, importing most of the raw materials and foodstuffs and exporting the manufactured products. Thus the imports include raw cotton, wool, hemp, metal ores, timber, tobacco, petrol, vegetable seeds and human provisions — chiefly grain, fruit and sugar. Owing to its position on the west coast, Liverpool is the main port for the Irish traffic. The port serves passengers bound for many parts of the world, though those destined for North America are most numerous. Industrial development in the city is concerned primarily with the processing and packing of food products, since facilities for heavy industries are limited, but there are large new industrial estates owned by the city at Speke, Kirkby and Aintree. Both the Anglican and Roman Catholic communities have been engaged in building fine new cathedrals this century.

● **lizards** The common lizard is the only reptile found in Ireland and is very common all over Great Britain. It lives in damp, heathy places and enjoys basking in the sun. The sand lizard is found only in southern England and inhabits dry, sandy heaths or dunes. The slow-worm is a legless lizard, snakelike in appearance, about 18 inches long.

● **Lomond, Loch** The largest lake in Great Britain and situated in Scotland. Loch Lomond is 24 miles long and extends from Ardlui in the north, where

Nelson's Column, Trafalgar Square – regarded as the very centre of Britain's great capital

its feeders rise near the River Tay, to Balloch in the south, where the River Leven flows out to the Clyde. The upper stretches of the lake occupy a steep-sided narrow valley, formed by ice, with mountains rising to over 3,000 feet on either side. The southern part of Loch Lomond widens out to about 5 miles and contains numerous large islands.

● **London** The capital of the United Kingdom and the premier city of the British Commonwealth. In 1965 a great reorganisation of the administrative areas in London took place. Before this date boundaries were difficult to define, since they consisted of metropolitan boroughs, non-county boroughs and many urban district councils besides the City of London, the County of London and Middlesex. In 1965 these broken 'pieces' were all combined under the Greater London

Council to form a well defined area of 620 square miles with a population in 1971 of 7,379,014. This area consisted not only of all the former 'pieces' but also of some of the urban areas of Kent, Surrey, Essex and Hertfordshire which have close connections with London. Greater London is now composed of 32 largely self-sufficient Greater London Boroughs, co-ordinated by the Greater London Council. Education is handled by a specially constituted committee of the Greater London Council called the Inner London Education Authority, and by each of the outer London boroughs. The capital is supplied by two airports — Gatwick and Heathrow — which handle an enormous volume of traffic, and plans for a third have been decided, for the Essex area of Foulness.

Although earlier settlements occurred along the banks of the Thames, it was the Romans who fixed the actual site of London and built Londinium on the north bank where, today, stands the City, the internationally important heart of the great metropolis. The small Roman commercial and trading centre managed to retain its functions during the Dark Ages, and its first Bishop was ordained in A.D. 604. After the Norman conquest and the building of the nucleus of the Tower of London by William I, the city grew rapidly, especially with the increase in maritime commerce, since it stands at the head of sea navigation on the Thames; by 1350 it must have had a population of some 40,000. The wealthy London merchants, with their well-organised guilds, became a powerful political force, possessing their own administration, independent of the Crown. Indeed they were physically separated from the monarch and government, in the Palaces of Westminster and St James, by the fields of Holborn and Charing Cross. In the 16th century, they supported expeditions of exploration to all parts of the world, and reaped the benefits with the increase in trade and the introduction of new commodities to the markets. These early activities laid the foundations of the present great 'entrepôt' trade, which involves goods from many countries being assembled in extensive warehouses in the Port of London and re-exported to the consuming countries. Hence the city became the chief money market of the world and the headquarters of Lloyd's, the famous insurance house. In addition, the Port of London handles imports for most parts of the country and exports many of the manufactured goods, especially the highly-specialised engineering products, for which Great Britain

is famous. The industries of the London area are mostly concerned with the making of light consumer goods, requiring pre-prepared materials and highly skilled labour for assembly. The few heavy industries are found along the lower reaches of the river — e.g., the steel and motor-car works at Dagenham, and numerous cement and paper works. Power for homes and factories is supplied by 30 large gas and electricity works, some of them farther upstream and served by barge.

The administrative functions of the capital are based on the City of Westminster, where stand the Houses of Parliament, Buckingham Palace (the chief town residence of the Queen), and the principal Government offices in Whitehall. Westminster Abbey has been the coronation church of the sovereign since 1066. The legal headquarters — the Law Courts and Inns of Court — are situated on the western boundary of the City, next door to the publishing houses and newspaper offices of Fleet Street. Bloomsbury, with the British Museum and the Senate House of the University, is the academic district, though its proximity to several main-line railway termini has also caused the establishment of many hotels. Many tourists come to see the sights of London — such as the Tower, St Paul's Cathedral, and Horse Guards Parade. They can visit numerous exhibitions, art galleries, museums and parks, and enjoy the pleasures of a concert at the Festival Hall or a play at one of the many theatres. London is a vital, busy metropolis, which continues to widen its influence over the surrounding countryside. The improvement in swift communications has enabled a vast number of people to live farther away from the congested districts, travelling daily to and from their work in London, which ranks among the three largest cities in the world. With its new concrete office blocks and tall, towering buildings, the city is taking on a new appearance, but the large acreage of parkland, for which London is famous, remains, to provide the citizens with a retreat from the busy streets and built-up areas which spread over most of the capital's 394,476 acres.

● **Londonderry** A county (804 square miles) of Northern Ireland, Londonderry extends westwards from the River Bann to the valley of the River Foyle. The northern boundary lies along the shores of Lough Foyle and the sea-coast, while inland the county includes parts of the Sperrin Mountains.

Fine architecture is centred on London's South Bank of the River Thames. To the left is the Royal Festival Hall

The population (174,658) is concentrated along the lowlands of the Bann valley and at the head of Lough Foyle. The towns of Londonderry (or Derry) (55,694) on the Foyle and Coleraine (13,960) on the Bann are the chief centres, especially of the linen industry.

● **Manchester** The largest commercial centre of northern England (population 541,468), with a rapidly growing ring of satellite towns. The Roman settlement Mancunium was built in A.D. 78 on the banks of the River Irwell, a tributary of the Mersey. In the Middle Ages, Manchester was a market town trading in wool and cloth; consequently, with its tradition in weaving, Manchester was able to transfer its attention to the new fibre, cotton, when first imported from the Middle East in the 17th century. Since that time, it has been the focus of the Lancashire cotton industry. The city has been made into a busy port by the Manchester Ship Canal, 36 miles long, which was opened in 1894, and enables ocean-going cargo ships up to 15,000 tons to penetrate 42 miles inland. This avoids trans-shipment of the bulky raw cotton at Liverpool, and hence is a saving of time and money in handling. A variety of other goods are imported — e.g., wheat, petrol, wood and wood pulp, steel and foodstuffs, many of which are distributed to the neighbouring industrial towns. Manchester is also the centre of an important engineering district, where the chief products are textile and electrical machinery. The city has a vital function as a shopping and cultural centre for a wide area, with its large high-class shops, theatres, art galleries, libraries and university.

The assembly line at a car-manufacturing factory in England's Midlands, the region in which a vast amount of Britain's industry is centred

● **Merionethshire** A mountainous county (660 square miles) of central Wales. The total population of 35,277 is found in the small towns of Dolgelly (6,561), Harlech and the slate-mining district of Ffestiniog (5,751), while Barmouth (2,103) and Bala (1,580) attract seasonal visitors.

● **Middlesbrough** With Billingham, Stockton-on-Tees and the seaside resort of Redcar, it forms part of the new County Borough of Teesside, created in 1968 for more efficient economic management of this important heavy industrial region of North Yorkshire and South Durham. Industry astride the River Tees includes several steel plants, two large heavy chemical complexes, and an oil refinery, besides several light industrial estates. Large quantities of pig iron are supplied to Sheffield and Birmingham factories and exported to other countries. The steel works make constructional girders for bridging, rails for railways, and plates for shipbuilding. Recently the estuary Tees has been widened and deepened for improved shipping facilities. The origins of heavy industry in this area are based on the 19th century mining of local ore, now worked out, which was smelted into iron and steel using coal from Durham. The whole area is set beneath the wild scenery of the North York Moors. The origins of heavy industry in this area are based on the 19th century mining of local ore, now worked out, which was smelted into iron and steel using coal from Durham.

● **Middlesex** Formerly, a very small county (232 square miles) on the north and west sides of the County of London, but now forming part of the Greater London Council area, and divided into a number of large London Boroughs. Although much of the area is urban, the outermost parts of Middlesex produce arable crops, especially vegetables for the London market, as a reminder of the county's agricultural past. The population mainly lives in suburban communities such as Harrow, Wembley and Uxbridge. London Airport (Heathrow) lies in Middlesex; now, however, the name is kept alive only as a postal address or in sport (e.g., Middlesex County Cricket Club).

● **Midlothian** A county (366 square miles) of central Scotland, extending inland from the southern shores of the Firth of Forth. The economy of the southern parts of the county — the Pentland, Lammermuir and Moorfoot Hills — is concerned with sheep-farming. The coastal areas support mixed farming and market gardening, influenced by the proximity of the capital city, Edinburgh. Midlothian is the second county in Scotland for pig-rearing. In the east is the Midlothian coalfield, and the mining towns of Tranent and Portobello, together with Leith (81,618), the port of Edinburgh, help to make the total population 595,631.

● **mole** The mole is about 6 inches long, with a one-inch long tail, and is covered by soft, dense, grey fur. It has a pointed nose and very small eyes and ears. Its legs are powerful for the mole spends most of its life in tunnels underground, where it eats many earthworms and wireworms.

● **Monmouthshire** Once an English county (542 square miles), but considered now as part of Wales. The agriculture resembles that of the adjacent counties, with the largest proportion, 44 per cent, under permanent grass. Many of the 461,459 inhabitants are employed in industry, for the large South Wales coalfield extends into Monmouth, and there are densely populated areas including places such as Ebbw Vale (26,049), Tredegar (17,976), Pontypool (37,014), Abergavenny (9,388), and Newport (112,048) at the mouth of the Usk. The county town is Monmouth (6,545).

● **Montgomeryshire** An inland county (797 square miles) of central Wales, though it reaches in the west to the Dovey estuary. It contains high ridges which form the watershed between the River Dovey, flowing westwards to Cardigan Bay, and the headwaters of the River Severn. Lake Vyrnwy, in the north, at the head of one of the Severn tributaries, supplies water to Birmingham. It is a hill-farming county with stock-rearing predominating, having the second largest number of cattle of any county in Wales, and being fifth in England and Wales for sheep. The towns are situated in the

eastern valleys, especially the Vale of Powis — Welshpool (6,705), Montgomery (968), the county town, and Newtown (6,122) small market towns in a county with a total population of only 42,761.

● **Morayshire (Elgin)** A county (476 square miles) of north-east Scotland, consisting mainly of the land between the lower parts of Strath Dearn (the valley of the River Findhorn) and Strath Spey. The coastal lowlands of the Moray Firth (Laich Moray) reach their maximum width in Moray. The chief (and county) town is Elgin (16,401), noted for its 14th-century cathedral. The population of 51,485 is distributed also in other centres, such as Grantown-on-Spey (1,601) in the extreme south, Forres (4,710) and Lossiemouth (5,681), a naval station on the coast.

● **motor-car industry** Of recent origin (Daimler built his first car at Coventry in 1896), the motor-car industry has grown and developed very rapidly. The output of vehicles mounted phenomenally from 95,000 in 1923 to 236,000 in 1930, and over two million vehicles in 1970. The building of motor-cars and other vehicles is concentrated in three main regions: (1) Birmingham and the Black Country, employing 40 per cent of the workers; (2) Greater London, 14 per cent; (3) South Lancashire and Manchester, 10 per cent. Other separate centres include Oxford, Derby, Luton, Glasgow, and South Wales. The locating factors for the motor-car industry are a supply of highly skilled labour, ease of assembly of the wide variety of raw materials and component parts needed in the construction of a motor vehicle, and easy export of motor vehicles. Such export, especially to countries in the dollar area, provides a valuable source of income for the United Kingdom.

● **mouse** The grey house mouse, a widespread pest, originally came from Central Asia. The harvest mouse is a tiny, yellowish animal, with a short, hairless, prehensile tail. It builds a nest of plaited grass on the stems of the corn. The short-tailed field-mouse is really a vole and has smaller eyes, a blunt nose, small ears and a short tail. The dormouse, so called because it sleeps all winter (dormeuse means sleeper), is found in oak or hazel woods. The long-tailed field-mouse often invades buildings in winter.

● **Munster** The south-western province (9,316 square miles; population 859,334) of the Irish Republic, consisting of 6 counties and including the important regional centres of Cork and Limerick. The estuary and lower reaches of the River Shannon, the great peninsulas and bays of Kerry, together with 'Killarney's lakes and fells', all lie within the province of Munster.

● **Nairnshire** A small county of 163 square miles, bordering the southern shore of the Moray Firth, in north-east Scotland. The small population of 9,000 is concentrated in the north along the routeways, and the chief town is Nairn (4,899).

● **Neagh, Lough** The largest lake in the British Isles, 154 square miles in area, Lough Neagh lies in a rift valley between the basaltic Antrim Mountains and the Sperrin Mountains in Northern Ireland. It is roughly rectangular in shape and is surrounded by lowlands floored by lacustrine deposits, which form rich, agricultural land. Lough Neath is drained by the northward-flowing River Bann.

● **Ness, Loch** Famed for the probably mythical monster which lives in its depths, Loch Ness (24 miles long) occupies part of the tectonic trench of Glen More, between the North-west Highlands and the Mondadhl'ath Mountains. The enclosing sides are steep and forest-covered, and the dark waters reach to a depth of 800 feet. The main road from Fort William to Inverness follows the western shore, and the loch provides a stretch of the continuous water from near Inverness south-westwards to Fort Augustus and then, linked by the Caledonian Canal, to Loch Lochy and Loch Linnhe and the Firth of Lorne.

● **Newcastle upon Tyne** The commercial and regional capital of north-east England (population

222,153). Newcastle (Monkchester) was an old Roman military station at the lowest bridging point and limit of sea navigation on the north bank of the River Tyne. Other advantages encouraged the city's rôle as a route centre — ease of communication with the west coast through the South Tyne Gap in the Pennines, and its situation on the eastern routeway to Scotland along the coastal plain of Northumberland. The city owes its fame to the coal trade, which began in the Middle Ages with the shipping of coal to London. The export of coal and coke from the highly productive Northumberland and Durham coalfield has remained the dominating activity of the Tyne until recent times. This abundant supply of fuel has resulted in the growth of many heavy industries. Newcastle and its adjoining towns on the river are noted for shipbuilding — cargo-boats, warships and, more recently, tankers. Associated industries are ship-repairing, marine turbine and electrical engineering, as well as chemicals. The city is the market and shopping centre for an area of dense population, in addition to its commercial and business interests connected with the local industries, and there are large trading estates, largely employing female labour.

● **newt** Newts are amphibians with tails. The *smooth newt*, 3 to 4 inches long, is the commonest. It is olive-green above and yellow-orange beneath, with black spots all over. The *palmate newt*, 2½ to 3 inches long, has a fine filament at the end of its tail, while the *crested newt*, 6 inches long, is dark greenish-brown above and orange spotted with black below.

● **new towns** As part of an overall scheme to assist areas of unemployment and to relieve the pressure on older established towns for housing and industry, twenty-eight new towns have been established in the United Kingdom, of which five are in Scotland, one in Wales and four in the north-east. Seven are sited in the outermost parts of the Greater London area. Actual total expenditure on them is estimated at £270 million, and by 1980 they will house over a million people. In 1961 they housed 436,000 people. Most are concerned with light industries.

● **nightingale** This shy little brown bird is a summer visitor. Arriving in late April, to nest in woods and copses in southern England, it is one of our best songsters.

● **Norfolk** A large agricultural county (2,054 square miles) of East Anglia. Most of the county is under 300 feet above sea level, with the chalky East Anglian Heights extending southwards from Hunstanton to form a pleasant undulating landscape and including the forested Brecklands, where sand overlays the chalk. Sixty-five per cent of the county is tilled land, mainly on a chalky boulder-clay with brown soils, and nearly a third of this grows barley and a sixth wheat. Norfolk is the major sugar-beet county in England, with 8 per cent of its area devoted to the crop. In this predominantly arable area the chief type of livestock is poultry, and the county produces 42 per cent of the nation's ducks. Norwich, the county town, and Great Yarmouth (52,860), an important fishing port, are the only two big urban centres. There are several rural market towns and villages with fine churches, the whole county having a total population of 616,427. The Norfolk Broads are an important tourist attraction.

● **Northampton** An industrial town (population 126,608) of the Midlands. Northampton stands on the banks of the River Nen, which flows into the Wash. Founded in 1189, it was a flourishing market town during the Middle Ages, noted for its leather-tanning industry, based on the abundant supply of skins and hides from the pastoral Midlands, oak from the forests, and soft water. Boot and shoe making, the main branch of the leather industry, now employs thousands of workers, and most of the hides are imported. In recent years, ironstone mining in the Jurassic limestone hills to the west has led to the development of an iron and steel industry in the area, and subsidiary metal and engineering works have been established in Northampton, making tools and machinery, especially for the boot and shoe industry.

● **Northamptonshire** A county in the eastern Midlands, 914 square miles in area. Fifty-two per cent of the area grows arable crops, a quarter producing wheat. Although mainly an agricultural county, there is increasing quarrying and mining of iron ore in the Liassic and Oolitic Uplands. The population totals 467,843. Apart from Northampton, other centres are Wellingborough (37,589) and Kettering (42,628).

● **Northern Ireland** An integral part of the United Kingdom. The country consists of six counties, totalling 5,238 square miles, and occupying the north-east corner of the island and the greater part of the old province of Ulster. When the southern counties of Ireland chose to become independent in 1919 (now Eire), the predominantly Protestant areas elected to remain linked with Great Britain, for, owing to its geographical proximity to the Scottish mainland, most of the early immigrants came from Scotland, bringing with them their own religion and cultural traditions. Today Northern Ireland has very close economic links with western Scotland; and movement of people has taken place in the opposite direction, too, for Glasgow has a large proportion of Irish inhabitants.

Northern Ireland had its own government for home affairs until March 1972, when it was suspended for a year whilst the country is ruled direct from Westminster in an effort to settle its political difficulties. The population of 1,525,187 is centred on Belfast, the capital, and several industrial towns in the Lagan and Bann valleys, in addition to Londonderry at the mouth of the River Foyle. The original industrial activity, the manufacture of textiles from agricultural products, has since ramified and expanded

Northern Ireland's famous Mountains of Mourne, County Down, rising above the green landscape at their foot

The Giant's Causeway is an unusual promontory of columnar basalt to be found on the north coast of County Antrim, in Northern Ireland

tremendously, leading to much greater prosperity, which should continue with the establishment of new light industries in development areas. Most productive are the food and tobacco industries, while the value of textile and engineering products is about £200 million annually. Unemployment is, however, a serious problem.

● **North Sea** A shallow body of water on the Continental Shelf, the North Sea is dotted with banks that are noted for their cod and herring fisheries. At the Dogger Bank, in the centre of the sea, the water is only 30 feet deep. Great seaports — London, Antwerp, Rotterdam, Bremen, Hamburg — have risen on the estuaries of rivers that empty into the North Sea. Drilling for oil and natural gas has recently begun on a large scale, and now a large section of England's gas consumption is from this natural source.

● **Northumberland** 2,019 square miles in area, Northumberland is the northernmost county of England and was once part of the province of Northumbria. The bleak moors of the northern Pennines give way in the east to a fertile coastal plain, which forms one of the major routeways to Scotland. Most of the 794,975 population live on the coalfield and in the Tyneside industrial towns, such as Tynemouth (68,861), North Shields and Newcastle itself, the county's administrative head-quarters.

● **North-west Highlands** The mountains of northern Scotland, west of Glen More. These resemble the Grampians, in that they are composed of metamorphic and igneous rocks, but they have not such an extensive area of land over 2,000 feet. Long sea-lochs penetrate the mountains along the west coast. The mountains of the islands of the Inner Hebrides, such as the Cuillin Hills of Skye, can be considered as part of the North-west Highlands. Population is dispersed and generally limited to the patches of lowland bordering the lochs, where animal husbandry is the most practised occupation. This is the region of the crofter, but in spite of increased tourism and improvements in the standard of living, the population continues to decrease, as people seek better jobs and more company in the towns further south.

● **Norwich** An ancient city (population 121,688) and the regional capital of East Anglia. Standing near the confluence of the Wensum and the Yare, Norwich was once a port for sea-going ships. The Normans built a castle for its defence and it also possesses a cathedral, the centre of the diocese. During the medieval period, Norwich served its agricultural district as a market town, and the city's merchants bought the local wool for processing. In the 17th and 18th centuries Norwich had become the greatest woollen manufacturing town in all England. The industry specialised in the making of worsteds, a skill which came with the immigrant Flemish weavers, and this monopoly persisted until supremacy in the industry was gained by the Yorkshire towns with the coming of the Industrial Revolution. The city's modern industries maintain their connection with the countryside, producing farm machinery and tools, boots and shoes of high quality, and many kinds of foodstuffs.

● **Nottingham** An industrial city of the north Midlands (population 299,758). Nottingham is situated on the River Trent, where the river leaves the Midlands to flow across the eastern plains to the Humber, and on the coalfield of the eastern Pennines. It was first an Anglo-Saxon settlement, and then the Normans built a castle on a commanding hill of red sandstone. Nottingham served through the centuries as a market town for the fertile agricultural district round about. In the 16th century, lace was a domestic occupation, but large-scale production came with the invention of factory machinery in the 19th century. The demand for lace and the prosperity of the industry fluctuated with changes in fashion and has declined since Edwardian times. The textile industry has increased the variety of its products to include hosiery, dyeing and knitwear. A certain amount of engineering is also carried on in Nottingham, such as the making of textile machinery, typewriters and bicycles. The city is also concerned with tobacco manufacture.

● **Nottinghamshire** A county (844 square miles) of the north-east Midlands of England. It lies on the eastern flanks of the southern Pennines and contains the lowlands of the middle Trent valley

(Belvoir Vale) and the Idle river near Retford. A half of the land is used for arable crops, a quarter is under permanent grass, and in the west is the famous Sherwood forest — much smaller than its original size. The county has a large section of the Yorkshire, Derbyshire and Nottinghamshire coalfields within its boundaries, particularly round Mansfield (57,598) and Worksop (36,034). Nottingham, the county town, commands the Trent valley, and farther downstream is the agricultural market town of Newark (24,610). These are the principal centres, containing many of the 974,640 population. The county, though about 125 miles from London, is well connected to the capital by fast trains from Newark or Nottingham, and by the A1 road and M1 motorway.

● **oak** The *common oak* (*Quercus pedunculata*), is found almost everywhere in Britain, especially on the clay and loam of southern England. A deciduous tree, 60 to 80 feet in height, with a stout bole and rugged bark, its boughs are crooked and much branched, ending in dense clusters of small, light-brown buds. The leaves are lobed, 2 to 4 inches long; the flowers, produced in April-May, consist of pendulous yellow male catkins, with female flowers borne separately near the ends of twigs. The fruits are acorns in stalked cups. The *durmast oak* (*Quercus sessiliflora*), is found farther west on the Silurian materials of Wales, and its growth habit is more erect. The leaves have no lobes, and the acorns no stalks. The wood is close grained and very durable.

● **Orkney Islands** A group of 90 islands, totalling 376 square miles in area, lying off the north coast of Scotland in latitude 59°N. The islands are composed of Old Red Sandstone, as is the neighbouring mainland of Caithness, from which they are separated by the Pentland Firth. About one third of the Orkneys are inhabited, and most of the population (17,075) are engaged in farming or fishing. Cattle-rearing for beef is the main activity, associated with rotation grass, oats and turnips. The summers are often too cool for the ripening of other cereal crops. The chief fishing port of Stromness (1,616) is noted for its herring and lobsters. Kirkwall (4,618), the chief town, is also on Pamona Island (the principal isle), and is connected with Wick, on the mainland, by a regular air-service. Scapa Flow, in the Orkneys, was formerly famed as the base for the British fleet from 1914 to 1919.

● **otter** The otter has become specialised for hunting in water. Three and a half feet long, it weighs about 20 pounds, has a small head with rounded ears, and is covered with soft grey under-fur mixed with stiffer brown hair. Its fore and hind feet are webbed and its tail acts as a powerful rudder. The mother spends much time training her family of three cubs to swim, dive and hunt. Otters are intelligent and playful, even when adult. Their chief food is fish, and they frequently travel miles to hunt in the sea. They do some damage to game fish in rivers, but this is offset by their killing of eels.

● **owl** All owls feed chiefly on rodents. The *tawny* or *brown owl* is the largest and best known, hunting at night. The *barn* or *screech owl* has a white face and underparts. It often nests in old buildings. The smaller *long-eared owl* is so called because of ear-like tufts of feathers on its head. The *little owl* is only about 8 inches long and hunts by day as well as night.

● **Oxford** An old university town and now, in addition, a modern industrial centre (population 108,564), the City of Oxford stands on a ridge between the Cherwell and the Thames, where the two rivers converge. The University of Oxford was founded in the 12th century and, since that time, has been noted throughout the country, and abroad, as a leading seat of learning. Oxford has many historical associations: in 1642, Charles I made Oxford his headquarters during the Civil War. The ancient college buildings have great charm and are a constant focus for foreign visitors. The university continues to maintain its traditions and high standard of scholarship. Oxford has become famous, too, for its growing industries; pressed-steel works, a vast motor-car factory, and the printing, book-binding and publishing trades, are major examples of the city's commercial life.

● **Oxfordshire** An irregularly shaped county of 749 square miles, extending between the Cotswolds and the London Basin near Reading. Nearly half of this agricultural county is arable land, with barley predominating (14 per cent of the total area). Oxford, the county town at the confluence of the Cherwell and the Thames, is the largest urban centre in a county which is predominantly rural and has a population of 380,814. Another important town is Banbury (29,216).

● **oyster-catcher** This handsome, black-and-white wader is about 16 inches long, with a red beak and pink legs. It is often seen in flocks on the north and west coasts. The oyster-catcher builds a nest on the shore from broken shells, pebbles and seaweed, in which it lays 2 to 4 cream-coloured eggs.

● **Peebles-shire** A mountainous inland county (347 square miles) of Scotland in the Southern Uplands. It includes the upper valley and headwaters of the River Tweed and its tributary, the Lyne. Sheep-rearing, for mutton and wool, is the major occupation, and in the valleys are centres of an old-established woollen industry. Peebles (5,881), the county town, and Innerleithen (2,216) are the two main places, and the total population amounts to only 13,675.

● **Pembrokeshire** A remote county (614 square miles) in south-west Wales. It is bounded by the sea on three sides, and the coastline is indented by St Bride's Bay and the drowned river valley of Milford Haven. With a higher proportion of lowland than most of the other Welsh counties, Pembroke has 33 per cent of its area devoted to arable crops, though permanent grass still covers the greatest amount of land (38 per cent). Besides agriculture, fishing is an important occupation, centred on Milford Haven (13,745), Pembroke (14,092) and Fishguard (4,898), which is also a passenger port for Ireland. Other important towns are St David's (1,595), Haverfordwest (9,101) and Tenby (4,985), and the total county population is 97,295. Milford Haven now has a large oil terminal and refinery.

● **Pennine Chain** The so-called 'backbone' of England, the Pennines extend from the South Tyne valley in the north to the Vale of Trent in the North Midlands. The highest point is Cross Fell (2,930 feet), a limestone mountain dominating the Eden valley. Large areas of the Pennine moors are over 2,000 feet above sea level. The South Pennine Moors are separated from the north by the Aire valley and, though less extensive, also rise to 2,088 feet in Kinder Scout. The Pennines are composed of carboniferous rocks, dipping eastwards from the faulted western margins. The carboniferous limestone formations once provided valuable minerals — e.g., lead, zinc, copper and barytes — but the flanking coal seams have a greater influence on the economy of the country. Now the Pennine moors provide soft water from reservoirs.

● **Perthshire** A large county of 2,493 square miles in central Scotland. The agricultural activities of Perthshire are varied and important; oats and potatoes are grown for industrial purposes; also

Perthshire is an important cattle-, pig- and sheep-rearing county. The lowland by the Firth of Tay, between Perth and Dundee, called the Carse of Gowrie, is the most productive area. The population of 127,138 is mainly concentrated in the lowlands, with Perth (43,051), the chief town, at the tidal limit of the Tay. Other notable centres are Blairgowrie (5,554), Crieff (5,604), Dunblane (4,499) and Aberfoyle (1,133). In addition, there are many small holiday resorts in the mountains, especially Callander (1,769), near the Trossachs.

● **pine** *Pinus sylvestris*, or Scots pine, is an evergreen conifer which, although a native of the Scottish Highlands, has been planted in many parts of Britain. The leaves, or 'needles', 2 to 3 inches long, grow in pairs. The trunk is reddish brown and coarsely fissured. Considerable areas of Britain have been planted with pines and other conifers. The wood is light, durable and easily worked. The tree attains its best development on sandy or dry soils.

● **plane** The plane tree, *Platanus acerifloria*, is not a British native tree and is not known in the wild state, but it has come to be associated with London, since it has proved to be exceedingly tolerant of smoke and fog. The smooth leaves are quickly washed by rain while the outer bark peels off, showing clean, young bark beneath. If allowed to grow freely, the plane tree may attain 90 feet in height. The leaves are large and fine-lobed, the fruits conspicuous hanging balls. It provides a timber highly favoured for furniture making.

● **Plymouth** The largest port on the south-west peninsula of England (population 239,314) and an important naval station. Plymouth is excellently placed, with a deep, sheltered harbour at the drowned confluence of two river valleys, the Tamar and the Plym. This south-Devon port has a traditional connection with ship-owners and seafaring men, and gained its Charter in 1439. In the 16th century, Sir Francis Drake sailed from the harbour on his expeditions against the Spaniards, and a little later the *Mayflower*, with its complement of colonists, sailed for the New World. The naval dockyards at Devonport were begun in 1690, and they contain an arsenal, ship-building and ship-repair yards. It is an important fishing base for the English Channel and Bay of Biscay.

● **Portsmouth** One of the chief ports of the Royal Navy (population 196,973), situated on the eastern bank of the Solent estuary, sheltered from the sea by the Isle of Wight and protected landwards by the chalk ridge of the Portsdown Hills, whose fortifications command the harbour. The city, composed of four towns — Portsea, Landport, Southsea and Portsmouth itself — is almost entirely concerned with the activities of the naval dockyard, which has facilities for building, repairing, arming and provisioning all kinds of warships.

● **rabbit** Rabbits are a serious pest to the farmer, doing enormous damage to crops. Under the 1947 Agriculture Act, farmers are required to keep down rabbits on their land. Myxamatosis, a virulent disease, has in recent years killed many rabbits, but a strain resistant to this disease is again well-established.

● **Radnorshire** A mountainous inland county (471 square miles) of central Wales. It has the smallest total population of any Welsh county, only 18,262, and there are no large towns. The county town, New Radnor, has 2,050 inhabitants.

● **railways** The first public railway to carry passengers opened in 1825 between Stockton and Darlington, though it was primarily meant for coal

transport. The 1840s were the main years for railway construction by numerous competing companies. The primary aim was to link up the large centres of population and join them to London, and gradually the network spread into the rural areas. Some towns virtually owe their existence to the coming of the railway — e.g., Folkestone (the Channel port), Grimsby, Fleetwood, and the railway junctions of Crewe and Swindon. Since the Second World War and nationalisation, considerable modernisation has been put in hand by British Rail: the introduction of many Diesel engines, to replace the old steam locomotives, and the electrification of some of the main lines. The length of track open to passenger traffic has been reduced, principally due to the closing of uneconomic branch lines serving country areas. Use of the railways is declining at present, largely due to the increase in ownership of private cars and other forms of road transport, but great efforts are being made to attract traffic to reorganised freight services and fast, long-distance passenger trains, often with facilities for transporting private cars.

● **Renfrewshire** A small Scottish county (240 square miles), forming part of the western Central Lowlands. It lies along the west banks of the lower course of the Firth of Clyde. The county contains most of the remote Renfrew Heights in the northwest. The majority of the 362,144 inhabitants are engaged in industry. Paisley (95,344) is the cotton-manufacturing town of Scotland, and Port Glasgow (22,399) and Greenock (69,004) on the Firth are noted for ship-building and repairing, together with other forms of engineering and heavy industry.

● **robin** The robin is a plump little bird which frequents our gardens, feeding on insects. The nest is often built in a can or old boot from dead leaves, grass and moss, and then lined with hair. The robin lays 5 to 7 white, red-spotted eggs.

● **Ross and Cromarty** A very large county (3,089 square miles) of northern Scotland. Most of the area is isolated, yet it contains beautiful scenery among the mountains, glens and sea-lochs of the indented coastline. The population is small, only numbering 58,267, and, in the main, widely scattered. Dingwall (4,233), near Cromarty Firth, is the county town, and other notable settlements are: Cromarty (480); Kyle of Lochalsh (1,525), the railway ferry-port for Skye; Ullapool; and Stornoway (5,153), on the Isle of Lewis.

● **Roxburghshire** A border county (666 square miles) of southern Scotland. The main boundary with England lies along the crest of the Cheviot Hills, and the county comprises the drainage basin of the River Teviot, principal tributary of the Tweed, and parts of the middle Tweed valley called Lauderdale. The population totals 42,000 — mostly engaged in farming, but with some employed in the woollen mills of Jedburgh (3,874), the chief town, and Melrose (2,188). Kelso (4,854) and Hawick (16,286) are famous for their important sheep-sales.

● **Rutlandshire** The smallest administrative county (152 square miles) in England. It is primarily concerned with agriculture, since 85 per cent of the total area is productive farmland (50 per cent arable). The population numbers 27,463, and the county town is Oakham (6,411).

● **Salford** The twin town of Manchester, Salford (130,641) is an independent county borough, although it is swallowed up in the western part of the great Manchester conurbation, separated largely by the River Irwell. Salford includes much of the important dockland area associated with the Manchester Ship Canal. Its primary interests are connected with the cotton industry, the manufacture of textile machinery, and the making of heavy machine-tools.

salmon The salmon, one of our largest fish, is prized both for eating and for the sport it provides. The eggs are laid in streams, where the young fish (or 'fry') stay for two years, when they become 5 inches long and are known as 'par'. After about eight months, the silvery 'smolt' go down the rivers to the estuaries for several weeks, to become acclimatised to the salt water. After several years in the sea, salmon return to the rivers as adult fish, 3 to 4 feet long, and make their way up the rivers to spawn.

Sca Fell This, the highest peak (3,310 feet) in England, is part of the central core of the Lake District mountains and is composed of very old volcanic rocks. Sca Fell is one among several peaks which are highly attractive to climbers because of the magnificent views they afford over the Lake District, the Irish Sea and the Isle of Man, which is visible on clear days.

Scilly Isles A group of 48 small granite islands, and numerous rocky reefs, resting on a submarine platform 25 miles from Land's End, in Cornwall. Only five islands are inhabited, the largest being St Mary's, about 2½ square miles in area. Several others are grouped near, after which the other isles in the group diminish in size south-westwards. The islands (population 2,428) enjoy the most equable climate in the British Isles; winter frosts are very rare and the summers are hot, for the islands lie south of the 50° parallel. Sub-tropical plants are grown, and garden roses and fuchsias flower in winter. The economy takes advantage of the mild climate and is based on the cultivation of flowers for the London market. The capital is Hugh Town, on St Mary's.

Scotland The country occupying the northern part of the island of Britain, Scotland extends from the Solway Firth to the Shetland Islands. Its area is 29,795 square miles, including the western islands. Much of Scotland is mountainous and forbidding; in the highland areas, settlement is found round the coast, and most of the 5,227,706 inhabitants are congregated in the Central Lowlands, extending from east to west between the Grampians and the Southern Uplands. Roman conquests extended into Scotland in A.D. 80, but the invaders had left by the close of the second century.

The name Scotland, or Scotia, derives from an Irish tribe which migrated to Argyll in the 6th century. From the same direction, St Columbia re-introduced Christianity, and by the 9th century the Celtic people of the north-west, the indigenous Picts and the Scots, had become united politically. Meanwhile, the Anglo-Saxons had penetrated into the eastern lowlands, but the two peoples of differing origins amalgamated to form the Kingdom of Scotland, with its capital at Dunkeld, Dunfermline and then Stirling. There was continuous conflict with England for 300 years, until at last a boundary was drawn through the Cheviot Hills; but raids were carried out from both sides, right into the 17th century. The two kingdoms were united by James VI of Scotland, who inherited the English crown in 1603, but Scotland continued to be independent, with its own government and Reformed Church. It was not until a century later, in 1707, that the Act of Union combined the two countries to form the Kingdom of Great Britain. Although benefiting economically from its union with England, Scotland retains many of its own institutions in local government, worship, the law and education. A number of people still speak the old Gaelic language in the communities of the highland glens and western islands — 76,500 all told. Most Scots are intensely proud of their inheritance and, though many have emigrated to the Commonwealth, membership of their family or clan remains important.

Today local government is vested in 33 civil counties and several large burghs (with Edinburgh the administrative capital). Eighty-three per cent

A view of the gardens on Princes Street, the main street of the ancient Scottish capital, Edinburgh

of the inhabitants live in urban settlements. This indicates in some measure the importance of industry in the economy of the country. Suitable agricultural land is limited to the lowlands, only occurring in very small patches in the highland zone. The latter, however, has very attractive scenery, and the resultant tourist industry brings considerable wealth to the Highlands, in addition to industries based on hydro-electric power, and, more recently, nuclear energy. The coalfields of the lowlands still support the largest number of people and, as in England, the manufactured products are exported to pay for foreign foodstuffs and raw materials.

Selkirkshire A small Scottish county (267 square miles) of the Southern Uplands, lying between Peebles and Roxburgh. It is nearly all high moorland, and contains only a short stretch of the Tweed valley in its north-east corner. The population of 20,868 are concentrated in the valley, in the largest woollen manufacturing centre of the region, Galashiels (12,605), and in the county town of Selkirk (5,687). Only small communities are to be found in the remote south-western areas; these are mainly concerned with sheep-farming, and catering for visitors to the beautiful St Mary's Loch and the Scott country. The large Ettrick Forest is found south of the River.

Severn River Rising on the slopes of Plynlimon (2,469 feet) in central Wales, the River Severn, 200 miles in length, follows a variable course to the Bristol Channel. It leaves the narrow valley of its straight upper course in the Vale of Powis, near the English border, to wind its way across the Shropshire Plain. At Shrewsbury the large meanders of the Severn nearly encircle the town, but farther east the course straightens and, with increased speed, the river flows through the Severn Gorge, between the Wrekin and the South Shropshire Hills. At this point the Severn is spanned by the first iron bridge, which was constructed in 1779. From Ironbridge the river follows a southerly direction across the western Midlands, to be joined by the Teme near Worcester and the Avon at Tewkesbury. This stretch of the Severn, and the land bordering the two tributaries, constitutes one of the richest agricultural districts of the British Isles. The mild climate of this sheltered area has encouraged market-gardening and fruit farming on a large scale. At Gloucester the Severn becomes tidal and, thereafter, describes many pronounced meanders before widening to form an estuary, now bridged near Chepstow, and bordered by the Vale of Berkeley.

Shannon River The longest river (224 miles) in the British Isles. The Shannon rises in the Iron Mountains of Eire, very near the Northern Ireland border. The small stream runs into Lough Allan, before commencing its course southwards across the central Irish plain. At the southern end of Lough Derg, the Shannon valley narrows, the gradient steepens and the river flows through a series of rapids at Killaloe. The head of water of 100 feet has been utilised by a hydro-electric power station at Ardnacrusha, from which electricity is distributed to the chief towns of Eire. Limerick stands at the tidal head of the Shannon estuary; there the valley turns westwards, extending for over 50 miles to the shores of the Atlantic Ocean.

Sheffield The chief centre of the special steel and cutlery industry in the British Isles (population 519,703), Sheffield is situated on the River Don, a tributary of the Ouse, where the river leaves the South Pennine Moors for the plain. It is in the centre of the great Yorkshire, Derbyshire and Nottinghamshire coalfields, in which iron ore was also mined, by using 'bell-pits'. This gave rise to a local iron industry, formerly based on water power and local charcoal. Soon there occurred specialisation in the making of knives and swords, and for these Sheffield became famous even during the Middle Ages. In 1853, the Bessemer converter for the large-scale production of steel was invented and, with the decline in the local supply of ore, higher-grade ores were imported from Spain and Sweden by rail and canal. The steel industry continued to expand, the products keeping pace with the times as swords and cutlasses were replaced by guns and shells. In addition, with the development in technical processes, special kinds of steel — e.g., stainless and special hard alloy types — were introduced to serve a variety of needs, as well as silverware. The continued production of a large number of specialised goods by highly skilled craftsmen has ensured increasing development and progress in Sheffield. The countryside to the west of the city is part of the Peak District National Park, and the built-up area has expanded southward into Derbyshire.

Shetland Islands (Zetland) A group of about one hundred islands situated 50 miles beyond the Orkneys, the Shetlands form the most northerly part of the British Isles. Sheep-rearing dominates the agricultural economy, and the islands are famous for their domestic woollen and knitted hosiery industry. The Shetlands were originally peopled from Scandinavia, and many of the old

'The Gateway to the World' is an apt title for Southampton – the great sea port on Britain's south coast

original settlements can be found. Herring fishing, another important industry, is based on Lerwick (6,107), the chief town. The total population is 17,298. Between the Shetlands and Orkneys lies Fair Isle, which is famous for its brightly patterned, hand-knitted articles, and also provides a bird sanctuary.

shipbuilding For the United Kingdom, a famous sea-faring nation since the late 15th century, ship-building has always been an important industry. In the days of wooden ships, building yards existed in many of the small ports all round the coasts. The essential requirements were a navigable waterway and ready supply of materials. When local timber was exhausted, it was imported from the Continent, especially southern Norway. The largest ship-building centres were the Thames and the Tyne, where there was constant demand for ships — merchantmen in the Thames and colliers in the Tyne. During the 19th century, the substitution of iron and then steel for wood meant that the ship-building yards near the iron and steel centres flourished and grew in importance at the expense of those places which were remote from sources of building materials. Hence the Tyne, Tees and Clyde soon became the major shipbuilding areas, and these also carry out much of the repair work. Other centres are Barrow, Belfast and Birkenhead.

shrew These tiny relatives of the mole can be distinguished from mice by their pointed snouts, shorter tails and shorter ears. They are mainly nocturnal and eat enormous quantities of insects, slugs, snails and other pests.

Shropshire The central English county of the Welsh borderlands (The Marches). Its 1,347 square miles contain the central part of the Severn valley and an eastward spur of the Cambrian Mountains, comprising the Longmynd and the Clee Hills. Shropshire is essentially an agricultural county, with 39 per cent of its area under perma-nent grass and 42 per cent used for arable crops. A distinctive breed of sheep is named after the Clun Hills on the western borders. The 336,934 inhabitants are mainly rural, with Shrewsbury (56,140), the county town, centrally situated.

Snowdon The highest mountain (3,560 feet) of England and Wales. It is the centre of a range of mountains in North Wales. Snowdon is a mass of volcanic rock eroded by glaciers on all sides, so that there are narrow, jagged ridges between deep, basin-like *cwms*. Some of the corries contain small lakes, or *llyns*. The ridge on the northern side of Snowdon is broader and is followed by a rack-and-pinion railway from Llanberis to the summit.

Somersetshire A large county (1,613 square miles) of south-west England. Somerset contains very many different types of landscape — e.g., the bleak heights of eastern Exmoor; the flat, marshy plains bordering Bridgwater Bay (the 'Somerset Levels'); the limestone massif of the Mendip Hills, and the deep, wooded gorges of the Avon near Bath. Over half the county is under permanent grass, with a much smaller proportion used for crops. This predominance of pasture-land is re-flected in the number of cattle, for the county is third in the country in its total of cattle and calves, and it has the greatest number of milking cows, indicating a high degree of specialisation in dairy-ing. The population numbers 681,974, and the chief towns include Bath (84,545), Taunton (37,373), Bridgwater (26,598) and Weston-super-Mare (50,492), a popular coastal resort.

Southampton The most extensive passenger port (population 214,826) on the south coast of Eng-land, Southampton is built on the peninsula of land between the tidal reaches of the Test and Itchen. From the confluence of the rivers to the Solent, the estuary known as Southampton Water is over a mile wide. Docks line both river water-fronts, and access to them by ocean-going vessels is assisted by multiple tides which lengthen the period of high water. The port accommodates the world's largest ocean liners, and is the terminus of the Cunard White Star ships which disembark passengers from North America for the fast train service over the short land route to London. Other shipping lines, serving the West Indies, South Africa and the Far East, use Southampton to avoid the difficult, time-consuming navigation of the Channel and the Thames, and thus it serves as an outport of London. Many new light industries have been established in the city.

Southern Uplands Mountains of southern Scot-land which extend right across the country. The highest peak is Merrick (2,764 feet) in the south-west, but several other points are over 2,000 feet. For the most part the Southern Uplands are com-posed of Silurian rocks, but some of the higher peaks and individual ridges, such as the Pentland Hills, consist of intrusive igneous rocks.

sparrow The *house sparrow*, related to the finches, is a common bird in both town and country. Intelligent and hardy, it raises several broods a year, nesting in large colonies. Sparrows often do much damage to young plants in gardens and, in the autumn, to cornfields. The *tree sparrow* is brighter in colour and more graceful. The *hedge sparrow*, or *dunnock*, is not a true sparrow at all, and is distinguished by its thin, pointed beak, designed for insect-eating.

Staffordshire A county (1,154 square miles) of the English Midlands, extending from the southern Pennines across the uplands of the Midland Gate, which separates southern England from the Che-shire Plain and the north. Staffordshire contains two major industrial areas located on coalfields; in the north, Stoke-on-Trent is the chief town of the Potteries and, in the south, Wolverhampton and West Bromwich (166,626) are part of the 'Black Country'. These two densely populated areas account for a large proportion of the 1,856,890 inhabitants.

starling About 8 inches long, this bird has a short tail and black plumage with a purplish, almost metallic, sheen. It is a common visitor to our gardens. In wintertime, thousands of starlings may roost in one place, often on a building, flying out during the day to feed on insects in the countryside.

Stirlingshire An irregularly shaped county (451 square miles) of central Scotland, extending from the eastern shores of Loch Lomond to the head of the Firth of Forth near Grangemouth. It contains the Campsie Fells and Lennox Hills, surrounded by lowlands of the Forth valley and of the tributary valleys of the Clyde, and the mountains of the Ben Lomond block. The agricultural activities are varied, but the limited permanent pasture repre-sents the largest area of improved land. Arable crops are grown on favourable soils on the Forth plains. Two large towns, Stirling (29,769), on the Forth, and Falkirk (37,587) share a good propor-tion of the 208,956 population. Stirling is the site of an ancient castle and of Scotland's newest University.

stoat A slender, red-brown creature, 16 inches long from its nose to its black tail-end, the stoat changes its coat to white in winter. It is very agile and hunts for sport as well as food. The stoat can be a serious nuisance to poultry farmers, but it also kills many rabbits and other rodent pests. Its rela-tive, the *weasel*, is smaller, lighter in colour, has no black tip to its tail and does not change to white in winter. The *pole-cat* and rare *pine-marten* are also relatives of the stoat.

Stoke-on-Trent A conurbation of the Stafford-shire Potteries (population 265,153), the City of Stoke-on-Trent now includes the neighbouring towns of Hanley, Burslem, Longton, Tunstall and Fenton. The pottery industry began with the use of local clay, found in the coal seams of the North Staffordshire coalfield, to produce ordinary earthenware. This was often carried out to supple-ment the earnings of farmers on comparatively poor small-holdings, and thus the organisation was essentially on a domestic basis. The growth of the pottery industry may be attributed to Josiah Wedg-wood, who built in 1769 the famous 'Etruria' factory, making high-grade porcelain. He also encouraged the construction of the Trent and Mersey Canal, connecting Stoke with Liverpool for the cheaper transport of imported finer clays. Today the city is much cleaner than of old, due to the introduction of electrically fired kilns.

Suffolk The second most important agricultural county (1,499 square miles) of East Anglia. It comprises roughly the land east of the chalk ridge of the East Anglian Heights, between the rivers Waveney and Stour, which form its boundaries. Much of the area is extremely fertile and 63 per cent supports arable crops. The climate encourages the growth of cereals — 12 per cent of the land grows wheat and 21 per cent barley, while sugar-beet, with 6 per cent, is also important. The population of 544,725 is mainly rural but there are several notable larger settlements: Bury St Edmunds (25,629), a market town in West Suffolk, and, in East Suffolk, Ipswich (122,814) on the Orwell estuary; Lowestoft (52,182), the famous fishing port in the north-east; and several growing holiday resorts on the coast, such as Southwold (1,992), Aldeburgh (2,793) and Felixstowe (18,888).

● **Sunderland** An industrial port (population 216,892) on the north-east coast of England. The town is at the mouth of the River Wear, which is bridged at this point across the steep-sided valley. Sunderland's main function is the exporting of coal, both coastwise to London and to foreign countries. There are large shipyards, specialising in collier and oil-tanker construction, and associated industries, such as the production of marine engines, machinery and ropes. Paper and flour mills, breweries and glass-ware works are other industries in the new industrial estates.

● **Surrey** One of the 'Home Counties' of south-east England, Surrey's 650 square miles extend from the winding banks of the Thames above London to the central part of the Weald. The county includes a long stretch of the chalky North Downs, which are dissected by the rivers Wey and Mole, flowing northwards to join the Thames. The soils are very variable, directly resulting from the numerous underlying rocks, but, nevertheless, at least 25 per cent of the land supports arable crops. Fast and regular electric train services have extended the London dormitories to Surrey towns such as Woking (75,771), Guildford (56,887), Dorking (22,354) and Reigate (56,088), and these centres account for a large proportion of the county's 999,588 population.

● **Sussex** An extensive county (1,457 square miles) of southern England, covering much of the fashionable South Coast. Most of the 1,241,332 population are concentrated in the towns along the coast, such as Brighton and Hove, Worthing (82,210), Eastbourne (70,495) and Hastings (72,169), but settlement is also marked along the railways, especially between Brighton and London. Older centres inland include Chichester (20,547), Arundel (2,392), Horsham (30,700) and Lewes (14,015), while the new town and airport at Gatwick are sited on the northern county boundary.

● **Sutherland** An extensive county (2,028 square miles) of northern Scotland, bordered on the north-west by the Atlantic Ocean and on the south-east by the North Sea. The county is one of the most thinly peopled areas in the British Isles, with a total population of only 13,053.

● **swallow** The swallow arrives in Britain in early April. It is a graceful bird, dark steel-blue in colour, with a long forked and pointed tail. It is often confused with the *house-martin*, which is smaller and has a less pointed tail. Both birds feed on insects while in flight, and build nests of mud, lined with grass and feathers, but that of the swallow is open at the top, while the house-martin builds under the eaves.

● **Swansea** The second port and industrial centre (population 172,566) of South Wales. Swansea stands at the mouth of the River Tawe, being the focus of valley routeways in the western part of the coalfield. Coal export is the chief function of the port, but handling of imported pig-iron and oil is also important. Metallurgical industries in Swansea include tinplate, copper, nickel and zinc works, in addition to the more usual iron and steel. Modern development is represented by the installation of oil refineries, and ship-repairing is also important. Swansea is a long-established settlement — called in Welsh, Abertawe — and it has a Norman castle.

● **sycamore** *Acer pseudo-platanus* is a native of central Europe which became naturalised in Britain at the time of the Tudors. It is a fast-growing tree with large, dark green, five-lobed leaves. The fruits, which hang in large clusters, consist of two single-seeded, winged portions which can be carried short distances by the wind and germinate easily.

● **Tay River** The longest river (117 miles) in Scotland. The Tay rises on Ben Lui (3,708 feet), and from Crianlarich flows in a north-easterly direction. This glaciated upper valley, deep and steep-sided, is occupied for much of its length by Loch Tay. Below Aberfeldy, the river turns southwards and, swollen by the waters of the Tummel from the north, flows to Dunkeld, where it leaves the highlands for the plains. Along its winding path across the vale of Strathmore, the Tay is joined by the Isla on the left bank and the Almond on the right. At Perth the river cuts between the Sidlaw and Ochil Hills, becoming tidal near its confluence with its longest tributary, the Earn. The Firth of Tay is crossed by the Tay Bridge, over 2 miles long, which carries the east-coast railway line, passing through Dundee at the northern end of the bridge, on its way to Aberdeen.

● **Teesside (see Middlesbrough)**

● **textile industry** The manufacture of woollen goods has been an important branch of the textile industry in the British Isles for hundreds of years. Spinning and weaving of woollen cloth was carried out in homes in many parts of the country, using local raw materials and supplying local needs. In the Middle Ages, many of the large market towns, especially in the West Country and East Anglia, had small woollen factories serving the neighbourhood. With the Industrial Revolution, woollen manufacturing became centralised in places where coal for fuel, soft water for washing and dyeing, and large quantities of imported raw wool, could be assembled together easily for processing. The

Milford Haven Oil Refinery, South Wales, showing (foreground) the marine terminal, with its 3,500-foot approach causeway

Salisbury Cathedral is particularly renowned for its spire, which reaches a height of 404 feet

West Riding of Yorkshire became the largest woollen and worsted manufacturing area. The cotton industry was introduced into Britain in the 17th century and became firmly established in Lancashire, where the raw cotton could be imported easily through Liverpool and Manchester. The linen industry was based on Belfast, near the locally grown supplies of flax, while the silk industry, declining since the introduction of many new synthetic fibres, was located in many scattered centres, which usually had a small woollen factory and a supply of skilled labour. Of all the textile industries, cotton is by far the largest. Today there are many man-made textiles, largely related to the chemical industry.

At Llangollen, in Wales, the Eisteddfod has become an international event

● **Thames River** The longest river (209 miles) in England, rising in the Cotswold Hills, only 15 miles from the Bristol Channel, the Thames flows in an easterly direction, joined by many tributaries — e.g., the Cherwell at Oxford, and the Kennet at Reading. Between these two, the Thames cuts through the chalk separating the White Horse Hills from the Chiltern Hills by a narrow, steep-sided valley known as the Goring Gap. Nearer London the river is joined by the Colne, and the Wey and Mole flowing in from the Downs. In its lower reaches, the Thames is a placid, slow-moving river, controlled in many places by locks to facilitate navigation and flowing through agricultural districts of varying kinds. At Teddington, 69 miles upstream from the mouth, the Thames becomes tidal. The mean tidal range of 21 feet at London Bridge permits ships to penetrate far inland from the sea, bringing passengers and merchandise to the Pool of London. The stretch of the river downstream from the Pool of London is a busy highway for all kinds of vessels, ranging from pleasure-steamers to barges, tugs and cargo vessels. With the increase in tonnage of ocean-going ships, docks have been built downstream from London at Tilbury and Gravesend, and thus large vessels can avoid the difficult navigation of the meanders and the narrow channel up to the London docks. Along its lower reaches, several oil harbours have been established.

● **thrush** The *song-thrush*, with its speckled breast and lovely song, is a popular bird in our gardens. Its mud-lined nest, containing sky-blue, black spotted eggs, is built in hedges and shrubs. Although the song-thrush may steal fruit, it helps by eating many slugs and snails, cracking their shells at a special stone, or 'anvil'.

● **tit** The tits (or titmice) are small, sprightly, acro-batic birds, all useful insect-hunters. The *blue tit* is a welcome visitor to most gardens. It nests in holes in trees or posts. The *great tit*, longer and less colourful than the blue tit, is also common in gardens. The tiny *long-tailed tit* builds a wonderful roofed nest of feathers, in which it may lay as many as 15 eggs.

● **toad** The *common toad* has a dry, warty skin, and is heavier and more squat in build than the frog. It lives on land, except when breeding, and hides in crevices or under stones during the day, coming out at night to catch insects, and eat worms and slugs.

● **Tweed River** The river rises on the slopes of Hart Fell (2,651 feet) in the Southern Uplands of Scotland, and flows nearly a hundred miles in a general easterly direction to the North Sea. The upper course of the river, winding considerably in a steep-sided valley, passes a number of woollen manufacturing towns. This industry is based on the sheep-rearing of the surrounding hills, and the river gives its name to the famous tweed produced in the region. The Tweed has one large tributary, the Teviot, while Kelso is noted for its sheep-sales. Downstream the river passes through a prosperous agricultural area, and for about 20 miles of its course the river forms the boundary between England and Scotland. At the mouth of the Tweed stands the fortress town of Berwick-upon-Tweed, in Northumberland.

● **Tyrone** The largest county (1,218 square miles) of Northern Ireland, which lies inland, extending westwards from Lough Neagh. The county is sparsely populated, with most of the 136,040 inhabitants centred in the towns of Omagh (10,350), Dungannon (6,494), Cookstown (4,964) and Strabane (7,786).

● **Ulster** The old province of Ulster (3,093 square miles) includes Northern Ireland (an integral part of the United Kingdom) and three counties in the Irish Republic. Of these, Donegal has a very narrow land connection with the rest of Eire, and most of its communications with the capital, Dublin, must pass through Northern Ireland. Some of the best Irish tweeds come from Donegal. The other two southern Irish counties of Ulster adjoin the more productive area of Leinster.

● **Wales** A principality and integral part of Great Britain, the 8,006 square miles of Wales are in the form of a broad peninsula projecting out between the Irish Sea and the Bristol Channel. Its landward boundary extends from the estuary of the Dee to the mouth of the Wye, if Monmouthshire is included. Much of Wales is mountainous country, part of the 'Highland Zone' of the British Isles, and the only lowlands of note are the island of Anglesey and the Lleyn Peninsula in the north, and the southern plains of Pembroke, Carmarthen and Glamorgan.

Wales was first peopled in the Bronze Age by Celtic tribes, who were gradually isolated from their Cornish and Scottish kinsmen by the continued pressure westwards of the Anglo-Saxons. Before this, Wales had been subjugated by the Romans in A.D. 78. In Norman times, the country was attacked repeatedly, the stages of conquest being marked by the numerous Norman castles situated in the borderlands and along the south coast. Owing to the difficulty of communication within the peninsula, Wales never became an independent state, yet the retention of the Welsh tongue has fostered a strong national spirit. The English settled in the valleys and established lines of trade and commerce with their homeland, and thus Wales became linked economically with England after the creation of the first Prince of Wales in 1301. There is a current wish among many Welsh people for some greater measure of freedom and self-government, with a corresponding increase in the use of the Welsh language and the maintenance of old traditions.

The country is divided into thirteen counties for the purposes of local administration, and the total population is 2,723,596. Most of these are concentrated in the two industrial areas which have developed on the South Wales and the Flintshire coalfields. The central part of the country is very thinly populated.

- **Warwickshire** A county (983 square miles) of the English Midlands, comprising the upper part of the Avon valley, a tributary of the Severn, the foothills of the Jurassic limestone country between the Cotswolds and the Northampton Heights, and part of the industrial 'Black Country'. The lowlands near the Avon are very fertile and have the greater share of the arable land, which amounts to 42 per cent of the county area. The population of 2,079,799 includes the city of Birmingham and neighbouring urban areas located on the coalfield in the north-west of the county. Other important centres are Coventry, Rugby (59,372), Leamington (44,989) and Warwick (18,289), with Stratford-on-Avon (19,449), Shakespeare's birthplace, the premier tourist town for foreign visitors.

- **West Lothian** A small county of central Scotland bordering the southern shores of the Firth of Forth and reaching inland for about 15 miles. It contains prosperous agricultural lowlands and also some interior uplands. The population of 108,474 is concentrated mainly along the plains, in Linlithgow (5,685) — the birthplace of Mary, Queen of Scots — and Bo'ness (12,858), an industrial port.

- **Westmorland** A rugged upland county (789 square miles) of north-west England. Most of the county lies above 600 feet and contains many of the Lake District mountains, the fells of Shap and a long stretch of the North Pennine Moors. Sheep- and cattle-rearing predominate in the agricultural economy, and most of the 72,724 population are scattered. The largest town is Kendal (21,572), which has superseded the old county town of Appleby, which, though receiving its Charter in 1179, still has a population of only 1,946.

- **whisky** An intoxicating spirit produced by distillation from malted barley. Whisky is made mainly in Scotland and Ireland. The distilleries are not concentrated in any special area, but may be found in most of the large Scottish burghs and in many of the small rural towns, especially those on the eastern side of Scotland, in the chief barley-growing regions. Whisky, the traditional drink of Scotland, is heavily taxed in the United Kingdom, but it is a very valuable export commodity, particularly to countries in the dollar-area. Good 'Scotch' whisky is in great demand in the United States and France.

- **Wigtownshire** A county in the extreme south-west of Scotland. Most of its 487 square miles are lowland, and part of the county — the Rhinn — is nearly separated from the mainland by the sea-loch Ryan and Luce Bay. The Mull of Galloway is only 20 miles from Northern Ireland across North Channel. Wigtownshire is an agricultural county, and a special breed of cattle, the belted Galloways, originated in the district. The small population of 27,335 is scattered, and the principal towns are Wigtown (1,118), a market town, and Stranraer (9,853), a packet station for Ireland.

- **Wiltshire** A large agricultural county (1,345 square miles) of central southern England. It extends from the upper Thames valley in the north, around Cricklade, to Cranborne Chase in the south and includes most of the Marlborough Downs, Salisbury Plain (containing Stonehenge) and the upper valleys of the Bristol Avon, the Vale of Malmesbury, and the Salisbury Avon rivers. Forty per cent of the land is arable, a third of this growing barley; and over a third is permanent grassland, supporting herds of dairy cows and large numbers of pigs and sheep. Most of the 486,048 population is rural, but there are several important towns, notably Salisbury (35,471) and Swindon (90,830, the railway centre), and the market towns of Marlborough (6,031), Warminster (13,593), Chippenham (18,662), Trowbridge (19,245) and Devizes (10,170), which latter have some industry, the last being the county headquarters.

- **Windermere** The longest lake (10 miles) of the Lake District and the largest (9 square miles) in England. Windermere occupies a narrow valley (as do most of the mountain valley lakes) on the southern side of the Cumbrian Mountains.

- **Wolverhampton** A large, and the westernmost, industrial town (population 268,847) of the Birmingham conurbation. Wolverhampton, lying just to the west of the South Staffordshire-Cannock Chase coalfield, owes its size to rapid development of industry, based on coal, after the Industrial Revolution. It owes its supremacy over the other satellites to its favourable position on the Midland canal network. Its specialised manufactures include cars, motor-cycles and bicycles, and metal goods of all kinds, particularly those made of copper and tin.

- **Worcestershire** A Midland county (699 square miles) of England occupying the plains of the Severn and Avon rivers. Primarily an agricultural county, with 42 per cent of the land arable and 35 per cent permanent grass, Worcestershire is the second county in England for acreage of orchards and small fruit (particularly apples), and third for hop production. The Vale of Evesham is the main fruit-growing area. The total population is 692,605. Some dwell in the urban districts in the north of the county, adjoining the industrial coalfields, but the minor industrial towns of Kidderminster (47,225), Redditch (40,775), and Worcester itself (73,445), house a high proportion.

- **wren** The wren is a very small brown bird weighing about ⅓ oz. The nest is a round ball with a small opening in the side, built near the ground.

- **yew** *Taxus baccata* is an evergreen tree with a much divided trunk and very dark-green, narrow leaves about 1 inch long. Male and female flowers are borne on separate trees, and the fruit is a seed surrounded by a fleshy red anis. The yew grows wild in abundance on the chalk and limestone of southern England, but is uncommon elsewhere. It is the only common tree to retain its old British name in modern English.

- **York** An historic city (population 104,500) of northern England, east of the Pennines. York stands at the old head of navigation of the River Ouse, commanding the corridor of lowland between the Pennines and the North York Moors. Founded as the Roman station of Eboracum in A.D. 71, it has always benefited from being on the main eastern routeway to Scotland. Constantine the Great was proclaimed Emperor there in A.D. 306, and York was the capital of Northumbria in the 7th century. The city was a major centre of the wool trade in the medieval period, when it was the focal point of the surrounding countryside and had direct access to the sea. At that time, too, York was a great ecclesiastical centre, being the seat of an archbishop, as it is today. The magnificent Minster dominates the narrow, winding streets, a fitting capital for the arch-diocese. The city lost much of its eminence in Tudor times, and it largely remains a quiet cultural centre with a new university. It is well suited to be the county town of Yorkshire, as it stands at the corner of the three Ridings. It has a considerable railway and light engineering industry. The making of chocolate and confectionery is the most important industry. A notable feature of the city is its Georgian mansions.

- **Yorkshire** The largest county in England, with an area of 6,090 square miles. For administrative purposes it is divided into three units: North Riding, East Riding and West Riding. Yorkshire covers a major portion of the north of England, and contains within its boundaries many varied types of countryside. The county contains a densely populated industrial area in the West Riding, which is chiefly engaged in woollen manufacturing, coalmining and iron- and steel-making. These occupy a large proportion of the 5,047,567 population in such towns as Leeds, Bradford, Huddersfield (130,964), Sheffield, Wakefield (59,650) and Barnsley (75,330). Other large centres of population are Teesside and Hull, with York, the old historic city, at the junction of the three Ridings. Northallerton (8,750) and Beverley (17,134) are the administrative centres of the North and East Ridings. Doncaster (82,505) is the main transport centre.

Windsor's clustered, whitewashed buildings, narrow bridge over the Thames, and towering castle in the background, help make it a great attraction for tourists

Europe

To understand the precise meaning of the word 'Europe', one must refer far back to the Assyrians, who divided the then-known world into two parts; the land towards the rising sun was named 'acu' (light), while the land over which the sun set was named 'ereb' (dark). The Greeks adopted these terms, modified, as Asia and Europe, and at first they were applied only to the coasts of Turkey and Greece respectively, though the two names were later retained, even when the full extent of both continents had been revealed.

Europe, with a total area of slightly less than 4 million square miles, is the second smallest of the seven continents. It adjoins the sea on three sides — north, west and south; only on the east does it have a land boundary — with Asia. Traditionally this boundary follows the Ural Mountains, the Ural River and the Caucasus. It has often been suggested that Europe is merely a peninsula of Asia, yet its history, peoples and cultures are quite different from those of Asia, even if some of the early re-peopling of Europe came from western Asia. Thus one is perfectly justified in considering Europe as a completely independent continent both physically and culturally.

The coast of Europe is very irregular, for deep seas and shallow inlets separate, in whole or in part, at least a third of the area of the Continent into islands and peninsulas. The largest islands are Great Britain, Ireland, Sicily, Sardinia, Corsica and Crete, and — a special case — Iceland. There are also many large peninsulas — from north to south: Kola, Finland, Scandinavia, Jutland, Iberia and Italy, and finally the Balkan-Greek area.

The seas and inlets to the north and west comprise the deep waters of the Bay of Biscay and the Norwegian Trench, with the shallower waters of the English Channel, the North and the Baltic Seas. However, the Mediterranean Sea to the south is really two large areas, the western portion to the north of the eastern, and both having relatively very deep portions — the Tyrrhenian and Ionian Seas — while the Adriatic is a relatively shallow, partially enclosed, northern offshoot.

As with the coastline and adjacent seas, so the geological layout of the land is varied and complex, while the story of the latest events of erosion and deposition which have modelled the present scenery has a fascination of its own.

The rocks within Europe represent virtually all the ages known to modern geological science. The oldest, the Pre-Cambrian rocks, are to be found in the Kola peninsula, in Finland, and in parts of Norway and Sweden, as the very core of the Fenno-Scandian Shield. Later movements of mountain

Wild Animals and Plants

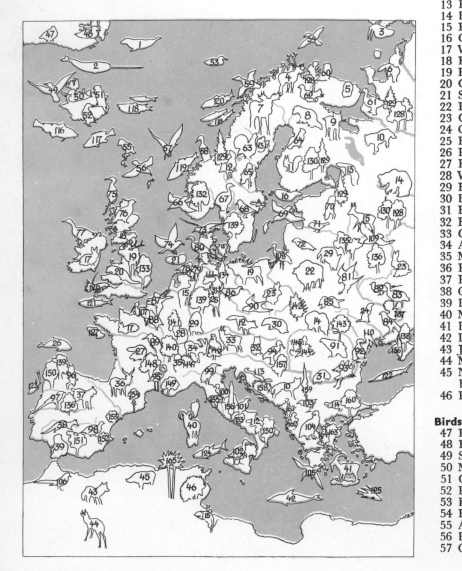

Mammals
1 Harp seal
2 Narwhal
3 Walrus
4 Reindeer
5 Lemming
6 Arctic fox
7 Elk
8 Glutton
9 Lynx
10 Wolf
11 Squirrel
12 Fox
13 Pine marten
14 Brown bear
15 Roe deer
16 Grey seal
17 Wild rabbit
18 Ermine
19 Red deer
20 Otter
21 Seal
22 European bison
23 Common hare
24 Ground squirrel
25 Fallow deer
26 Porpoise
27 Polecat
28 Wildcat
29 European wild boar
30 Badger
31 Hedgehog
32 Hamster
33 Chamois
34 Alpine ibex
35 Marmot
36 Pyrenean ibex
37 Pardine lynx
38 Genet
39 Barbary ape
40 Mouflon
41 Bezoar goat
42 Dolphin
43 Jackal
44 Mhorr gazelle
45 North African wild boar
46 Porcupine

Birds
47 Ptarmigan
48 Eider duck
49 Skua
50 Merganser
51 Gyrfalcon
52 Razor-billed auk
53 Red-throated loon
54 Fulmar
55 Atlantic puffin
56 Black-backed gull
57 Glaucous gull
58 Guillemot
59 Velvet scoter
60 Snowy owl
61 White-fronted goose
62 Black grouse
63 Capercaillie
64 Waxwing
65 Bullfinch
66 Yellow-legged gull
67 Greylag
68 Brambling
69 Great black-backed gull
70 Sparrow hawk
71 Blue titmouse
72 Crossbill
73 Common tern
74 Herring gull
75 Gannet
76 Red grouse
77 Brant goose
78 Oyster-catcher
79 Avocet
80 Sheldrake
81 Red-footed falcon
82 Pallas' sand grouse
83 Bustard
84 Pallid harrier
85 Hooded crow
86 Pheasant
87 Mallard duck
88 Partridge
89 Heron
90 Peregrine falcon
91 Golden eagle
92 Cormorant
93 Egret
94 Spoonbill
95 Flamingo
96 Pygmy owl
97 Blue magpie
98 Pin-tailed sand grouse
99 Bittern
100 Bald coot
101 Red-legged partridge
102 Glossy ibis
103 Pygmy moorhen
104 Griffon vulture
105 Caspian tern
106 Mauretanian magpie
107 White stork
108 Black stork
109 Buzzard
110 Pelican

Reptiles and Amphibians
111 Common European viper
112 Green lizard
113 Aesculapius snake
114 Land tortoise
115 Chameleon

Fishes and other marine life
116 Cod
117 Rosefish
118 Herring
119 Coal-fish
120 Cusk
121 Mackerel
122 Sturgeon
123 Sardine
124 Tuna
125 Flying fish
126 Lobster
127 Oyster

Plants
128 Birch
129 Spruce
130 Common pine
131 Cowberry
132 Beech
133 Ash
134 Juniper
135 Willow
136 Durmast oak
137 Sunflower
138 Elm
139 Common oak
140 Hornbeam
141 Fir
142 Larch
143 Austrian pine
144 Horseradish
145 Pasqueflower
146 Swiss pine
147 Edelweiss
148 Aspen
149 Olive tree
150 Chestnut
151 Cork oak
152 Orange tree
153 Lemon tree
154 Aleppo pine
155 Stone pine
156 Cypress
157 Lilac
158 Broom
159 Serbian spruce
160 Horse chestnut
161 Oleander
162 Thyme
163 Olive tree
164 Agave
165 Date palm

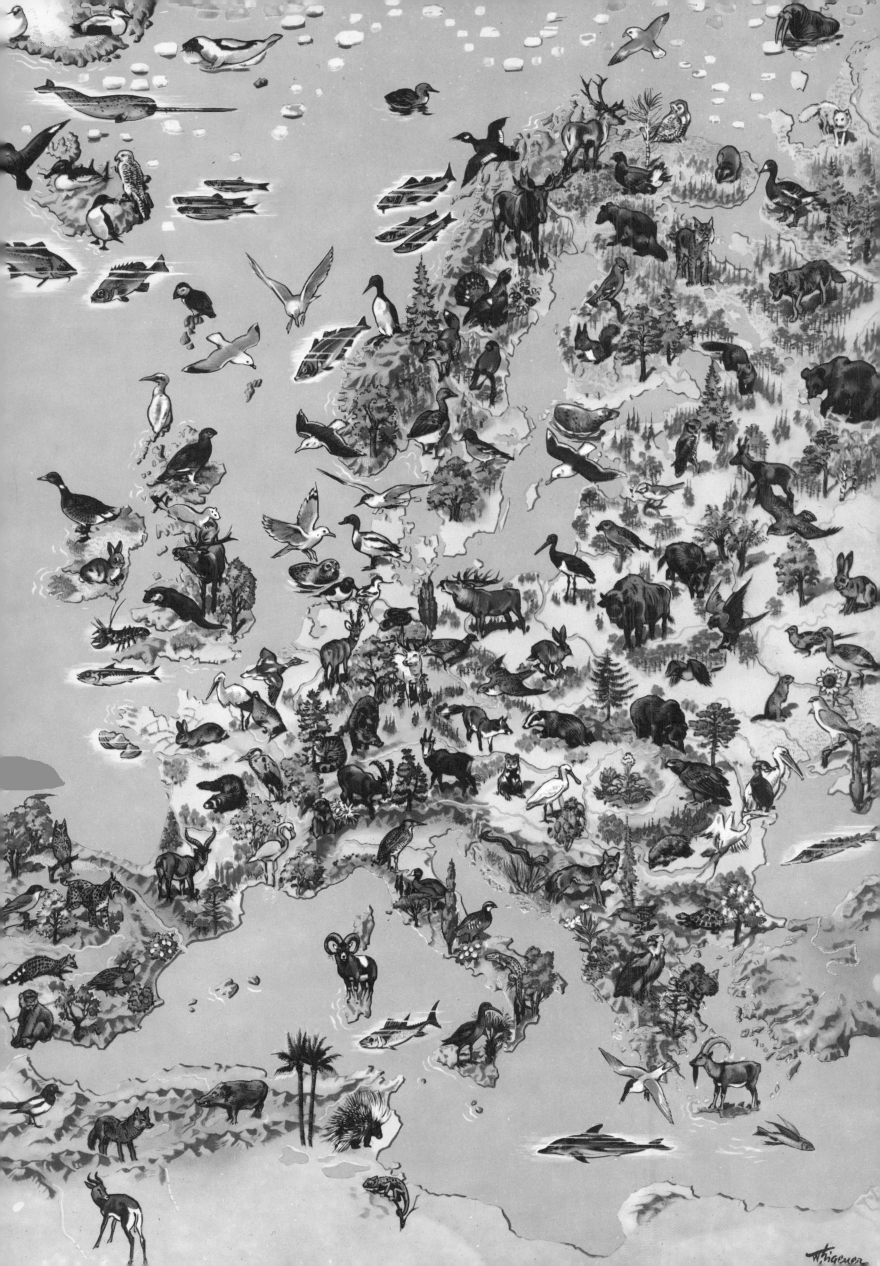

building — the Caledonian orogeny of Silurian times — formed mountains in north and west Norway, north-west Scotland and north England, and in Ireland. Yet later movements of great complexity to the south — the Hercynian and Variscan foldings — formed mountains in western and southern Europe: northern Ireland, Cornwall, Britanny, the central Meseta of Spain, central France, and in Corsica and Sardinia. Parts of central Europe also provide evidence of Variscan mountain building, though today the features are much subdued — the Ardennes, the Rhine and Greek plateaus, the Rhodope and Ural Mountains, and the hills of north Dobregea, in Romania. In parts, too, the materials of these movements are now overlaid by later sediments — as with the London-Brabant platform, found at a depth of 1,000 feet under London.

Many of the former Caledonian mountains and the Fenno-Scandinavian Shield have been heavily glaciated, creating many lakes and fjords, among other distinctive land forms, while the central portion of Europe is a great plain, stretching from the Strait of Dover and broadening eastwards into western Russia. It is partly founded on glacial and alluvial deposits, while its most productive southern parts are based on soils formed on deep layers of loess.

Central Europe is bordered to the south by higher portions of Hercynian ranges and then the most recent mountain ranges of imposing appearance, the Alps, which were almost entirely uplifted during Tertiary times and consist of materials dating from this era. Such ranges ring and interpenetrate with the northern parts of the Mediterranean Sea, and to the south-west lie the Atlas ranges. Among these complex mountains are found Europe's highest peaks and ranges — Sierra Nevada, Cantabrian

and Pyrenees, Alps, Apennines, Dinaric Alps of Yugoslavia, Balkan of Bulgaria, Carpathians, Pindus of Greece, and the Caucasus.

Streams and rivers rise in these generally well-watered mountains and hills and, flowing towards lowlands and the sea, they transport material which builds up flood plains and rich alluvium. The valleys and lowlands adjacent to these rivers are well populated, while many rivers have added importance in providing power or transport facilities, and have played a considerable role in the industrial development of Europe. Today man has many uses for rivers, as a source of water for irrigation, for use in steel industries, and as a means of disposal of the waste of urban areas.

The largest and most important rivers are the Volga and the Dnieper in Russia, the Danube in central and south-east Europe, the Po in Italy, the Loire and Seine in France, the Rhine in West Germany and the Netherlands, the Elbe in Germany, and the Thames in England. The Volga and its tributaries are the basis of transport in the U.S.S.R., carrying a half of all goods transported in Russia. In addition to rivers, a number of lakes are found in Europe, equal to 2 per cent of the total area. The largest are in Russia — Ladoga and Onega — and Finland and Sweden are both rich in lakes, the latter with Vanern and Vattern in central Sweden. Yet no part of Western Europe is less than 150 miles from the sea coast.

Europe is divided into many states and has many different ethnic, cultural and religious groups of peoples. Basic reasons for this political and linguistic diversity are hard to find (more than 70 languages are spoken within Europe). One reason lies in the many complex movements of peoples into and within Europe, with many invasions and displacements of people; another reason is the great geographical variation of Europe, with mountains enclosing and protecting lowland basins and the presence of other 'niches', such as mountain valleys and islands. Apart from Soviet Russia, France and Spain are the largest States with 213,000 and 191,000 square miles respectively. Next

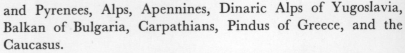

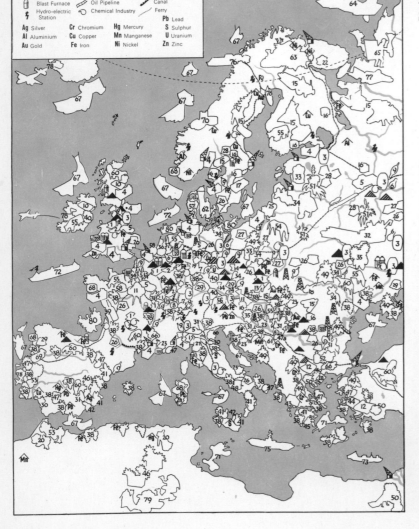

Production, Mineral Resources and Trade

Industries

1 Iron
2 Steel
3 Machinery
4 Shipyard
5 Car industry
6 Electrical goods
7 Optical goods
8 Watches
9 Textile industry
10 Linen
11 Fashions
12 Carpets
13 Shoes
14 Glass
15 Lumber
16 Paper mill
17 Matches
18 Salt
19 Potash
20 Phosphate
21 Marble
22 Apatite
23 Bauxite
24 Graphite
25 Amber

Agricultural Products

26 Wheat
27 Rye
28 Oats
29 Barley
30 Rice
31 Maize
32 Combine-harvester
33 Potatoes
34 Sugar beets
35 Sunflowers
36 Vegetables
37 Tulips
38 Wine
39 Brandy
40 Beer
41 Oranges
42 Lemons
43 Currants
44 Sultana grapes
45 Figs
46 Dates
47 Olives
47a Plums
48 Canned goods
49 Tobacco
50 Cotton
51 Flax
52 Rose oil
53 Cork oak

Livestock and Animal Products

54 Horses
55 Cattle
56 Dairy cattle
57 Butter
58 Cheese
59 Eggs
60 Sheep
61 Pigs
62 Meat products
63 Reindeer
64 Seal hunting
65 Furs
66 Silk culture
67 Fishing
68 Fish canneries
69 Tinned sardines
70 Fish canneries
71 Sponge fishing

Transportation and Trade

72 Passenger liner
73 Oil-tanker
74 Ferryboat
75 Aircraft-carrier
76 Ore exports
77 Lumber exports
78 Major airport
79 Caravan
80 Seaside resort

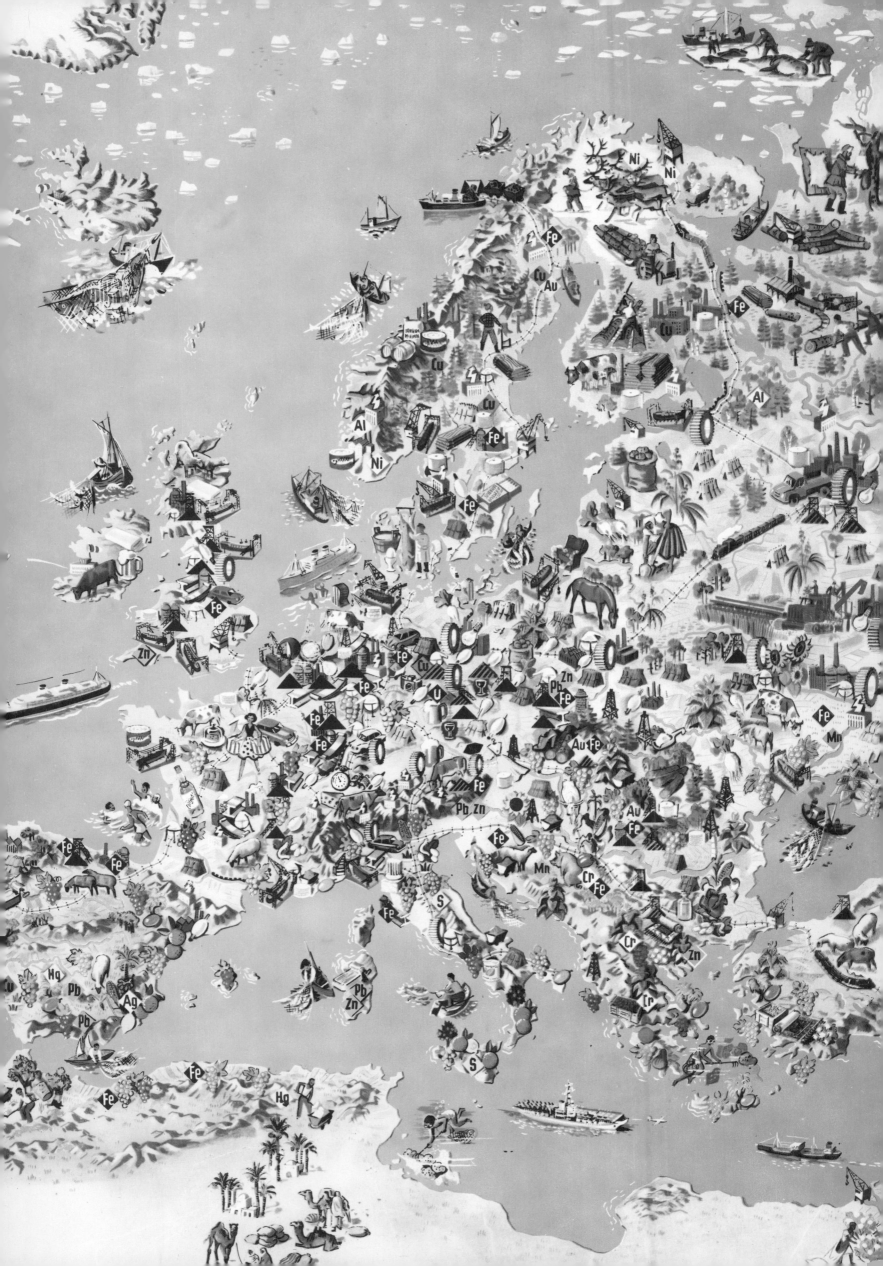

in order comes Sweden: 174,000 square miles. Norway, Poland and Finland are all larger than the United Kingdom which, with 93,000 square miles, is a little smaller than the German Federal Republic (95,707 square miles). Europe can also boast several 'lilliput' States — San Marino, Liechtenstein, Monaco, Andorra and the Vatican State — all less than 200 square miles in area.

Despite the relatively localised and dense populations of certain parts of Asia, Europe is without doubt the most densely peopled of the world's Continents. Its population of about 440 million exceeds that of Africa or the Americas, and its most populated parts are Belgium, Netherlands and south-east England.

Even during the Ice Age, Europe was inhabited, first by 'Heidelberg man' (Palaeanthropus heidelbergensis) and later, at the end of the Ice Age, by peoples who belonged to presently existing and therefore different types, termed Homo neandertalensis. Remains of Neandertal man are found in many parts of Europe and south-west Asia, and a special European race developed. This disappeared quite suddenly after the last glaciation, and Homo Sapiens ('modern man') appears equally suddenly, first as Aurignacian, later as Cro-magnon man. Physiognomic traces of the latter can still be seen among the people of Westphalia and of Dalarn, in Sweden. Traces of these early peoples include their tools and cave art, from which we can see that they led the life of hunters and gatherers. At the present time nearly all the peoples of Europe belong to one major group, the Europides, yet differences of physique and mentality are large within the group, as may be appreciated when comparing a Swede with a Spaniard.

The climate of Europe is, to a great degree, dominated by the proximity of the sea and especially of the warm Gulf Stream and its off-shoot, the North Atlantic Drift, which renders the climate of Western Europe much milder than normal for the latitude. Hence, on the same latitude as Newcastle, eskimos live in Labrador, while harbours which are warmed by the waters of the North Atlantic Drift are ice free all the year round, even in the northernmost parts of Norway — in turn on the same latitude as Scoresby Sound in Greenland and the northern parts of Alaska. Only in northernmost Russia can true Arctic climates be found, while most of Europe lies in the temperate zone, with a coastal climate in West Europe, while a continental climate obtains over most of Russia, Finland, Poland and Hungary. Rainfalls are highest in Western Europe and on the Alpine mountain ranges, and decrease gradually towards the east, and with the exception of the Mediterranean region with its winter rain, precipitation occurs at all seasons.

The northern Arctic zone is marked by a long, hard winter and a brief, cool summer, during which many plants grow quickly and provide nourishment for great flocks of birds which here rear their young, in late summer migrating southwards to milder climes and returning the following spring. Many animals migrate in similar fashion and many also hunt in groups or flocks — for example, lemmings, wolves and foxes.

A distinct Arctic milieu is the tundra; this is marked by lakes and peat bogs, and a plant life largely composed of mosses and lichen. In winter the water is frozen — even at considerable depths in the ground — yet, in summer, only a shallow surface layer thaws out, while the lower layers are still frozen (permafrost). The melted ground ice, or rain, cannot penetrate into the ground, and summer ground conditions are therefore very wet. There is no woodland in the Arctic zone, only sparse gnarled dwarf shrubs. Only farther south in the temperate zone are these supplemented by aspen, birch, hazel and conifers. Nearly all of the European temperate zone was once covered by forest, in the northern part by coniferous trees, to the south by deciduous trees. Solely in Eastern Europe, where the rainfall is lower, is steppe and wooded-steppe to be found. The original forest is now cleared from most parts of the lowland to make room for farming land. Only in Northern Europe and in some mountain regions does forest still dominate the scene.

The clearance of the woodland has had a great effect on the animal life, many species having almost disappeared. This is true of the wild horse, while the last aurochs, the forebear of our domesticated cattle, was killed in 1627. It must not be confused with the European bison, which still lived, wild, in Poland and the Caucasus, until shortly after the First World War. A number now survive in zoos or in reserves in Sweden and Poland. The elk, the largest deer in Europe, has also suffered badly, for it vanished from Central Europe during the Second World War and is now found only in Sweden, Finland and Russia. In similar fashion, the bear, lynx, wildcat and wolf have declined in numbers and are limited in their spread within Europe. Bird-life, too, has altered and, as with the animals, it is the larger types which have suffered most; such is the case with the lammergeier, the golden eagle, the black stork, bustard and stone curlew, which have become most rare over much of Central Europe.

This gradual disappearance of wild birds and animals is viewed with alarm, and attempts have been made to introduce and establish new breeds. Among others the pheasant and roe deer comprise quite a large proportion of the wild fauna, and in many places wild sheep — moufflon — are established. Other

The modern Saint Egrève power station at Grenoble, in south-east France

animals and birds have been able to adapt themselves to the changed conditions without the deliberate help of man, especially many rodents, such as the mouse and the rat; the house sparrow is also a case in point. Fortunately areas can still be found in Europe where plant and animal life can develop without being disturbed, especially in Northern Europe, as well as in the high mountain areas, or on small islands, or in marshy areas, most of which are now protected in order to conserve the animals and plants.

The Mediterranean region is partly situated in subtropical latitudes. The rain mainly falls in winter, so that plant life must protect itself against drought during the hot, dry summer. The plants do this by means of their pointed or thick-skinned leaves. This is the area of the *maquis*, gnarled bushes, cypress trees, stone pines, oleander, laurel, evergreen oak and many bulbous plants, all blossoming in the spring. Among the other warmth-loving plants of this region are the lemon, the orange, the olive, fig and sweet chestnut.

The cultivated area — over half the total area — of Europe, is annually sown with many types of grain, root or vegetable crops. Yet Europe is quite unable to grow all the food she needs. To balance the large amount of food imported to meet this need, and the large amounts of industrial raw materials, too, European countries must export large amounts of industrial produce. We live in an industrial age and it really began with James Watt's invention of the steam engine in 1769. Almost a century later, von Siemens showed the world how to harness electrical energy, and with this new impulse was coupled the development of the internal-combustion engine by Lenoir and also by von Langen, a development which was completed by the work of Rudolf Diesel. By then, man had many constant sources of energy and was no longer dependent on the vagaries of wind and water.

Just as the Great Age of geographical exploration commenced in Europe in the 15th century, so this new development started in Europe and spread rapidly to all other accessible parts of the world. Many of the more than 60 million emigrants who left Europe in the century after 1820 played an important part in this spread of technical knowledge.

Before 1900 Europe controlled about 90 per cent of world industrial production and 70 per cent of world trade. Great industrial centres had grown up, and in many European countries this growth was the result of intensive migration from, and depopulation of, rural areas. Yet industry and farming both improved at these times. Good agriculture is born in towns and, while industry in part used farm products, and required food from the land, in turn it supplied machinery and capital to agriculture.

The two World Wars jeopardised this development, and Western Europe was restored largely with the help of Marshall Aid. In order to prevent a similar catastrophe from ever happening again, many politicians feel that a United States of Europe should be set up. Precursors of this are already in existence — the Iron and Steel Community, the Common Market (the Six) and the European Free Trade Area (the Seven).

Though Europe's highly developed economy is based largely on industry, agriculture still has a large role to play, for the hitherto great increases in Europe's population have prompted a many-sided effort to improve the quality and quantity of food produced by agriculture. Improved methods of cultivation, of fertilising the soil, of crop and stock breeding, of pest control, and of rationalisation of the farm labour force, all have led to increased yields per acre or lower costs of production. Higher yields of milk and meat are also universal, while new methods of marketing, transport and refrigeration all assist the optimum use of Europe's limited farm area.

The timber industry is also of great importance in many parts of Europe, especially in Scandinavia and Finland and in the Alpine areas, because elsewhere in Europe large areas have been cleared for farmland, often as long ago as prehistoric times, for building, shipbuilding — as by the Vikings in southwest Norway — and heating. The forests of today are carefully managed and provide timber for furniture, constructional purposes, and pulp and paper making. Especially in Sweden

An evening scene on the island-studded, mountainous coast of Yugoslavia

Boating is a big holiday attraction on the Yugoslav island of Rab

there is large-scale production of hardboard and other prepared by-products.

The fishing industry is also important in that, in the North Atlantic, there are large and rich fishing grounds, especially near Lofoten and close to the Faeroes and Iceland, which supply all Europe. The produce is landed mainly in British, Norwegian and Danish harbours, and distributed — fresh, frozen or dried — to many parts over the excellent transport network which Europe possesses, and which largely exists to meet the manifold needs of Europe's industrial and populous regions. This close contact with the sea, and with one another, has always been a strong stimulus to exploration and trade from Europe to other parts of our globe.

The varied outline of the coast of Europe has led to the development of large ports, especially Rotterdam and its extension, Europort, at the outlet of the Rhine. Close rivals are Antwerp and Gent, while London, Liverpool, Le Havre and Hamburg are other great ports of Western Europe. In Southern Europe, Genoa and Marseilles control a great part of their countries' exports through the Mediterranean, both to the west and to Asia and the far east.

Athens, the capital of Greece, lies at the foot of the Acropolis, its ancient citadel

The Moorish Giralda at Seville, in Spain

●**Aachen**, population 177,642, is an historic town in West Germany close to the Belgian border. Its warm sulphurous springs have been known since Roman times. Charlemagne, in the 8th century, made it his residence and founded the great Cathedral which is his burial place. All German kings were crowned in Aachen until the 16th century. Later, many historical events took place there, usually related to its French name Aix-la-Chapelle. Today it is an important railway centre with considerable textile and machinery industries.

●**Aalborg**, with a population of over 100,000, is Denmark's fourth largest town, and most important provincial port. Situated in northern Jutland, it has a cement industry, and is noted for its production of 'snaps' (or akvavit), and for its Lim Fjord oysters.

●**Aarhus** is the second town of Denmark, with 187,342 people. It has a large harbour, a modern university, and widely diversified engineering and chemical industries.

●**Adriatic Sea** a long, relatively shallow arm of the Mediterranean separating Italy from Yugoslavia. The Italian coast is low and without good harbours, while the Dalmatian coast is mountainous, and rich in attractive islands, bays and headlands which form a tourists' paradise. In the north is the delta of the Po and other Alpine rivers, and the two most important ports, Trieste and Venezia (Venice). Other ports are Ancona, Bari and Brindisi in Italy, and Rijeka, Split and Dubrovnik in Yugoslavia.

●**Åland Islands**, situated to the south-west of Finland, of which only 80 of a total of 6,550 islands are inhabited. The chief town is Mariehamn. The inhabitants speak Swedish, though the islands belong to Finland.

●**Albania** A small mountainous country and People's Republic, situated between Yugoslavia and Greece. The coast is marshy but cultivated, though the cultivated area comprises only 15 per cent of the total. Maize, tobacco, cotton, fruit, vine

and sugar beet are the main produce, while sheep and goats are ubiquitous. Over half of the country's 2 million inhabitants are Moslem, and they speak a language related to ancient Illyrian and quite unrelated to any other modern language. The capital is Tirana (169,000) with its outport Durrës (53,000). The country became independent of Turkish rule, which had commenced in 1467, only in 1912. It is not without mineral wealth — oil, copper, chrome, iron and lignite being mined, largely for export.

● **alder** The alder tree is found in Europe, America, eastern Asia, Asia Minor and North Africa. In Europe the common alder is best known. It forms coppices on marshy ground and moors. The leaves are roundish and unevenly toothed on the margin. Staminate and pistillate flowers grow as catkins. After pollination the short male catkins remain as round woody cones. Another species, the white alder, occurs in moist places in mountains. Its bark is silvery-grey; that of the common alder is black and fissured. The alder timber is not hard and durable, yet is very resistant to water, and it is used in the construction of mines and underwater installations, and for toys and wooden shoes.

● **Alpine passes** In Switzerland, France, Italy and Austria there are Alpine passes for rail and road traffic between Central and Southern Europe. The Brenner Pass, attaining a height of only 4,495 feet, did not require tunnelling and was already in use during the Middle Ages, and has been crossed by a railway since 1867. All other Alpine railways necessitated the construction of tunnels. The oldest of these routes (1854) crosses the Semmering Pass by a 1-mile-long tunnel. In 1872—82 the St Gotthard tunnel (9¼ miles long) was constructed, and in 1898—1906 the Simplon tunnel (12 miles long). Other important railway routes are the tunnels through the Mont Cenis (7½ miles), the Lötschberg (9 miles), and the Arlberg (6.3 miles) Passes. The longest road tunnel in the world (7½ miles) was bored jointly by French and Italian enterprise under Mont Blanc, and completed in 1961. The highest Alpine road crosses the Stilfser Joch (9,024 feet), approached on the north side by forty-eight hairpin bends. The Grossglockner Road rises to 8,480 feet. Other high-altitude roads are those across the St Gotthard (6,926 feet), the Great St Bernard (6,768 feet) and the Furka Pass (7,976 feet). These road passes are dangerous or impassable in winter, and in recent times all-the-year-round traffic has been assured by means of road tunnels or rail-ferries.

● **Alps** These mountains are the highest in Europe, and extend as an arc from the Mediterranean near Nice, through France, Italy, Switzerland, Liechtenstein, Germany and Austria to Vienna and Yugoslavia. The arc is at least 100 miles wide, and its highest point is Mont Blanc (15,781 feet). The Alps are complex recent fold mountains, dating from Tertiary times. The range is divided into different parts or groups of peaks, the largest being the western and the eastern Alps, the boundary between them being a line from Lake Constance to Lake Como. Among the most well-known parts are the Hohe Tauern, with the Grossglockner as the highest peak (12,461 feet); the limestone Dolomites; the Wallis Alps, with the Matterhorn (14,780 feet) and Monte Rosa (15,200 feet); the Bernese Oberland, with the Jungfrau (13,763 feet) and Finsteraarhorn (14,022 feet). Several of Europe's largest rivers rise in the Alps — the Po, the Rhône and several tributaries of the Danube. The water power in these rivers is used for hydroelectricity, and this gives rise to industries in both valleys and adjacent lowlands. Otherwise the Alpine economy is based on agriculture, dairying, forestry, mining (iron, lead, zinc and copper), and a well-developed tourist industry. Even though the Alps form a natural barrier between Central and Southern Europe, they are crossed by a network of communications, and modern aircraft have introduced a new and important means of transport across the mountain range.

● **Amsterdam** is the largest city of the Netherlands (1,040,395 people) and the second largest port. It lies by a bay, the Ij, the southwestern-most portion of the former Zuider Zee. It was established on a foundation of wooden piles in unstable mud, and is criss-crossed by many canals bordered by narrow streets. A city of over 400 bridges, and known as the Venice of the North, it is a commercial centre with world-wide connections and is renowned for its financial and historical connections, and its manufacture of tropical imports and diamonds. It is connected to the North Sea by a large canal, finished in 1876, and in the future, with the completion of the Ijsselmeer scheme, it will form the node of Randstadt Holland. It is also connected to the intensive traffic on the Rhine. The city also has oil refineries, shipbuilding, and other metal industries. The town is an important cultural centre, with two universities, an Art Academy, and many libraries and museums, including one for the paintings of Rembrandt. The city was founded as a Norman fort and joined the Hanseatic League in 1370, but it really flourished in the 17th and 18th centuries with the East Indian trade.

● **Andalusia** One of the southernmost parts of Europe and with a very sunny climate, it consists of the plain of the Gaudalquivir, bordered and sheltered by the Sierra Morena to the north and the Sierra Nevada to the south. Large areas of rich black soil are irrigated, and these support huertas (market gardens), some of which grow sub-tropical crops, and also orchards of oranges, figs, almonds, the mulberry and, above all else, olives, for this region produces a third of Spain's olive crop. Farther east, near Córdoba, large crops of wheat are grown. Other crops are rice, cotton and sugar cane, while sherry from Jerez, near Cadiz, is a world-famed fortified wine. In uncultivated sub-arid plains and in the hills, large herds are kept, for black bulls and horses are reared here for the ring. The mountains, too, are rich in mineral deposits — copper, iron, uranium, lead and zinc. The largest cities are Seville, Córdoba, Granada and Cadiz, with many Moorish palaces and other buildings, especially the Alhambra of Granada and the Giralda of Seville, as examples of the cultural richness of Moorish times. These times ended only in 1492, the year that Columbus rediscovered America, and yet greater wealth was to come to Andalusia during later decades.

● **Andorra** A mountainous pocket state in the eastern Pyrenees, with a population of 18,000 in 1971. Both France and Spain have voting rights in this Republic. The population, which is Catalan-speaking, rear sheep and goats, and there is some agriculture, industry and tourism. Government is by a council of 24 members elected by heads of families. The capital is Andorra la Vieille, with 8,000 inhabitants.

Ruins of the mighty Parthenon, ancient Greek temple to the goddess Athena which crowns the Acropolis, overlooking Athens

Neuschwanstein Castle stands high on a peak overlooking Germany's beautiful lake Alpsee, in the province of Bavaria

Antwerp is the second city of Belgium, with a population, including suburbs, of 919,840. The chief seaport, it lies on the right bank of the Schelde, about 50 miles from the open sea. It is the outport for parts of Western Germany and for Brussels and the Kempen coalfield. It is the starting point of a motorway to Vienna and has many industries — oil refining, ore smelting, metal works, textiles and a diamond industry. The Normans first built a castle on the site in the 9th century, and Antwerp came to have great commercial importance in the 15th century, for Europe's first stock exchange opened here in 1460. The city then had almost a quarter of a million inhabitants and became an art-centre, with Rubens as its leader. After Spanish occupation, Antwerp's second period of importance began in 1860, when Belgium recovered the right to free navigation on the Schelde.

Gran Sasso d'Italia. The Apennines have long since been deforested and are covered by *maquis* (brushwood). Yet wine and olives are produced, and there are many large isolated villages in the area.

Aragon The area watered by the Ebro in north-eastern Spain and lying between the Pyrenees and the Iberian Mountains. The area is generally only sparsely populated, for the climate is warm and dry in summer, and cold in winter, and the soils are sandy, rocky, or in parts saline. Sheep and goats are reared extensively and there is some irrigation of wheat, vine, fruit and sugar beet crops near the river. The kingdom of Aragon was founded in 1035 with a view to hindering the northward penetration of the Moorish invaders. In later years its rule extended to southern France,

Sicily and Naples, while it was linked to Castile by the marriage of Ferdinand and Isabella in 1479. Zaragoza is the territory's largest city.

Ardennes A forested plateau in southern Belgium and extending into Luxembourg and north-east France. Its greatest elevation is 2,300 feet. To the north it is bordered by the Sambre-Meuse depression, in which lie the towns of Charleroi, Namur and Liege Formerly rich in coal and ores, the area now features light industry and textiles. A battle-ground in both world wars, it is a favoured tourist area, with rivers, woods, spas and caves.

ash This tree can reach heights of 125 feet, and is slender, with an open crown and greyish bark. The timber is hard and elastic and is therefore used to make tool-shafts, skis, oars, and other poles which must combine strength and durability. It was much favoured by prehistoric man, for the leaves could be used as fodder for his animals.

Assisi A small town, south-east of Perugia in central Italy (25,000 inhabitants), and famous as the birthplace of St Francis. The church, built where he was buried in the 13th century, is a centre for countless pilgrims.

Athens The capital of modern Greece, Athens lies in the plain of Attica by the 500-foot-high Acropolis and has 1.9 million inhabitants, if its seaport, Piraeus, is included. This metropolis controls the country's industry and commerce, and much of the marketing of the agricultural produce — tobacco, corriander, raisins and olive oil. It is also responsible for the import of petroleum, timber and manufactured goods. The modern city dates from the 1850s, from the rebirth of the Greek nation. On the Acropolis stand remains of temples, amphitheatres and statues from ancient Hellas, whose classical civilisation both spread into, and later inspired the western world in its development of democracy and culture. The most imposing remains are those of the Parthenon, symbol

Barbary ape of Gibraltar

ape, Barbary This large, powerful, light-brown creature is the only monkey at large in Europe. It is found on the Rock of Gibraltar and in north-western Africa. Also known as the magot, this strong tailless monkey belongs to the genus of the macacas.

Apennines Fold mountains stretching down the Italian peninsula from the plains of the Po to the Strait of Messina. Their highest parts are the Abruzzi Mountains, which reach 9,561 feet in the

A picturesque village clings to the pine-covered slopes of Germany's Bavarian Alps

of the glory that was Greece. This white marble temple, surrounded by 46 Doric columns, was built during the 'golden age' of Pericles and dedicated to Athena, the city's patron goddess. Athens reached the peak of her glory in the 5th century B.C., after defeating the Persians at Marathon. Democracy flourished under Pericles, and the names of Socrates, Aristotle and Plato are for ever linked with the city and its culture. The rivalry between Athens and Sparta led to the Peloponnesian War (431—404 B.C.) in which Athens was temporarily subdued, but the city's power did not finally wane until the Macedonian conquest of Greece in 338 B.C. By the middle of the 2nd century B.C., Athens had declined to the status of a Roman dependency. It remained within the Byzantine Empire until the Crusades, then came under Turkish rule in 1458.

● **Atlantic Ocean** This, the world's second largest ocean, has the same name as the Atlas Mountains, and the lost Continent Atlantis, all derived from the Greek god, Atlas. It has an area of 32 million square miles (10 times the size of the United States), separating the Americas (the New World) from Europe and Africa (the Old World). Shaped like an hour-glass, the Atlantic is narrowest (less than 2,000 miles wide) between the western bulge of Africa and the north-eastern coast of Brazil. At the latitude of the United States and western Europe, it is about 3,000 miles wide, a distance which the fastest ocean liners can cover in less than four days. Aeroplane travel across the North Atlantic is enjoying increasing popularity; with the arrival of commercial jets the ocean could be spanned in about six hours, and supersonic jets will cut this time approximately in half. The greatest depth recorded is the Milwaukee Deep (30,250 feet), off the island of Puerto Rico in the Caribbean Sea. The Gulf Stream (best known of the currents that circulate in the Atlantic Ocean) flows out of the Gulf of Mexico through the Straits of Florida, parallels the coast of the south-eastern United States, and widens as it

crosses the ocean and reaches France, while the North Atlantic Drift washes Great Britain and Norway, its warm waters having a moderating effect on the climate of western Europe. The Labrador Current, on the other hand, carries cold Arctic waters, together with icebergs carved off the Greenland glaciers, southward into the North Atlantic shipping-lanes. Its clash with the warmer currents moving up from the south produces dense fogs off Newfoundland. Another cold current, the Benguela Current, washes the south-western coast of Africa before moving westward across the Atlantic.

Beginning in the 7th century A.D., sailors from Scandinavia are known to have ventured into the Atlantic; they probably reached North America around the year A.D. 1000. In the 15th century, Portuguese navigators opened trade routes along the coast of Africa. Then, following the voyages of Columbus, the North Atlantic was destined to become the most travelled shipping route in the world. The ocean was first crossed by air in 1919 by Captain John Alcock and Lieutenant Arthur Whitten-Brown, and in 1927 Lindbergh completed his famous solo flight from New York to Paris. From north to south, in the centre of the Atlantic Ocean, is a submarine ridge on which several islands are sited: Iceland, the Azores, Ascension Island, Tristan da Cunha, Gough Island and Bouvet Island.

● **Austria** A mountainous republic of central Europe, with an area of 32,000 square miles and a population of 7,073,807. Its capital is Vienna. Before World War I, Austria was the heart of the Austro-Hungarian Empire, which was eight times as large as Austria itself. Now Austria consists of nine autonomous provinces: Vorarlberg and Tirol (in the west), Salzburg, Upper Austria, Kärnten, Burgenland, Steiermark, Lower Austria and Vienna. The population, 98 per cent German-speaking, is unevenly distributed. Only 30 per cent live in the Alps, which cover 60 per cent of the country's area. Vienna alone contains one-fourth of the total population. Dairying in the mountains and crop growing in the plains do not meet the nation's food needs and Austria depends on grain imports. In exchange she exports industrial products based on mineral resources (iron ore, lead, zinc, petroleum), lumber and paper. Austria is a world source of high grade graphite. Hydro-electric stations provide power for the country with a surplus for export. The Danube is important for transport. Tourism, attracted by Viennese and Alpine resorts, provides a major source of income. Austria was annexed to Germany in 1938, during Hitler's regime. After World War II, in 1945, the victorious Big Four (Britain, France, the Soviet Union and the United States) divided the country into four occupied zones. Foreign troops were not withdrawn until 1955, when a state treaty restored Austria's independence.

● **Azores** An island group (888 square miles; population 330,000) in the North Atlantic Ocean, 1,000 miles west of Portugal, to which they belong. Scattered over 300 miles of ocean, the Azores are mountainous, and all but one of the nine larger islands show evidence of their volcanic origins in the form of craters, lava flows and small geysers. The Azores are important primarily because of their location astride transatlantic traffic lanes. Two modern airports were built during World War II, when the Azores served as an Allied air and naval base. Tourists enjoy the year-round mildness of the islands' climate and the almost tropic lushness of the vegetation, with bananas, oranges, pineapples and vines. Ponta Delgada (30,000 inhabitants), on São Miguel Island, is the chief seaport. Portuguese settlement of the Azores began in the mid-15th century, about a century after they first appeared on a medieval map of the 'world' and when they were still unpopulated.

● **Azov, Sea of** An arm of the Black Sea, from which it is separated by the Crimea. It takes its name from the old town of Azov on the delta of the Don River. The shallow sea (nowhere deeper than 50 feet) contains only 1 per cent salt, and therefore freezes over in the winter while the saltier Black Sea remains almost ice-free. It is an important fishing ground. Main Soviet ports are Zhadanov, Rostov and Kerch.

● **Balearic Islands** An island group (2,000 square miles; population 443,327) in the western Mediterranean off the coast of Spain, to which they belong. Majorca and Minorca are the two main islands; much of their surface is mountainous. Almonds, olives and grapes are grown on the sunny, *maquis* (brushwood)-clad slopes overlooking the marvellously blue sea. Their scenery and an exceptionally mild climate have made the islands a popular tourist resort for much of northern Europe. Palma (population 208,127) on Majorca is the principal resort town. In Moorish times (8th—12th centuries) the islands served as a base for pirates preying on Mediterranean shipping.

● **Balkan Peninsula** The third of the southerly projecting European peninsulas, which lies between the Black Sea on the east and the Adriatic Sea on the west. It includes Romania, Bulgaria, Greece, Albania and Yugoslavia. Balkan is a Turkish word meaning 'mountain'. The peninsula takes its name from the Balkan Mountains, which form the east-west backbone of Bulgaria, rising to 7,800 feet. In many parts farming is the most important activity, and though many places are still very poorly developed, industrialisation has increased greatly since 1945.

● **Baltic Sea** This large inland sea of northern Europe has an area of 166,000 square miles, including its two arms, the Gulf of Bothnia and the Gulf of Finland. The Baltic Sea is connected with the Atlantic Ocean through the Straits of Denmark. It is a relatively shallow sea, rarely exceeding 500 feet in depth. Its salt content decreases to such a degree that it is composed of virtually fresh water in its eastern arms. Large sections of the sea freeze when winters are exceptionally cold. The northern coasts are generally rocky and abound in tiny islands known as skerries. The southern coasts are often lined with sand dunes. The chief ports of the Baltic Sea, which is almost tideless, are: Kiel and Lübeck in West Germany; Rostock in East Germany; Szczecin and Gdansk-Gdynia in Poland; Kaliningrad, Riga and Leningrad in the Soviet Union; Helsinki in Finland; Stockholm and Malmö in Sweden; and Copenhagen in Denmark.

● **Barcelona** Spain's second city (population 1,759,148) and its leading industrial centre; it is a well-equipped modern seaport on the Mediterranean Sea which handles 90 per cent of Spain's imports, especially coal, oil and cotton. Textile mills dominate the industrial scene, but machinery and chemicals are gaining steadily in importance. Barcelona exports cloth, wine, cork and fruit, and imports coal and cotton for its manufacturing plants. The city is more than 2,000 years old and has been occupied by the Romans, the Visigoths, the Moors, and the Franks under Charlemagne. After the 12th century it flourished as the capital of the kings of Aragon. The population of Barcelona has frequently resisted the rule of the Madrid government. Catalan (the language of the region known in history as Catalonia) is widely spoken; it is akin to Provençal, spoken in south-eastern France. Water power is now much utilised in the mountains inland.

The Danube at Budapest, Hungary, seen from the ancient fortress of Buda

Bari A seaport of southern Italy on the Adriatic Sea. It is the chief city (population 352,425) of Apulia, the fertile agricultural region of southern Italy. Bari's trade includes the shipment of almonds, olive oil, lentils, tobacco and dried peas — all locally grown. Long known as one of the poorest parts of Italy, the Bari region has benefited from post-war development projects and is attracting an increasing number of tourists. A university was founded in 1924.

Barley and an ear

barley This grain is one of the oldest cultivated cereals, as indicated by finds in tombs and caves. Barley is hardy and can resist drought and frost. It is thus planted in the oases of the Sahara as well as in the far north as six-row barley, where no other cereal will grow. In mountain areas barley can be cultivated up to heights of 12,000 feet. There are several cultivated sub-races of barley. The flower of barley is an ear with long spikes. The small ears containing the grains are arranged in two or six rows. Barley is used for domestic cooking and is made into semolina and coffee substitute. It also serves for the manufacture of extract of malt, malt sugar and sweets. A special variety, malting barley, is used in brewing. Much barley is also used as fodder for livestock.

Basel (Basle) A leading commercial city (370,000 inhabitants) of Switzerland at the junction of several international rail lines and with a harbour on the Rhine River, which, leaving Switzerland below Basel, is navigable from there to the North Sea. The city has many diverse industries and is an important printing and banking centre. It was founded by the Romans, became a free city of the Holy Roman Empire in the 11th century, and joined the Swiss Confederation in 1501. Its university dates from 1460. The population is Protestant and German-speaking.

Basque Country An area of northern Spain and south-western France extending across the Pyrenees into the Cantabrian Mountains along the shores of the Bay of Biscay. Many Basques still speak their old language, which is not related to any other tongue, and have jealously guarded their ancient customs. For centuries they have insisted on controlling their local affairs without interference from the Spanish and French governments. The typical Basque head-dress is the beret.

Bavaria is the largest of the West German states (27,200 square miles) with a population of over 10.5 million. It is located on the south German plateau, by the northern slopes of the Bavarian Alps, which reach their highest point (9,700 feet) in the Zugspitze. Munich, internationally known for its beer, is the capital city and Bavaria's leading cultural centre. Bayreuth has acquired world renown for its Wagner opera festivals; the towns of Rothenburg and Dinkelsbühl have been preserved as examples of medieval architecture; and, in the Alps, tourists visit the scenic lakes and resorts of Garmisch-Partenkirchen and Oberammergau (known for its Passion play). Bavaria was ruled by a long line of dukes (later kings) from the 12th century until 1918. At the time of the Reformation it remained firmly Roman Catholic. It now forms a self-governing state within the German Federal Republic.

Beech trees and a nut

beech One of the largest trees of north-west Europe, it has a closed growth, casting dense shade in which very little undergrowth can thrive. The nuts are edible and the timber is much used in furniture making, and for parquet floors.

beer One of the most common alcoholic beverages. The main raw materials used in making beer are barley and hops. The barley is soaked in water until it sprouts, producing so-called malt (germinated grain). Hops are then added to give the characteristic flavour of beer. The resulting brew is fermented through the addition of yeast and aged for two to three months; carbon dioxide is injected, and the beer is ready for bottling or canning. Beer is made in virtually all countries of the world. The leading producers are Britain, the United States, West Germany, Belgium and Australia.

Belgium A kingdom of north-western Europe, small in area (11,800 square miles) but, next to the Netherlands, the most densely populated country on the continent. Of its 9.6 million people, more than half speak Flemish, a tongue akin to Dutch; French is spoken by the Walloons (of Latin stock) who live predominantly in southern Belgium. The language border runs just south of Brussels, the bilingual capital of this highly cultured nation. The North Sea coast is unbroken and sandy — affording more bathing resorts (such as the one at Ostend) than sheltered harbours. Antwerp, Belgium's chief seaport, lies near the mouth of the Schelde River, which crosses Dutch territory before reaching the open sea. The Meuse River separates the rolling farming lands to the north-west from the heavily wooded Ardennes plateau in the southeast. Belgium's main crops are fodder grains, beets, flax and potatoes; livestock raising and dairying are important. Much more significant, however, is the country's industrial output, based on coal mining and iron and steel milling. Steel products are fabricated in Brussels (machinery, railway equipment), Antwerp (shipyards), and in the Meuse valley, notably at Liége and Charleroi. The centuries-old textile industry (once renowned for its lace and tapestries) now produces linen, wool and synthetic fibres. Antwerp rivals Amsterdam as a centre of the diamond trade. The historic towns of Gent and Bruges, with their well-preserved old buildings and maze of canals, look much as they did during the Middle Ages, though Gent is now much industrialised.

Belgium lies at the crossroads of overland and air communications in Europe and has the world's densest railway network. It formed the historic buffer-zone and battle-ground between France and Germany in recent times, while Julius Caesar mentioned the country in his account of the conquest of Gaul. In the Middle Ages, Belgian cities became wealthy and semi-independent under a succession of foreign rulers. Passing from the Dukes of Burgundy to Spain, Austria and France, Belgium was finally united with the Netherlands in 1815. It declared its independence in 1830 and installed a German prince as King Leopold I. The country was overrun by Germany during both world wars. In 1947 Belgium entered into a customs agreement with neighbouring Luxembourg and the Netherlands, called the Benelux Union. Its former valuable African possession, the Congo, 75 times as large as the homeland and infinitely richer in natural resources, was made independent in 1960. The territory of Ruanda-Urundi, also in central Africa, was administered by Belgium under a United Nations trusteeship, but it, too, is now independent.

Benelux A word coined in 1947 to describe the progressive economic union of three countries of north-western Europe — Belgium, the Netherlands and Luxembourg, now part of the Common Market.

Beograd (Belgrade) Capital of Yugoslavia since 1918. A city of 843,209, Belgrade lies on a hill overlooking the Sava River, just west of its junction with the Danube. Belgrade, whose name means 'white town', is an important transportation centre on rail lines linking central Europe with the Balkans. Because of its strategic position it has been exposed to frequent attack in the past. Its last Turkish garrison left in 1867. Under Yugoslav rule, the city has developed into a modern metropolis and is the commercial centre of the country.

The spires of Chartres Cathedral soar high above the rooftops of the old French city

The Brandenburg Gate, in Berlin

Berlin The capital of Germany until 1945. With its universities, scientific institutes, museums, libraries and famous theatres, Berlin was the foremost educational and artistic centre of Germany and one of the leading cities in Europe, even though it is not an ancient foundation. It was also important in the manufacture of garments and electrical goods, and in the printing and publishing industries. Since World War II, the city's position has declined because of the partition of Germany — Berlin is now divided into a western sector (population: 2,134,256) and an eastern sector (1,083,856). West Berlin is considered part of West Germany, from which it is separated by 70 miles of East German territory. East Berlin is the capital of East Germany. Allied bombings during World War II destroyed 30 per cent of the city and up to 60 per cent of its central business district. Many famous buildings, and monuments such as the Brandenburg Gate, have been rebuilt or repaired. Joint four-nation rule of the city (established after the war by Britain, France, the Soviet Union and the U.S.A.) ceased in 1948, and Berlin is now divided into two parts — East and West — each separately administered. Despite its great extent, Berlin is not completely urban, for large parks and broad streets beautify the city — among them the famous Kurfüstendamm, the Unter den Linden, Friedrichstrasse, Karl Marx Allee and others.

Berne The federal capital of Switzerland (since 1848). A favourite tourist centre, sited on the river Aare, Berne has preserved its medieval inner town which dates from the 12th century. Here is the bears' den, whose live brown bears symbolise the independence of Switzerland. The graceful clock tower is the city's chief landmark. The snow-covered summits of the Bernese Alps rise along the southern horizon. Berne has been part of the Swiss Confederation since 1353. German is the language of most of the city's 260,600 people.

Bilbao An important port, and industrial and commercial city (population 400,505), of northern Spain on a deep inlet in the Bay of Biscay. Nearby iron mines supply the city's steel mills and shipyards and provide ore for export, chiefly to Britain. Bilbao also has chemical plants, an oil refinery and machine shops. Most of the population is Basque.

Biscay, Bay of An inlet of the Atlantic Ocean, off western Europe, formed by the north coast of Spain and the west coast of France meeting at right angles where the Pyrenees reach the sea. The bay is noted for sudden severe storms whipped up by north-west winds; tides are among the highest in the world — up to 40 feet.

bison The bison (vicent) is the original wild bull, which used to live in all European forests. By the advance of civilisation and by deforestation the bison was exterminated, except for some hundred specimens in the Caucasus and some single animals in zoological gardens or game preserves. The few remaining animals are protected by law and carefully tended. In the pine-forests of the Caucasus the bisons live in the higher regions; during the summer in moist thickets, where they feed on grass, leaves and tree bark. The animal stands about 6 feet high at the shoulder and only about 4 feet high at the hind legs. The body is about 10 feet long and covered with thick, shaggy hair; it can weigh up to 100 stone. The large head has a high forehead; the small horns curve sideways and upwards. In spite of its heavy body, the bison is remarkably agile and is able to swim. Male animals live singly and join the much smaller females for mating. A young calf is born every second year.

bittern The bittern belongs to the family of herons. It is found in Europe, Asia and North Africa. It lives hidden in reed swamps and migrates south during the winter. Its shape is thick-set and clumsy, the neck long and thick, the plumage mottled brown and buff; only the upper head is quite black. It is 28 inches long and its wings have a span of 4 feet. The male utters a booming cry like the lowing of an ox. The bittern feeds on fish, frogs, snakes and small animals.

Black Sea A large inland sea between Europe and Asia, with an area of 160,000 square miles. It is connected with the Mediterranean through the Turkish Straits (Bosporus, Sea of Marmara and Dardanelles). Its greatest depth is 7,400 feet. The salt content of the water ranges from 1.8 per cent at the top to 2.2 per cent at great depths. Marine life exists only down to a depth of 500 feet, for sufficient oxygen is lacking at greater depths. The Black Sea is ice-free in winter, except for its northwest coast.

Bologna Industrial and commercial centre of northern Italy, situated in the Po River valley at the foot of the Apennines. Due to its location at the head of two mountain passes, Bologna (population 490,000) commands the most direct route to Rome and southern Italy. With its arcaded streets and old town hall, the city has preserved some of the flavour of a medieval market town. Its university, which dates from the year 1088, was one of the great centres of learning and book publishing in the Middle Ages.

Bonn An old German city and, since 1949, the capital of the German Federal Republic (West Germany). It lies on the hilly left bank of the Rhine where the river issues from a scenic gorge. The city's population has grown to 299,376, due to expanding government activity. The university was founded in 1818. The archbishops of Cologne, who were powerful princes of the Holy Roman Empire, transferred their seat to Bonn in 1263 and remained there for 500 years. In 1794 the city was captured by Napoleon. It was returned to Prussia in 1815. The house where Beethoven was born is now a museum.

Bordeaux A seaport (population 555,152) of south-western France at the mouth of the Garonne River (which here widens into a 60-mile-long estuary emptying into the Bay of Biscay). It lies at the centre of a world-famous region of vineyards, whose red and white 'name' wines are handled from Bordeaux. The most well-known wines are Médoc, Graves, Sauternes and St Emilion. The city has many attractive boulevards, an old university (1441) and several art collections. Its importance as a trading centre dates from the Middle Ages when it was controlled by England for three centuries (1154—1453). The Third Republic was proclaimed in Bordeaux in 1871. In 1914, and again in 1940, the city was the seat of the provisional wartime government of France. Industries include shipbuilding, oil refining, metals and cement.

Bornholm This island in the Baltic has an area of 215 square miles and consists of a block of granite rising to 535 feet, with steep cliffs to the north. The western and southern parts are lowland covered with deposits of glacial drift and used for agriculture. The population of 47,405 have also developed a prosperous ceramic industry based on kaolin. The island belongs to Denmark, and is famous for tourism and for its smoked fish industry.

Bosporus The easternmost of the Turkish Straits, linking the Black Sea with the Sea of Marmara and, via the Dardanelles, with the Aegean Sea. Istanbul controls the southern entrance to the strait, which is 17 miles long but less than 2 miles wide. Both the Bosporus and the Dardanelles have long been tremendously important strategically, for whoever controls the straits can shut off the only entrance to the Black Sea. It is now controlled by Turkey, though there is international agreement to free transit.

Bothnian Gulf The northern part of the Baltic Sea between Swedish Norrland and Finland. Its waters are almost fresh, and are frozen for almost half the year.

Bratislava A city of Czechoslovakia, on the Danube River; population: 281,000. It is the capital of Slovakia, which is an autonomous part of Czechoslovakia. Bratislava has oil-refining and chemical industries, produces cables, other electrical goods and ceramics, and processes foods. The centre of the city lies on the plain along the left bank of the Danube. Residential areas compete with vineyards on surrounding hills. Germans, formerly one-third of the population, called the city Pressburg. From 1526—1784 Bratislava was the capital of Hapsburg Hungary, and Hungarian kings were crowned there until 1830. The city is now an important route centre, and has many centres of learning and technical institutes. It is near to the Austrian and Hungarian borders, downstream from Vienna.

Bremen Together with its port of Bremerhaven, Bremen is West Germany's second largest seaport, outranked only by Hamburg. The combined population of the two cities, which are situated 35 miles apart at the mouth of the Weser River, is 755,977. Bremen, by far the larger of the two, is an industrial centre noted for its tobacco factories, motor-car works, machine shops and shipyards. It imports cotton, wool, tobacco, rice, coffee, and timber for Germany's thriving cities. Bremerhaven, founded in 1827 to accommodate the largest transatlantic liners, soon became the traditional point of departure for European emigrants. Germany's oldest seaboard city, Bremen was established in the 9th century and for many centuries was ruled by its archbishops. In the 13th century it became a leading member of the Hanseatic League, and even today its official name includes the words 'free Hansa city'. Numerous medieval buildings in the Old Town were severely damaged during World War II. After the armistice of 1945, Bremen became the chief supply depot of the U.S. occupation forces in Germany. Together with its outport, it now constitutes the smallest state within the German Federal Republic.

Brittany The peninsula of western France jutting out into the Atlantic Ocean between the English Channel and the Bay of Biscay. The rocky, picturesque coast was settled by Celtic refugees from Britain (hence the name Brittany) about the year 450 A.D. Throughout the Middle Ages the hardy Bretons fought to preserve their independence, but in 1491 they were joined to France by a royal marriage. To this day, however, they have held to their local traditions (including old-fashioned costumes and the language of their forebears). The inland city of Rennes (192,782) is the cultural capital of Brittany, while the seaport of

Brest (169,279) — almost completely destroyed during World War II — remains the chief base for France's Atlantic fleet. Tourists flock to Brittany, attracted by the quaintness of its fishing villages, the mystery of its prehistoric stone monuments, the richly adorned religious shrines, and the lacework and earthenware produced by the people. It supplies Paris with horticultural produce and fish.

Brno Second largest city of Czechoslovakia, in Moravia, with a population of 335,000. Brno has a diversified machine industry, producing tractors, Diesel engines, turbines and ball-bearings. Other important industries are woollens and leather. The old town, dominated by a medieval castle, is separated from the newer suburbs by broad boulevards. Just east of Brno is the site of the battle of Austerlitz, one of Napoleon's great victories (1805).

broom The home of most species of broom is Iberia, though it grows on sandy heath-land in the British Isles. Its flowers are yellow or white. The plant's twigs are used to make brooms, baskets and mats.

Bruges (Brugge) An old lace-manufacturing and trading centre (population 51,463) of Belgium near the North Sea. When it was founded, over a thousand years ago, Bruges was a seaport. But the sea has since receded and the bay (Et Zwin) has filled with silt. The city now lies 7 miles inland and is linked to its outport, Zeebrugge, by a canal. A Venice in miniature, Bruges has innumerable bridges and more waterways than streets. Its showpiece is a medieval belfry.

Brussels Capital of Belgium, with a French- and Flemish-speaking population of over one million people. Long known for its lace, Brussels is now a modern manufacturing centre with textile mills, assembly plants and chemical works. The city's central square is dominated by the 14th-century town hall, flanked by medieval guild halls. Nearby, in the heart of Brussels, close to the River Schelde, is the world's first commercial heliport (i.e., landing place for helicopters). Founded in the 10th century, Brussels grew from a wool-trading town into a world-famous centre for carpets, tapestries, and lace manufacture. It was ruled by the dukes of Burgundy, then in succession by Spain, Austria and France. When Belgium broke loose from the Netherlands in 1830, King Leopold I established his residence in Brussels. In 1958, Brussels played host to the first post-war World Fair. It is the cultural centre of Belgium, and has many museums and art galleries. It houses the headquarters of the Common Market.

Bucharest Capital of Romania since 1861, with a population of 1,475,050. The country's only large city, Bucharest is situated in the centre of the rich farmlands of the Walachian plain. Broad streets, parks and large business buildings give the city's central section the appearance of a modern metropolis, and a distinct Parisian flavour. The industrial suburbs, close to the railways which encircle the city, have been expanded in recent years. Large skyscraper flats intermingle with old low houses of peasant type which are gradually being cleared away. Intensive horticulture and farming surround the city, which has many industries based on farm produce, and large colourful markets. Bucharest owes much of its industrial importance to the nearby Ploesti oilfield, with which it is connected by pipelines.

Budapest Capital of Hungary, on the Danube River. It has a population of 1,940,000. The city consists of the old fortress town of Buda on the right bank, and of the newer commercial and

industrial sections of Pest, on the left bank, and on the island of Csepel. The three sections, linked by six bridges across the Danube, were merged into one city in 1872. Budapest accounts for two-thirds of Hungary's industries, dominates Hungarian affairs, and functions as the country's administrative and cultural centre. In World War II, Budapest was the scene of a great battle, in which Soviet troops besieged the German-occupied city. Two-thirds of its buildings were destroyed or damaged, and the population was reduced to 833,000.

Bulgaria This Balkan People's Republic, with an area of 43,000 square miles, consists of four natural regions; the North Bulgarian plain along the Danube, the Balkan Mountains, the Maritsa plain of eastern Rumelia and the Rhodope Mountains. The two mountain ranges merge in the west around Sofia, the capital. South of the Balkan mountains is a much warmer climatic area. Maize, wheat, tobacco, grapes, tomatoes and cotton are grown in the fertile lowlands on collectivized farms, some of which are irrigated. Sheep and goats are raised on the mountain slopes. Bulgaria has a steel mill near Sofia and lead-zinc mines in the Rhodope Mountains. In addition to ores, the country exports tobacco, cement, canned goods and the famous rose oil, used in perfume. The country is relatively poor in minerals, but has some salt, oil, and iron ore. Its 8.3 million people are mainly Eastern Orthodox; there is a small Turkish Moslem minority. The Bulgars migrated into their present area from Asia in the 7th century, and adopted the language and culture of the Slavs. The country was under Turkish rule for almost 500 years before it became independent in 1908. Since the Second World War, Bulgaria has adopted a Socialist form of government.

Burgundy A wine-growing region of central France; its traditional capital is Dijon. Some of the finest vineyards are found on a hill range called the Côte d'Or (i.e., the golden ridge). The famous white Chablis wines are also products of Burgundy. The first kingdom of Burgundy dates from the 5th century A.D., when a Germanic tribe settled in the of Burgundy, for varying periods of time, ruled most of Belgium, the Netherlands and north-eastern France. The end of Burgundy as an independent state came in 1477 when Charles the Bold was killed in battle at Nancy by the Swiss.

butter Butter is made from the cream of cow's milk by churning. Its fat content is approximately 87 per cent. Two and a half to three gallons of milk yield one pound of butter. Butter is a product of the temperate zone and is mainly traded there. The chief exporting countries are Denmark, the Netherlands, Australia and New Zealand. Great Britain is the world's largest importer of butter.

buzzard This bird of prey hardly occurs outside Europe. The colour varies — some are dark brown (nearly black), others are light in colour. The bird's nest has a diameter of 24—32 inches. Three to four eggs are laid. The buzzard feeds mainly on mice, rats, frogs, insects and snakes.

Cádiz A Spanish seaport (population 137,925) on the Atlantic, north-west of the Strait of Gibraltar. It was founded by the Phoenicians about 1100 B.C., and was held in turn by the Carthaginians, Romans, the various barbarian tribes and the Moors. Columbus sailed from here on his second voyage to America. The city thrived in the 16th and 17th centuries when it traded with the Spanish colonies in the New World. It is now a frequent port-of-call for ships plying the Mediterranean. It exports sherry and wine, salt, olives and cork. Cádiz is noted for its mild winters (all-year-round bathing is possible) and for its gay, palm-lined streets.

canals are artificial waterways connecting seas or navigable rivers and lakes — for example, the St Lawrence Seaway. Sea canals are either open waterways between seas of equal levels; (Suez Canal); or closed canals with locks where the water level varies with the tides (Kiel Canal); or are constructed where differences in height have to be overcome (Panama Canal). Inland canals usually pass over water-sheds connecting rivers, so they require flights of locks and sluice-gates for lifting or lowering ships, boats or barges. Central Europe has a dense network of west-east canals linking the north-flowing rivers. Holland and parts of Italy are also famous for their canals.

Carcassonne A well-preserved medieval city of south-western France, whose double ramparts, fifty turrets, churches and houses make it one of France's leading tourist attractions. It lies on the Canal du Midi between the Aude and Garonne rivers.

Carpathians An arc-shaped mountain range, extending more than 800 miles from the eastern end of the Alps to the lower Danube. The Carpathians are densely forested and of medium height (about 6,000 feet). Only in the High Tatras, an Alpine resort area on the Polish-Czechoslovak border, do the peaks rise higher than 8,000 feet into permanent snowfields. The Carpathians form a natural barrier between the Vistula and Dniester river basins in the north and east, on the one hand, and the Danube-Tisza basin of Hungary and Transylvania, on the other. The ranges are rich in minerals, while the Romanian part has more wild volcanic scenery and is more densely forested.

Castile Historic region of central Spain occupying a barren and monotonous tableland known as the Meseta. To the north lies Old Castile, separated from New Castile in the upper Tagus area by the central Sierras of Spain. Because of elevation (2,500 feet) and remoteness from the sea, the Castiles have cold winters and very hot summers, and frequently suffer from prolonged droughts. For centuries the dry grasslands have been grazed by sheep and goats, and much of the thin soil has been eroded for lack of a vegetal cover. Cereals, potatoes and forage crops are grown in sheltered spots where the underground water table is close to the surface. The drought-resistant olive tree does well in the south. Castile became a self-governing kingdom in 1035. Its name derives from the numerous castles built by Christian noblemen against Moorish attacks. By the marriage of Ferdinand and Isabella (the Catholic rulers) the two leading kingdoms of the Iberian Peninsula, Castile and Aragon, were at last united in 1479. Madrid has been the chief city of Castile since the 16th century when Philip II made it his capital. The Castilian dialect has evolved as the literary language of Spain, the 'King's English' of the Spanish-speaking world.

Catania A seaport on the Mediterranean and the second largest city (population 412,721) of Sicily, in a fertile plain at the foot of Mt Etna. It was founded in the 8th century B.C., then passed into Greek hands and later became a Roman colony. The city has been threatened repeatedly by earthquakes and by violent eruptions of Mt Etna, notably in 1669 when it was ringed by a fiery flow of lava. Catania's chief industry is the processing of locally mined sulphur, and tourism is developing.

cement One of the most important building materials of the modern industrial economy. It is produced by burning a mixture of clay and limestone. Concrete is made by mixing cement, sand and gravel with water and allowing the mixture to harden. The largest producers are the U.S.A., the U.S.S.R., West Germany, Japan, Italy, France and Great Britain.

ceramics Ceramics are products made from burnt clay. The so-called fine ceramics, distinguished according to the raw material and the finishing process, are terracotta, majolica (faience), earthenware, stone-ware and porcelain. They are used for the manufacture of household china, luxury goods, tiles and kitchen sinks.

Cevennes This mountain range forms the steep and dissected south-eastern edge of the French Central Plateau, and reaches its highest elevation in Mont Mézenc (5,755 feet). Descending from the cold and sparsely populated plateau through grassy slopes, beechwoods and vineyards, one reaches the highly cultivated Rhône Valley with its southerly character. The cold wind from the Cevennes, the mistral, can do great harm to the vineyards. In the coal-fields on the eastern edge of the mountains, heavy industry has developed, especially at St. Etienne and Le Creusot.

chamois This goat-like animal is found in the Alps, high above the timber line. Elusive and swift-footed, it is a prized quarry for the hunter. It is able to make high leaps and to land safely on treacherous mountain ledges. The chamois is easily recognised by its horns, which rise straight up and then hook abruptly backwards. The soft, pliant leather known as 'shammy' was originally made from the hide of the chamois.

Champagne An historic region of north-eastern France, its western part being famous throughout the world for sparkling white wines. The cathedral city of Rheims is the chief processing centre, where the wine is aged in limestone caverns. Except for its vineyards, western Champagne is a barren, sparsely settled district in which grass provides a meagre pasture for sheep and goats.

Chartres A small French market-town (population 28,750) 50 miles south-west of Paris. Its Gothic cathedral, built in the 11—13th centuries, with matchless sculptures and stained-glass windows, is one of the great masterpieces of medieval architecture. Its two graceful spires overlook the gently rolling countryside.

Cherbourg A transatlantic seaport (population 38,262) of north-western France, on the English Channel, less than 100 miles south of Southampton, England. Its harbour was heavily damaged in World War II during the Allied invasion of Normandy (1944).

chestnut, sweet The sweet chestnut grows to a height of 110 feet and has a dark-grey bark. The flowers appear in June/July. The slender, yellowish catkins bear staminate flowers. Its fruit — the chestnut, or marron — is covered with a brown leathery skin enclosed in a prickly envelope. The home of the sweet chestnut is in southern Europe, North Africa and western Asia.

chicory A common European plant cultivated for its root and as a winter salad plant. The roots, when roasted and ground, serve as a substitute or flavouring for coffee.

clock-making industry The clock-making industry developed when accurate time-measuring instruments became essential in a variety of fields — for example, astronomy, navigation and industry. Clocks actuated by springs or weights gradually reached a high standard of perfection, but are today frequently replaced by electric clocks which have better time-keeping properties. The latest developments are in electric oscillatory circuits, which are independent of mechanical disturbance and precise to within thousandths of a second. The most extensive clock-making industry is found in the U.S.A., but Switzerland is still leading in the manufacture of watches, and Britain in the manufacture of ships' chronometers. Germany, France and Italy also produce efficient clocks and watches.

cod This fish, up to 5 feet long, lives in the North Atlantic and the Pacific. The skin is olive-green to brown, mottled with dark spots. The cod is a deepwater fish which is caught mainly near Iceland and off the coast of Lofoten and Newfoundland. It is dried or cured and is also used to produce cod-liver oil.

Cognac This is a brandy named after the French town of Cognac in south-west France. It is manufactured entirely from the end products of wine-making in many parts of southern France, and true Cognac is a highly distilled product, matured in wood.

Cologne (Köln) An historic city (population 866,308) of West Germany, on the Rhine. It was founded in A.D. 50 as an outpost of the Roman empire. Since Napoleonic times, Cologne has been a hub of western Europe's trade and communications by rail and sea. The first railway bridge across the Rhine was built here in the mid-19th century. Its industries specialise in Diesel engines and road and rail vehicles, armaments and electro-technical equipment. The pharmaceutical industry dates back to 1700, when it first produced the widely known *eau de Cologne*. The city's river port will admit small sea-going ships which maintain a regular service to several North Sea ports. Heavily bombed during World War II, Cologne lost most of its medieval inner city, which has since undergone redevelopment with pedestrian precincts. However, the splendid Gothic cathedral escaped with only minor damage. The city's medieval importance can be ascribed to the influence of its powerful archbishops, who became princes of the Holy Roman Empire. Though its cathedral was begun in 1248, it was completed only in 1880.

Constance, Lake One of western Europe's largest lakes (200 square miles; 40 miles long), it lies on the border of West Germany, Austria and Switzerland. The Rhine flows into and out of it, the lake acting as a regulator for its seasonally high and low flows. Popular resorts on the shore are Constance (Germany), Bregenz (Austria), and Rorschach (Switzerland). The attractive town of Lindau lies on an island in the lake.

Chicory

continental shelf This forms the outer margin of the continents, submerged under shallow seas. The outer edge is usually at 600 feet under sea level, bounded by the continental slope down to the oceanic platform at about 2½ miles depth. Wide shelf-seas are situated north of Siberia and off the east coast of America. The British Isles lie on the British Shelf, which also includes the North Sea. Altogether the continental shelves of the Earth cover an area of 11 million square miles, i.e., 7.8 per cent of the ocean surface. During the Ice Age, the continental shelf was mostly dry land, for much water was locked up in the ice sheets, and it is covered with sand and gravel, while on the ocean bed there is only very fine clay. The great rivers of the continents have cut gorges up to 3,000 feet deep into the shelf border (Indus, Ganges, Hudson, Mississippi). Shelf areas are usually rich fishing grounds (Newfoundland, North Sea, Iceland, Alaska). The presence of Continental shelves has enabled drilling rigs to be set up in relatively shallow waters.

Copenhagen is the capital of Denmark and, with its suburbs and the now-enclosed town of Frederiksberg, forms the only million-population city of Scandinavia (1,377,605). It is one of the most attractive cities of Europe, with a wealth of old buildings and a picturesque central core. It is strategically situated on The Sound, a narrow stretch of water joining the Baltic with the Kattegat. It is partly a free port and has large shipyards, oil refineries and machine shops on the island of Amager to the south-east, on which the airport is situated. Plans are afoot to replace the ferries to south Sweden with a long bridge to Malmö, which is less than 20 miles away. The city is well-known for its porcelain, glassware, furniture, jewellery, silverware and brewing industries. Limited within its defensive walls until 1864, Copenhagen has now spread over the country to the west, and has large parks and high-class residential quarters to the north. Many of the buildings in central Copenhagen are splendid examples of Renaissance architecture: the Stock Exchange, Regensen — the students' hostel — and many of the Royal Palaces, most instigated by Christian IV. It is extremely popular with tourists, two main attractions being the Tivoli Gardens — an amusement park of great enchantment — and Strøget, a winding street in the centre of the city between the Town Hall and the harbour, now closed to traffic and forming a shopping precinct.

Córdoba A city (population 231,641) of Andalusia famed for its Moorish splendour, especially the Alcazar. Its mosque, now a cathedral, was one of the great religious centres of Islam; it was built between the 8th and the 10th centuries A.D. Captured by the Moors in 711, Córdoba soon became a world centre of Moslem art and culture; goat-skin leather, silver, and gold were worked by skilled artisans. In 1236 Ferdinand III of Castile took the city from the Moors, and its prosperity soon declined, never to be regained. Today, its historic monuments are tourist attractions.

cork oak Cork is obtained from the evergreen cork oak, grown in the Mediterranean region. The bark is first stripped when the tree is fifteen or twenty years old, and thereafter every eight or ten years until the tree is 200 years old. Cork is used for bottle stoppers, life-buoys, and in the production of linoleum and shoe soles. The chief producers are Portugal, Spain and the Atlas lands of North Africa.

Cork oak

Corsica A mountainous island (3,400 square miles) belonging to France, in the western Mediterranean north of Sardinia. Its 269,831 inhabitants speak an Italian dialect and cherish many old-fashioned customs, among them the *vendetta*, a bloody feud between rival families. The dense shrubbery (called *maquis*) which covers the island offers concealment to outlaws, for whom Corsica was notorious. The French Resistance workers during World War II derived their name from this shrubbery and became known as the *Maquis*. The chief towns are Ajaccio, the birthplace of Napoleon Bonaparte; Bastia, a fishing and air port; and Bonifacio, facing the island of Sardinia. Corsica was permanently annexed to France in 1796. The chief products are wine, olives, chestnuts and citrus fruit.

Cracow Largest city (population 571,000) of southern Poland, on the upper Vistula River. This 1,000-year-old city became the residence of the kings of Poland in the 14th century. A famous European university, the Jagallonian, founded in 1364, a cathedral, and other medieval buildings, date from that period. Cracow is dominated by a hill called the Wawel, where the kings and other great Poles are buried. The city was the capital of the Republic of Cracow from 1815 to 1846. The city was part of Austria-Hungary during the late 19th century. It escaped destruction in World War II. Since 1949, the large steel mills of Nowa Huta have been built in Cracow's eastern suburbs.

Crete Largest of the Greek islands in the Mediterranean, guarding the entrance to the Aegean Sea. It is 160 miles long, 10 to 35 miles wide, and predominantly mountainous. Mount Ida, 8,196 feet, is the highest point, while the north coast has many good harbours, with Heraklion (Candia) the main city. Its 500,000 people eke out a meagre livelihood on the island's small patches of cultivable land. The climate is sub-tropical, and vines, olives, cotton, almonds and citrus fruits are grown and exported. The Minoan civilisation, known to us from excavations at Cnossos, flourished on the island of Crete more than 3,000 years ago. Here, according to Greek legend, Daedalus built the labyrinth in which the monster Minotaur was confined. During World War II, Crete was seized by German forces in an airborne invasion. Previously it was controlled by Romans, Arabs, Greeks, Venetians and Turks.

crossbill The bright-red crossbills are very lively, gregarious birds, the size of a sparrow. They live in coniferous forests in mountain areas and feed on pine seeds, which they extract from the cones by means of their crossed bills. They inhabit trees and are very rarely seen on the ground.

cypress An evergreen tree of the Mediterranean region, with a tall, slender appearance, dark-green scale-like leaves and a durable wood. The cypress is among the longest-living trees, often attaining 2,000 years.

Czechoslovakia This Socialist Republic of Central Europe, with an area of 50,000 square miles and a population of 14.3 million, was created in 1918 out of parts of Austria-Hungary. Its people, basically Czech and Slovak (speaking two related Slavic languages), originally included a large German minority in a fringe area round the borders with Germany. These Germans were expelled after Germany's defeat in 1945. Czechoslovakia consists of three major regions: the Bohemian basin (Čechy), centred on Prague (Praha), the national capital; Moravia, drained by the Morava River, a tributary of the Danube; and Slovakia (Slovensko), in the Carpathian Mountains. The country's highly productive agricultural economy produces grain, sugar beets, hops and malt. Czechoslovakia has coal and iron ore resources in the Erz Gebirge providing the basis for a steel industry centred in

Newly cut logs afloat on the Paijanne, one of the many lakes which stud Finland's vast forests

Gdansk, an important Polish seaport on the Baltic Sea, was formerly the Free City of Danzig

Ostrava. Other ores found are those of copper, gold, lead and graphite, as well as asbestos and kaolin. Forestry is also important. The country is a leading exporter of machinery and other manufactured goods. Glass, porcelain, pencils and the beer of Pilsen are typical products. Czechoslovak resorts, such as Karlovy Vary, are world famous. Czechs are, for the most part, Roman Catholics. Since World War II, Czechoslovakia has adopted a Socialist form of government.

● **dairy products** About 40 per cent of all the milk produced in the world is consumed in liquid form. Another 40 per cent is converted into butter, 10 per cent (skimmed) into cheese, and the rest is fed to livestock or utilised for other products, such as condensed milk, powdered milk and ice cream. Butter is the fatty part of milk that separates when cream or milk is agitated and churned. Two and a half to three gallons of milk yield one pound of butter. Milk contains proteins, sugar, vitamins, fats and dissolved mineral matter. The United States and the Soviet Union, which are the leading butter producers, consume their butter at home. Among the trading nations, New Zealand, Denmark, Australia and the Netherlands are the exporters, and Britain is the chief importer. Most of the world's cheese is made from skimmed milk, which remains after cream has been separated from whole milk. There are about 500 varieties of cheese, with each country having its own characteristic speciality. Other dairy products are made from curdled or fermented milk; for example, cottage cheese and yogurt.

● **Danube River** Second longest river in Europe, after the Volga. It rises in the Black Forest of south-western Germany and flows 1,750 miles to the Black Sea. It traverses Bavaria and Austria, borders Czechoslovakia, then flows through Hungary and Yugoslavia, and forms the border between Romania and Bulgaria, before entering its delta and three distributaries, the northernmost being the present Romanian-Soviet boundary. The upper course of the Danube is famous for its scenery and its many historic and literary associations. Below Vienna, the Danube is a meandering waterway of the plains. It is interrupted only by the rapids in the Iron Gate (the gorge on the Yugoslav-Romanian border where the river breaks through the Carpathian Mountains). The Danube is an important traffic artery, but its volume of commerce has been curtailed by the many political frontiers it crosses along its route, and because it flows into a sea that is far from the world's main trade routes. It is navigable by barge from Regens-

burg and has a canal connection to the Rhine. The main ports are in Romania, at Galati and Braila.

● **Dardanelles** At their narrowest, less than a mile in width, the straits of the Dardanelles link the Aegean Sea to that of Marmara and, as the Bosporus, separate Europe from Asia. The Greeks called these straits 'Hellespont', and both Xerxes and Alexander the Great led their armies across them. Turkish since 1356, they are a vital and strategic 'eye of a needle' for passages between the Black and the Mediterranean Seas. They will always be associated in Britain with the unfortunate campaign during the First World War, when attempts to seize control of the Dardanelles ended in failure, after initially successful landings on the Gallipoli Peninsula by British, Australian and New Zealand troops.

● **deer, fallow** The fallow deer is smaller than the red deer and differs from it by its palmate antlers and long tail. Its colour varies: some are reddish brown with white spots; some nearly white; others dark brown. Its original home was Persia, Mesopotamia, Asia Minor and North Africa, but the fallow deer was brought to Europe in very ancient times. It is still fairly widespread in the British Isles but is almost extinct in its real homelands.

● **Delft** (83,698 inhabitants in 1970). A town in the Netherlands, south-east of The Hague, which is famous for its faience and porcelain, especially from the mid-17th to mid-18th centuries. It is also known through its famous artist, Jan Vermeer (van Delft), who found a wealth of subjects in the fine houses, beautiful lime trees and canals within the town centre in the Middle Ages. Today, Delft houses the internationally known Technical University of the Netherlands.

● **Denmark** A small kingdom (16,600 square miles; population 4.9 million) of north-western Europe whose territory, consisting of the Jutland peninsula and a large number of low-lying islands, lies between the main mass of the continent and the Scandinavian Peninsula. At its closest point, Denmark — classified as a Scandinavian country — is only 3 miles from Sweden. The narrows and straits that separate Denmark from Scandinavia proper (they are known as the Skagerrak, the Kattegat, the Belts and The Sound) form navigable passages between the North Sea and the Baltic Sea. The principal islands are Sjealand (Zealand), on which Copenhagen — the capital — is located, and Fyn

(Fünen). Far to the east lies the island of Bornholm, a noted Danish resort. More than three-quarters of Denmark is farmland, and Denmark is recognised throughout the world for the efficiency and productivity of its agriculture. Until 1958, dairy farming constituted the chief source of wealth and of exports revenue, including bacon, butter, eggs, condensed milk, live cattle, and several distinctive brands of cheese as its main products. Cattle and pig rearing is carried on in close association with the production of barley and fodder root crops, for there is little pasture land. Most of the marketing of produce and the purchase of fertilisers, seed and equipment is done co-operatively. Denmark also has a large merchant marine and a modern, mechanised fishing fleet which frequents the Baltic and North Sea banks.

The Danes are predominantly Lutheran and their language is Teutonic. Almost one quarter of the population lives in and around Copenhagen, the country's main industrial centre, where machinery (Diesel engines), textiles and high-class furnishings and jewellery are produced. A thousand years ago Denmark was a powerful nation. Under King Canute (11th century) it ruled much of England and Norway, and in the 14th century it extended its sway over large parts of northern Europe. The personal union of Denmark, Norway and Sweden under a Danish monarch lasted until 1520, when Sweden broke away to form an independent kingdom. Norway, however, remained under Danish rule until 1814. In the mid-19th century Denmark fought two wars with Prussia over Schleswig-Holstein, losing it in 1864. In 1920, however, a popular vote returned part of Slesvig (Schleswig) to Denmark. The country remained neutral during World War I; in 1917 it sold the Virgin Islands, its only possession in the western hemisphere, to the United States. During World War II Denmark was occupied by Germany until the armistice of 1945. In that year Iceland formed an independent republic. The Faeroe Islands, in the North Atlantic Ocean, continue to recognise the king as their sovereign but have substantial self-government, while Greenland is still a part of Denmark. Since 1950 industrialisation in Denmark has been very rapid, mainly in specialised engineering, textiles, chemical and pharmaceutical, furniture and food industries, so that industrial produce is now a more important export than dairy produce, and industry now employs more people than farming.

● **diamond trade** Diamonds are mined in many parts of Africa—notably South Africa, South-West Africa, Botswana, Zaire, Angola, Tanzania, Ghana and Sierra Leone—and in Russia, Brazil, Venezuela, Guyana, Indonesia and India. More than 85% of the world's newly mined diamonds are sold in London, through the De Beers' Central Selling Organisation, in such a way as to maintain stable prices irrespective of demand. By weight 80% of the diamonds produced are used in industry and only 20% are of sufficiently high quality to be used for jewellery. These gem diamonds, used for jewellery, are cut and polished by highly skilled workers in the world's major diamond cutting centres, namely Antwerp, New York, Tel Aviv, Bombay, London and Amsterdam. Because diamonds are the hardest known substance, the industrial qualities play an invaluable part in modern science and technology. The application and uses of these diamonds are particularly evident in precision engineering, as a drilling material, stone cutting saws and boring tools.

● **Dinaric Alps** form the mountain range east of the Adriatic coast. The western part forms islands, peninsulas and gulfs. The interior shows barren hills, limestone formations and gorges. Rivers often run in long subterranean caves; this is called the Karst, in north-west Yugoslavia. The rainwater produces sharp ribs in the denuded limestone.

Golden Eagle

which lie between deep clefts. A characteristic feature of the Karst area is its stalactite caves. Faults produce numerous depressions on the surface. In these *polja* and *dolina* the eroded red soil accumulates and allows modest cultivation in the midst of grey rocks and under-developed shrubs. The *polja* appear like oases in a sun-scorched stone-desert. One of the most beautiful caves is near Postojna, in the frontier region between the Alps and Karst. It is 2½ miles long, and the labyrinth of subterranean grottoes and passages has a length of 13 miles.

Dortmund A city (population 648,883) of West Germany in the industrial Ruhr region. It is the centre of a coal and iron-mining district which supplies coke works, blast furnaces and steel mills in the area. It is a busy inland port on the Dortmund-Ems Canal, which gives the Ruhr direct access to the North Sea and by-passes the Netherlands. It was formerly famous for its breweries.

Dresden The third largest city (population 501,184) of East Germany, on the Elbe River. It consists of the old historic city of Saxony on the left bank and a new industrial section on the right. It has a large river traffic and is an important rail centre for traffic to Poland and Prague. Industries are many and varied: electrical goods, precision instruments, cameras and typewriters are among the city's products. As the royal residence of the kings of Saxony, Dresden became a famous artistic and cultural centre. Many of its famous historic buildings, in baroque or rococo style, were destroyed by bombing in World War II. The world-famous art museum known as the Zwinger is among the structures rebuilt after the war. The surrounding area is rich agricultural land.

Duisburg West Germany's largest inland port on the Rhine, serving the industrial Ruhr district. It can be reached by ocean-going ships which bring iron ore, petroleum, timber and raw materials to the steel mills and chemical plants that dominate the landscape. It manufactures a quarter of West Germany's iron and steel. Heavily damaged by Allied air raids during World War II, Duisburg is once again the busiest trans-shipping centre on the Rhine and Europe's largest inland port. Its population has again risen to 457,891.

Düsseldorf The leading commercial centre (population 680,806) of the Ruhr district of West Germany, with a deep-water harbour on the Rhine 20 miles north of Cologne. Its factories produce steel products, textiles, chemicals and machinery (DKW cars). As a centre of German war industry, Düsseldorf was severely damaged by Allied air attacks during World War II. After the war it was designated as the capital of North Rhine-Westphalia, the most populous (17.1 million people) of

the German Federal Republic's constituent states. It is a cultural and congress centre, famous for its exhibitions.

● **eagle, golden** The largest of the typical eagles, this magnificent bird ranges over the mountains of Europe and Asia. It has a wingspread of more than six feet. The golden eagle plunges after its prey with great force, attacking even large animals when pressed by hunger.

● **Ebro River** Spain's longest river (575 miles), the Ebro flows into the Mediterranean south-west of Barcelona. It rises in the Cantabrian Mountains, crossing the arid plains of Aragon, and waters the fields and orchards of Saragossa through miles of canals and irrigation ditches. The delta is marshy and silted, but is partially reclaimed for rice cultivation. Power plants have been built on the river's headwaters. The Iberian Peninsula (occupied by Spain and Portugal) was named after the Ebro (Iberus, in Latin).

● **edelweiss** A small perennial herb of the alpine regions, growing just below the snow line in the Alps, Pyrenees and Carpathians. It has white hairy leaves, the highest of which surround a cluster of five or six flowers. Its blossom is the national flower of Switzerland.

Edelweiss

● **Elbe River** A major stream of central Europe, 700 miles long. It rises in Czechoslovakia as the

Labe and flows past Dresden, Magdeburg and Hamburg in Germany to the North Sea. An important European waterway, the Elbe is linked by canals with the Rhine and the Oder Rivers. Its 60-mile-long estuary on the North Sea is used by ocean-going vessels as far as Hamburg. The normally heavy traffic on the Elbe has been sharply reduced since World War II because of the political division of Germany.

● **electric power** Large-scale production of electricity began at the turn of the 20th century and has been a characteristic of modern industrial development. There are three main types of electric power station: thermal, hydro-electric and nuclear. Thermal stations use coal, oil, natural gas or other fuels to raise steam. Electricity is then produced by generators driven by steam turbines. Such stations are usually located near fuel sources. In atomic power plants, the heat needed to raise steam is produced by atomic reactors. Hydro-electric power stations use falling water to drive water turbines, which in turn drive power generators. The required head, or force, of water on the turbines can be produced either by a great waterfall or by some other large volume of swiftly moving water. The main power-producing countries are also the leading industrial nations — the United States, the Soviet Union, Britain, West Germany and France. Some mountainous countries, such as Switzerland, Sweden and Norway, derive nearly all of their power from hydro-electric stations; others, such as Britain and Belgium, from coal-fed thermal stations.

● **elm** This is a high tree, with fan-like branches and a distinctive patterned bark. The fruit (manna) is a circular seed in the centre of a thin wing. There are three forms — the Wych elm, common in Scotland, the field elms, and the Dutch elm. All are widely distributed in Europe, requiring a deep rich soil, and the elm's waterproof timber is used in dock construction and ship-building.

● **Essen** The great steel-manufacturing centre (population 696,905) of West Germany, dominating the Ruhr heavy-industry district. Coal-mines

Gibraltar, the British citadel at the entrance to the Mediterranean Sea

form a ring around the city, the deepest and newest to the north. In 1810, the Krupp family — builders of Europe's largest industrial empire — established the first steel mill in Essen. The city's phenomenal growth continued until World War II, when Allied bombers selected it as one of their main targets. After the war, however, it took Essen less than a decade to rebuild many of its shattered plants and to restore Germany's position as Europe's leading steelmaker. The city has many large suburbs and estates built by the Krupps for their workers.

● **European Common Market** An economic union agreed upon by the signing of the Treaty of Rome in 1957 by six European nations: France, German Federal Republic, Italy, Belgium, the Netherlands, and Luxembourg. The formation of the Common Market or European Economic Community (E.E.C.) has been the first real attempt to unite western Europe economically.

In the progress towards unity have come such things as the reduction or abolition of tariffs against each other's exports, fewer restrictions on factory building in each other's countries, international agricultural co-operation, oil pipe lines and electrical grid systems across national frontiers, and free movement of labour (with welfare and housing benefits) and tourists between member countries. All this has resulted in one vast and potentially wealthy industrial region stretching from Northern Italy to the Ruhr region of Germany. To counteract regional imbalances, the European Investment Bank has helped finance projects designed to reduce population movement to the large central areas.

The European Free Trade Association (Outer Seven) grew out of the inability of Great Britain, Austria, Switzerland, Portugal, Denmark, Norway and Sweden to gain entry to the Common Market, and confines itself to the adoption of a common tariff.

In 1972, however, the 'doors' of the Common Market had been opened and the United Kingdom, Irish Republic, Denmark and Norway all signed a preliminary Treaty of entry in Brussels.

● **Faeroes** (meaning sheep-islands) are a group of 24 rugged, basaltic islands (540 square miles; population 38,527) in the North Atlantic Ocean between Iceland and Scotland. Settled by Norsemen in the 9th century, the Faeroes have been part of the kingdom of Denmark since the end of the 14th century. They obtained local self-rule in 1948, and are reviving their native language, which is a mixture of Icelandic and Norwegian. Fishing, whaling and sheep-raising are the principal occupations on these gale-swept islands, whose harbours remain ice-free all the year round. The main town is Torshavn (7,500). Since 1968 they have been included in E.F.T.A.

● **falcon, Iceland** This falcon belongs to the race of Gyrfalcons and is found in Iceland. Its body is compact, the bill well developed, the legs long and strong. The plumage is greyish-white, streaked with black.

● **Finland (Suomi)** An independent republic (130,000 square miles; population 4.7 million) of northern Europe, bordering on the Soviet Union. In the south and west, the country faces two arms of the Baltic Sea: the Gulf of Finland and the Gulf of Bothnia. By the peace treaty of 1947, Finland surrendered part of her territory to the U.S.S.R., notably her outlet to the Arctic Ocean at the far-northern port of Petsamo (now called Petjenga) and the industrial city of Viipuri (now called Vyborg) at the approaches to Leningrad. The northern third of Finland lies within the Arctic Circle, barren lands of the midnight sun inhabited by semi-nomadic Lapps and their large herds of reindeer. The highest point is Halditjokko, near the Norwegian border. From there the land falls

gradually south to the southern part of the country, which is dotted with thousands of interconnected lakes, formed by retreating glaciers during the Ice Age, and heavily forested. The lakes are used for

Lumber rafts in Finland

timber rafting and, wherever possible, for the generation of hydro-electric power. A very small part of Finland in the south-west is suitable for cultivation, but over a third of the area is covered with high-quality timber, the nation's richest natural resource. Lumber, wood products, pulp and paper are exported to the United Kingdom, the Soviet Union, Germany, and even the United States. Helsinki, the modern capital, is the leading manufacturing centre; Finnish glassware and ceramics enjoy a growing reputation in the United Kingdom and the United States. The Finns, a people of central Asian origin, came to this northern land early in the Christian era. They were ruled by the Swedes from the 12th century until 1809, when Finland became a grand duchy within the Russian Empire. The Bolshevik revolution of 1917 marked the end of Russian domination, and in 1919 the country finally achieved its independence. During World War II, Finland conducted two unsuccessful campaigns against the Soviet Union, first independently in 1939—40, and again in 1941 as Germany's ally. About one-tenth of the population of Finland speak Swedish, especially in the Aland Islands, which lie at Sweden's doorstep in the Baltic Sea. Finland possesses Europe's largest copper reserve at Outukumpu, though most of her exports comprise forest produce. The largest imports are metals, machinery and oil, as well as foodstuffs.

The three largest cities, with their metropolitan areas all in the south, are Helsinki (804,256 inhabitants), Tampere (217,311) and Turku (220,340).

● **fisheries** Prehistoric evidence shows that from very ancient times man has used the enormous resources of the sea and rivers to supplement his food. The importance of fisheries in food economy has grown steadily and will continue to grow as the world's population increases. While inland fisheries, in rivers, lakes and ponds, only provide local supplies, apart from salmon and trout, sea fisheries have taken over the supply of inland areas, as the transport of fresh fish has been speeded up and a variety of fish preserves is now available. Sea-fishing is either restricted to coastal areas (coastal fisheries) or ranges, as deep-sea fishing, across the oceans. Within the territorial waters (three-mile limit) fishing is only permitted to the natives of a particular country. Most countries have extended this limit to 12 miles, in view of increasing international agreement. As the most desirable fish collect at definite seasonal periods at certain fishing grounds, large fishing fleets assemble in these areas, such as the Dogger Bank in the North Sea, the Grand Banks of Newfoundland and the Barents Sea. The trawlers of each nation are accompanied by naval vessels, which give protection, medical service and maintain communications with the home land. To locate the shoals, modern electronic devices are now used. In order to preserve the stock of fish, protected areas and closed seasons have been introduced in sea and inland fisheries. In rivers, lakes and ponds fish have been cultivated for a long time. These provide mainly valuable species, such as trout and carp. The natural stock of fish in rivers has been harmed by the waste waters of certain industries and has in some areas been more or less destroyed. Regulation and canalisation of rivers has also caused damage. For fish migrating up the rivers to spawn, such as salmon, special steps are erected near weirs and locks so that they can pass these obstructions. The foremost fishing nation is Japan, which depends on the resources of the sea for a population restricted to a small area of cultivated land. In the Pacific region the Soviet Union takes second place. In Europe, Norway, Great Britain and Germany have the biggest landings of fish, then France, Spain and Italy.

● **fish preserving** Because of its perishable nature fish is preserved by salting, pickling, smoking, steaming, heating in oil, drying and freezing.

The historic town of Dubrovnik, on the Adriatic coast of Yugoslavia, has become a popular seaside resort, attracting visitors from all over Europe

Commercially, herring preserves are most important. These are mainly smoked as kippers or bloaters, or salted. Related species are sprats, which are smoked, and sardines, which are salted and cooked in oil and canned. Shell-fish and crustaceans are also canned.

fjord or fiord A long, narrow inlet of the sea, with steep rocky sides. Fjords are especially common along the coasts of Norway, West Scotland, Greenland and Alaska. Glaciers descending from the adjacent mountains carved deep valleys along the coast, and the sea later invaded the lower ends of these valleys, forming the present fjords when the ice melted.

Lyse Fjord, east of Stavanger, Norway

flax One of the world's major fibre plants, flax is grown commercially both for its seed and its fibre. The seed yields linseed oil, used in painting, and linseed cake, a cattle feed. The long, silky bast fibre, obtained from the stalk, is used in the making of linen.

Florence An historic city (population 459,058) of north-central Italy, situated in the fertile Arno River valley amidst the olive-clad hills of the Apennines. As the cradle of the Italian Renaissance, Florence is one of the richest art centres of the world, a living museum of the works of Michelangelo, Leonardo da Vinci, Raphael, Donatello, Giotto, Cellini, Botticelli and other great masters of painting, sculpture and architecture. The city's most famous buildings date from the 13th—16th centuries, and range in style from Gothic to Renaissance to flowering Baroque. They include the Gothic cathedral, with its impressive dome, a separate campanile (bell tower) designed by Giotto, and the baptistry whose famous doors were carved by Ghiberti and Pisano; the church of San Lorenzo, which contains the tombs of the Medici family by Michelangelo; the imposing city hall (Palazzo della Signoria); and two rambling 16th-century palaces (Uffizi and Pitti), which house priceless collections of paintings. The ancient Ponte Vecchio (whose roadway is lined with small shops built into the stone structure) spans the Arno River; it was the only Florentine bridge spared from destruction in World War II. Florence became an important trading centre for silk and wool around 1200 A.D. It was the scene of bloody rivalry between the Guelphs and the Ghibellines which resulted, among other things, in the banishment of Dante. Under the rule of the Medici, Florence grew into the 'golden city' of the Renaissance, the unquestioned leader of Europe's cultural revival. In 1569 it became the capital of the grand duchy of Tuscany, which came under Hapsburg rule in the 18th century. Between 1865 and 1870, Florence was the capital of the newly formed kingdom of Italy.

Among the hills of Brittany lies the little French town of Dinan, a few miles inland from the English Channel coast

föhn wind The föhn wind is a warm mountain wind, blowing down the northern Alpine valleys on about thirty days each year. Air rising over the southern Alps gives rain and heat is liberated. On descending on the northern side the air becomes rapidly warmer, and helps to thaw the winter snows.

France the second largest country of Europe, after Russia, lies between the Atlantic Ocean and the Mediterranean Sea. Its area is 213,000 square miles and its population 49,778,540. The capital is Paris. France displays great variety in its landscapes, ranging from the marshes and dunes of the north and west, to the high peaks of the Alps in the south-east, and the Pyrenees Mountains in the south. Much of France is bordered by the sea, whereas its well-defined natural land frontiers have accounted in part for the relative stability of French territory throughout the last 300 years. In contrast to the high border ranges, the interior of France contains uplands of medium elevation, including the Central Massif (one of France's most isolated regions of low productivity); the wooded Vosges, in the north-east; and the low hills of Brittany and Normandy. These interior uplands surround the river basins of the Seine, the Loire, the Garonne and the Rhône Rivers, which are connected by a network of navigable tributaries and canals. Because of France's west coast situation on the Atlantic, and the influence of the North Atlantic Drift, the country's climate is largely maritime, with mild winters and cool summers. Yet fashionable resorts along the south coast bring native and foreign visitors to France throughout the year. France is one of the leading wine producers of the world, accounting for about 30 per cent of the world's total output. The names of wine-growing regions (Champagne, Burgundy, Rhône Valley, Bordeaux) are well known. About one-fourth of the population derives its living from farming. Wheat is grown in fertile northern soils, maize in the south. Sugar beet is also widely cultivated, France having over 100 sugar-beet factories producing about 850,000 tons of sugar per year. Cattle rearing is important in all parts of France, while sheep and horses are bred in various parts. In the south, rice, citrus fruit and other subtropical crops are grown. Except for the silk-milling industry in the Lyon area, and other isolated pockets round Southern towns, French industry is concentrated in the northern parts of the country. There, coal and iron deposits provide the basis for heavy industries at Lille, Roubaix and other centres. Recently a large steel smelting complex

has been established at Dunkerque with all the advantages of a coastal site. Domestic bauxite deposits provide raw material for a large aluminium industry in the south, where extensive deposits of natural gas and sulphur are now being mined at Lacq in the foothills of the Pyrenees. Hydro-electric stations produce about half of France's power supply. The country's large ports are Marseille on the Mediterranean: Bordeaux on the Atlantic; and Cherbourg and Le Havre on the English Channel. The largest towns are Paris, Marseille, Lyon, Toulouse, Bordeaux, Nice, Nantes and Strasbourg.

The recorded history of France begins with the Roman conquest under Julius Caesar about 55 B.C., when the country was known as Gaul. France was part of the empire of Charlemagne in A.D. 800. Later the Capetian dynasty established an increasingly powerful royal authority. The Valois dynasty succeeded to the throne in 1328, but its claim was disputed by England. This provoked the Hundred Years' War (1337—1453), from which France, roused by Joan of Arc, finally emerged victorious. The Reformation in the 16th century brought ferocious conflicts between Catholics and Protestants. A centralised royal régime reached its peak under Louis XIV, who extended the French overseas empire to Canada, Louisiana and India. The excesses of Louis XV, intolerable tax burdens, the rise of an intellectual movement and a series of disastrous wars led to the French Revolution (1789) and the ultimate emergence of Napoleon Bonaparte. After his brief though spectacular conquest of most of Europe, France was reduced essentially to its present limits. During the 19th century successive restorations of the monarchy, alternating with revolutions (1830, 1848, 1871), eventually terminated in the establishment of the Third Republic, which lasted until World War II. Since the war, proclamation of a Fourth Republic led to the return to power of General de Gaulle as President of France.

Frankfurt-am-Main An historic trading and financial centre (population 660,410) of West Germany, at the hub of the Rhine-Main industrial district. Here are the headquarters of West Germany's largest chemical concern, the country's leading publishing houses (many transferred from Leipzig, the pre-war publishing capital), the German Stock Exchange, and a semi-annual trade fair whose origins have been traced to the Middle Ages. Frankfurt's airport serves all major international airlines. The canalised Main River gives Frankfurt access to the Rhine; it is one of the country's most important inland waterways. In World War II, the medieval Old City was almost completely destroyed by Allied air-raids. But some of the historic buildings — including the 15th-century city hall (known as the *Römer*), the church of St Paul, and the birthplace of Goethe — have been rebuilt. Frankfurt dates from Roman times. In the 8th century it became one of Charlemagne's residences, and in the 12th century it was chosen as the city where Holy Roman Emperors were elected and (after 1562) crowned.

● **Frankfurt-an-der-Oder** The main German border town on the Oder-Neisse line, which now separates Poland from East Germany. A medieval trade centre, Frankfurt owed its importance to its location at a ford across the Oder. Its population is over 58,000.

● **Frisian Islands** A low-lying chain of sandy islands in the North Sea off the coast of the Netherlands (West Frisian), West Germany (East Frisian) and Denmark (North Frisian). Their wave-cut shores, dune-bordered, are retreating towards the mainland, and periodic floods have cut down the size of the islands. The Frisian people, who speak a Low German dialect, earn their living by fishing and by means of the tourist trade. The Wadden Sea between the islands and the mainlands is very shallow and could be reclaimed.

● **fulmar** This white or silvery grey bird lives in the Arctic Sea; further south it is rare. It breeds on solitary islands and on rocks — e.g., near Iceland and Greenland. Its tasty eggs serve as food. It swims well, but moves clumsily on shore.

● **Gdansk** Polish city (population 370,000) on the Baltic Sea. With its twin city of Gdynia (population 182,000), Gdansk is Poland's leading seaport. It is situated on an arm of the Vistula delta and serves as a trans-shipping point for Vistula steamers. Possession of Gdansk has been disputed through history by the Poles and the Germans, who call it Danzig. Under German influence from 1309 to the 16th century it became a member of the Hanseatic League before passing to Poland in 1600. After the partition of Poland in 1793, the city reverted to Prussia. Between World Wars I and II, the Free City of Danzig was an autonomous state. Hitler's demand for the reunion of Danzig with Germany was an immediate cause of the German invasion of Poland in 1939 and of the outbreak of World War II. The city centre, with buildings dating from the Hanseatic period, gabled houses and narrow winding streets, was destroyed in the war. The 14th-century St Mary's Church survived. It is now a large port, with many industries.

● **genet** The European genet belongs to the family of civets, related to the cat family and distinguished by an unusually long and thin body. From head to tail end the animal can measure up to 3 feet, while its height is only 6 inches. The genet's home is in North Africa and the Iberian Peninsula.

● **Geneva** The principal city with suburbs (population 314,900) of French-speaking Switzerland, and one of the truly cosmopolitan centres of the world. It has been the headquarters of the International Red Cross since 1864, and of the World Council of Churches since 1948. The League of Nations, established in 1920, also had its seat at Geneva. Since the end of World War II, the marble Palace of Nations, built for the League, has housed several agencies of the United Nations (whose headquarters is in New York). It has been estimated that about one-third of Geneva's population is made up of foreign nationals who work there. The beautifully laid-out city is sited at the western end of Lake Geneva and is divided into

two sections by the Rhone River, which flows out of the lake, dividing the city. Geneva lies in a small 'pocket' of Swiss territory hemmed in on three sides by France, the spectacular peaks of the Alps and the crests of the Jura Mountains. On a clear day the snowcapped summit of Mont Blanc (15,800 feet) can be seen from the lakeshore boulevards. Watchmaking is the city's best-known industry. Geneva was founded in Roman times. Calvin lived at Geneva in the 16th century and made it the centre of the Reformation. In the 18th century the city attracted some of Europe's great writers and philosophers. It joined Switzerland in 1815, after having been annexed to France by Napoleon.

● **Genoa** Italy's primary seaport (population 842,000) and one of the biggest shipping centres in the Mediterranean. It lies at the foot of the Apennine Mountains, flanked by the resorts and beaches of the Italian Riviera. Roads and railways from the industrial centres (Milan, Turin) of northern Italy reach Genoa through passes in the mountains. Wine, olive oil, silk and motor-cars (Fiat) are exported. Shipbuilding is the chief industry. Genoa is the home port of Italy's growing merchant marine; it has a maritime tradition that dates back to the 11th century. As a powerful city-state, Genoa took part in the Crusades, played an important role in developing trade with the Orient, and defeated Pisa — her rival in the western Mediterranean — in 1284; but, in 1380, Genoa was subdued by her new competitor, Venice. By the middle of the 18th century, the city had lost all its outlying possessions; Corsica, the last, was ceded to France. After being occupied by Napoleon, Genoa and surrounding Liguria were united with the kingdom of Sardinia in 1815. Christopher Columbus was born in Genoa in 1451, and there is an ancient University, founded in 1243.

● **Gent** The principal textile centre (population 151,614) of Belgium with a port on the Scheldt River, linked to the North Sea by a navigable canal. As the historic capital of Flanders, Gent has preserved its medieval appearance, notably the 12th-century castle of its powerful counts and the Gothic cathedral of St Baaf, which contains a famous altarpiece (the *Adoration of the Lamb*) by van Eyck, dating from 1432.

● **Germany** Country of central Europe, extending from the Alps to the North and Baltic Seas. Germany consists of four major natural regions: the North German plain, mainly agricultural (potatoes, rye and sugar beets); the central industrial low uplands, well populated, including the Ruhr, Harz Mountains, Thuringia and the Bohemian Forest on the Czech border — this includes much of the Rhine valley and Black Forest; the southern uplands of Bavaria, with a prosperous farm economy; and the Alps themselves. These natural regions are traversed by some of Europe's greatest navigable rivers: the Rhine, the Elbe and the Oder in the north, and the Danube in the south. Germany's climate is under the influence of air-masses from the Atlantic Ocean, producing a temperate humid climate. The history of the modern German state dates from the Franco-Prussian War of 1870—71, when Prussia realised its long struggle for hegemony in Germany. The German states, of which Prussia, Saxony and Bavaria were the leaders, were united in the newly created German Empire, and King William I of Prussia was proclaimed Emperor. The aggressive foreign policy of his successor, William II (Kaiser Wilhelm), and the militarisation of Germany, soon became a threat to peace. The Triple Entente (England, France, Russia) faced Germany and its allies in World War I. In 1918 a Social Democratic revolution swept the Emperor from power. At the peace

conference of Versailles, Germany lost all its colonies, Alsace-Lorraine and some eastern territories, as well as North Slesvig (Schleswig). The early years of the post-war republic were marked by political unrest, unemployment and inflation. The depression of 1929 paved the way for the Nazi coup of 1933. Hitler centralised every aspect of German life, enforced a police state and pursued a policy of racial extermination against the Jews. His aggressive foreign policy and remilitarisation led to the Second World War. By the spring of 1945, Germany had been defeated again by an alliance of Britain, France, the Soviet Union and the United States, together with the British Commonwealth and many other nations. At the Potsdam Conference in August, 1945, German territory east of the Oder and Neisse Rivers was placed under Polish administration, as was the southern part of East Prussia. The north section of East Prussia was transferred to the Soviet Union. The rest of Germany was divided into four occupation zones — American, British, French and Russian. Since 1949, the country has been formally divided into two States: East Germany and West Germany (*see below*).

● **East Germany (Democratic Republic)** has an area of 42,000 square miles and a population of 17,074,504. Its capital is East Berlin. East Germany has a Socialist form of government and is known as the German Democratic Republic. Like West Germany, the eastern state is an importer of raw materials and an exporter of manufactured goods, for the most part machinery of all kinds. Agriculture is broadly based, while mineral resources include lignite — which is used as the basis for a major chemical industry and for generating electric power — and potash, a fertiliser. Optical goods are also a characteristic product of East Germany. A pipeline from the Oder to near Halle carries Soviet oil directly to the industrial centre of Europe. The chief industrial cities are Leipzig and Dresden. Neither German state is a member of the United Nations, and the issue of German reunification remains one of the great political problems still unresolved in world affairs.

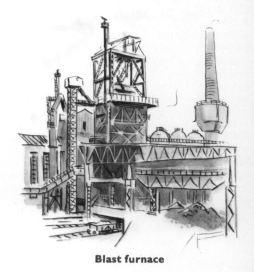

Blast furnace

● **West Germany (Federal Republic)**, the larger and more populous of the two states, has an area of 95,000 square miles and a population of 54 million. Its capital is Bonn and it comprises ten Republics (Länder). West Germany is a Western-type democracy, officially known as the German Federal Republic. As a result of a rapid postwar recovery, it is in second place in industrial output among the world's non-Communist nations (after the United States). An extremely large part of West Germany's industrial might is concentrated in the Ruhr Basin, with its many coal and its steel industries. West Germany imports raw materials, especially iron ore from Sweden, and semi-manufactured goods. It exports fabricated products, notably machinery, ships, motor-cars, electrical goods and chemicals. Agriculture is very highly developed. West Germany's leading cities are: Hamburg (the principal seaport), Munich, Cologne, Essen, Frankfurt-am-Main, Düsseldorf, Stuttgart, Dortmund and Hanover. West Berlin is closely tied politically to West Germany.

Gibraltar A strategic tongue of land, 2¼ square miles in area, at the southern tip of Spain, overlooking the Mediterranean approaches to the Strait of Gibraltar. The Rock — an impressive limestone cliff honey-combed with tunnels and caves — rises sheerly 1,396 feet above the breakwater-sheltered port of Gibraltar (population 26,000). It has been a British crown colony since 1704, having a large harbour and being an important naval base.

glass Glass is made by melting together finely ground sand, soda and lime. It is a solidified fluid and there are several hundred different types of glass with differing properties. The demand for glass in the building, lighting and optical industries has greatly increased its production.

goose, greylag This bird is the ancestor of our domestic goose. It is the only species of wild goose which breeds in the British Isles. It winters in southern Europe and Africa. At the end of February or the beginning of March it returns. It feeds mainly on plant matter such as leaves, seeds and roots. In fields near its breeding-grounds it occasionally causes damage to crops. It is grey, with red legs and beak.

Göteborg Sweden's chief seaport (population 446,875) on the Kattegat (a strait linking the North Sea with the Baltic Sea), opposite the northern tip of Jutland. Its shipyards are the largest in Scandinavia. Göteborg was founded in 1619 and acquired considerable commercial importance during Napoleon's blockade of the continent; at that time it served as Britain's major trade centre with the mainland of Europe. A 17th-century fortress guards the entrance to the harbour. The Göta Canal, which begins here, serves as Sweden's principal artery of inland navigation. Industries include car manufacture, ball-bearings, chemicals and textiles.

Gotland The largest island in the Baltic Sea, with an area of 1,220 square miles and a population of 54,093 (1969). Most of the inhabitants live in Visby, an old port and Hanse city. The soils are fertile and the climate mild, so early vegetables are grown for the Stockholm market.

Granada An historic city (population 170,127) of southern Spain at the foot of the Sierra Nevada. It is one of the great tourist centres of Europe. The magnificent Alhambra castle is the finest monument of Moorish kings during the 13th and 14th centuries. The old quarter of the city has narrow, crooked streets and windowless, whitewashed houses like those of a North African town. A prosperous trade centre in the Middle Ages, Granada was famous for its tapestries, rugs, leather goods, iron and copper-ware, which were sold throughout Europe. Granada was the last stronghold of Moorish power in Spain; it was finally conquered by the Catholic monarchs, Ferdinand and Isabella, in 1492.

graphite This is a dark-grey soft mineral consisting of pure carbon. It is used in the manufacture of pencils, crucibles and electrodes. The most important graphite deposits are in Siberia, Ceylon,

Mexico and Madagascar. In central Europe graphite deposits are mined in Passau, Lower Austria, Steiermark and in the Bohemian massif.

Graz A city of southern Austria with paper, glass, textile and metalworking industries. It is the capital of Steiermark, one of Austria's most scenic Alpine provinces. A 15th-century fortress in ruins and a handsome clock tower (1561) are the city's landmarks. Its population is 237,000. Some of the country's largest steel mills are in the Mur River valley, 25 miles to the north.

great bustard The great bustard is the largest European land bird. It can be more than 3 feet long; head and neck are bluish-grey, the back is rust coloured with white bands. The male is larger and more strikingly coloured than the female. The bustard prefers treeless plains, such as the Hungarian Puszta and the Russian steppes. The nest is built in cornfields, and it feeds on seeds, grains, green plants, and insects. Apart from the great bustard there are in Europe some smaller species, but they also avoid forests.

Greece (Hellas) A kingdom of south-eastern Europe, in the southernmost part of the Balkan Peninsula. It includes many islands in the Ionian and Aegean Seas. Greece has an area of 51,000 square miles and a population of 8.6 million people. Its capital is Athens, the only other large city being Salonika. The Greek mainland is split by the Gulf of Corinth, where a canal cuts off the southern peninsula of the Peloponnesus. The country is predominantly mountainous and the rocky coast is deeply penetrated by gulfs. The highest peak is Olympus, 9,573 feet. Lowlands are few, mainly in Macedonia, Thrace, Thessaly and Epirus. A climate of the Mediterranean type (rainy winters, dry summers) favours the growing of cotton, tobacco, vines, olives and citrus fruit, which make up the country's chief export crops. Only 30 per cent of the land is cultivated, though its produce feeds more than 60 per cent of the Greek population. Numerous livestock include goats and sheep. Industrial development suffers from a lack of mineral fuels, except some oil in West Central Greece, but consists of textiles, food and household goods. In addition to its specialised commercial crops, Greece exports cement, iron ore, magnesite, chromite and other minerals. Tourist traffic, attracted by the remains of ancient Greece, compensates for an unfavourable balance of trade. In addition, a large shipping fleet helps to restore the balance. Ancient Greek civilisation reached its peak in the 5th century B.C. Its sculpture, architecture, poetry, drama and philosophy became the foundation of Western culture. Greece fell to the Romans, and later became part of the Byzantine Empire until the Turkish conquest in the 15th century. The Greek war of independence (1821—29) overthrew Turkish domination and led to the establishment of a modern Greek state in the year 1830.

green lizard The home of this lizard is in the countries of southern Europe, where it reaches a length of 2 feet, and is one of the most frequent species of lizards. It feeds on insects, mainly grasshoppers.

Gulf Stream This is an ocean current of the northern Atlantic Ocean. It originates from the northern equatorial current. The trade winds drive a great bulk of water into the Caribbean Sea and further north into the Gulf of Mexico, partly between the Antilles and partly on the eastern side of these islands. The Gulf Stream leaves the Gulf of Mexico through the Straits of Florida as the 'Florida Stream', which has a temperature of 75°F, and transports a quantity of water 12,000 times that

moved by the Mississippi-Missouri at a speed of 5½ m.p.h. The Florida and Antilles Streams combine in the region of the Bahamas and continue as the Gulf Stream. This first runs along the coast of North America, then turns east and crosses the whole Atlantic. It submerges below the Arctic Sea. Near the British Isles, where the Irminger current branches off towards the west coast of Iceland, the temperature is still 12.8°C. Because of the Gulf Stream and its offshoot, the North Atlantic Drift, the mean temperature of northern Europe is approximately 18°F higher than that of other regions at the same latitude, keeping the west-facing coasts ice-free throughout the year.

gull, black-headed The black-headed gull inhabits the northern seas of Europe, and is found in winter on the North Sea and Baltic Sea. Its bill and legs are yellow, the body is white, and the upper part of the wings black. It feeds on fish, robs other sea birds of their eggs and searches the beaches for all kinds of sea animals.

Haarlem A city (population 238,608) of the Netherlands, between Amsterdam and the North Sea. Tulip bulbs grown in the surrounding fields are exported throughout the world. Chartered in the 13th century, Haarlem is noted for its medieval gabled houses, its city hall, and the famous organ in the Grote Kerk.

Hague, The A handsomely laid-out residential city (population 719,426) of the Netherlands and the seat of its government. It lies near the North Sea coast amid several waterways. Here the Queen resides, and the legislature sits in the 13th-century Binnenhof, and here most government business is transacted, even though Amsterdam is the constitutional capital of the country. The Hague has been the scene of many peace conferences; since 1945 it has been the seat of the International Court of Justice, which works within the framework of the United Nations. Nearby Scheveningen is a well-known seaside resort.

Halle City of East Germany, in Saxony; its population is 259,957. Halle is a railway centre on the navigable Saale River (a tributary of the Elbe). It is the centre of a lignite-mining region, and produces railway wagons, mining machinery, paints

A corner of Lisbon, capital city of Portugal

and cement. It also has a sugar refinery. An old German city dating from the 10th century, Halle has long been known for its university (1694), its publishing trade and its museums.

● **Hamburg** West Germany's premier port and, next to Berlin, the country's largest city (population 1,817,073), with a vast harbour on the lower Elbe River. It was built at the point where cargo from ocean-going ships must be transferred to river barges or overland transport. Its industries are, therefore, chiefly concerned with processing of imported raw materials, such as coffee, flour, tobacco, petroleum, rubber, cotton and wool. Shipbuilding, long the city's chief industry, has been revived, following almost total destruction during World War II. Between 1940 and 1945 Hamburg was subjected to frequent air raids, including one in which the centre of the city was set afire. By 1955 it had been substantially rebuilt. However, the city's trade with the hinterland remains impaired, due to the political partition of Germany which placed the upper course of the Elbe River within East Germany. Other industries are electrical machinery, marine engineering and chemicals. Hamburg's growth began with the establishment of the Hanseatic League in the 13th century. The core, Altstadt, is on the right bank, while Neustadt is sited at the junction of the Alster and Elbe, and linked with the suburbs of Wilhelmsburg and Harburg by bridges and a tunnel. Together with Altona and Wandsbeck, Hamburg covers an area of over 200 square miles. Its trade with the Indies, and later with the New World, gave it a leading position among North Sea ports. In 1510 it was declared a free city of the Holy Roman Empire, and even today its official name includes the words 'free and Hanseatic city'. Hamburg now forms a constituent state of the German Federal Republic.

● **Hammerfest** The world's northernmost city (population 6,000), on the northern coast of Norway at latitude 70° N. Its fishing port is ice-free all the year round because of the warming influence of the North Atlantic Drift, which reaches the shores of the Arctic Ocean. There is continuous sunlight from the middle of May until the end of July, and it is continuously dark between November 22 and January 22. The town has been inhabited for almost 200 years, and depends on fishing and whaling.

● **Hanover** An industrial city (population 517,783) of West Germany, on the Mittelland canal linking the Elbe and Weser. It lies 60 miles south-east of Bremen on the river Leine. Its factories specialise in heavy machinery and rubber products. The old town, with its Renaissance buildings, was gutted by Allied bombs during World War II. After the war it became the capital of Lower Saxony, now one of the constituent states of the German Federal Republic (West Germany).

● **Haparanda** This is the most northerly port of Sweden (3,400 inhabitants in 1961) and is a frontier station near the mouth of the Torne river. It has an important meteorological station.

● **harbour** Harbours are natural or artificially made basins or bays offering protected anchorage for ships with facilities for loading and unloading. Natural harbours are mostly situated in bays, near sea inlets or on river estuaries. Artificial harbours are created by building breakwaters and strong embankments (quays), and by excavating harbour basins. As the movement of ships in narrow harbour basins is difficult, special precautions are required. All large ships are tugged within harbour waters. For unloading and loading, cranes are installed on the dockside, and large harbours are equipped with floating cranes for heavy goods; they can lift

several hundred tons. Cargo is either stored in warehouses or loaded directly on railway trucks which can run on tracks right up to the ship. Recently special container lorries have been introduced which can be driven straight on to cargo and ferry ships. In addition, barges are used for unloading; they come alongside the ship and are loaded with the ship's own loading gear. For special ships — e.g., tankers — special installations are provided, mostly in a reserved part of the harbour, as the inflammable cargo has to be kept apart from the general harbour traffic. The charges for the use of loading and unloading equipment vary according to the size of the ship and the duration of anchorage; shipping companies prefer harbours where loading and unloading can be dealt with quickly.

● **hare** Numerous species of hare are spread all over Europe and now penetrate beyond the Urals. They are also found in Asia Minor, the Middle East and Africa. The animal lives in open country, avoiding woods, and searches for its food at dusk, hiding during daylight in hollows or in thickets.

● **Havre, Le** The principal transatlantic seaport of France (population 247,374), on the English Channel at the mouth of the Seine River and about 100 miles from Paris. A passenger terminal and oil refineries have been built since the war.

● **hazel** This tree is usually small, 10—16 feet high, and bushy. The nuts are edible. The tree usually occurs in hedgerows, or as an understorey to the oak. It is widespread in Europe, North Africa and Asia Minor.

● **Hekla** This volcano (height approximately 5,107 feet) is situated in the south of Iceland. It is a ridge about 4½ miles long, consisting of young volcanic material which was ejected from a fissure running from south-west to north-east. Since the year 1100 there have been twenty-four eruptions, the last in 1947—48.

● **Heligoland** This island has an area of approximately 160 acres and lies near the Elbe estuary, 43 miles from Cuxhaven. Its steep red cliffs consist of Bunter sandstone and are 180 feet high. It is about one mile long and one-third of a mile in width. After much war damage and its use as a bombing target by the British R.A.F. after the war, Heligoland's settlement was rebuilt on the southern lowland (Unterland). Its 3,000 inhabitants live by fishing and tourism.

● **Helsinki** The attractive, modern capital (population 804,256) of Finland, with a sheltered harbour (icebound for four months) on the Gulf of Finland. It lies less than 200 miles from Leningrad, the Soviet Union's main port on the Baltic. The city's growth dates from 1812, when it became the capital of a semi-independent grand duchy under the rule of the Russian Tsar. Helsinki became Finland's chief manufacturing centre (textiles, paper, plywood, glass and pottery) after World War II, when the industrial city of Viipuri (now called Vyborg) passed to the Soviet Union. The 1952 Olympic Games were held in Helsinki.

● **heron** The plumage of this stork-sized bird is grey; the wings and three long crest-feathers are greyish-black. In flight the long neck is bent like an 'S'. The heron is found in Africa, Asia and Europe up to a latitude of 60° N. It lives near shallow waters and feeds on fish, frogs, snakes and snails. It nests in colonies on high trees.

● **heron, white** This bird is frequently seen in south-eastern Europe, Africa, and central and

southern Asia. It lives near shallow waters, but preferably in large and deserted swamp areas, such as the swamps of the Danube in Hungary and Romania. It has a slender build and a beautiful brilliant white plumage. The particularly striking feathers on its back are eagerly collected. They were once used as decoration for ladies' hats.

● **herring fisheries** The annual catch of the herring fisheries — five million tons — is shared mainly between the Norwegian, German, Dutch and Scottish fishing fleets. The best catching-grounds are the North Sea, and the waters near Iceland and Labrador. During the day herrings are caught with the ground draw-net; during the evening, when they rise to the upper layers, with drift-nets. In the North Sea, herrings are caught with drift-nets from May to December, and the fish are immediately cured on the vessels, which are specially equipped for the purpose.

● **herring gull** This duck-sized bird lives in large groups in the southern Arctic Ocean and the North Sea. In winter it occasionally migrates far south. The plumage is white, the wings and upper back are pearl-grey, and the wing-tips black. The strong yellow bill has a red mark.

● **Holland (North and South)** Two coastal provinces which form the richest part of the Netherlands, with fertile soil and many industrial and commercial towns.

● **hops** The common hop is cultivated widely. It grows as a wild plant everywhere in the northern temperate zone, in hedges, thickets and on river banks. The hop is a twining plant; the leaves are hand-shaped, with three to five lobes and hairy stalks; the flowers are unobtrusive, greenish. On the leaves of the ovaries and on the seed envelope are small, bright yellow, globular glands (strobiles) containing a bitter substance. This lupulin is of great importance in the brewing of beer, as it gives the beer an agreeable bitter taste and makes it more durable. Because of this the lupulin hop was cultivated as early as the Middle Ages. In early autumn, the strobiles are gathered, dried and brought to market in large sacks.

● **horse-chestnut** A beautiful tree which grows to a height of 60 to 90 feet; its stem diameter can attain 3 feet. The wood is not very durable. Before the Ice Age the chestnut was found all over central Europe, but was then restricted to a small region in the Balkans. Its present widespread distribution in temperate regions is due to man, as heavy seeds prevented its natural spread. Other species are found in North America and East Asia.

● **Hungary** This central European republic, with a population of 10.3 million, has an area of 36,000 square miles. Its capital is Budapest. Hungary is largely a lowland basin enclosed by the Carpathian Mountains, the Dinaric Alps and the Alps. Its main water arteries are the Danube and its tributary, the Tisza. Because of its isolation from the sea, Hungary has a continental climate. The broad, rolling fields of the Hungarian plain are treeless, partly saline steppes, known as *pusztas*. Huge herds of cattle and horses once grazed there. Nowadays, most of the area is cultivated, mainly with wheat, maize and sugar beets, vegetables (including red peppers) and tobacco. Industry, concentrated in Budapest, produces foodstuffs, metals and textiles. Bauxite, the ore of aluminium, oil and lignite are the only important mineral resources. The Hungarians, also known as Magyars, settled in the Danubian basin in the 9th century, having come from central Asia. Their language is related to that of the Finns and Siberian tribes. Two-thirds of the population is Roman

Catholic; the rest are Protestant. Hungary flourished as an independent kingdom from 1001 until the 14th century, fell to the Turks in the 16th, and was joined to Austria circa 1700. Modern independence dates from 1918. Since World War II the country has adopted a Socialist form of government. Apart from Budapest, the largest towns are Miskolcz (173,000) and Debrecan (155,000).

hydrogenation plant This is a chemical plant in which coal and coal products are transformed into petrol and heavy oils by the action of hydrogen. The process requires high pressure and high temperatures and is assisted by the use of catalysts such as finely divided platinum, nickel or iron.

ibex, Alpine The Alpine ibex is a relative of the domestic goat. Formerly it was widespread in the High Alps. Today it has become very rare as a result of hunting by man, and only continuous protection can prevent its extermination. This robust animal is one of the best mountain climbers among mammals. The well-developed antlers of the male reach a length of 3 feet and a weight of 3¼ lbs. The females live in herds, the males often singly, only joining the herd during the mating period from December to January; then there are embittered fights between rivals, with noisy collisions of antlers.

Iceland An independent island republic (40,000 square miles; population 203,442) in the North Atlantic Ocean, just south of the Arctic Circle. It is the westernmost state of Europe. Its capital and only large city is Reykjavik 81,476). The centre of Iceland consists of a bleak, almost uninhabited plateau, with glaciers in the south and east. There are over 100 volcanoes, many of them active. Fishing for cod and herring, fish processing (meal, cod-liver oil, etc.) and sheep-raising are the main occupations of Icelanders. Over 90 per cent of the exports are fish produce. Heat from geysers and warm springs is used for industry, domestic heating and in glasshouses, and the volcanic phenomena are in themselves a tourist attraction.
The first Norse and Celtic settlers arrived in A.D. 874, and in A.D. 930 an independent government was set up. Iceland was ruled by Norway between 1262 and 1380, then passed to Denmark. It recovered its independence in 1918, but continued to recognise the King of Denmark as its sovereign. Allied forces occupied the island in World War II; the U.S.A. built a large air-base at Keflavik, now an international air traffic centre. The union with Denmark was disolved and a republic was proclaimed in 1944.

Inn, River The source of the Inn (320 miles) lies above the Maloja Pass in the Swiss Engadin, at a height of 8,184 feet. The river passes through the Tyrol in a north-easterly direction and runs into the Danube at Passau, to which it brings more water than the Danube itself carries. The lower part of the Inn forms the border between Germany and Austria. At the point of intersection of the Inn with the Brenner route lies Innsbruck (102,000 inhabitants).

Innsbruck A tourist centre of western Austria on the Inn River (a tributary of the Danube), at the junction of major rail lines and highways. Hemmed in by Alpine ranges, the city is a gateway for mountain-climbing and winter-sports enthusiasts. The less athletic visitors ride cable-cars to several vantage points which offer magnificent views of the Austrian Alps.

iron ore occurs in numerous minerals containing iron compounds such as oxides, carbonates, silicates, sulphides and phosphates, which have an iron content of over 30 per cent and can thus be called iron ores. The highest percentage (70 per cent) is found in the Swedish ores, known as magnetite. Up to 70 per cent occurs in red haematite, 60 per cent in brown haematite, and 50 per cent in spathic iron ores.

iron production In order to extract metallic iron the metal has to be separated from the other components of the ore. This is done in iron-works, where the ore is crushed and mixed with limestone. It is then heated and melted in a blast-furnace, together with coke. The slag formed in the furnace is used for the manufacture of various types of bricks. The pig-iron is hard and brittle when extracted from the furnace, and cannot be forged or welded because of its high content of carbon (2—6 per cent). By reducing this to less than 1.5 per cent, the pig-iron is converted into steel. This is done in a Bessemer Converter, where part of the carbon is removed from the liquid pig-iron by an air stream. Other varieties of the process are the Thomas Process, and the open-hearth process after Siemens-Martin. The steel thus produced is malleable and can be forged, rolled and drawn.

Istanbul Largest city of Turkey, on the Bosporus. Its population is 2,247,630. Its name was officially changed from Constantinople to Istanbul in 1930. As Constantinople, the city was one of the most famous capitals in world history. It was founded in A.D. 330 by Emperor Constantine as the capital of the Roman Empire. The largest and most splendid city of the Middle Ages, it had about one million inhabitants in its greatest period in the 10th century. It declined with the Byzantine Empire and was almost depopulated when it fell to the Turks in 1453. Under the sultans of the Ottoman Empire, the city flourished once again as one of the great political and commercial centres of Europe. In modern Turkey, it continued as the nation's economic focus. Although the capital was moved to Ankara in 1923, Istanbul handles most of Turkey's imports and a large part of its exports. It has shipbuilding and consumer goods industries. Skyscrapers alternate with ancient mosques, and marble palaces with slums. Among the city's famous sights is the Hagia Sophia (Sta Sophia), originally a Byzantine church, later a mosque, and now a museum.

Italy A republic of southern Europe, penetrating as a narrow peninsula into the Mediterranean Sea. It has an area of 116,000 square miles and a population of 54.4 million. The capital is Rome. Along its northern borders, Italy is separated by the Alps from the rest of Europe. South of the Alps lies the Po River plain. Here, in an area covering only 15 per cent of the whole country, centres Italy's economic life, with 40 per cent of its population. The fertile Po plain yields most of the country's farm production. The Alpine slopes are used for fruit growing and grazing, and supply hydro-electric power (Italy lacks mineral fuels). The industrial centres of the Po plain are Milan and Turin. Well-developed agricultural land grows wheat (for pasta), sugar beet, tomatoes, rice and mulberries, and there is considerable dairying and cheese production. The deforested Apennine range forms the backbone of the Italian peninsula south of the Po. In contrast to the prosperous North, the southern areas of Italy are economically backward, although recently development projects have been carried out in this area and the economy is improving. Central and southern Italy contain the great cultural and historic centres of Florence, Pisa, Rome and Naples. The large Italian islands of Sicily and Sardinia share the backwardness of the South, although these have a large share of the country's sulphur, mercury and oil deposits. Italy has to import most industrial raw materials, including coal, petroleum, metals and foodstuffs. The principal exports are subtropical fruit, winter vegetables, and consumer goods such as textiles, hats, motor-cars, ships, typewriters, silver, olive oil, wine and cheese. A large tourist trade, attracted by Venice, Rome, Florence and other historic and resort towns, helps compensate the unfavourable balance of trade. Much of the tourism passes through Genoa, the leading seaport. Italy was the heart of the Roman Empire, which lasted for about 1000 years (500 B.C.—A.D. 500). Later the peninsula disintegrated into sometimes powerful city-states (Venice and Genoa), and duchies and kingdoms (Sardinia, Naples). In 1861 Italy emerged as a modern, united state. It acquired African colonies (Eritrea, Somaliland, Libya) and sided with the Allies in the First World War. Mussolini's Fascist dictatorship, which began in 1922, ultimately placed Italy on the side of Germany and Japan in World War II. Italy lost its colonial possessions and became a Western-type democracy after the war. Emigration has hardly alleviated the pressure of population and many Italians now live in the U.S.A., Switzerland, South America and Australia.

The tiny principality of Monaco (8 sq. miles) is located on the Mediterranean coast of France

The Midnight Sun is seen at Narvik, in northern Norway

● **juniper** The juniper is a pyramid-shaped evergreen coniferous shrub. The ripe berries are dark blue and are eaten by many birds. They are also used in the kitchen, in medicine and in making gin. The juniper is the most widespread conifer of all, occurring all over the northern hemisphere.

● **Jura** A mountain range of western Europe, extending about 160 miles along the Franco-Swiss border. It rises to 5,650 feet in the Crêt de la Neige, and is heavily wooded. Communication across the Jura is difficult because there are no low passes. Woodworking and watchmaking are the main activities of the skilled, French-speaking people who have lived in these mountains for many generations.

● **Karl Marx Stadt** City of East Germany, in Saxony; its population is 298,543. Formerly known as Chemnitz, this industrial city is the centre of the East German cotton textile and knitwear industry. It also produces textile machines, office equipment and bicycles. Its industrial growth dates from the 17th century. It was renamed after Karl Marx in 1953.

● **Karlsruhe** A city (population 257,144) of West Germany near the right bank of the Rhine, north of Stuttgart. Its chemical and metal industries are once more in full operation, after their virtual destruction during World War II. The town was founded only in 1715.

● **Kiel** A Baltic seaport (population 269,106) of West Germany; until 1945 Germany's principal naval base. Its large shipyards were dismantled after World War II, but commercial fishing vessels are still built there. The 60-mile-long Kiel Canal links the Baltic with the North Sea along the base of the Jutland peninsula. Though much damaged, the town still retains some of its ancient buildings and is the capital of Schleswig-Holstein.

● **Lapland** A region of northern Scandinavia, mostly within the Arctic Circle. It covers the northern parts of Norway, Sweden and Finland, and reaches into Soviet territory in the Kola Peninsula. Mountainous in the west, Lapland is strewn with lakes and bogs, and covered with tundra in the Finnish and Soviet portion of its Arctic wilderness. Lapland is rich in minerals — iron mines in northern Sweden (Kiruna und Gällivare), nickel and apatite in the Soviet sector, and gold in many stream channels. Fisheries are carried on in the Arctic Ocean, which is ice-free for most of the year along the coast, except in the White Sea, thanks to the moderating influence of the North Atlantic Drift. The reindeer is the main source of food and transport for the native Lapps, who lead a nomadic life, though many are now settled. The Finnish area is known as Lappmark.

● **Leipzig** Largest city of East Germany, apart from Berlin, with a population of 585,803. It is the economic and cultural centre of Saxony, sited on the Elster, and a major transportation hub. Its main railway station is the largest in Germany. Leipzig is best known for its annual trade fair, which attracts industrial exhibitors from all over the world. Its traditional industries have been printing, publishing and the fur trade. Machinery plants produce printing presses, farm implements, cranes and power shovels. Leipzig has many musical associations. Bach was a cantor of the St Thomas' Church choir, and Wagner was born there. The Gewandhaus, an old guild hall, has been used since 1743 for symphony concerts. The University, founded in 1409, is the oldest in Germany.

● **lemming** Lemmings are mouse-like rodents with short tails and yellowish-brown fur, blotched with black. Some species live in the tundra regions of Europe, Asia and North America. They feed on grass, lichens, tree-bark and roots. Their nests are made of dry grass, or they cut tunnels into the thick moss or lichen cover of the ground. There they also find their food under the snow in winter. Litters of up to ten are born twice a year. In good summers they multiply more prolifically and then start a great migration, for which the Scandinavian lemmings are well known. Countless swarms descend into the low-lying regions, crossing snowfields, swimming rivers and lakes, climbing rocks. Predatory birds and animals follow these swarms and live, in such years, more or less exclusively on lemmings. Most of the lemmings die on the way.

● **lemon** The most important citrus fruit is the lemon, used in the kitchen and for making many types of soft drinks. The lemon was probably first cultivated in Persia; then the Arabs brought it, via Sicily, to southern Europe. Today the lemon is cultivated widely in the Mediterranean area and in the southern states of the U.S.A. The harvest begins in Sicily in October or November, and in northern Italy in the beginning of February. One tree produces 800 to 1,200 — sometimes 2,000 — lemons per year.

● **Liechtenstein** A small, independent principality of central Europe on the upper Rhine, just south of Lake Constance, between Austria and Switzerland. It is 15 miles long, 5 miles wide, and beautifully situated amid the Alps. Its German-speaking population of 27,758 lives on dairying, the manufacture of pottery, leather goods and precision instruments, and by the frequent issue of colourful stamps. In fact the last 30 years have seen a rapid change from an agricultural economy to a highly industrialised one. This has encouraged the immigration of many foreign European workers. The lovely 16th-century castle at Vaduz (the chief town, with 3,400 inhabitants) is the residence of the ruling prince. Founded in 1719, though its history goes back to 1342, and its boundaries to 1434, Liechtenstein became independent in 1866 and remained neutral through both world wars. It is linked economically with Switzerland.

● **Liége** An industrial city (population, if its suburbs are included, of 621,935) of Belgium, on the Meuse River. Its iron and steel works are served by railways and river barges. Liége is the cultural centre of the French-speaking part of Belgium. Its fortifications temporarily checked the German advance in World War I. The transport system around Liége is now even further improved by the opening of the Baudouin motorway from Antwerp to Aachen.

● **lignite** A low-grade coal, also known as brown coal. Because of its high moisture content and low heat value, lignite is not worth transporting far from the mines, or open-cast workings. It is used in electric power stations and as a raw material for synthetic fuels and other chemicals. Lignite is usually mined with power shovels from open cuts. The leading producers of lignite are East Germany and the Soviet Union.

● **Linz** An industrial city (population 195,978) of Austria, with steel mills, machine factories, and shipyards on the Danube River. It was founded by the Romans.

● **Lisbon** The capital (population, with conurbation, 1,034,141) of Portugal on the wide estuary of the Tagus River, one of the most spacious and best-sheltered natural harbours on the Atlantic coast of Europe. Its exports include all of Portugal's main products: wine, olive oil, cork, sub-tropical fruit, sardines and other fish products. Tourists stay here on their way to the Portuguese Riviera, centred on nearby Estoril. Since World War II, Lisbon has become an important air traffic centre for transatlantic flights to South America. The city is built on seven hills, and its rise as a trading centre dates from the late 15th century when the Portuguese extended their empire to Africa and India. Between 1580 and 1640 it came under Spanish rule; the Spanish Armada sailed from its harbour in 1588. A disastrous earthquake destroyed the city in 1755 and killed 30,000 people. It was later rebuilt along modern lines, with streets laid out in a typical gridiron pattern.

● **lobster** The lobster is related to the crayfish. It reaches a length of about 20 inches. The European lobster occurs from Norway to the Mediterranean. It is caught in baskets ('pots') containing shredded crabs as bait. Apart from the European lobster, the American lobster and the Norwegian lobster are known. The latter only grows to a length of one foot but has a better taste than the common lobster.

● **Lodz** Second largest city of Poland, with a population of 751,000. Lodz is the centre of the Polish textile and clothing industry. The city was established in the 19th century by German weavers who were brought there by the Russian government. It is a typical factory town with a checkerboard pattern of narrow streets. Only its southern section has open spaces with parks and villas.

● **Loire River** France's longest river (600 miles) rises in the central Plateau and flows north, then west, reaching the Atlantic Ocean at the shipbuilding centre of Saint-Nazaire. The seaport of

Nantes, 30 miles above the river's mouth, is accessible for ocean-going ships only at high tide. The wide valley of the Loire is noted for its wines and for its historic castles (*châteaux*), notably those of Chambord, Blois and Chenonceaux. The Loire is linked to both the Seine and Rhône by canals.

Lübeck An old city (population 242,191) of West Germany and its chief Baltic seaport, about 40 miles north-east of Hamburg. The East German border is only a few miles away. Lubeck achieved great commercial prosperity during the Middle Ages when it became the head of the Hanseatic League; as such it controlled the entire Baltic and North Sea trade. Despite heavy World War II damage, the inner city has preserved its medieval character. Its commercial activity, however, has been impaired by postwar changes in the economic and political composition of Europe. This recalls its earlier decline, when the Hanseatic commerce widened westward from the Baltic, and Lübeck stagnated at the expense of Hamburg and Bremen.

Luxembourg or **Luxemburg** An independent state between Western Germany, France and Belgium. Since 1815, it has been a Grand Duchy whose sovereign is a member of the House of Nassau. It owes its economic importance to extensive iron ore deposits in the south and a steel industry on a scale comparable to that of much larger nations. The capital, Luxembourg, is the seat of the European Coal and Steel Community. Radio Luxembourg is a well-known commercial broadcasting station. In spite of intensive agriculture and livestock-rearing, much food must be imported. In 1947 Luxembourg entered into a customs union with Belgium and the Netherlands (the Benelux Union). The country's population of 338,500 speaks French, German and a distinctive German dialect called Letzeburgesch. Although it had been declared a neutral territory in 1867, Luxembourg was occupied by Germany in both world wars. In 1948 it abandoned its neutrality and joined the North Atlantic Treaty Organisation.

Lyons A manufacturing city (population 1,074,823) of central France, at the junction of the Saône and Rhone rivers. Its traditional textile industry (formerly silk, now rayon and other synthetic fibres) is supplemented by chemical plants and metal-works. Lyons is an important communications centre for traffic between Paris, Switzerland and the Mediterranean. Its excellent restaurants draw gourmets and tourists. Founded as a Roman colony, Lyons soon became the chief city of Gaul. The silk industry dates from the late Middle Ages, when silkworms were raised in the Rhone valley south of the city. Much is now imported from Japan. A well-attended trade fair is held in Lyons every year.

Madrid The capital (population 3,030,689) of Spain, located in the centre of the country on the bleak central plateau — the Meseta — at an elevation of 2,000 feet. Despite its harsh winters and torrid summers, Madrid has become the focal point of the country's political and artistic life. Its broad, tree-lined avenues and squares, its luxurious 18th-century palaces, its wealth of churches and its fine museums (notably the Prado, which is recognised as having one of the outstanding collections in the world) compare favourably with their counterparts in other European capitals, even though the city is not among the oldest. The city owes its rise to Philip II, who brought his court to Madrid in 1561. In modern times, the city has benefited from the arrival of railways which converge on Madrid from all directions. Madrid was heavily damaged during the Spanish Civil War (1936–39). The Franco government brought new industries to the city and rebuilt its residential suburbs.

Magdeburg A city of East Germany, sited at a major crossing-point of the Elbe River; its population is 269,690. Magdeburg manufactures heavy machinery, such as steel mills, dredging equipment, steam shovels and heavy machine tools. The city was 70 per cent destroyed by bombing in the Second World War, but its 13th-century cathedral has been rebuilt. Magdeburg also has an important sugar-refining industry.

Main River The most important and largest German tributary of the Rhine, the 300-mile-long Main (canalised for much of its length) serves several industrial centres of West Germany, including the cities of Würzburg and Frankfurt. It reaches the Rhine's right bank opposite the river-port of Mainz, provides hydro-electric power and is linked by canal to the Danube.

Málaga A garden city (population 350,977) on the Mediterranean shore of southern Spain. Its mild winter climate, beaches and luxurious flora have made it a popular resort for sun-seeking tourists. The irrigated vineyards in the surrounding plain produce the sweet Málaga wine of international repute. Lemons, oranges, figs, almonds and olives are among the city's other exports. Under Moorish rule, during the Middle Ages, Málaga served as the seaport for Granada. The Catholic Kings recaptured it from the infidels in 1487. Málaga is the birthplace of Picasso. There are several industries based on ores mined in the nearby mountains.

Malmö An industrial city (population 258,311) of southern Sweden, the third largest in Sweden and the main port for southern Sweden, on The Sound (a strait linking the Baltic Sea with the North Sea) opposite Copenhagen, Denmark. A train and air ferry connects the two cities. Malmö has shipyards, sugar refineries and textile mills. Founded in the 12th century, the city has a medieval castle and many fine 16th-century houses. It has been ruled by Sweden since 1658 and was formerly under Danish control.

Malta A small island in the central Mediterranean, about 60 miles from the southern tip of Sicily, with an area of 120 square miles and a population of 322,000. It is now an independent nation within the British Commonwealth. For long a bastion of the Royal Navy between Europe and Africa, Malta had a great naval dockyard, now completely converted for commercial use. Malta has a varied agriculture, and a growing tourist trade. The main town and capital is Valletta (15,547). Neighbouring islands belonging to Malta are Gozo and Comino. The language is Maltese.

Mannheim-Ludwigshafen Twin cities (population 505,618) of West Germany, on opposite banks of the Rhine at the inflow of the Neckar River. A busy trans-shipment centre, this riverport handles millions of tons of cargo destined for the Ruhr, for the seaports at the mouth of the Rhine, and for upstream cities in France and Switzerland. The cities have six railway stations between them. Both Mannheim and Ludwigshafen are leading centres of Germany's diversified chemical industry.

maple This family of trees and shrubs includes many species and occurs only in the northern hemisphere. In Great Britain, the sycamore, the common maple and the Norway maple are best known. The Norway maple is 60–80 feet high, with hand-shaped leaves, mostly divided into five lobes. The Norway maple grows mainly in lowland forests. The sycamore, also about 80 feet high, develops pendulous panicles. The common maple, which also occurs as a shrub, grows to a height of 30–60 feet. Its timber is used as veneer.

marble This is a crystalline limestone used by sculptors for decorative stones and in industry. It occurs as white, yellow, red, green and black marble. It is found in many countries: Italy (Carrara, Siena, Verona, Trento); Austria (Carinthia, Untersberg); France (Boulogne, Dijon, Marseilles); Sweden; Greece (islands of Tinos and Skyros); and in the U.S.A. (Vermont). As the use of marble is decreasing, the world deposits are no longer fully exploited.

margarine Margarine is an edible fat made from plant and animal fats with the addition of milk, egg-yolk, lecithine and vitamins. Plant fats used are cocoa and palm-kernel fat, and ground-nut, soya-bean and sun-flower oil, cole-seed and cottonseed oil. Most of the animal fat added is whale oil. Liquid fats have to be hardened and chemically purified. The U.S.A. produces 22 per cent of the world's output, Western Germany 18 per cent, the Soviet Union 14 per cent and Great Britain 10 per cent. Smaller producing countries are the Netherlands (7 per cent), East Germany (5 per cent), and the Scandinavian countries (about 3 per cent each).

Marmara, Sea of This sea lies between European and Asiatic Turkey. In the east it is connected with the Black Sea through the Bosporus; in the west with the Aegean Sea through the Dardanelles. Istanbul (Constantinople) lies at the entrance to the Bosporus. The sea is named after an island which is famed for its marble.

Windmills are often seen in the Netherlands

In the heart of Paris, looking from the Louvre across the Tuileries Gardens to the Champs Élysée, crowned by the Arc de Triomphe

marmot The European marmot, or Alpine marmot, lives in high mountains. In the eastern European plain a larger species, the Siberian marmot, occurs. The Alpine marmot is found in the Carpathians, the Pyrenees and the Alps at altitudes of 5,200 to 9,900 feet, just below the eternal snow limit. It prefers lonely regions, where it hibernates during at least eight months in its frost-proof burrow. Its main enemy is the eagle. When in danger the animal whistles loudly and then disappears quickly into its burrow. This rodent, about the size of a hare, feeds on Alpine plants, herbs and roots.

Marseilles The chief Mediterranean seaport of France and the country's third largest conurbation (population 964,412), with a long history of commerce. Wines and fruit are imported from North Africa, tropical staples and spices from the Far East and West Africa. Raw material imports for industrial purposes include tobacco, silk, cotton, skins, oil seeds, oil and coal. Soap is produced here by blending domestic and Tunisian olive oil with perfumes obtained from local flower gardens. The city also produces chemical fertilisers and sprays for use in vineyards, machinery for ships, and glass. In addition there are large shipyards, and nearby are several petroleum refineries. Marseilles is France's oldest city but has only a few relics of the past, notably a large white Byzantine church surmounting a hill near the centre of the town. A typically southern port, Marseilles is a gay, noisy city, full of sailors and containing a large number of people from North Africa. The residents of Marseilles speak a French dialect mixed with Italian and other foreign words, and are described by other Frenchmen as rugged individualists and braggarts.

About 600 B.C., Greeks from Asia Minor settled the site on this broad bay of the western Mediterranean. The town, then known as Massaia, was taken by Rome in 48 B.C. and called Massilia. Changing hands frequently during the Middle Ages, the city finally became part of France at the end of the 15th century. The opening-up of Algeria during 1830—37, followed by the opening of the Suez Canal (1869), gave Marseilles a commanding lead over French ports on the Atlantic Ocean.

marten, pine The pine marten has a valuable fur. It lives in most forests in Europe and spreads into Asia. On trees and steep rocks it is an excellent climber, and surpasses even the squirrel in speed and dexterity. Squirrels are its favourite prey. Otherwise it feeds on any type of animal from the mouse to the small fawn, as long as it can cope with them. In captivity the pine marten becomes tame and affectionate. It is bred on farms because of its fine, thick fur. Continuous persecution by man has reduced the wild marten to the verge of extinction.

Mediterranean Sea A land-locked sea of the Old World, bordering on Southern Europe, North Africa, and south-western regions of Asia. Together with the Black Sea (with which it is connected by the Turkish straits) it covers 1,145,000 square miles, almost one-third the area of Europe. The narrow Strait of Gibraltar provides a link to the Atlantic Ocean, and the Suez Canal gives access to the Red Sea and the Indian Ocean. The peninsulas of Southern Europe divide the Mediterranean into several arms (e.g. Adriatic Sea, Ionian Sea, Tyrrhenian Sea, Aegean Sea). The Mediterranean is less than 100 miles wide between Sicily and Tunisia. Its western portion contains the islands of Sardinia (Italy) and Corsica (France), as well as the Balearic Islands off the east coast of Spain. In the eastern Mediterranean, Crete (a part of Greece) and Cyprus are the only significant islands, but the Aegean Sea is dotted with hundreds of island groups stretched out between the coasts of Greece and Turkey. Apart from the Black Sea, only a few large rivers flow into the Mediterranean Sea: the Ebro in northern Spain, the Rhône, the Po, the Varda and Maritsa in Greece, and the Nile in Egypt. This, coupled with a high temperature and evaporation, gives a high salt content, up to 4 per cent in the eastern half. Hence, many lagoons on the coasts can be used for salt production. The fish-life is much poorer than in the Atlantic, only tuna, mackerel and anchovies being of importance.

From the dawn of history the Mediterranean has served as an avenue, if not the centre, of trade and conquest. The Phoenicians explored its most distant shores, and later Carthage, Greece and Rome fought for its control. The Romans, whose empire at one time extended from one end of the sea to the other, called it *mare nostrum* (i.e., 'our sea'), a term revived by the Italians under Mussolini before World War II. The principal modern seaports on the Mediterranean are: Barcelona (Spain); Marseilles (France); Genoa, Naples and Trieste (Italy); Piraeus, the port of Athens (Greece); Istanbul (Turkey); Beirut (Lebanon); Haifa and Tel Aviv-Jaffa (Israel); Alexandria (Egypt); Tunis (Tunisia); Algiers and Oran (Algeria). Great Britain controls the western entrance to the Mediterranean at Gibraltar and its central channel at the island of Malta.

melon Melons belong to the gourd family, and, as with the related cucumbers, the various types differ in taste and appearance. The sweet melon from the East Indies is highly favoured for its delicate flavour. From ancient times they have been cultivated in the Mediterranean area, and in tropical Africa and Asia. The fruits are large, globular or ovoid, with a green or yellow skin; the flesh is pink or yellowish, very juicy and varies in sweetness.

mercury The only metal that is liquid at room temperature and is very dense (SG:13.6). Its principal uses are in the electrical industry for mercury-arc rectifiers (which convert alternating into direct current), in mercury-vapour lamps and in thermometers. Mercury is also used in medicine and dentistry, and to extract gold and silver from their ores. Almost all the world's mercury is obtained from the mineral cinnabar. The leading producers are Spain, Italy, Yugoslavia and the U.S.A. (California).

Messina A seaport and ancient University city (population 272,312) of Sicily, facing Italy across a strait two to ten miles wide. It ships citrus fruit, wine and olive oil to the mainland. The fishing and silk industries are important. The town was destroyed by an earthquake in 1908.

Milan Italy's second largest city (population 1,701,612), its leading financial and industrial centre, and hub of communications in the Po Valley. It commands the routes through the Alps to Switzerland, and to the resorts on Lakes Como, Lugano and Maggiore. Milan has long had a reputation as the chief silk market of Europe and as a music-publishing centre. Its modern factories specialise in transport equipment, office machinery, chemicals and foodstuffs Outstanding among the city's many old buildings are the Gothic white-marble cathedral (14th century), with its 2,000 finely sculptured pinnacles and statues, completed in 1813, and the world-famous La Scala opera house. During the Middle Ages, Milan was ruled by the powerful Visconti and Sforza families. Then, after a long period of Spanish, French and Austrian domination, the city was united with the kingdom of Sardinia (1859) and incorporated into Italy in 1861. Milan was heavily damaged during World War II. Since the war, many people have migrated to Milan from the poorer areas of southern Italy.

milk Milk contains proteins, lactose, vitamins, finely divided fat, and minerals dissolved in water. It thus possesses all body-building materials and is a perfect food, the nutritious value of which rises with the fat content. To prepare milk for human consumption, the raw cow's milk is purified by centrifuging, brought to a prescribed fat content, pasteurised, and sometimes irradiated with ultra-violet rays. The excess fat is left behind as cream and, from this, butter, cheese, cream cheese and yoghurt are made. By evaporating full-grade milk with the addition of sugar, condensed milk or powdered milk is produced.

mining This term describes all the operations for the prospecting, opening-up, production and preparation of useful mineral deposits, such as coal, ores, rocks, sand, earths, salts and oil. If deposits are close to or at the surface they are worked by opencast mining; if at great depth, shafts and horizontal galleries are used. As soon as geological prospecting has located deposits, confirmed by searching operations in the surrounding rock, production is started. The ore is transported to the bottom of the shaft by small trains, and from there brought to the surface. The supply of fresh air and the removal of dangerous gases is effected by special ventilation shafts. Any subsoil water is collected at the deepest point of the shaft and removed by compression pumps.

mistral The mistral and bora are cold, dry, mountain winds. They occur in winter in regions where mountains descend towards a warm sea. Above the cold mountains, atmospheric pressure is high; while above the warmer sea, pressure is low. Air therefore flows towards the sea, and is not warmed because the distance through which it falls is short. The mistral in the Rhône Valley is formed by an exchange of air between the cold hinterland of the Central Plateau and the warm Gulf of Lions. It blows through the Rhône Valley, at a speed of 30 to 60 m.p.h., on at least fifty days each year. The bora is the mountain wind of the Adriatic coast of Yugoslavia. This autumn gale has sufficient force to destroy windows and roof slates.

● **Monaco** The Principality of Monaco is a small territory of 373 acres on the French Riviera between Nice and the Italian border. Independent Monaco thrives on the booming tourist business. The famous gambling casino of Monte Carlo has been in operation since 1856. The population of 23,035 pays no income tax. Ever since the 13th century, Monaco has been ruled by a member of the Grimaldi family. The old town of Monaco is perched on a rocky headland that projects into the blue Mediterranean; its 16th-century castle and a noted oceanographic institute overlook the attractive harbour, which is adjoined by the Condamine, a luxury trading centre.

● **Moselle River** A 320-mile-long tributary of the Rhine River in West Germany. It rises in the western side of the Vosges Mountains of eastern France, flows past Metz and through its deep valley between the Eifel and the Hunsrück, reaching the Rhine at Coblenz. Barges carrying coal and iron ore ply the river between French Lorraine, the Saar and the Ruhr — centres of Western Europe's steel industry. The vineyards of the noted Moselle wines are on the steep slopes of its lower course, between Trier and Coblenz.

● **motorways** These highways are restricted to motor vehicles and have double or triple carriageways. The advantage of the motorway lies in the absence of crossings so that high speeds can be achieved. The densest networks of completed motorways are found in Germany (autobahns) and in the United States (highways). Many other countries have started construction.

● **Munich** The chief city (population 1,326,331) of Bavaria, West Germany, in the northern foothills of the Alps on the banks of the Isar River. Long known for its beer and its wooden handicrafts, Munich also has specialised industries producing machinery, precision tools and instruments. Founded in the 12th century as a salt-trading centre, Munich has been the capital of Bavaria for over 700 years. Due to the interest and good taste of its rulers, the city grew into a cultural centre. It is the home of West Germany's largest university, numerous museums, art galleries and theatres. In the 20th century, however, Munich witnessed the birth of the National Socialist movement and Hitler's rise to power. In World War II, many of the city's finest buildings were damaged by Allied air raids; among the casualties were the beautiful Liebfrauenkirche, 1468—88 (the Church of Our Lady), and the Pinakothek, whose invaluable art collection was fortunately preserved.

● **Nantes** A major seaport (population 393,731) of western France near the mouth of the Loire River on the Atlantic Ocean. It imports tropical hardwoods, oils and fibres from France's former possessions in Africa. The modern harbour can be reached by ocean-going vessels at high tide. The outport of Saint-Nazaire, 30 miles to the west, is France's leading shipbuilding centre. The Edict of Nantes, giving protection to the Huguenots (Protestants), was issued here by Henry IV of France in 1598. Its revocation in 1685 was followed by bloody religious persecutions.

Hradčany Castle, embracing the Cathedral, towers above the roof-tops of the old city of Prague, capital of Czechoslovakia

● **Naples** The principal seaport (population 1,276,824) of southern Italy, situated on a beautiful bay of the Mediterranean Sea within view of cone-shaped Vesuvius, the only active volcano on the European mainland. Naples exports such typical products of Italy as macaroni, olive oil, fruit and cheese, as well as gloves and textiles. Famous for the gaiety of its songs and festivals, Naples is a noisy city, and nowhere in Europe is street life more crowded or more confused, especially in the narrow lanes that lead to the tiers of whitewashed, flat-roofed houses stacked up above the bay. Naples has a long and checkered history that began in 326 B.C. with the Roman occupation of an ancient Greek colony on this site. In 1282, Naples became the capital of a kingdom of the same name, over which France, Spain and Austria fought in later years. In 1816, Naples and Sicily were merged into the Kingdom of the Two Sicilies which, in turn, was incorporated into the newly created independent Italy in 1860. The port of Naples suffered severe damage in World War II. Naples has a university founded in 1224, and a famous vulcanological institute. There are many modern industries, including iron, textiles and foodstuffs.

● **Narvik** Situated on the Ofot Fjord in Norway, it is the main shipping port (14,400 inhabitants) for the Swedish iron-ores from Kiruna, which reach the port by railway. Twenty thousand tons of ore can be loaded there in sixteen hours. The harbour is always ice-free. The town was completely reconstructed after the war.

● **Neckar** This river is 222 miles long, rising in the eastern Black Forest and joining the Rhine at Mannheim. It was formerly used for floating wood down to the Rhine from the Black Forest. By canalisation it was made navigable for 1,200-ton ships. Thus the industrial area of Württemberg was provided with an efficient waterway and Heilbronn became an important trans-shipping port. The beauties of the Neckar Valley, above romantic Heidelberg, attract many tourists.

● **Netherlands** (population 12,957,621). A kingdom of north-west Europe, generally — though incorrectly — known as Holland, which is, in fact, the name of a coastal region divided into two provinces (North and South). A flat, low-lying country of 13,000 square miles, the Netherlands is bordered by the North Sea, from which have been wrested thousands of fertile acres for agriculture. A large part of the Netherlands is embraced by the Rhine-Maas delta. The 'Delta project', due for completion in 1980, consists of a scheme to build barrages across the arms of this delta to form more *polder* land and create fresh water reservoirs. Almost 5,000 miles of canals link the Rhine — Western Europe's most travelled waterway — with all the larger Dutch cities. Rotterdam, the country's leading seaport, handles the transfer of goods from river barges to ocean-going ships and vice versa, and has been enlarged by the construction of Europoort. Amsterdam, the legal capital of the Netherlands, also has a deep-water harbour and a direct canal connection to the North Sea. The daily business of government is carried on at The Hague, a fine residential city containing the royal palace. Since a quarter of the country lies below sea level, it has had to be protected by an intricate system of dikes, ditches and pumping stations, and by a 20-mile-long dam across the entrance to the Ijssel Meer, a former arm of the sea, drained and reclaimed for cultivation. The new land thus created — the Dutch call these areas *polders* — has been taken over by small farmers, though certain areas in the south will be used for industry. The Netherlands is Europe's most densely settled country. Its rapidly growing population speaks Dutch (Low German). Trade has always been the principal activity of the hard-working Dutchmen. Agricultural exports (condensed milk, Gouda and Edam cheeses, butter, and greenhouse fruits and vegetables) are in great demand in Western Europe and the United States. The Netherlands is also an industrial nation, known for radio and electronic products, textiles, bicycles and ships. The country refines its own petroleum and has immense reserves of natural gas; it contributes the output of its steel mills to the European Coal and Steel Community. Since 1947, it has been linked in an increasingly important economic union (the Benelux Union) with Belgium and Luxembourg, and has since become a member of the Common Market.

The Low Countries, of which the Netherlands is the largest, have had a turbulent history in the European struggle for power. They passed from the dukes of Burgundy to Austria, and then to Spain. With the growing strength of Protestantism, the northern provinces declared their independence in 1579. Soon the Dutch began their far-flung trading operations, which resulted in the conquest of the East Indies and the founding of Nieuw Amsterdam (now known as New York) in 1612. After the fall of Napoleon, the Low Countries were united under William I of the House of Orange, whose heirs have ruled the Netherlands ever since. Belgium broke away to form a kingdom of its own in 1830. The Netherlands remained neutral in World War I; but, during the last war, the country was occupied by Germany. Little is left of its once powerful colonial empire. In the Far East, the Dutch East Indies (with the exception of West New Guinea) federated in 1949 to form the independent Republic of Indonesia and, in 1963, Dutch territory in New Guinea (West Irian) also joined the federation. In the western hemisphere, the Netherlands Antilles (with the oil-refining islands of Curaçao and Aruba) and the mainland territory of Surinam (Dutch Guiana) are united with the Netherlands under one crown.

● **Nice** The largest resort centre (population 392,635) of the French Riviera, beautifully situated on the Mediterranean at the foot of the southern Alps. Nice lives off the winter tourist trade, but it also manufactures perfumes and soap, and ships Mediterranean fruits and flowers to the less-favoured parts of France. The Mardi Gras festival is celebrated as lustily here as it is in New Orleans. Nice was a Greek colony in the 6th century B.C. It was ceded to France by the King of Sardinia in 1860.

● **Normandy** This region in northern France on the lower Seine derives its name from the Normans (Vikings). On its white-cliffed coast, there are many well-known seaside resorts. Inland, in the east, there is fertile agricultural land and a rich fruit-growing area with large hedges surrounding the fields. In the west, cattle-breeding is predominant. Le Havre (247,374 inhabitants in 1962) is the main import harbour for Paris, mainly for coffee, oil and cotton. In the area of Rouen (population 369,793), an extensive textile and chemical industry has developed.

● **North Cape (Nordkapp)** The most northerly promontory of the European Continent, on the island of Magerö, Norway, at a latitude of 71° 10′ 21″ N. The Cape rises steeply from the sea to a height of 1,013 feet. Nordkyn, further east, and also in Norway, is the most northerly point of the European Mainland, at 71° 8′ 1″ N.

● **Norway** A kingdom (125,000 square miles; population 3,866,468) of northern Europe, occupying a narrow strip of land in the mountainous western part of the Scandinavian Peninsula, over a distance equal to that from Newcastle-on-Tyne to Rome. Its capital, Oslo, faces Denmark to the south. With its deep, steep-sided fjords, Norway's North Sea coastline ranks among Europe's scenic wonders. Cruise ships take tourists beyond the Arctic Circle into the land of the midnight sun, where Hammerfest is the world's northernmost city. Norway has a very efficient and inexpensive electric railway system from Oslo to Bodo in the north west. In the far north, where Norway borders on Finland and the Soviet Union, the nomadic Lapps drive their herds of reindeer across moors and tundra. More than two-thirds of Norway is so high, with rugged peaks or bleak plateaux, some covered with snow and ice-fields (broeer), and so inaccessible, that it is uninhabitable. Some of the people, Lutheran in religion and speaking a Teutonic language, live in the deep, narrow valleys between mountain ranges and around the fjords, where every village has its fishing boats. Forests (chiefly pine) and fisheries are the country's principal natural resources. Forest

products include paper and cellulose. Cod, herring, halibut and mackerel form the bulk of the catch and are exported fresh, salted, dried or canned. Norway's whaling fleet, from Sandefjord, now operates in Antarctic waters; its merchant marine is the third largest in the world, after those of the United States and the United Kingdom. Because of its long coastline and the difficulty of overland transport, the country has always been dependent on coastal shipping. Cheap electric power, produced by harnessing the swift waters of Norway's mountain streams, has attracted such power-hungry industries as aluminium refining and the manufacturing of nitrate fertilisers. The main export items are base metals (titanium, nickel, copper and silver), fishery products, paper and pulp. Since only 3 per cent of the land is cultivated, Norway is forced to import food products as well as fodder for its livestock. All of the larger cities are seaports (Oslo, Bergen, Trondheim and Stavanger), and most of the people live near Oslo or in the south-east.

The Norwegians' seafaring tradition dates from the 8th and 9th centuries, when Vikings raided the British Isles, and Norsemen settled in Ireland and along the coast of Normandy. In the 13th century Norway extended its rule to the Shetland and Orkney Islands off the Scottish coast, and to Greenland and Iceland in the far north. Norway and Sweden were united in 1319. Between 1380 and 1814, Norway was ruled by the Kings of Denmark. Complete independence was not achieved until 1905, when a Danish prince became King of Norway. Neutral during World War I, Norway was invaded by Germany in 1940 and remained occupied throughout World War II, despite active local resistance. The Norwegian government was transferred to London, and most of its merchant marine continued to operate in the service of the Allies. Norway's overseas possessions include Svalbard and Jan Mayen islands in the Arctic Ocean, and several small islands in the Antarctic. Norway has long been an active participant in the exploration of the polar areas.

● **Nuremberg (Nürnberg)** An old city (population 477,108) of Bavaria, West Germany, less than 100 miles north of Munich. It is the centre of Germany's toy industry, which also produces for the export market. Nuremberg gingerbread enjoys an unrivalled reputation. The city's diversified metal industry produces engines, machine tools, radio parts, optical instruments, hardware and office equipment. The historic old town, an almost

perfect example of medieval architecture, was heavily bombed during World War II.

● **oak** The oak varies greatly in shape and form. Usually about 80 feet high, its crown is open and its growth is often crooked. The tree's bark is thick and rugged, and its leaves only appear late in spring. The oak-seed, or acorn, is produced in large numbers and is a favourite food for pigs. The oak is widespread in Europe and in other parts of the world. Oak timber was formerly used in charcoal and for barrel production, and its bark for tanning. It was formerly said that the oak had so many uses by man, it touched his life at every point from cradle to coffin.

● **oats** An important feed grain, oats thrive in a moist, cool climate and are less demanding in soil requirements than either wheat or barley. In volume, oats rank second only to maize as a fodder crop; almost the whole supply is consumed as animal feed. A small part of the best grades is made into oatmeal and breakfast foods. The Soviet Union and the United States each plant about 30 per cent of the world's oat acreage.

● **Odense** The third-largest city of Denmark (132,978 inhabitants) and the second major industrial town, with shipyards and a port linked to the Kattegat by canal. It has many old buildings, and Hans Andersen, writer of the famous fairy tales, and Carl Nielsen, the Danish national composer, were born there.

● **Oder River** Central European river, 560 miles long. It forms part of the so-called Oder—Neisse line, separating East Germany and Poland since the Second World War. The Oder River rises in the Sudeten Mountains in Czechoslovakia. It flows past Ostrava, Wroclaw, and along the East German-Polish border, past Frankfurt, to the Baltic Sea at Szczecin. The Oder is an important waterway between the Baltic and the Upper Silesian industrial area. Canals link it with the Elbe and the Vistula.

● **olive** An evergreen tree of the Mediterranean region, with a low, gnarled trunk and silvery

The upper course of Germany's scenic river Rhine flows past terraced vineyards and medieval castles

The ancient Roman Forum and the Colosseum are part of the archaeological treasures which attract large numbers of tourists to modern Rome

leaves. Its fruit is one of the world's important sources of vegetable oil. Virtually the entire supply comes from the Mediterranean countries, with Spain, Italy, Greece and Portugal in the forefront. Olive oil needs no refining after extraction. It is the most expensive of the edible oils and is used in cooking, soap manufacture and other, including technical, processes. The olive tree is a slow-growing, unusually long-lived plant, still producing after 500 years. In the wars of ancient times it was customary for the victors to destroy the olive orchards of the defeated, thus inflicting great damage lasting for decades. For that reason an olive branch became a sign of peace.

Olympus Highest mountain of Greece, in Macedonia near the Aegean Sea. Its summit, 9,600 feet above sea level, is usually hidden by clouds. The ancient Greeks believed Olympus to be the home of the Olympian gods, presided over by Zeus.

Oporto Portugal's second city (population 693,170), an Atlantic seaport at the mouth of the Duero River. The grapes from which the world-famous port wine is made are grown on the steep slopes overlooking the city. British merchants established the wine trade during the 17th century; it has flourished ever since. The city's Portuguese name is Pôrto.

optical industry This branch of industry is closely connected with the precision machinery industries. It manufactures optical instruments and apparatus, in which German firms especially have achieved world fame, such as cameras, microscopes, cine-technical equipment and binoculars. Well-known German firms include Zeiss, Leitz, Voigtländer and Agfa. Other firms important in this industrial field are the American Kodak and some French and Swiss firms. In post-war years Japanese firms have also achieved prominence.

orange The sweet orange is cultivated mainly in southern Italy and Sicily, the southern coastal regions of the Iberian Peninsula, in North Africa, Israel, California, East Asia, Australia, South Africa, and everywhere in the tropics. According to their origin, oranges vary in appearance, taste and size. Special favourites are the blood oranges, with dark-red tissue and reddish skin, and the navel oranges, which seem to contain a small

daughter-fruit under a navel-shaped disc. Jaffa oranges are large and seedless and have a thick skin. The orange tree resembles the lemon tree, but its stem, flowers and leaves grow larger. The former name, China Orange, indicates its Chinese origin.

Oslo Capital (population 487,363) of Norway and seaport on ice-free Oslo Fjord, a deep inlet of the Skagerrak. Founded 900 years ago, and known as Kristiana from 1625 to 1925, Oslo is now a modern city, with a brand-new city hall, many street statues and fine museums. The older part of Oslo was founded on the Akers river, using its water-power. Akershus fortress, a 14th-century royal residence, overlooks the busy harbour. The present royal palace, built in 1848, is in the centre of the city. Oslo exports lumber, paper products and fish. The industrial suburbs were absorbed into the city in 1948. Many museums and larger houses are situated on the peninsula of Bygdøy.

Ostrava City of Czechoslovakia, on the Oder River, in Silesia; its population is 272,000. Ostrava is the centre of a highly industrialised region, producing coal, iron and steel, heavy machinery and chemicals. The city is situated on the historic border between Moravia and Silesia. Until recently it consisted of two separate cities — Moravian and Silesian Ostrava.

oyster Oysters occur everywhere in the sea. Commercially important is the common oyster, which is found in all the seas of Europe, except in the Baltic with its low salt content. The oyster lives in firmly grounded beds in shallow lagoons, where tidal currents provide it with 'fresh' water and sufficient food. As oyster consumption is steadily rising, oysters are now bred artificially on an increasing scale, especially on the Atlantic coast of France. The main enemy of the oyster-beds is the starfish, which eats oysters and often destroys large quantities.

Palermo A seaport and the largest city (population 659,177) of Sicily with a sheltered harbour on the Tyrrhenian Sea. A fertile coastal plain, called the 'golden shell' (Conca d'Oro), surrounds Palermo with orange and lemon groves against a backdrop of barren limestone hills. The town has many fine boulevards, churches and palaces. Metal, textile and chemical industries are well developed. Exports include citrus fruits, olive oil and sulphur.

Paris The capital of France has a population of 2.6 million, but with its immediate suburbs it occupies nearly all of the Seine department (one of France's 90 political divisions) and embraces nearly 8 million people. Situated on the winding Seine River, at the heart of the fertile Paris basin and only 90 miles from the Channel coast, Paris is the administrative, commercial, industrial and cultural centre of France. Its riverport handles more bulk than any other French port. Railways lead to the city's seven major terminals from all parts of the country, like spokes to the hub of a wheel, and its two international airports, Orly and Le Bourget, make Paris the leading communications centre of western Europe. Most of the heavier industries (motor-cars, chemicals) are concentrated in northern suburbs along the bends of the Seine; the city itself specialises in luxury products (fashions, perfumes, jewellery) for which it is justly famous. Paris is the 'city of light' not only because its sumptuous monuments and impressive boulevards are illuminated at night, but because it has been a world leader in art and thought for many centuries.

The right bank of the Seine is the centre of business and amusements. There is to be found the avenue of the Champs Elysées, one of the world's best-known thoroughfares, leading from the Arc de Triomphe (Napoleon's victory arch at the Place de l'Etoile, a circle upon which twelve avenues converge) to the Place de la Concorde with its Egyptian obelisk. There, too, are the 19th-century Opera House, the Louvre (with its invaluable collection of paintings), and the theatre which houses the Comédie Française. Rue de la Paix (with its pavement cafés) and Place Vendôme lie at the centre of the most fashionable shopping district. The bohemian and night-club district of Montmartre occupies the city's highest hill, topped by the striking church of Sacre Coeur. The left bank of the Seine is the intellectual and government quarter of Paris. The old Latin Quarter, for many centuries the retreat of university students, and the once-aristocratic Faubourg Saint-Germain are the best-known left-bank districts. There, too, is the Sorbonne (founded in 1150), the Panthéon, the Hôtel des Invalides (where Napoleon is buried), and the 984-foot-high Eiffel Tower, the city's landmark along the banks of the Seine. The oldest part of Paris is the Ile de la Cité, a small island largely occupied by the Palais de Justice and the renowned cathedral of Nôtre Dame. It is connected with the smaller Île Saint-Louis, occupied by the once-elegant homes of Parisians of the 17th and 18th centuries.

After Caesar's conquest of Gaul, the fishing village on the Île de la Cité spread to the left bank and acquired considerable importance under the late Roman emperors. The Merovingian kings made Paris their capital, and Charlemagne turned it into a centre of medieval learning, circa 800 A.D. Paris was occupied by the English during the Hundred Years War, and suffered from famine and the Black Death. Reconquered from the English in 1436 (six years after Joan of Arc had been captured while attempting to take it), Paris recovered quickly. In 1572 it witnessed the massacre of St Bartholomew's Day. Under Louis XIII and Cardinal Richelieu, Paris became the political centre of Europe. Louis XIV transferred his residence to the sumptuous palace at Versailles, but Louis XVI and his wife, Marie Antoinette, were brought back to the city by an angry mob of Parisians, ready to launch the French Revolution (1789). The storming of the Bastille, the city's hated fortress and prison for political prisoners, marked the actual beginning of this bloody revolt. In 1804, Napoleon was crowned Emperor at Nôtre Dame Cathedral. In 1814, and again in 1815, the city was occupied by Napoleon's victorious enemies, but Paris once again flourished under the restored Bourbon kings. Both the July Revolution of 1830 and the February Revolution of 1848 were centred in Paris, and their repercussions were felt throughout the rest of Europe. The city fell to German forces in 1871, at the end of the

Switzerland's famous skiing resort – St Moritz

Franco-Prussian War, but its economy recovered under the Third Republic. During World War I, German long-range guns shelled the city, but Paris remained in Allied hands. In 1940, however, the city was captured by German armies, being liberated by Free-French and some American forces in 1944. The large number of treaties and other political agreements that were signed in Paris are only one of the indications of the city's importance through the ages.

- **partridge** The partridge lives all over Europe, except in the far north. This brown-coloured bird likes open country and prefers the plain to the mountains. It builds its nest in fields under bushes and thickets, and feeds mainly on field crops. Its flight is clumsy and it rarely settles in trees.

- **peat** consists of partly decomposed vegetable matter. It is cut out of bogs and dried for use as fuel in electric power stations. The Soviet Union and Ireland are the world's leading peat-users.

- **Peloponnesus** The southernmost peninsula of Greece whose narrow link to the mainland is cut by the Corinth Canal. The Peloponnesus is a mountainous, deforested and barren land inhabited by 1 million people, who raise goats and grow currants, olives and wine-grapes. Patras, a seaport on the Gulf of Corinth, is the chief city. The area was a centre of culture in former times, for Sparta and Epidaurus were sited here.

- **peregrine falcon** The peregrine falcon is slate-grey on its upper parts; it is a predatory bird, with a wing-span of over 3 feet. It lives in the far north and migrates from there all over Europe, Asia and America in autumn, often pursuing migrating birds far to the south. It lives in forests, building its nest on steep rocks or in large trees. The bird is very shy and extremely agile, strong and daring, catching its prey in flight.

- **pharmaceutical industry** In former times, dried plant matter (flowers, leaves, bark and roots), as well as their aqueous or alcoholic extracts, were used for the prevention and healing of diseases. With the development of chemistry a tremendous revolution took place. After years of research, science succeeded in producing chemical drugs for curing diseases that so far seemed incurable. Day by day scientific research produces new drugs with an ever-widening field of application.

- **pheasant** This bird is beautifully coloured and has a long, narrow tail of striking appearance. It is the size of a domestic hen. In Europe there are two species: the pheasant and the ring-necked pheasant. They are very similar in appearance and live in thick undergrowth near fields, avoiding the forest. The pheasant does not fly well and is exposed to many dangers. Its worst enemy is the fox.

- **pig, wild** The European wild pig is a relative of the domestic pig. Its body is, however, more thick-set and its hair thicker and dark. The head is more elongated, the ears are erect, and the tusks are strongly developed and protrude from the mouth. The grown-up male is called a boar, the female a sow. Wild pigs live in moist, marshy and wooded country and often combine in groups called droves. They eat whatever they find. As they turn up the ground in meadows and fields, they often cause much damage. Wild pigs are quick runners and excellent swimmers.

- **pine, Aleppo** This pine-tree grows to a height of about 50 feet and develops, when older, a parasol-like shape. In the eastern Mediterranean region it plays an important part in the afforestation of bare slopes, especially in the Karst and dune areas of the Adriatic coastlands. Its timber is widely used; the resin and young seeds serve in Greece and in the Orient for the preservation of wine (resinous wine). The bark is used in tanning.

Stone Pine

- **pine, stone** The stone pine grows in the Alps and the Carpathians at heights of 4,900—8,200 feet and, together with the larch, forms the timber-line. It does not grow naturally in the plains but is planted as an ornamental tree. Its height rarely exceeds 75 feet. Its needles form clusters of five on the short shoots. The timber is of high quality and is used for the better type of cabinet-making, and for wood-carvings.

- **Pisa** An Italian walled city (population 103,011) on the Arno River near the shore of the Ligurian Sea. Pisa owes its fame to the Leaning Tower, the top of which (180 feet above the ground) slants 16 feet from the perpendicular position. This tower was built in 1174—1350 as a clock tower for the fine white-marble cathedral nearby. In the 11th and 12th centuries Pisa grew into a maritime republic whose power rivalled that of Genoa and Venice. It is the birthplace of Galileo and has a university dating from 1338.

- **plums** This name is used for a number of plants belonging to the species of stone-fruit. Among them are: the common plum, the greengage, the mirabelle, the cherry-plum and the damson. The most important is the common plum, which came originally from the Near East. This tasty fruit was greatly appreciated by the Romans. It is mostly cultivated in the Balkans, especially in Serbia, and from there large quantities of dried plums are exported as prunes. Plums are also used for the manufacture of spirits (Slivovits).

- **Po River** The longest river (400 miles) of Italy flows from the Alps (near the French border) to the Adriatic Sea (south of Venice) across a wide, level plain where most of the country's wheat, rice and maize are grown. Although parts of the Po Valley are poorly drained with many anastomosing channels, it is densely settled and fringed by such important cities as Milan, Turin, Bologna, Padua and Verona.

- **Poland** Eastern European country with an area of 120,000 square miles (the size of the British Isles) and a population of 32.67 million. Its capital is Warsaw (1¼ million people). Poland is predominantly a morainic lowland drained by the Vistula and Oder Rivers. Only along the southern border does the country rise in the Sudeten and Carpathian Mountains. Poles, a Roman Catholic, Slavonic people, make up more than 90 per cent of the population. In agriculture, rye is by far the most important grain crop. Potatoes, cucumbers and sugar beets are also widely grown, along with wheat and tobacco. Dairying is important. Since World War II, Poland has contained almost the entire Upper Silesian industrial district, producing coal, steel and zinc. The Silesian coal-mines and the shipyards along the Baltic coast supply a large part of Poland's exports. Poland was a leading European power in the 15th and 16th centuries. It was partitioned among Prussia, Austria and Russia in the late 18th century and revived as a modern State after World War I. After World War II, Poland ceded its eastern territories to the Soviet Union, but gained the former German territories on the Oder—Neisse line. Poland adopted a Socialist form of government after her liberation in 1945. The main exports are coal and coke, machinery, cement and timber.

- **polecat** The polecat is distinguished from its relatives by its emission of a fetid odour. It is about 2 feet long and has chestnut-coloured fur. Its home is the temperate zone of Europe and central Asia. Its food consists of small rodents, frogs and snakes. The polecat prefers the neighbourhood of farms, where it raids the poultry yards.

- **porpoise** The porpoise occurs on the coasts of all northern seas and also in the Mediterranean. It sometimes appears in the lower reaches of large rivers. Its back is dark brown, its belly white, and it is 5 feet long. In the spring, one to two young are born; these are fed and guided by their mother for one year. The porpoise feeds mainly on herrings and does much damage to fisheries.

- **Portugal** A small country (34,200 square miles; population 9.6 million) on the south-western seaboard of Europe, bounded by the Atlantic Ocean to the west and south, and Spain to the east and north. Except for its capital, Lisbon, Portugal is one of the more backward nations of Europe, with almost half its people illiterate. Portuguese is a Romance language related to Spanish. Portugal's rugged hills and mountains are cut by the narrow valleys of swift rivers that drain from the Spanish Meseta: the Duero reaches the Atlantic at the city of Oporto, the centre of Portugal's famous port-wine district; the Tagus enters the sea at Lisbon, where it provides one of Western Europe's largest and most sheltered natural harbours. Although there is little fertile land, almost two-thirds of the country's population is engaged in agriculture. Wheat and maize are the leading crops but do not meet the nation's needs, and grain has to be imported. The wooded slopes of the interior yield Portugal's chief export, cork, for which the United States is the main customer. In addition to port, Portugal also exports sparkling wines, sweet muscatel from the south coast, brandy, and choice wines from the island of Madeira. Sardines and tuna are canned for export. Portugal's mineral resources are not fully developed, but iron, tin, pyrites, kaolin and tungsten ore are mined. Several new hydro-electric stations provide power for the country's growing processing industries.

The year 1140 marks the beginning of Portugal's history as an independent state. With the reign of King Henry the Navigator, Portugal rose to the rank of a great colonial power. By blazing the sea route around Africa to India, it took away Venice's lucrative trade with the East. Then it shared with Spain in the division of the New World. The Portuguese ruled Brazil until the beginning of the 19th century, enlarged their holdings along the African coast, and settled Madeira and the Azores, two groups of islands in the Atlantic that now form part of metropolitan Portugal. The country lost its position of leadership during the 17th century when, for a time, it passed under Spanish rule. Napoleon's armies invaded Portugal in 1806, but were soon ousted with the help of British forces under the Duke of Wellington. Considerable unrest prevailed throughout the 19th century, and in 1910 a republic was proclaimed. For 300 years Portugal has been a faithful ally of Great Britain, its traditional trading partner. However, it remained neutral during World War II, and was turned into a centre for international espionage on a grand scale. Military bases were granted to the Allies in the Azores.

Because of its venturesome 14th- and 15th-century navigators, Portugal still has overseas possessions far larger than the area of the homeland. They include Angola, Mozambique and Portuguese Guinea on the African continent; the Cape Verde Islands, and the islands of São Tomé and Príncipe, off the Atlantic coast of Africa; the port of Macao on the south China coast; and Portuguese Timor in the Indonesian archipelago, north of Australia.

● **Potsdam** City (population 110,750) of East Germany, adjoining West Berlin. An old garrison town and residence of the kings of Prussia, Potsdam has many parks and palaces, including the 18th-century Sans Souci of Frederick the Great. Babelsberg, a suburb, contains a locomotive factory and the East German film studios. Leaders of the victorious Allied powers met in the city for the Potsdam Conference of 1945.

● **power station** This is a plant for the production of electric current. The current-producing generators are driven by coal, oil or water, and lately also by atomic energy. In the Larderello plant, near Mount Vesuvius, volcanic energy is used. Wind-driven generators are rare. The exploitation of the water-cycle for the production of electric power has led to special types of plants: the tidal power stations in Brittany, and in Canada and the U.S.A. (Passamaquoddy Bay, Fundy Bay), and the large plant exploiting water strata of varying temperature on the Ivory Coast (Abidyan); while the plant at Shottesh-Shergi, in Algiers, uses the gradient of underground water.

● **Poznan** Industrial city of western Poland; its population is 460,000. It is the centre of rich farm-lands along the Warthe River, a tributary of the Oder. Poznan processes the farm products of the surrounding fertile area, and manufactures loco-motives, agricultural implements and fertilisers. The city is one of Poland's oldest towns, dating from the 10th century. Its modern industrial development dates from the 19th century, when it was part of Germany.

● **Prague** Capital of Czechoslovakia, in Bohemia, on the Vltava River (a tributary of the Elbe). Its population is 1,034,000. The city is dominated by Hradčany Hill, on the left bank, surmounted by a 1,000-year-old castle and St Vitus' Cathedral (1344). The Charles Bridge, one of eleven across the Vltava, leads to the Old Town, with tall, narrow, gabled houses built by German colonists in the 13th century. The New Town, the business district, adjoining the Old Town on the south, dates from the 14th century, when medieval Prague was at the height of its prosperity. Prague, a treasure house of baroque architecture, has been called the 'golden city of a hundred spires'. Engineering industries in outlying suburbs produce cars, rolling stock, aeroplanes, machine tools and heavy machinery. Among the city's traditional products are gloves, glass and smoked meats. An old political centre of Bohemia, Prague was the second city of Europe, after Paris, during the 14th century. It declined in the 15th century, at the time of the Hussite wars between the Czechs and Germans.

● **ptarmigan** This bird is the size of a partridge, with a plump body and short legs which are completely covered with hairlike feathers. In winter the plumage is of a brilliant white, except for the black-tipped tail-feathers; in summer it is rust-coloured. The ptarmigan lives on the moors of Scandinavia, East Prussia, Poland and the Baltic States, and also in Siberia, North America and Greenland. It feeds at night and hides during the day. It is highly valued by hunters.

● **Pyrenees** A high mountain range along the border between France and Spain, the Pyrenees form an effective barrier between the Iberian Peninsula and the rest of continental Europe. With only a few passes in the mountain crest, the Pyrenees extend almost 300 miles from the shores of the Mediterranean to the Atlantic Ocean. Many of the summits are covered with snow; the highest peaks in the Maladetta Massif exceed 11,000 feet. Railways skirt the Pyrenees on both sides, while highways that cross the scenic passes are snow-bound for much of the year. On the French side, the Pyrenees have been attracting a growing number of tourists.

● **rabbit** Distinguished from the hare by its smaller size and shorter ears, the rabbit lives mainly in colonies in warrens, and feeds on grass and crops. It reached pest dimensions in Britain and Australia before being affected by myxomatosis. The young are born in litters of 3—12 every six to eight weeks. Many types of tame rabbit are also reared for their skins and their meat.

● **Reykjavik** Capital, largest town and principal fishing centre (population 81,476) of Iceland, on the island's south-western coast, on the bay called Faxafjoi. It exports herring and cod-liver oil, fish meal and sheepskins. Nearby hot springs are tapped for the city's heating system. The town was founded in 874, but consisted of a single large farm until the 1750s, when a clothing factory was established. The cathedral was built in 1874 and its university in 1911. Its airport is called Keflavik. Today it is extremely modern and prosperous looking.

● **Rheims** (also spelled Reims) An historic city (population 167,830) of north-eastern France at the centre of the Champagne wine-growing region. The splendid Gothic cathedral (begun in 1211) is a French national shrine. For centuries it was the coronation place of the kings of France; in 1429, Charles VII was crowned here in the presence of Joan of Arc. The cathedral was damaged by German shells in 1870 and again during World War I. It was restored with American aid. The city suffered further damage in World War II. But on 7th May, 1945, it witnessed the unconditional surrender of Germany to the Allies.

● **Rhine River** Rising near Graubunden, near St Gotthard in the Swiss Alps, and flowing 800 miles north across the most densely populated and industrialised parts of Western Europe, the Rhine stands out as the most important commercial waterway of the continent. In Germany, where it flows for half of its length, the river is as much a national symbol as is the Thames in England. In the Netherlands, the Rhine's delta is being reclaimed gradually. From its mouth on the North Sea, ocean-going ships sail upstream as far as Cologne, while river barges are able to reach Basel, Switzerland, almost 700 miles inland. In its upper course, the Rhine flows through Lake Constance; it forms the German-Swiss border as far as Basel, then the Franco-German frontier for over 100 miles. In Germany it receives its main tributaries — the Neckar, Main and Moselle — each an important waterway in its own right. Before reaching the Netherlands, the Rhine flows past the steel towns of the Ruhr. Rotterdam is the chief seaport at the river's mouth. The main inland ports are Duisburg (which handles coal and iron for the Ruhr), Dusseldorf, Cologne, Bonn, Mainz, Mannheim-Ludwigshafen — in West Germany — and Strasbourg in France. A far-reaching system of canals also links the Rhine with other navigable rivers of Central Europe, notably the Danube and the Elbe. Tourists visit the famed Rhine gorge above Bonn, where ruined medieval fortresses and towns, and carefully terraced vineyards, look down upon the swiftly flowing waters. The Rhine has often served as a natural line of defence through Europe's turbulent history.

Scene at Seville's bullring, in Spain

Rhodes A Greek island of 540 square miles in the Aegean Sea, though only 12 miles off the Turkish coast of Asia Minor. It is the largest of the Dodecanese island group, with a population of 60,000. Fishing, citrus fruit production and tourism are the main sources of livelihood.

Rhône River This swift river of south-eastern France rises in the Rhône glacier of the Swiss Alps, flows through a picturesque mountain valley of southern Switzerland into Lake Geneva and, upon entering France, is harnessed for electric power by one of Europe's most impressive concrete dams. It then flows on to Lyons, turns southward, and reaches the Mediterranean after skirting the historic cities of Avignon and Arles. Another power dam spans the river in its lower course. The valley of the Rhône below Lyons is the chief railway and highway route between Paris and the Mediterranean; its lower slopes are lined with vineyards, orchards and olive groves. The river's delta is very marshy and is gradually being reclaimed.

Riviera A coastal strip of south-eastern France and northern Italy on the Mediterranean Sea, at the foot of the Alps and the Apennines. This scenic region, with its mild winter climate, exotic plants and mountain-fringed beaches, rates as one of the world's great holiday areas. Its fashionable hotels, private villas and quaint fishing villages offer accommodation and amusements for tourists of every taste and means. Nice (in France) and Genoa (in Italy) are the largest cities of the Riviera, but there are dozens of other resorts along the rocky shore of the deep-blue Mediterranean between Toulouse and Spezia. These include Cannes and Antibes in France, the Principality of Monaco with the famous casino of Monte Carlo, and the Italian part, which consists of the Riviera di Ponente with San Remo, Ospedaletti and Bordighera and the Riviera di Levante with Genova, Rapallo and Spezia. On the French Riviera (also known as the *Côte d'Azur*), a scenic highway links the principal resorts.

roe-deer Roe-deer live everywhere in Europe, from the British Isles to Asia and from the Mediterranean coast to central Sweden. They like woodlands, but also occur in large forests, as long as there is sufficient undergrowth. The male is called a roe-buck, the female a doe, and the young (of spotted appearance) a fawn. In summer these graceful animals live in families; in winter, in large herds. During the day, roe-deer stay hidden, then, at nightfall, they emerge to feed on fields, grassland and young tree-shoots.

Romania A Balkan country on the Black Sea; its area is 92,000 square miles (larger than Great Britain) and its population is 20.14 million. The capital is Bucharest. The Romanians speak a Romance language with Slavic elements, and trace their origin to the settlers of the Roman province of Dacia in the 2nd century A.D. They are chiefly Orthodox Catholics. Romania is crossed by the arc-shaped Carpathian and Bihar mountains, which enclose the uplands of Transylvania — very similar to Central European landscapes. South and east of the mountains are the fertile lowlands of Walachia, Moldavia and Dobregea, the latter being rather dry. These are Romania's agricultural areas, producing wheat and maize. In the foothills of the forested Carpathians are Romania's oilfields, the leading East European producers outside the Soviet Union. The main refining centre is Ploesti. A pipe-line leads to the Black Sea port of Constanta. In addition to oil products and grain, Romania exports manganese, wood products and machinery. Since the Second World War, the country has adopted a Socialist form of government. Wine is grown in the foothill areas, and industrialisation is proceeding rapidly. The Danube is used by ocean-going ships as far as Braila.

Rome The capital of Italy, its largest city (population 2,731,397), and the See of the Pope *(see Vatican)*. Called 'The Eternal City', Rome is one of the world's richest places in history and art, and one of its great cultural and religious centres. It lies on both banks of the winding Tiber River, 15 miles from the Tyrrhenian Sea, and an equal distance from the barren hills of the Apennines. Because of a low and marshy coastline, Rome does not have a good seaport, and most of its foreign trade is channelled through Naples, 120 miles away. Modern Rome has become a city of diversified industries and its suburbs have mushroomed with colourful blocks of flats. But the tourist trade overshadows all other economic activity, as visitors lend continued support to the old saying that 'all roads lead to Rome'.

Ancient Rome was built on the east bank of the Tiber on seven hills rising from the marshy lowland of the Campagna. The seven hills are the Palatine, Capitoline, Aventine, Quirinal, Viminal, Esquiline and Caelian. The traditional story tells of the founding of Rome by Romulus (who, with his brother Remus, had been suckled by a she-wolf) in 753 B.C. — the date from which Roman historians reckoned the city's history. It was probably the Etruscans who civilised Rome and established its control over the surrounding region, called Latium. About 500 B.C., the Romans overthrew their foreign rulers and established the Roman republic, to last four centuries. Under the rule of the Senate, Rome began her march to world supremacy. In the 4th and 3rd centuries B.C., the city came into full contact with Greek civilisation, which brought about many changes in Roman life. In the course of its conquest, Rome defeated Carthage, her chief rival, in the Punic Wars. Greece and Egypt came under Roman control in the 2nd century B.C. Julius Caesar, a popular democratic leader, became master of Rome in 70 B.C., brought the Near Eastern shores of the Mediterranean under Roman dominion, and achieved great personal fame during the Gallic Wars, in the territory that is now France. Caesar's assassination, in 44 B.C., resulted in anarchy, out of which emerged the Roman Empire under Augustus Caesar. Augustus brought a long period of peace to the city, extended the Empire to the North Sea and into eastern Europe as far as the Danube delta, and built the great system of Roman roads, many of which are still in use.

St Peter's, in the Vatican City, Rome

Throughout the Roman Empire the Christians expanded steadily, despite persecutions. In the face of constant danger, they worshipped in the open, even in Rome, where the catacombs housed not only graves but also churches. In the 3rd and 4th centuries A.D., the Empire was gradually divided, through internal dissension, into a Western and an Eastern part — the latter with its capital at Byzantium, since renamed Constantinople, and now called Istanbul. In the 5th century, the weakened Empire was attacked by Germanic tribes, and the last Emperors moved their capital away from 'The Eternal City'. In this general disintegration the Popes, originally the Bishops of Rome, greatly increased their power, and thus restored to the city some of the importance it was losing as a political centre. The end of the Roman Empire came in A.D. 476, when the last Emperor was deposed by the invading barbarians. Although the fall of Rome came about gradually, the Italian peninsula did not recover from the event until the middle of the 19th century. Its history throughout the Middle Ages and the beginning of the modern period is bewildering in its detail, as a result of the country's fragmentation into numerous self-governing units. Beginning in the 15th century, the Popes strengthened their rule over the city and over the Papal States. Italy was proclaimed an independent kingdom in 1862, but Rome did not become its capital until 1871, when the Pope was forced to surrender his temporal powers. The subsequent conflict between the Pope and the King

Málaga is a Mediterranean port on the south coast of Spain

was not solved until the signing in 1929 of the Lateran Treaty, which gave the Pope sovereignty over Vatican City. The Fascist march on Rome (1922) brought Mussolini to power. Since World War II, Italy's President and republican government rule the country from Rome in place of the former kings.

Among the city's most famous sites, apart from Vatican City, are: the Colosseum; the ruins of the ancient Forum Romanum and the Emperors' Fora; the Arch of Constantine and the Baths of Caracalla; the beautiful Renaissance buildings designed by Michelangelo on the Capitoline Hill; the impressive but ornate monument to King Victor Emmanuel II; and the Palazzo Venezia, a Renaissance palace from the balcony of which Mussolini used to address the Roman crowds.

Among the countless churches of Rome, there are five patriarchal basilicas — St Peter's (the world's largest), St John Lateran, St Mary Major, St Lawrence's Outside the Walls, and St Paul's Outside the Walls. Most of the city's churches occupy the sites of martyrs' tombs.

Rotterdam The chief seaport (population 1,061,253) of the Netherlands, on an arm of the Rhine delta with access to the North Sea by the New Waterway. At Rotterdam goods are transferred from ocean-going vessels to the fleet of steamers and barges that serve inland cities in Germany and France, and as far up the Rhine as Basel, Switzerland. In addition to many miles of wharves and warehouses, there are shipyards, oil refineries, grain elevators, and other facilities to handle vast quantities of bulk cargo. Rotterdam's commercial importance dates from the completion of the New Waterway (1872). In World War II, the entire centre of the city was destroyed by a savage German air raid, a few hours after the Dutch surrender in 1940. It has been rebuilt along modern lines. The city is the central point of Dutch motorways, and on the southern side of the Waterway a vast new oil harbour, as well as the Europoort, is being built.

Ruhr Major industrial and coalmining region of West Germany, often compared to the equally smoky and densely built-up industrial north of England. From Duisburg, the region's huge inland port on the Rhine, to Dortmund (30 miles to the east) the Ruhr is an industrial area with collieries, steel mills, machine works and chemical works alternating with green belts; Essen is the largest city and Düsseldorf (a few miles upstream on the Rhine) is the business centre of the Ruhr. Other busy industrial centres of the district are Bochum, Gelsenkirchen, Oberhausen and Wuppertal, which is renowned for its textiles. Despite heavy destruction, the Ruhr is once again the leading steel centre of western Europe, while mining is stretching out into the deeper coal layers further north. Yet much of the northern Ruhr is fertile farmland on deep layers of loess — the Börde country. The southern part is hillier. The region is also linked to the North Sea by the Dortmund-Ems Canal.

rye Except for wheat, this is the only grain commonly used to make bread. It demands less of the soil than does wheat and is therefore grown predominantly in the cool, moist areas of northern and central Europe, which have poor, acid soils. Rye is also used as a substitute for coffee, in the manufacture of whisky and as a feed for poultry and farm animals. The leading rye-producing countries are the Soviet Union, Poland, Germany, Argentina and Czechoslovakia.

Saar A territory (990 square miles; population 1.1 million) of West Germany, on the French border. Crossed by the Saar River (a tributary of the Moselle), the region has rich coal deposits and produces pig iron, steel and chemicals. Long a disputed area between France and Germany, the Saar was detached from Germany after World War I and placed under the League of Nations. In 1935, at Hitler's urging, it voted for reunion with Germany. After World War II, in 1945, it was organised into a self-governing territory, economically united with France. A popular vote in 1955 demanded its return to Germany, which was accomplished in 1957. However, the territory continues to supply coal to the nearby steel mills of French Lorraine under the supervision of the European Coal and Steel Community. The chief city of the Saar is Saarbrücken (population 130,765).

salmon The salmon reaches a length of about 5 feet. Like the trout, it is well adapted to swimming in swiftly-moving water. It feeds on small fish and crabs. The salmon lives in the North Atlantic and the adjacent seas, and migrates widely. Thus, torn-off fishing gear of foreign origin is often found in their mouths. Salmon do not feed in fresh water but subsist on their reserves, mainly fat. During the spawning season their silvery-grey colour changes to red.

Salzburg A cultural and tourist centre (population 108,114) of Austria, near the Bavarian border, and Mozart's birthplace. Picturesquely situated at the foot of a 900-year-old fortress, Salzburg is a city of beautiful churches, episcopal palaces and monasteries. The annual music and opera festival, started in 1926, attracts visitors from all over the world. The scenic Salzkammergut alpine resort district lies a few miles to the east.

San Marino A tiny State (25 square miles) on the slopes of the Apennines, entirely surrounded by Italian territory. With a population of 16,500 (mostly Italians), San Marino is the oldest republic in the world, having maintained its independence for more than 15 centuries. Wine, barley, skins, pottery and building stone are 'exported' to the nearby city of Rimini, on the Adriatic Sea. The sale of postage stamps to collectors is one of the main sources of revenue.

Saragossa (in Spanish, **Zaragoza**) An old city (population 439,451) of north-eastern Spain on the Ebro River, which is spanned by a 15th-century arched stone bridge. Grapes, sugar beets and fruit are grown in irrigated fields and gardens that resemble an oasis in the midst of a dry, barren landscape.

Rye and an ear

sardine A small marine fish of the herring kind. The name 'sardine' is given to the young of the pilchard, and also to other related small herrings, when preserved in oil. The sardine has a length of four to eight inches, and its home is off Sardinia and along the Atlantic coast between Gibraltar and the south coast of England. The main sardine-canning nations are Portugal and France.

Sardinia An Italian island (9,200 square miles) in the Mediterranean, just south of Corsica and about 160 miles south-west of Rome across the Tyrrhenian Sea. The mountainous interior, covered by *maquis* (brushwood) and cork oak woodland, is not suitable for agriculture, in which half of the population is engaged; where conditions allow, wheat, vines, olives and citrus fruit are grown. Fishing, sheep and goat-raising, and mining (lead, zinc, coal and copper) provide a scanty living for the island's subsisting population of 1,419,362. Cagliari is the chief trade centre (223,002 people).

Scandinavia A peninsula (300,000 square miles; population 11.6 million) of northern Europe comprising the countries of Norway and Sweden. The rugged, fjord-cut west coast fronts on the North Sea and North Atlantic; the level east coast is washed by the Baltic Sea and its northern arm, the Gulf of Bothnia. In the south, a chain of straits (called the Skagerrak, Kattegat, and The Sound) separate the Scandinavian Peninsula from the mainland of Europe. Politically, however, the term 'Scandinavia' usually refers to Sweden, Norway *and* Denmark — three countries which were once united under one crown, which speak related languages, and which enjoy a common cultural heritage. Finland, whose language is of Asian rather than Teutonic origin, is sometimes listed among the Scandinavian countries. It shares with Sweden and Norway the northernmost part of the peninsula (north of the Arctic Circle), which includes the lake- and tundra-covered wastes of Lapland. During the Pleistocene period Scandinavia was covered by a solid mass of ice, the retreat of which left lakes, waterfalls, fjords and moraines scattered over the landscape.

seal, grey As its name indicates, this seal is grey in colour; it can be recognised by its long snout. The grey seal is about 8 feet long and feeds mainly on fish, for which it sometimes dives to a depth of 300 feet. Grey seals occur on the North Atlantic coasts, the European coasts, on the islands in the North Atlantic and in the Baltic Sea. They are hunted for their oil; the fur is of minor value.

seal, harp This large seal is still found in large herds on drifting ice in the North Atlantic. It is also known as the saddle-backed seal, from the characteristic markings on the yellowish coat of the male. More than 100,000 harp seals are taken every year in the Arctic; both for their oil and their skins.

Seine River This 500-mile-long stream of north-central France rises near Dijon, flows through the city of Paris in a wide loop, and winds its way to the English Channel at Le Havre. Ocean-going ships are able to reach Rouen, 75 miles upstream. With its numerous tributaries (including the Yonne, the Marne and the Oise) the Seine drains the Paris basin, France's largest and most productive agricultural region. Canals link the Seine with other French rivers, with the Rhine, the Sihelde and the Sambre.

Seville Spain's fourth-largest city (population 622,145), the leading commercial and cultural centre of Andalusia, and a river port on the Guadalquivir, 50 miles from the Gulf of Cadiz and the Atlantic Ocean. It exports wine, olives, cork, Mediterranean fruit, and mercury. It also produces armaments and tobacco. The city is surrounded by beautiful gardens and fertile, irrigated orchards and vineyards. Its gay fiestas and unique Moorish architecture attract crowds of tourists.

Regatta of gondolas on Venice's Grand Canal

The streets are narrow and winding; they are lined with low, whitewashed houses with flower-decked patios which cannot be seen from the outside. Fine, wrought-iron balconies decorate the more prosperous homes. Seville's famous buildings include the 12th-century Moorish palace, an immense Gothic cathedral hung with the works of many Spanish masters, and the Giralda — a graceful 12th-century minaret which reaches 300 feet into the sky and is the city's landmark. Seville has been an important centre since Roman times. The Moors occupied it from 712 to 1248. Columbus sailed from there to discover America. Later the city's exclusive trade with the new Spanish colonies brought prosperity.

● **Sicily** The largest island (10,000 square miles) in the Mediterranean Sea, separated from the Italian mainland by the two-mile-wide Strait of Messina. Despite its triangular shape it is often described as the 'football' about to be kicked by the Italian 'boot'. A mountainous island, Sicily is topped by Mt Etna (10,700 feet high), an active volcano with over 250 recorded eruptions since Roman times. Vineyards, and citrus and olive groves, cling to the sunny slopes, whose natural forest cover was felled either by the Greeks or the Romans. Most of Italy's sulphur is mined in Sicily and there are reserves of salt and of petrol at Ragusa. The island is densely settled by a growing population of 4.7 million. The chief cities are Palermo, Catania and Messina.

● **Sierra Nevada** A snow-capped mountain range in southern Spain running parallel to the Mediterranean coast of Andalusia. Mulhacén (11,411 feet) is the highest summit in Spain. Its southern slopes are covered with vineyards, olive groves and citrus orchards. The city of Málaga lies on the sea at its southern foot, while Granada lies on the north slope; both cities are much frequented by tourists.

● **Sofia** Capital of Bulgaria, with a population of 868,200. The city is situated in a small upland basin, near the junction of the Balkan and Rhodope Mountains. Sofia is a transportation centre on railway lines leading from Central Europe to Turkey. Industries in the city, and industrial districts formerly included in it, account for one-fourth of the country's total industrial output. The city flourished under the First Bulgarian Kingdom (8th—11th centuries) and under the Second Kingdom (13th—14th centuries). Sofia fell to the Turks

in 1386, and became the capital of modern Bulgaria in 1879.

● **Sogne Fjord** This is one of the largest fjords of Norway. Fjords are trough-shaped valleys which were cut into the rock, deepened by glaciers and subsequently drowned. They are often branching and winding. The Sogne Fjord has a length of 124 miles and is 3½ to 5 miles wide. Its greatest depth is 4,000 feet, but at its mouth, over a submarine rock-sill, it is only 400 feet deep. On its banks, mountains rise to nearly 6,000 feet; yet an important fruit-growing area of Norway occurs on the middle reaches in low-lying, sheltered parts.

● **Spain** Nominally a kingdom, Spain occupies ⅚ of the Iberian Peninsula, in the south-western corner of Europe. It has an area of 194,000 square miles and a population of 32.4 million. The Pyrenees form an effective barrier along the French border, and even rail communications along the Atlantic and Mediterranean coasts are made difficult by the difference in gauge between the Spanish and other European railways. The massive interior of Spain is occupied by a barren tableland, known as the Meseta, which rises to about 2,000 feet above sea level, and is noted for its cold winters and torrid summers. Madrid, the capital, is the only large city on the plateau and is surrounded by sparsely populated lands where sheep-raising is the main source of income. Most of the other cities are either seaports (Barcelona, Valencia and Malaga on the Mediterranean; Cadiz, Santander and Bilbao on the Atlantic) or inland centres, surrounded by fertile, irrigated areas, such as Seville, Córdoba and Granada in Andalusia, and Saragossa in the otherwise arid Ebro River valley of north-east Spain. Primarily an agricultural country, Spain grows wheat, barley and maize for domestic consumption, but these have to be supplemented by imports. Grapes and olives are the leading industrial crops. Vineyards, found notably in Andalusia, yield the famed sherry (from Jerez) and Málaga wines. Olives and olive oil, grapes and wine, cork, almonds and fruit (oranges, figs, melons) make up more than half of Spain's exports. There are fisheries on the north-west coast in Galicia, and canned fish (tunny, sardines, anchovies) are exported. Iron, the main mineral export, is either smelted in the Bilbao industrial area or shipped to Britain. Copper, mercury, lead and phosphate are other important minerals, copper being mined in the south at Rio Tinto. Since petroleum is almost entirely lacking, industry depends largely on hydro-electric power.

The earliest inhabitants of Spain were the Iberians, the Basques and the Celts. The Phoenicians established colonies there, followed by the Greeks, Carthaginians and Romans. From A.D. 400 to 700, Spain was overrun by Germanic invaders, including the Vandals and the Visigoths. In 711 the Moors invaded Spain from North Africa. The Moors, who stimulated arts, industry and agriculture, were gradually driven from their Spanish holdings by Christian reconquest. They were finally expelled from Granada in 1492 by Ferdinand and Isabella, who by their marriage merged Castile and Aragon, founding a united Spain. The discovery of America by Columbus, under Spanish sponsorship, led to an enormous expansion of the Spanish Empire. By the 16th century it included almost all of the Americas and the Philippines. The defeat of the Armada in its attempted conquest of England in 1588 marked the beginning of Spain's decline as a major power. In the 19th century Spain lost nearly all her overseas possessions, of which she now retains only Spanish Sahara (Rio de Oro and Saguia el Hamra), and the Canary Islands, off the north-west African coast. A republic, established in Spain in 1931, ended in the great civil war of 1936–39. The regime of Francisco Franco emerged victorious. Despite its sympathies for the German-Italian axis in World War II, Spain remained neutral during that conflict. It was admitted to the United Nations in 1955. Under a 1953 accord, the United States has built military bases in Spain.

● **sponge-fishing** Sponge-fishing is practised mainly on the Mediterranean coasts. The sponge animals are detached from the sea-bed by divers, dried in the air, and then washed until only the skeleton remains. The manufacture of artificial sponges from rubber and plastics has had an adverse effect on the sponge-fishing trade.

● **Stockholm** The capital and largest city (population 747,490) of Sweden, beautifully situated on 13 islands and several peninsulas at the outlet of Lake Mälar. Because of its many canals and waterways (linking Lake Mälar with the Baltic Sea), Stockholm — like Amsterdam — is often described as 'the Venice of the North'. Except for its medieval centre, Staden Mellem Broarna (the town between the bridges; i.e., on an island) with narrow twisting streets, and many buildings in Baroque style, Stockholm is the model of a well-planned modern city. Among its noteworthy public buildings are the 17th-century hall of nobles, the 18th-century royal palace, a large medieval church, the parliament (called Riksdag), and the striking 20th-century town hall. Stockholm is the centre of Sweden's highly specialised machine and electrical equipment industry. Stockholm was founded in 1252, and the city was soon involved in the commercial activities of the Hanseatic League. The modern Swedish nation was established in 1523, after Gustavus Vasa had led a revolt against the city's Danish masters. Since 1901, Stockholm has been the scene of the annual Nobel Prize awards and has a renowned zoo-park, Skansen, to the east. To east and west are many summer-houses by the sea or lake shore. Stockholm city and Stockholm county have been united giving a total population of 1,459,800.

● **stork, white** The white stork of Eurasia is the best-known member of the stork family. It has white plumage with black wing-feathers; the bill and legs are red. In northern Europe this bird builds its huge nest of sticks on the roofs of buildings. The white stork is one of Europe's best-loved birds. Its long association with man was probably the basis for the legend that the stork brings babies.

Strasbourg Cathedral

● **Strasbourg** An historic garrison city of eastern France, only three miles from the left bank of the Rhine (and on its tributary, the Ill River) facing Germany. Its busy riverport trades in Alsatian wines, vegetables, potash, coal and iron ore. The city is noted for its metal industries, its beer, and a food delicacy — *pâté de foie gras* (fattened goose-liver paste with truffles). Strasbourg's landmark is the single 500-foot spire of its beautiful medieval cathedral. An important crossroad since Roman times, the city has had a turbulent history in the contest for power between France and Germany. German is still widely spoken throughout Alsace — the border province of which Strasbourg (population 334,668) is the traditional capital. The city is an important cultural centre and is the meeting place of the Council of Europe.

sturgeon This long fish, covered with tough skin and five rows of bony plates, is famous for its eggs, which are eaten as caviar. Most sturgeons are salt-water fish, which enter large rivers in the spring to lay their eggs; some live permanently in streams and lakes. The Atlantic sturgeon is found on both sides of the North Atlantic. The sterlet and the beluga furnish the famous Russian caviar, while the Danube delta is also an important catching area.

Sturgeon

Stuttgart A railway centre (population 628,412) of West Germany, about half-way between Frankfurt and Munich. The old city lies in a narrow basin on the river Neckar, surrounded by verdant hills on which attractive residential districts are perched. The industrial suburbs, including huge motor-car factories (Mercedes), electrical machine shops, textiles and chemical plants, escaped with minor war damage. Stuttgart has a well-earned reputation as a leading publishing centre; it is also known for its manufacture of precision and optical instruments. For many centuries the city was the residence of the counts of Württemberg.

sugar beets Until 1800, sugar was made from sugar cane only, and Europe depended on the West Indies and Brazil for its sugar supplies. The Napoleonic wars interrupted this import, which was largely controlled by England. Napoleon therefore encouraged the cultivation of sugar beets, which have now become Europe's principal source of sugar. In the beet-sugar factories, the beets are washed and sliced into thin, long pieces, and the juice is then extracted. It is purified, condensed and, finally, crystallised into sugar. The world's leading sugar beet producers are the Soviet Union, the United States, West and East Germany, France and Poland.

sunflower This stately plant is found in many gardens and its large flower has been likened to a small sun. Its home is in tropical America. In the Balkans and in southern Russia, it is cultivated in large fields in order to produce the oil from its seeds, which is used for human consumption and technical purposes.

Sweden With an area of 175,000 square miles, this kingdom of Northern Europe occupies ⅘ of the Scandinavian peninsula. Its population is 8 million. Sweden extends almost 1,000 miles, north-south, along the Baltic Sea; its greatest width is 300 miles. One-seventh of the country lies within the Arctic Circle, where the midnight sun shines in mid-summer. Sweden can be divided into: the forested northern plateau, sloping east to a narrow coastal plain and divided by many river valleys, much used for hydro-electric power; the central lowland around the large lakes Vanern and Vättern, and eastwards to Stockholm and Uppsala; Småland, a forested upland; and Skåne, a fertile farming district in the extreme south. Almost 57 per cent of the country is forested; lumbering, paper and pulp-milling are major

industries and supply 40 per cent of exports. Although cultivated land amounts to only 9 per cent of the total area, modern farming obtains high yields of grain, sugar beets, flax and potatoes. High-grade iron ore, mined in the Kiruna area, is exported and also supplies the steel industry of central Sweden. Stainless steel cutlery is a characteristic product in the industrial towns of the central lowlands. Ships, armaments, ball-bearings and electrical goods are also manufactured. Industry is based largely on power supplies from hydro-electric power stations, which provide ⅔ of the nation's electric power supply. The largest cities are Stockholm, the capital, Göteborg and Malmö. Social progress has kept pace with industrial development. Sweden has one of the highest standards of living in the world, with an abundant life accessible to all. Except for 30,000 Finns and 7,000 Lapps in the extreme north, the population is uniformly of Swedish stock. The established church is Lutheran.

Sweden acquired Finland in the 12th century, but was joined to Norway and Denmark during the 15th century. Sweden asserted its independence under the Vasa dynasty in the 16th century and became a leading European nation. At the zenith of its power, Sweden intervened in the Thirty Years War (1618—48) and acquired large areas on the European continent. Defeat in the Nordic War (1700—21) against Russia forced Sweden to give up its territorial gains, and to accept the position of a second-class power. Since the Napoleonic Wars, Sweden has pursued a neutral policy. It joined the United Nations in 1946.

Switzerland Mountainous country of Central Europe, with an area of 16,000 square miles and a population of 5½ million. The capital is Berne. Switzerland consists of three well-defined regions: the low Jura mountain range, occupying 10 per cent of the total area; the Mittelland, or Swiss Plateau (30 per cent); and the Alps (60 per cent). The beautiful Alpine landscape attracts tourists from all nations, and provides an important source of revenue. More than half the Swiss population is concentrated in the so-called plateau, a country of rolling foothills, rich in forests and water-power resources. The plateau contains some of the leading cities, including Zurich, Geneva and Berne. The only major city outside this region is Basel, a major riverport on the Rhine. Switzerland imports food and industrial raw materials in return for the famous Swiss exports. These include milk products (chocolate, cheese, condensed milk), watches and precision machinery, as well as textiles, toys and pharmaceutical products. Switzerland is a country of many languages. About 75 per cent of the population speak German, 20 per cent French, 4 per cent Italian and 1 per cent Romansch. The Swiss Confederation started in 1291 as a defensive union against Austria. Originally made up of three cantons, the country now includes 25 such areas, which have preserved a great deal of self-rule. Since the 16th century, Switzerland has pursued a strict policy of neutrality, and is not even a member of the United Nations. However, many international organisations have their headquarters in Switzerland, notably in Geneva.

Szczecin Baltic port of Poland, at the mouth of the Oder River; its population is 335,000. After 700 years of German settlement and development, the city (called Stettin by the Germans) passed to Poland as a result of the Second World War. Szczecin has a large shipbuilding industry, and paper and pulp mills. The city functions as a seaport for Czechoslovakia, which ships goods on barges down the Oder River, as well as exporting Polish coal.

tanning The basic process of the leather-manufacturing industries. Hides are treated with solutions of tanning substances to make them soft, resistant and durable. While untanned hides

become parchment-like when dry, the tanning process transforms them into leather by the intake of tanning materials. Tanning with plant materials produces a tough, durable and water-proof leather used in the manufacture of shoe soles and driving belts. Soft and durable leather is produced by tanning with minerals such as alum and chromium-salts. It is used for the uppers of shoes. Treatment with oil and fats produces the flexible chamoised leather used for articles of clothing.

tern, common The neck and the upper head of the common tern are black, the body white and the wings grey. The tail is deeply forked. This small sea-bird is found in Europe, Asia and North America, frequently migrating far to the south.

timber industry The timber industry uses wood as its raw material. There exist at present roughly 10,000 different uses for wood, which is usually worked by machines in factories. Apart from its direct use in building and mining, timber is used for sleepers, furniture, domestic appliances and toys; wood pulp is made into plywood and, by chemical treatment, into cellulose, paper and hard-board; it also forms the basic material for the manufacture of artificial wool fibre and rayon. Of the annual yield in timber, 57 per cent is used in industry (building 33 per cent, paper and pulp 13 per cent, railways 2 per cent, mining 3 per cent, and other industries 6 per cent). The remaining 43 per cent serves as fuel.

tit, blue Blue tits occur everywhere in Europe, except in the far west; also in North Africa, and central and northern regions of Asia. The upper parts are bluish-green; head, wings and tail are blue; the under parts are yellow. The blue tit lives in woods and gardens, rarely in coniferous forests. It roosts mostly in holes in trees, which it makes itself. The blue tit is a very active, agile bird, feeding on insects and their eggs, and also on seeds.

Toledo A city (population 46,000) of Spain, on the Tagus River, south of Madrid. Built on the slopes of a high granite hill, it is one of Spain's most famous cities because of its history and architecture. It flourished under Moorish rule (after the 8th century) and as the capital of Spain (from 1085 to 1560). Its fine-tempered swords were highly prized throughout Europe. Among Toledo's buildings are the 13th-century cathedral and the Alcazar, a 16th-century palace built on a rise overlooking the city. The painter El Greco was one of Toledo's most famous residents.

Toulouse A city (population 439,764) of south-western France, on the Garonne River. It has a 700-year-old university and several medieval churches, of which the oldest contains the tomb of St Thomas Aquinas. The counts of Toulouse once ruled most of southern France and attracted the best troubadours (medieval ballad singers) to their court. A rich agricultural region surrounds the city. The city produces aircraft, textiles, shoes, fertilisers and tobacco. Its university dates from 1203.

Transylvania Region of central Romania, enclosed by the arc of the Carpathian Mountains and crossed by three rivers — the Somesul, Muresul and Oltul. The fertile loess-derived soil of this hilly basin produces wheat, maize, fruit and wine. In addition to Romanians, the population of Transylvania is made up of Hungarians and Germans, who settled here in the 12th century. The area was part of Hungary before World War I and again during World War II. Cattle-rearing is important, as is forestry, and many ores are mined, including iron, copper, gold, lead and zinc. The chief town is Cluj (202,715 inhabitants).

Trieste An Italian seaport (population 278,370) at the head of the Adriatic Sea, 70 miles east of Venice. Its shipyards were built before World War I, when Trieste belonged to Austria and served as the chief outlet for Central European trade. Its commercial importance declined after 1919, when it became part of Italy, and even more after 1947, when it was incorporated into the Free Territory of Trieste (together with 200 square miles of surrounding territory), created under a provision of the Italian peace treaty. Allied troops occupied the city, while Yugoslav forces took over the rural hinterland. In 1954 the city was returned to Italian administration.

tulips There are about fifty species of tulip, and they all occur in the temperate zone of Europe and Asia. The garden tulip, which has developed from various strains, has been a favourite for centuries. It appears in a variety of colours and shapes, so that its cultivation is worthwhile and rewarding. The Turks brought the tulip to Constantinople and from there to Vienna in the 16th century. The name is said to derive from the Turkish word *tulipan* (turban) and refers to the shape of the flower. In the Netherlands, the popularity of this flower was rather exaggerated in the 16th century, and special bulbs were sold for exorbitant prices. Holland is still famous for her tulip fields. Apart from the garden tulip there is a wild species which grows in orchards, parks and meadows. The flower of this is greenish-yellow outside and yellow inside. It is thought that this was originally a cultivated flower which gradually reverted to wild life.

tunny fish The tunny fish is a giant of the mackerel family. Its length reaches 9 to 12 feet, and it weighs between 600 and 1,200 pounds. The tunny fish lives in the Mediterranean at great depths, and only comes to the surface and near the seashore for spawning. Then the fishermen go out and catch it in nets. The flesh is tender and tasty, and is sold salted or preserved in oil.

Turin Italy's motor-car-manufacturing centre, on the River Po at the foot of the Alps. There are large hydro-electric power plants in the nearby mountain valleys. Turin, with a population of 1,177,039, is also a hub of communications with France and Switzerland. Other industries include textile, rubber, electrical and chemical goods. For centuries the city was ruled by the counts of Savoy; it became the capital of the kingdom of Sardinia (which comprised the island of Sardinia and most of north-western Italy) in 1720, and during the early 19th century was at the centre of the movement for Italian independence. The birth of a united kingdom of Italy was proclaimed in Turin's Palazzo Carignano in 1860, and it was the country's capital for the next five years.

Utrecht An old city (population 278,966) of the Netherlands, 20 miles south-east of Amsterdam. It is the main railway centre of Holland, has several large metal-fabricating plants, and is the seat of insurance companies and the national mint. Canals criss-cross the inner town. The Utrecht Fair is an annual event that dates back to the 12th century. The Union of Utrecht (1579) laid the foundation for Dutch independence from Spain. The treaty which ended the War of the Spanish Succession was signed in Utrecht in 1713.

Valencia Spain's third-largest city (population 624,227), Valencia is a seaport on the Mediterranean, bordered by irrigated rice fields, vineyards, orchards and citrus groves. There are a growing number of industries, including ship-building and metal-working. The 'valencia' orange, tobacco and early vegetables are the main export items. Other specialities are silk, soap, lace, ladies' fans, liqueurs and brandies. Valencia is a city of

fiestas, and famous for its colourful flower-markets. It has a Gothic cathedral and a university dating from 1441, and many fine churches.

Vatican City Sovereign state (population 1,000) within the city limits of Rome, Italy, over which the Pope is the absolute ruler. The area (109 acres), on the right bank of the Tiber River, has been closely associated with the history of the Roman Catholic Church since the time of the martyrdom of St Peter. It embraces the papal residence, St Peter's Church, the famous library and art collections, and the Vatican Gardens. Vatican City issues its own postage stamps, and exercises rights over a number of religious buildings outside its walls, including the Pope's summer villa at nearby Castel Gandolfo. The State is the smallest in the world, with its own railway station, coins and radio station. It is much visited by pilgrims and tourists.

Venice Italy's famed city of canals is built on 120 small islands in a lagoon of the Adriatic Sea, north of the Po River delta. It is connected with the mainland, 2½ miles away, by motor-car and railway causeways. The city's canals, crossed by as many as 400 bridges, replace the streets of ordinary towns. The principal traffic artery, the Grand Canal, curves through Venice from the modern railway station to the Piazza San Marco, a huge square, inhabited by many pigeons, to which tourists flock in large numbers to visit the ornate church of St Mark's, the clock tower, and the Campanile (bell tower). Adjoining the square is the Palace of the Doges (residence of the medieval rulers of Venice) and the Bridge of Sighs, over which prisoners used to be led to their cells. The Grand Canal is lined with sumptuous palaces, built hundreds of years ago by the city's wealthy merchants. During the latter part of the Middle Ages, Venice was the centre of European commerce with the Orient; it successfully competed with Genoa (1380) and established strategic bases in the eastern Mediterranean, including Constantinople. However, its trading monopoly was broken at the end of the 15th century, when Portuguese navigators discovered a route to India around southern Africa. The city's present population is 367,631; its tourist trade is all-important. The Lido, a fashionable bathing resort on the sandbar which encloses the Lagoon of Venice, is reached by ferry-boat. Venetian glassware, blown and cast in many colours, has been the city's most famous product for many centuries.

Vesuvius The only active volcano on the mainland of Europe, overlooking the Bay of Naples in southern Italy. A violent eruption in A.D. 79 buried the Roman cities of Pompeii and Herculaneum under a thick blanket of volcanic ash, causing the loss of 2,000 lives. The ruins of Pompeii were rediscovered in the 18th century in an excellent state of preservation, giving the modern world much information about life in Roman times. Several other destructive eruptions have been recorded in the past 300 years. The approximate height of Vesuvius is 4,000 feet.

Vienna The capital (population 1,627,566) of Austria, beautifully situated on the Danube River by the rolling hills of the Vienna Woods (Wienerwald). Until World War I, it was the residence of the Hapsburgs, Austria's royal dynasty, and the capital of the powerful Austro-Hungarian Empire. Although Austria is now a small country, Vienna has retained much of the splendour and cultural leadership of its imperial days. Almost one-third of the country's population lives here, at the crossroads of Central Europe. Vienna lies at the head of deep-draught navigation on the lower Danube. The city's industries are diversified, ranging from machinery, textiles and furniture to such luxury items as leather goods and jewellery. The annual

trade fair attracts buyers from afar. St Stephen's Cathedral, the city's 800-year-old landmark, is a fine Gothic structure with a single tall spire. The inner town, with its crooked, narrow streets and small shops, is encircled by a wide, tree-lined boulevard (the Ringstrasse), laid out on the site of the former city walls. Haydn, Mozart, Beethoven, Schubert and Brahms lived and composed much of the world's greatest music here, and Johann Strauss gave Vienna the waltz. In the centre of the town is the Hofburg, the former palace, which now contains museums, offices and the Spanish Riding School.

Vienna began as a military outpost of the Roman Empire. In the 12th century it became the seat of the dukes of Austria, and in 1278 it came under the House of Hapsburg, whose last reigning monarch died in 1916. Twice, in 1529 and 1683, the Turks reached the gates of Vienna in their attempt to conquer Europe, and twice the city stopped them by its heroic defence. Napoleon occupied Vienna in 1805 and again in 1809, but the Congress of Vienna (1814–15) promptly divided his conquests among his former enemies. In 1938, Hitler marched into Vienna unopposed. The Russian army recaptured the city in 1945, and during the next ten years it was jointly occupied by American, British, French and Russian forces. In 1955 Austria regained its independence, and Vienna reverted to its leisurely way of life.

viper, common The common viper, or adder, is a common poisonous snake. Colour and markings are extremely variable, but dark zigzag stripes running down the whole length of the middle of the back are usually very distinct. The snake measures approximately two feet in length, and occurs all over Northern and Central Europe and temperate Asia. Its main food is frogs, lizards and, especially, mice, for which reason the viper could be considered useful. The common viper is the only poisonous snake in Great Britain. It is not as dangerous as is often assumed, for a viper's bite rarely leads to complications, though serum is essential. It attacks man only in self-defence.

Vistula River Principal stream of Poland, 680 miles long. It rises in the Carpathian Mountains, and flows north past Cracow and Warsaw to the Baltic Sea. It is navigable and is linked by canals with the Oder and Pripet Rivers.

Warsaw Capital of Poland, on the Vistula River; its population is almost 1.3 million. The city became the capital of Poland at the end of the 16th century, succeeding Cracow. Warsaw developed on the left bank of the Vistula, where the absence of marshes gave an easy crossing. Between the two world wars, the city became the commercial and intellectual centre of modern Poland. Warsaw fell to the Germans in 1939. Uprisings — first by Jews, who had been enclosed in a ghetto, and later by other Poles — resulted in the virtual destruction of Warsaw during the war. Industries include the manufacture of foodstuffs, motor-cars and steel.

Weser River This 470-mile-long river of West Germany is navigable from the junction of its two headstreams (the Fulda and the Werra) to the North Sea. Bremen may be reached by ocean-going ships at high tide. Canals connect the Weser with the Rhine and the Elbe, West Germany's principal inland waterways.

wheat The world's principal grain, wheat occupies a larger acreage than any other crop. An area twice as large as that of maize or rice is sown in wheat. The best wheat-growing regions are the grasslands of the Northern Hemisphere (in the United States, Canada and the Soviet Union) and of the Southern Hemisphere (Argentina and Australia). About 57 per cent of the total wheat acreage is in winter wheat, which is planted in the autumn and harvested in the summer. In areas where winters are too cold, wheat is sown in the spring and harvested in the autumn. About one-fifth of all the wheat grown enters into international trade. The principal exporters are the United States and Canada, the chief importers Britain and West Germany.

● **whooping swan** or **whooper** Found in the swamps of central Siberia, northern Russia, Finland and Iceland. In the autumn it migrates southward and spends the winter in more southerly parts of Europe, occasionally going much farther south. The whooper feeds on fruit, seeds, leaves, water-weed, grass and roots.

● **Wiesbaden** A famous spa (population 260,614) of West Germany, with a nearby riverport on the right bank of the Rhine, 20 miles west of Frankfurt-am-Main. The healing qualities of its warm springs were known to the Romans, who piped their waters into specially built bath-houses. Though nearly destroyed during World War II, Wiesbaden has recovered its industrial importance as a chemical and boat-building centre. The capital of Hessen, it has large museums, and is famed for its libraries and printing and publishing firms.

● **wild cat** The wild cat is dangerous in proportion to its size (3—4 feet long). It hunts at night for small mammals and birds, and frequently invades poultry-yards, pigeon-houses and pheasantries. The damage done is somewhat compensated for by the number of mice it destroys. During the day, the wild cat hides in burrows or sleeps in trees. The home of the wild cat is in central and southern areas of Europe, and also western Asia. In populated areas, it is more or less extinct.

rich farming area. It possesses a large railway-wagon factory, and chemical, electro-technical and wool and linen industries. Wroclaw was two-thirds destroyed during World War II and is still far short of its pre-war population of more than 600,000. The city possesses a university, founded in 1702, a Gothic City Hall, and a castle as well as a cathedral, both founded in the 12th century.

● **Yugoslavia** A mountainous Balkan country of 100,000 square miles, with a population of 20.5 million. Its capital is Belgrade (843,209). Yugoslavia, whose name means South Slavia, did not exist before the First World War. It was formed in 1918 as a union of the south Slavic peoples: the Serbs, Croats, Slovenes and Macedonians. The cultural influences of former rulers are still strong in parts of the country: Italian along the Dalmatian coast of the Adriatic Sea; Central European in Slovenia and Croatia; Turkish Moslem in Bosnia, Serbia and Macedonia. Grapes, olives, tobacco and fruit are grown in sunny Dalmatia and Macedonia. The bare Dinaric Alps, rising behind the sub-tropical coast, drop in the north-east to the fertile plain of the Sava and the Danube. There are to be found Yugoslavia's maize and wheat fields. Two-thirds of the country's population is engaged in agriculture. Industry has been developed increasingly in recent years on the basis of the country's rich mineral resources. These consist chiefly of non-ferrous ores (copper, lead, zinc, chrome). Yugoslavia exports bauxite, cement and mercury, fruits (especially prunes), timber, eggs and tobacco. Since World War II, Yugoslavia has adopted a Socialist form of government. The official language is Serbo-Croat.

● **Zagreb** Second-largest city of Yugoslavia, in Croatia; its population is 821,651. Zagreb manufactures diversified products including machinery,

woollen goods, wood products and processed foods. The city consists of three sections: the Capitol hill, with a Gothic cathedral founded in the 11th century; the older upper town of the Croatian nobility; and the newer lower town, with commercial establishments, which developed in the 19th century.

● **Zuider Zee** An embayed coastal region of the Netherlands, partially reclaimed from the North Sea. At one time it was a lake; then, in 1287, a flood broke through the coastal barrier, joining the lake to the North Sea and leaving a string of islands across its entrance. Beginning in 1923, the Dutch undertook a huge project to reclaim part of the area, draining it and turning it into productive cropland. A dike across the narrow entrance prevents recurrent flooding. Except for a small fresh-water lake, the Ijsselmeer, the region now consists of *polders* — level areas of reclaimed land divided by embankments and cut by small drainage canals. The *polders* provide food for the country's rapidly-growing population, and are included in a zonation plan for urban, industrial and rural planning, as well as new transport routes east and north-east of Amsterdam, with a new town, Lelystad, created on the eastern polder of Oost Flevoland. In 1967 Zuidelijk Flevoland polder was completed.

● **Zurich** The largest city (population 674,400) of Switzerland, and its financial and publishing centre with far-flung banking and trade connections. Textiles, paper, chocolate and radios are among the many products of the city's factories. As the gateway to the Alpine reaches of the upper Rhine valley, Zurich is also a major tourist resort. It lies at the north end of the Lake of Zurich (25 miles long), whose southern shores are fringed by the foothills of the Alps.

Vineyards beside the Rhine

● **wine** About 80 per cent of the world's grapes are grown for wine. The rest are consumed as table grapes and raisins. The most important wine-producing countries are those around the Mediterranean Sea, France, Italy, Algeria, Spain and Portugal. France is both the largest exporter and the largest importer of wine. Wine has many and varied kinds, and the wine of each region, even each vineyard, has a distinctive character. There are many factors affecting the final product: the type of grape, degree of ripeness, soil character, amount of sunshine received, fermentation, bottling processes and others. Wine may be roughly divided into table wines (red and white), and fortified wines, with added alcohol. Some wine is distilled and cognac is made from the spirit.

● **Wroclaw** Largest city (514,000) of Polish Silesia, on the Oder River. When it belonged to Germany, prior to 1945, it was called Breslau. The city is an important industrial and commercial centre in a

St Stephen's Cathedral stands at the centre of Vienna, capital of Austria

Asia

Even though Europe has a 2,000-mile-long land boundary with Asia, marked in part by the narrow Ural mountains, which reach up to 6,000 feet, few Europeans had looked eastward into northern or central Asia even as late as the 15th century, and first-hand knowledge of these areas was scanty in the extreme. Adventurous merchants from the Russian trading city of Novgorod had penetrated to the Ob River by the end of the 15th century in search of furs, but this mighty Siberian river marked the boundary of European discovery, and beyond lay an unknown world. Yet, much earlier, this same area of central Asia, between the Altai and Tien Shan, is regarded as being the place of origin of many north and east European peoples who had migrated westwards.

In 1581, a Russian fur-trader named Stroganov had hired a band of Cossacks to protect the trade from warlike Tartars. Their subjugation of the Tartars marked the real beginning of Russian rule in north-west Asia. The Cossack leader Yermak conquered the Tartar capital of Sibir, near Tobolsk on the Irtysh River, and this led to further Cossack penetration of Siberia during the next century. Wooden forts (*ostrogs*) were built, and the Cossack settlers were followed by hunters and merchants, attracted by the fur trade. In 1632, Yakutsk — far to the east on the Lena River — had been founded, and the Okhotsk Sea had been reached by 1640. This remarkable search for skins was carried through despite the difficult terrain — impenetrable forest, swampy land, cold winters, wild animals, great distances — and the local peoples, who resisted the eastward movement. Even with modern equipment, exploration in far north-eastern Siberia is difficult.

North Asia borders on the Arctic Ocean along a 3,000-mile front, with the Polar Ice Pack reaching almost to the coast in summer on the north-east. The natural eastern boundary is with the Bering and Okhotsk Seas, separated from the Pacific by the island arcs of the Aleutian and Kurile Islands, while the Sikhote Alin region of far south-east U.S.S.R. borders on the Sea of Japan.

In the south, North Asia is sharply demarcated from South Asia by natural boundaries, with almost unbroken mountain ranges stretching from the Caspian to the Okhotsk Seas. Within these mountain fastnesses, small, previously independent republics exist. In the west the peaty waterlogged lowlands of the Ob, and the salt deserts of Kazakh and Karakum proved effective barriers to eastward movement, limiting it to a narrow band in the steppes of northern Kazakhstan in the latitude of

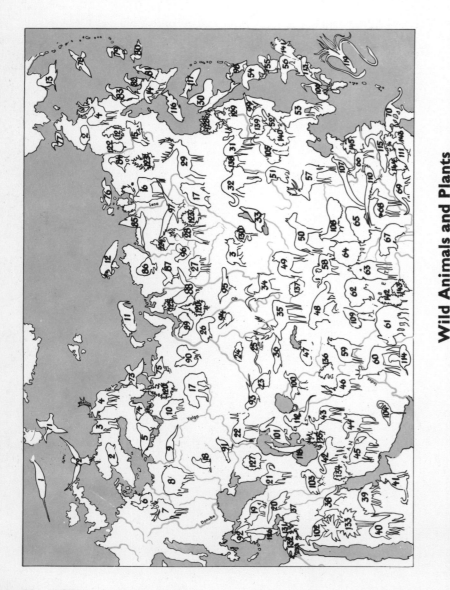

Wild Animals and Plants

Mammals
1 Narwhal
2 Lemming
3 Lynx
4 Reindeer
5 Grey seal
6 Common hare
7 Red deer
8 European bison
9 Otter
10 European wild boar
11 Walrus
12 Bearded seal
13 Fur seal
14 Silver fox
15 Sable
16 Elk
17 Brown bear
18 Ground squirrel
19 Przewalski's horse
20 Ichneumon
21 Red sheep
22 Coral
23 Bobac
24 Pika
25 Big-eared jerboa
26 Beaver
27 Wolf
28 Siberian red deer
29 Altai wapiti
30 Sea lion
31 Sika deer

32 Manchurian tiger
33 Baikal hair seal
34 Siberian ibex
35 Maral
36 Tiger polecat
37 Golden hamster
38 Caracal (Persian lynx)
39 Striped hyena
40 Beatrix antelope
41 Cheetah
42 Persian leopard
43 Goitered gazelle
44 Onager
45 Bezoar goat
46 Markhor
47 Manul
48 Ounce
49 Koulan
50 Amur badger
51 Flying squirrel
52 Red squirrel
53 Glutton
54 Japanese macaque
55 Japanese black bear
56 Père David's deer
57 Argali
58 Tahr
59 Nilgai
60 Indian rhinoceros
61

62 Himalayan black bear
63 Kiang
64 Yak
65 Takin
66 Water deer
67 Panda
68 Musk deer
69 Indian civet cat
70 Clouded leopard

Birds
71 Eider duck
72 Herring gull
73 Great black-backed gull
74 Brant
75 Bean goose
76 Spectacled eider
77 Yellow-billed loon
78 Fulmar
79 Puffin
80 Steller's eider duck
81 Guillemot
82 Auk
83 Steller's sea eagle
84 Ptarmigan
85 Whistling swan
86 Snowy owl
87 Bluethroat
88 Eagle owl
89 Black grouse

90 Capercaillie
91 White-winged lark
92 Griffon vulture
93 Sand grouse
94 Azure titmouse
95 Siberian jay
96 Hazel grouse
97 Osprey
98 Cormorant
99 Coal titmouse
100 Macqueen's bustard
101 White pelican
102 Egyptian vulture
103 Hooded vulture
104 Flamingo
105 Lilford's crane
106 White-necked crane
107 Reeves' pheasant
108 Blue-eared pheasant
109 Black-necked crane
110 Golden pheasant
111 Cabot's tragopan

Reptiles and Amphibians
112 Desert Monitor
113 Giant salamander
114 Indian cobra
115 Chinese alligator

Fishes and other marine life
116 Cod
117 Salmon
118 Sturgeon
119 Giant squid

Plants
120 Spruce
121 Siberian stone pine
122 Alder
123 Larch
124 Birch
125 Bilberry
126 Cypress
127 Beech
128 Alder buckthorn
129 Dog rose
130 Scotch pine
131 Olive tree
132 Cedar of Lebanon
133 Date palm
134 Fig tree
135 Tragacanth
136 Edelweiss
137 Saxaul
138 Walnut
139 Maple
140 Oak
141 Bamboo
142 Cedar
143 Rhododendron
144 Camphor tree
145 Mulberry tree
146 Gingko tree

Omsk, and this is the route which earlier peoples had followed westwards — the Huns and Mongols, who had invaded much of eastern and central Europe. Hence North Asia may be regarded as a closed territory, with its only access to the sea through Vladivostok, for the northern coasts are ice-bound for much of the year, though large modern ice-breakers prolong the ice-free conditions.

Much of northern Asia, with its vast plains, alluvial lowlands and low plateau, forms a two-dimensional landscape of great monotony. For example, the town of Omsk, though it is 1,000 miles distant from the sea, is only 250 feet above sea level. Only to the north and east of the Lena are high mountains to be found, while the Putorana Plateau north of the Yenisey, in north-central Siberia, reaches to 5,000 feet. The Verkhoyansk and Cherski Mountains in the far north-east reach to 12,000 feet, and the settlement of Verkhoyansk is a notorious frost hollow. The Kamchatka peninsula is the site of active volcanoes, including Klyuchevskaya reaching to 15,912 feet.

North Asia includes Siberia, a vast territory which covers over 4 million square miles, an area greater than that of Europe, while the steppes and deserts of the south-west cover a further 1½ million square miles. The climates of these areas are extreme, with no amelioration from the sea, while the summer of northern Asia marks the thawing of the surface soil which, however, is kept moist due to the presence of impenetrable permafrost beneath. Whoever hears the name Siberia surely thinks first of cold — and not without reason, for the coldest part of the Northern hemisphere lies, not at the North Pole, as might be supposed, but in the mountain basins of north-east Siberia. The settlement of Oimyakon, on the upper Indigirka River, has recorded −56·6 °C (with an average for the coldest month of −77·7 °C). Snow lies from October to March, although only thinly, for the precipitation is low, often less than 20 inches per annum. Yet, as with all extreme continental climates, the brief summer can have very high temperatures, and the thermometer may reach 90°F, for nowhere else in the world are the seasonal extremes so great.

The extremely cold prolonged winter causes the accumulation of cold in the subsoil, which is permanently frozen to considerable depths, from 5 feet in the south to 2,000 feet in the north. The southern limits of this zone of ground freezing — and short summer thaw — are from the lower course of the Ob in the west, then southwards to Lake Baykal, placing all of east-central and east Siberia under permafrost. Since there are few paved roads, the thawed layer produces muddy, almost glutinous conditions, so that travel is often impossible for much of the early part of summer, and house foundations must be built with care.

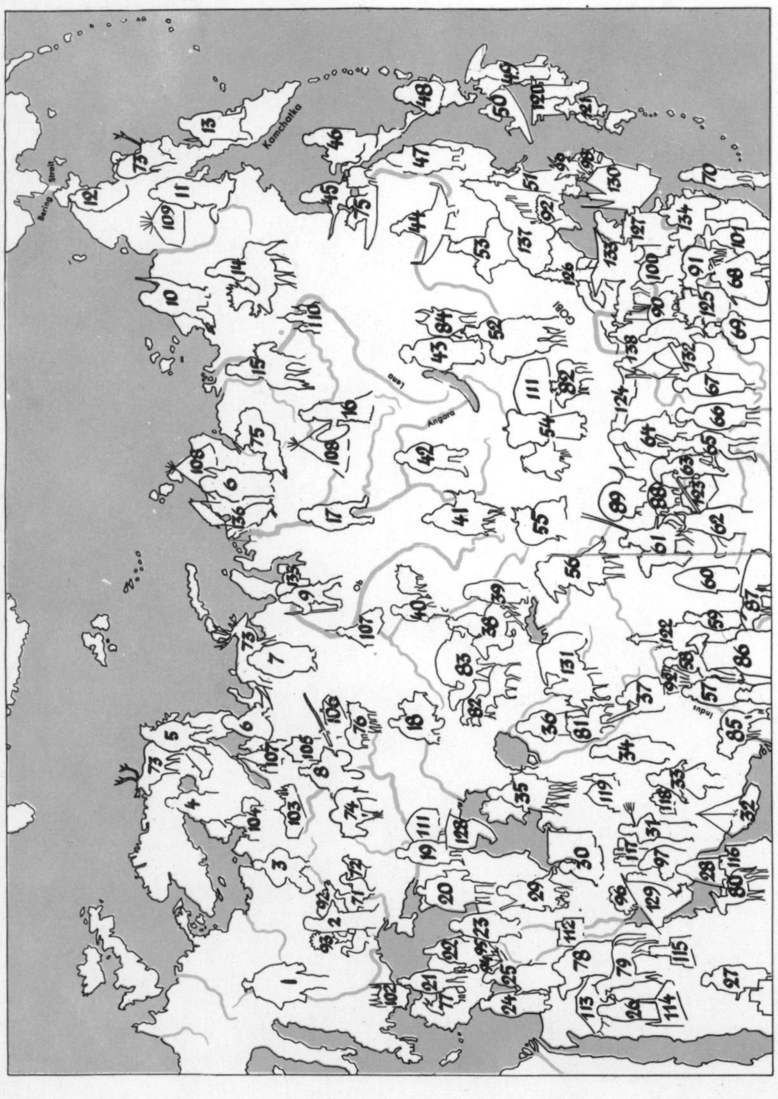

Peoples, Domestic Animals and Useful Plants

Peoples in Traditional Costumes

1 Hungarian cowboy
2 Ukrainian peasant woman
3 Pole — dancing the cracovienne
4 Finnish bard
5 Lapp
6 Nenets (Samoyed)
7 Mansi (Vogul)
8 Russian
9 Khanty (Ostyak)
10 Odul (Yukagir) hunter
11 Luoravetlan (Chukcha) hunter
12 Nymylen (Koryak)
13 Itelmen (Kamchadal)
14 Evenki (Tungus)
15 Yakut
16 Evenki shaman
17 Siberian from the Yenisei country
18 Russian with samovar
19 Kalmyk

20 Cherkess (Circassian)
21 Osmanli Turk
22 Turk smoking a hookah (water-pipe)
23 Armenian
24 Jew in 18th-century costume
25 Arab
26 Bedouin
27 Yemenite
28 Arab woman from Muscat
29 Kurd
30 Afghan raw-weaver
31 Iranian farmer
32 Pearl divers
33 Beluchi
34 Afghan
35 Turkmen
36 Uzbek
37 Afridi
38 Kirghiz
39 Kirghiz woman
40 Tobolsk Tartar
41 Altai Tartar
42 Karagass
43 Buryat
44 Nanai (Gold)

45 Nivkh (Gilyak)
46 Orok hunter
47 Orochon
48 Ainu
49 Japanese woman
50 Japanese fisherman with cormorants
51 Korean
52 Mongol riding a camel
53 Manchu Mongol
54 Mongol woman
55 Kalmyk woman
56 Uigur with trained falcon
57 Rajput
58 Oad
59 Western Hindu
60 Nepalese monk
61 Tibetan
62 Bhutanese dancer
63 Buddhist monk
64 Ngolok Tibetan
65 Naga
66 Kachin woman
67 Yi (Lolo)
68 Chinese poultry vendor
69 Chinese actor

70 Kaoshan

Domestic Animals

71 Geese
72 Chickens
73 Reindeer
74 West Russian cart-horse
75 Sledge dogs
76 Ox and hog
77 Angora goat
78 Dromedary camel
79 Arab horse
80 Muscat donkey
81 Karakul sheep
82 Fat-tail sheep
83 Bactrian camel
84 Buryat cattle
85 Sind zebu cattle
86 Ceremonial elephant of a maharaja
87 Buffalo cart
88 Pack sheep
89 Yak
90 Masked pig
91 Zebu cattle

Useful Plants

92 Wheat
93 Sunflower
94 Durra
95 Barley
96 Plums, figs, oranges
97 Roses in Shiraz
98 Soya-beans
99 Millet
100 Rice
101 Tea-picker

Characteristic Landmarks

102 Sultan Ahmed Mosque in Istanbul
103 Kremlin in Moscow
104 St. Isaac's Cathedral
104 St. Isaac's Cathedral in Leningrad
105 Old watch-tower in Gorki
106 Russian log cabin
107 Russian wooden church
108 Pole tent
109 Circular tent
110 Cathedral in Yakuts
111 Yurt
112 Ishtar gate in Babylon
113 Bedouin tent
114 The Kaaba in Mecca
115 Royal palace in Riyadh
116 Old Portuguese fort in Muscat
117 Ruins of Persepolis
118 Ruins of ancient city in Afghanistan
119 Meshed, Iranian pilgrimage centre
120 Shinto gate
121 Temple lantern
122 Lamaist shrine (chorten)
123 The Potala, palace of the Dalai Lama
124 Great Wall of China
125 Belltower of a Chinese temple
126 Pagoda
127 Chinese gate

Transportation and Trade

128 Caspian fishing boat
129 Dhow
130 Junk
131 Araba (travelling coach)
132 Wind-driven wheelbarrow
133 Chinese travelling coach
134 Jinricksha

Miscellaneous

135 Fish traps
136 Fish-drying rack and slain grey seal
137 Soya-bean cart
138 Treadmill

The duration and intensity of the Siberian winter is such as to influence the use of the large rivers — the Ob, the Yenisey and the Lena — for navigation, for they are frozen up for much of the year: ten months at their mouths, six months at latitude 60°N. Most of the rivers of Siberia flow northwards, hence their lower stretches freeze first and thaw last, causing vast areas to be inundated by flood waters at various times of the year. Fortunately, the sea areas are only sparsely populated. Uses other than navigation have been mooted for these giant streams. Vast river diversions have been proposed by Russian engineers, damming the northward flowing streams and diverting the water to the south, to irrigate the drier areas. It was also supposed that these vast reservoirs would themselves lead to an amelioration of the climate.

The zones of vegetation within Siberia are largely a reflection of the climatic regions. Tundra occurs along the Arctic coasts; and for 150-200 miles inland, a treeless zone exists, with some dwarf birch or willow as the dominant species in the most favourable parts. The great amount of surface water produced by the thaw of the ground ice and of the rivers creates vast swamps each year, for it cannot soak into the permafrosted subsoil, and very little is evaporated in the early summer.

Southwards of the tundra lies the great forest belt known as taiga, widening towards the east (see map p. 73). Virtually the whole of Siberia is a vast forest of conifers, dark and impenetrable because of its tangled undergrowth of fallen trees and branches. Spruce and pine are found in western Siberia, with larch dominating in the east. Mixed woodland occurs in the Soviet Far East in the Amur basin, north of Vladivostok in the cool, monsoonal lands. In these forests live bears, sables, martens and the ermine, the furs of which are sought at least as avidly today as in the days of the first Cossack colonisers and trappers. Large peaty swamps are also widespread, especially in the Irtysh-Ob lowlands of western Siberia, where the land is so flat that natural drainage is extremely slow.

South and south-west of the forest belt are the drier areas, which provide a sharp contrast to the rest of northern Asia. Travelling southwards, away from the coniferous forest, we first meet deciduous woodlands, and wooded steppes with large collective farms. Gradually the trees disappear and the steppe grasslands appear, now almost entirely under cultivation, with grain crops growing on the deep fertile black soils called *chernozem*, one of the most important wheat-growing areas in the world.

The present population of North Asia, that is Asiatic Russia, beyond the Urals, is about 40 million, of which 30 millions are Russians who have colonised the area, while only 10 millions are the original North Asiatic peoples. The Russians have mainly settled along the narrow, elongated belt of land comprising the grass-steppe and the southern margins of the Siberian forest, which in reality corresponds to the Trans-Siberian Railway, which was built at the turn of the century. This corresponds to the towns of Omsk, Novosibirsk and Tomsk-Krasnoyarsk, with some movement southwards towards the Altai and Semipalatinsk.

New areas of cultivation and new industries and mining followed the coming of the railway, for southern Siberia is rich in minerals, especially iron, zinc and aluminium. Thus a thin wedge of modern industry and land use has been driven, in the space of sixty years, between the forest dwellers to the north and the nomadic herders and oasis farmers of the sub-arid lands to the south. The forest dwellers have many differing languages and characteristics, and many are related to the Finns, Lapps,

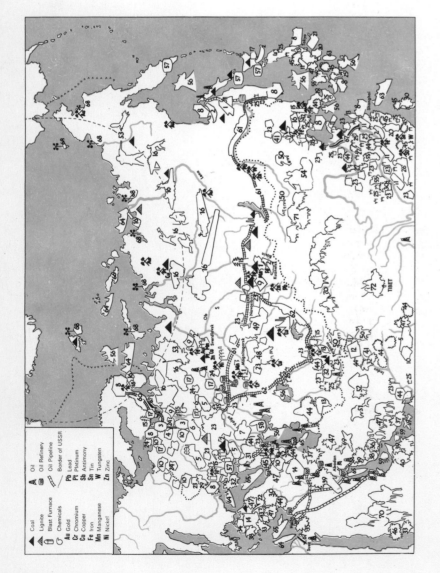

Production, Mineral Resources and Trade

Industries
1 Iron foundries
2 Steel manufacture
3 Machinery industry
4 Electrical goods
5 Locomotives and rolling stock
6 Car industry
7 Tractor industry
8 Shipyard
9 Aluminium
10 Textile industry
11 Silk industry
12 Cashmere shawl
13 Cotton mill
14 Carpet mill
15 Hydro-electric station
16 Lumber
17 Paper mill
18 Apatite
19 Graphite
20 Chinaware
21 Lacquerware
22 Meerschaum pipes

Agricultural and Animal Products
23 Wheat
24 Rye
25 Rice
26 Rice farmer
27 Millet
28 Kaoliang
29 Sugar beets
30 Sugar cane
31 Sunflowers
32 Fruit
33 Wine
34 Raisins
35 Jaffa oranges
36 Oranges
37 Peaches
38 Figs
39 Dates
40 Mangoes
41 Walnuts
42 Soya-beans
43 Onions
44 Cotton
45 Tea
46 Coffee
47 Tobacco
48 Cattle-raising
49 Dairying
50 Sheep and goat herding
51 Karakul sheep
52 Persian lamb
53 Fur-trapping
54 Hides and wool
55 Silk-raising
56 Fisheries
57 Fish canning
58 Caviar
59 Pearl oysters

Transportation and Trade
60 Moscow-Murmansk railway
61 Trans-Siberian railway
62 Kuibyshev-Tashkent-Novosibirsk railway
63 Passenger liner
64 Freighter
65 Tanker
66 Icebreaker
67 Canal
68 Arctic observation station
69 Passenger plane
70 Camel caravan
71 Yak caravan
72 Tibetans riding yaks

Eskimos or even to some of the Indian peoples of North America. They engage in hunting for furs and skins, reindeer-herding, fishing or forestry, while in recent times many have migrated to work in the modern industrial areas. In the drier southern areas, most of the people are of Turkish origin, living in Turkestan ('land of the Turks'), and even there the traditional economy is being varied by irrigation, and cotton and rice are being produced.

The development and settlement in North Asia is a story of pioneer living and a witness to man's urge to conquer nature. Yet, despite the achievements of Soviet industry and agriculture in developing the rich natural resources of Siberia, there are still serious obstacles to be overcome, both in organisation and in the natural world. The cold winters and vast distances imply that the centre of gravity of economic life and the main area of population increase can be expected to remain in European Russia within the foreseeable future.

In contrast to North Asia, South Asia is the seat of many old cultures and varied civilisations — for example, in Mesopotamia (Iraq) around the Tigris and Euphrates Rivers, around the Indus River (Pakistan), and in China and South-East Asia.

Trade between Europe and South Asia has existed for almost five centuries, even before the Portuguese navigator Vasco da Gama found a sea route to India around Africa in 1498, for overland routes to India and China had existed earlier and continued almost uninterruptedly through the Middle Ages, dating back before the birth of Christ. Yet, despite this trade, few Europeans had a clear picture of the mystical Orient before Marco Polo visited the Far East in the 13th century. The son of a Venetian merchant, Marco in the first place came to the court of the Mongol ruler of China and undertook various missions for him in eastern Asia. On his return to Italy, Marco Polo wrote a report on all that he had seen and experienced, and this was the first reliable description of that part of Asia. Nevertheless, it is remarkable that contemporary Europe could hardly bring itself to believe most of what he had written.

The Near East is a part of South Asia, lying closest to Europe and forming a bridge between Europe and the Middle East. It is via the Middle East that Europe earlier received Asiatic wares, which came by caravans on the Silk Route, ending in Izmir on the Aegean Sea, where goods were trans-shipped to Europe. The caravan route to Izmir crossed the Armenian highlands, the highest point of which is Mount Ararat (16,945 feet). From these highlands mountain ranges extend westward to enclose the inland plateau of Turkey, and south-eastward to border the Iranian Highlands (Iran).

The Near East has an area of 2 million square miles, with a population of over 70 million people. It is bordered by six seas:

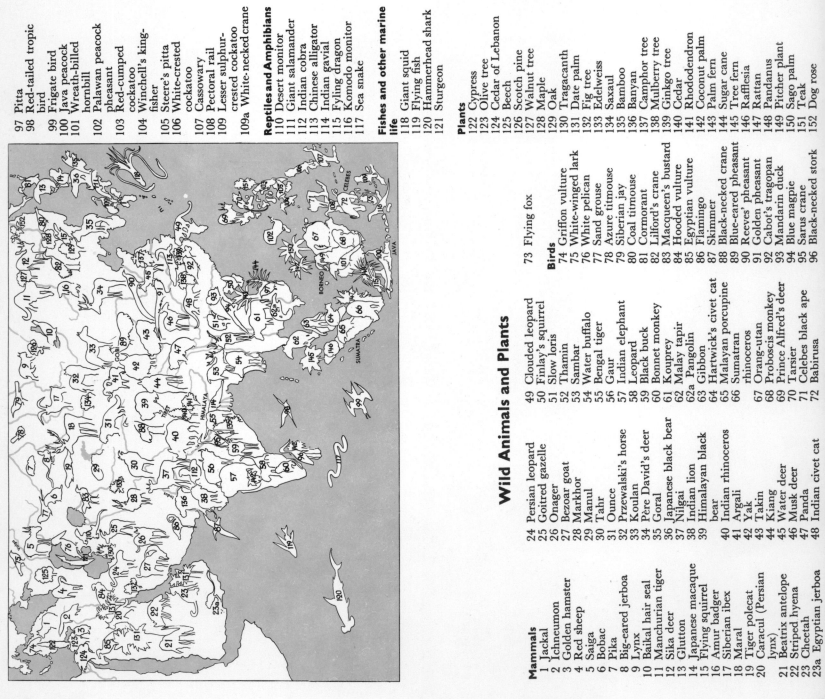

Wild Animals and Plants

Mammals
1 Jackal
2 Ichneumon
3 Golden hamster
4 Red sheep
5 Saiga
6 Bobac
7 Pika
8 Big-eared jerboa
9 Lynx
10 Baikal hair seal
11 Manchurian tiger
12 Sika deer
13 Glutton
14 Japanese macaque
15 Flying squirrel
16 Amur badger
17 Siberian ibex
18 Maral
19 Tiger polecat
20 Caracul (Persian lynx)
21 Beatrix antelope
22 Striped hyena
23 Cheetah
23a Egyptian jerboa
24 Persian leopard
25 Goitred gazelle
26 Onager
27 Bezoar goat
28 Markhor
29 Manul
30 Tahr
31 Ounce
32 Przewalski's horse
33 Koulan
34 Père David's deer
35 Goral
36 Japanese black bear
37 Nilgai
38 Indian lion
39 Himalayan black bear
40 Indian rhinoceros
41 Argali
42 Yak
43 Takin
44 Kiang
45 Water deer
46 Musk deer
47 Panda
48 Indian civet cat
49 Clouded leopard
50 Finlay's squirrel
51 Slow loris
52 Thamin
53 Sambar
54 Water buffalo
55 Bengal tiger
56 Gaur
57 Indian elephant
58 Leopard
59 Black buck
60 Bonnet monkey
61 Kouprey
62 Malay tapir
62a Pangolin
63 Gibbon
64 Hartwick's civet cat
65 Malayan porcupine
66 Sumatran rhinoceros
67 Orang-utan
68 Proboscis monkey
69 Prince Alfred's deer
70 Tarsier
71 Celebes black ape
72 Babirusa
73 Flying fox

Birds
74 Griffon vulture
75 White-winged lark
76 White pelican
77 Sand grouse
78 Azure titmouse
79 Siberian jay
80 Coal titmouse
81 Cormorant
82 Lilford's crane
83 Macqueen's bustard
84 Hooded vulture
85 Egyptian vulture
86 Flamingo
87 Skimmer
88 Black-necked crane
89 Blue-eared pheasant
90 Reeves' pheasant
91 Golden pheasant
92 Cabot's tragopan
93 Mandarin duck
94 Blue magpie
95 Sarus crane
96 Black-necked stork
97 Pitta
98 Red-tailed tropic bird
99 Frigate bird
100 Java peacock
101 Wreath-billed hornbill
102 Palawan peacock pheasant
103 Red-rumped cockatoo
104 Winchell's king-fisher
105 Steere's pitta
106 White-crested cockatoo
107 Cassowary
108 Pectoral rail
109 Lesser sulphur-crested cockatoo
109a White-necked crane

Reptiles and Amphibians
110 Desert monitor
111 Giant salamander
112 Indian cobra
113 Chinese alligator
114 Indian gavial
115 Fyling dragon
116 Komodo monitor
117 Sea snake

Fishes and other marine life
118 Giant squid
119 Flying fish
120 Hammerhead shark
121 Sturgeon

Plants
122 Cypress
123 Olive tree
124 Cedar of Lebanon
125 Beech
126 Scotch pine
127 Walnut tree
128 Maple
129 Oak
130 Tragacanth
131 Date palm
132 Fig tree
133 Edelweiss
134 Saxaul
135 Bamboo
136 Banyan
137 Camphor tree
138 Mulberry tree
139 Ginkgo tree
140 Cedar
141 Rhododendron
142 Coconut palm
143 Palm fern
144 Sugar cane
145 Tree fern
146 Rafflesia
147 Rattan
148 Pandanus
149 Pitcher plant
150 Sago palm
151 Teak
152 Dog rose

the Caspian Sea, the Black Sea, the Aegean Sea, the eastern Mediterranean Sea, the Red Sea, and the Arabian Sea (a part of the Indian Ocean). The northern mountainous part of the Middle East is joined to the Arabian peninsula by the lowland of Mesopotamia, a name which, in Greek, means 'the land between the rivers', that is the rivers Tigris and Euphrates.

The Mesopotamian lowland was more than the link between India and Europe, it was the cradle of many ancient and highly-developed civilisations. Nineveh, near Mosul on the Tigris in northern Iraq, was the capital of the Assyrian empire, which flourished about 650 B.C. and united the whole of the Near East and Egypt. The Tower of Babel, where, according to biblical authority, the greatest confusion of languages occurred, stood on the Euphrates at Babylon, a city which was the centre of the Babylonian empire two thousand years before Christ. The Sumerian civilisation existed at an even earlier date; its capital, Ur, has been excavated in southernmost Mesopotamia.

The Near East is almost entirely a part of the great hot arid belt which extends from the North African Sahara north-eastwards to the deserts of Central Asia. Some rain falls on the marginal mountain ranges of Turkey and Iran, and also, to a lesser degree, on the mountains of Yemen.

The Arabian Peninsula is largely occupied by the State of Saudi Arabia, one of the most thinly populated countries of the world, for it consists almost entirely of hot desert. Arid steppe and desert also cover the southern half of the State of Israel, and nine-tenths of the nations of Syria and Jordan. Here river courses are usually dry, and water-flow normally occurs only for brief periods, but with great intensity, after the violent rain-storms which are typical of the eastern Mediterranean. Drinking water is a great problem in western Asia; for example, in the little oil-rich sheikhdom of Kuwait, on the Persian Gulf,

drinking water is obtained by the distillation of sea water. Aridity and heat are the dominant climatic traits in the Near East.

The greater proportion of the population of the Middle East are Arabs, Turks or Persians, whose religion is Islam, founded by Mohammed. The Holy City of Islam is Mecca, the birthplace of Mohammed. From Mecca the faith of Islam has spread over a large area, extending from West and North Africa to the Pacific, and embracing more than 200 million believers.

Peoples, Domestic Animals and Useful Plants

Peoples in Traditional Costumes
1 Osmanli Turk
2 Turk smoking hookah (water-pipe)
3 Armenian
4 Cherkess (Circassian)
5 Kalmyk
6 Russian with samovar
7 Tobolsk Tartar
8 Kirghiz
9 Kirghiz woman
10 Turkmen
11 Jew in 18th-century costume
12 Arab
13 Kurd
14 Bedouin
15 Yemenite
16 Arab fisherman
17 Afghan rug-weaver
18 Iranian farmer
19 Beluchi
20 Afghan
21 Arab woman from Muscat
22 Pearl divers
23 Uzbek
24 Afridi
25 Uigur with trained falcon
26 Altai Tartar
27 Kalmyk woman
28 Karagass
29 Buryat
30 Nanai (Gold)
31 Orochon
32 Ainu
33 Mongol woman
34 Mongol mounted on camel
35 Manchu Mongol
36 Korean
37 Tibetan
38 Ngolok Tibetan
39 Buddhist monk
40 Rajput
41 Oad
42 Western Hindu
43 Nepalese woman
44 Bhutanese dancer
45 Naga
46 Kachin woman
47 Yi (Lolo)
48 Chinese poultry-vendor
49 Chinese actor
50 Kaoshan
51 Japanese fisherman with cormorants
52 Japanese woman
53 Bhil
54 Indian snake-charmer
55 Fakir lying on bed of spikes
56 Kurumba
57 Singhalese
58 Vedda
59 Palm-oil carrier
60 Indian potter
61 Burman
62 Padaung woman
63 Lahu woman
64 Annamese mandarin
65 Annamese priest
66 Coolie
67 Temple dancer in Thailand
68 Burman woman
69 Cambodian musicians
70 Sempang with blow-pipe
71 Malay
72 Batak
73 Sumatran pepper-vendor
74 Igorot
75 Bagobo
76 Sulu
77 Punan
78 Dyak
79 Kulawi
80 Javanese dancer
81 Balinese dancer
82 Blanket weaver
83 Timorese

Characteristic Landmarks
134 Yurt
135 Ishtar gate in Babylon
136 Bedouin tent
137 The Kaaba in Mecca
138 Royal palace in Riyadh
139 South Arabian palace
140 Meshed, Iranian pilgrimage centre
141 Ruins of Persepolis
142 Ruins of ancient city in Afghanistan
143 Old Portuguese fort in Muscat
144 Pagoda
145 Great Wall of China
146 Lamaist shrine (chorten)
147 The Potala, palace of the Dalai Lama
148 Chinese gate
149 Belltower of Chinese temple
150 Shinto gate
151 Temple lantern
152 Temple gate in Madura
153 Temple in Benares
154 Burmese temple
155 Shwe Dagon Pagoda in Rangoon
156 Wat Arun temple in Bangkok
157 Angkor Wat
158 Pile dwelling in Nicobar Islands
159 Sumatran community house
160 Pile dwelling
161 Log cabin

Domestic Animals
84 Angora goat
85 Fat-tail sheep
86 Bactrian camel
87 Dromedary camel
88 Arab horse
89 Muscat donkey
90 Karakul sheep
91 Sind zebu cattle
92 Buryat cattle
93 Yak
94 Pack sheep
95 Donkey
96 Ceremonial elephant of a maharaja
97 Water buffalo
98 Masked pig
99 Zebu cattle
100 Nellore zebu cattle
101 Batak pony

Useful Plants
102 Durra
103 Barley
104 Date palm
105 Plums, figs, oranges
106 Roses in Shiraz
107 Wheat
108 Millet
109 Soya-beans
110 Rice paddies
111 Rice plants
112 Rice
113 Tea picker
114 Cotton
115 Coconut palm
116 Jute
117 Opium poppy
118 Tobacco
119 Sugar cane
120 Sago palm

Transportation and Trade
121 Caspian fishing boat
122 Dhow
123 Araba (travelling coach)
124 Buffalo cart
125 Chinese travelling coach
126 Junk
127 Wind-driven wheel-barrow
128 Jinricksha
129 Annamese cart
130 Sampan
131 Houseboat of Mergui Archipelago
132 Moro outrigger
133 Malay proa

Miscellaneous
162 Soya-bean cart
163 Treadmill
164 Rice threshing
165 Village idol

Afghanistan, the homeland of the Afghans, is the easternmost country of the Middle East and,.at the same time, the transition zone from southern Asia, the Indian sub-continent and Turkestan, for here the ancient trade routes from China and India met to proceed to Europe. The trade route led to India via the Khyber Pass, a gateway which offered the only access through the high mountain barriers of the Sulaiman Mountains. This pass was used by ancient conquerors — the Emperor Darius of ancient Persia; Alexander the Great and his Macedonian legionaries, and the Mongol hordes of Genghis Khan.

Southernmost Asia is protected on its northern side by some of the world's highest and wildest mountains, among them Mount Everest, 29,028 feet high. South of this complex range of mountains, emerging fanlike from the knot of the Pamirs, lies the Indian sub-continent, a land of contrasts, stretching from the snowclad peaks of the Himalayas to the hot, tropical Malabar coast, and from the salt deserts of Pakistan to the monsoonal rain forests of Assam. Surrounded by the Indian Ocean and protected to the north by the high Himalayas, the main part of northern India consists of the Ganges lowland, a densely populated region, while India's southern portion, triangular in shape, mainly consists of a high basalt plateau — the Deccan — sloping down from its highest parts in the Western Ghats, eastwards to the low sandy Coast of Coromandel.

The climate of southern Asia is dominated by the monsoon, during which, for half the year, the wind blows off the land, generally from the north towards the south; for the remaining six months, the wind directions are almost exactly reversed in many areas, the winds blowing and air masses moving from the south, off the ocean.

Agricultural activity, transport and many other aspects of economic life are affected, if not even controlled, by the great seasonal changes of climatic conditions. The great contrast is not one of temperature, as prevails in Europe, but of rainfall, with a dry season from January until June and, in India especially, a wet season extending from June in the south, with the coming of the south-west monsoon, and a little later with very heavy rains in north-east India, especially in the Ganges Delta and the mountains of Assam.

In Assam especially, the rainfall is extremely high, with up to 40 feet of rain per year. If the south-west (wet) monsoon is late in arriving, crop failure may result, leading to lack of food supplies, hunger, and even famine. The dry period, beginning with a cool period early in the calendar year, continues until the oppressive heat of June, and the prevailing north-east winds of this period were also responsible for the early colonisation of East Africa by Arabs. With the change of wind, these early traders sailed home, aided by the south-west winds.

In the Far East, the south-west monsoon is less well marked, in seasonality and in wind direction, and the summer rainfall is supplemented by typhoons. Very heavy falls of rain provoke widespread floods in China and, during the rainy season, the discharge of water by the great rivers of China — the Hwang-ho, and Yangtze — increases as much as tenfold. Major works of river-control by dams, channel duplication and regulation, and controlled flooding, are being undertaken to lessen this great and age-old scourge.

To the north of India and in the innermost western parts of China lies the vast central Asiatic highland, which is overlooked and interspersed with high and rugged mountain ranges. From the Pamir knot radiate the ranges of Himalaya and Karakorum, across the lands of Jammu and Kashmir, and the

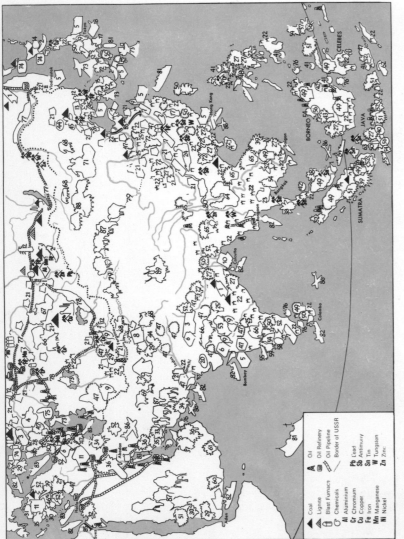

Production, Mineral Resources and Trade

Industries and Handicrafts
1 Iron foundries
2 Steel industry
3 Locomotives and rolling stock
4 Tractor industry
5 Shipyard
6 Textile industry
7 Silk industry
8 Cashmere shawl
9 Cotton mill
10 Jute
11 Carpet mill
12 Hydro-electricstation
13 Lumber
14 Paper mill
15 Graphite
16 Ruby
17 Chinaware
18 Lacquerware
19 Meerschaum pipes
20 Salines

Agricultural and Animal Products
21 Wheat
22 Rice
23 Rice mills
24 Rice farmer
25 Millet
26 Kaoliang
27 Sugar cane
28 Sunflowers
29 Fruit
30 Wine
31 Raisins
32 Jaffa oranges
33 Oranges
34 Peaches
35 Figs
36 Dates
37 Mango
38 Bananas
39 Pineapple
40 Melon
41 Copra
42 Coconuts
43 Sago palm
44 Walnuts
45 Soya-beans
46 Onions
47 Cotton
48 Hemp
49 Natural rubber
50 Tea
51 Coffee
52 Tobacco
53 Opium poppy
54 Pepper
55 Cinnamon
56 Cloves
57 Nutmeg
58 Cardamom
59 Ginger
60 Frankincense
61 Myrrh
62 Sandalwood
63 Cinchona bark
64 Teak
65 Bamboo
66 Cattle raising
67 Dairying
68 Sheep and goat raising
69 Karakul sheep
70 Persian lamb
71 Hides and wool
72 Silk raising
73 Fishing
74 Fish canning
75 Caviar
76 Pearl oysters

Transportation and Trade
77 Trans-Siberian railway
78 Kuibyshev-Tashkent-Novosibirsk railway
79 Silk Road
80 Burma Road
81 Passenger liner
82 Freighter
83 Tanker
84 Warship
85 Canal
86 Passenger plane
87 Camel caravan
88 Yak caravan
89 Tibetans riding yaks

Main Ports and Their Exports
Aden—Bunker coal
Bangkok—Rice
Bombay—Cotton
Colombo—Tea, rubber, cinnamon
Hong Kong—Silk
Calcutta—Jute, tea
Karachi—Cotton, wheat
Manila—Sugar, hemp
Rangoon—Rice, coconuts
Saigon—Rice

Coal
Lignite
Blast Furnaces
Chemicals
Al Aluminium
Cr Chromium
Cu Copper
Fe Iron
Mn Manganese
Ni Nickel
Oil
Oil Refinery
Oil Pipeline
Border of USSR
Pb Lead
Sb Antimony
Sn Tin
W Tungsten
Zn Zinc

Kunlun and Tien-shan, which last divides Sinkiang (China) into the Tarim basin and Dzungaria.

Tibet is the highest-lying region of the world. To the east it gives way to the Tanglha Mountains, and southwards to the high ranges and deep gorges of Yunnan and northern Burma. In contrast to these almost empty areas, eastern Asia is densely populated, especially around the Chinese rivers of the Hwang-ho and Yangtze-Kiang, which were formerly centres of flourishing cultures and well-developed agriculture. Here the monsoons are from the north-west and the south-east; the former — the winter monsoon — coming from Mongolia, is bitingly cold, while that in summer is very humid.

Off the eastern coast of Asia lie chains of islands, the principal group constituting Japan. Other large island groups off the south-east coast are the Philippines and Indonesia, all of which are mountainous and volcanic, the island of Java alone having over a hundred volcanoes. These island arcs also experience frequent earthquakes, and such manifestations witness both to the crustal instability of the region and to the vast forces, acting on the boundary of the Pacific, which have been building mountains since Tertiary times. Noteworthy features of this part of the globe are the vast oceanic deeps and trenches, some of greater depth than the world's highest mountains.

In marked contrast to North Asia's 40 million people, South Asia has a population of 1,600 million, but this is partly the result of much better living conditions, at least as far as intensive use of the land is concerned, especially with the possibility of growing two or three crops each year on the same land. One may also find some explanation of the great difference in numbers of people in the fact that numerous early civilisations arose in southern Asia.

Southern Asia includes the two most populous regions of the world: China, with more than 700 million inhabitants, and India with over 400 million people. Roughly 70 per cent of the people of India work on the land, many living in small villages of less than 500 inhabitants; yet in many Indian regions, especially the lower Ganges, the density of population is greater than in many of the highly industrialised urban communities of the western world — densities reaching up to 10,000 people per square mile in highly productive rural areas, and 300,000 per square mile in urban districts. Both India and China are seeking to mitigate their great problems of over-population, though from very different and opposed ideologies. Measures of birth control, internal colonisation, industrialisation and land reallotment all lead to increased use of resources or control of population increase. The pressure of population on the land is often so great that, though the primary problem of gaining enough food to eat is a major concern, it is now being realised that more people can be supported and nourished from an industrial plant than from the produce of even a large area of rich farmland. However, even some of the smaller nations of South-East Asia, not yet faced with over-population, are turning to industrialisation, and the problem of population pressure is not solely the problem of the nations concerned, but is one of the most intractable facing the world political scene. The degree of success eventually achieved by the two competing systems of China and India in solving the problem is one of the greatest issues of our times.

●**Abadan** Petroleum-refining centre in the Iranian lowlands at the head of the Persian Gulf (population 270,726). The city has one of the world's largest refineries, linked by pipelines with nearby oil-fields, and to its oil harbour.

●**Aden** A former crown colony, now part of the new Democratic Republic of the Yemen. At the south-western corner of the Arabian peninsula, Aden guards the southern entrance to the Red Sea. It was a major port of call and refuelling station for ships using the Suez Canal, until the canal's closure in 1967. It is still an important port for loading oil. Together with the former Federation of South Arabia and a number of sultanates and emirates, it is now part of the Democratic Republic of the Yemen, 61,800 square miles in extent, with a population of 1½ million. It has a frontier with the Yemen Arab Republic and a coastline extending eastwards along the Gulf of Aden. The capital is Madinet Al-Shaab (formerly Al Ittahad), and Aden is still a main centre, with a population of 285,000. Subsistence agriculture is the main occupation, although there is a lucrative business in cotton exports. Outside the fertile districts, the land is mountainous or desert, and the people in nomadic communities, depending on livestock to survive.

●**Afghanistan** A land-locked Moslem kingdom of south-western Asia, between Pakistan, Iran and the Soviet Union, and sharing a short boundary with China. Afghanistan has an area of 250,000 square miles and a population estimated at between 10 million and 16 million, the latter an Afghan estimate and the former a more cautious figure. The capital is Kabul (435,000 people). Afghanistan consists of the rugged central highlands of the Hindu Kush and surrounding plateaux, much of which are desert. Half of the cultivated area in the lower-land is irrigated by rivers descending from the central mountains. The longest of these is the Helmand, site of a water-development project. Wheat is the most important food crop and is sown over nearly half the total available acreage. Cotton and sugar beet, grown in the northern part of the country, supply new processing industries. Fresh and dried fruit (pomegranates, peaches, raisins and dried apricots) are exported. Livestock raising, yielding karakul skins and wool, rivals crops in importance among the largely nomad population. Afghanistan's exports (karakul skins, fruit, wool, cotton, hides and carpets) are shipped by road and rail through the port of Karachi, in Pakistan. Half of its population is Afghan, a quarter Tadzhik and 11 per cent Uzbek. Pushtu (the language of the Afghans) and the related Persian are the official languages. Camel and mule caravans still play a major role in transportation. There are no railways and few good roads. Its mineral resources so far are little developed. Some coal is mined and natural gas from the north is piped to the Soviet Union. Through much of its history, Afghanistan has been under the sway of neighbouring powers, yet an Afghan dynasty ruled from the 10th to the 12th century, extending its control to cover large parts of Persia and the Punjab. Modern Afghanistan emerged as a nation in the late 18th century, and preserved its independence as a nation despite British and Russian attempts at penetration. Afghanistan has been developing its economy recently with American and Soviet loans, and pursues a neutral policy in world affairs.

●**Agra** City of northern India, 120 miles south-east of Delhi (population 509,000). As a result of it being the capital in the Mogul kingdom from 1526 to 1857, the city has many beautiful buildings, especially famous being the mosques and the Taj Mahal, one of the most impressive structures of the Moslem world. It was built from 1632 to 1650 by the Mogul ruler Shah Jehan as a memorial to his wife.

●**Ahmadabad** The main city of Gujarat, north-west India, 275 miles north-west of Bombay (population 1,149,918). One of India's largest cotton-milling centres, it is second only to Bombay, and is the cultural capital of the Gujarat people, one of India's leading language groups.

●**Aldan River** A 1,400-mile-long tributary of the Lena River, in north-eastern Siberia, rising in the Aldan Plateau and flowing through uninhabited forest land. Only its lower valley has farm settlements.

At Agra stands the Taj Mahal. Constructed of white marble, this mausoleum was erected in memory of Shah Jehan's wife, who died in 1629

Aleppo City of northern Syria (population 425,467). The centre of a rich grain and cotton district, Aleppo was situated on the ancient caravan route which crossed Syria on the way to Baghdad. One of the largest cities of the Arab world for many years, it has now acquired industries such as textiles and cement.

Allahabad Commercial and university city of India, 350 miles south-east of Delhi; (population 411,955). Great Hindu religious festivals are held here, attracting millions of pilgrims.

Alma-Ata Capital (population 730,000) of the Soviet republic of Kazakhstan. The city is situated at an elevation of 3,000 feet, amid shady apple orchards which contrast greatly with the arid steppe to the north. Alma-Ata (which means 'father of apples') was founded as the Russian frontier fortress Verny ('faithful') in 1854. It has developed into an industrial centre producing heavy machine tools, farm machinery parts, textiles and food products. A university and Scientific Academy were founded in 1934.

Altai Mountains A mountain system of Central Asia, where the borders of the Soviet Union, the Mongolian People's Republic and China meet. It rises to 15,000 feet in Mount Belukha. Forests of larch, stone-pine and spruce cover its slopes, especially on the northern slopes, which experience higher rainfall, and where the Ob River has its source. The southern parts of the mountains are more desert-like. The main centre of the Russian atomic industry is at Ust-Kamenogorsk in the Altai mountains.

Amoy (Sze-ming) Port of south-east China, on the Strait of Formosa (population 224,300). Amoy was one of the first Chinese ports opened to trade with the British and Dutch in the 18th century. In the 19th century, Amoy had a flourishing tea trade and served as the port of departure for Chinese emigrants to South-East Asia. Amoy was reached by a new railway in 1957.

Amritsar City of north-west India, in the Punjab, near to the boundary with Pakistan (population 376,000). Amritsar is the religious centre (the Golden Temple) of the Sikhs, a Hindu religious sect. It is famous for the weaving of carpets and shawls.

Amu Darya River Great river (1,600 miles long) of Central Asia, rising in the Pamirs and flowing into the Aral Sea. Its upper course forms the border between the Soviet Union and Afghanistan. In the lower reaches, its waters are used for irrigation. Navigation is hindered by sand-banks in the low-water winter season, when the river carries only one-sixth of its maximum summer volume.

Amur River A great river of the Far East (2,800 miles long), second only to the Yangtze in eastern Asia. The Amur and its tributaries form the Soviet-Chinese border for almost 2,000 miles. Navigation is hindered by the long ice season (November to April) and by silt at the river's

mouth in the Okhotsk Sea. The Russians and Chinese are planning to improve navigation and to build hydro-electric plants along its course.

Andaman Islands A chain of islands in the Bay of Bengal, south of Burma. They belong to India and separate the Andaman Sea from the Bay of Bengal. Copra is the main product. The largest town is Port Blair. Together with the Nicobar Islands to the south, the total population is 63,548.

Angara River or **Upper Tunguska** A river of southern Siberia, rising in Lake Baikal and flowing 1,100 miles to the Yenisey. A large, regular flow of water throughout the year and a steep gradient make the Angara ideal for hydro-electric development. The Bratsk power station (in the river's middle course) is one of the world's largest. A relatively smaller hydro-electric plant is at Irkutsk.

Angkor A vast collection of ruins in Cambodia, dating from the 9th—12th centuries, and the site of the capital of a Khmer (Cambodian) empire. The best preserved monument is Angkor Wat, a temple consisting of five towers surrounded by a moated wall. The ruins were discovered in thick jungle in 1860 and have been converted into a park.

angora goat This variety of the domestic goat is to be found mainly in the Middle East, but is also bred in South Africa and Australia. Its colour is usually white, and the long, silky hair is used in the finest cloth and wool manufacture under the name of mohair.

Ankara formerly Angora and Ankyra, has been the capital of Turkey since 1923. The creator of modern Turkey, Kemal Atatürk, chose it on account of its central situation and in an attempt to break the old Ottoman traditions of Istanbul as a capital. Apart from the ruins of an old cliff-top fortress, Ankara is now a modern city, with broad streets and new buildings. Formerly a small town, trading in angora goat skins, it has grown more than fifteen-fold since the end of World War I. Its population (with suburbs) is 2,208,791 (1970) and today it has a well-developed industrial base, with textiles, machinery and chemicals. Its university was founded in 1933.

An-shan is the largest steel centre of China, in Manchuria (population 805,000). It is situated 60 miles south-west of Shen-Yang (Mukden), on the railway to Lu-ta. Steel production first started there in 1918 and was greatly expanded under Japanese rule (1931—45), then by the Chinese Communist administration after 1949.

An-tung Industrial city of China, in Manchuria (population 360,000). On the Yalu River, which forms the border between China and North Korea, An-tung's industries — non-ferrous metals, lumber, paper, matches and rayon — gain their energy from the large hydro-electric plant of Su-pung, also on the Yalu.

Aqaba, Gulf of An arm of the Red Sea between the Sinai Peninsula of Egypt and Saudi Arabia. A very narrow segment of its northern end is shared by Israel's port of Eilat and Jordan's port

of Aqaba (Akaba). The Arabs' refusal to allow free passage to shipping bound for Israel through the Gulf created a major political crisis in 1967.

Arabs A Moslem people of Semitic origin, originally settled in the Arabian Peninsula (Saudi Arabia). After the rise of Islam in the 7th century, the Arabs rapidly spread through North Africa, South Asia as far as Indonesia, and into southern Europe and East Africa, reaching their greatest power about 750. The purpose behind their expansion was the spread of the Islamic faith, though this was aided by its policy of blending with, rather than disturbing, the existing cultures. The Arabic colonisation and spread of Islam gave the Arabs much geographical knowledge, and long before Vasco da Gama discovered the sea route to India in 1498, the Arabs had full control of the navigation and rich trade of the Indian Ocean. Most of the Arab possessions came under the Turkish Ottoman Empire during the 16th century; but, after World War I, Arab States were established in North Africa and the Middle East. These were Egypt, Iraq, Saudi Arabia and Syria; Palestine and Transjordan also emerged, largely under British control. During, and especially after, World War II, yet more Islamic countries — formerly colonial territories — achieved full independence: Morocco, Algeria, Tunisia, Libya, Sudan, Lebanon, Pakistan and Indonesia. In 1958, an attempt was made to unite the Arab world, and Egypt and Syria federated as the United Arab Republic, but this union was dissolved a few years later. Recently the Arab world has been drawn together by hostilities against Israel.

Aral Sea A large (25,000 square miles) salt lake of Soviet Central Asia in the Turansteppe which receives both the Amu Darya and the Syr Darya Rivers, but has no outlet. Its average depth is 50 feet, reaching to 220 feet. Frozen in its northern part for three months of the year, the lake is situated in sparsely settled desert east of the Caspian. Navigation is unimportant, but there are some fisheries.

Ararat The highest mountain of Turkey (16,945 feet), near to the borders with Iran and the Soviet Union. According to the Old Testament, Noah stranded the Ark on Mount Ararat after the Great Flood.

Archangel A Soviet town near to the mouth of the northern Dvina River, which flows into the White Sea. It was formerly Russia's chief port, but has long been overtaken by Leningrad. Nevertheless, Archangel is still the chief harbour for the export of timber, and an important fishing harbour, though it is ice-bound from November to April. The vast forests around the town determine its commercial activity and industries — sawmills, skin and leather industries, shipbuilding and fish preserving, as well as oil-refining. The town has 343,000 inhabitants.

Armenia A Soviet republic of Transcaucasia, bordering on Turkey and Iran. With an area of 11,500 square miles, it has a population of 2.5 million. The capital is Erivan. Most of the usable land of this mountainous country is in pasture. Irrigated valleys support cotton, sugar beets, vineyards and orchards. Industry is based in part on farm products (canned goods, brandy) and on ores (copper, molybdenum, aluminium). Volcanic tuff (a building stone) and pumice are two Armenian rocks of industrial value. Armenians, who make up 80 per cent of the population, are a Caucasian people of Christian Orthodox religion. They use a peculiar

In Asia Minor, camel caravans like the one pictured above cross the broad Anatolian Plateau, near Ankara, the capital of Turkey

alphabet developed in the 4th century and have distinctive facial features. Armenia, an independent state in the 1st century B.C. and again in the 10th A.D., was later divided between the Turks and the Persians. The section conquered by the Russians in the 19th century became the present Soviet republic in 1936. As a result of persecution by the Turks in 1895 and 1914, about one million sought refuge abroad. Of the world's present Armenian population of 3 million, all but one-fourth live in the Soviet Union.

● **Ashkhabad** Capital of the Soviet Republic of Turkmenistan, near the Iranian border (population 253,000). Situated in an earthquake zone, its buildings are built low to reduce damage. Nevertheless, a great tremor in 1948 virtually levelled the city. Ashkhabad's industries include glass, textiles and food. The surrounding area is a fertile oasis.

● **Astrakhan** A Russian city (population 411,000) which stands on an island in the Volga delta, on the left bank of the main distributary. It is the centre of the world-famous sturgeon fisheries, and distributes petrol and salt. Astrakhan is linked by rail to Saratov, though its harbour is becoming shallower because of the lowering of the Caspian and the lessened flow of the Volga after damming.

● **Azerbaijan** A Soviet republic (population 5.1 million) of Transcaucasia, on the Caspian Sea, with an area of 33,000 square miles. The capital is Baku. It is a dry steppe lowland, known as the Kura River plain, which is ringed by the Caucasus and other mountain ranges. Seventy per cent of the land is irrigated, and on this cotton is very important. Agriculture, which requires irrigation, yields cotton, tobacco, fruit, wine and silk. Sheep graze on the unirrigated lowland in winter and on mountain slopes in summer. Industry is based largely on mineral resources, especially the petroleum field of Baku, as well as iron ore and aluminium. The Azerbaijani people, 60 per cent of the total population, are a Moslem group speaking a language closely related to Turkish. There are also many Russians and Armenians in the area, which was long disputed between Turkey and Iran. It passed to Russia in the early 20th century. The name Azerbaijan is also applied to a province of Iran immediately south of Soviet Azerbaijan.

● **Azov, Sea of** An arm of the Black Sea, separated from it by the peninsula of the Crimea (Krym). The name derives from the old town of Azov in the delta of the Don. Because of the vast amounts of river water entering the sea, its salt content is only 1 per cent and it freezes readily. It is rich in fish and has many fishing harbours, the largest being Zhdanov, Rostov, and Kerch with its iron mines. Despite the sea's size, its maximum depth is only 50 feet.

● **Baghdad** Capital of Iraq since 1921, on the Tigris River. The sprawling city (population 850,000) extends for 15 miles along both banks of the historic Tigris. Industry is largely confined to bazaar crafts, such as textiles, metals and food-stuffs. The old part of the town lies on the right bank around a large mosque. On the left bank is the modern section, with parks and broad avenues. Baghdad was founded in the 8th century by the caliphs (Moslem rulers) as a natural crossing point of the Mesopotamian plain, where the Tigris and the Euphrates approach to within 20 miles of each other. Under the caliph Harun-al-Rashid (786–809), Baghdad was the centre of the far-flung Moslem world. It was the home of scholars and artists, and a city of great wealth with 2 million inhabitants. Its glory is reflected in the stories of the Thousand and One Nights. The city was sacked by the Mongols in the 13th century, and occupied by the Turks from 1638 to 1917. It did not regain importance until modern times.

● **Bahrain** Arab island sheikdom (population 200,000) in the Persian Gulf, off the Arabian Peninsula. It has an area of 230 square miles. The capital is Manama (population 79,098). A British protectorate after 1861, it has been an important petroleum producer since 1934, and is now an independent State no longer relying on British protection since troop withdrawal in 1971. Its refinery also processes crude oil from the nearby Saudi Arabian fields. Bahrain is rich in archaeological remains.

● **Baikal, Lake** This large, 400-mile-long lake of southern Siberia covers an area of 12,000 square miles. It is the world's deepest lake, reaching 5,700 feet in its central portion. Because of the huge

volume of water that has to be cooled, and because of violent autumn storms which mix the water, the lake does not freeze over until January. The ice, up to four feet thick, remains until May. Lake Baikal's water is remarkably clear, despite its many affluents, while it has only one outlet, the Angara River. Its fauna, including the Baikal hair seal, has many unique forms.

● **Baku** Capital of the Soviet republic of Azerbaijan, Baku is famous as one of the world's oldest petroleum centres. Greater Baku (population 1,261,000) includes the entire oil-rich Apsheron Peninsula, on the Caspian Sea, and its offshore oil-wells. The city proper, with 636,000 people, lies on a semi-circular bay on the southern shore of the peninsula. The port, one of the most important on the Caspian Sea, is sheltered against the strong north-easter that blows in the late autumn and winter; Baku means 'city of winds'. The surrounding oil-fields were the world's leading producers of petroleum around 1900. They continued to yield 70 per cent of the Soviet Union's petroleum until World War II. Since then Baku's oil production has declined, and the Soviet Union obtains most of its supply from new oil-fields between the Volga and the Urals.

● **Bali** One of the volcanic Lesser Sunda Islands of Indonesia, just east of Java (approximate population 1 million). Although relatively small (2,200 square miles), Bali is culturally and economically one of the most important islands of Indonesia. The Balinese, a Malay group closely related to the Javanese, grow rice, maize and sugar cane, and engage in handicraft industries. Unlike Java, which is Moslem, Bali has retained Indonesia's original Hindu religion. The Balinese often gather in their village temples to attend festivals and religious dances noted for their masks and costumes. The women of Bali are also known for their beauty and grace.

● **Balkhash** City of Soviet Kazakhstan (population 62,000). One of the Soviet Union's leading copper-mining and smelting centres, it was founded in 1936. The city is situated on the north shore of Lake Balkhash (6,700 square miles), a shallow, elongated salt lake, with a maximum depth of 85 feet. The Ili River flows into it at its eastern end.

● **bamboo** A woody, treelike grass of the tropics and sub-tropics. Its hollow stems, which attain a diameter of six inches, are a hard, durable building material. Smaller stalks are used in making furniture, tent poles, fishing rods and ski sticks. The youngest bamboo shoots are edible. Bamboo fibres are woven into mats or used as raw material in paper making. Bamboos grow rapidly, perhaps more than 2 feet per day, and attain heights of 130 feet.

Bamboo

● **Bandung** City (population 1 million) of western Java, in Indonesia, situated in a fertile highland basin enclosed by a ring of volcanoes. Plantation

A young Djanger dancer in Bali, Indonesia

agriculture specialises in cinchona (for the production of quinine), tea and rubber. Bandung is best known for the conference of 23 Asian and 6 African nations that met there in April, 1955, and condemned colonisation and racial discrimination, while planning the economic, cultural and political improvement of their nations.

Bangalore City (population 905,134) of southern India, 180 miles west of Madras, beautifully laid out with numerous parks and wide streets. It is distinguished by a large number of modern industries: aircraft plants, electrical appliances and plastics. Bangalore is the capital of Mysore.

Bangkok The capital (population 2,300,000) of Thailand and a port on the Chao Phrayo (Menan) River, 15 miles from the Gulf of Siam. Great sandbanks across the shallow, winding river restrict traffic to small ocean-going ships. Although it is the most modern city in Thailand and has many foreign business concerns, it still retains a distinct Thai appearance. With ornate Buddhist temples, among them the 200-foot-high pagoda of Wat-Chi'ang, and royal palaces at its centre, the city has expanded into modern business districts and parks. Industries, found mainly in the suburbs, include rice, paper and sawmills, an oil refinery and railway workshops. A large Chinese population plays an important role in the city's commercial life, as elsewhere in South-East Asia. Across the river is Thonburi, which is sometimes regarded as part of the Bangkok urban area (population 1,540,300). Bangkok was founded in 1782, when it succeeded the older capital of Ayutthaya, situated 40 miles farther north. Bangkok's Siamese name is Krung Thep.

Barnaul City (population 439,000) of southwestern Siberia, on the upper Ob River. A vital railway centre linked with cotton-growing in Central Asia, Barnaul has become the leading cotton-textile producer of Siberia. Boilers, Diesel engines and machine tools are also made here.

Barnaul was founded in 1738 and, even earlier, was a Siberian gold and silver producer.

Basra Chief port (population 327,000) of Iraq, situated on the combined mouth of the Tigris and Euphrates Rivers, the Shatt al Arab, 75 miles from the Persian Gulf. It is the centre of Iraq's date-growing region, and dates are its leading export product, providing 80 per cent of the total supply of dates on the world market.

Beirut Capital of Lebanon, and a major seaport (population 600,000) on the Mediterranean Sea. With few industries, Beirut has achieved eminence as a commercial centre, handling a large part of the transit trade to and from the Middle East. Its picturesque site attracts many tourists. Two well-known foreign universities (American Protestant and French Catholic) are there.

Benares Vanarasi City (population 574,000) of northern India, on the Ganges, and one of Hinduism's most sacred places. Thousands of pilgrims daily crowd the city's ghats (bathing stairs) to bathe in, or drink of, the holy river. Benares has a large handicraft industry of silk, brocade and brassware, catering mainly to the pilgrim trade. On the southern outskirts is a famous Hindu university, founded in 1916.

Bengal A region (population over 60 million) divided between India and Bangladesh, in the Ganges-Brahmaputra delta; a leading rice- and jute-growing area. It is located on the Bay of Bengal, an arm of the Indian Ocean. The partition of British India left most of the jute fields in Bangladesh, and the jute mills, around Calcutta, in India; hence new factories have been built in Bangladesh. The people of Bengal speak the Bengali language, which is derived in part from Sanscrit.

Bering Sea This northernmost section of the Pacific Ocean is bordered on the south by the Aleutian Islands. It is deep in its south-western part (to almost 16,000 feet) and quite shallow in the north-east. The entire Bering Sea region is marked by volcanic activity, especially in Kamchatka and the Aleutians. To the north, the Bering Strait leads into the Arctic Ocean, separating Alaska from Siberia. The 50-mile-wide strait was discovered in 1648 by the Cossack Dezhnev, but both strait and sea were named after Vitus Bering, a Danish navigator in Russian service, who reached the area in 1728.

Bezoar goat

bezoar goat A wild goat of the Middle East. The male is recognised by its long curved horns. It lives in flocks in remote mountains, feeding on the sparse grass. In the stomach of this goat the bezoar stone is found, consisting of tightly matted hair cemented together, which in former times was considered to have medicinal properties, especially as an antidote for poisoning.

Bhutan A small Himalayan State (population 1 million) under Indian protection and bordering Tibet, Sikkim and India, with an area of 18,000 square miles. Its capital is Bumtang (Punakha). One of the most isolated countries in the world, Bhutan is rarely visited by outsiders. Its people are related to the Tibetans, and live on agriculture (rice, maize, millet) and livestock (yaks, elephants, ponies) only now being developed, thanks to financial aid from India.

Bombay The second largest city (population 4,152,056) of India, on the west coast, with an excellent natural harbour and favourable location facing Europe, advantages which have made it the traditional gateway to India. Situated on a peninsula jutting into the Arabian Sea, its east side, facing the protected harbour, has extensive quays, docks and warehouses. On the west, looking out on the ocean, are residential districts. An industrial zone with cotton mills, railway workshops and other factories lies in the northern part of the city. Bombay is the centre of India's cotton-milling industry, producing chiefly factory yarn for the country's handicraft weavers. Bombay was first acquired by the Portuguese around 1530 and passed to Britain in 1661. The city's Haffkine Institute is widely known for its research on tropical diseases. The university was founded in 1857.

Borneo Largest island in the Malay Archipelago and the third largest in the world (after Greenland and New Guinea). Divided between Malaysia and Indonesia (plus the British-protected State of Brunei), its area is 287,000 square miles (three times the size of Great Britain) and its population 5,800,000. Although the mountainous interior rises to more than 13,000 feet in Mount Kinabalu, the island is tropical lowland, for the most part, covered with rain forest and vast swamps. Large navigable rivers are the only routes into the wild interior, where the primitive Dyak people live. The island's dense tropical forests and swamps have restricted economic development largely to coastal areas, where immigrant Malays, Javanese and Chinese have developed rubber, coconut and pepper crops for export. Petroleum is the only

Mosque in the main square of Baghdad, Iraq

SOUTH ASIA

Scale 1:30,000,000 0 100 200 300 400 500 Miles

● CALCUTTA Cities over 1,000,000 population.
● Kobe Cities of 250,000- 1,000,000 population.
○ Malacca Cities under 250,000 population.
⊛ Capitals of Countries

Depths in feet:

over 650 | 0-650

Heights in feet:

Below sea level | 0-650 | 650-1650 | 1650-4900 | over 4900 | Salt lake | Desert

Intermittent streams Wadi Canals Swamps
Railroads Head of navigation

important natural resource so far discovered.

Indonesian Borneo, which the Indonesians call **Kalimantan**, comprises three-fourths of the total area, with a population of 4½ million. Its economic areas are limited to the petroleum-rich south-east coast (around Bandjermasin, the capital) and the west coast (around Pontianak).

Along the north coast Borneo consists of three parts: **Sarawak**, an elongated area, with a population of 933,609; **Sabah**, formerly British North Borneo, with a population of 622,480; and the tiny protectorate of **Brunei**, with 130,000 people. Rubber, tropical hardwoods, copra and petroleum are the principal exports of this area. Sabah and Sarawak are now members of the Federation of Malaysia.

● **Brahmaputra River** One of the great rivers of southern Asia; 1,800 miles long. It rises in Tibet and flows first to the north of the Himalayas, and then through Assam and Bangladesh to the Bay of Bengal, forming a vast joint delta with the Ganges. The river is navigable for 800 miles in its lower course. Brahmaputra means 'son of Brahma', who is one of the great Hindu gods.

● **Buddhism** One of the world's great religions (over 500 million people), founded in the 6th century B.C. by the Hindu prince Siddhartha Gautama, known as the Buddha or 'Enlightened One'. It teaches that life is full of suffering, and that supreme happiness and peace of mind (nirvana) can be achieved only through self-denial of all desires and passions. Although Buddhism began in India, it has been largely replaced there by Hinduism. There are now two major divisions of Buddhism; the earlier Hinayana form, which stresses monastery life and is practised in Ceylon, Burma and Thailand, and the later Mahayana form, which has made Buddha into a god and is practised in China and Japan.

Water buffaloes

● **buffalo, water** The wild water buffalo, or carabao, is savage and extremely dangerous. The domesticated animal, on the other hand, is so gentle that it can be driven in herds by small children. Tamed at least as early as 3000 B.C., it has become the most important draft animal of southern Asia, especially in rice-growing areas.

● **Bukhara** One of the famous cities of Central Asia, now in Soviet Uzbekistan. Its population is 57,000. Bukhara (or Bokhara) flourished in the 10th century on the caravan route to India and China, dealing in costly silks and brocades, jewels and carpets.

● **Burma** Republic of South-East Asia, between Bangladesh, India, China, Laos and Thailand. It has an area of 260,000 square miles and a population of 27.58 million. The capital is Rangoon.

Wharves and warehouses line the river-front of the Chao Phrayo River at Bangkok, Thailand. Behind them stands a Buddhist temple

Burma is cut off from its neighbours by high mountain ranges that enclose the country in the shape of a giant horse-shoe. Within this mountain barrier is the heart of Burma, formed by the valleys of the Irrawaddy and its tributaries. Rice is sown over 70 per cent of the total arable land, and the Irrawaddy delta is one of the few rice areas of Asia where the grain is cultivated on a large commercial scale, making Burma the world's leading rice exporter, rivalled only by Thailand. Other export crops are cotton and rubber, plus teak, which is felled in the forests of the inland hills. Petroleum, lead-zinc and tin-tungsten ores are also exported. Burma's foreign trade is chiefly with Japan, Britain and India. The Burmese, who make up two-thirds of the population, are a Mongolian race of Buddhist religion. Their language, related to Tibetan, uses the Pali alphabet of the sacred Buddhist writings. Non-Burmese peoples are settled in the surrounding mountains. A unified Burmese state existed in the 11th and 12th centuries before being crushed by the Mongols under Kublai Khan. From 1886 to 1937, Burma was a province of British India; but, after Japanese occupation during World War II, Burma won complete independence from Britain in 1948. Formally known as the Union of Burma, the independent republic includes autonomous states for non-Burmese peoples of the hill lands. In international affairs, the Burmese Government has followed a neutral course between East and West.

● **Burma Road** 700-mile-long highway between Burma and the city of Kunming, China, built in 1937—38. The Burma Road served as a vital supply route for the Chinese during the Sino-Japanese War and World War II.

● **Buryats** A Mongol people living in the Soviet Union, around Lake Baikal. Numbering about 300,000, the Buryats are primarily nomadic livestock herders, but also engage in farming and fur hunting. They form an autonomous republic, with its capital at Ulan-Ude (population 254,000).

● **Calcutta** Largest city (population 2,900,000; with suburbs, 5,600,000) and port of India, in Bengal, on an arm of the Ganges delta, near the Bay of Bengal. Although about 80 miles from the sea, this tropical metropolis can be reached by large ocean-going ships. Calcutta is one of India's leading manufacturing centres. Concentrated here are the country's jute mills, which process jute from both India and Bangladesh. Jute is exported as well as the tea of Assam. Calcutta is the economic

centre of north-east India and the site of a university dating from 1857 and the National Library. Founded by Britain in 1690, it grew rapidly as an outlet for India's raw materials. The city was the capital of British India from 1772 until 1912, when the seat of government was moved to Delhi.

● **Cambodia** (Khmer Republic) Country of South-East Asia, on the bay of Siam, bordered by Thailand, Laos and South Vietnam. It has an area of 70,000 square miles and a population of 6 million. The capital is Pnom-penh (population 600,000). Cambodia is a vast alluvial plain traversed by the Mekong. Rice, the main food crop, takes up 80 per cent of the cultivated land. Rubber and pepper are grown for export. Industries include oil refining, cigarettes, metal works, glassware, and food preparation. Cambodians, or Khmers, comprise 90 per cent of the population. The rest consists of Vietnamese and Chinese. The Khmer people formed a powerful empire in the 10th and 11th centuries with their capital at Angkor. Later Cambodia came under the influence of both Siam and Annam (Vietnam). The French protectorate, dating from 1863, lasted until 1954, when Cambodia became independent. In 1970 the neutral Prince Sihanouk was overthrown and shortly after the Americans extended the Vietnam War into Cambodian territory, for a few months. In October 1970 Cambodia became a Republic known as the Khmer Republic.

● **camel, Bactrian** This two-humped camel of Central Asia is not so slender, handsome or speedy as the African dromedary, but it is stronger and more heavily built, with long, shaggy hair that permits it to withstand the cold winters of Asia. It can still be found wild, but is largely tamed.

Camphor tree

camphor A large evergreen tree of the Far East, growing to a height of 160 feet. Its wood and bark yield the fragrant substance known as camphor, which is used in medicine and in the making of celluloid. About half of the world's supply of camphor comes from Formosa. Clothes kept in chests of camphor wood are protected against moths and termites.

Canton Kwang-chow is the largest city (population 3 million) of southern China, at the northern edge of the Si-kiang's delta. A major transportation centre, Canton is linked by railway northward with Wuhan and Peking, and south-eastward with Hong Kong. Canton's port of Whampoa, on the south-east outskirts, is accessible to ocean-going vessels. Its varied industries include textiles, cement, paper, tobacco and canned goods. The city's educational institutions include the important university. After the overthrow of the Manchu dynasty in 1911, Canton was a major revolutionary centre and produced the Kuomintang, under the leadership of Sun Yat-sen. From here the Nationalists under Chiang Kai-shek advanced northward in the middle 1920s to establish their capital at Nanking and win control of most of China. Canton had trade contacts with Arabs and Hindus as early as the 10th century, and was one of the first Chinese ports to be visited by European traders. Canton was the scene of Chinese-British incidents, in 1841 and 1856, that led to the First and Second Opium Wars, which subjected China to increased European control.

Caspian Sea The largest lake in the world, with an area of 164,000 square miles. It is shared by the Soviet Union (with 80 per cent of the coastline) and Iran. It is shallow at its northern end, where it has a low salt content and freezes for two to three months a year. In the south, the sea reaches a maximum depth of 3,200 feet. Its water level — 92 feet below that of mean ocean level — has been falling in recent years because, in the dry climate, more water evaporates from the sea than is replaced by the influent fresh water of the Volga and other rivers. In former times, the Caspian extended far to the north in the salt steppes of West Kazakh.

Caucasus This great mountain system of the Soviet Union extends 750 miles from the Black Sea to the Caspian, and is both higher and broader than the Alps. It rises to the 18,480-foot-high Mount Elbrus, separating the southern Russian steppe from sub-tropical Transcaucasia and traditionally marking the boundary of Europe with Asia. Although railways must skirt the range, the Caucasus contains a few high passes. The most important is used by the Georgian Military Road between Ordzhonikidze and Tiflis. Among the area's rich mineral resources are the petroleum fields of Baku, Grozny and Maikop, the manganese of Georgia, and tungsten, molybdenum, copper and coal. The numerous invasions and migrations that swept over the Caucasus in antiquity and the Middle Ages have left a great complexity of peoples, and over 40 languages are spoken by various small ethnic groups at the present time.

caviar The salted black fish eggs of the sturgeon, considered a great delicacy. Southern European Russia, the home of the sturgeon in the Volga and Caspian Sea, used to have a world monopoly of caviar production. A similar product is now also made from other fish eggs in the United States and Canada, and from the pink eggs of the carp in Rumania.

cedar A stately, coniferous tree, native to Asia Minor. The famous cedars of Lebanon yielded construction timber used in antiquity for the building of temples (Solomon's) and ships. The few remaining trees, which grow to a height of 130 feet, are now strictly protected. Many cedars are now planted in parts of temperate Europe.

Cedar

Celebes An island of Indonesia to the east of Borneo, known in Indonesian as Sulawesi. Its 70,000 square miles are densely forested, largely mountainous and volcanic, and support a population of 7.5 million. The greatest concentration is in the north-eastern Minahassa Peninsula and around Macassar, the largest city, in the south. Fertile volcanic-ash soils yield rice for food, and coffee, corn and coconuts for exports.

Ceylon An island State to the south-east of India, in the Indian Ocean. It has an area of 25,000 square miles and a population of 11,992,000. The capital is Colombo. Ceylon has been an independent country within the British Commonwealth since 1948. The pear-shaped island, 270 miles long and 140 miles wide, consists of a central mountain mass surrounded by a broad coastal plain, the highest mountain being Pidurutalagala (8,279 feet). Rice is the staple food crop. Coconuts, rubber and tea are grown for export. Ceylon is second among the world's tea exporters (after India) and fourth among rubber producers (after Malaya, Indonesia and Thailand). There are few modern manufacturing industries. More than 40 per cent of the island's factories engage in the processing of coconut products; many others are small tea and tobacco factories. Graphite and diamonds are the only important mineral resources. Ceylon trades chiefly with Britain, China and Australia. Tea, rubber and copra are exchanged for food and manufactured goods. The mixed population consists of 70 per cent Sinhalese; 12 per cent Tamils; 6 per cent Moors and Burghers. The original inhabitants, known as the Veddas, were conquered in the 6th century by the Sinhalese, a Buddhist people of partly Indo-European origin. They were followed by the Tamils, a Hindu people of southern India, who gradually pushed the Sinhalese into the southern part of the island. The island was visited in the 12th and 13th centuries by Arab traders, whose descendants are now known as Moors. The Portuguese arrived in the early 16th century — many Ceylonese have Portuguese family names — followed in 1658 by the Dutch, whose descendants are known as Burghers. In 1796, Britain won control of Ceylon, governing it as a crown colony from 1798 until 1948. Since 1948, independent Ceylon has pursued a neutral policy in world affairs. In 1972, Ceylon became known as Sri Lanka.

Chang-chun City of China, in central Manchuria. Chang-chun (population 1,800,000) is a vital railway centre on the main line between Harbin and Shen-yang (Mukden). Its industries process agricultural goods from the surrounding fertile Manchurian countryside, and in recent years a truck factory, and a locomotive and railway wagon plant, have been built. Chang-chun has many educational and research institutions and one of China's film studios. As the capital of Japanese-ruled Manchuria from 1932 to 1945, Chang-chun was known as Hsin-king, which means 'new capital', and was greatly enlarged and modernised with broad avenues, large parks, sports grounds, and new public buildings and dwellings.

Chang-sha City (population 650,600) of central China, south of the Yangtze River, at the centre of China's main rice-growing region. It ships tea, lumber, tung oil via the Siang-kiang, and has a smelter for antimony, lead and zinc.

Cheetah

cheetah This big, spotted cat is one of the fastest land animals, able to run at a speed of 45 miles an hour. Found in the grasslands of Africa and southern Asia, the long-legged cheetah can be trained for hunting and is, therefore, sometimes known as the hunting leopard.

A golden figure of Buddha in a Bangkok pagoda

Devout Buddhists contribute gold-leaf for the adornment of pagodas at Rangoon, in Burma

● **Chelyabinsk** One of the largest Soviet cities in the Ural region, on the eastern Siberian side. Its population has risen from 59,000 in 1926 to 874,000 in 44 years. Founded in 1745, Chelyabinsk became a base for the settlement of Siberia around 1900. In the Soviet period it has become an industrial centre, largely because of the presence of vast lignite deposits used to generate cheap electric power. Chelyabinsk produces iron and steel, ferro-alloys, zinc, tractors and machine tools.

● **Cheng-chow** City (population 766,000) of northern China, in the Yellow River plain. A relatively new city, it owes its rise to the railway, as it is situated at the crossing of the main north-south and east-west lines of China. In recent years it has become a major cotton-milling centre, processing the raw cotton grown in the surrounding countryside.

● **Cheng-tu** City (population 1,107,000) of southwest China, in the Szechwan basin; linked by railway with Chungking and (since 1957) with northwest China. Cheng-tu is the centre of a rich irrigated agricultural region. Its industries include textiles, processed foods and chemicals. Railway workshops and the production of farm machinery and machine tools were added in recent years.

● **China** The world's most populous country (population estimates vary from 700 to 746 million) and, with its 4,300,000 square miles — extending from the Pacific coast to the Central Asian deserts — the second largest in area after the U.S.S.R. The capital is Peking. The Chinese People's Republic, as it has been called, since 1949, when the Communist government took over, includes historic China proper and the outlying regions of Manchuria, Inner Mongolia, Sinkiang and Tibet. One of China's large off-shore islands, Hainan, belongs to the mainland People's Republic, while the other, Formosa, has been a refuge for the Chinese Nationalists since 1949. Most of the country's population is concentrated in China proper, which includes the great Yellow River plain, the Yangtze River valley and the hill country of South China. These regions (particularly the two river basins) are China's most important agricultural areas. Wheat is the key crop in the warm temperate north, together with cotton, tobacco, maize and ground nuts, and rice in the sub-tropical south, along with the soya bean, sugar cane and tea. Of the outlying regions, Manchuria is China's greatest asset, having fertile black soil with wheat, maize, millet and soya bean crops, and a highly developed industry based on coal and steel. Elsewhere in interior China, nomadic herding and oasis agriculture (cotton, silk, fruit) support the sparse population of Inner Mongolia, Sinkiang and Tibet. The Chinese, who make up 94 per cent of the country's population, speak regional dialects, of which the Mandarin of Peking is the most important; yet the spoken dialects are often incomprehensible to other peoples, although all dialect groups use the same written language, which consists of symbols representing entire words. Sponsored by the Chinese Communist government, the Latin alphabet is gradually being introduced, and the nation-wide use of Mandarin is being promoted. Non-Chinese minority groups, who live mainly in the outer regions, include the Uigurs of Sinkiang, the Tibetans and the Mongols.

Although three-quarters of the population lives on farms and is employed in agriculture, China has more large cities than any other nation. Over 18 urban centres now contain more than 1 million people, including Shanghai, Peking, Tientsin, Shen-yang (Mukden), Chungking, Canton, Wuhan, Harbin and Nanking. Industry is concentrated in southern Manchuria and elsewhere along the coast. In recent years, more industries have been developed and much land brought under cultivation in the interior, in conjunction with new rail construction. Rail lines lead to the Soviet Union through Mongolia and Sinkiang, but since the recent Russian-Chinese disagreements 80 per cent of China's trade is now with non-Communist countries like Japan. China has most of the raw materials necessary for the foundation of industries on a large scale, and both mining and industry have developed greatly since 1949. Among China's traditional industries are those of paper-making, porcelain and silk.

China exports ores (tungsten, antimony, tin, mercury, molybdenum), fibres (wool, raw silk, jute) and farm products (soya beans, peanuts, tea, tung oil, hog bristles and skins). In return, China imports steel, rice, petroleum products and industrial equipment.

China's history is told in terms of dynasties, each starting with a strong ruler, gradually declining under the pressure of revolts and invasions, to be succeeded by the next. The original home of the Chinese people was in the Yellow River (Hwang-Ho) valley. According to tradition, the first dynasty began in 2200 B.C. The Chou dynasty (1122—249 B.C.) produced the great Chinese philosophers, including Confucius (Kung-futse). The Tsin dynasty, in the 3rd century B.C., was the first to unite the country and complete the Great Wall. The Han dynasty (206 B.C.—A.D. 221) was marked by wars with the Huns, the first contacts with Rome, and the official introduction of Buddhism. Poetry, literature and philosophy flourished under the Tang (618—907) and the Sung (960—1279) dynasties. In the early 13th century began the great Mongol conquest under Genghis Khan. His descendants conquered all of China and set up the Mongol dynasty under Kublai Khan. The realm of this great Mongol ruler was visited by Marco Polo. Under the Ming dynasty (1368—1644), the first European traders and missionaries arrived in China. In the 17th century, the Manchu tribes of Manchuria founded the last of the imperial dynasties, the Manchu dynasty (1644—1912). In the mid-19th century, large-scale European penetration of China commenced, with several nations vying for territorial and economic concessions. Weakened by foreign pressure and domestic revolts, the Manchu dynasty was overthrown by the 1912 revolution, led by Sun Yat-sen. After a period of internal strife, Chiang Kai-shek unified the country in 1928 under Nationalist rule. In 1931, China lost Manchuria to Japan, and in 1937 began the Sino-Japanese war, which continued into the Second World War and led to Japanese occupation of China's most important economic areas. The rift between the Chinese Nationalists and Mao Tse-tung's Communists, which began in the 1920s, widened after the defeat of Japan in 1945, and full-scale civil war developed. Though aided by the United States, the Nationalists were expelled from the Chinese mainland in 1949 and sought refuge in Formosa (Taiwan). The Chinese Communist government has concentrated its efforts on economic development since it came to power. Agriculture has been collectivised, industry nationalised, and the traditional Chinese way of life has given way to a more regimented system designed to transform China into a great world power. China is now becoming an active country in world affairs for after many years of isolation and hostilities with Russia and the U.S.A., she is now a member of the United Nations and for the first time in history opened her country to the President of the United States of America and the rest of the world with television cameras in 1972.

● **Chinese Wall** The Great Wall of China was built in the 3rd century B.C. to defend China against the warlike nomads of what is now Mongolia. It is

The Great Wall of China

20 feet wide at the base and up to 40 feet high, with 50-foot towers at frequent intervals. It extends about 1,500 miles from the Yellow Sea into Central Asia, and is best preserved in its eastern section, where it is faced with granite blocks and bricks. It has often been rebuilt and improved; the most recent occasions were in the 15th and 16th centuries, and by the Communist government in recent years.

● **Chita** City of the Transbaikal region of southern Siberia (population 244,000). Locomotive and wagon shops on the Trans-Siberian railway are situated at Chita, as well as sawmills, and a meat-packing plant.

Chittagong Port city of Bangladesh, on the Bay of Bengal (population 150,000; with suburbs 364,205). It has developed rapidly since the partition of India as an outlet for the products (chiefly jute), which formerly moved through Calcutta. The harbour of Chalna was made in 1950 to relieve crowding in the port of Chittagong.

chrome Probably best known for its use in the electroplating of motor-car fittings and domestic utensils, the metal's main industrial application is in the making of stainless steels. Chrome ore, called chromite, is used in furnace bricks and in the chemical industry. Leading chrome producers are the Soviet Union, South Africa, Rhodesia and Turkey. With the exception of the Soviet Union, all the world's big steel producers are dependent on imports of chrome.

Chukchi Peninsula The north-easternmost point of Siberia, facing Alaska across the Bering Strait. It is named after the native Chukchi, a Siberian tribe engaged in reindeer raising and fishing in the treeless tundra.

Chungking (Pahsien) Largest city (population 2,121,000) of south-west China, on the Yangtze River — widely known during World War II, when it was the capital (1937—45) of wartime China. At that time it enjoyed an economic boom, acquiring many industries (steel, machinery, textiles). Coal is mined in the northern outskirts. Since 1957, Chungking has been linked by rail with the rest of China. Its river port is the head of regular navigation on the Yangtze River.

Cinnamon

cinnamon The highly aromatic bark of several kinds of Asian trees and shrubs belonging to the laurel family. Its distinctive flavour makes it widely popular as a spice. White cinnamon comes only from tropical North America.

cobra, Indian This snake, also known as the spectacled cobra, is the most dangerous poisonous snake of southern Asia. Like all cobras it is able to spread its elastic skin around its head, forming a kind of hood. The hood is ornamented with two joined eye-like markings, forming the 'spectacles'. It is usually about 5 feet long, and its venom is a rapidly acting nerve-poison, which yearly kills many people. The King cobra lacks the 'spectacles', and reaches a length of 16 feet.

Colombo Capital of Sri Lanka (formerly Ceylon), on the densely populated south-west coast (population 511,644). Its location at the southern tip of the Indian peninsula has made it a natural shipping and transportation centre on the route between Europe and the Far East, being principal port-of-call in the Indian Ocean between Aden and Singapore. Colombo exports tea, rubber and coconuts. Countries of the British Commonwealth, meeting there in 1950, formulated the Colombo Plan for the economic development of the countries of South and South-East Asia. The city has many temples, a mosque and a university, founded in 1942.

Crimea A large peninsula of the Ukraine between the Azov and Black Seas. It is connected to the mainland by the narrow Perekop isthmus. The northern part contains the dry steppelands which produce wheat, barley, sunflowers and tobacco. The climate over this northern part, three-quarters of the total area, has cold winters and hot, dry summers. Towards the south, the land rises to the barren limestone mountains, while the south-east coast has a Riviera-type climate, with sub-tropical crops of fruit and vines; tourism is popular, including the towns of Yalta and other resorts. The largest towns there are Simferopol (250,000) and Sevastopol (229,000), a naval base. The town of Kerch, to the east, is famous for its iron mines. The Crimea was occupied in turn by Phoenician, Greek and Roman traders; later by Genoese, Turks and Tartars. Crimea came into Russian hands in 1783, and from 1853—56 was the scene of the war between Russia, Turkey, Britain and France.

Cyprus An island republic within the British Commonwealth, situated in the eastern Mediterranean Sea (population 630,000; area 3,570 square miles). The capital is Nicosia (114,000). Since the abandonment of the Suez Canal zone, Cyprus has become an important British military base in the eastern Mediterranean. The population is four-fifths Greek and one-fifth Turkish. Fairly rich in minerals, Cyprus has been known since ancient times for its copper. The word copper, in fact, is derived from Cyprus. Other minerals are asbestos, chrome and iron pyrites. Besides these minerals, Cyprus also exports carobs (a Mediterranean fruit also known as St John's bread), wine, and other fruit. Conquered by the Turks in 1571, Cyprus came under British control in 1878. In recent years, a large section of the Greek Cypriot majority has agitated for union (Enosis) with Greece, and there has been a bitter dispute between the Greek and Turkish communities.

Dacca Largest city and capital of Bangladesh; (population 556,712); a commercial centre in the rice- and jute-growing area of the Ganges-Brahmaputra delta. After the partition of India, Dacca became the capital of East Pakistan. It has large textile factories and its university was founded in 1921.

Dairen (Ta-lien) Port city of China in southern Manchuria and one of Manchuria's leading manufacturing centres, second only to Mukden. It produces chemicals (soda, fertilisers), machine tools, and electrical machinery. There are shipyards, a car-building plant and an oil refinery. The port, situated on a deep, sheltered bay, is ice-free all the year, and lies on a peninsula jutting into the Yellow Sea. It ships Manchuria's farm products, especially soya beans and wheat. Founded by the Russians in 1898, the city passed to the Japanese in 1905, who named it Dairen (its Chinese name is Ta-lien) and developed it into a modern industrial city. Under Chinese Communist rule, since 1949, Dairen is part of the joint municipal district of Port Arthur-Dairen, known in Chinese as Lü-ta, with a combined population of 3,600,000.

Damascus Capital of Syria, 50 miles east of Beirut (Lebanon); its population is 557,253. Damascus is one of the oldest towns in the world and is situated in an irrigated fruit-orchard area, in which the white towers of the city form a picturesque contrast against the green of the trees. The city is built up around the large mosque of the early caliphs. The Barada, one of the biblical rivers of Damascus, divides the city into an old town and a modern section. The name of Damascus has been associated in history with the city's characteristic products, such as the figured fabric known as damask, and hard, elastic steel used in Damascus sword blades. Modern Damascus owed its importance to the fertility of the surrounding countryside and to the rise of the Syrian state. It flourished as a centre of the Moslem realm before the caliphs moved their capital to Baghdad in the 8th century, and was sited originally at the meeting place of caravan routes.

Dead Sea Salt lake on the border of Jordan and Israel. Its surface is 1,292 feet below sea level, making it the lowest elevation on earth. It receives the Jordan River but has no outlet. No fish can live in it because of its high salt content (24 per cent), which is many times that of the ocean. Salt deposits at the southern Israeli end of the lake yield potash, nitrates and bromine.

Delhi City (population 2,409,000) of central India adjoining the city of New Delhi (population over 300,000), especially built (1912—29) as the capital of India. New Delhi is a modern city of broad thoroughfares laid out in symmetrical pattern. Many government buildings and official residences are here. The older city of Delhi, by contrast, is a busy, crowded commercial and transportation centre on the main routes from the Ganges plain to the Punjab region. The gracefully domed Jami Masjid, one of the world's greatest mosques, dates from the 17th century, when Delhi was the capital of the Moslem Mogul empire. Delhi was the capital of British India from 1912 to 1931, when New Delhi was inaugurated.

Dezhnev, Cape Siberian headland of the Chukchi Peninsula, on the Bering Strait opposite Alaska. It is named after the Cossack Dezhnev, who in 1648, discovered the cape.

Dhahran United States air-base in Saudi Arabia on the Persian Gulf, and the centre of the country's petroleum industry. Its population is 50,000. Nearby is the oil refinery and loading port of Ras Tanura and the commercial port of Damman.

The Great Mosque at Damascus, in Syria, was originally a Roman temple

Dnepropetrovsk (863,000 people) is an important iron, steel and machinery producing town on the Dnieper River in the southern Ukraine, between Krivoi Rog and Donbas, from which iron ore and coal are obtained. Manganese is obtained from Nikopol, and there are large supplies of energy available from the hydro-electric plants of Zaporozhe, south of the town, from natural gas and the thermal station to the east (Pridneprovskoye). The town was founded by Catherine the Great and Potomkin in 1783 with the name Ekaterinoslav, which it was called until 1926, and lay in newly colonised steppe, won from the Turks. The town specialises in the metal industries requiring a great deal of electricity, such as aluminium refining and ferro-alloy manufacture.

Dniester A 900-mile-long river in the Ukraine and Moldavian Republic. It has its source in the northern Carpathians and reaches the Black Sea near to Odessa. Between the wars, the river marked the boundary between the Soviet Union and Romania.

Don This is the third longest river of European Russia, almost 1300 miles in length. It rises at a height of only 590 feet above sea level in the central Russian plateau, east of Tula and south of Moscow, and it has its mouth in the Sea of Azov. A short canal connects the river with the Volga near to Volgograd, over a distance of about 60 miles. Downstream from this canal is a vast reservoir-lake, created recently. The Don is not a useful river for navigation, because of its low gradient and very low summer flows — hence 'And Quiet flows the Don'.

Donbas An abbreviated term denoting the Donets coal basin, which in 1913 produced nearly 80 per cent of Russia's coal, but now only a third, for new fields have been opened in Siberia. Nevertheless, it is still the main coalfield and industrial area in western Russia, producing 199 million tons of coal in 1967. It lies on the Donets, a tributary of the Don, and its most important towns are Donetsk (q.v.), Makejevka (393,000), Gorlovka (335,000) and Lugansk (363,000). Industrial development began in 1870, with the use of coal by the railways of Russia. Half of Russia's coking coal comes from the Donbas, and heavy chemicals and glass are produced. A limiting factor in industrial development is the low rainfall and lack of water supplies.

Donetsk, formerly Stalino (879,000 inhabitants) — and before that (until 1925) Yuzorka (named after a Welshman, John Hughes, who set up the first coke-fired furnace in Russia in 1870) — is the largest city of the Donbas region. It has many coal mines, metal works and chemical plants.

Dushanbe, formerly Stalinabad, is the capital of the Soviet Republic of Tadzhikistan. From a small village, the settlement developed after 1929 into a modern city with 374,000 inhabitants. The industries are based on textiles and foodstuffs, and the city is the natural, cultural and political centre of the republic.

Dvina is the name given to two rivers in the western area of Russia. The northern Dvina is 1,200 miles long and is formed by two rivers: the Vychegda, rising in the northern Urals, and the Sukhona, flowing from the Vologda lake region. The northern Dvina flows to the White Sea, near Archangel. The shorter western Dvina (650 miles in length) rises near to the source of the Volga, but flows westwards through Byelorussia and Lithuania to join the Baltic in the Gulf of Riga.

Dyak a people of the island of Borneo in Indonesia, related to the Malays. Formerly notorious for their head-hunting practices, they hunt with blowgun and poisoned arrow, and grow rice in forest clearings. Their pile dwellings stand along river banks.

Dzungaria A mountain-ringed steppe in the Chinese province of Sinkiang, north of the Tien-Shan, inhabited largely by Kazakh (Cossack) herders. There are agricultural oases along its southern edge bordering the Tien-Shan. The largest oasis contains the city of Urumchi, the capital of Sinkiang. The Dzungarian Gates, a natural pass through the western mountains, were used by the Huns, the Mongols and other peoples in their migrations toward Europe. The gateway is now used by a new railway linking China and the Soviet Union.

elephant, Indian This Asiatic elephant is found in India and most of South-East Asia. It is somewhat smaller than its African cousin and has less conspicuous ears. Indian elephants have been domesticated since ancient times, and used for work in peace and war. Working elephants are employed chiefly for moving logs and in heavy construction work.

Indian elephants at work

Erivan (Yerevan) Capital (population 767,000) of the Soviet Republic of Armenia, on the Turkish border; situated in a fertile valley at the foot of Mount Ararat. Erivan accounts for more than half of Armenia's industrial output, which includes synthetic rubber, tyres, plastics, power generators, auto parts and watches. An aluminium plant takes its power from hydro-electric stations on the Zanga River, which flows through the city. Erivan produces the well-known Armenian brandies.

Estonia (U.S.S.R., Europe) is one of the smallest of the Soviet Republics, with an area of 17,800 square miles, only Armenia and Moldavia being smaller. It has a population of 1,400,000 — the smallest of all the Republics. On account of its northerly site, it has the least favourable climate of the three Baltic republics, and is bordered by the Gulf of Finland, the Gulf of Riga and the Baltic Sea. The coastline is largely marshy, with many low islands, the largest being Saaremaa and Hiiumaa, and low limestone cliffs to the north. The inland parts of the country are made up of productive soils on glacial drift, but with many lakes and peaty areas. The highest point is Munamagi (1,054 feet) in the south-east. Estonia was and is the most forward of the Baltic Republics, with emphasis on agriculture, formerly developed by the Prussian 'Baltic barons' and, though now collectivised, bearing close resemblance to the Danish model. Industry is based on textiles, especially linen, and both forestry and fishing are important. The capital is Tallinn (363,000 population); it is practically ice-free, and is concerned with machinery and phosphate production. Energy comes from oil shales and from an electric station at Narva, on the Baltic.

The population is largely Protestant, speaking a language similar to Finnish. Estonia was conquered by the Danes in 1219, and later came under German and Swedish control. Between 1721 and 1918, it was part of Russia, and was independent only from 1918 to 1940.

Euphrates River One of the two great rivers of Mesopotamia; 1,700 miles long. It rises in eastern Turkey and flows south-east through Syria and Iraq to the Persian Gulf, uniting at its mouth with the Tigris River. Although longer than the Tigris, the Euphrates carries less water and plays a less significant part in irrigation.

Fergana Valley A mountain-ringed basin of Soviet Central Asia, shared by the Uzbek, Tadzhik and Kirghiz Republics. Irrigated oases in the valley, which is traversed by the Syr Darya River, have been centres of civilisation since antiquity. With a densely settled population of 3½ million, the Fergana Valley is a leading producer of cotton and silk. Coal, petroleum and other minerals are

This Japanese woman is playing the banjo-like samisen. In the background is Fujiyama, a 12,395 ft. extinct volcano, which is Japan's highest mountain

mined along the mountain margins. The city of Fergana, in the valley, has cotton and silk mills and an oil refinery. Its population is about 84,000.

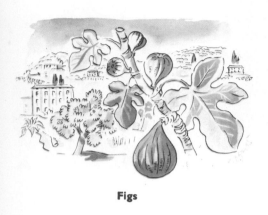

Figs

● **fig**   The fig tree, native to the Middle East, is now cultivated all over the warmer parts of the world, though originating in the Mediterranean region. The pear-shaped fruit is eaten fresh, or is preserved or dried. To ensure the ripening and improve the flavour of the edible fig, a wild fig, known as caprifigus, must be introduced into fig orchards. The caprifigus harbours a small insect known as the fig wasp, which is the agent in the pollination of the cultivated figs.

● **flying dragon**   This lizard of South-East Asia is equipped with a thin membrane of skin, supported by false ribs extending beyond the body. By spreading the membrane, which is folded back at rest, the flying dragon can glide as far as sixty feet at a time. The lizard spends virtually its entire life in trees.

Flying dragon

● **Foochow**   City (population 553,000) of south-east China, on the Strait of Formosa. Although situated on the lower Min River, it is not accessible to ocean-going vessels because of mudbanks. It was reached by a railway in 1958. Foochow was first opened to foreign trade in 1842, and developed rapidly as China's leading tea-shipping centre. River silting and the decrease in demand for Chinese tea has caused Foochow to decline. The city has paper-, cane sugar- and tea-factories.

● **Formosa** (Taiwan)   Largest island off the Chinese coast, with an area of 13,800 square miles and a population of 14,420,000. The capital is Taipei, with a population of 1,700,000. The elongated island was called Formosa ('the beautiful') by the Portuguese, who discovered it in 1590. The Chinese and the Japanese call it Taiwan. Forested mountain ranges, rising to Hsinkao (13,113 feet), traverse the island from north to south, and decline gently to the broad western coastal plain, where most of the population and economy are concentrated, and where rice, sugar cane, tea and pineapples are the

principal crops. The mountain forests yield much of the world's camphor. In addition to the processing of farm products, there are machinery, aluminium, oil-refining and cement industries in the larger cities, which include Taipei, Tainan, Taichung, and the two ports of Keelung and Kaohsiung. Formosa's population is almost entirely Chinese. Under Japanese control, from 1895 to 1945, the island economy was modernised and industrialised. After World War II, Formosa was returned to Chinese rule; but, since 1949, the island has been the refuge of Chiang Kai-shek's Nationalist Government of China, which also controls the Pescadores island group, in the Formosa Strait, and the small Chinese offshore islands of Quemoy and Matsu.

● **Frunze**   Capital of the Soviet Republic of Kirghizia, in Central Asia; its population is 431,000. It is situated in the centre of the irrigated Chu River valley, at the foot of the Tien Shan mountain system. Machinery factories, a woollen mill and a meat-packing plant are among its industries. The city was named after a Bolshevik general.

● **Fujiyama**   The highest mountain (12,395 feet) of Japan, 60 miles south-west of Tokyo. A dormant volcano, it is famous for its beautiful symmetry and is a common subject of Japanese art. Sacred since ancient times and a national symbol, Fujiyama is visited each year by thousands of pilgrims and tourists. The snow-capped volcano last erupted in the year 1707.

Fujiyama

● **furs**   The fur trade played an important role in the development of the northern regions of the world. It was a search for furs that drove the Cossacks eastward through Siberia in the late 16th and early 17th centuries. Similarly, fur traders of the Hudson's Bay Company opened up the Canadian interior after the mid-17th century. Fur-bearing animals are still economically important for the peoples of Canada and Siberia. Furs are tanned like leather and dyed according to the current fashion. The most valuable furs are those of the ermine, sable, mink, fox and fur seal. Many fur-bearing animals are now raised on fur farms. The principal fur-trade centres are New York and Montreal in North America, and London, Copenhagen and Leningrad in Europe.

● **Fu-shun**   One of China's greatest coal-mining centres (population 1 million) in southern Manchuria; situated just east of Mukden. Oil shale is mined there, and converted into petroleum products. Other industries include aluminium, chemical and steel plants, and the manufacture of electrical and mining machinery.

● **Ganges River**   Sacred river of the Hindus, in northern India; 1,600 miles long. It rises in the western Himalayas, north of Nanda Devi, and flows south-eastward through the densely populated Ganges plain, forming a vast joint delta with the Brahmaputra River on the Bay of Bengal. On the Ganges are the holy cities of Allahabad and Benares.

● **Georgia**   A Soviet Republic of Transcaucasia; (area 29,400 square miles; population 4,700,000). The capital is Tiflis. Georgia is overshadowed along its northern border by the Caucasus, and abuts on Turkey in the south. The densely populated western part of the republic, on the Black Sea, has a humid, subtropical climate unusual for the Soviet Union, and this makes Georgia popular as a tourist resort. This area is the ancient Colchis, where Jason landed in search of the Golden Fleece. It is the only major Soviet producer of tea, lemons and tangerines, tung oil and high grades of tobacco. Elsewhere in Georgia, wine, fruit and silk are important products. One of the world's largest deposits of manganese is at Chiatura. Coal is also mined. Manufacturing industries produce iron and steel, chemical fertiliser, lorries, and other machinery. Georgians are a people of Christian

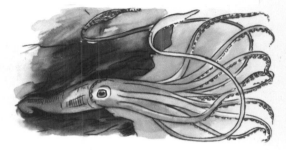

Giant squid

Malaya rubber plantation; trees are tapped daily

Orthodox religion, speaking a Caucasian language. An independent kingdom in the early Middle Ages, it passed to Russia early in the 19th century.

● **giant squid** This ten-armed relative of the octopus is not only the largest mollusc, but the largest invertebrate animal. Its body may reach a length of 20 feet, with 35-foot-long tentacles — a total length of 55 feet.

Gibbon

● **gibbon** This ape of South-East Asia is only three feet high. It is the smallest of the great apes and has the lowest intelligence. It moves most easily through trees, swinging swiftly from branch to branch, for it has long arms and fingers. On the ground it appears awkward and moves with difficulty. The gibbon has a tremendous voice, and its ear-splitting shrieks can be heard a mile away. Gibbons vary in colour and size, for there are many types.

Ginkgo tree

● **ginkgo** The tall ginkgo tree of China and Japan is the only survivor of an early family of plants. It has been preserved as an ornamental plant in parks and temple enclosures. The ginkgo bears peculiar fan-shaped leaves and edible nuts.

● **Goa** A former Portuguese possession on the west coast of India, south of Bombay. Goa was the remains of Portugal's extensive holdings in India during the 15th and 16th centuries, being under Portuguese rule from 1510 to 1961, when India seized the territory.

● **Gobi** A great desert of sand and gravel in east-central Asia, forming part of Outer Mongolia and in part belonging to China (Inner Mongolia). Its grassy sections are used by Mongol herdsmen. The desert was crossed by an ancient caravan route linking Russia and China. In recent years, this has been superseded by a major railway line.

● **Gorki** A town, with 1,170,000 inhabitants, which until 1932 was called Nijni-Novgorod, and is an ancient, historic city, founded in 1221 at the extreme east of the old Russian lands, at the confluence of the Oka and Volga. Its picturesque old town quarter is built on a hill dominated by a 16th-century castle (kremlin). Along the river is a larger industrial area, concerned with the production of cars, Diesel engines, machinery and ships. Maxim Gorki was born in the town, which came to be named after him. In former times the famous trade fair could call upon furs from Siberia, tea from China, silks, cotton and carpets from Turkestan, and wine from the south.

● **Haifa** Chief seaport (population 214,500) of Israel, on the Mediterranean Sea, and an industrial centre with an oil refinery, textile mills, chemical and metal industries, cement works and rubber factories. The harbour was built between 1929 and 1936, and oil and citrus fruits are exported, for Haifa is the terminal of an oil pipeline from Kirkuk.

● **Hai-nan** Second-largest island off the China coast, in the South China Sea (13,000 square miles; population 3 million) bordering the Bay of Ton-king. Hai-nan has a tropical climate, favouring the cultivation of coffee, rubber, bananas and other tropical fruit. There are large coal mines.

● **hammerhead shark** This shark has one of the most peculiar heads in the fish kingdom. Its eyes and nostrils are in the two long, squared-off projections of the skull. The hammerhead, which reaches a length of 13 feet, is found in all warm oceans, where it feeds on other sharks, skates and sting-rays.

Haifa, an Israeli port on the Mediterranean coast, seen from the slopes of Mount Carmel

Hammerhead shark

● **hamster, golden** This Syrian rodent, golden brown in colour, is one of the most popular pets. It is noted for its rapid rate of reproduction, and is therefore widely used as a laboratory animal. Its period of gestation (16 days) is the shortest among the higher mammals.

Golden hamster

● **Hangchow** City (population 784,000) of eastern China, 100 miles south-west of Shanghai; situated in an area producing silk, tea, cotton and jute. Its industries include silk mills, tea factories and a large jute mill. One of China's oldest cities, Hangchow is situated in a charming natural setting on the shore of scenic West Lake and at the foot of high wooded hills. Its view attracts tourists and painters.

● **Hanoi** Capital (population 850,000) of North Vietnam, situated in the heart of the Red River delta. Since the establishment of the new State of North Vietnam, Hanoi has greatly expanded as a political and administrative centre. Its trade is orientated almost entirely towards China, with which it is linked by two railways. Except for a new machinery plant, Hanoi's industry consists mainly of handicraft shops. A railway leads from Hanoi to the port of Haiphong (population 369,000), which handles a large part of North Vietnam's exports: mainly coal and non-ferrous ores. Haiphong's industries include cement, fish canning and fertilisers (phosphates).

● **Harbin (Pin-kiang)** Industrial city (population 1.6 million) of China, in northern Manchuria, and a railway centre and important river port on the Sungari River (a tributary of the Amur). A vast complex of food-processing plants produces flour, beet sugar, and soya-bean products. A linen mill, and factories making electrical machinery and precision instruments, have been added in recent years. The city was founded by the Russians in 1897. It still has a marked Russian appearance, and a sizeable Russian population.

● **hemp** A tall herb, native to Asia, but now cultivated throughout the world. Its tough bast fibre is used for making canvas, sails, cordage and floor coverings. The chief hemp fibre producers are the Soviet Union, India, Italy and Yugoslavia. Hemp seed yields an oil used in soap and varnish manufacture. An Indian variety of hemp yields narcotic drugs. Manila hemp is also important.

Himalayas Loftiest mountain range in the world, separating the virtually uninhabited Tibetan highlands from the densely populated Ganges plain of northern India. The mountains extend about 1,500 miles from the Indus River (the Pamirs) to the Brahmaputra River (Assam). Their highest point is Mount Everest (29,028 feet). The Himalayas are an important climatic barrier, separating the cold Asian air of the north from the warm, moist winds of the south. Himalaya means 'dwelling place of the snows'.

Hinduism The social and religious system of the Hindus in India. It involves belief in a trinity of gods, consisting of Brahma the Creator, Vishnu the Preserver, and Siva the Destroyer. The social system of Hinduism is based on caste, now officially renounced in India, where there are over 400 million Hindus.

Hiroshima City (population 504,000) of Japan, on the island of Honshu. It was the first city to be struck by an atom bomb, on 6th August, 1945. The blast destroyed all buildings within a radius of two miles from the explosion centre. About 36 per cent of the population, or 145,000 persons, were killed or injured. The city has been largely rebuilt in post-war years. The dropping of the bomb is commemorated by the Peace Tower, unveiled in 1947. The city's industries are concerned with textiles (cotton and silk).

Hong Kong British crown colony in southern China, 90 miles south-east of Canton. With 390 square miles, and a population of 4,039,000, the colony consists of the rocky offshore island of Hong Kong, on which the capital of Victoria is situated, and the so-called New Territories on the mainland, including the Kowloon Peninsula. Most of the population, almost entirely Chinese, is concentrated in the urban complex of Victoria and Kowloon, on both sides of Hong Kong harbour. The island passed to Britain in 1841, with Kowloon added in 1860, and the New Territories were leased in 1898 for 99 years. Since the mid-19th century, Hong Kong has become one of the leading commercial centres of South-East Asia, containing the headquarters of large banks and corporations, and 18,899 factories in 1970. Its deep-water port has traditionally handled a large part of the transit trade with China. Its airport is one of the main international air centres in Asia. Since the coming of the Communist government in China, Hong Kong and its railway to Canton have been the only gateway to the Chinese mainland from the West.

Hyderabad City (population 1,619,000) of southern India. An industrial centre, with textile mills and a locomotive and railway-wagon plant, Hyderabad was the capital of the former State of Hyderabad. The State was annexed by force in 1948 and was dissolved in 1956. Another city of Hyderabad (population 250,000) is situated in the Indus valley of Pakistan, 90 miles north-east of Karachi.

India One of the great nations of Asia — a triangular peninsula jutting southward into the Indian Ocean. India (population 546,955,944) is the second most populous country in the world (after China). Its area is 1,100,000 square miles and the capital is New Delhi. India won its independence from Britain in 1947. Since 1950,

Shipping from all over the world lies at anchor in the magnificent harbour at Hong Kong, the British possession on the south coast of China

it has been a republic within the British Commonwealth. Separated from the rest of Asia by the lofty mountain barrier of the Himalayas, India

Indian snake-charmer

includes the densely populated alluvial plain of the Ganges (north) and the Deccan plateau (south). India has a tropical climate; the south-west monsoon (June to September) brings most of the country's rainfall. On its timely arrival and duration depends the success of the Indian harvest. About 70 per cent of India's population is engaged in agriculture. Land reforms are gradually easing the traditional landlord system, under which large landowners controlled most of the acreage, and rented it to tenant farmers. Although four-fifths of the land is sown in grain, India must still import much of its food supply. The principal food crops are rice (in the Ganges valley), wheat, millet and maize. Sugar cane, cotton, tobacco and oilseeds are also grown, and a fifth of the cropped area is irrigated. Tea from the Assam hills makes India the world's leading tea exporter. Although India has enormous numbers of cattle (60 animals for every 100 persons), they are used primarily as draught animals. Indian cattle — poorly bred and inadequately fed — are among the least productive in the world. Since Hindu religious traditions forbid slaughtering cows, and as their milk yield is low, they are economically useful for their hides only; consequently, hides are a large export item.

Iron ore and coal resources provide the basis for India's steel industry in the north-eastern part of the country. Other minerals, mined chiefly for export, include manganese, mica, ilmenite and monazite. Manufacturing is predominantly devoted to food processing and light consumer goods. Textiles, especially cotton (concentrated in the Bombay region), account for nearly a third of factory employment. Handicraft industries play a major role in cotton weaving, pottery and tobacco.

The largest cities are Calcutta, Bombay and Madras (all of them major ports), and Delhi.

India is a multi-national country with a large number (845) of language groups. English and Hindi are the official languages. Hindi, which is an Indo-European tongue derived from Sanscrit, is spoken in northern India. Its spread as a national language is being resisted in southern India, where the ancient Tamil and Telugu languages are deeply rooted. Although most of the Moslems who lived in India before it was partitioned are now in Pakistan, India still has a 10 per cent Moslem population. The majority (85 per cent) follow the Hindu religion.

The lowland of the Ganges (Hindustan) was the cradle of several old civilisations, and before British rule began the country's complex early history saw two outstanding periods of unification. The first was in the 3rd century B.C., when the Emperor Asoka established a powerful Hindu-Buddhist state which dominated eastern Asia. The second was from the 16th to the 18th century, when invading Moslems established the strong Mogul empire. Vasco da Gama first led the Portuguese to India in 1498. A British-French struggle for supremacy in India ended in British victory and, by the early 19th century, the British were firmly entrenched in India. British rule was marked by a period of railway construction and commercialised (irrigated) agriculture, starting in the second half of the 19th century. After the First World War,

A view of the lofty Himalayas, the mountain range which contains 29,028 ft. Mt Everest

Hindu temple in the modern city of Jaipur, in northern India

Oil pipeline

a nationalist independence movement, led by Mahatma Gandhi, spread to all parts of India. Although both Moslems and Hindus sought independence, the Moslems feared their rights would be ignored by the Hindu majority. When independence was finally granted, in 1947, Moslem demands led to partition of former British India into the two States of India and Pakistan. After independence, Nehru led India on a course of gradual economic development and neutrality in world affairs. The Indian name for their nation is Bharat.

● **Indian Ocean** With an area of 28 million square miles, the Indian Ocean is the smallest of the three great oceans of the world. It is traversed by one of the world's main shipping routes, leading from the Suez Canal, through the Red Sea, past Aden and Colombo, to Singapore and the Far East. Its greatest depth is 24,440 feet, in the Java Trench, south of Java, and its average depth is 13,000 feet. On the south coast of Asia, the Indian Ocean creates two great indentations: the Arabian Sea and the Bay of Bengal.

● **Indo-China** The eastern portion of the large South-East Asian Peninsula, which is also shared by Thailand and Burma. Colonised in the 19th century by France, it consisted of Cambodia, Laos, Cochin China, Annam and Tonkin. After World War II, during which it was occupied by the Japanese, the Annamese nationalist revolt in Vietnam led to the Indo-China War between the French and the Communist-led nationalists of Vietnam. The Geneva armistice that ended the war in 1954 resulted in the division of Indo-China into four independent states: Cambodia, Laos, North Vietnam and South Vietnam.

● **Indonesia** Archipelago and republic (population 118 million) of South-East Asia, extending 3,000 miles east-west between the Pacific and Indian oceans, Indonesia's total area is 575,000 square miles. The capital is Jakarta. The country includes the Greater Sunda Islands (Java, Sumatra, Celebes and the southern part of Borneo), the Lesser Sunda Islands (which include Bali and Lombok), the Moluccas, western Timor, and many smaller islands; in 1963, West New Guinea, now called West Irian, was ceded to Indonesia by the Dutch. Indonesia lies in the humid tropics astride the Equator, and where the mountainous, volcanic, heavily wooded mountain slopes have been cleared, they support large plantations of tobacco, rubber, tea, coffee, sugar cane and cinchona. Rice and tapioca, grown in the fertile coastal plains, are the principal food crops. Other products are spices (including pepper), palm oil and copra. The forests yield tropical hardwoods (teak, ebony). The principal mineral products are tin, mined on the islands of Bangka and Billiton, and petroleum, from Sumatra and Borneo. Leading exports — chiefly to the United States, the Netherlands and Japan — are rubber, petroleum, copra and tin.

Indonesians are predominantly of Malay stock and are Moslem in religion; and the Indonesian language is a variant of Malay. Chinese emigrants form a large minority. In its early history, Indonesia came under the influence of Indian culture, and Hindu-Buddhist empires first reached Sumatra, and later Java. In the 15th century, with the arrival of Arab traders, Islam replaced Buddhism as the dominant religion. During the 16th and 17th centuries, the Javanese empire fell prey to Portuguese, British and Dutch colonialism. The Dutch ousted their rivals and created the Netherlands East Indies, one of Europe's richest colonial empires.

The Indonesian independence movement was spurred during Japanese occupation in World War II. After a confused period of alternating hostilities and negotiations with the Dutch, Indonesia was recognised as a sovereign country in 1949, though President Sukarno had proclaimed independence in 1945. He then faced the task of consolidating the wide-flung islands into a unified State.

● **Indus River** One of the great rivers of southern Asia; 1,900 miles long. It rises in Tibet, and flows through Kashmir and Pakistan to the Arabian Sea. In Pakistan, it traverses a large arid region, where agriculture is possible only because its waters are used for irrigation. The Indus is of little importance for transportation. The Indus valley was the centre of some of the earliest civilisations.

● **Iran** Moslem kingdom of south-western Asia, between the Caspian Sea and the Persian Gulf (630,000 square miles; population 25,781,090). The capital is Teheran. Iran — its official name — is also widely known, in English, as Persia. Its King is called the Shah. The country consists of a vast central plateau (4,000 feet high), ringed by great mountain arcs that keep out moisture-bearing winds; consequently, most of the country is covered with dry steppe, desert or salt flats. Except for parts of Azerbaijan and the humid subtropical coast on the Caspian Sea, agriculture requires irrigation. Wheat and barley are the main food crops; rice is grown where irrigation is possible. The commercial crops, grown mainly in the Caspian area, include cotton, tea, tobacco, fruits and nuts. Sheep and goats yield wool and hides. Sturgeon and caviar are Caspian fishery products. Iran is one of the major petroleum countries of south-western Asia, with deposits concentrated in the south-western part of the country, around the refining centre of Abadan. Aside from crude petroleum and refined products (the country's chief source of wealth), Iran also exports rugs, cotton, rice, wool, hides and dried fruit. Nearly all the country's foreign trade is seaborne, passing chiefly through Persian Gulf ports. The country's chief trade partners are the United Kingdom, West Germany and the United States. Iran has large untapped reserves of iron, copper, lead, chromite, coal and salt.

More than half of the country's population are Persians, who speak an Indo-European language and use the Arabic alphabet. The rest of the population is made up of Azerbaijan Turks (20 per cent), Kurds, and various other groups. Persia emerged as a great world power in antiquity under the Emperors Cyrus and Darius, before falling to Alexander the Great in 328 B.C. The country came under Arab rule in the 7th century and fell to the Mongols in the 13th. A new Persian dynasty rose in the 16th century, flourishing under Abbas the Great (1587—1628). The present Pahlevi dynasty was founded in 1925 by Riza Shah. During World War II, Iran was accused of pro-German activity and was occupied (1941—46) by Soviet and British troops. Iran's largest cities are Teheran, Tabriz, Isfahan, Meshed, Abadan and Shiraz.

● **Iraq** Moslem republic of south-western Asia; (170,000 square miles; population 8,765,915). The capital is Baghdad. Iraq, watered by the Tigris

Young girls draw water at the communal well, in a small agricultural town in southern India

Part of the city of Jerusalem, capital of Israel and a religious centre for Christians, Jews and Mohammedans.

and Euphrates Rivers, occupies the historic region of Mesopotamia, which means 'between the rivers', the Tigris-Euphrates lowland, bordered to the north-east by the rugged highlands, peopled by the Kurdish people; and to the south-west, deserts, inhabited by nomadic Bedouin tribes. Wheat, barley and rice are the chief food crops, produced entirely under irrigation. Cotton, tobacco and fruit are also raised. Iraq is the world's greatest grower of date palms, which provide food, spirit (arrack), matting, textile fibres, rope and building material. Iraq furnishes 80 per cent of all the dates in world trade. Their export value is exceeded only by petroleum. Iraq's oil-fields, centred on Kirkuk in the north-eastern part of the country, send their output by pipeline to refineries and loading ports on the Mediterranean Sea in Lebanon and Syria. The country's other exports (dates, barley, wool) move through the Persian Gulf port of Basra. Its population is 75 per cent Arabian, 15 per cent Kurdish, and partly Persians. Islam is the dominant religion, with three-fifths of the population belonging to the Shiite sect.

Among the earliest empires of historic Mesopotamia was the Sumerian, followed by the Babylonian and Assyrian periods. Among its ruined cities were Ur, Babylon and Nineveh. The region flourished again after the 8th century A.D. as the country of the Arab caliphs of Baghdad. The Mongols arrived in the 13th century (1258) and destroyed the ancient irrigation systems. The region fell to the Ottoman Turks in 1534. After World War I, the independent kingdom of Iraq was founded in 1920, but remained under British influence until 1932. A coup in July, 1958, ended the monarchy under King Faisal and established Iraq as a republic.

● **Irkutsk** City (population 451,000) of southern Siberia, on the Angara River, 40 miles from Lake Baikal. Founded in 1683, it became one of the early administrative and trading centres of Siberia. In the Soviet period, Irkutsk has developed a metal industry based on the ores from the nearby mines (coal, iron, bauxite, and other minerals used in special steel production). It also has sawmills and fur factories. More recently, hydro-electric projects along the Angara River have attracted new power-consuming industries, such as the smelting of aluminium.

● **Irrawaddy River** Main stream and economic life-line of Burma. One of the great rivers of South-East Asia, 1,300 miles long, it runs the full length of Burma from north to south and is navigable as far north as Mandalay. Its wide delta is a rich rice-growing area. Petroleum barges and teakwood rafts account for most of the downstream traffic.

● **Irtysh River** Longest tributary of the Ob River in Siberia, 2,800 miles long; rising in China's Sinkiang Province, in the Altai Mountains, and flowing north-west to the Ob, past Semipalatinsk, Omsk and Tobolsk. Hydro-electric projects along its upper course supply power for the lead-zinc industry in the Altai Mountains. The town of Khanty-Mansisk lies at the confluence of the Ob and Irtysh.

● **Isfahan** City (population 575,000) of Iran, 200 miles south of Teheran; centre of an agricultural region, with textile mills (cotton, silk, wool) and weapon and ceramic industries. Its great mosque and other buildings, decorated with mosaics and coloured tiles, date from the 17th century, when Isfahan was the capital of Persia under Abbas the Great, and later, from 1600 to 1749.

● **Islam** One of the world's great religions, founded in the 7th century by Mohammed. His followers are called Moslems. Islam requires belief in one god (Allah), in Mohammed as the Prophet who speaks for Allah, and in the Koran as the sacred scripture. Islam developed both as a religious and as a social movement, rapidly carried by the Arabs through North Africa, Asia and into southern Europe. It reached its greatest power from the 7th to the 9th century. There are now more than 500 million Moslems in the world, from West Africa to the Philippines. About 90 per cent belong to the orthodox Sunnite sect, which accepts the legality of Mohammed's immediate successors. The Shiite sect, found chiefly in Iran and Iraq, regards Ali, Mohammed's son-in-law, as the Prophet's legitimate successor. The holy cities of Islam are Mecca and Medina, and are centres of pilgrimage.

● **Israel** Jewish republic (8,000 square miles; population 2,999,000, largely former Jewish refugees) in the Middle East, on the Mediterranean Sea. The capital is Jerusalem, in the western (newer part) of the city. Israel was established in 1948, as the result of Zionist aspirations for an independent state in Palestine, the historic homeland of the Jews. Extending for more than 100 miles along the sea, Israel consists of a coastal plain; central highlands, reaching to over 4,000 feet in Jarmak; part of the Jordan River valley, including the Dead Sea and Sea of Tiberias; and the Negev Desert in the south, reaching to the Gulf of Aqaba. The population and economic activities are concentrated in the coastal plain, which contains the cities of Tel Aviv, Jaffa and Haifa. Oranges, wine and olives are the principal export crops, often grown in kibbutz, which are communal collective settlements. Other exports include textiles, cement and machinery. Israel must import part of its food requirements and many of the raw materials for its rapidly developing manufactures. Potash, copper and petroleum are among its mineral resources. Chief trade partners are the United States, Britain and West Germany. Jews make up 90 per cent of the country's population; Arabs include about 165,000 Moslems and 70,000 Christians. Hebrew is the nation's official language. Since 1948, the population has been increasing at a rate of more than 100,000 a year. Proclamation of the new State led to the Arab-Israeli War, and although hostilities were terminated by a truce under United Nations auspices in 1949, an official state of war has continued to exist between Israel and the Arab nations. Tension has been particularly high along the borders of Egypt, Jordan and Syria, especially in 1956, and open war broke out in 1967. Since then no settlement has been reached, and outbreaks of fighting occur frequently.

● **Izmir** City (population 520,686) of south-west Turkey; widely known as Smyrna. A fine natural port on the Aegean Sea, it handles most of Turkey's exports, including raisins, figs (Smyrna figs), carpets, tobacco, silk, olives, and ores of chrome and manganese. An early centre of Christianity in Asia Minor, the city was a focus of Greek culture, even under Ottoman rule. After World War I, Greek forces tried to seize control of the city and its surrounding area, but were expelled by the Turks, at which time most of its Greek population returned to Greece. Izmir is a noted university centre.

● **Jakarta** Capital and largest city (population 4.75 million) of Indonesia, on the north coast of Java, consisting of two sections: an old town with traditional Javanese, Chinese and Arab quarters, and a modern residential area built by the Dutch. Although it is Indonesia's political and educational centre, it does not have as great an industrial development as Surabaya. Under Dutch rule (1619 — 1949), the city was known as Batavia. Rubber, sugar, tea and tin are exported.

● **Jamshedpur** Iron and steel centre (population 332,000) of India, 140 miles west of Calcutta. Its steel plant, Tata-works, opened in 1911, is one of the largest in Asia.

● **Japan** The Land of the Rising Sun, called Nippon or Nihon in Japanese, consists of one of the large island groups off the coast of eastern Asia. Its total area of 140,000 square miles includes four main islands — Honshu, Hokkaido, Kyushu and Shikoku — and hundreds of small (and some uninhabited) islets. Its total population is 104.6 million. The capital is Tokyo, the world's largest city. In Japan, where no point on the islands is farther than 100 miles from the coast, the sea and the mountains are never far apart. Rivers are short, swift and usually not navigable, but they play a major role in the generation of hydro-electric power and in irrigation. More than three-fourths of the total land area is mountainous, including some volcanoes of which Fujiyama is best known.

Japan lies in one of the world's most active earthquake zones, and minor shocks are an almost daily occurrence. The Japanese, a people of Mongolian race, speak a language unrelated to any other known language. It is written with Chinese characters and with a system of syllabic symbols dating from the 8th or 9th century. Buddhism and Shintoism are the chief religions. The population is concentrated (at one of the highest densities in the world) in small plains along the coast and in interior mountain basins. Among the largest cities are Tokyo, Osaka, Nagoya, Kyoto, Yokohama and Kobe. Although only 15 per cent of the country is arable, the Japanese manage, through intensive cultivation, to produce nearly 80 per cent of their food needs. Rice is by far the main crop. Others are fruit, mulberry trees (for raising silk-worms), tea, tobacco, potatoes, barley and sweet potatoes. Coastal and deep-sea fisheries and other seafoods contribute a large part of the national diet. Japan's fishermen take a larger catch from the sea than any other nation in the world.

Until recently a third of the population derived its income from agriculture, but this is now reduced to about one ninth. The Japanese economy is primarily industrial, with emphasis on most manufacturing. Because of a lack of textiles and natural resources, Japan must import its fuels (coking coal, petroleum), industrial raw materials (iron ore and non-ferrous metals) and fibres. In return it exports textiles (cotton, wool and silk), steel, machinery, chemicals and specialised products, such as porcelain and lacquer-ware. Japan is also one of the world's leading shipbuilding

nations, and lately has won a reputation for its optical instruments, radios and cameras.

The country's early history is lost in legend, one of which states that Japan was founded by Jimmu Tenno in 660 B.C. During the 6th century, in early contacts with China, Buddhism was introduced, and Chinese art, written language and philosophy left a permanent imprint. The growth of a provincial gentry resulted in a feudal system in which successive dynasties of shoguns (military governors) usurped the power of the emperors. The rule of the shoguns lasted from 1186 to 1867. In 1854, Commodore Perry forced the opening of trade with the West. In 1867, the shogun was compelled to resign, and power was restored to the Emperor. The nation embraced the technological civilisation of the West and, in a short time, became a modern world power. Victories over China in 1895 and Russia in 1905 were followed by Japan's annexation of Korea in 1910. During World War I, former German islands in the Pacific were added to the Imperial realm. An increasingly aggressive policy, fostered by military leaders, led to the seizure of Manchuria in 1931 and the Sino-Japanese war of 1937. Japan drifted into the

Japanese family

Fascist 'camp' and became a fully fledged partner of the Axis powers. On 7th December, 1941, Japan opened hostilities against the United States and Britain, striking at Pearl Harbour, Singapore, the Philippines and other Pacific areas. Initial successes brought Japan to the gates of India, but by the end of 1942 the tide had begun to turn. Island by island, the Allies fought their way towards Japan. The war's conclusion was hastened by the dropping of atomic bombs on Hiroshima and Nagasaki. At the close of the war Japan's

Empire was reduced to the home islands. Military occupation of Japan under General Douglas MacArthur ended in 1951, but, under a mutual accord, United States troops remained. Japan's foreign policy is generally favourable towards the Western powers. In 1956, Japan became a member of the United Nations.

● **Java** Smallest of the Greater Sunda Islands, Java (50,000 square miles; population 74 million) is the political and economic core of the Republic of Indonesia. Although Java makes up less than one-tenth of the total area of the country, it contains 60 per cent of the total population. The long, narrow volcanic island (650 miles long, 100 miles wide) is covered with luxuriant tropical vegetation. Although even mountain slopes are converted into terraced rice fields, food must be imported. The fertile coastal plain produces coffee, tobacco, sisal and sugar cane. Over a hundred volcanoes, some of them still active, rise to more than 10,000 feet. The largest cities are Jakarta (the Indonesian capital), Surabaya and Bandung.

● **Jerusalem** Historic city of Palestine — a holy place for Christians, Jews and Moslems alike. Situated in the Judaean hills, about 35 miles from the Mediterranean Sea, Jerusalem was divided between Israel and Jordan in 1948, but was taken over by Israel in the 1967 war.

The Old City of Jerusalem (population 60,000) contains almost all the holy places of the three faiths. In the Christian quarter, in the north-west, are the Church of the Holy Sepulchre and the Via Dolorosa. The Moslem quarter, in the east, contains the Moslems' Dome of the Rock and the Jews' Wailing Wall.

The New City of Jerusalem (population 283,100 in 1971) is the capital of Israel, and includes the Israeli Parliament, government offices, public buildings, industrial establishments and the university.

● **Jews** Term originally applied to members of the tribe of Judah of the ancient Israelites of Palestine. Later, it was used to include all Israelites. The destruction of Jerusalem by the Romans (70 A.D.) led to the dispersion of Jews throughout the world. Because of traditions going back over the centuries, Jews are regarded on the one hand as a religious entity, and on the other hand as an ethnic group. Two groups can be distinguished: the Ashkenazim, descendants of central and eastern European Jews; and the Sephardim, descendants of Spanish-Portuguese Jews. Some Ashkenazim speak Yiddish, derived chiefly from medieval German and written in the Hebrew alphabet. Some Sephardim speak a mixed Spanish-Hebrew language. The Zionist movement of the late 19th century, calling for the return of Jews to Palestine, led to the establishment of the state of Israel in 1948, where Hebrew, a Semitic tongue related to Arabic, has been revived as a modern language. Of the entire world population of 11 million Jews, over 5 million are in the United States, over 2 million in the Soviet Union and more than 2 million in Israel.

● **Jogjakarta** City (population 312,000) of Java, in Indonesia, and seat of an old sultan, whose vast 18th-century palace forms the centre of the town, which is situated at the foot of the volcano Merapi and was heavily damaged by an eruption in 1867. For a short time after World War II, it was the capital of the new Republic of Indonesia, while the Dutch still held Jakarta. The city has a large university.

● **Jordan** Arab kingdom (37,000 square miles; population 2.2 million) of the Middle East, adjoining Israel, Saudi Arabia, Iraq and Syria. The capital is Amman (population 330,000). As a result of the Arab-Israeli War of 1948-49, the new nation was

Istanbul, formerly Constantinople and one-time capital of Turkey, stands on the Golden Horn peninsula, where the Bosporus enters the Sea of Marmara

created, combining two areas: the original kingdom of Transjordan (east of the Jordan River), carved out of the Ottoman Empire after World War I; and the east-central part of former Palestine (west of the Jordan), which had been designated by the United Nations as Arab territory and had been occupied by Jordanian troops in 1948. Only 10 per cent of the country is under cultivation; wheat and barley are the chief grain crops. Most of the eastern section of the country is desert. Phosphates are the principal mineral resource, mined for export.

●**jungle fowl** A wild bird of India from which the many varieties of domestic chickens are believed to be descended. Domesticated thousands of years ago in India, it gave rise to the modern commercial varieties, raised either for their egg-laying or for their meat.

●**junk** The characteristic vessel of Far Eastern waters, having a high stern, flat bottom and square sails spread by battens. Coastal junks, which displace about 400 tons, usually have three masts. River junks are single-masters. Despite their heavy-set look, they are highly sea-worthy craft.

Jute

●**jute** An Indian plant of the linden family, yielding a tough bast fibre. Jute, which is injured by moisture, is used mainly for making cheap, strong sacks and burlap (coarse canvas), as well as for twine, and tarpaulin and linoleum backing. Almost the entire world supply is grown in Bengal: about one-third from West Bengal in India, and two-thirds from East Bengal in Bangladesh.

●**Kabul** Capital (population 435,000) of Afghanistan, at the western end of the Khyber Pass route. Sited in a triangular valley in the eastern part of the country, Kabul is linked by this major trade route to India, making it an important commercial centre.

●**Kaifeng** One of China's ancient capitals (10th to 12th century) near the Yellow River; its population is 299,100. In modern times it has been increasingly supplanted by the railway \and industrial centre of Chengchow.

●**Kalgan** City (population 230,000) of northern China, on the old trade route to Mongolia. Known as Chang-kia-kow to the Chinese; flour and oil-seed mills and a new mining-machinery plant are there.

●**Kalinin,** before 1932 called Tver, was founded north-west of Moscow in the 12th century as a trading station on the Upper Volga at the head of navigation and on the trade route from Central Russia to the Baltic Sea. It is now an industrial centre making textiles, leather and railway rolling stock and has a population of 345,000. It is also a very important timber centre.

●**Kaliningrad** is the Soviet Union's most important Baltic port on the Bay of Gdansk, and was formerly the Königsberg of East Prussia. It has a population of 297,000 and was founded in 1255. In the 16th and 17th centuries, Kaliningrad was the seat of the Prussian dukes and kings. The northern part of East Prussia came under Soviet control in 1946. The city has a castle dating from 1255 and a university founded in 1544. It now has many industries, with shipyards, machinery, paper and timber industries, and fishing is important. The port is connected to the open sea by a 20-mile-long canal, and is virtually ice-free.

●**Kama** the largest of the tributaries of the Volga, over 1,200 miles in length, and the main traffic artery for the industrial towns of the western Urals. The largest riverport is Perm, which can deal with quite large ships. There is a canal connection with the Northern Dvina, and there are many hydro-electric plants on the river.

●**Kamchatka** Large peninsula of north-eastern Siberia, on the Pacific Ocean, separating the Bering Sea from the Sea of Okhotsk. Along the centre of the peninsula extends a chain of active volcanoes, rising to more than 15,700 feet in the Klyuchevskaya Sopka, and there are many hot springs and geysers. The economy is based almost entirely on fisheries, and the coast has many fish-canning plants, as well as floating crab canneries. Out of a total population of 200,000, over a half lives in Petropavlovsk, the chief city.

●**Kanpur** Industrial city (population 984,000) of northern India, on the Ganges River, and a leading textile centre, with cotton, wool and jute mills. Chemicals, cement and machinery are also manufactured here.

●**Kaoh-siung** City of southern Formosa, with a population of about 663,388. It is an industrial centre, producing aluminium, chemical fertiliser and cement. There is an oil refinery.

●**Karachi** Former capital (population 2 million) of Pakistan, and a port on the Arabian Sea, north-west of the Indus River delta. Situated in a coastal oasis between the desert and the sea, Karachi is the shipping point for Pakistan's exports (wheat, cotton, hides). It also serves as a port for land-locked Afghanistan. British traders began to develop Karachi in the second half of the 19th century as the port for what was then north-west India. Later the city became a major air traffic centre on international airlines from Europe to the Far East and Australia. With the establishment of Pakistan in 1947, Karachi experienced enormous expansion as the political centre of the new country, but the capital functions have since been moved to Islamabad.

●**Karaganda** Industrial city of the Soviet republic of Kazakhstan. Founded about 1930 in a large coal basin, Karaganda rose to a population of 522,000 within 40 years. The urban area is made up of a central city and as many as 50 mining settlements. In addition to its coal mines, Karaganda has a mining machinery plant. The north-western suburb of Temir-Tau has a power plant, and a large iron and steel mill. Part of the development of Karaganda was achieved with prison labour.

●**Karakoram Mountains** One of the world's highest mountain systems, in Kashmir, at the western end of the Himalayas. It contains the peak

Buddhist priests (bonzes) at Nikko, in Japan

K² (28,250 feet), and many other high summits and great glaciers.

●**karakul sheep** A broad-tailed, rather small sheep of Central Asia, raised for its lambskin fur. Karakul fur is obtained from the tightly curled, glossy black coat of the newborn lambs. Various types are known as Persian lamb or astrakhan.

●**Karelia** is a border region between Finland and the Soviet Union. The Russian part consists of the Karelian ASSR, with 714,000 inhabitants and an area of 69,720 square miles. Its capital is Petrozavodsk. The republic contains nearly 44,000 lakes, which are rich in fish; but the vast forests, covering 70 per cent of the area, and mineral deposits, are the basis of the economy. Quartz, marble, mica, granite, andores of zinc, lead, silver, copper, molybdenum, tin and iron are quarried or mined. Industries are concerned with timber, furniture, paper and pulp. The Karelian Peninsula is that part between the Gulf of Finland and Lake Ladoga. This productive area belonged to Finland until 1940, when it was adjoined to Russia. It was then recaptured by the Finns in 1941, and in 1945 was retaken by the U.S.S.R. The main city and port is Vyborg (Viipuri).

●**Kashgar (Shu-fu)** City (population 100,000) in the western part of China's Sinkiang Province, at the foot of the Tien Shan. Situated in a large oasis, Kashgar is the political and economic centre of the southern part of Sinkiang.

●**Kashmir** A mountain country of Asia (82,000 square miles, population 4,500,000) at the western end of the Himalayas. Upon the partition of British India in 1947, both Pakistan and India claimed Kashmir, which has a 77-per-cent Moslem population, with a pro-Indian ruler and Hindu ruling class. Armed hostilities between India and Pakistan were ended in January 1949 by a United Nations-sponsored truce. Since then Kashmir has remained divided between India and Pakistan, and negotiations leading to a final solution have made no progress. In 1965, friction became so

A crowd of turbaned Afghans assemble in Kabul to witness their king's coronation parade

great that open warfare broke out for a short time between the rival claimants to Kashmir; this only ceased after determined intervention by the United Nations. Indian Kashmir, which includes the greater part, is centred on the beautiful Vale of Kashmir, with its capital, Srinagar (population 285,000). Here is where most of the cultivated land is located, and where grain and fruit are grown. Handicraft industries produce fine woollens (cashmere shawls) and many other products.

● **Kazakhstan** An Asian republic of the Soviet Union, between China and the Caspian Sea. Its area of one million square miles has a population of 12.9 million. The capital is Alma-Ata. Kazakhstan consists of three distinct natural zones: a northern belt of steppe, where wheat and other grains are grown; a central short grass and bush area, where livestock herding is the principal activity, and a southern zone of irrigated oases, producing cotton, sugar beets, rice, fruit and tobacco.

The area is well-known for its sheep, which produce an excellent wool. Industry is based on rich mineral resources: coal and wolfram (Karaganda), iron and steel, oil and non-ferrous metals. Kazakhstan produces two-thirds of the Soviet Union's copper, lead and zinc ores. The Kazakhs, who make up less than a third of the population, are a Turkish-Moslem people, originally nomadic herdsmen. The rest of the population is composed of Russians and Ukrainians, who live in cities and on the northern wheat farms. In addition to the 3 million Kazakhs of the Soviet Union, nearly half a million live in the Dzungarian section of China's Sinkiang Province. North-western and central Kazakhstan passed to Russian control in the first half of the 18th century; the south-east followed in the mid-19th century. Since 1936, Kazakhstan has been the fifth union republic of the Soviet Union.

● **Kazan** is an old trading centre on the Volga, with a population of 869,000 (1970), at the northern end of the vast new lake of the Great Volga Scheme, and the capital of the Tartar A.S.S.R. A fortified outpost, with a Kremlin rivalling that of Moscow, it possesses a large university and many industries, including metals, car manufacture, chemicals, synthetic rubber, textiles and typewriters. It marks the crossing of river

transport with the railway line from Moscow to Sverdlovsk.

● **Kemerovo** One of the industrial cities of the Kuznetsk Basin, in Siberia, north of the Altai. Its population is 385,000. Kemerovo has large coke and chemical industries.

● **Khabarovsk** Largest city (population 322,000) of the Soviet Far East, at the confluence of the Amur and Ussuri rivers, near to the Manchurian border. Founded in 1858, Khabarovsk owes its importance to its location at the crossing of the Trans-Siberian railway and important waterways. It has an oil refinery for crude petroleum carried by pipeline from Sakhalin, shipyards, machine-tool and farm-machinery factories, as well as chemical plants.

● **Kharkov** is the sixth-largest city of the Soviet Union, in the Ukraine, with a population of 1,223,000 in 1970, and founded in the 17th century. The city is an important rail and air centre with many large industrial plants, for machinery, tractors, Diesel locomotives, turbines, machine-tools and textiles, and also mining equipment. The university was founded in 1805, and there are many centres for technical education and research. The city was the capital of the Ukraine from 1919 to 1934, a position now held by Kiev. It is connected to Moscow, the Donbas and the southern seaports, and has a densely populated countryside surrounding it.

● **Khyber Pass** Famous gateway through the mountains between Pakistan and Afghanistan. Winding for over 30 miles through barren, rugged cliffs, and reaching to 4,000 feet, it connects the Pakistan city of Peshawar with Kabul, the Afghan capital. The Khyber Pass has been used for centuries by the invaders of India, among them Alexander the Great, Genghis Khan, Babur Khan and Nadir Shar. Britain obtained control over the pass in 1879 and fought several small wars against the hostile Afridi tribes of the area.

● **Kiev** is situated on the Dnieper and became the capital of the Ukraine in 1934. With a population

of 1,632,000, it is the third-largest city in the Soviet Union. Kiev was an important trading station as early as the 8th century, and from 882 until 1169 was the capital of Russia. Eclipsed under the Tartar conquest, its modern development dates from 1800, when it became a banking and commercial centre controlling the sugar and grain production of the Ukraine. During the present century, industrialisation came in, with leather, tobacco, printing and heavy engineering industries, including coaches and motorcycles. An important cultural centre, with a university founded in 1834, it has many religious buildings, an abbey (now a museum) and the Cathedral of St Sophia, dating from 1037.

● **Kirghizia** A Central Asian republic (76,000 square miles; population 2,900,000) of the Soviet Union, in the Tien Shan mountain system. The capital is Frunze. Kirghizia is a mountain country with broad, grassy highland valleys separated by east-west-oriented ranges. Livestock raising (sheep, beef cattle, horses) is the most important occupation, only 7 to 8 per cent of its area being suitable for crops. In addition to wheat and other grains, Kirghizia produces sugar beets, cotton and other fibres. Mineral industries are based on coal, mercury, antimony and lead resources. The Kirghiz, a Turkish-Moslem people related to the Kazakhs, make up 40 per cent of the population. The rest consist of Russians, Uzbeks and Ukrainians. In addition to the 1.2 million Kirghiz living in the Soviet Union, almost 100,000 live across the border in China's Sinkiang Province. Kirghizia passed to Russian control in the second half of the 19th century. It has been a union republic of the Soviet Union since 1936.

● **Ki-rin** Industrial city (population 510,000) of China, in central Manchuria, situated 60 miles east of Changchun, on the upper Sungari River. Formerly Ki-rin was a timber centre, with sawmills, match and paper factories. The construction of the large Fengman hydro-electric station, on the Sungari River, has attracted a large complex of chemical plants which use the cheap electric power.

● **Kobe** One of the two largest ports (population 1,217,000) of Japan, the other being Yokohama. Kobe is the port for the large Osaka industrial area, on a bay in southern Honshu, and has shipyards, steel and rolling-stock plants. Kobe also produces electrical goods and rubber products, and possesses chemical industries.

● **Kola Peninsula** Lying in the Soviet Union, between the White Sea and the Barents Sea, the terrain is of tundra and coniferous forest. The rocks are among the oldest in the world (3,500 million years), are rich in minerals, such as apatite, nickel, iron, copper, bauxite and mica. Nearly 90 per cent of the people live in the towns and are engaged in mining, forestry or fishing. The largest towns are the ice-free port of Murmansk (309,000 people) and Kirovsk, a mining centre.

● **Kolyma River** A river of north-eastern Siberia, flowing 1,200 miles north to the Arctic Ocean. A large gold-mining area in its upper course has been developed, largely with forced labour, in an area where the average January temperature drops to 40 degrees below zero, or more.

● **Komsomolsk** A city (population 218,000) of the Soviet Far East, on the Amur River, built in 1932 by the Komsomol, the Communist youth organisation. Industries include a steel plant, shipyards, lumber mills and an oil refinery.

Korea Asian peninsula between the Sea of Japan and the Yellow Sea (85,000 square miles; population 45.36 million in 1970). The Korean peninsula, almost 500 miles long and 200 miles wide, has a deeply indented coastline, a mountain range near the east coast, and fertile lowlands along the west coast. Koreans belong to the Mongolian race, and their language, which uses either Chinese characters or a phonetic alphabet invented in the 15th century, is not known to be related to any other.

Early Korean history is that of a succession of kingdoms similar to the dynasties of China. The Silla kingdom, supported by China's Tang dynasty, flourished from the 7th to the 9th centuries. It was followed in the 10th century by the Koryu kingdom, from which the name Korea is derived. The country was under Mongol rule from 1231 to 1363. The Yi dynasty was founded in 1392 with the support of the Chinese Ming Dynasty. Korea resisted a Japanese invasion in the late 16th century, but became a vassal of China's Tsing dynasty. Thereafter, Korea was known as the Hermit Kingdom, because of its policy of strict isolation from the outside world. Trade agreements signed with Japan (1876) and the United States (1882) finally

Houseboats on Dal Lake at Srinagar, in the Vale of Kashmir

Korean man

re-opened Korea to the outside world. After the Sino-Japanese War (1894—95), Russia and Japan carved out zones of influence. With a Japanese victory over Russia in 1905, all of Korea became a Japanese protectorate, and was annexed in 1910 as the province of Chosen. Korea was then developed economically and industrially as an integral part of the Japanese economy until 1945.

After the end of World War II, Korea was occupied by Soviet and United States forces, the former north and the latter south of the 38th parallel. Co-operation between the two zones, leading to unification of the country, proved impossible, and in 1948 the division of the country was formalised, creating two antagonistic regimes. The Korean war, which erupted in June 1950, led to the intervention of the United States and other members of the United Nations on the South Korean side, and of Communist China on the North Korean side. Much fighting wrought tremendous destruction throughout the peninsula, but the front line became stabilised slightly north of the 38th parallel. An armistice was signed in July, 1953, at Panmunjom.

● **North Korea** Officially known as the Korean People's Democratic Republic (49,000 square miles; population 13.9 million), its capital is at Pyong-yang. North Korea's Communist regime, led by Kim Il Sung, controls the greater part of the peninsula's industrial resources (coal, steel, non-ferrous ores, chemicals, textiles, hydro-electric power and machinery), and half the cultivated land, on which rice, maize and other grains are raised. North Korea has the iron ore and nearly all the metallurgical works of the peninsula. Oil, manganese tungsten, lead and copper are also mined. Agriculture has been collectivised, industry

is largely state-owned, and most trade is carried on with the Soviet Union and other Communist nations.

● **South Korea** Officially known as the Republic of Korea (36,000 square miles; population 31.4 million) has its capital at Seoul. Formerly led by Syngman Rhee, it is an ally of the United States. South Korea contains the greater part of Korea's rice lands. Other crops include cotton, tobacco, hemp and ramie. Raw silk, fruit and wine are produced. The largest cities in the south, in addition to Seoul, are Pusan and Taegu. Industries are concerned with foodstuffs, silk and cement. Minerals include coal and one of the world's largest deposits of tungsten.

● **Krakatoa** Small volcanic isle between Java and Sumatra, known for its great eruption of August 27, 1883. The explosion, which blew up two-thirds of the island, could be heard as far away as the Philippines and Japan, and scattered volcanic ash over a large part of the world, for it ascended for a height of 18 miles into the atmosphere.

● **Krasnodar** A town on the river Kuban, northwest of the Caucasus on the well-cultivated Kuban plains. An administrative, commercial and industrial centre, and a railway junction. It has a population of 465,000, engaged in food processing, machine industries and oil refining. The city was founded in the early 18th century and became the capital of the Kuban cossacks.

● **Krasnoyarsk** Siberian city (population 648,000) at the crossing of the Yenisei River and the Trans-Siberian railway. Founded in the 17th century, it has become a major industrial city during the Soviet period. Its factories produce machinery and equipment for Siberia's mines, hydro-electric projects and timber manufacture. Krasnoyarsk also builds locomotives, river boats and harvester combines. A large aluminium plant arose in the late 1950s.

● **Krivoy Rog** is the most important iron-ore region in the southern Ukraine, on the Ingules, a tributary of the Dnieper. It had a population of 573,000 in 1970 and is really a conurbation of small mining towns, comprising a belt, 30 miles in length, along the river. About half of Russia's iron ore comes from this area, and is sent to the Donbas coal-mining region, over 200 miles away. However, some is used in the furnaces, and iron and steel manufacture are increasing.

● **Kuban** River of the Soviet Union, rising near Elbrus, in the Caucasus, and flowing to a point, near Krasnodar, on the Aral Sea. The lower course forms plainlands which are one of the main farming areas of the U.S.S.R.

● **Kuibyshev** An industrial city with a population of 1,047,000 in western Russia, at the confluence of the Samara with the Volga river. Named after a Soviet leader in 1935, it was formerly the wheat trading town of Samara and is an important route centre. Industries include milling, brewing, machine tools, watches and agricultural machinery. It is now an oil-refining centre and has an aircraft industry. Water power is much used, from one of the world's largest hydro-plants on the Volga. It was the centre of administration during the war of 1941—45, emphasising its distance from Europe and its nodality for communication with Siberia and Kazakhstan.

● **Kun-lun** A great mountain system of Central Asia, in China, forming the northern edge of the Tibetan highlands. The Kun-lun extend about 1,000 miles from west to east and rise to about

A busy street scene in Karachi, Pakistan — cars, bicycles, camels and pedestrians

24,000 feet. The Yangtze-Kiang and the Hwang-Ho both rise in the eastern part of the Kun-lun.

● **Kun-ming** City (population 880,000) of southwest China. During World War II, Kun-ming was the terminus of the famous Burma Road and one of the centres of Chinese resistance against the Japanese.

● **Kurds** A fiercely independent Moslem people of the Middle East, related to the Persians. They number 3 million, and inhabit Kurdistan (country of the Kurds), a region divided among Iran, Iraq and Turkey. Most now live by agriculture, though formerly a nomadic people.

● **Kuriles** An arc-shaped chain of volcanic islands in the North Pacific, extending 650 miles from Kamchatka to Japan. The climate is cold and stormy, though with many fogs. The sparse population engages in fishing and fish canning. Under Japanese control after 1875, they passed to the Soviet Union in 1945. The Kuriles separate the Sea of Okhotsk from the Pacific Ocean.

● **Kursk** With 284,000 inhabitants, Kursk is an old-established city, founded in the 11th century as a staging post on the salt route from the Black Sea. At the centre of a vast agricultural region, now specialising in wheat and sugar beet, Kursk's industries are concerned with farm machinery and food preparation. In the late 1950s, a start was made on the exploitation of large iron-ore deposits, and the city is an important railway junction. The iron deposits are at great depth and of low quality.

● **Kuwait** Independent Arab sheikhdom (6,000 square miles; population in 1969 was 733,000, of which 315,190 were non-Kuwaits) on the Persian Gulf, formerly under British protection. The capital is the town of Kuwait (population 150,000). Since 1946, when oil production began, Kuwait has become the third largest petroleum producer of the Middle East and the seventh largest in the

The Ukrainian city of Kiev, in the Soviet Union, stands on the right bank of the broad Dnieper

Lake Ritsa, Georgian resort in the Caucasus region of the U.S.S.R.

world. Oil revenues have led to the erection of fine schools, hospitals, roads and irrigation works.

● **Kuznetsk Basin** Industrial region of Siberia, east of Novosibirsk. It has the largest coal deposits of the Soviet Union and produces 15 per cent of the country's coal. The principal cities of the highly urbanised area are Novokuznetsk, Kemerovo and Prokopyevsk. The development of the Kuznetsk Basin as one of the Soviet Union's great coal and steel districts began in the 1930s.

● **Kyoto** One of the largest cities (population 1,365,000) of Japan, on the island of Honshu. Kyoto, whose name means 'capital city', was the capital of Japan's emperors from about 800 A.D. until 1868, when Tokyo was accorded this status. Of all Japan's large cities, Kyoto has remained relatively non-industrialised, and it escaped bombing during World War II. It is the centre of the country's handicraft industries, including silk fabrics and brocades, embroidery, porcelain and lacquerware. Kyoto is also a cultural centre, and is visited by many pilgrims.

● **Lahore** Largest city (population 850,000) of the Punjab, Pakistan, in the centre of a rich wheat and cotton district, and at the crossing of major railways. The old town contains mosques and other landmarks from the Mogul period of the the 16th and 17th centuries. To the south and east are the modern sections of the city, dating from the British period. Lahore is the site of Punjab University, one of the chief educational centres of Pakistan, and is the seat of the Judiciary. It is also a route centre for both the Ganges and Indus lowlands.

● **Lanchow** City (population 699,000) of northwest China, situated on the upper Yellow River. Lanchow has long been a major transportation centre on the route between China and Central Asia. From here a railway now leads towards Sinkiang and the Soviet Union. A machinery plant, making equipment for the petroleum industry, an oil refinery, and textile and chemical industries, are sited here.

● **Laos** Kingdom of South-East Asia (91,000 square miles; population 2,700,000) on the Indo-Chinese peninsula. The capital is Vientiane (population 150,000), though the royal seat is at Luang Prabang (22,000 inhabitants). Laos is an under-developed country of wooded mountain ranges and plateaux, cut by narrow valleys and gorges descending to the Mekong River. Rice is the chief food crop. Coffee, tea, cotton and tobacco are grown for export. Tropical hardwoods are also exported, as is tin, which makes up half of the total export value.

Two-thirds of the foreign trade of landlocked Laos moves through Cambodia and South Vietnam; one-third through Thailand. The Laotians, who make up most of the population, are closely related to the Thais of Thailand. Buddhism is the dominant religion. Long under Thai influence, Laos passed to French control in 1893. Together with the other States of former French Indo-China, Laos became independent in 1954. It has pursued a neutral policy in world affairs, but is periodically disturbed by civil war.

● **Latvia** (U.S.S.R., Europe) One of the Baltic countries, now a Soviet republic. Its area is 24,695 square miles and its population is 2,400,000. Latvia has three main ports: Riga, the capital, with 733,000 inhabitants, is the largest town of the three Baltic republics; Liyepaya (71,000) and Daugavpils (65,000) are much smaller. The Gulf of Riga partially divides the country into a southwestern part, Kurland, and an eastern part, Livland, including the lower basin of the Southern Dvina. The terrain is mainly low moraine, with many lakes and bogs, a quarter of it covered by forest. The river provides water power, and peat is used for fuel. Coal, oil and metals are imported for industry, largely concerned with foodstuffs, textiles (linen), timber and electrical equipment. Farming is well developed, with oats, barley, rye, potatoes, flax and sugar beet, and dairying is very important. The population consists of 62 per cent Latvians and 27 per cent Russians. The country has been in the possession of Germans, Swedes, Poles and Russians, the last since the 18th century. Latvia was independent from 1918 until 1940.

● **Lebanon** Smallest (4,000 square miles; population 2,179,000) of the Arab nations of the Middle East, on the Mediterranean Sea. The capital is Beirut. The bare Lebanon mountains extend the length of the small country, separating the fertile Bekaa valley from the narrow coastal plains. Lebanon does not grow enough food for its population, for only a quarter is cultivated, so it must import grain and sugar, in addition to manufactured goods. In return, Lebanon exports citrus and other fruits, tobacco, olives, wool, cement and handicraft articles. The tourist and transit trades, to and from other countries in the Middle East, play a major role in the Lebanese economy. Oil pipelines from Iraq and Saudi Arabia terminate at Lebanese ports. Unlike other Arab nations, which are almost entirely Moslem, Lebanon is 53 per cent Christian and 47 per cent Moslem. A majority of the Syrian Christians belong to the Maronite sect. Most of Lebanon's history has been closely associated with that of Syria, for until recently the two countries were known as the Levant States. After the First World War, they were placed under French control, which ended in 1944, when Lebanon became an independent republic, though it had declared itself so in 1941.

Lena is one of the largest Siberian rivers, at least 2.800 miles in length. It rises near Lake Baikal and flows in a large curve through the sparsely peopled Yakut A.S.S.R., before forming a large delta in the Laptev Sea. At Yakutsk, it is 4 miles wide, and the river is up to 7 miles wide in its lower course. Gold is mined in its eastern tributary, the Aldan. The River Lena is frozen over from October to June.

The Potala, Lhasa

Leningrad The second largest city of the Soviet Union. Formerly known as St Petersburg and then Petrograd, Leningrad was Russia's capital until 1917, and is still its most important port, with a population of 3,950,000. Leningrad lies at the mouth of the Neva, at the head of the Gulf of Finland, actually built upon piles on a muddy delta containing more than a hundred islands, with nearly 400 bridges connecting the city's various parts. Peter the Great founded the city (of St Petersburg) in 1703, and it became the Russian capital in 1712. It has good communications by rail and water with inland areas. From the early 18th century date the many fine palaces, squares and buildings, which are now used as museums or scientific institutes. Leningrad is a large industrial city, with shipbuilding and the manufacture of marine turbines, transport equipment, tractors, textiles, chemicals and paper. Leningrad was among the first ports of eastern Europe to feel

the effects of the Industrial Revolution, and later was the centre of the political revolution which introduced Communism to Russia. Today there are other Soviet ports in the Baltic Republics, but Leningrad is still very important, despite the fact that the port is frozen up for 2—3 months each year.

Lhasa Capital of Tibet, with a population of about 50,000. Lhasa is situated on a high plateau at an elevation of 12,000 feet. For centuries Lhasa was the Forbidden City, which only a very few foreigners dared to visit, because of its remoteness and the traditional hostility of the Tibetans. Lhasa is the holy city of the Lamaist religion (a form of Buddhism) and a pilgrimage centre for its followers. High above the city rises the golden-roofed Potala palace, the home of the Dalai Lama until 1959, when the Chinese Communist government in Peking took over administration of the country.

Lithuania (U.S.S.R., Europe) A Soviet Republic, and the southernmost and largest of the Baltic States. It has an area of 26,173 square miles and a population of 3,100,000. Lithuania has a short sandy coastline and undulating ridges of terminal moraine, rich in lakes and peat bogs. It is drained by the River Niemen, which floods during the spring. 'High' Lithuania, in the east, reaches to just over 1,000 feet. The largest town is the present capital, Vilnius (372,000 inhabitants), the former capital from 1918 to 1940 being Kaunas (306,000). The population is 80 per cent Lithuanians, and some Latvians, with their own allied languages. Agriculture is well developed, the farmers living in dispersed villages or on collective farms, cultivating half the land area, mainly with rye, oats,

Lotus blossom

Many fishermen of China live in crowded colonies of houseboats and sampans on rivers and in the harbours of cities

China's 1,400-mile Great Wall dates from 200 B.C.

potatoes, vegetables, flax, and fodder grasses for the livestock and poultry rearing, which are intensive. Since the Second World War, industry has grown rapidly, including textiles, shipbuilding and linen, and the main port of the country is Klaypeda (Memel) with a population of 140,000 Lithuania was one of the greatest nations of Europe in the 14th century, for it reached from the Baltic Sea as far as the Black Sea. Later it united with Poland and, in 1795, was taken over by Russia. Lithuania was independent between the two World Wars.

lotus A large-flowered water-lily of southern Asia. It is the sacred flower of Buddhism, representing the earth and beauty. The rootstock is edible.

Lo-yang One of China's ancient capitals, in the Yellow River plain; its population is 171,200. Lo-yang was the capital of several dynasties from the 8th century B.C. to the 10th century A.D. It was supplanted by Kaifeng in the 12th century. In recent years, ancient Lo-yang has undergone an industrial rebirth, for modern factories have been built to produce tractors, ballbearings and mining machinery.

Lucknow City of northern India, its population being 662,000. Lucknow is a transportation hub and industrial centre, producing paper, carpets, electrical supplies and optical goods. As the principal city of Uttar Pradesh, it has many beautiful old buildings and a University. The buildings include the Maharaja-palace, the white marble palace, Inimbra, and the Palace of Pearl.

Lü-ta — see Dairen.

Lvov (Lwów) 553,000 people. A frontier town, now sited in north-westernmost Ukraine on the foreland of the northern Carpathians. It was founded in 1270 on the route from Kiev to western Europe and was known as Lemberg by the Germans, for it was part of the Austro-Hungarian Empire after 1772. Its university was founded in

1656. Between the two World Wars, the city was in Poland. Originally a trading centre, industry is now well-developed, producing mining and farm machinery, omnibuses and processed foods.

● **lynx** This large wild cat, found in Northern Asia and North America, is a resident of the northern forests. Its broad feet and strong legs enable it to move easily over snowy terrain. The lynx prowls the woods at night and preys on small mammals and birds.

● **Macao** Portuguese possession in southern China, with an area of 6 square miles and a population of 169,000. The territory, south of Canton, consists of the town of Macao (where most of the Chinese population are located) and of a few small offshore islands. Macao is a fishing centre, and there is some transit trade with China. It has been under Portuguese control since 1557, and flourished as a port for China's foreign trade throughout the 18th century. Since the mid-19th century, it has been eclipsed by the rise of Hong Kong, 40 miles to the east.

● **Macassar** Largest city (population 510,000) of Celebes, Indonesia. The island's products (palm oil, coffee and copra) are collected here for export. It is a trans-shipment port for goods from Borneo, brought in small coastal vessels across the 150-mile-wide Macassar Strait. Its people are known as seafarers and play an active part in the inter-island trade that binds Indonesia together.

● **Madras** Largest city (population 2,208,000) and port on the east coast of southern India. Madras extends for miles along the flat, stormy Coromandel coast. Its shipping uses a large artificial harbour. It is the centre of southern India's largest cotton industry, with spinning mills and handlooms. Hides and skins are processed into leather here or exported. Madras was the chief British settlement of the east coast in the 17th century. Its university dates from 1857. Silk and chemical industries are new developments.

● **Madura** City (population 425,000) of southern India; 250 miles south-west of Madras. Madura has cotton and silk industries, and a large Dravidian temple built during the 14th to 17th centuries.

● **Magadan** Port (population 55,000) on the Sea of Okhotsk, in north-eastern Siberia. A new city, dating from the 1930s, Magadan is the gateway to the gold-fields of the Kolyma River area. The city

In Kyoto, Japan, street processions are held in July to celebrate the Shinto religious Gion Festival

has a truck-repair plant, a fish cannery, and a glass factory. A motor highway leads north to the mines.

● **Magnitogorsk** Soviet steel city in the Urals. It was founded in 1930 at the foot of Magnetic Mountain, a huge iron-ore deposit after which the city was named. The steel plant that rose here became the greatest in the Soviet Union, and the population of the city increased to 146,000 by 1939, and 364,000 by 1970. Early work at Magnitogorsk was assisted by Western engineers.

● **Malacca** City on the west coast of Malaya; its population is 50,000. One of the oldest towns on the Malay Peninsula, Malacca was founded by Malays, circa 1400, and became the leading political and trade centre of the region. Malacca's pre-eminence continued under the rule of the Portuguese, who arrived in 1511, and the Dutch, after 1641; but the rise of British-owned Penang caused Malacca to decline in the late 18th century. One of the Straits Settlements before the Second World War, Malacca has since become part of the new State of Malaya. The Straits Settlements were so called after the Strait of Malacca, which separates the Malay Peninsula from Sumatra.

● **Malaya** A Federation of 11 States of South-East Asia, on the Malay Peninsula; its area is 50,000 square miles; population 8.89 million. The capital is Kuala Lumpur (316,000 people). Since 1957, Malaya has been an independent federated nation within the British Commonwealth. The dense tropical jungle that covers most of Malaya has been cleared in the north and along the west coast. Here rice is raised, which meets only one-third of the country's food needs. Agriculture is chiefly devoted to export crops, particularly rubber, copra, palm oil and pineapples. Rubber plantations cover 65 per cent of the total area under cultivation and support one-third of the working population. Malaya is one of the world's largest rubber producers. Next to rubber, tin is Malaya's leading product. Iron ore and bauxite are also exported. Singapore handles most of Malaya's foreign trade. The largest centres within Malaya itself are Kuala Lumpur and the port of George Town (on Penang Island), the latter having more than 235,000 inhabitants. Only half of the country's population consists of Malays, a Moslem people using Arabic script. Chinese immigrants make up almost 40 per cent, and Indians (mostly Tamils) slightly over 10 per cent. The Malay Peninsula came under Hindu influence early, being dominated by Sumatra in the 8th century. The 15th century saw the rise of the kingdom of Malacca, which introduced Islam. The first Europeans to establish trade centres in Malaya were the Portuguese in the 16th century, followed by the Dutch in the 17th, and, finally, by the British after 1786. Under British rule, Malaya was divided into the British crown colony of the Straits Settlements (Singapore, Penang and Malacca) and the Malay States, under British protection. After the Second World War, Britain combined all Malayan areas (except Singapore) into a union, or federation, that gradually rose from being a colony (in 1946) to independence (in 1957). It now forms the nucleus of the Federation of Malaysia, formed in 1963, which contains Malaya, Sarawak and Sabah. Formerly a member of the Federation, Singapore seceded in 1965, to become an entirely independent State.

● **Malay Archipelago** Name of the vast island region between South-East Asia and Australia. Most of the island group is divided between Indonesia and the Philippines.

● **Maldive Islands** A chain of coral islets in the

Korean peasants harvest rice by hand. The stalks sometimes grow to a height of more than six feet

Indian Ocean, south-west of Ceylon. The Maldives, which have a population of 96,432, are a Moslem sultanate, under British protection since 1887 and now fully independent and a Republic since 1968. They live by trading, seafaring, fishing and agriculture, growing coconuts, millet, fruit and nuts. The capital is Male, with 10,875 inhabitants.

• **Manchuria** Large region (600,000 square miles; population 73 million) of north-eastern China, long disputed among China, Russia and Japan. Since the early 20th century, Manchuria has become a great pioneering country of expanding agriculture. Virgin prairie is being gradually put under the plough, especially in the north; the principal crops being soya beans, kaoliang (a sorghum), millet, wheat and maize. Agricultural development has been accompanied by industrial expansion, with steel mills at An-shan and Pen-ki, coal-mines at Fushun, and supply manufacturing industries at Shen-yang, Lü-ta (Port Arthur-Dairen) and Harbin. Manchuria was the country of the Manchu people, who conquered China in the 17th century and founded the Manchu dynasty. The modern development of Manchuria began about 1900 in connection with railway construction by the Russians. As a result of Japan's victory in the Russo-Japanese war, in 1905, southern Manchuria came under Japanese influence. Industrialisation and settlement by the Chinese continued after the Chinese revolution of 1911. From 1931 to 1945, all Manchuria was ruled by Japan as the nominally independent state of Manchukuo.

• **Mandalay** Second city (population 360,000) of Burma, in the central part of the country. It was the last capital of the Burmese kings, up until its capture by British troops in 1885. The city suffered heavy damage during World War II, when it fell to the Japanese (1942 to 1945). Mandalay is well-known for its temples and pagodas, and is the religious capital of Burma.

• **manganese** A ferro-alloy which is unique, because it is indispensable in the production of every kind of steel. It is used to remove oxygen and sulphur. The Soviet Union is the only major steel-producing nation with domestic manganese resources. Other leading producers are India, Ghana and South Africa.

• **Manila** Former capital and chief port of the Philippines, with a population of 1,582,000. One of its eastern suburbs is Quezon City (585,100), named after the first President. Quezon City was officially designated as the capital in 1948, but the government continues to function in Manila. Divided into two sections by the short Pasig River, Manila's south side consists of Intramuros, the old walled city. On the north bank stands its newer section, containing most of the large industrial establishments of the Philippines, processing rice, sugar cane, tobacco, coconuts, hemp and other products. Manila was founded in 1571; its Santo Tomas University dates from 1611. During the Spanish-American War (1898), Admiral Dewey defeated the Spanish fleet in Manila Bay. In World War II, the city was heavily bombed by the Japanese in 1941, and further damaged in the battle for its recapture in 1945. Most of the historic buildings, dating from the 400 years of Spanish rule, were destroyed.

• **Mecca** Religious centre of the Moslem world, in the Hejaz hills of Saudi Arabia; its population is 250,000. Mecca is the birthplace of Mohammed and the site of the Kaaba, foremost shrine of Moslem pilgrimage. The Kaaba is a small cube-shaped building, in the court of the Great Mosque, which contains the sacred black stone. Pilgrims

The Kaaba in Mecca

kiss the stone and walk seven times around the Kaaba itself as part of their devotions. About 100,000 Moslems from all over the world visit Mecca yearly in the pilgrimage, known as the *hadj*. Its harbour is Djidda, the largest port of Saudi Arabia.

• **Medan** Largest city (population 360,000) of Sumatra, in Indonesia, on the north-east coast. It is at the centre of the most populated part of the island. Medan itself is situated 15 miles from the sea, on the shallow Deli River. Rubber, tobacco, coffee, tea and palm oil are produced. Its export trade is handled by the outer port of Belawan.

• **Medina** City (population 60,000) of Saudi Arabia and one of the sacred cities of the Moslem world — second only to Mecca, 200 miles to the south. Mohammed fled from Mecca in A.D. 622 and came to Medina, where he was successful in establishing the nucleus of the Moslem world community. The flight, known as the *hegira*, is the initial date in the Moslem calendar. Medina is the site of Mohammed's grave.

• **Mekong River** A great river of South-East Asia; 2,600 miles long. It rises in the eastern Tibetan highlands and flows southward through China, Laos, Cambodia and South Vietnam to the South China Sea near Saigon, in its large delta, a densely populated rice-producing area. Canyon-like gorges make its upper course largely unnavigable. The greater part of the boundary between Laos and Thailand is formed by the Mekong.

• **Meshed** City (population 417,171) of north-east Iran, 450 miles east of Teheran. It is a major pilgrimage centre for Shiite Moslems, who visit the golden-domed shrine of one of the founders of their

sect. The city was reached in 1957 by a railway from Teheran. It is a famous carpet-producing centre.

• **Moldavia** (U.S.S.R., Europe) Soviet Republic, situated between the Ukraine and Romania; founded in 1940 from the former Moldavian A.S.S.R. (itself founded in 1924 and Russian-held since 1812) and Bessarabia, which was gained from Romania. The western boundary is the Prut River and, to the south, the northern arm of the Danube delta. Moldavia has an area of 13,012 square miles and a population of 3.6 million inhabitants, mostly Moldavian, of mixed Romanian-Slavonic origin. The language is similar to Romanian, though written in Russian script. The land consists largely of fertile black soils (*chernozem*), which, coupled with a mild climate, provide excellent conditions for the production of wine and fruit, giving rise to fruit-canning and viticulture; indeed, Moldavia is the leading wine-producer of the Soviet Union. Other crops are sugar beet, sunflowers, tobacco, and flowers such as roses and lavender, which are used to produce perfumes and oils. Maize and winter wheat can be grown, and live-stock rearing is important. The capital of the Republic is Kishinev (357,000 inhabitants).

• **Moluccas** An Indonesian island group between Celebes and West Irian, with an area of about 35,000 square miles and a population of over 700,000. The Moluccas used to be known as the Spice Islands, because of their pepper, cloves, nutmeg and cinnamon. The spice trade flourished particularly from the 15th to the 17th century, and is still important, together with sago, timber, pearls, rice and copra.

• **Mongolia** A large region of north-central Asia, between Siberia's Lake Baikal and China proper, with an area of 1,200,000 square miles. It is a high plateau, consisting largely of the Gobi desert region, and is the country of the Mongols, who number about 5 million and speak a language (Mongol) that is probably related to the Turkic languages. The Mongols are mainly nomadic herders, raising sheep, goats, cattle, horses and camels. Hides and wool are the principal products. During the 12th and 13th centuries, under Genghis Khan and his successors, the Mongols conquered a vast empire that included most of Asia and extended far into eastern Europe. Later, most of the Mongols gradually passed under Chinese rule. The two traditional divisions of Mongolia are: Inner Mongolia, where Chinese rule has been relatively firm; and Outer Mongolia, now the People's Republic of Mongolia, where Russian influence has been much stronger.

The busy Neva River at Leningrad, U.S.S.R., a Baltic port which is ice-free for seven months of the year, and therefore of vital importance to Russia

Inner Mongolia has been made an autonomous region by the Chinese Communists. Its area of 600,000 square miles equals that of Outer Mongolia, but Inner Mongolia's population of more than 13 million includes a majority to the ratio of 10 to 1 over the Mongols. The Chinese are farmers along the margins of the desert, especially in the irrigated belt along the great northward bend of the Yellow River (Hwang Ho) near to Paotow, site of a new steel plant and the largest city. The Mongols are herders in the dry steppe and the desert. Inner Mongolia includes the rich timber lands of the Khingan Mountains. The regional capital is Huhehot (population 148,000), whose name means 'blue city' in Mongol.

Outer Mongolia has been known since 1924 as the Mongolian People's Republic, and gained independence from China in 1921. It has an area of 600,000 square miles and a population of 1.2 million. The capital is Ulan Bator (population 254,000). Livestock herding is by far the most important economic activity, even though large areas are now being brought under the plough. Small deposits of gold and oil are exploited. Some coal is mined near Ulan Bator. A railway that forms a new link between Russia and China was built in 1956. In 1961, Mongolia was admitted to the United Nations.

● **monsoon** This term is derived from an Arabic word meaning 'season'. It applies to the periodic winds that completely reverse their prevailing direction from season to season. Monsoons are most prominent in South and East Asia. In the summer, intense heating of the Asian mainland produces a low-pressure area over the continent, causing warm, moist sea winds to blow from the south-west. In the winter, as the land cools, a high-pressure area is established over the Asian mainland and causes a cold, dry wind to blow from the north-east toward the sea. In India and China, the timely arrival of the rainy summer monsoon may often mean the difference between drought and a plentiful harvest.

● **Moscow** is the capital of the Soviet Union and its largest city, with a population exceeding 5 million in 1959. Immediately around it are other large industrial towns, such as Perovo and Babushkin. In 1960, the boundaries of the city were extended and its area now exceeds 340 square miles, with a population of over 7 million. Moscow is the centre of an extensive network of roads and railways and, as the city lies on the River Moskva — with the construction of the Moscow—Volga Canal in the 1930s, and the Mariinsk Canal (Volga Baltic Waterway) — it can be reached by river vessels and barges from the White, Baltic and Black Seas.

Moscow has grown up around the Kremlin, a walled citadel which contains government palaces, cathedrals, and museums. Adjoining it is Red Square, a military parade-ground, where the tomb of Lenin is situated. Moscow's street plan is largely radiai, connected with wide, circular boulevards. A fine underground railway system was constructed in the 1930s and is being expanded. Moscow's industries are an epitome of the whole region around it: machine tools, precision instruments, motor vehicles, food processing and distilling, textiles and clothing, and printing. Soviet education and culture are also largely centralised in the capital. Moscow's new university building, 32 stories high, lies in the new south-western part of the city, and there are many technical institutes. Other cultural centres are the Bolshoi Theatre, the Moscow Art Theatre and the Tretyakov Art Gallery.

Moscow was founded in 1147, and was the capital of Russia from the 14th century until the seat of government was moved to St Petersburg (Leningrad) in 1712, resuming its status as capital after the 1917 Revolution. Moscow was burned down by Napoleon in 1812, but was not taken by the Germans in 1941. Its position as the capital of the U.S.S.R. is somewhat far removed from the

vast new lands beyond the Urals. The Moscow coal-field nearby is a large metal-producing area.

● **Mount Everest** Highest point in the world, in the Himalayas; its elevation is 29,028 feet. The mountain, situated on the border between Nepal and Tibet, attracted mountain climbers after 1921. After many unsuccessful attempts, the top was finally reached by a British expedition under Sir John Hunt in 1953, the successful climbers being Edmund Hillary and Sherpa Tenzing.

● **Mukden** — see Shenyang.

Mulberry branch with silkworm

● **mulberry** A widely cultivated tree bearing an edible raspberry-like fruit. There are three types: the red mulberry of the eastern United States, the black mulberry of Iran, and the white mulberry of the Far East. The white mulberry's leaves serve as food for silkworms. Silk-growers harvest the leaves three to four times a year.

● **Murmansk** A town with 309,000 inhabitants which is, along with Norilsk in Siberia, the world's northernmost town. Murmansk is situated on the northern part of the Kila peninsula at 69°N latitude, corresponding to northern Alaska, and it is the most important Russian port on the Barents Sea, being virtually ice-free because of the North Atlantic drift. Murmansk was founded during the Great War in 1915, but still had only 9,000 inhabitants in 1926. Its main industries are fishing and shipbuilding. The port is a naval base, exports apatite from nearby mines, and has a railway link with Leningrad.

● **Nagasaki** City of Japan, on the island of Kyushu; its population is 405,000. Nagasaki was one of the two Japanese cities destroyed by atomic bombs in August 1945 (Hiroshima was the first). It is now rebuilt, and is again an important trading and industrial centre. The oldest foreign-trade port of Japan, Nagasaki was visited by Portuguese, Spanish and Dutch traders as early as the 16th century. During the period of Japan's isolation, Dutch traders were confined to the island of Dejima, in Nagasaki Bay. Western influences, such as Christianity and science, first entered Japan through Nagasaki. The city's industries include shipyards and fish- and fruit-canning plants; canned tangerines are a speciality.

● **Nagoya** Third largest city of Japan, on the island of Honshu; its population is 1,935,000. Nagoya is a major industrial centre. In addition to its traditional products (cotton goods, clocks and watches), Nagoya produces ships, railway rolling stock, motor-cars, and many kinds of machinery and chemicals.

● **Nagpur** City (population 643,000) of central India, situated at the crossing of major railways. It is the outlet for India's manganese ore, which is mined nearby. Cotton mills, and paper and timber industries, are also located at Nagpur.

● **Nanking** City (population 1,419,000) of eastern China, on the lower Yangtze River. Nanking was the capital of China under the Nationalist regime from 1928 to 1949. Its name means 'southern capital', while Peking means 'northern capital'. Nanking occupies a site where many of China's ancient cities have stood, the present city dating from the 14th century, and its older portions are surrounded by a wall more than 20 miles long. Its streets are lined with fine examples of Chinese architecture, while the picturesque, hilly surroundings contain parks, lakes and hot springs. Tombs of the early Ming emperors, who had their capital here (1368—1431), and a memorial honouring Dr Sun Yat Sen (1867—1925), the father of the Chinese Republic, are outside the city walls. Nanking's industries are found in the suburb of Pukow, across the Yangtze. They are, namely: cotton and satin mills, chemical plants, electrical goods, and machine tool and camera factories. Nanking's educational institutions include China's oldest University and the Purple Mountain Observatory, which date from 1385.

● **Negev** A desert area in southern Israel, occupying more than half of the country. The northern margins of the Negev are gradually being irrigated and colonised, thanks to the Yarkon-Negev water pipeline, part of the National Water Carrier Project, which will carry water from the Sea of Galilee to the South. A highway leads through the desert from Beersheba, its northern gateway, to the port of Eilat, on the Gulf of Aqaba, at its southern tip. An oil pipeline goes from Eilat to Haifa. Copper and oil are found in the Negev.

● **Nepal** Mountain kingdom (56,000 square miles; population 9.5 million) of southern Asia, in the Himalayas. The capital is Katmandu (population 195,260). Nepal extends from the snow-capped peaks of the Himalayas on the Tibetan border to a swampy jungle along the Indian frontier. Nepal is an under-developed country, trading small amounts of hardwoods, hides and farm products (rice, jute, oil-seeds, cane sugar) for Indian manufactured goods. But it does have five hydroelectric power stations which help to run new chemical, jute, leather and sugar industries. Nepal's medicinal herbs are sold throughout the world. The population is made up of the Newari people, related to the Tibetans, and the Gurkha ruling group, whose language is derived from Sanscrit. The Gurkha warriors conquered Nepal in 1769, and the modern Gurkha soldier serves in the British and Indian armies, earning a great deal of foreign currency for Nepal. Until recently, Nepal was a feudal monarchy that followed a strict policy of isolation. After the partition of India, Nepal established relations with other nations and formed a constitutional monarchy. The first road from India to Katmandu was completed in 1953, and is the way of import for textiles, salt, oil and many other goods from India.

Nicobar Islands A chain of islands in the Bay of Bengal, south of the Andaman Islands. Part of India, the Nicobars are inhabited by a primitive Malay people living in round pile-dwellings.

● **Nizhni Tagil** Steel centre (population, 378,000) in the Ural Mountains of the Soviet Union. It is situated at the foot of Blagodat Mountain, an iron-ore deposit. Nizhni Tagil has two steel plants: an old one, founded in 1725, which was reconstructed in the Soviet period, and a huge new plant built in the 1940s. Other industries are a cement factory, a coke-chemical plant and a railway-wagon shop, while platinum is mined nearby.

● **Norilsk** Industrial city (population 136,000) of northern Siberia, near the Yenisei River. It is situated in an area where the average January temperature is 20°C below zero. Founded in the late 1930s at the site of copper and nickel mines, the early part of its development was achieved with forced labour.

Novokuznetsk is a new town, founded in 1934, near to the little town of Kuznetsk in the Kuznetsk basin, and had 499,000 inhabitants in 1970. It is the largest steel centre of Siberia, and has aluminium and chemical industries.

Novosibirsk Largest city (population 1,161,000) of Siberia, situated where the Trans-Siberian railway crosses the Ob River, and founded in the 1890s during the construction of the railway. It grew rapidly, out-stripping the older Siberian cities. In the Soviet period, Novosibirsk has become a major producer of machinery, fabricating steel supplied by the nearby Kuznetsk Basin. Heavy machine tools, presses and mining equipment are made here, as are power generators for Siberia's new hydro-electric stations. One of these stations has been built just south of Novosibirsk on the Ob River. The city, whose name means New Siberia, typifies the industrial development of Siberia during the Soviet period. Among Novosibirsk's sights are the railway station (the largest in Siberia), and the huge dome of the opera house. A new 'science city' rose on the city's southern outskirts in the late 1950s. It contains schools and research institutions working for Siberia's development.

Nutmeg

nutmeg One of the major spices native to the Moluccas, the traditional Spice Islands of Indonesia. It is the hard, strongly flavoured seed of the nutmeg tree, usually used in pulverised form, which is now also cultivated elsewhere in Indonesia, as well as in the West Indies and Brazil.

Ob River A great Siberian river, rising in the Altai Mountains and flowing 2,700 miles north to the Arctic Ocean. Most of its course lies in the flat West Siberian plain, where the Ob (sometimes as much as 25 miles wide) winds its way slowly through uninhabited marshy woodlands. It is navigable, except during the winter, when it freezes from November to June. The Irtysh River is its longest tributary, and Novosibirsk its main river port.

Odessa is situated on the Black Sea coast, on a marine terrace rising suddenly up to a height of 150 feet above sea level. Founded in 1795, after the defeat of the Turks, it is now, with a population of 822,000, the fifth largest city of the Ukraine. For long it has been the main export centre for the grain, oilseeds and sugar produced in the Black Earth region of the Ukraine. Today the city extends for 6 miles along the Black Sea coast and is a much-visited tourist centre with mineral baths. It has shipyards, metal and chemical works, and spinning mills. Odessa also has oil refineries and flour mills. Odessa was the centre of the 1905 uprising and played a leading part in the Revolution of 1917—20.

Okhotsk, Sea of An arm of the North Pacific, on the Siberian coast. It is bounded by Kamchatka and the Kuriles in the east, and Sakhalin Island in the west. The coldest part of the Pacific basin, it generally freezes over in its northern section during the winter. Foggy weather frequently hinders shipping using its ports, of which Magadan is the largest. The sea is rich in salmon and in crabs, especially along the Kamchatka coast.

Oman Arab region (82,000 square miles; population 750,000) in the south-east corner of the Arabian Peninsula. The capital is Muscat (6,000), but it has lost its importance to Matrah (14,000). In the fertile areas grow the famous Batinah dates, fruit, and sugar cane. Oil is drilled on a commercial scale. In 1956 an unsuccessful uprising resulted in armed clashes. The area was under British protection for nearly a century, and in 1970 it became an independent sovereign state known as the Sultanate of Oman.

Omsk A Siberian city (population 821,000) at the crossing of the Trans-Siberian railway and the Irtysh River. Situated in the heart of West Siberia's farm belt, Omsk grew up around an old fortress (founded in 1716) and was chartered in 1804. It developed rapidly in the early 20th century, after the railway had made Western Siberia accessible to new settlers. The industries of Omsk produce farm machinery, locomotives and rolling stock. The city processes lumber, floated along the Irtysh River, and the farm products (wheat, butter) of the surrounding countryside. Its oil refinery is supplied with crude petroleum brought by pipe-line from Tuymazy, in European Russia.

Opium poppy

opium poppy A tall herb cultivated since antiquity as the source of opium. The drug consists of the dried milky juice of the poppy and is obtained from the unripe seed capsules of the plant. Opium contains morphine, codeine and other narcotics used in medicine to relieve pain and induce sleep. The plant mainly belongs to Central Asia and the western parts of the Middle East. Its growth is limited and carefully controlled in an effort to stop narcotic trafficking and addiction.

Orangutan

orangutan Of all the great apes, it is best adapted to life in trees, for its armspread reaches seven-and-a-half feet, enabling the animal to swing easily from branch to branch. The orangutan is easily recognised by its long brick-red hair, weighs up to 200 pounds, and dwells in the tropical forests of Borneo and Sumatra, living entirely on fruit.

Osaka Second largest city (population 3.15 million) of Japan, on the south coast of the island of Honshu. Centre of an industrial belt that includes Kobe and other cities, Osaka's industries include textiles, ship-building, steel, machinery and chemicals. A large town even in the 16th century, Osaka has many canals.

Padang City (population 325,000) on the west coast of Sumatra, Indonesia. It is the port for a fertile highland area with volcanic soils which produce tobacco, coffee and coconuts. A railway leads to the highland town of Bukittinggi and to nearby coal-mines.

Pakistan This was a Moslem republic (365,000 square miles population 94 million) of South Asia, consisting of a Western section and an Eastern section, separated by 1,000 miles of Indian territory, until 1972, when, after a short war the Eastern territory established its independence and became known as Bangladesh. This situation arose because social and political conditions were becoming more favourable to the Eastern section than the Western section. Thus the latter territory brought troops into the east, captured the leaders and indulged in guerilla warfare. This resulted in 10 million East Pakistanis pouring into India giving that country a large refugee problem. On behalf of these refugees and for her own political reasons India intervened, sending troops to both East and West Pakistan to force a withdrawal by the West Pakistan soldiers. This move was successful — hence the new country of Bangladesh.

The origin of the united Pakistan was in the 1930s when India had the idea for it to become the Moslem homeland of India. The supporters of the scheme coined the name Pakistan using the initials of Punjab, Afghania and Kashmir plus

St Basil's Cathedral, in Red Square, Moscow

the ending 'stan' which means 'land'. Since Pak is also the Urdu word for spiritually pure or clean, Pakistan also means 'land of the pure'. The state was created in 1947, at the time when British India was partitioned. Among the problems that faced the new state were the settlement of Moslem refugees from India, and the replacement of non-Moslem administrators who had left for India.

Bangladesh (55,126 sq miles) population 51 million. The capital is Dacca and Bengali is the language spoken by the majority. Bangladesh lies in the humid tropical delta of the Ganges and Brahmaputra Rivers, where there is too much water. Rice is the staple food crop, and tea and jute are grown for export. Bangladesh accounts for 80% of the world's jute production. Agriculture employs 82% of the population and 64% of the land area is under cultivation. Bangladesh is also a great fish producing nation. Its industries include jute, sugar and paper mills, aluminium works, hosiery and fertiliser factories, and a shipyard. There is natural gas as Titas.

(West) Pakistan (310,403 square miles; population 43 million). It is a hot, dry region traversed by the life-giving Indus River and enclosed by rugged mountain ranges. Its economy, based on irrigated agriculture, produces wheat and cotton. Cattle and sheep raising yield wool and hides. There is some mining of coal, salt, petroleum, chrome, limestone and gypsum. Industry employs 10 per cent of the population in cottage textile industries, chocolate, tanning and paint factories. The largest city and port is Karachi with a population of over 2 million. The new capital is at Islamabad near Rawalpindi. The population of West Pakistan speaks Urdu, a language closely related to the Hindi of India but employing the Arabic alphabet. Relations with India have been dominated by disputes over Kashmir, water rights on the Indus River, and recently India's support for Bangladesh against them.

● **Palembang** Largest city (population 528,000) of southern Sumatra, in Indonesia. It is the economic centre for nearby rubber plantations and oil-fields. The city has large oil refineries.

● **Palestine** Historical Biblical region of the Middle East, between the Mediterranean Sea and the Jordan River. Regarded as the Holy Land by Jews, Christians and Moslems, Palestine has had a complex history. Because of its strategic position on the route from Egypt to Mesopotamia it was a prize sought by many empires. It was the site of the early Hebrew kingdoms, whose rule ended with the Roman conquest in 63 B.C. Palestine came under the Moslems in the 7th century, and gradually declined in importance after 1517, until the end of Ottoman Turkish rule during World War I. After 1920, the country was under British administration, though strife between Jews — who had begun to immigrate in 1870 — and Arabs soon developed. In 1947, the United Nations General Assembly recommended the partition of Palestine into independent Jewish and Arab States. Britain withdrew in 1948, and the Jewish State of Israel was formed. As a result of the Arab-Israeli war of 1948—49, most of the area allocated to the Arab State passed to Jordan. Relations between Jews and Arabs are still extremely strained, following the outbreak of hostilities in June, 1967, and a final political settlement in the area is still awaited (1972).

● **Pamir** means 'the roof of the world', and is a Central Asian highland plateau, with an average elevation of 10,000 feet. The Pamir is the central hub of the great Asian mountain systems: the Himalayas, extending towards the south-east; the Tien Shan, toward the north-east; the Kun-lun to the east; and the Hindu Kush, towards the south-west. The Pamir is part of the Tadzhik Republic of the Soviet Union. Its sparse population of 60,000 combine meagre agriculture and sheep- and goat-raising.

● **Paotow** City (population 500,000) of Inner Mongolia, on the great Yellow River and situated on a railway from Peking. It was, for a long time, a trade centre for Mongol hides and wool with a population of about 80,000. The new Chinese steel industry and coal deposits account for Paotow's recent enormous increase in population.

● **paper** In antiquity, the stem of the papyrus plant — growing in the Nile swamps of Egypt — was converted into a paperlike material. Later, an Asiatic paper-mulberry provided the Chinese and Japanese with a substance considerably nearer to modern paper; people also used cotton and linen rags as raw material. Today, most paper is made from wood. First, small logs are reduced to pulp by mechanical or chemical methods. The resulting slurry is converted into continuous sheets of paper by a 100-foot-long machine that draws off water, and presses and dries the sheets to form paper. About 20 per cent of all the pulp products are newsprint and 35 per cent are paperboard. Leading producers of newsprint are the United States, Canada, Britain, Sweden and Germany. Canada, which accounts for 50 per cent of the world's supply, is by far the largest exporter. Both the United States and Britain import newsprint. The United States produces two-thirds of the world's paperboard.

● **peanut** The peanut, also known as the groundnut, is an annual herb with yellow flowers; it belongs to the pea family. Its flower stalks bend down after pollination and push the pods into the ground, where they ripen. The ripe pod contains two oil-rich seeds, the size of hazelnuts. Originally from Brazil, it was brought to Africa over a century ago. There it is now cultivated on a commercial scale. Peanuts are also grown in India, China and in the United States. In good soils and with careful cultivation, yields as high as 70 cwts per acre can be obtained. The oil extracted from unshelled peanuts is used for margarine and as an edible oil. The press cake is a high-grade livestock feed.

Pearl fishing

● **pearl fishing** A pearl is a hard, smooth mass deposited around a foreign particle inside the shell of molluscs, such as pearl oysters. The oysters are found in most warm seas in the vicinity of coasts on underwater rock ledges. Since many of the natural oyster banks have been exhausted, most pearls are now obtained from cultivated beds. In pearl culture, practised in Japan especially, foreign particles are inserted, and the oysters are then left in the water in large wire baskets for about two years before being opened.

● **Pechora** A river of north European Russia, rising in the northern Urals. It is over 1,000 miles long and reaches the Barents Sea at Naryan-Mar. It flows through uninhabited forestland, and is frozen for four months of the year, while its mouth is frozen for a much longer period. The Pechora's upper course is used for the transport of coal, ore and timber.

● **Peking** Capital (population 7 million) of China, situated in the North China plain. It lies about 70 miles from its port of Tientsin, and near natural gateways to Mongolia and Manchuria. Peking proper consists of two adjoining walled cities: the Inner City (the Manchu city), dating from the 15th century, and the Outer City to the south, built a century later. Inside the Inner City was the Imperial City; and that, in turn, enclosed the walled and moated Forbidden City. The Forbidden City, which was the emperor's palace, is now

Moscow lines both banks of the Moskva River. The park of the Kremlin is seen in the foreground

a museum. Modern government offices stand just west of the Palace Museum, around two lakes. South of the former palace is Tien-an-Men (Gate of Heavenly Peace), where Chinese leaders review parades on holidays. South-east of the Palace Museum is the former Legation Quarter, with department stores, hotels and theatres. The Outer City, south of the Inner City, contains business districts and the Temple of Heaven, set in a park. In modern times, Peking has expanded beyond its walls, particularly toward the former Summer Palace (now a park) in the north-west. The city limits of Peking now include a rural population of 2 million farmers. The city's industries include a steel plant, a railway-wagon factory, cotton mills, and plants producing machinery, matches, glass and cement. Peking is famous for its handicrafts (enamelware, embroidery, carved ivory and jade). The city is China's leading educational centre. Three universities — Peking, Tsinghwa and Central University — are situated in the north-western suburbs. Since the earliest days of China's history there has been a city where Peking now stands. As one capital was destroyed, another rose on the same site. Kublai Khan, the Mongol emperor of China, had a capital here, visited by Marco Polo, circa 1275. Peking (which means 'northern capital') was China's capital for 500 years under the Ming and Manchu emperors. Under the Nationalist regime (after 1928), the seat of government was established at Nanking ('southern capital'). During that period, Peking was known as Peiping, which means 'northern peace'. In 1949, the Chinese Communists made it once again the national capital.

● **Penang Island** (110 square miles; population 778,747) lies off the west coast of the Malay Peninsula. On its north-east coast is the city of George Town (population 300,000), the site of the first British settlement in Malaya, founded in 1786. It succeeded Malacca as the regional trade centre, but was in turn supplanted by Singapore in the mid-19th century. One of the Straits Settlements before World War II, the State of Penang has since become one of the 11 States of Malaya, and thus one of the 13 States which comprise the Federation of Malaysia.

● **Penki** Important industrial city (population 449,000) of China, in southern Manchuria; situated on the railway leading from Shenyang to North Korea. It has large coal-mines, and coke-chemical and steel plants.

Pepper

● **pepper** The world's most important spice, obtained from the berry (peppercorn) of a tropical shrub which is native to Indonesia. The dried, unripe berries yield black pepper, and the dried, ripe seeds provide white pepper. Its pungent taste is caused by a resin in the peppercorn. Indonesia furnishes about 70 per cent of the world's supply.

● **Perm** A town with 850,000 inhabitants, and situated west of the Urals as the main port on the Kama River. It was founded in 1780 as the centre

for the administration of the Ural region, and it was an important centre for access to Siberia before the coming of the trans-continental railway. Industries include machinery and shipbuilding, mining gear, and chemical works. A vast new hydro-electric scheme nearby was completed in 1954. The city was known as Molotov from 1940 to 1957, a name now applied to one of its modern suburbs.

● **Persepolis** Ancient capital of Persia, 30 miles north-east of modern Shiraz. It was founded in 500 B.C. by Darius the Great, and ruined 200 years later by Alexander the Great, during his conquest of Persia. The ruins include the remains of palaces standing on a platform that is reached by a great stairway.

● **Persian Gulf** An arm of the Indian Ocean between Iran (Persia) and the Arabian Peninsula. It is known for its oppressively hot and humid summer climate, and for its pearl fisheries. The Persian Gulf has, in recent years, become a major traffic lane for tankers carrying petroleum from the rich oil-fields of Iran, Iraq, Kuwait, Saudi Arabia and Bahrein, especially to Europe.

● **Philippines** Island republic (115,000 square miles; population 37 million) of South-East Asia, in the Pacific Ocean. The capital is Quezon City, officially, but government affairs are still carried on in Manila. Largest of the 7,100 islands are Luzon, with almost half of the total population, Mindanao, Samar, Negroes, Palawan, Panay, Mindoro, Leyte and Cebu. The islands are mostly of volcanic origin on three or four mountain chains, and earthquakes and eruptions are frequent. The highest point is Apo, 9,690 feet, on Mindanao. There is a humid tropical climate and naturally fertile soil. Many of the small islands have no population and are unnamed. The principal food crops are rice and maize. Exports include copra and coconut oil, cane sugar, abaca (Manila hemp), timber, iron and chrome ores, canned pineapples and tobacco. There are few large industrial establishments in the country. More than half of the foreign trade is with the United States.

Most of the people of the Philippines belong to the Malay-Polynesian language group and are known as Filipinos. They constitute the only Christian nation in this part of the world, for Roman Catholicism, a heritage of the islands' Spanish conquerors, is professed by about four-fifths of the population. The Christian Filipinos are divided into eight ethnic groups, differing from each other in language and culture. The largest are the Visayans (in the islands between Luzon and Mindanao), and the Tagalogs and Ilocanos in Luzon. In addition to English and Spanish, Tagalog, akin to Malay, has been made a national language. The Moro people of Mindanao are Moslems, and there are some pagan peoples in the north.

The first Europeans to visit the Philippines were those of the globe-circling expedition of Magellan, who was killed here in 1521. The Spaniards conquered the islands later in the 16th century, and named them after King Philip II of Spain in 1542.

Masked pigs

In 1898, the United States acquired the islands as a result of the Spanish-American War. Under increasing pressure for independence, the Commonwealth of the Philippines was established in 1935, with Manuel Quezon as its first President. After a period of United States tutelage, interrupted by Japanese occupation during World War II, the Philippines became an entirely independent republic in 1946.

● **pig, masked** A Far Eastern breed of the domestic pig, with deeply furrowed faces and loose jowls. Sows are remarkable for their large litters of 15 to 20 piglets.

● **pitcher plant** An insect-eating plant of the tropical forests of South-East Asia (especially Borneo and Sumatra). Its leaves form pitcher-like containers, in which captured insects are digested in an acid secretion.

● **platinum** A greyish-white rare metal, noted for its resistance to ordinary acids and to heat. It is used in jewellery, in dentistry, in the chemical industry (for laboratory crucibles) and in the electrical industry (for contact points). Most of the world's platinum is mined in the Urals of the Soviet Union and in the Sudbury nickel district of Canada; Colombia and South Africa are other producers.

● **Poona** City of India, 75 miles south-east of Bombay. The city is an industrial centre (population 721,000), with cotton and carpet mills, and chemical and ordnance factories.

● **Port Arthur** Naval base (population 126,000) of China on the Yellow Sea, in southern Manchuria. Originally developed by Russia, it passed to Japan in 1905. After World War II, it was a joint Soviet-Chinese naval base until 1954, when the Russians withdrew. Port Arthur (called Lüshun in Chinese) forms a joint municipality with Dairen (Talien), and is known as Lüshun-Talien, or Lü-ta.

● **Prokopyevsk** Large coal-mining town (population 275,000) in the Kuznetsk Basin of Siberia. Its mines produce about one-fourth of all the coal obtained from the basin.

● **Punjab** A region divided between India and Pakistan. The Punjab (a word meaning 'five rivers') is named from the five tributaries of the Indus River, whose waters are used to irrigate the region. The Punjab is a major wheat, sugar cane and cotton-growing area. Its largest city is Lahore, in Pakistan. The people of the Punjab speak the Punjabi language, partly derived from Sanscrit.

● **Pusan** Second largest city (population 1,878,000) of South Korea, on the south coast. Pusan is the Korean port nearest to Japan, from which it is separated by a strait more than 100 miles wide. It is the country's chief trading centre.

● **Pyongyang** Capital (population 1,500,000) of North Korea, on the Taedong River. It is the processing city for a large agricultural district. Most of its industries produce food and consumer goods. South-west of Pyongyang is the Yellow Sea port of Nampo, where a zinc-smelter operates.

● **Qatar** Independent sheikhdom (4,000 square miles; population 130,000), on the Persian Gulf, in special treaty relations with Britain but no longer protected by her. The capital is Doha (population 100,000). Oil was struck there in 1939, and Qatar has been a commercial producer of petroleum since World War II.

Buddhist pagoda (temple) in Peking, China

●**Rangoon** Capital of Burma and a leading port (population 1,758,731) of South-East Asia. It ranks next to Bombay and Calcutta among seaports on the Indian Ocean. Rangoon handles 80 per cent of Burma's trade, exporting rice, teakwood and petroleum. Its overseas shipping has given it a cosmopolitan air. Rangoon is the most modern and westernised town in the country, and lies on an arm of the Irrawaddy delta. Among the city's sights is the great Shwe Dagon Pagoda (the Golden Pagoda), one of the best-known temples in the Buddhist world. During World War II, the city suffered more from bombing than any other Asian capital, except Manila. Its post-war recovery was slowed by civil war in the hinterland.

Reindeer moss

●**reindeer moss** A grey, branched lichen growing widely in the northern tundra. During the winter, when it is perhaps the only plant to survive under the snow, patches of reindeer moss supply food for the caribou and the domesticated reindeer.

Indian rhinoceros

●**rhinoceros, Indian** This one-horned rhino is the largest found in Asia. A big male may weigh two tons. Its range is now largely restricted to the jungle at the foot of the Himalayas.

Rice

●**rice** The staple food grain for over a half of the world's population. It constitutes 70 to 90 per cent of the diet of Asians; failure of the rice crop means famine for millions. Rice grains consist almost entirely of starch; only the hull (or husk) contains vitamins. Milled rice — the kind most widely used for human consumption — has had the hulls rubbed off. People who eat only this polished rice are subject to vitamin-deficiency diseases, such as beriberi, which shows a lack of vitamin B, and need fruits and vegetables to supplement their diet.

. Rice culture is a most laborious process. Seedlings are raised in special seedbeds and are transplanted, by hand, into flooded fields. As the harvest approaches, the fields are drained, and the rice is left to ripen. Areas favoured with high temperatures and plenty of water yield several rice crops a year. Rice yields more food per unit of land than any other crop, except potatoes. It may be grown year after year on the same land, and it requires only a small percentage of the yield to be saved for use as seed for next year's crop. Besides its use as food, rice also provides straw for: thatching roofs; fuel, feed and fertiliser; making footwear and baskets; paper-making. It can be used to make alcoholic beverages, such as saké and arak. In the United States and other countries outside Asia, rice is grown using modern mechanised methods. The world's largest rice producers are China, India, Japan and Pakistan, but these populous countries consume their entire supply and have no surplus for export. Only about 5 per cent of the world's rice supply enters into international trade. The largest exporters are Burma, Thailand, Laos, Vietnam and the United States. The major importers are India, Malaya and Ceylon.

●**Riga** (733,000 inhabitants in 1970) is the capital of the Soviet Republic of Latvia and is sited at the mouth of the Western Dvina, where it flows into the Bay of Riga. Seventy per cent of the Republic's industry is located in the city, including electrical machinery, motors, turbines, superphosphate fertilisers and foodstuffs. Riga is a centre of rail and road routes, for it is the next largest Soviet port on the Baltic Sea, after Leningrad. The city was founded in 1201, and grew into an important Hansestadt (i.e., Hanse town, belonging to the Hanseatic League of international trading cities — 13th to 17th centuries); the castle, guildhalls, and churches from the 14th and 15th centuries, still survive in the old town on the right bank. The Gothic cathedral dates from 1215—26.

Riga has had a chequered history, being controlled by Poland after 1591, by Sweden after 1621, under Russian domination from 1710—1917, independent until 1940, and thereafter under the Soviet Union. Riga's beach resorts, among pine-clad dunes west of the city, attract many visitors from Russia and Eastern Europe.

●**Rostov-on-Don** is a city in Soviet Russia on the Don River, about 30 miles from its mouth at the north-eastern corner of the Sea of Azov. It had a population of 789,000 in 1970. Rostov is an important traffic centre, situated at a crossing point on the river, and with routes to the Caucasus oil area. The city is well industrialised, for it is near to

the Donbas and, being also near to the rich grain-lands of the steppe, it specialises in agricultural machinery and foodstuff industries, as well as tobacco and footwear. The city was founded in the late 18th century, and the construction of the new 63-mile-long Don-Volga canal in 1952 has stimulated Rostov's activities, especially as a port, providing transport of coal to Volgograd, and also establishing a link between the Baltic-Black Sea river and canal route.

●**rubber** During the 19th century, rubber was produced only in the Amazon valley of Brazil by tapping wild rubber trees, known by their scientific name: *Hevea brasiliensis*. In 1876, the British brought seeds of the wild rubber tree to the Botanical Gardens in London, and thence to South-East Asia, where large rubber plantations were established. As the world demand for rubber increased, the more efficient British plantations easily captured the world market. Today, more than 90 per cent of the world's natural rubber comes from South-East Asia, with Malaya and Indonesia accounting for most of the output.

Rubber is obtained by making daily incisions in the bark of the tree and letting the milky juice, or latex, flow into an attached container. The juice is then thickened and cured by smoking, and is ready for export. In the importing countries, further processing involves the adding of chemicals, such as sulphur, and vulcanising (a heat treatment under pressure in a mould).

Synthetic rubber production has been promoted by countries that have not had easy access to the natural rubber of South-East Asia. They include the Soviet Union, and (during World War II) the United States and Nazi Germany. Synthetic rubber is produced largely from petroleum and petroleum gases. Other methods use lime and coke or grain and potato alcohol as raw materials. The world's leading rubber consumers are: the United States, which uses two-thirds natural and one-third synthetic rubber; Britain and West Germany (chiefly natural rubber); and the Soviet Union (chiefly synthetic). About four-fifths of the rubber is used in motor-car tyres.

●**Russia** A name commonly applied to the entire Soviet Union (*see separate article*), and originally referring to the Realm of the Tsar. Before that, Russia was a term describing the land controlled by the Swedes (*russer*), and is best limited today to the European part of the U.S.S.R. Strictly-speaking, too, the Russian Soviet Federated Socialist Republic (R.S.F.S.R.) is 'Russia', and is by far the largest and most populous of the fifteen republics of the Soviet Union. Its area is 6,600,000 square miles — twice that of the United States — and its population is 241 million; the capital is Moscow. The R.S.F.S.R. consists of European Russia and vast Siberia, where only 25 million people live. Russians are a Slavic people of Eastern Orthodox religion, while the rest are largely non-Russians, and live in autonomous republics or regions within the R.S.F.S.R.

●**Ryukyu Island** Island chain extending in an arc between Japan and Formosa, with a total area of 1,300 square miles and a population of 934,176. The capital is Naha, on the large island of Okinawa and with a population of 257,177. The principal products of the islands are sugar cane and sweet potatoes, Panama hats and textiles. Long contested by China and Japan, the Ryukyus passed to Japan in 1879. Since 1945, the Ryukyus have been under United States military administration, with self-government since 1962, and Okinawa has been developed into a major U.S. air and naval base.

●**sable** This famous Russian marten has been hunted for centuries for its precious fur, and is now found chiefly in the forests of north-eastern Siberia. The soft, delicate fur, coloured grey-brown, is

Sampan

among the most highly valued in the world. It was the search for the sable that led the Russians to the conquest of Siberia in the late 16th and early 17th centuries.

● **saiga** This odd-looking goat antelope is at home in West Central Asia, in the open country of the Kirghiz Steppes, U.S.S.R., which are severely cold in winter, and hot and dusty in summer. The saiga's ugly, swollen nose is believed to be especially adapted to this kind of environment: its many small, hair-lined channels filter the dust and warm the cold air before it reaches the lungs. It has a close fur, and mainly lives on the plants which grow in the saline steppes.

● **Saigon** Capital of South Vietnam, on the edge of the Mekong River delta; the city's population, with that of its Chinese-dominated twin city of Cholon, is 2 million (1966). Saigon is a port of the South China Sea, and is reached by a winding tidal stream, accessible to large ocean-going vessels. A small village at the time of the French conquest in 1859, Saigon is now very much like a French town in atmosphere and layout. It has a university, large government buildings and department stores. Saigon's trade and industry are based on rice. Nearly all of South Vietnam's rice exports pass through the port and its mills.

● **Sakhalin** Elongated island (30,000 square miles; population 700,000) off the Pacific coast of Siberia, north of Japan. The capital is Yuzhno-Sakhalinsk (population 79,000). Principal products are lumber and paper, fish, coal and petroleum. The island was settled in the late 18th and the 19th centuries by the Japanese (in the south) and Russians (in the north). In 1875, the entire island passed under Russian control, but the Japanese regained the southern half in 1905. Since the end of World War II, all of Sakhalin has been under Soviet rule. Almost all the Japanese have left the southern population centres and have been replaced by Russian settlers.

● **salt** Such a valuable commodity, in Asia as elsewhere, that there are records of salt being used as money in Tibet. The average person consumes about 12 pounds of salt per year. Salt is also a major industrial raw material, used in the making of basic chemicals such as soda ash and caustic soda, and chlorine compounds. Salt (its chemical name is sodium chloride) is found in natural deposits, either as rock salt or as a brine. In warm countries, salt is recovered from sea water through evaporation. The leading producers are the United States, the Soviet Union, China and Britain.

● **Samarkand** A great ancient city of Central Asia, now in the Uzbek Republic of the Soviet Union. Its population is 267,000. Samarkand was conquered by Alexander the Great in 329 B.C. Later, in the 9th and 10th centuries, it became a centre of Islamic and Arab culture. In 1220, the city

was destroyed by Genghis Khan, but flourished after 1370 as the capital of Tamerlane, who decorated the city with magnificent mosques, gardens and palaces. Soviet Samarkand has silk mills, a phosphate fertiliser plant and a tractor parts factory.

● **sampan** A small river and harbour vessel of the Far East, propelled by a single scull over the stern and provided with mat shelters. Sampans are widely used as year-round residences in crowded Asian cities.

● **Saudi Arabia** Arab kingdom (600,000 square miles; 6 million inhabitants) occupying most of the Arabian Peninsula. The capital is Riyadh (population 300,000). This desert country consists of two historic regions: the Hejaz highlands, rising to 9,000 feet along the Red Sea coast, and the Nejd desert plateau, sloping eastward to the Persian Gulf. The traditional economy of the country is one of oasis agriculture (dates, grains) and nomadic animal husbandry (dromedaries, sheep and goats). However, since the late 1930s, Saudi Arabia has become one of the world's leading producers of petroleum. The oil-fields are concentrated near the coast of the Persian Gulf, around the seaport of Dhahran. Crude oil is piped to refineries at Ras Tanura and Bahrain island as well as being exported. Other leading towns are the religious centres of Mecca and Medina, in Hejaz, which attract Moslem pilgrims from all over the world. Saudi Arabia was established in 1932, after Ibn Saud, an Arab Bedouin ruler, had conquered most of the peninsula from rival Arab leaders.

● **seal, Baikal** One of the few types of seal found in inland lakes of northern Asia. The seal is normally an ocean dweller, but it is believed that the Baikal seal dates from the end of the Ice Age, when the Arctic Ocean reached as far south as Lake Baikal.

● **Semarang** City and port (population 521,000) on the north coast of Java, Indonesia. It is an industrial centre. Semarang's hinterland, with a large Chinese population, produces sugar cane, rubber and coffee for export.

● **Seoul (Kyongsong)** Is the capital (population 5,509,993) of South Korea, on the Han River. Seoul is the historic capital of Korea, established by the Yi dynasty in the 14th century. It is the centre of a densely populated farm region, with food-processing, textile, paper and machinery industries. Its Yellow Sea port is the more important industrial centre of Inchon (population 402,000), while Seoul is also a railway centre.

● **Shanghai** Largest city (population 10,000,000) of China. In 1842, when Shanghai was opened to foreign trade, it was an unimportant fishing port on the Whangpoo River (a tidal inlet of the Yangtze estuary). Within 100 years, it became the fourth largest city in the world, after New York, Tokyo and London. The city's phenomenal growth is due to its location at the gateway to the Yangtze basin of central China and to the extensive development of Western economic interests in China. Shanghai is China's leading manufacturing centre, accounting for the production of one-third of the country's cotton cloth and consumer goods. Under the Communist regime, some of Shanghai's industries have been moved to other cities to achieve a more equal distribution of industrial production. However, other industries, such as rolled steel, tyres and machine tools, have been expanded. Shanghai's business district is the former International Settlement, where broad streets and handsome boulevards are lined with imposing buildings (business houses, hotels and department stores). The Bund (which runs along the waterfront) is the best-known thoroughfare. Industries are concentrated in the Hongkew section, north-east of the

Imperial tombs (Ming Dynasty 1368–1644) near Peking, in northern China

Settlement, and in Pootung, across the Whangpoo. The wharf-lined river, a busy shipping route, must be dredged to admit ocean-going vessels. The city centre is surrounded by an 11th century wall.

● **Shenyang** Industrial city (population 4,000,000) of China, in southern Manchuria. Formerly known as Mukden, Shenyang is a large rail centre and manufacturing city. It produces many kinds of machinery, electrical goods, chemicals, steel, textiles and food products. Many of its raw materials, such as coal and steel, come from the nearby cities of Fu-shun, An-shan and Pen-ki. Modern industrial development began about 1900, in connection with the building of Manchuria's railways. In 1905, Russia's interests in the area passed to the Japanese. Shenyang consists of: an old Chinese section; a new city of broad, straight avenues near the railway station; and the western part, a vast residential and industrial district beyond the railway, built under Japanese rule.

● **Shiraz** City (population 1,500,000) of southern Iran, 120 miles from the Persian Gulf. Situated in a farming area specialising in sugar-beet and wine growing, Shiraz is famous for its roses and gardens. It is the birthplace of two great Persian poets: Sadi (13th century) and Hafiz (14th century). Many of the city's fine buildings date from the 18th century, when, for a brief period, it was the capital of Persia. Nearby are the ruins of Persepolis.

● **Siam** — see **Thailand.**

● **Sian** City (population 1,500,000 of north-west China, 600 miles south-west of Peking. Sian is the centre of a cotton-growing area in the Wei River valley, a tributary of the Hwang-Ho, and the site of large cotton mills and other industries. Nearby coal-fields support a metal industry. The city is the starting point of the Silk Route, and has many archaeological and historical remains.

● **Siberia** A vast forested region of northern Asia, forming part of the Russian Federated Republic of the Soviet Union. Most of Siberia's 5 million square miles, extending from the Urals to the Pacific, are virtually uninhabited forest (see 'taiga'). The area's population (25 million) is concentrated in a narrow belt along the Trans-Siberian

Silver fox

railway, at the southern edge of the forest. Siberia's main cities (Omsk, Novosibirsk, Krasnoyarsk, Irkutsk, Khabarovsk) are situated at points where the railway crosses the great rivers which rise in the mountains of Central Asia and flow to the Arctic Ocean, or, in the case of the Amur, into the Pacific Ocean (Irtysh, Ob, Yenisei, Angara, Amur). Between the Urals and the Yenisei is the Great Siberian Lowland, traversed by the Ob and its tributary, the Irtysh. The majority of Siberia's economic activities (wheat and dairy farming, coal-mining, steel smelting, manufacturing) are concentrated in the railway zone, for Siberia is very rich in minerals — coal, iron, gold, copper, lead and zinc. Most of the population consists of settlers from European Russia. Native Siberian peoples, numbering a few hundred thousand, engage in fishing, reindeer-raising, fur hunting and, in some cases, farming the forest clearings. The Russians first penetrated across the Urals into Siberia in 1581, when the Cossack leader Yermak conquered the Tartar region of Sibir (near modern Tobolsk). The Cossack adventurers moved quickly eastward by land and river, and reached the Pacific, at Okhotsk, in 1640. Siberia, was used as a penal colony and a place of exile. Tribute in furs was exacted from the native tribes. Russian settlement began in the 19th century, with construction of the railway. In the Soviet period, the economic development of Siberia gathered momentum remarkably.

● **Sikkim**   A small Himalayan State (2,700 square miles; population 162,189) under Indian protection. The capital is Gangtok. Its peoples are related to the Tibetans. Sikkim's importance lay in the fact that it was crossed by the trade route between India and Tibet. Sikkim's people live by agriculture in the valleys, and by yak-breeding.

● **Silk Road**   The historic route through Central Asia over which Chinese silk was carried to Europe in antiquity and during the Middle Ages. In modern times, this route became a lorry road, linking the Soviet Union and China. In the late 1950s, a railway was begun along the same route.

● **silver fox**   A variety of the red fox, raised on fox farms for its fur. It is one of three colour variations of the red fox — the two others are the black fox and the cross fox, with a dark cross on its back. All three may turn up in one litter of cubs. The fur is extremely valuable.

● **Sinai Peninsula**   A region of Egypt, between the Gulfs of Suez and Aqaba at the northern end of the Red Sea. It is a largely a desert area inhabited by nomadic Bedouin herdsmen. Petroleum is obtained along the coast of the Gulf of Suez. In the southern part, the Sinai Mountains reach to over 8,000 feet. Since 1967, Israel has occupied this territory as far as the Suez Canal.

● **Singapore**   A group of islands forming an independent State off the southern tip of the Malay Peninsula. It consists of Singapore Island (224 square miles; 2,033,500 people) and several small adjacent islands. The city of Singapore, one of the great commercial centres of South-East Asia and one of the largest transit ports of the world, lies on the south coast of Singapore Island, with a population of 1 million. Singapore exports most of its rubber and tin, and even imports some of Indonesia's exports (petroleum, tin and rubber) for re-export. Singapore is a typical example of what is known as an *entrepôt* port, its main functions being those of handling, forwarding, shipping, re-shipping, breaking bulk, sorting, distributing and collecting. Its processing industries — far less important than its commission trade — include a large tin-smelter, rubber factories and pineapple canneries. The development of Singapore is associated with the name of T.S. Raffles, an official of the British East India Company, who picked the small fishing village of Singapore to establish a trade station on the route to the Far East. A policy of free trade, plus encouragement to settlers and the advantageous location of Singapore, promoted its rapid rise in the 19th century. One of the most decisive factors in the growth of Singapore has been the flow of Chinese immigration. It was encouraged by the British, who considered the Chinese settlers business-like and hard-working. Chinese now make up 76 per cent of the population; Malays make up only 12 per cent; and Indians and Pakistanis 8 per cent. Singapore was one of the Straits Settlements before World War II. In 1946, it was set up as a British colony separate from Malaya, but joined her — together with Sabah and Sarawak — in the Federation of Malaysia, when it was set up within the British Commonwealth in 1963. Then, in 1965, Singapore broke away from the Federation as an independent State, but British bases are retained there.

● **Sinkiang**   Largest autonomous province (660,000 square miles; population 8,000,000) of China, in Central Asia. The capital is Urumchi (population 140,700). The mighty Tien Shan mountain system divides this desert province into two regions: Dzungaria in the north, and the Tarim basin (East Turkestan) in the south. Most of the inhabitants live in oases along the north foot of the Tien Shan and around the Tarim basin, which reaches to elevations more than 500 feet below sea level, growing cotton and wheat, and raising mulberries (for silk production) on irrigated land. The development of mineral resources (petroleum and rare metals) is expected to be speeded up with the completion of the new railway linking the Soviet Union and China, through Sinkiang, along the historic Silk Road.

Snowy owl

● **snowy owl**   This is one of the few owls that hunt by day, for it needs to do this during the Arctic summer of the tundras, when the sun does not set.

● **Soochow**   City (population 474,000) of eastern China, in the Yangtze delta. Soochow, which is 50 miles west of Shanghai, is an old textile centre, specialising in silk goods. Its traditional cotton industry has been supplanted by the modern mills of Wusih, 25 miles north-west of Soochow.

● **Soviet Union**   Country of eastern Europe and northern Asia, known officially as the Union of Soviet Socialist Republics (U.S.S.R.). The capital is Moscow. Its area (8,600,000 square miles — three times the size of the United States) makes the Soviet Union the largest nation in the world, forming one-eighth of the land surface of the world. In population (220 million) it is third after China and India. The Soviet Union consists of 15 union republics. The largest is the Russian Soviet Federated Socialist Republic (R.S.F.S.R.), which extends through most of Soviet Europe and Asia. Along the western border of the European U.S.S.R. are the Republics of Estonia, Latvia, Lithuania, Byelorussia, the Ukraine and Moldavia. To the South are the Transcaucasian Republics of Armenia, Azerbaijan and Georgia. The Republic of Kazakhstan, and the Central Asian Republics of Kirghizia, Uzbekistan, Tadzhikistan and Turkmenia, are in Asia. *(See separate articles for each.)*

Although half of its borders are on the sea, the Soviet Union is primarily a land power. Its coastline faces either the frozen seas of the Arctic Ocean, or nearly enclosed seas (Black, Baltic) that lead to the open oceans through straits controlled by other nations (Turkey, Denmark-Sweden, respectively). Most of the Soviet Union's rivers, moreover, flow either into closed seas or into the Arctic Ocean; and, in addition, many of them are frozen for a large part of the year. There are only

Rice – the staple food of many millions of Asian people – has to be grown where there is fresh water to submerge the fields

The Yangtze runs 3,400 miles past Chungking, Wuhan and Nanking. Near Shanghai, crowded with sampans and houseboats, it empties into the East China Sea, or Tung Hai, part of the Pacific Ocean

two ice-free harbours, Vladivostok and Murmansk.

The Soviet Union, therefore, relies heavily on railways and canals for its internal transportation. The length of its railway system (75,000 miles) is second only to that of the United States.

The Soviet Union shows a great variety of climates and contains four major zones of vegetation: the tundra along the Arctic Ocean; the taiga (coniferous forest), which covers the northern half of European Russia and almost all of Siberia; the steppes (grasslands), extending in a relatively narrow belt along the southern margins of the forest; and the shrub and desert, covering most of central Asia, east of the Caspian Sea.

The country's population and most of its economic activity are concentrated in a triangle (with Moscow at its centre) roughly connecting the cities of Leningrad, Odessa and Sverdlovsk. This area contains a zone of mixed coniferous and deciduous forest, as well as most of the country's large cities, and the greater part of its fertile farmlands on the steppes. The rest of the country is either too cold for large-scale settlement (as in Siberia) or too dry (as in the deserts of Central Asia). Less than 25 million people live in Siberia, and only 15 million in the Central Asian Republics. Yet great attempts are being made to extend the cultivated lands of Russia in these two areas, as well as develop the mineral deposits.

Russians, a Slavic people using the Cyrillic alphabet, make up slightly more than half of the Soviet Union's population. Together with the two other Slavic groups (Ukrainians and Byelorussians), the Russians account for 75 per cent. The rest of the total is made up of such varying language groups as the Turkic peoples of Central Asia, the Finnic peoples of northern European Russia and Siberia, and the Mongol-speaking peoples of the south-east. The Soviet Union's principal crops are wheat and sugar beet, grown in the black soil of the steppe zone, and cotton in irrigated fields in Central Asia. The Soviet Union is very well endowed with mineral resources and has become an industrial power second only to the United States. Heavy industry is concentrated in the Urals, and in the Kuznetsk and Donbas. Domestic coal and

oil are used for power, and more and more Hydroelectric stations are being established.

The Soviet Union succeeded the old Russian Empire as a result of the Bolshevik Revolution of 1917. The first Russian State flourished in the 11th century around Kiev. Inroads by nomadic steppe-dwellers drove the Russians deeper into the forest zone around Moscow, where a new State was established in the 14th century. The Muscovite State expanded rapidly, especially under Ivan the Terrible in the 16th century, and under Peter the Great in the early 18th century. Cossacks drove through Siberia, beginning in 1581, and reached the Pacific by 1640. Under Catherine the Great, in the late 18th century, Russia expanded westward and southward to the Black Sea. In the second half of the 19th century, Russian control was extended into Central Asia.

The Soviet State that emerged from the 1917 Revolution was first led by Lenin and then by Stalin. Its policy of authoritarian one-party rule, collectivisation of agriculture, and State control of industry, served as a model for other countries that adopted Communism after World War II. During that war, the Soviet Union, in alliance with Britain, the U.S.A. and other nations, defeated the Germans, who had driven deep into European Russia. After the war, the Soviet Union and the United States became the two leading world powers. Their interests came increasingly into conflict, giving rise to the period of international tension known as the 'cold war'. After Stalin's death, in 1953, succeeding Soviet governments introduced a series of progressive new policies. More contacts were permitted with other nations and world tension was lessened. In 1963 a pact was signed banning the use of nuclear weapons. However, in recent years tensions have increased again over relations with China and over trouble spots like the Middle East.

● **soya bean** A bushy annual herb, native to Asia and growing to a height of two feet. Its roots penetrate up to six feet into the ground, making the plant relatively drought-resistant. Soya beans

yield not only an edible vegetable oil (also used in soap, paints and linoleum), but also soya-bean flour and cake, which is a high-protein animal feed. Its shoots are a prized delicacy. Before World War II, China and Manchuria (then under Japanese control) accounted for almost 90 per cent of the world's soya-bean crop. Since the war, production has been about evenly divided between China and the United States.

● **steppe** Name given to the grasslands of Eurasia, consisting of level, generally treeless plains. It reaches its greatest extent in a broad belt stretching from the lower Danube through the Ukraine into Western Siberia. Hardly any of the steppe remains

Bear-hunting in the pine forests of Siberia, a vast region in the U.S.S.R.

Sampans and barges crowd the busy waterfront at Singapore, an independent island-city State at the southern tip of the Malay Peninsula

in its natural state, for it is now cultivated and constitutes one of the largest wheat-growing regions in the world.

● **Sumatra** Second largest island of Indonesia, to the north-west of Java. Its area is more than 160,000 square miles (almost the size of Sweden) and its population 19.7 million. Mountain ranges rising to more than 10,000 feet traverse the entire island along the west coast, including Kerintji (13,805 feet). The low east-coast plain is covered with tropical mangrove swamps. The population, concentrated in the cooler highlands, grows rubber, spices, coffee, tea and tobacco for export. Rice is raised for domestic food needs. The Sumatrans are Moslems, except for the Batak people, who are Christian. The island is Indonesia's principal petroleum producer, and has some coal, iron and gold mines. Sumatra was the centre of a flourishing Hindu kingdom in the 8th century, but later fell under the control of the Javanese. The largest cities of Sumatra are Medan (in the north), Padang (on the west coast) and Palembang (in the south).

● **Sunda Islands** Name given to islands of the Malay Archipelago forming part of the Republic of Indonesia. The Greater Sunda Islands are Borneo, Celebes, Java and Sumatra. The Lesser Sunda Islands, which form a chain east of Java, include Bali, Lombok, Sumbawa, Sumba, Flores and Timor. The only non-Indonesian sections are Portuguese (eastern) Timor and parts of northern Borneo (Brunei, Sabah and Sarawak). The islands are largely mountainous and volcanic, and they experience many earthquakes; yet they have many fertile lowlands, and Java is among the most densely peopled lands of the earth.

● **sunflower** This tall plant is so called because of the form and colour of its large yellow-rayed flower. It is widely cultivated in the Soviet Union, the Balkans and Argentina for its seeds — a source of vegetable oil and cattle feed.

● **Surabaya** Second largest city (population 1,300,000) of Indonesia, in north-eastern Java. One of Indonesia's leading ports and industrial centres, Surabaya's industries include shipbuilding, textiles, machinery and oil refining. The port is also used as a naval base.

● **Sverdlovsk** Largest Soviet city of the Urals (population 1,026,000), situated on the Iset River where the mountain range is easily crossed by transportation routes. The city was founded in 1721 and named Yekaterinburg, after the Russian Empress Catherine I. In the Soviet period, Sverdlovsk (renamed after an early Soviet leader) has become a major machine-building centre, producing heavy equipment for steel, chemical and electrical industries. The city has a university, a mining school, and the Urals branch of the Soviet Academy of Sciences. Unlike most Russian cities, Sverdlovsk has a regular street plan, laid out amid picturesque lakes and pine-covered hills. Nicholas II (the last Russian czar) and his family were executed here in 1918, during the civil war.

● **Syr Darya** One of the great rivers of Central Asia, rising in the Tien Shan, near the Chinese border, and flowing to the Aral Sea; 1,650 miles long. Its upper course irrigates the rich Fergana Valley, and is used to generate power in several hydro-electric plants. The lower course, in the desert near the Aral Sea, freezes for several months in winter.

● **Syria** Country (66,000 square miles; population 5,700,000) of the Middle East, formerly and briefly federated with Egypt as the United Arab Republic. Its capital is Damascus. Most of the country in the centre and the south-east is covered by desert, where Bedouin tribes raise sheep, goats and camels. Population and economic activities are located near the Mediterranean coast, in the hilly western part of the country. There, cotton and tobacco are raised for export, and wheat, barley, millet and sugar beet for home use. Railways link the major cities of Aleppo, Homs, Hama and the port of Latakia with Damascus. Syria's population, predominantly Arab, is 85 per cent Moslem and 15 per cent Catholic and Orthodox Christian. Syria was formerly a French mandated territory, and under Turkish domination before World War I. It first became independent during the Second World War. Oil and natural gas have been discovered in the Jezirah region.

● **Tabriz** City (population 468,459) of north-west Iran, in Azerbaijan; has rug-weaving, cotton and wool industries. Long contested between Turkey and Persia, Tabriz has been in the traditional Russian zone of influence since the 19th century.

The city is linked by rail with the Soviet Union and with Teheran.

● **Tadzhikistan** A Soviet Republic (55,000 square miles; population 2,900,000) of Central Asia, bordering on Afghanistan and China. The capital is Dushanbe. Tadzhikistan consists of a series of high mountain ranges (including the Pamirs) that enclose fertile cotton-growing valleys. Only 10 per cent of the total area is cultivated for wheat, barley, sugar cane, jute, rice and citrus fruits; it requires irrigation in its desert lowlands. Tadzhikistan is a major produce rof non-ferrous metals (lead, zinc, tungsten). In cotton production, the republic is second only to Uzbekistan in the Soviet Union. Silk, rice, essential oils (geranium) and dried fruit are other products. Tadzhiks, a Moslem people speaking an Iranian language, make up 53 per cent of the population. Other groups are Uzbeks (24 per cent) and Russians (15 per cent).

● **Taegu** City (population 870,000) of South Korea, on the Pusan-Seoul railway. It has a large silk and cotton-milling industry.

● **taiga** Name given to the great coniferous forest land of Siberia, bordered in the north by the Arctic tundra and in the south by the steppe. The principal trees are pine, spruce and larch. The taiga contains many swampy areas. During the spring, much of the land is flooded by northward-flowing rivers whose lower courses, near the Arctic Ocean, remain frozen.

● **Taipei** Capital (population 1,700,000) of Formosa (Taiwan); founded by Chinese settlers in the early 18th century. It was greatly expanded under Japanese rule, between 1895 and 1945. It has machinery and food-processing industries. Taipei's seaport is Keelung (population 220,000), exporting tea, camphor and timber. Taipei is now the capital of Nationalist China.

● **Taiyuan** City (population 1,020,000) of northern China, 250 miles south-west of Peking. Taiyuan is the capital and economic centre of the province of Shansi. Its industrial growth advanced rapidly in recent years, with the expansion of its steel and machinery industries.

● **Tallinn, (Reval)** This is the capital and most important port of Estonia, with 363,000 inhabitants. It lies on the Gulf of Finland and, despite many sieges, has kept its old buildings, most worthy of note being the 13th-century castle, the 14th-century Town Hall and the 12th-century cathedral. Tallinn, meaning in Estonian 'Danes' Town', was founded in 1219 by Valdemar, but later came under Hanseatic control. In 1561, the Swedes won control of Tallinn, and then the Russians in 1710, when it became a naval base. The city was linked by rail to St Petersburg in 1870, and its modernisation commenced. Today it has thriving

Malay tapir

industries, among which are shipbuilding yards, and textile, paper and metal works.

● **Tangshan** Industrial city (population 800,000) of northern China, on the railway from Peking to Manchuria. Tangshan is the centre of the Kailan coal basin. Steel, coke chemicals and cement are major products. Large power stations, burning Kailan coal, feed electricity to Peking and Tientsin.

● **tapir, Malay** Creature of the Malay Peninsula, standing three and a half feet at the shoulder and weighing 500 pounds. Its coat is almost evenly divided — a light grey hind part and a black front — giving the animal an effective protective colouring.

● **Tarim Basin** A desert region of East Turkestan, Central Asia, in China's Sinkiang Province. Its more than 4 million inhabitants live in a ring of oases around the basin. They are predominantly Uigurs, a Moslem people speaking a Turkic language. The River Tarim flows in the basin, into the Lop-Nor lake. In the surrounding mountains — Kun-lun, Pamir, Tien Shan — there are gold, zinc and copper mines.

● **tarsier** This odd-looking monkey-like creature of Indonesia and the Philippines is only six inches long. It has enormous owl-like eyes, and adhesive pads on fingers and toes enabling it to cling to tree branches. With its long hind legs and short fore limbs, the tarsier hops about like a kangaroo or a frog.

● **Tartars** A Moslem people, speaking a Turkic language, settled chiefly in the Soviet Union. The greatest concentration of Tartars is found in the Volga valley around Kazan (Volga Tartars). Another large group, formerly settled in the Crimea, was exiled to Central Asia after World War II, because of alleged collaboration with the German invaders. Some Tartars live in the area of Tobolsk and elsewhere in Siberia. The Tartars are believed to have come to Russia at the time of the Mongol invasions of the 13th century. After the collapse of part of the Mongol empire known as the Golden Horde, Tartar khanates (principalities) were formed in the 15th century at Kazan, Astrakhan and in Siberia, and these fell to the Russians in the 16th century.

● **Tashkent** Largest city (population 1,385,000) of Soviet Central Asia, in the Uzbek Republic, of which it is the capital. Situated in an ancient oasis at the western end of the Tien Shan, Tashkent was the metropolis of Central Asia even before the Russian conquest in 1865. The city became the capital of Russian Turkestan. Its modern development began about 1898, when it was reached by railway. Tashkent consists of an old Oriental city, whose narrow, dusty alleyways have been partly modernised, and a new Russian city near the railway station. Tashkent's industries, particularly machine shops, received great impetus during World War II, when many plants from European Russia were moved here. The city produces cotton-pickers and other farm machinery, power shovels, mining equipment, electrical goods, and machinery for the cotton gins and oilseed mills of Central Asia. Tashkent is the seat of the Central Asian University and of the Soviet Union's cotton research institute.

● **tea** An evergreen shrub with large, fragrant white flowers, which grows best in hilly country, in a humid, sub-tropical climate. The China tea bush grows to a height of 10 to 20 feet and matures early, while the Assam variety grows twice as high, has larger leaves and matures later; yet in plantations shrubs are kept less than 6 feet high. The tea harvest, which can begin after two years of growth, consists of plucking leaves and leaf buds fifteen to twenty-four times a year. Teas are classified as green, black or oolong. Green tea is dried immediately after picking and thus retains its original

Tea shrub

colour. Black tea is fermented before drying. Some tea is perfumed by using dried flowers or by chemical means. Oolong tea is only partly fermented, steamed and pressed into bricklike shapes, especially in Central Asia. China was formerly the greatest producer of tea, but today the largest crop is grown and exported by commercial estates in India (Assam) and Ceylon. Other tea-producing nations are Japan, Indonesia, and the Soviet Republic of Georgia.

● **Teheran** Capital (population 3,150,000) of Iran, at the foot of the Elburz Mountains. Teheran is the transportation centre of the country, with railways going south-west to the Persian Gulf, north-west to Tabriz and north-east to Meshed. The centre of the city is the Rose Garden, with a royal throne hall and a museum containing the jewelled Peacock Throne. South of this are the crooked, narrow streets and bazaars of the old town. The northern part of the city contains broad, tree-lined avenues and modern buildings. One-third of Iran's industries, including metal-works, chemical and textile plants, are in Teheran. The city's growth dates from 1788, when it became the capital of Iran (Persia).

● **Tel Aviv** City of Israel, in the coastal plain on the Mediterranean Sea; its population is 382,900 (including adjoining Jaffa). Tel Aviv developed after 1909 as a Jewish suburb of the old Arab orange-shipping port of Jaffa. Tel Aviv rapidly expanded into a modern city, and is now the largest city of Israel, with a large share of the country's manufacturing industries. Although the Israeli capital was moved from here to Jerusalem in 1950, most foreign ambassadors still reside in Tel Aviv, and many cultural and educational institutes are there.

● **Thailand** Kingdom (200,000 square miles; population 32 million) of South-East Asia; its population includes 75 per cent Thai and 20 per cent Chinese peoples. The capital is Bangkok. Long known as Siam, the country changed its name to Thailand in 1939, back to Siam in 1945, and once more to Thailand in 1949. The densely populated alluvial plain of the Chao Phraya River, also known simply as Menam (the Thai word for river), runs through the heart of the country's great rice-producing region. In the wooded northern and eastern highlands, domesticated elephants are used in cutting teak and other tropical hardwoods. In the eastern plateau country, greater stress is put on livestock raising. The southern peninsula part of Thailand is noted for its rubber, coconuts and mineral resources (tin, tungsten, antimony). Thailand's surplus rice, rubber and tin make up 70 to 80 per cent of the total value of exports. Foreign trade, which passes largely through Bangkok, is carried on chiefly with Japan and the United States.

The language, which belongs to the Indo-Chinese group, uses a peculiar alphabet probably derived from Cambodia. The Thai State succeeded the Khmer (Cambodian) Empire as a leading power in the 14th century, and flourished until defeated by the Burmese in the 18th century. After the coming of the Europeans in the 19th century, Thailand managed to remain independent in the face of growing French influence in Indo-China, and British gains in Malaya and Burma. In an effort to resist European advances, Thailand undertook a programme of progressive modernisation during the second half of the 19th century. During World War II, Thailand sided with Japan (in 1942) and temporarily annexed parts of Laos, Cambodia, Malaya and Burma. In the post-war period, Thailand has become an ally of the United States.

● **Tibet** Autonomous province (580,000 square miles; population 1,300,000) of China. The capital is Lhasa. With an average elevation of 13,000 to 15,000 feet, Tibet is the highest region of the world. It is a vast, high plateau between the Kunlun mountain system and the Himalayas. Mountains running from east to west divide the region into arid basins covered with sparse steppe grass, stony deserts or salt lakes. Some crops are raised in the river valleys of southern Tibet, where the population is concentrated. Elsewhere nomadic Tibetans raise yaks, which provide almost all their food, clothing and shelter. Tibetans, a distinct Mongolian type, are of the Lamaist (Buddhist) religion. About 10 per cent of the population consists of lamas (or monks) living in monasteries. Since the 17th century, Tibet has been ruled by the Dalai Lama, the

Fortress of St Peter and St Paul in Leningrad (formerly St Petersburg), Russia's largest seaport

Russia's 'breadbaskets' are found in Siberia and in the vast, 'black-earth' cornfields of the Ukraine

high priest of Lamaism. In the past, Chinese authority (which replaced Mongol rule over Tibet in the 18th century) has been largely nominal. From 1912 to 1950, Tibet was virtually independent, and permitted Britain to keep trading posts there. In 1950, the Chinese Communist government established suzerainty over Tibet and made it a part of China. The Dalai Lama fled to India in 1959.

● **Tien Shan** Great mountain system of Central Asia, whose name means 'heavenly mountains' in Chinese. It extends more than 1,000 miles from the River Syr Darya in the Soviet Union to the Gobi Desert in China. The highest point is Pobeda (Victory) Peak (24,400 feet), which was discovered by the Russians in World War II on the Soviet-Chinese border. Some agriculture is practised in mountain valleys and in the basin of the mountain lake named Issyk-Kul, where wheat and opium-poppies are grown. More important is the grazing of livestock by Kirghiz herders on high mountain pastures.

● **Tientsin** Port city (population 4,000,000) of northern China, situated 70 miles south-east of Peking, on the railway leading to Manchuria. Tientsin is a major manufacturing centre, producing steel, tractors, bicycles and chemicals, in addition to its traditional textiles, food and paper products. The city is not accessible to ocean-going vessels. Large ships use the new outer port at Ta-ku. Tientsin developed as a commercial city in the mid-19th century, when the British and French opened it to foreign trade.

● **Tiflis (Tbilisi)** Capital (population 889,000) of the Soviet Transcaucasian Republic of Georgia, situated in the valley of the Kura River, in the centre of Transcaucasia. Tiflis is a transportation centre of routes linking the Black Sea with the Caspian, and of the Georgian Military Road, which leads north across the Caucasus. The city's name in Georgian is Tbilisi, which means 'hot water', on account of the hot sulphur springs used there since ancient times for health cures and for the tanning of leather. The city's industries produce fine woollens, silks, sparkling wines, and

machinery for the textile, tea, wine and petroleum industries. To the south-east is the Georgian steel city of Rustavi (population 53,000), founded in the 1940s.

● **Tigris River** One of the great rivers of Mesopotamia, in modern Iraq; 1,200 miles long. It rises in Turkey and flows south-east past Baghdad to the Persian Gulf. At its mouth, the river joins the Euphrates. Though shorter than the Euphrates, the Tigris is much swifter and carries a larger volume of water. Dams and irrigation works along the Tigris furnish much of the water for Iraq's crops.

● **timber** Forests cover nearly one-third of the earth's surface, or an area twice as large as all the land under cultivation. There are two major types: the coniferous forests of the north, and the broad-leaved hardwoods of the temperate and tropical zones. Vast coniferous forests stretch right across northern Asia (in the U.S.S.R.), and tropical rain-forests are found in many parts of south-eastern Asia. The northern softwoods go mainly into industrial uses (saw-logs, plywood, pulpwood); the rest is used as firewood. In the case of the hardwoods, most is used for fuel. Indirect applications of timber include fibreboard, paper (including newsprint) and paperboard. Wood pulp is also a basic raw material in the making of artificial fibres, such as rayon. The world's leading wood producers are the United States, the Soviet Union and Canada (mainly softwoods), and Brazil (hardwoods). Canada, Sweden and Finland have a large surplus for export.

● **Timor** Largest and easternmost of the Lesser Sunda Islands, with an area of 13,000 square miles and a population of 1 million. The island is divided between Indonesia and Portugal. Copra, tobacco, coffee and sandalwood are the chief exports.

● **Tokyo** Capital of Japan and now the largest city in the world. The city proper, consisting of 23 boroughs, has a population of 8,832,647. Greater Tokyo, which has an area of 785 square miles, has

a population of 11,480,000. At its centre are the moated Imperial Palace grounds, around which major thoroughfares form a radial pattern. South of the palace grounds lies the government district. To the east is the Marunouchi business district, with huge modern concrete buildings surrounding Tokyo Central Station. Nearby is the Ginza, the amusement and shopping area. In the northern part of Tokyo is Ueno Park, with its zoo, museums and art galleries. Industries include shipyards, motor-car and aircraft plants, machinery, textile and chemical factories. Tokyo, which was formerly called Yedo, owes its rise to the Tokugawa shoguns (military governors) of Japan, who made the city their headquarters in 1603, while Kyoto remained the imperial capital. In the late 18th century, Yedo had a population of 1,400,000, making it one of the world's largest cities at that date. With the restoration of imperial power in 1868, the emperor moved his capital from Kyoto to Yedo, which he renamed Tokyo ('eastern capital'). The disastrous earthquake of 1923, and fire in 1925, destroyed nearly half the city, which was then rebuilt along modern lines. In World War II, Tokyo was devastated by bombing, and its population reduced from the war 6½ million to 3 million. Post-war recovery has been rapid. The Olympic games were held in Tokyo in 1964, and Expo '70 took place in Tokyo in 1970.

● **Tomsk** Old Siberian city, established in 1604 as a gold mining centre on the Tom River, a tributary of the Ob; population 339,000 Tomsk is a Siberian education centre, with a university founded in 1888. Lumber mills, and factories making mining equipment, chemicals and electric motors, are sited there.

● **Transcaucasia** A region of the Soviet Union, south of the Caucasus, between the Black Sea and the Caspian Sea. It is divided into the three Soviet Republics of Georgia, Armenia and Azerbaijan.

● **Trans-Siberian Railway** The only land transportation route crossing Siberia from west to east, along the southern margins of the forest zone. The railway, built between 1891 and 1902, is the focus of Siberia's economic development and settlement. Nearly all the large cities are situated on it: Sverdlovsk, Omsk, Novosibirsk, Krasnoyarsk, Irkutsk, Khabarovsk, Vladivostok. The original line ran through Manchuria, where it was called the Chinese Eastern Railway, though, during the years 1908—16, an all-Russian link was completed along the Amur River. The Trans-Siberian has been double-tracked in the Soviet period, and large sections were electrified in the 1950s. The Trans-Siberian express now takes 8¼ days to cover the 5,800 miles between Moscow and Vladivostok.

● **Tsinan** City (population 862,000) of northern China, near the Yellow River. The centre of a rich agricultural region producing wheat and soya beans, it is linked by railway with the port of Tsingtao.

● **Tsingtao** Chinese port (population 1,121,000) on the Yellow Sea, on the south coast of the Shantung Peninsula. It exports peanuts and tobacco from the fertile hinterland and is an important fishing centre. The city's industries include cotton mills, a locomotive and car-building plant, and shipyards. In World War I, the city was seized by the Japanese for a time, but they surrendered it to China in 1922.

● **Tula** (462,000 people) lies south of Moscow, in the vast lignite- and coal-field in that area, and specialises in metal working. The city developed quite rapidly in the 17th century, based on minor iron-ore deposits, though it was founded much earlier, in the 12th century. First products were armaments for the State, and traditional products are samovars and sewing machines.

- **tungsten** The principal use of tungsten, which has the highest point of fusion (337°C) of all metals, is in the making of high-speed tool steels. It also forms the filament of light bulbs and the super-hard alloy, tungsten carbide, a substitute for diamond drills. The world's leading producers are China, Portugal, the United States, Bolivia and Burma.

Sancta Sophia, Istanbul

- **Turkey** Country (300,000 square miles; population 35.6 million) of Asia and Europe, consisting of a small part of the Balkan Peninsula, and of Asia Minor)Anatolia). The two sections are separated by the Turkish Straits (the Bosporus, the Sea of Marmara, and the Dardanelles). The capital is Ankara. European Turkey amounts to no more than 3 per cent of the country's area, and holds 8 per cent of the population in and around Istanbul. Asiatic Turkey has fertile coastal strips, backed by steep ranges that enclose the vast steppe-like central uplands, which are sub-arid with many saline lakes. Highest among the marginal

Interior of the 'Blue Mosque', Istanbul

ranges are the Taurus and Pontic Mountains. Agriculture and animal husbandry support 80 per cent of the population and supply 80 per cent of the exports. The leading commercial crops are raisins, figs, tobacco, filberts, walnuts and cotton. In recent years, a large part of former grazing land has been sown with grain, so that Turkey now has a small surplus for export. Coal, iron ore and petroleum resources are adequate for Turkey's needs, while chromite, lead and zinc ores are exported. Bauxite production began in 1966. Industries are of recent origin and produce manufactured goods for the country's own use. The largest cities are Istanbul (the former Constantinople), Ankara (the new capital of modern Turkey) and Izmir (also called Smyrna), a leading port.

Turkey was the heart of the Ottoman Empire, a vast State established by the Osmanli Turks, who invaded the Middle East from Central Asia. The empire rose in the 14th century and reached its peak in the 16th century. The expansion of Russia became an increasingly serious challenge in the 18th century. As a result of World War I, in which Turkey fought on the side of Germany, the empire disintegrated. After the war, a modern Turkish Republic asserted itself in 1923, under the leadership of Kemal Ataturk. Turkey was neutral in World War II and joined N.A.T.O. during the post-war years. Turkey is in an earthquake-prone area and has had several severe tremors in the last few years, killing many people.

Mahouts (drivers) guiding Indian elephants as they roll huge teak logs near Bangkok, Thailand

- **Turkmenia** One of the Soviet Republics (187,000 square miles; population 2,200,000) of Central Asia. The capital is Ashkhabad. About 85 per cent of Turkmenia is uninhabited sandy desert known as Kara Kum (black sands). Irrigated agriculture is practised along the few rivers (Amu Darya, Murgab, Tedzhen) and along the new Kara Kum Canal, which links the Amu Darya with the Murgab and Tedzhen oases. Cotton and lucerne, grown in rotation, are the chief crops. Karakul sheep and camels graze on sparse desert pastures. Turkmen riding horses are famous. Industry is based on rich mineral resources (petroleum, coal, sulphur) and on farm products (cotton, silk and carpet mills). Population is concentrated in the oases, and along the railway linking the port of Krasnovodsk with the rest of Central Asia. The Turkmen, who make up 60 per cent of the total, are Moslems speaking a language akin to Turkish. Other population groups are Russians (17 per cent), Uzbeks and Kazakhs.

- **typhoon** A term, which means 'big wind' (tai-fun) in Chinese, applied to the tropical cyclone of the China Seas. Like all tropical cyclones, a typhoon brings winds of tremendous strength and torrential rain, causing widespread destruction. These storms are most frequent in late summer and early autumn. The coastal areas of South China and the Philippines are commonly affected.

- **Ufa** A city on the south-western slopes of the Ural mountains and capital of the Bashkir Autonomous Republic, the inhabitants of which are a Moslem people, speaking a Turkish language. Ufa was founded in 1586 as a Russian fortress in the campaign against the Tartars and Bashkirs. Today, with a population of 773,000, the city has a petroleum refinery, deriving oil from the Volga-Ural field; it manufactures electrical goods, and has engine plants and textile factories. Ufa has expanded rapidly in recent years and absorbed the new town of Chernikovsk, close by.

- **Ukraine** (U.S.S.R., Europe) is the third largest Soviet Republic, with an area of 230,000 square miles (population 47.1 million). Its capital is Kiev. It is largely a lowland steppe, extending from the Pripet Marshes to the Black Sea and from the eastern Carpathians to the Don River. Rich black soils (chernozem) yield wheat, rye, sugar beets, sunflowers, maize and cotton. The Ukraine also contains the Crimea, with its fruit and wine production, and the Donbas, with its coal, iron ore, steel mills and other mineral deposits.

The Ukrainians (meaning 'border people') are Slavs of Orthodox faith, with a Russian culture and traditions, but also some Polish influences, for the Ukraine belonged to Poland until the 17th century, and the land west of the Dnieper until 1793. The 1938 boundaries of the Ukraine did not correspond with the distribution of Ukrainian speech, and territory was added in 1945 from some countries of eastern Europe. The Ukraine is, perhaps, the most densely peopled and economically developed part of the Soviet Union.

- **United Arab Emirates** These are a group of seven Arab sheikdoms which form part of the Persian Gulf States, with Bahrain and Qatar. British forces had exclusive protectorate rights from the 19th century until their ultimate withdrawal in 1971. The United Arab Emirates have a population of 180,000 and an area of 32,300 square miles. Dubai (population 60,000) is the

A native of Uzbekistan rides into market at Tashkent, capital of the Uzbek Republic

largest town, and Abu Dhabi is one of the states which has expanded greatly (55,000), and enriched itself through oil production. Traditionally pearling, fishing and trading were chief occupations, but more and more people are drifting to the urban settlements in the desert where oil is the chief employer.

● **Ural** The name of a mountain range and a river of the Soviet Union, together forming the conventional border between Europe and Asia. The Urals extend north-south for 1,300 miles, rising to 6,184 feet in Narodnaja. In the middle section, the mountains are relatively low and are easily crossed by transportation routes. The Urals are rich in mineral resources and have become one of the industrial regions of the Soviet Union, especially since World War II. The largest cities, each with a population of 500,000 or more, are Sverdlovsk, Chelyabinsk, Perm and Ufa. The northern Urals were first reached in the 12th century by Russian fur-hunters from Novgorod; but the mountains were not crossed until 1581, when the Cossack Yermak led an expedition into Siberia. Mineral industries (iron, copper) flourished under Peter the Great, but declined during the Industrial Revolution as the Donets Basin became more important in European Russia. Under the Soviet regime, the Urals have become a modern industrial area with oil-fields nearby.

● **Uzbekistan** The most populous Soviet Republic of Central Asia (157,000 square miles; population 12 million), stretching from west of the Aral Sea as far as the western Tien-shan. It is largely desert. The capital is Tashkent. Occupying one-third of Soviet Central Asia, the Uzbek Republic contains 60 per cent of its population, three-fourths of the industry and more than half of the cultivated land. It is also the leading Soviet producer of cotton, natural silk, rice, dried fruit and karakul skins. Population and economic activity are concentrated in the oases of Tashkent, Fergana, Samarkand and Bukhara, and the valley of the Amu Darya. In addition to farm products, industry exploits rich mineral resources, including coal, oil, copper, lead and zinc. Among the republic's new industrial cities are: Chirchik (electro-chemicals), Begovat (steel), Angren (coal) and Almalyk (copper and other non-ferrous metals). Uzbeks, a Moslem people speaking a Turkic language, make up two-thirds of the population. They are skilled cotton, silk and fruit growers. Russians account for 14 per cent of the population.

● **Valdai Hills** form an area of morainic deposits overlying a limestone ridge between Leningrad and Moscow, their highest point being Kamennik, which reaches to 1,050 feet. The Volga, Dnieper and western Dvina all have their source in the Valdai Hills.

● **Verkhoyansk** Small town of north-eastern Siberia, known as one of the coldest places in the world. A temperature of 92 degrees Fahrenheit below zero has been recorded here. Verkhoyansk was founded in 1638 and became a fur-trading post. In the Soviet period, tin-mines have been developed nearby.

● **Vietnam** An area of South-East Asia, on the South China Sea. It extends in a narrow band along the east coast of the Indo-China peninsula. The country consists of two large delta lowlands on the Red River (in the north) and on the Mekong River (in the south), which are linked by a long, narrow mountainous backbone. Population and economic activities (mainly agricultural) are concentrated in the two delta lowlands. The country's tropical monsoon climate favours rice growing, especially in the Mekong delta. Other crops are rubber, tea and coffee. Minerals (coal, tin, chrome, phosphates) are restricted to the north. Vietnamese, who comprise more than 80 per cent of the population, are a Mongolian race of Chinese culture, Buddhist religion and Indo-Chinese language, using the Latin alphabet. In the highlands are a number of minority groups; the cities, especially in the south, have a large Chinese population. Before World War II, Vietnam was divided into three French colonial areas: Cochin China in the south, Annam in the centre, and Tonking in the north. They were French protectorates between 1862—84. After World War II, in which these areas were occupied by the Japanese, a Communist-led nationalist revolt resisted the return of French rule. The revolt led to the Indo-China War between the French and the nationalists, which lasted from 1946 to 1954. The Geneva armistice of 1954 partitioned Vietnam along the 17th parallel.

Fighting continued in the South between factions favouring a Communist government as in the North and those opposing it. In 1964 America moved in massive troops to destroy the Communist Vietcong, but victory was not forthcoming and in 1970 the war spread to Cambodia for some months. Despite plans to withdraw American troops, the war continues.

● **North Vietnam**, officially called the Democratic Republic of Vietnam, has a Communist government. It has an area of 64,000 square miles and a population of 18.8 million. The capital is Hanoi. The Red River (Song-kai) delta is the economic heart of North Vietnam, whose rice crop is barely sufficient to feed the population, 90 per cent of which lives in rural settlements. North Vietnam's foreign trade is carried out almost entirely with other Communist nations. North Vietnam exports coal, non-ferrous ores, timber, coffee, tea and handicraft articles, in return for petroleum products and manufactured goods. Industry is nationalised and agriculture has been collectivised.

● **South Vietnam**, officially called the Republic of Vietnam, has an area of 63,000 square miles and a population of 15.1 million. The capital is Saigon. The Mekong delta, where the population is concentrated, is a major rice-exporting area. Rubber, tea and coffee are also exported. South Vietnam's leading trade partners are France, the United States and Japan. The population is largely Buddhist, but Roman Catholicism is also strong.

● **Vilnius (Vilna)** is the capital of the Soviet Republic of Lithuania and one of the most disputed cities of Europe, for it carried out its present function throughout the Middle Ages, then passed to Russia in 1795 and to Poland in 1920, though it had been the centre of Lithuanian independence for three years previously. Its university dates from 1578, and the city — with 372,000 people today — had 214,000 inhabitants in 1918; it was a centre of Jewish culture between the wars. The city's population is largely of Polish origin, the people of the surrounding countryside being dominantly Lithuanian.

● **Vladivostok** Soviet Far Eastern port (population 442,000) at the Pacific end of the Trans-Siberian railway. It is situated on slopes, descending in the form of an amphitheatre to the Golden Horn, a natural harbour. Icebreakers are used in winter to keep the port accessible to ships all the year round. Vladivostok has shipyards and fish canneries, and manufactures mining equipment. It is the base for fishing, whaling and crabbing fleets operating in the Soviet Far East. Founded by the Russians in 1860, the port became a naval base after Russia lost Port Arthur to Japan in 1905. Since the 1950s, most of Vladivostok's merchant shipping functions have been shifted to the new port of Nakhodka (population 54,000), 60 miles farther south-east, with its sheltered, ice-free natural harbour.

● **Volga River** The largest in Europe and the Soviet Union; 2,400 miles long. It has its source in the Valdai Hills, and flows into the Caspian Sea by way of a large delta. It is navigable along most of its course, and now serves several lake reservoirs of vast length, together with power stations at Rybinsk, Gorki, Kuibyshev and Volgograd. The Volga carries more than a half of all the freight moved on Soviet waterways, especially oil, grain, salt and fish upstream, while timber is the main downstream cargo. The river is connected by canals to Moscow, Leningrad and the Don River, so that one can sail direct from the Baltic to the Black Sea, and the legendary 'Volga boatman' has made way for Diesel tugs and powered barges.

● **Volgograd**, the former city of Stalingrad, and before that Tsaritsyn, had a population of 818,000 in 1959. The city lies on the Volga river, in the south-east part of the most heavily populated region of European Russia, facing the desert steppe of the Caspian depression. The city stretches for forty miles in a narrow belt along the right bank of the Volga. Volgograd is one of the main machinery-manufacturing centres of the U.S.S.R., producing

Tokyo, vast capital city of Japan, presents a colourful, neon-lighted appearance at night

steel, tractors, river vessels, aluminium and chemicals, as well as refining petroleum. The Volga-Don canal joins the river to the south of the city. To the north of Volgograd lies one of the world's largest hydro-electric stations. The Battle of Stalingrad, fought during the winter of 1942—43, made the city world renowned; the defeat of the German armies ended their advance eastwards and was a turning point in the war, for over 300,000 German troops were encircled and captured. The city has since been entirely rebuilt.

Vorkuta The urban centre of the Pechora coalfield. The town has a population of 70,000, while the coalfield yielded 17½ million tons of coal in 1960. The town lies north of the Arctic Circle, at the very north of the Urals, and is linked by rail to the Pechora River and, further south-west, to Kotlas, on the North Dvina.

Voronezh, with 660,000 inhabitants, lies midway between Moscow and Rostov, and is the largest city of the 'black earth' region. It is a machine-manufacturing centre, specialising in farm, foodstuff and electrical machinery. There is a large synthetic-rubber plant. The city was founded in 1586 as a Russian fortified post, while Peter the Great built warships there in 1694 during his campaign against the Turks. The city quadrupled its population between 1926 and 1959, as it developed into an important administrative, cultural and industrial centre. The water communications of Voronezh have declined, and it is now a rail centre.

White Sea An arm of the Barents Sea, in north-west European Russia. Shipping is active during the brief ice-free season from May to November, while the principal port is Archangel, and there are excellent fishing grounds in the western part. A canal to the Baltic was opened in the 1930s.

Wu-han This metropolis of Central China, on the Yangtze River, consists of three cities: Hankow, Hanyang and Wuchang. The total population of the tri-city area, administered as a single city, is 2,146,000. Hankow, the largest section, is now linked by a bridge across the Han River with Hanyang, and Hanyang, in turn, is connected by a great Yangtze bridge (completed in 1957) with Wuchang. Wu-han is a major transportation and industrial centre. It lies midway between Peking and Canton on China's main north-south railway, and its port, though 600 miles from the sea, is accessible to ocean-going vessels. Most of the city's commercial activities and many industries are concentrated in Hankow, which was opened to foreign trade in 1858. Its rapid development was spurred by Western business interests. Hanyang has many industries, including a large cotton mill. Wuchang, on the south bank of the Yangtze, has preserved its traditional Chinese appearance. It contains two universities. Wu-han's greatest industrial project, a large steel plant, is rising east of Wuchang.

Wusih City (population 600,000) of eastern China, in the Yangtze delta. Wusih is a large cotton-milling centre, whose modern machine methods have supplanted the traditional textile centre of Soochow.

yak An ox-like animal, still found in the wild state in remote parts of the Tibetan plateau. The yak is, however, better known as the domesticated animal of the Tibetans, whom it serves as a source of milk, meat and fat, leather and hair, and as a beast of burden.

Yakuts A Turkish-speaking people of eastern Siberia, in the basin of the Lena River. Numbering about 250,000, the Yakuts engage in grain farming, cattle and horse raising and, to the north, reindeer herding. With Russian settlers and other Siberian tribes, the Yakuts form an autonomous Soviet Republic (Yakutsk), with its capital at Yakutsk. In the Middle Ages, the Yakuts fled from their earlier homeland near Lake Baikal.

Yakutsk City of eastern Siberia, on the Lena River; (population 74,000). Yakutsk was founded in 1632, as the Cossacks advanced through Siberia. It became an early centre for exiles and is now the capital of the Yakut Autonomous Republic (Yakutsk). The city, which consists almost entirely of wooden buildings, is situated in the heart of the Yakut farming area. Its trade is mainly concerned with skins, furs and timber.

Yangtze River Longest river of China and, after the Ob-Irtysh, of Asia, too, flowing 3,400 miles from the Tibetan highlands to the East China Sea, north of Shanghai. The Yangtze is by far the most important of China's navigable rivers. Along its course are many of the country's great cities: Chungking, the head of navigation; Wuhan, which can be reached by ocean-going vessels, though 600 miles from the sea; Nanking; and Shanghai, near its mouth. The Yangtze flows through the lake-filled rice-growing basin of central China. Cotton, soya beans, tobacco and other crops are grown. Its valley is one of the most densely populated regions in the world. Like the Yellow River, the Yangtze presents a flood threat during the summer monsoon. Flood reservoirs have been built in recent years to divert excess water. Long-range plans call for the construction of a huge dam in the Yangtze gorges (between Chungking and Wuhan), where rapids now endanger navigation.

Yellow River One of the great rivers of China, flowing 2,900 miles from the Tibetan highlands to the Yellow Sea, north of the Shantung peninsula. At one time, its mouth was south of the peninsula. The Yellow River owes its name to the yellowish silt brought down from the loess (fine loam) lands in its middle course. After the river emerges from the mountains and enters lower ground, its speed is reduced, and the silt load is deposited. Over the years, the Yellow River has built up the fertile North China plain. In its lower course, the Yellow River has to be contained by dikes, and so flows in a channel above the surrounding countryside. Because of lack of flood control, the Yellow River presents a constant threat in the high-water stage, during the rainy summer monsoon. For the rest of the year it carries little water and is not navigable. Lack of navigation and the flood danger have kept cities away from the river banks. The cities of Kaifeng and Tsinan, near the lower course, have to be protected by dikes. A flood control programme, undertaken in recent years, includes the construction of large dams in the upper course of the river, to regulate its seasonal flow. The river was once known as 'China's Sorrow', because of the disastrous floods it caused.

Yellow Sea An arm of the Pacific Ocean, between Korea and North China. The Yellow River empties into this sea. The main ports of the Yellow Sea are: Inchon and Nampo in Korea; Lü-ta, Tientsin and Tsingtao in China.

Yemen Arab Republic Arab State (75,000 square miles; population 5,300,000) of the Middle East, in the south-west corner of the Arabian Peninsula. The capital is Taiz (population 100,000). Yemen consists of a narrow coastal plain and the interior highlands, where most of the population and economic activities are concentrated. The highlands' climate is unusually cool and moist for the Arabian Peninsula, and favours agriculture. Coffee, hides and dried fruit, Yemen's leading exports, move through the port of Hodeida, on the Red Sea. The country's Moslem population belongs to the Shiite sect in the highlands and the Sunnite sect on the coastal plain. Yemen's Jews, who numbered about 50,000, have emigrated to Israel. Although traditionally opposed to foreign penetration, Yemen became more active in world affairs after World War II. It pressed its claims against the Aden Protectorate, joined the United Nations in 1947, and formed a close alliance with the United Arab Republic in 1958. The king was deposed in 1962, and a republic declared. Since then, however, civil war has disturbed the Yemen. In 1967 Egyptian troops withdrew, and in 1970 a first permanent constitution was announced.

Yenisei River One of the great Siberian rivers flowing northward to the Arctic Ocean; 2,400 miles long. The Yenisei rises in the foothills of the Altai Mountains, in the Mongolian People's Republic, and flows north past Krasnoyarsk and Igarka. Ice covers the lower reaches of the river from the end of October to mid-June, leaving only a four-month navigation season. Large hydro-electric projects, including one near Krasnoyarsk, open a great industrial potential for the Yenisei valley and those of its tributaries, the Tunguska and Angara.

Yokohama Large city port (population 1,980,000) of Japan, just south of Tokyo. Yokohama was visited in 1854 by Commodore Perry, and was the first Japanese port opened to foreign trade in modern times. Like Tokyo, Yokohama was heavily damaged both in the 1923 earthquake and by bombing raids in 1945, during World War II. The city has large metal-industrial concerns.

yurt A light, movable tent, consisting of skins or felt stretched over a lattice framework. It is used by the Kirghiz and other nomadic herders of Central Asia.

Kirghiz yurt

Zaporozhye is an industrial city of the Ukraine, with a population of 658,000. Sited on the Dnieper, it is concerned with steel, aluminium and chemical manufacture, and derives electricity from a large dam, first built in 1932, but reconstructed after the war. The city had a small population (56,000) in 1926; its enormous growth since then provides evidence of the great migration from the rural areas to the towns which has taken place during the Soviet period.

zebu The humped cattle of India, also known as Brahman (after the Hindu god Brahma, to whom the sacred cattle are dedicated). The zebu are probably of aurochs stock, and were domesticated in Asia by 4,000 B.C., though some are still to be found in the wild. They differ from European cattle in having a large fatty hump, a big dewlap, short horns and long ears. The humped cattle have been introduced into Texas and other places, where they have been crossed with other breeds, producing a variety resistant to disease.

Africa

The continent of Africa (12 million square miles; population estimated to be approaching 280 million) ranks second among the seven continents in area, and fourth in population. It is surrounded by important ocean routes of traffic, and flanked by the world's two principal land masses — Eurasia and the Americas. Africa straddles the equator far enough, north and south, to be intersected by both the Tropic of Cancer ($23\frac{1}{2}°$N) and the Tropic of Capricorn ($23\frac{1}{2}°$ S). Its northernmost point (in Tunisia) is about the same distance from the equator — roughly 2,500 miles — as Cape Agulhas at the southern tip of the continent. At its north-western corner, by the Strait of Gibraltar, Africa is only nine miles from Europe, and the two continents are intervisible. Nor is it far removed from Saudi Arabia across the Bab-el-Mandel Straits in the east.

More than any other continent, Africa is a land of the tropics, with more than 9 million square miles (three times the area of the United States) lying in the zone of perpetual summer. Here the rays of the sun at midday are vertical or near-vertical every day of the year. It is the warmest of all continents, and its seasonal differences are best described in terms of rainy and dry periods.

The African rain forest is found in the Congo Basin and along the Gulf of Guinea. Its climate is monotonously hot and humid, and daily downpours are the rule. The forest is dense and luxuriant; it consists of tall trees that form a solid canopy above an under-storey of smaller trees. It is the home of tree-dwelling animals, notably monkeys and apes. Climbing plants and vines abound, rendering travel along the ground tedious and difficult.

The savanna is a zone of transition between the tropical rain forest and the desert, to the north as well as to the south of the equator. Its vegetation ranges from low grass and thornbushes in the vicinity of the desert, to tall grasses, shrubs, and trees near the rain forest. Its climate is noted for a well-defined dry season, which lengthens as one proceeds further away from the equatorial belt. The treeless portion of the savanna is the home of such herbivorous animals as the antelopes, the giraffe, the elephant, and the zebra; and also the carnivorous lion.

The Sahara, which extends from the Atlantic to the Red Sea, and the Kalahari, in south-western Africa, are two of the continent's most thoroughly dry regions, and it is not unusual for years to go by without a drop of rain falling, though many parts have slight rain annually. Most of the rivers that reach the desert from the more humid regions either disappear in the sands or terminate in shallow lakes without outlets to the sea. Only two African rivers, the Nile and the Orange, succeed in crossing the deserts to the sea.

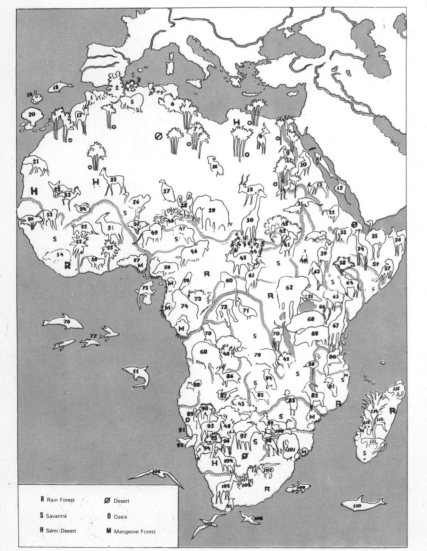

R Rain Forest   Ø Desert
S Savanna   O Oasis
H Semi-Desert   M Mangrove Forest

Wild Animals and Plants

Mammals

1 Barbary ape
4 Yellow jackal*
5 Barbary lion
6 Crested porcupine
8 Loder's gazelle
10 Sabre-horned oryx
13 Soemmering's gazelle
15 Addax
16 Aoudad
17 Mhorr gazelle
18 Porpoise*
21 Spotted hyena*
22 Fennec
25 Dama gazelle
29 Forest elephant
30 Nubian giraffe
32 Gelada baboon
33 Hamadryas baboon
34 Gerenuk
36 Somali wild ass
37 Cheetah*
30 Grevy zebra
45 Bongo
46 Congo buffalo
47 Leopard*
49 Lion*
51 Giant eland
52 Aardvark*
53 Hussar monkey
54 Pygmy hippopotamus
56 Diana monkey
58 Bush pig
60 Brazza's monkey
61 Okapi
62 Bush elephant
64 Beisa oryx
65 Blue gnu
67 Masai giraffe
68 Hippopotamus*
69 Cape buffalo
70 Lechwe
72 Chimpanzee
74 Gorilla
76 Bottle-nosed dolphin*

79 Black rhinoceros*
80 Guereza
82 Sable antelope*
85 Yellow-backed duiker
86 Bushbuck
88 Common duiker
92 Cape seal
93 Greater kudu*
96 Springbok
97 Roan antelope*
99 Hartebeest*
100 Cape hunting dog*
101 White rhinoceros*
102 Klipspringer*
104 Hartmann zebra
105 Bontebok
110 Killer whale*
111 Fossa
113 Ring-tailed lemur
115 Ruffed lemur

Birds

9 Sacred Egyptian ibis
14 Abdim's stork
23 Secretary bird*
26 North African ostrich
27 Eared vulture*
28 Flamingo*
35 South African ostrich
41 Shoebill
42 Saddle-billed stork
59 Grey parrot
63 Marabou*
71 Congo peacock
78 Bateleur eagle*
81 Wedge-tailed hornbill
83 Crowned crane*
84 Crowned hawk eagle
87 Grey touraco
91 Jackass penguin

98 Paradise crane
106 Wandering albatross*
107 Sooty albatross*
108 Cape pigeon*
112 Vasa parrot

Reptiles and Amphibians

24 Rhinoceros viper
31 Nile crocodile

Fishes

11 Blue shark*
12 Sting-ray*
77 Flying fish*
109 Coelacanth

Plants

2 Cedar*
3 Dwarf fan palm*
7 Date palm
19 Indian fig*
20 Dragon tree*
38 Coffee shrub*
43 Papyrus*
44 Bamboo*
48 Baobab*
50 Acacia*
55 Oil palm
57 Mangrove*
66 Giant lobelia
73 Cardamom
89 Pachypodium
90 Aloe*
94 Weltwitschia
95 Aloe dichotoma*
103 Spurge*
114 Traveller's tree

Miscellaneous

40 Termite mound

Plants and animals designated with an asterisk (*) have a wide distribution. Others are found only where pictured.

Only a century ago most of 'the dark continent', apart from Egypt and North Africa, remained unexplored.

Ancient Egypt was the transfer point for goods from distant India and China. Alexandria was a thriving commercial centre as early as 300 B.C. Farther west, in present-day Tunisia, the historic city of Carthage had grown up under the Phoenicians in the 6th century B.C. It may have had a population of 700,000 more than 2,000 years ago, protected by its tripled city walls.

After the defeat of Carthage, in 146 B.C., the Romans established a province on the North African shore facing Sicily. They called it 'Province Afri' — the name later given to the entire continent. Most of the northern rim of Africa became part of the Roman Empire, and its main granary.

Europe's contacts with Africa were interrupted in A.D. 697 by the Arab conquest of North Africa. No Europeans were allowed to set foot on Moslem soil. Thus, through the Middle Ages, through the centuries of overseas explorations, and until the end of the 18th century, the interior of Africa remained virtually unknown. In the north, the Sahara was an effective barrier. Elsewhere, Africa's virtually unbroken coastline offered no more than a few sheltered harbours, access to the interior being impeded by fever-infested and marshy tropical forests, and by a highland escarpment a short distance inland from the coast. Furthermore, most of the continent's rivers form falls or rapids, making them unnavigable where they break through the highland rim on their way to the sea.

Two Scottish explorers, James Bruce (1730—94) and Mungo Park (1771—1806) were among the first white men to venture deep into the continent. Bruce, entering from the east, spent five years in Ethiopia, discovered the source of the Blue Nile in 1770, and followed the river downstream until it joined the White Nile at Khartoum. But nearly a century was to pass before another British explorer, John Speke (1827—64), solved the riddle of the source of the White Nile, which was at Lake Victoria.

Mungo Park set out in 1795 from Gambia, on the west coast of Africa, to find the Niger, but he was killed before he reached the river's mouth.

Although the spirit of adventure and the quest for knowledge drove men of all nations into the uncharted interior, the desire to halt the slave trade was the main reason for opening up tropical Africa in the 19th century. David Livingstone (1813—73), another Scotsman, 'devoted thirty years of his life to missionary work among the natives and to fighting the slave trade in Central Africa'. So reads the epitaph on his tombstone of black granite in Westminster Abbey. He traversed the interior of southern Africa and Bechuanaland, discovering the Zambezi River and its spectacular Victoria Falls, the headwaters of the Congo, and Lake Malawi, or Nyasa as it used to be called. So keen were his endeavours against the slave trade that he refused requests to return home, and he died of yellow fever in the Bangweulu jungles, while seeking the source of the Nile.

Livingstone's work was continued by Henry Stanley (1841—1904), the journalist who had been sent to find him when he had been presumed lost in 1871. They met at Ujiji, near Lake Tanganyika. Stanley found the connection between the river

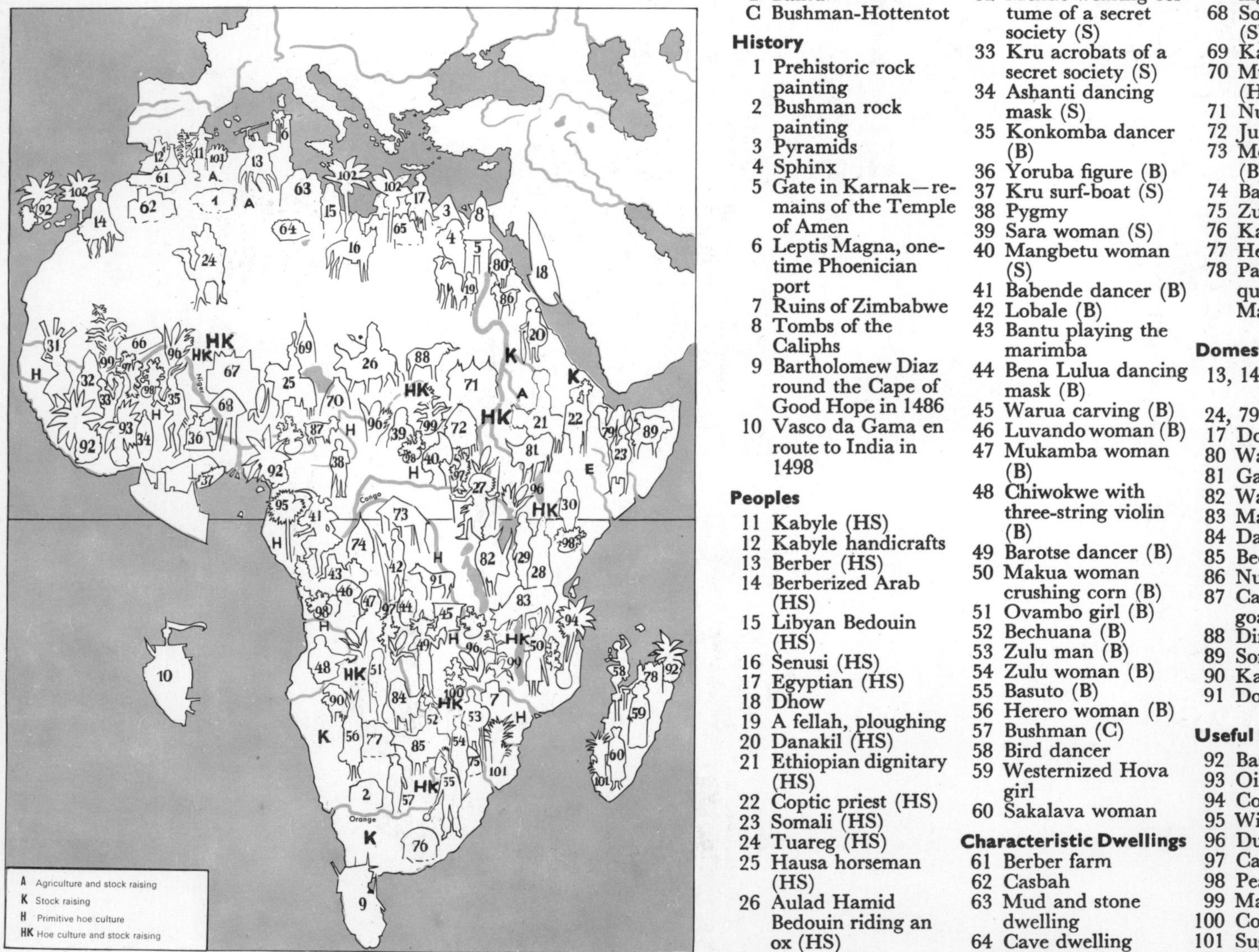

Peoples, Domestic Animals and Useful Plants

Language Families
HS Hamito-Semitic
S Sudanic
B Bantu
C Bushman-Hottentot

History
1 Prehistoric rock painting
2 Bushman rock painting
3 Pyramids
4 Sphinx
5 Gate in Karnak—remains of the Temple of Amen
6 Leptis Magna, one-time Phoenician port
7 Ruins of Zimbabwe
8 Tombs of the Caliphs
9 Bartholomew Diaz round the Cape of Good Hope in 1486
10 Vasco da Gama en route to India in 1498

Peoples
11 Kabyle (HS)
12 Kabyle handicrafts
13 Berber (HS)
14 Berberized Arab (HS)
15 Libyan Bedouin (HS)
16 Senusi (HS)
17 Egyptian (HS)
18 Dhow
19 A fellah, ploughing
20 Danakil (HS)
21 Ethiopian dignitary (HS)
22 Coptic priest (HS)
23 Somali (HS)
24 Tuareg (HS)
25 Hausa horseman (HS)
26 Aulad Hamid Bedouin riding an ox (HS)
27 Watusi (B)
28 Masai man (S)

29 Masai woman (S)
30 Wakamba (B)
31 Pepel dancer (S)
32 Mende wearing costume of a secret society (S)
33 Kru acrobats of a secret society (S)
34 Ashanti dancing mask (S)
35 Konkomba dancer (B)
36 Yoruba figure (B)
37 Kru surf-boat (S)
38 Pygmy
39 Sara woman (S)
40 Mangbetu woman (S)
41 Babende dancer (B)
42 Lobale (B)
43 Bantu playing the marimba
44 Bena Lulua dancing mask (B)
45 Warua carving (B)
46 Luvando woman (B)
47 Mukamba woman (B)
48 Chiwokwe with three-string violin (B)
49 Barotse dancer (B)
50 Makua woman crushing corn (B)
51 Ovambo girl (B)
52 Bechuana (B)
53 Zulu man (B)
54 Zulu woman (B)
55 Basuto (B)
56 Herero woman (B)
57 Bushman (C)
58 Bird dancer
59 Westernized Hova girl
60 Sakalava woman

Characteristic Dwellings
61 Berber farm
62 Casbah
63 Mud and stone dwelling
64 Cave dwelling
65 Mud mosque in Augila oasis

66 Fisherman's hut on the Niger
67 Painted mud dwelling in Tessaoua
68 Sokoto pile dwelling (S)
69 Kanuri hut
70 Musgu mud hut (HS)
71 Nuba huts (S)
72 Jur pile dwelling (S)
73 Mongo pile dwelling (B)
74 Banunu hut (B)
75 Zulu hut (B)
76 Kaffir hut (B)
77 Herero hut (B)
78 Palace of the last queen of Madagascar

Domestic Animals
13, 14, 16, 25 Berber horse
24, 79 Dromedary
17 Donkey
80 Water buffalo
81 Galla cattle
82 Watusi cattle
83 Masai cattle
84 Damara cattle
85 Bechuana cattle
86 Nubian goat
87 Cameroons dwarf goat
88 Dinka sheep
89 Somali sheep
90 Karakul sheep
91 Dog

Useful Plants
92 Banana
93 Oil palm
94 Coconut palm
95 Wine palm
96 Durra
97 Cassava
98 Peanut
99 Maize
100 Cotton
101 Sugar cane
102 Date palm
103 Wheat

A Agriculture and stock raising
K Stock raising
H Primitive hoe culture
HK Hoe culture and stock raising

systems of the continent, so important if they were to be used for trade. Between 1874 and 1877, he explored equatorial Africa, tracing the course of the Congo despite dense jungles and hostile tribes. His later explorations, made for King Leopold II of Belgium, led to the establishment (1885) of the Congo Free State (later the Belgian Congo, and now an independent republic). The natives called him Bula Matari, the crusher of rocks. Apart from English, French and American explorers, many Germans also made journeys into Africa. Heinrich Barth (1821—1865) traversed Africa from Lake Chad to the Niger, while Gerhard Rohlfs (1831—96) explored the Saharan oases. He was the first European to travel by land from the Mediterranean to the Gulf of Guinea. Gustav Nachtigal (1834—85) discovered the Tibesti Mountains and journeyed from Chad into the eastern Sudan. Many other men, from many lands, achieved less fame, for their researches were more localised, or else they were lost without trace, killed by hostile natives or by disease.

A new era in the settlement and exploitation of Africa began in 1869. With the opening of the Suez Canal and the discovery of diamonds in South Africa, several European powers started scrambling for lands in Africa.

On the eve of World War I, the continent was under European rule from Cairo to the Cape, and from Dakar in the west to the 'horn' of Italian Somaliland in the east. Only Abyssinia, now better known as Ethiopia, and the Negro republic of Liberia existed as independent African nations.

After the war, the erstwhile German colonies were turned over to the newly created League of Nations and their administration entrusted to four European powers: Togoland and the Cameroons were split up between Britain and France, South-West Africa was mandated to the Union of South Africa, and former German East Africa came under British rule (as Tanganyika), except for tiny Ruanda-Urundi, entrusted to Belgium through the Congo.

Between the two world wars, Italy was the only European power to enlarge its African holdings, by defeating Ethiopia in a war (1935—36) that the League of Nations had been unable to stop. Her empire did not survive World War II, however, and two new nations — The Libyan Arab Republic and Republic of Somalia — have risen from its ashes.

Today, 'the dark continent' is well-explored and mapped, carved up into separately governed areas, and well on its way to playing an increasingly important part in world affairs. Although Africa is almost the last continent where European countries are holding on to their colonies and dependencies, self-government and nationhood are becoming the goal of an ever-growing number of Africans. In West Africa, the Gold Coast (renamed Ghana) achieved independence within the British Commonwealth in 1957, and Nigeria has had complete and Federal self-government since 1960. Farther south, the two Rhodesias and Nyasaland were joined together in the Central African Federation (1953), in which the native African was slowly receiving greater recognition and representation, though this has now split up into Zambia (Northern Rhodesia), Rhodesia (Southern Rhodesia) and Malawi (Nyasaland).

In North Africa, Libya (1951), Morocco and Tunisia (1956), and the Sudan (1956), have achieved their independence; Ethiopia, free once again from Italian rule, joined former Italian Eritrea in a federation headed by the Ethiopian emperor; the Somali Republic (known as Italian Somaliland before World War II) became independent in 1960; and the Arab peoples of Moslem Algeria became independent of French

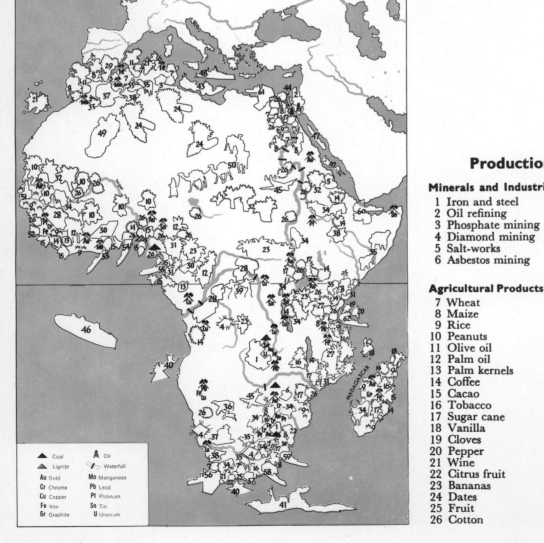

Production, Mineral Resources and Trade

Minerals and Industries
1 Iron and steel
2 Oil refining
3 Phosphate mining
4 Diamond mining
5 Salt-works
6 Asbestos mining

Agricultural Products
7 Wheat
8 Maize
9 Rice
10 Peanuts
11 Olive oil
12 Palm oil
13 Palm kernels
14 Coffee
15 Cacao
16 Tobacco
17 Sugar cane
18 Vanilla
19 Cloves
20 Pepper
21 Wine
22 Citrus fruit
23 Bananas
24 Dates
25 Fruit
26 Cotton

27 Sisal
28 Rubber
29 Cork
30 Timber
31 Coconuts, copra
32 Gum arabic
33 Esparto grass

Livestock and Animal Products
34 Cattle
35 Sheep
36 Karakul sheep
37 Wool
38 Skins
39 Ivory
40 Fishing
41 Whaling
42 Pearl diving
43 Sponge fishing

Transportation and Trade
44 Suez Canal
45 Transport plane
46 Passenger ship
47 Tanker
48 Naval base—Malta
49 Desert bus

50 Caravan
51 Bathurst—air centre exports peanuts
52 Freetown—exports palm kernels
53 Accra—exports gold, timber, cacao, manganese
54 Lagos—exports cacao, palm kernels, palm oil
55 Douala—exports hardwoods
56 Cape Town—exports skins, wool, gold, diamonds
57 Port Elizabeth—exports wool, hides, fruit, diamonds
58 East London—exports wool
59 Durban—exports manganese, coal, chrome
60 Djibouti—exports coffee
61 Alexandria—exports cotton
62 Zanzibar—exports cloves

rule in 1962, after a long and bitter war for their freedom.

Egypt, which obtained its independence from Turkey after World War I, took control of the strategic Suez Canal in 1956, and set out to lead the Arab countries of the Near East away from dependence upon Western Powers. Egypt's expansionist policy took an important step forward in 1958, when Syria joined Egypt — followed later by the Yemen — to form the United Arab Republic under President Nasser's leadership, but this has not been carried through. Except in the Republic of South Africa, the Portuguese possessions (Angola, Mozambique and Guinea), Rhodesia, and the territory of the Spanish Sahara, where the policy of white supremacy is straining race relations, the era of European domination is drawing to a close. The 'wind of change' has achieved the independence of many other African nations since 1960, some not without internal strife, especially in the Congo, and in Rwanda and Burundi. Most French-held nations achieved independence in 1960, while certain free nations have combined to form Federations, notably Tanzania (Tanganyika and Zanzibar), Mali (now broken up) and Ethiopia. The last remaining British responsibility in Africa was Swaziland, which gained its independence in 1968. Spain and Portugal still have possessions in Africa, and several critical problems remain to be solved: the controversial South African policy of *apartheid*, by which white and black communities are kept completely separate and are not allowed to mix: and the future of Rhodesia's government by Europeans — a relatively small minority of the population — in the face of world-wide opposition, since the country's unilateral declaration of independence (UDI) in 1965, and subsequent complete break with Britain in 1970. Negotiations for a settlement were proceeding by 1972.

When colonisation began, less than a hundred years ago, the Europeans met natives whose way of life seemed primitive by Western standards. They were hunters and food gatherers, or nomadic shepherds, always on the move with their herds. Their tribal organisation and customs had little in common with Western views about government, law, or earning a livelihood.

Although many aspects of native culture have been preserved, European civilisation has had a tremendous impact on Africa.

Tropical diseases have been brought under control in many parts of the continent. Malaria, the most widespread of all diseases, can now be checked simply by spraying wide areas with DDT. Africa's population is growing rapidly — from about 120 million in 1900 to approximately 280 million today. At least two-thirds of Africa's peoples are Negroes, with Europeans and Asians in the minority everywhere. Only in North Africa is another ethnic group — represented by the Arabs and the Berbers — in the majority.

Africa has thus become a land of changes and contrasts. Modern cities have risen within sight of tribal villages; plantations, where rubber, coffee and cacao are grown under efficient management, have been carved out of the bush or jungle; copper, tin, iron, gold, diamonds, and even uranium, are mined in the interior of the continent, and railways have been built to transport these raw materials to the nearest seaport; rivers have been dammed to control floods and irrigate downstream areas, and also to provide hydro-electric power for Africa's new industries; aircraft span the continent, flying over deserts and tropical forests; and schools and universities have been established to educate the African leaders of tomorrow.

The new African States have strong interests in politics, policies and trade. Similarly, though outward looking, internal colonisation of their countries has been facilitated by development of measures protecting men and animals against insects and bacteria. Missionaries and others have developed schools and hospitals, though Europeans have not done this without much greater rewards, for many have received more than they have ever given, especially in highly prized minerals and ores, such as copper, for Katanga (a province of the ex-Belgian Congo) and Zambia supply a quarter of the world's copper needs, and South Africa and Katanga supply more than half the world's diamonds and gold.

Despite great development and natural wealth, Africa is still largely undeveloped, and many of its peoples are poor and undernourished. Serious deficiencies remain, in road and rail transport, large harbours, schools and universities, as well as great problems of social differences and a high birth rate.

African huts beside the giant Voortrekker Monument, which stands near Pretoria and commemorates South African pioneers of 1835–43

AFRICA

Scale 1:30,000,000
0 100 200 300 400 500 Miles

♣ ALEXANDRIA *Cities over* 1,000,000 *population*
⊙ Algiers *Cities of 250,000 - 1,000,000 population*
○ Luanda *Cities under* 250,000 *population*
◉ *Capitals of Countries*

Depths in feet: Heights in feet:

over 650   0-650   Below   0-650 650-1650 1650-4900 over 4900
                         sea level

~~~ *Intermittent streams*   ✕✕✕ *Wadi*   ▦ *Salt Lake*   ▨ *Desert*
⌐ *Head of navigation* ─── *Railroads* ─── *Canals* ☲ *Swamp, marsh*

aardvark An African animal the size of a pig, with a long snout, large donkey-like ears and a thick tail. Aardvarks destroy termite mounds with their powerful claws, sweeping up the insects with long, sticky tongues. Their name 'aardvark' is a word meaning 'earth pig'. Aardvarks live in deep holes during the daytime.

acacia A plant of the mimosa family; it is either a woody shrub or a tree, often thorny. Many acacia plants are important because of hardwood, tanning extracts and gums made from them. The flat-topped acacia is the characteristic tree of the African savanna.

Accra The capital of Ghana, with a population of 663,880. This is served by a new deep water port, Tema, built in 1962, 17 miles from the city. Cacao, timber, manganese and gold are the chief exports. Though Ghana was formerly a British colony, Danes settled on the Gold Coast and built the Christiansborg Castle.

Addis Ababa The capital of Ethiopia. This sprawling city of 644,190 inhabitants lies more than 8,000 feet above sea level, in rugged high-lands. The emperor's palace stands above all. Mingled in the streets are modern motor-cars and herds of sheep, city folk in Western clothing and poor villagers carrying produce to market. A rail-way connects Addis Ababa with the port of Djibouti 500 miles away on the Bay of Aden.

Afrikaans The language spoken by the Boers of South Africa. English and Afrikaans are the two official languages of the Republic of South Africa.

albatross, sooty An albatross of the Southern Atlantic and Indian Oceans, often seen from pas-senger liners. It has a sooty-brown plumage and a wedge-shaped tail.

albatross, wandering A large ocean bird, mainly white with black wing-tips. It is 45 to 50 inches long and has a wing span of 10 to 12 feet.

Alexandria The chief port of Egypt and the second-largest city (1,513,000 people) in Africa. It lies on the Mediterranean at the western edge of the Nile delta. Most of the Republic's foreign trade moves through Alexandria. Cotton, grown in the Nile Valley of Egypt and in the Sudan, is the chief export. Founded in 332 B.C. by Alexander the Great, it was for three centuries the leading commercial city of the Mediterranean, and a cultural centre with a renowned university and library. Captured from the Egyptians by Julius Caesar in 47 B.C., Alexandria prospered under the Roman Empire. In modern times its importance was helped by its proximity to the Suez Canal, until the canal's closure in 1967.

Algeria A country of northern Africa (popula-tion 13.2 million) extending southwards from the Mediterranean to the heart of the Sahara, and adjoining Morocco and Tunisia. The Atlas Mountains stretch across Algeria, parallel to the rugged coastline. Northern Algeria (85,000 square miles) is more settled, and economically more important, than the vast desert region of 750,000 square miles south of the Atlas; but recent oil and mineral discoveries in the desert have increased its value.

The narrow coastal plains and the lower slopes of the northern Atlas ranges are intensively farmed, principal crops being wheat, wine grapes, citrus fruit, and early vegetables for sale in France. Algeria also exports iron ore and phosphate rock for fertilisers. The chief seaports are Algiers, the capital, and Oran, a naval base. Only 10 per cent of Algeria's population is non-Moslem, predomi-nantly French. About a third of the cultivated land is owned by European farmers, who began settling there more than a century ago. Algeria was ruled by the French from 1830 until 1962, but is now an independent republic.

Algiers The chief city (population 943,000) of Algeria and once a stronghold of the Barbary pirates. It trades actively with Marseilles, France's chief port, across the Mediterranean. Wine, fruits, winter vegetables, cereals, cork and wool are ship-ped there. Around the city's excellent natural harbour is an old Moslem quarter, where narrow, crooked lanes separate clusters of crowded, windowless houses. The Casbah, a 16th-century fortress-quarter, built by the Turks, overlooks the ancient city.

Angola 'Portuguese West Africa' A Portu-guese overseas province in south-western Africa, fourteen times the size of Portugal. Its 480,000 square miles are only sparsely settled with about 5 million people. The natives, Bantu Negroes, grow maize, groundnuts, cassava, rice, and castor seed. The south coast has some oyster-fishing. In the south-east, a few tribes of Bushmen remain. The Portuguese, avoiding the hot coastal lowland, have coffee plantations on the interior plateau. Cotton and sugar plantations also are found at lower elevations. The uplands of Angola remained almost inaccessible until the completion, in 1929, of the Benguela Railway. This connects Lobito, one of the best natural harbours on the west coast of Africa, with mining centres of Katanga (Congo). Shorter railways tap the interior from the ports of Luanda (the territory's capital) and Moçamedes. Angola's coastline was discovered by Portuguese navigators in 1482. For over two centuries, slaves were rounded up in Angola and shipped to Brazil. Political and armed attempts to gain independence have been suppressed.

antelope, roan An antelope that can travel at a strong, brisk gallop like that of a horse. The male has a grizzled roan coat. The ribbed horns, rela-tively short and strong, are curved backward. The roan favours open upland regions.

antelope, sable The most stately of the antelopes. It arches its neck when running, and its superb sickle-shaped horns, sweeping back from the face, may reach 5 feet in length. The lustrous coat is deep mahogany or black, with white markings about the flanks.

antelopes A group of hollow-horned ruminants renowned for grace and speed. They are popular as game; their meat is tasty, and their skin easily tanned; the horns are carved into utensils or used as spearpoints. Africa's many varieties of antelope include some with spiral horns — kudu, bushbuck, eland and bongo. Duikers are small antelopes of the bush country. Water-loving antelopes include water-buck, lechwe and reedbuck. Sable and roan antelopes are strong, stately animals that deport themselves like horses. Antelopes with straight horns include the oryxes and the addax. Harte-beest, gnu and bontebok are antelopes with long, narrow faces. Smaller are the gazelle, the gerenuk and the klipspringer.

apes A group of mammals including the gibbons, orangutans, gorillas and chimpanzees. They are the largest and most highly developed of the primates. Apes are tree-dwellers. On the ground, they can stand or walk half erect.

ass, Somali wild A handsome, strongly built animal which is probably the ancestor of our domesticated donkey. It stands about 4½ feet at the shoulder, and has a reputation for great speed and sure-footedness. Low, stony hill country is its home.

Aswan A town of 48,000 people in Egypt, near the First Cataract of the Nile. Three miles up-stream, a 1¼-mile-long dam was built by British engineers in 1902, to provide year-round water supply for Egypt's farms. In summer, the muddy floodwaters are allowed to pass through the open gates of the dam. In early autumn, the gates are closed and the water level rises. During the dry season — April to June — the waters gradually move through irrigation canals to the fields. Since the Aswan Dam cannot be raised higher, the Egyptians have built the so-called High Dam at a point 5 miles above the present one; this will be 350 feet high and nearly 2 miles wide.

By the shores of the Mediterranean, near Bougie, Algeria, an Arab shepherd boy tends his flock

Atlas Mountains A system situated in Morocco, Algeria and Tunisia, in north-west Africa. They were folded at the same time as the Alps of Europe. Three ranges are found in Morocco: the Rif, the High and the Anti Atlas. To the east, only two are found: the Tell and the Sahara Atlas. The highest peak is in the High Atlas: Ojebel Toubkal, reaching to 13,661 feet. Between the eastern ranges lies the High Plateau, with salt lakes in the Shott region. The mountains contain iron, oil, lead, zinc, coal and other metals, as yet largely unexploited.

baboons The largest, most powerful and most savage of the monkeys. These 'dog-faced' animals walk on all-fours, with tail erect. They live in well-organised herds and travel far in search of food. Well-known baboons are the gelada, quite sinister-looking, and the hamadryad, with its long mane of silvery hair.

Bantu The language spoken by most of the native peoples of the southern half of Africa. Bantu has many dialects, and the peoples who speak them number about 50 million. These people, grouped into about 200 tribes, show a very wide range of physical characteristics and follow different ways of life.

baobab A mighty plant, also known as the monkey-bread tree, with a trunk that often reaches 35 feet in thickness. The fruit is like a gourd. The soft wood is fashioned into canoes, and the bark into cloth and ropes; leaves are eaten as a vegetable, and the fruit yields a tart beverage. Even the oil-rich seed is edible.

Bedouins Arab nomads of the deserts of North Africa and Arabia. They raise camels, sheep, horses and goats, and serve as caravan drivers. The Aulad Hamid are Bedouins dwelling in oases of the Libyan Desert.

Beira A seaport (50,000 people) of Portuguese East Africa (Mozambique) on the Indian Ocean. Two railways — one from Zambia, Rhodesia and the Congo, and the other from Malawi — reach the sea at Beira. Copper, lead, chrome and other minerals are shipped to Europe and North America.

Benguela One of the first Portuguese settlements in West Africa, founded in 1617. The **Benguela**

Current travels north along the coast of South-West Africa and Angola. The cold water chills the warm sea air; its moisture condenses, forming dense fogs along the coast — hence the dry climate of nearby land areas.

Berbers A Hamitic people (about 5 million) of north-west Africa. They are probably descendants of the original population, mixed with the Arabs who came in the 7th century. Unlike the nomadic Arabs, Berbers like farm and town life, with the exception of the Tuaregs. Many of them have strongly resisted all European penetration of their inland fastnesses.

Boers Descendants of Dutch settlers in South Africa. The name means 'farmers', and the people concerned are more properly called Afrikaners. They first arrived in 1652. After the British came, about 1800, the Boers moved inland on the Great Trek (1835—36). The Boers founded the Transvaal, Orange Free State, and Natal, but lost their independence to Britain in the Boer War (1899 —1902), being incorporated into the Union of South Africa (1909). The Boers keep their traditions and are very active in running the country, now proclaimed the Republic of South Africa.

bongo An antelope of the bamboo forests of West Africa. It has spiral horns and a rich chestnut-red coat with white vertical stripes. Hard to find, the bongo is a prize for hunters.

bontebok A now rare antelope of southern Africa, with a long, narrow face and short, S-shaped horns. It wears a purplish-red coat and has a white face and rump. Its name means 'spotted buck' in Dutch.

Botswana Formerly the British protectorate of Bechuanaland, Botswana became independent within the Commonwealth in October, 1966, and adopted Gaberones as its capital. The country lies between Zambia, Rhodesia, the Republic of South Africa and the Portuguese territory of Angola. Three times the size of Great Britain, Botswana contains 275,000 square miles, and its population of 535,000 tribal Bantus is scattered over this vast area of entirely native-owned land. The largest town is Kanye (37,000).

buffalo, Cape A heavily-built black buffalo. Big-game hunters call it the most dangerous hoofed

animal in the world. An old bull, nearly 5 feet tall, has massive horns as much as 3½ feet wide. The Cape buffalo once roamed in large herds through East and South Africa. It now survives largely in wildlife reserves.

Burundi A monarchy in Africa, between the Congo and Tanzania, and south of Rwanda. The population of 3,500,000 is largely Bantu. Formerly known as Urundi and under Belgian administration, it became independent in 1962. The country exports coffee, cotton and vegetable oil, tobacco and minerals. The capital is Bujumbura, with a population of 100,000.

bushbuck An antelope with spiral horns; also known as the harnessed antelope, because of the pure-white stripes on its russet-coloured coat. Shy in the wild, it is aggressive in captivity.

Bushmen Descendants of the original population of southern Africa. Driven into the desert by Bantu Negroes (moving south) and Europeans (moving north), today they are almost extinct. Survivors live by food-gathering and hunting. Cave and rock paintings in many parts of Africa show where they once lived. The language of Bushmen, like that of Hottentots, is characterised by peculiar clicking sounds.

cacao A plant native to tropical South America, now grown mainly in West Africa, notably Ghana. The tree grows to a height of 15 to 50 feet, bearing its seedpods on the stem. Its fleshy, yellow fruits mature throughout the year and contain 40—80 seeds, which are fermented to eliminate a bitter taste, then dried, roasted and ground. Cacao (cocoa) butter, pressed from the seeds, is used in cosmetics and soap. The cake that remains is used for chocolate. Nearly the whole of the production is exported from Ghana, Nigeria, Ivory Coast, Cameroun and Brazil. The chief importers are the U.S.A., Netherlands and Great Britain.

Cairo The capital of Egypt, and the largest city in Africa. On the right bank of the Nile, at the head of the wide delta, it is a city of contrasts, with crowded areas of Arabic-style, windowless buildings, and modern apartment and business districts, accompanied by many parks. The population is over 3.3 million. The streets are busy, except around midday in July, when temperatures are 43.3 °C or more in the shade. July is also the time of the Nile flood. The pyramids of Giza are 20 minutes away, at the edge of the desert on the other side of the river. The pyramids and sphinx are about 6 miles from Giza itself. Ruined Memphis, capital of the Old Kingdom of ancient Egypt, is a few miles upstream. Cairo has the world's oldest university, founded in 987.

Cameroun is a republic lying at the head of the Gulf of Guinea and stretching inland as far as Lake Chad; population 5.7 million and area 143,500 square miles. A German colony until the First World War, the Cameroons were then split into French and English mandated zones. Since 1960, the French part has been an independent republic (Cameroun), while the smaller British part divided in 1961, the northern region joining Nigeria and the southern region uniting with Cameroun. The capital of the Republic is Yaounde (130,000), and the largest port is Duala (210,000), which exports coffee, bananas, cacao, palm oil and tropical hardwoods. There is a large water-power site at Edea, and an aluminium industry.

Canary Islands A group of Spanish islands in the Atlantic Ocean, opposite southern Morocco. Home

The port of Cape Town, South Africa, is spread out at the foot of Table Mountain (3,567 ft)

African elephants, feeding on grass, leaves, twigs and fruits, sometimes eat half a ton per day

of the canary bird, the seven main islands (population 909,000) are the tops of volcanoes rising from the ocean floor. The highest reaches 12,200 feet above sea level. Some have extinct volcanic craters; smoke rises from others. The climate is mild throughout the year. Rain is light; crops must be irrigated. Bananas, citrus fruit, vegetables and tobacco are the main products. In winter, many Europeans and Americans come to enjoy the warmth and colourful sub-tropical vegetation, but today it has mainly summer visitors. The Canaries have been a possession of Spain since the 15th century.

● **Cape of Good Hope** An historic tongue of land near the southern tip of Africa. It guided early European navigators on their way to India. The Portuguese sailor Bartholomew Diaz discovered the route round the Cape in 1486, which he called Cabo Tormentoso. The southern tip of Africa is actually Cape Agulhas.

● **Cape Town** Largest passenger port of the Republic of South Africa, founded by the Dutch in 1652. A resort city, noted for its mild climate and its beauty, it is the seat of the Republic's legislature. Over 750,000 people live there. The flat top of Table Mountain, at 3,549 feet, is reached by an aerial cable-car.

● **Casablanca (Dar el Baida)** is Morocco's principal seaport and largest city. It has grown from a fishing hamlet to a metropolis of 1,177,000 in less than 50 years. Casablanca is now the fourth-largest city in Africa, after Cairo, Alexandria and Johannesburg. Large warehouses, grain elevators, harbour installations, single-storey factories, broad boulevards and tall office buildings give Casablanca a modern appearance.

● **casbah** (Arabic, *qasaba*, 'fortress') is the name given to the old citadels in the Atlas Mountains of North Africa. The casbah, overlooking a town, served as a refuge for the people of the countryside. The best-known casbah is in the city of Algiers; it includes an old section of hilly, winding alleyways.

● **Central African Republic** Formerly the region of Ubangi-Chari in French Equatorial Africa, but an independent republic since 1960. Largely composed of savanna, this land-locked country exports cotton, coffee, diamonds and groundnuts. It has an area of 234,000 square miles and a population of 1,466,000, largely Bantu or Sudan Negroes. The capital is Bangui, with 150,000 inhabitants.

● **Chad** A republic of central Africa and a land-locked State, south of Libya and between Niger and the Sudan. It has an area of 487,920 square miles and a population of 3,500,000, mainly Arabs or Sudan Negroes. Lake Chad lies in the west of the territory, and most of the land is desert or dry savanna, with the Tibesti Mountains in the far north, and the low-lying Bodelé depression adjacent to it. The capital is Fort Lamy, with 132,500 inhabitants, sited on the Chari river, which flows north-westwards to Lake Chad. The country exports cotton, groundnuts and animal products.

● **chimpanzee** An ape — the most manlike of the ape family. In the tropical forest of Africa, chimpanzees travel in small groups and feed on wild fruit. They can stand and walk upright, but generally travel on all-fours, with hands doubled up. Chimpanzees in captivity are used as experimental animals in the study of human diseases, and for psychological studies.

● **cobalt** A silver-white metal used in alloys for high-speed cutting tools and jet engine parts. About 80 per cent of the world's cobalt comes from the Congo and Zambia.

● **coelacanth** *Latimeria chalumna*. A fringe-finned, bony seafish. Hailed as a 'missing link', it is

thought that all back-boned land animals are probably descended from this fish. The first living coelacanth was found near Madagascar in 1938; several more were caught in 1952.

● **Comoro Islands** A group of small islands in the Indian Ocean, 300 miles north of Madagascar. They belong to France. About 275,227 people, most of them Moslem, grow spices, essential oils, and sugar. Copra, the dried meat of the coconut, and vanilla are the principal exports.

● **Congo** Within the 900,000 square miles of this vast republic, formerly the Belgian Congo, lies the vast Congo basin, the heart of tropical Africa. Kinshasa (population 1,225,720) the capital city, is a river port on the mighty Congo, whose tributaries and head-waters extend to the far reaches of the territory.

Half the country is covered by dense tropical vegetation, or rain forest. Most of the highly productive mines are in the province of Katanga, along the southern rim of the Congo basin. There, in the city of Lubumbashi is a prosperous copper industry and diamond mines. Manganese, cobalt, tin, gold and uranium are also mined in the Congo. Development of these valuable resources was slowed by lack of transport facilities, but today the output of the mines is transported by rail to Lobito, in Angola, or by rail and via the Congo River. Other exports include palm oil, palm kernels, cotton, coffee, and animal skins and hides.

The 21.6 million people mostly keep their tribal way of life. They grow their own crops — maize, cassava, sweet potatoes and plantains. Some have gone to work in the Belgian-owned mines, factories and plantations; 70,000 Belgians formerly ran the country.

The territory was explored by Livingstone and later by Stanley. It was the private possession of King Leopold II until 1908, when he turned it over to the Belgian government. During World War II, the Belgian Congo supplied the United States with uranium. After a long period of internal strife between Katanga and the rest of the country, itself far from united — and, more recently, an uprising in the north-eastern part of the land — progress has been made towards the establishment of a stable national administration in Kinshasa capable of asserting authority throughout the Congo. In 1971, the Congo was re-named Zaire.

● **Congo, Republic of** Formerly the French Congo, this is a smaller republic to the north of the Congo River, reaching the coast at Pointe Noire, and stretching for over a thousand miles north-eastwards. It has an area of 130,000 square miles and a population of 900,000, largely Bantu. The boundary with the Congolese Republic is formed by the Congo and Ubangi rivers. The land largely consists of tropical rain forest and mountains or highland. The Republic was formerly part of French Equatorial Africa, and became independent in 1960. It exports timber, palm oil, copra and ores. The capital is Brazzaville (population 156,000).

● **Congo River** One of the world's longest rivers (2,900 miles), second in Africa only to the Nile, and exceeding it in discharge. Even the source streams of the Congo are important rivers: the Luapula, which passes through Lakes Bangweulu and Mweru, and Lualaba. With its numerous tributaries, the Congo drains 1½ million square miles. In places, the stream is several miles wide and splits up into a number of channels. Before reaching the sea, the Congo cuts through the Guinea highlands and tumbles over Livingstone Falls.

It is navigable for ocean-going ships as far as Boma and Matadi, 100 miles from the sea. A 250-mile railway between Matadi and Kinshasa by-passes Livingstone Falls; other railway lines by-pass rapids farther upstream — the entire Congo basin can thus be crossed by combined rail and river travel. In 1971, the river Congo was re-named Zaire.

● **Copts** Descendants of ancient Egyptians who kept their Christian religion after the coming of Islam in the 7th century A.D. The Coptic Church, founded in the 5th century, is headed by the Patriarch of Alexandria, who has his seat in Cairo. The sect numbers about 2 million, and has a large following in Ethiopia. Coptic speech is ancient Egyptian and Hamitic, and is written with Greek characters. Though the language died out in the 17th century, it remains in a liturgical form.

● **crane, crowned** A species of crane, perhaps the most beautiful of all, with a dense crest of golden plumes and scarlet patches on its cheeks.

● **crane, paradise** A pale-grey crane of southern Africa, with an unusually large head and a tuft of long, drooping plumes hanging from its chest.

● **crocodile, Nile** A crocodile of the rivers of eastern Africa. During the day it suns itself on sandbanks, and at night floats in streams and lakes, always on the lookout for fishes or water birds. Sighting a victim, the creature dives and reappears directly under its prey. The crocodile will attack human beings, but does not pursue them out of the water.

In Europe in the Middle Ages, this reptile was considered a symbol of hypocrisy, because it shed 'crocodile tears' while devouring its victim. Actually, the crocodile secretes a saline solution from glands in its snout, to aid its digestion. The female lays 30 to 100 eggs in a dry place, covering them with sand, and the eggs are incubated by the sun. After 7—12 weeks, the young emerge, and the mother leads them to water. New-born crocodiles are 10 inches long; adults, about 18 feet. The Nile crocodile was considered to be holy by the Ancient Egyptians.

● **Dahomey** A republic, independent since 1960, on the Gulf of Guinea between Nigeria and Togo. This territory of 45,000 square miles has 2.37 million people. Porto-Novo (74,500 people) is the seat of government, Cotonou (111,000 people) the principal port and commercial city. Several short railway lines reach inland. Maize, cassava and sweet potatoes are the chief crops, and palm oil and kernels are shipped abroad.

● **Dakar** The former capital of French West Africa. Its 474,000 people include 20,000 Europeans. The harbour can take ocean liners and big warships. The busy international airport is the last stop for aircraft crossing the Atlantic to Brazil, less than 2,000 miles away. Opposite the port lies the rocky island of Gorée, which has been in French hands since 1677. For almost 200 years, African slaves were transported from Gorée to the West Indies and North America. The university was founded in 1946. Dakar is now the capital of the Republic of Senegal.

● **Dar es Salaam** (Arabic, 'haven of peace') The capital of Tanzania, on a bay of the Indian Ocean sheltered by a coral reef. The population of 163,000 is three-quarter African and one-quarter Indian; Europeans number less than 4,500. Large coconut groves surround the city. A railway leads west across Tanzania — one branch to Mwanza, on Lake Victoria, the other to Kigoma on Lake Tanganyika.

● **dates** — see **palm, date.**

● **desert** A region of very little rain and very little vegetation. The largest deserts are deep in the continents, far from moist ocean air. In the northern hemisphere, the largest desert belt runs across northern Africa to the Middle East, Iran and Pakistan; it includes the Sahara (largest of all deserts), the Arabian Desert, and the Thar of India and Pakistan. In the southern hemisphere, desert areas are smaller and (except for the Namib Desert in South-West Africa and the Atacama along the west coast of South America) not as dry as the Sahara.

Deserts are not restricted to warm areas; the Gobi, in China, the dry areas in central Turkestan, and the Great American Desert of the southwestern United States, occur in temperate latitudes. Hot, sunny days and cold nights are desert characteristics. Except for oases, mining settlements and military outposts, deserts are usually empty, for they cannot support a permanent population.

● **dhow** An old-fashioned sailing boat of the Nile and the east coast of Africa. Rigged with dark-coloured triangular sails, known as lateen sails, they are slow and have small holding capacity. They are gradually being replaced by power-boats.

● **diamond** A crystallised form of pure carbon and the hardest naturally formed mineral known. The best-quality diamonds are cut into gems. Inferior ones are used in cutting and drilling tools. Diamonds were first produced in India, then in Brazil (early 18th century) and South Africa (late 19th century). Most gem diamonds now come from the Republic of South Africa, and most industrial diamonds from the Congo.

In diamond mining, the diamond-bearing earth is brought to the surface, crushed, and sorted over greased tables to which the diamonds adhere while other rock material passes on. The diamonds are then cleaned and graded for sale. Gem diamonds are cut and polished in Europe.

Cape hunting dogs

● **Djibouti** A port on the Gulf of Aden in eastern Africa. It is the capital of The Afars and Issas, and has about 62,000 people. It is the terminus of the railway from Addis Ababa, capital of Ethiopia.

● **dog, Cape hunting** A wild dog, the size of a large Alsatian, as fierce as the hyena. It lives in packs of about 15. When hunting its prey (chiefly antelopes), the pack works in relays to pursue the swiftest of animals to exhaustion.

● **dragon tree** A tree of the Canary Islands yielding a variety of 'dragon's-blood'. It grows to a height of 40 feet or more and attains a great age. Dragon's-blood is a dark-red resin used in varnishes; it was used medicinally in the Middle Ages.

Dromedary

● **dromedary** The single-hump camel of the hot and arid regions of North Africa and Arabia; also known as the Arabian camel. Without this 'ship of the desert', vast sandy regions would be uninhabitable by man. The camel is sad-eyed, ungainly and slow-moving, full of complaints and objections; but it can endure great heat, carry burdens, and travel long distances. Its hump is a storage place for fat, and its stomach is a water reservoir; these enable the camel to go a long time without food or drink. The camel was domesticated as much as 5,000 years ago; it no longer exists wild. It has been introduced into South Africa, Australia and America.

● **Duala** A seaport of 210,000 people in the Cameroun Republic on the Gulf of Guinea. From the equatorial forest, a railway brings hardwoods, coffee, cacao, palm oil and ivory for export. The city has a modern woodworking industry.

Duiker

● **duiker** A small antelope, with short spiked horns, of the forest and bush country. Its name ('diver' in Afrikaans) comes from the duiker's habit of diving into underbrush when alarmed.

● **Durban** A leading seaport of the South African Republic, on the Indian Ocean. It is a port for the mines and industries of the Witwatersrand district, around Johannesburg. Manganese, chrome and coal are exported; also sugar cane. Durban is the chief city of Natal province and is growing rapidly. Its 682,000 people include many Indians from Asia. Durban's university was founded in 1909. The city is a noted holiday resort.

● **durra** A grain sorghum, the most important food cereal of the arid regions of Africa and Asia. It can be grown in slightly salty, dry soil. The plant grows to 20 feet. Some varieties are grown for green manure, others for syrup from their sweet stalks; some are made into whisk brooms. Grain grown under tropical conditions lacks gluten, which makes dough sticky, so durra flour cannot be used for bread. The grain is ground coarsely or pulverised, and is eaten as mush (in Africa) or as flat cakes (in Asia).

● **eagle, crowned** A magnificent bird of the tropical forest of central Africa. Warlike chieftains prize its feathers and huge claws. This eagle feeds on monkeys, diving upon them from its aerial vantage-point.

● **Egypt** An independent republic in north-east Africa, on the land bridge leading to Asia. There one of the world's oldest civilisations grew up. Although mostly desert, the country has a population of 30.9 million that is rapidly increasing. Almost all Egypt's people live in the long, 10-mile-wide oasis of the Nile River, between Aswan and Cairo, and in the delta of the Nile below the capital city. The population is crowded into a thirtieth of Egypt's total area of 390,000 square miles. Even on the farm lands of the delta, there are over 1,000 persons per square mile.

The empty desert stretches east and west of the steep hills between which the Nile River flows. For thousands of years, Egyptian peasants have watered their small patches of land with the Nile's waters. Primitive water-wheels and treadmills have been used since ancient times. Nowadays, canals and giant dams, such as the one at Aswan, provide water throughout the year. Irrigation pumps bring water to the cotton fields of Lower Egypt (the Nile delta) and to the sugar-cane plantations of Upper Egypt (the Nile valley above Cairo). Part of the grain Egypt needs must be imported, because Egypt concentrates on raising cotton to sell abroad.

The growing population can no longer live solely by agriculture, for land beyond the steep sides of the Nile valley cannot be watered for crops. Egypt is therefore developing more industries, mostly in Cairo, Alexandria, and other cities of the delta. More than 40 per cent of all industrial workers are in the textile industry. Rice-growing in the delta has started a rice-milling industry. The famous Egyptian cigarettes are made with Macedonian tobacco. There are sugar mills and date-drying plants. Refineries at Suez and Alexandria process oil from the Sinai Peninsula.

The Suez Canal lies entirely in Egypt. At its northern end is Port Said. The canal was once one of the most important waterways in the world, but by the time it closed in 1967, ships could sail round the cape in almost as short a time as it took to pass through the canal.

Egypt already had an advanced culture over 6,000 years ago, and Memphis was the capital as early as 3400 B.C. Ancient Egypt reached its peak about 2900 B.C., the age of the great Pyramids. Its history was told on limestone slabs inscribed with hieroglyphics, the pictorial alphabet of the Egyptians. The temples of Luxor and Karnak date from approximately 1500 B.C.

Ancient Egypt was repeatedly invaded, its people mingling with the conquerors. Alexander the Great took Egypt in 332 B.C., and his general, Ptolemy, founded an empire that lasted two centuries. Then came the period of Roman rule and of Queen Cleopatra's attempt to regain independence for Egypt. The country became part of the Arab world in the 7th century A.D.; it was conquered by the Turks in 1517 and occupied by Napoleon, 1798—1801.

The modern history of Egypt began in 1805, when Mohammed Ali became pasha (or ruler). This one-time Albanian soldier modernised the country and founded the line of rulers which lasted until 1952, when King Farouk was forced to abdicate. After completion of the Suez Canal in 1869, Britain controlled Egypt until 1922. Since then, Egypt has been independent. Under the leadership of President Gamal Abdel Nasser, Egypt merged with Syria in 1958, to form the United Arab Republic, which the Yemen joined later. This union was broken up in 1962. Since 1968, Egypt has concentrated her energies on a series of battles with Israel.

● **eland** The largest of all antelopes. Reddish brown, ox-like, and heavy (2,200 pounds), with spiral horns thicker than those of most antelopes; it is generally a forest dweller in highland areas.

● **elephant** The largest land-dwelling animal. Elephants live in Africa and Asia. They have powerful limbs, incisors (teeth) developed into ivory tusks, and a snout prolonged into a proboscis, or trunk. Elephants eat tree branches, gather fruit with the trunk, and dig for roots and tubers with the tusks. They like to drink and bathe, using their trunks as sprays. Contrary to popular belief,

Esparto grass

Fennec

elephants live only about as long as man. They used to roam freely across the African savanna, but now are reduced to a few herds in certain areas. Elephants — chiefly the Indian species — have been tamed since antiquity as work animals and for war; they have also been hunted — particularly in Africa — for their ivory tusks, which may be 6 feet long and weigh up to 200 lbs.

The common African or bush elephant, the largest, reaches a height of 12 feet and may weigh 6 tons. The African pygmy or forest elephant, about 7 feet high, has small, rounded ears. It frequents the tropical rain forest. The Asian or Indian elephant, about 9 feet tall, has smaller ears than African types. The elephant's large ears are vital for cooling purposes.

● **Elisabethville (now Lubumbashi)** The chief city of the Katanga mining district, at a height of 5,000 feet. With about 170,000 inhabitants, it is one of the most modern centres of tropical Africa, with the head offices o several large mining enterprises. More than 10,000 Europeans enjoy the mild highland climate thefre. Copper-smelter process ore mined in the region. Since 1960, there has been much civil unrest in the area.

● **Eritrea** A former Italian colony on the Red Sea. It now forms a province in the Federation of Ethiopia and Eritrea. Of the 60,000 skilled Italian farmers and craftsmen who came to Eritrea before World War II, some have remained among the two million natives of this 46,000-square-mile country. The Italians built fine roads, one connecting Asmara (178,537), the capital city (almost 8,000 feet above sea level), with Massawa, on the Red Sea, one of the hottest places on Earth.

● **esparto grass** A wild grass of North Africa, where it is also known as alfa, or halfa, grass. Its dried leaves and stems yield fibres for weaving and pulp for paper.

● **Ethiopia** An independent nation in north-east Africa; formerly known as Abyssinia. It is ruled by an emperor. With 400,000 square miles of rugged, wild land, Ethiopia is as large as France and Spain combined. The central highlands rise to 15,000 feet and give rise to numerous streams, including the Blue Nile, which rises from Lake Tana. Ethiopia has small amounts of gold, potash and salt, and its production of textiles, cement and food is increasing. Most of the 22.6 million Ethiopians live in the highlands; they avoid the steamy tropical forests and the scorching coast along the Red Sea. Most are peasants, and at least half are Gallas, a dark-coloured people of the southern highlands. The highland zone was the original home of the coffee plant; it also produces wheat, barley and vegetables.

The noblemen, who rule the country like feudal lords of the Middle Ages, are a Coptic Christian people, the Amhara. Ethiopia is economically backward; it lacks modern means of transport, and local rulers do not want control by the central

Women of mainland Tanzania come to market balancing bunches of green bananas on their heads

government. The only railway links Addis Ababa, the capital, with Djibouti, in The Afars and the Issas. Camels, mules and donkeys are still used to carry heavy loads across mountain and desert. In 1935—36, Ethiopia was invaded by Italian armies and incorporated in Italian East Africa, but the British ousted the Italian army in 1941. In 1952, the former Italian colony Eritrea became part of the Federation of Ethiopia and Eritrea, and now has provincial status.

● **fennec** A dainty North African fox, with ears a quarter of the length of its 15-inch body. Its home is the Sahara, where the fennec stays in its burrow by day, but comes out at night to hunt lizards and other small prey.

● **Fez** The principal religious centre of Morocco, and the main trading and industrial centre of northern Morocco. This city of 249,000 inhabitants lies at the foot of the Atlas Mountains. It is a traditional seat of the sultan, the country's ruler. The city was founded in A.D. 808, and has a Moslem university dating from the Middle Ages. Surrounded by orchards and groves, the city contains more than 100 mosques, among which is the Karubin mosque. The brimless red felt hat worn by many Moslems was named after Fez.

Fishermen draw their boats up on the beach at Pram Pram, a tiny village near Accra, on the Ghana coast, which was once called the 'Gold Coast'

Flamingos

● **flamingo** A tall, slim, white or pink bird of shallow coastal lagoons. When feeding, it puts its head low and nearly upside down, using the upper half of its oddly bent bill as a scoop in mud and shallow water. A comb-like sieve in the bill separates the tiny aquatic creatures that the bird scoops up. Flamingos live in large colonies and build their nests on pillar-like mud mounds. There are four species, which live in Africa, a part of Asia, in the West Indies, and the Andes.

Fossa

● **fossa** An odd civet-like animal of the cat family, found in Madagascar. Its body is about 2½ feet in length, and its slender tail almost as long. With

its sharp, retractable claws, the fossa attacks poultry, sheep and young cattle.

● **French Territory of the Afars and Issas** (formerly French Somaliland) lies near to the southern entrance to the Red Sea. It has a population of 125,000, and area of 9,000 square miles, and its capital is the port of Djibouti (62,000).

● **Fulani** One of the largest tribal groups of West Africa. They live in scattered areas between the Senegal and Nigeria, tending their large herds of cattle. The Fulani ruled much of West Africa (Sokoto) until the Europeans came in the 19th century. They are light-skinned Hamitic Moslem people.

● **Gabon** has an area of 101,400 square miles and a population of 475,000, largely Bantu, but with some pygmies. It is an independent republic, founded in 1960, and is mountainous, with the river Ogoué flowing westwards; near to this river lies Lambaréné, where the late Dr Albert Schweitzer had his hospital. The capital is Libreville (73,000 people), the port of export for palm oil, timber, rubber, mineral oil, and uranium and iron ores.

● **Gambia** A former British possession in West Africa, and one of the oldest on the continent. This land of 4,000 square miles and 315,486 people consists of narrow strips on both banks of the Gambia River and of the island at the river's mouth, where the capital, Bathurst (27,809), is located. Large quantities of groundnuts are shipped down-river and exported. Gambia became independent on 18th February, 1965.

● **gazelle** A delicate, small antelope, one of the fastest mammals on Earth. Most gazelles are at home in the hottest and driest parts of North Africa. Their lyre-shaped, ringed horns curve backward and upward. The sandy-brown coat makes them inconspicuous in desert regions. The largest gazelle varieties, 36 inches at the shoulder, are the dama and the mhorr.

● **gerenuk** A gazelle-like antelope of East Africa, with a long, slender, giraffe-like neck. It stands on

its hind legs to feed on high branches. The horns curve forward at the tip.

● **Ghana** (formerly **Gold Coast**) A member of the British Commonwealth of Nations, and the first of Britain's African colonies to achieve full independence (1957). This 92,000-square-mile country (population 8.5 million) includes former British Togoland, a United Nations trust territory until 1957. 'Gold Coast' was the name given by early gold and slave traders to this strip of coastline along the Gulf of Guinea. In the 17th and 18th centuries, British, Dutch and Danish slave-traders picked up human cargoes there. Britain, late in the 19th century, took the entire coast. Then, in 1901, Britain became protector of the Ashanti kingdom inland and occupied the Northern Territories, north of the Volta River.

Today, the country is the world's largest producer of cacao beans, mostly grown by thousands of enterprising small native farmers. Independent Ghana began in 1966 to use its huge deposits of high-grade bauxite for aluminium manufacturing. To this end, a dam on the Volta River, a large hydro-electric plant, new rail connections, and a new port (Tema) near the mouth of the Volta, have been built. Harbours are few because of the relatively unbroken coastline. At Accra, the capital city, surf-boats and lighters used to carry freight to ships anchored off-shore. At Sekondi-Takoradi (population 161,000) an artificial harbour has been built. Exports from this port include hardwoods, gold, manganese, bauxite and cacao. There is a railway to Kumasi (342,900 people), the chief city of Ashanti, in the midst of the cacao-growing district. Ghana is the name of an African kingdom said to have existed in the area between the 9th and 13th centuries.

● **giraffe** The tallest of mammals. The average giraffe carries its head 16 feet above the ground. It feeds on high-growing leaves, and, to reach food near the ground, must spread its forelegs wide. The giraffe's large, dark-brown eyes, with their soulful expression, are very keen, but the animal has no voice. On its forehead, the giraffe bears two or more horn-like bosses covered with skin. It is a swift runner. Most surviving giraffes are found in eastern Africa.

gnu (or **wildebeest**) A large antelope, with a horselike body and a long, melancholy face. It likes to cavort, kicking with its hind limbs and snorting. The most common types are the blue (brindled) and the white-bearded gnus. They are found mainly in southern and eastern Africa.

goat, Nubian A goat of Upper Egypt. It is generally hornless and short-haired, and has long, drooping ears.

gold The heavy, yellow, precious metal used as an international measure of value. Most countries base their money on gold, and half of the world's gold production is used for coin or bullion to back up such monetary systems. The other half is used for ornaments, in dentistry, and in industry.

Gold occurs almost always in the native state — not mixed with other substances. It is found either as lodes or veins embedded in quartz (lode gold), or as dust, grains or nuggets in weathered deposits (placer gold). Gold-bearing rock from lodes or veins is first ground, and then washed or treated chemically to separate out the gold. Placer gold is extracted from sand or silt in large washing plants.

The world's leading gold producers are the Republic of South Africa, the Soviet Union, Canada, and the United States. South Africa alone contributes half of the world's total output.

gorilla The largest of the man-like apes. Standing about 6 feet and weighing 500 pounds, strong and ferocious in appearance, gorillas are not dangerous unless attacked. They feed on fruits and vegetables, and never kill to eat. When threatened, the male snarls at the intruder and beats his chest with his fists. Gorillas lead a nomadic life, travelling in small family groups in the rain forests, but are now very rare. They make camp by building a crude nest in a tree, and move on the next day. Gorillas walk on all fours, leaning on their knuckles.

guenon The commonest monkey of Africa, distinguished by slender body, long legs, very long, straight tail, and short face. Guenons are good-natured and friendly, and fond of showing their teeth in grimaces. They used to be trained by organ-grinders to beg for pennies. Wild guenons live in large droves led by an old male. There are about 80 different forms, each distinctively coloured.

guereza A monkey with a long coat of silky fur and a long tail ending in a bushy brush. The popularity of 'monkey fur' for women's clothing at the end of the 19th century, almost caused this animal's extinction. Fortunately, the vogue passed, and the guereza now lives in peace in the rain forests of highland East Africa.

Guinea The coastal area along the Gulf of Guinea, West Africa. In the past, this name was applied to the British, French, Portuguese and Spanish shore possessions from Senegal to Angola. The Niger River delta divides Upper (northern) from Lower (southern) Guinea. Sections of the Guinea coast were named Grain Coast, Ivory Coast, Gold Coast and Slave Coast. Today, these regions could be named Palm-Oil Coast, Peanut Coast or Cacao Coast — after their products. Rainfall is heavy, and tropical vegetation is lush along the coast and on several islands which belong in part to Spain (Fernando Po, Annobón), and in part to Portugal (São Tomé and Principe).

The Guinea Republic (95,000 square miles; population 3.8 million) was formerly part of French West Africa. Its chief city, Conakry (120,000 people), lies at the ocean end of a railway which extends inland, for several hundred miles, to Kankan. Diamonds are found, and bauxite shipped to Canadian smelters. The territory is mainly highland, though cattle-rearing and tropical fruit production are carried on. The country became completely independent in 1958.

Portuguese Guinea (population 550,000) is a small, unhealthy, undeveloped section of West Africa. Its chief town, Bissau (20,000 people), lies in an isolated and swampy stretch of coast. Portuguese since 1879, the territory's products are rice and palm oil.

Republic of Equatorial Guinea (formerly **Spanish Guinea**) A small state including the mainland territory of Rio Muni (10,000 square miles; population 230,000) and the off-shore islands of Fernando Po and Annobon (80,000). The country became independent in 1968.

gum arabic A colourless gum, obtained from several types of acacia in north-east Africa. It is used in adhesives, and in the textile and ceramic industries. The Sudan is the world's leading supplier of gum arabic.

Hamites The native peoples of northern Africa. They have a stronger Caucasoid (white) racial strain than the peoples of the southern half of the continent, the vast majority of whom are Negroid. Since the peoples have intermixed, it is easier to distinguish between them by language and custom than by race. In general, the Hamites include the peoples speaking Arabic, Berber, the Cushitic languages of the eastern 'horn' of Africa, and the Chad tongues of the Hausa. The term is derived from Ham, Noah's youngest son.

hartebeest An antelope that looks like a long-faced cow. It has an ungainly body and stout, backward-curving horns. Timid and retiring, it is among the fastest of the large antelopes. The figure of the hartebeest adorned ancient Roman coins, symbolising Rome's African holdings. It is one of the fastest antelopes, living in the savanna lands.

Hausa A Negro people of northern Nigeria. They were an early trading nation, founding cities and states. Their language became the trade tongue of the Sudan. They are largely Moslem, and famous for their skill in handicrafts.

hippopotamus The largest living land animal, except for the elephant. Its name, from Greek, means 'river horse', but it is not like a horse; it is, in fact, a relative of the pig. The body is round and bulky, with legs so short that the big belly barely misses the ground. A full-grown animal may weigh 4 tons. Since the tiny, bulging eyes are high on the head, and the nostrils on top of the snout, the animal when swimming can breathe and see with only the very top of its face above water. It feeds chiefly on reeds and grasses, but comes ashore at night to raid fields and gardens. The hippopotamus can stay under water as long as ten minutes without coming up to breathe. A baby hippo generally rides on its mother's back, even under water. The gigantic mouth of a hippo, when opened to its widest, is an awe-inspiring sight. The old saying that hippos 'sweat blood' is false; the 'blood' is just a brownish oil produced by the skin when dry.

hippopotamus, pygmy A small hippo of the deep forests of Liberia and Sierra Leone. It spends more time on land than its big relative, which weighs about 14 times as much as this 300-pound midget. The pygmy hippo was regarded by many as an imaginary creature until the first specimens were brought out of Africa in 1912.

hornbill, wedge-tailed A West African hornbill with black plumage. Only the tips of its long tail-feathers are white.

Hottentots Descendants of the original population of South Africa. Together with the Bushmen, the Hottentots speak the so-called 'click' languages; these employ peculiar clicking sounds which are found nowhere else in the world. Unlike the hunting, food-gathering Bushmen, the Hottentots have a cattle economy. Most are in the Republic of South Africa.

hyena, spotted The best known of the hyenas, and considered one of the most gruesome members of the animal kingdom. The size of a large dog, this animal has a massive, ugly head, and hind legs shorter than the front limbs. It preys on feeble, injured or old animals. When attacked, it feigns death to avoid fighting. A well-known eater of carrion, the hyena may find a carcass only after vultures have picked it clean of flesh; then the hyena's powerful jaws will crack and crush the bones. By day, it sleeps in burrows, and at sunset the animal begins to hunt, uttering the chilling, diabolical cackle which has earned it the name of 'laughing hyena'.

ibis, sacred A white bird, with naked black head and lacy black tail-plumes. The ancient Egyptians portrayed Thoth, their god of wisdom and learning, as ibis-headed. Mummified bodies of this ibis have been found in Egyptian tombs.

Ibo The chief tribal group of south-eastern Nigeria. They speak one of the Bantu languages. Living in small village communities, the Ibo people sell the oil and kernels of the palm tree.

ivory The dentine of the tusks of male African elephants. Easily shaped by carving and machining, ivory is widely used for utensils and ornaments. Indian elephants yield ivory of inferior grade. Walrus tusks are used as a substitute for genuine ivory. The hunting of elephants for ivory is now strictly regulated, to save them from extinction.

Ivory Coast The name given by early traders to the coast along the Gulf of Guinea between present-day Liberia and Ghana. It was formerly part of French West Africa, but became independent in 1960. Cacao is the chief export; the forests yield mahogany and ebony. Although elephants still inhabit the jungle, ivory is no longer an important commercial product. From Abidjan (282,000 people), the chief city, a navigation canal runs to the sea, and a railway runs to inland towns in the territory of Upper Volta. The Republic has a population of 3.84 million, and an area of 124,000 square miles.

jackal, yellow A mammal that looks like a wolf, but is smaller and more slender, with larger ears and a sharp-pointed face. It is found from eastern Europe and northern Africa through to southern Asia.

Johannesburg The largest city of southern Africa, and the industrial and commercial centre of the Republic of South Africa. It was founded in 1886, and the gold-mining region known as the Witwatersrand (shortened to: the 'Rand') grew around it. Roads, railways and three airports now make the city the transportation centre of the Republic. Only two-fifths of the population of 1,370,000 is white. Many of the natives who work in the deep mines were brought to the Rand from the native reservations and from neighbouring countries. Some of the worst slums have now been cleared to provide better housing conditions for natives.

Kabyles The Berbers of the Atlas Mountains of Algeria, about 1 million in number. They are farmers, growing field crops and fruit, and have led the national independence movement in Algeria.

Kaffir A name (Arabic, 'unbeliever') applied by Moslems to all infidels, but more specifically to the Bantu Negroes of southern Africa. The male Kaffirs raise livestock, and work in mines and factories. They number 6 to 7 million. They call themselves 'ama', plus their tribal name — for example, 'ama-zulu'. The women till the land, and families live in circular huts which, grouped together within an enclosure, form a kraal (village).

Kalahari Desert A dry and sandy upland in southern Africa, mainly in Bechuanaland, between the upper Zambezi and Orange rivers. There, Hottentots graze their sheep and cattle on scanty bunchgrass, and a few Bushmen still roam in search of wild game. In the northern Kalahari are a few dry, salt-covered lake-beds.

Kenya A republic and former British colony in eastern Africa. Kenya has an area of about 225,000 square miles and is crossed by the equator. Only the coast and southern highlands are well populated. The northern part, a dry region, rises gradually from the coast towards the Ethiopian border. The population of over 10.9 million is mostly African, with about 37,000 Asians, 27,000 Arabs (most of them in the port of Mombasa), and 40,000 Europeans, who prefer the cooler uplands. Nairobi, the modern capital, lies more than 5,000 feet above sea level, amid European-operated farms which are gradually being bought out for transference to African ownership. The presence of European farmers and the shortage of land for the natives, together with a growing desire for majority-rule and independence, led to the Mau Mau rebellion of 1952—56.

Kenya exports coffee, cotton, sisal, tea, tobacco, hides and some minerals, via the excellent harbour of Mombasa, and on to Lake Victoria and Uganda (Entebbe). Elephants, zebras, giraffes and antelopes may be seen from the railway near Nairobi. Its wildlife has made Kenya a favourite ground for hunting expeditions (safaris). As in other parts of Africa, Game Reserves have been created to protect wild animals, and these are visited by parties armed with cameras instead of guns. Kenya achieved independence on 12th December, 1963.

Khartoum The capital city of the Sudan, 1,000 miles south of Cairo, at the junction of the White and the Blue Nile, and founded in 1823 for trade between Egypt and southern Africa. This city of 135,000 people is surrounded by desert, except for an extensive cotton-growing district in the south. The modern commercial centre lies on the left bank of the Blue Nile, and this contains government buildings and shops of Arab traders. Northwest is the native town of Omdurman, with its crowded, unsanitary mud huts. Together, the population reaches 312,000. In the streets of Khartoum, Arabs from the north mix with Negroes from the south.

Kikuyu A Bantu Negro tribe of the Kenya highlands. In 1952, they formed the Mau Mau terrorist movement and rose against European settlers in Kenya.

Kilimanjaro The highest mountain (19,565 feet) of Africa, Kilimanjaro is a huge snow-capped volcano, visible for hundreds of miles across the East African plateau. It lies just south of the equator in Tanzania. There are coffee plantations on its lower slopes. Sisal is grown near the mountain's arid base. Its summit was first reached in the year 1889.

Native villages in South Africa are called 'kraals'. The thatched huts are built of clay

Kimberley A city (population 96,300) in the Republic of South Africa known as the diamond capital of the world. Diamonds were first discovered there in 1871. Most of the mining is done at depths greater than 3,000 feet. The long-range future of Kimberley's diamond industry may be in doubt, because a process to produce artificial diamonds at low cost has been developed in the United States. The Republic of South Africa still counts diamonds among its leading exports. Asbestos, manganese and wolfram are also mined, and, in addition, Kimberley has a large cattle market.

klipspringer (Afrikaans, 'rock-jumper') A small African antelope of rough, rocky country. Surefooted as a mountain goat, the klipspringer leaps from crag to crag, and bounds up steep cliffs as if it were flying. Its hoofs, small and long, can be put so close together that the animal can stand on a point of rock the size of a large coin.

kola nuts The brown, bitter nuts of the kola (or cola) tree, native to tropical Africa. They contain the same stimulants as coffee and cocoa, and yield an extract used in 'cola' drinks.

kraal A village of South African natives, especially of the Kaffirs, sometimes surrounded by a stockade. The word 'kraal', which also means enclosure for cattle, is related to the word 'corral'.

Kru A Sudanese Negro people of Liberia, noted for their skill as boatmen. They are employed along the surf-ridden coast of West Africa in the transfer of cargo to and from ships by small boat.

kudu One of the stateliest-looking antelopes in Africa. The magnificent corkscrew horns of the male stand nearly vertical, sweeping up in wide spirals as long as 60 inches. The kudu is greyish-brown, with vertical white stripes.

Lagos The capital of Nigeria, on the Gulf of Guinea. The city (population 364,000) and its

modern seaport are on an island in a coastal lagoon; a shipping channel has been dredged to the open sea. Palm oil, palm kernels, cacao, copra and cotton are shipped out at Lagos. A slave market existed there until the 19th century. Since then, religious missions and the colonial government have built schools and hospitals, and the city has an important airport.

lechwe A small antelope, usually found in shallow water, where it is preyed upon by crocodiles. It is at home in the swamps of the upper Zambezi River.

lemur A little monkey with a fox-like face. Lowest of the primates, most lemurs live in the forests of Madagascar. They move stealthily about, mostly at night, and that may be why they were named 'lemur' — a Latin word for 'ghost'. The ruffed lemur, or vari, has a conspicuous ruff on the sides of its neck. At dawn, the creature sits up and extends its arms towards the sun, as if in prayer. The ring-tailed lemur, or catta, is not a forest dweller. It prefers the dry, rocky regions of western Madagascar.

leopard (or panther) A large, wily, savage member of the cat family, found in both Africa and Asia. Most familiar is the yellowish, black-spotted leopard, but there is also a black leopard. Both

Leopard

black and spotted cubs may be born in the same litter. The leopard's fondness for dogs' flesh sometimes brings it close to human dwellings. Climbing and lurking in trees, the leopard is active mostly in the darkness. This intelligent hunter has been known to resort to trickery to make a kill.

● **Leopoldville** (now **Kinshasi**) The capital of the Congo. It is a modern city of 360,000 inhabitants. Many of the new office buildings are air-conditioned, and the residential distrist is laid out attractively along the banks of the Niger, which forms a lake (Stanley Pool) there. The sprawling African town consists of clay and adobe houses, with wattle fences. River boats navigate the Congo and its tributaries above Kinshasi. Detouring around the rapids and falls below the city, a railway connects Kinshasi with Matadi, a port reached by ocean-going ships. Founded by Stanley in 1887, the city was named after King Leopold II. It has many industries and an important airfield.

● **Leptis Magna** An ancient Phoenician seaport in Tripolitania. It declined after the coming of the Arabs in the 7th century. The ruins were excavated about 1920 near Homs, Libya.

● **Lesotho** Formerly the British protectorate of Basutoland, became independent within the Commonwealth in October, 1966. The capital and seat of government of this small kingdom (11,716 square miles; population 969,634) is at Maseru, with 8,000 inhabitants. Completely surrounded by the Republic of South Africa, Lesotho lies at the head of the Orange River, enclosed on the south by the Drakensburg Mountains, and is a mountainous plateau. Mainly an agricultural people, the Basutos produce maize, wool and mohair; but erosion, caused by excessive grazing, continues despite large soil conservation, and many people are forced to find work in the mines and cities of South Africa.

● **Liberia** An independent country on the West African coast, founded in 1822 as a small settlement of freed slaves from the United States. After many hardships, the little colony proclaimed itself a free and independent republic in 1847. The constitution and form of government today are patterned on those of the United States, but the right to own property is limited to persons of African descent.

This tropical land (42,000 square miles), with year-round high temperatures and 160 inches of rainfall per year, has about 1 million people — mostly back-country tribesmen. The chief source of wealth is rubber, grown on large American plantations. Other American companies mine iron ore in the hills, 40 miles south of Monrovia, the country's capital (100,000 inhabitants). A railway connects the mine with the port. Liberia has no good roads, and only the main streets in Monrovia are paved. The country needs capital to build schools and hospitals, open up the interior, and help farmers to grow more and better crops.

● **Libya** An independent republic (population 1,800,000) in northern Africa, on the Mediterranean Sea. Mostly barren desert, it includes the provinces of Tripolitania, Cyrenaica, and the Fezzan, totalling 670,000 square miles. There are, on the average, only 2 inhabitants per square mile — mostly Arabs, with a number of Berbers in the western hill areas, and some 40,000 Italians along the coast of Tripolitania.

The two main cities, Tripoli (245,000) and Benghazi (140,000) both serve as the capital. Long a Turkish province, Libya was taken by the Italians in 1911—12. They built new roads, deepened harbours, and introduced modern ways of cultivating the dry land. In World War II, after

Leptis Magna – ruins near Homs, Libya

heavy see-saw fighting, the Allies took Libya from the German and Italian armies. In 1951, the ruler of the Senusi, a Moslem tribe of Cyrenaica, became king of an independent Libya, with the assistance of the United Nations. In 1969 he was deposed and Libya became the Libyan Arab Republic.

● **lion** The largest member of the cat family. The King of the Beasts looks the part — in its size, dignified and noble face, and long, stately mane. Unlike the other big cats, it has a comparatively friendly disposition, loves company, and moves about in groups of five or six. Lions kill only when hungry, never needlessly. They usually prey on antelopes and zebras, and share their meals amiably in groups. A lion will turn on his own kind only during the breeding season, when he must win his mate. Four cubs are the average number in a litter. They do not kill for themselves until they are a year old. Since the lion mostly inhabits comparatively open country, over which civilisation is advancing, it has suffered more from man than has the tiger, which has vast areas of jungle to hide in.

● **Livingstone** A town of 30,000 people in Zambia, near the famous Victoria Falls of the Zambezi River. The falls were discovered in 1855 by David Livingstone. The two-mile-wide river falls 350 feet into a gorge, and then flows through a narrow opening — 'the Boiling Pot' — in the vertical wall of cliffs. A 650-foot rail and road bridge spans the Zambezi canyon below the falls. The railway leads north to the Zambian Copper Belt, and south-east to Bulawayo, in Rhodesia.

● **Lourenço Marques** The capital of Mozambique (Portuguese East Africa). This city of 100,000 has a fine harbour on the Indian Ocean, and is linked by rail with the Transvaal, a province of the Republic of South Africa. It is the home of Portuguese, English, French, South Africans, and immigrants from India, as well as natives. The city has food-processing industries, and exports coal and cotton.

● **Madeira** A small Portuguese island of about 300 square miles in the Atlantic Ocean, 400 miles west of Morocco. The population is over 300,000. This favourite resort of European tourists has a spring-like climate the year round. Sugar cane, oranges, bananas, avocado pears, and many early vegetables, are grown on neat terraces along the steep hillsides. The city of Funchal (55,000 people), founded by the Portuguese in 1421, lies on a beautiful bay amid flowering shrubs and sub-tropical trees.

● **Malagasy (Madagascar)** The fifth-largest island in the world (after Greenland, New Guinea, Borneo and Baffin Land). It lies in the Indian Ocean, off the south-east coast of Africa. This republic is rugged, and the eastern portion has a truly moist tropical climate. The total area is about 228,000 square miles. The chief crops are grown in the central highlands — coffee, vanilla, cloves and pepper. The Hova people are the main tribe of eastern Madagascar; they are prosperous

and educated. On the African (west) side, the population is predominantly Negro. The French took over the island as a protectorate in 1895; they built roads and railways, and introduced new methods of agriculture; independence was gained in 1960. The chief towns are Tananarive (population 322,000), the highland capital, and the east-coast port, Tamatave (50,500). The total population is over 6.7 million.

● **Malawi** An independent republic of south-east Africa, formerly called Nyasaland and previously part of the now defunct Central African Federation. The country is entirely agricultural, the chief cash or export crops being tobacco, tea, cotton, sisal and groundnuts. Its Bantu population numbers about 4 million and there are 7,000 Europeans. Although the town of Blantyre is the largest place (109,461), situated in the cool Shire highlands, Zomba (19,666) has been acting as the capital, which is to be moved to a new site nearer to Lake Malawi. A railway leads from the south-western shores of the lake at Salima to Blantyre, and thence to Beira, in Mozambique. Lake Malawi is the third largest of the great lakes of East Africa, and has a widely fluctuating water level. It is from 15 to 50 miles wide and over 2,300 feet deep.

● **Mali** An independent republic in former French West Africa, with a large area of 582,437 square miles. Mali extends from 11°W eastwards into the upper Niger valley, and north into the western Sahara. It has a population of 4,700,000— mainly Tuaregs, Moors, Fulani and Sudan Negroes. Mali exports groundnuts, rice, gum arabic and cattle. The capital is Bamako (170,000 people) on the uppermost Niger, near to the border with the Republic of Guinea. Timbuktu is another centre of importance.

● **Mangbetu** A Negro people of the north-eastern Congo. They live near the Uele River, a tributary of the Ubangi. The Mangbetu still follow the custom of shaping heads by binding the skulls of children. They are largely an agricultural people, also famous for their wood and ivory carvings. Formerly they were cannibalistic and took part in the slave trade.

● **marabou** A stork of Africa and India, known also as the 'adjutant'. The bare head and neck, and loose folds of pinkish skin hanging from the throat, are distinctive features. Marabous eat small birds, frogs and carrion, so they are protected by villagers. The lonely appearance of a single marabou accounts for the name, derived from the Arabic word for 'hermit'.

● **Marrakesh** The principal inland city of southern Morocco. The narrow, crooked streets of the old part of this city of 264,300 inhabitants are full of people and domestic animals. In the colourful bazaar, a tremendous variety of merchandise is on display. Most of the trading takes place in front of the shops. The city rarely has any rain, though the snow-capped peaks of the High Atlas are always on the horizon. The place was founded in 1062, and a 12th-century mosque towers over Marrakesh. The Arab and Berber inhabitants have made fine leather goods and carpets for generations. The surrounding land is a fertile oasis.

● **Masai** A nomadic Negro warrior people of East Africa with Hamitic speech. They live on the milk of their cattle, and do not raise crops. Largely untouched by civilisation, and intensely proud of their way of life, the Masai live in reserves assigned to them in southern Kenya and northern Tanzania. The women wear metal rings on their arms, ankles and necks. Masai clothing consists of ox-skins.

A Masai and a Pygmy

● **Mau Mau** A secret society of the Kikuyu tribe, in Kenya. It was formed to expel Europeans and win 'Africa for the Africans'. Vast European land-holdings, unemployment in towns, and inadequate social services, were some of the native grievances which gave rise to the Mau Mau movement. After 1952, Mau Mau terrorism died down, as some of its leaders were caught and the British-controlled government gave more privileges to the Africans.

● **Mauritania** The independent Islamic Republic (since 1960) of Mauritania is in north-west Africa, bordering on the Atlantic, with its port and capital at Nouakchott (20,000 people). By far the largest part of the area of 322,240 square miles is desert and dry steppe, where most of the population of about 1 million live by cattle-raising. The population is largely Moorish, with a Negroid mixture in the south. There are rich mineral resources — iron ore at Fort Gouraud, and copper at Akjoujt in the north. The main exports are iron and copper ore, cattle, salt and fish.

● **Mauritius** An island in the Indian Ocean, 720 square miles in extent. Formerly a British crown colony, it became independent in 1968. With a population of 870,000, it has a density of more than 900 people per square mile. Two-thirds of them are descended from immigrants brought from India during the last century to work on sugar plantations; the other inhabitants are descendants of European immigrants or African slaves. The chief city is Port Louis, with a population of 139,300. Since sugar is the island's only commercial crop, the islanders suffer when the world price of sugar is low or the harvest is bad. In some years, there is no crop at all, for Mauritius lies in the path of tropical hurricanes. Mauritius was held by the French from 1715 to 1810, and French is still spoken alongside English. Including Rodrigues and all the other island dependencies of the colony, Mauritius has a population of over 890,000. A new British colony formed in 1965 — British Indian Ocean Territory — is made up of islands (Chagos Archipelago, Aldabra, Farquhar and Des Roches) formerly administered by Mauritius and the Seychelles.

● **millet** Any of a group of drought-resistant cereals and forage grasses. Millet is grown in Africa as a food crop. True millet, or proso millet, is widely cultivated in the Soviet Union, where it is used for a thick porridge (*kasha*). Italian millet, or fox-tail millet, is grown in the Middle East and in Manchuria. Pearl millet, or cat-tail millet, is a staple crop in India and in the African Sudan. Millets, and particularly pearl millet, are often confused with sorghum. Sugar and syrup can be obtained from some millets.

● **monkey, Metternich's** A white-limbed guereza monkey, discovered in 1941 on the island of Fernando Po, in the Gulf of Guinea. It lives on the slopes of the island's Santa Isabel Peak.

● **Morocco** An independent kingdom in north-western Africa, facing the Mediterranean Sea in the north and the Atlantic to the west. The African shore of the Strait of Gibraltar is in Morocco. The country's area of 170,000 square miles has a rapidly growing population of over 15 million, including 12 million Moslems. Independent since the early Middle Ages, Morocco was ruled by Berber kings (sultans), who invaded Spain during the Middle Ages (Moors). After European countries became interested in the area, Morocco was divided between France and Spain in 1912, and Tangier became an international city in 1923. During this period, the sultan remained the figure-head ruler. Newly independent Morocco became a member of the United Nations in 1956. The sultan, now given the title 'king', resides in Rabat, but also visits his palaces in Fez, Marrakesh and Meknes.

The area formerly under Spain is a rugged coastal strip with little farmland, but former French Morocco grows cereals, olives, almonds, citrus fruit and figs. Forests yield cork, lumber, and pit-props for the mines. Phosphate rock (for fertiliser), iron ore, manganese, lead, zinc and cobalt are mined.

Morocco's industries, established with French capital, include sardine canning, processing of fruits and vegetables, and textile manufacturing. The French built good roads from the major cities to isolated villages in the Atlas Mountains. All the seaports (Casablanca, Fedala, Safi, Mogador, Agadir) have modern installations, and long breakwaters against the Atlantic surf. Agadir was largely destroyed by an earthquake in 1960.

● **Mozambique** (or **Portuguese East Africa**) A Portuguese overseas province (population 6,600,000) on the Indian Ocean, opposite the island of Madagascar. The territory covers nearly 300,000 square miles. Along the north coast and in the valley of the Zambezi River, in the territory of Manica, and in the Limpopo valley, there are several plantations run by Europeans, Indians and Chinese. The chief crops are sugar cane, sisal, coconuts, tea and tobacco. The main towns are all seaports: Lourenço Marques, the capital; Beira, which has a railway link to Rhodesia, Malawi and Zambia; and the city of Mozambique, in the north, which Vasco de Gama visited in 1498.

● **Nairobi** The capital of Kenya, Nairobi lies 5,500 feet above sea level, halfway between two giant volcanoes, Mount Kenya (17,040 feet) and Kilimanjaro (19,565 feet). An attractive modern city of 509,000, with a large European colony (19,180), and 67,000 Asiatics, it lies almost on the equator, yet has a healthy, cool, upland climate. It specialises in outfitting hunting expeditions (safaris) into the African bush. Big game (lions, giraffes, hippos) abounds in the vicinity. Nairobi was founded in 1899, and even as late as 1948 had only 50,000 inhabitants.

● **Negroes** A dark-skinned people native to Africa. They tend to be long-skulled, kinky-haired, and tall, with full and prominent lips, but individuals differ widely. Long relatively isolated in Africa from other peoples, some Negro groups nevertheless developed a high degree of language, crafts and social organisation. Many were taken for slavery in the 18th and 19th centuries and shipped to the New World, where they mixed with American Indians and the European settlers.

Whereas northern Africa is dominated by peoples of the Caucasoid (white) race, Africa, south of the Sahara, is regarded as Negro Africa. The Bushmen, Hottentots and Pygmies are special Negro types; they appear to be remnants of the original African peoples. African Negroes generally engage in farming, stock-raising, or a combination of both. Farming predominates in areas of heavier rainfall, and cattle-herding in the drier savanna regions. Political organisation was once highly developed among some Negro groups, particularly in West Africa, but these confederations of states were replaced by European colonies in the 19th century. The Negro republic of Liberia was founded in Africa by Negroes from America in 1847. Since the Second World War, the peoples of former British colonies in West Africa, notably Ghana and Nigeria, led the drive for independence.

Like Negroes in the United States, the Negroes in Africa are demanding equality of opportunity with the European, and are making some progress towards that goal. Recent years have seen great unrest in southern Africa, where a large number of people of European origin continue to resist Negro efforts to achieve equality.

● **Niger Republic** is situated in the Sudan and Sahara, and consists of savanna and desert respectively. It has an area of 484,000 square miles

Rhinoceros, means 'horn-nosed'. Some Asian rhinos have one horn, but in Africa they all have two

Palm trees growing around ancient Egyptian ruins, at an oasis near Luxor, in the Nile valley

and a population of 3,600,000, principally composed of the Tuareg, Fulani, Hausa and Jerma peoples, while there are also some 3,000 Europeans. Exploration and occupation of the country by the French occurred between 1891 and 1914, and the country attained full independence in 1960. Niger exports tin, groundnuts, gum arabic and salt. The capital is Niamey (70,000), on the Niger River. Large uranium deposits are being mined, and a uranium ore concentrate plant opened in 1970.

Niger River Third-longest river in Africa, the Niger rises in the Fouta Djallon highlands, less than 200 miles from the west coast. It swings northeast through the Mali Republic towards the Sahara, then south-east into Nigeria, and south to the Gulf of Guinea. Its marshy delta, along 200 miles of coastline, occupies 14,000 square miles. The upper Niger, above Timbuktu, overflows between August and December, its floodwaters being directed into cotton and rice fields. Flat-bottomed ships can move up the Niger and its chief tributary, the Benue, for part of the year; but the Niger is not as important a waterway as the Congo or the Nile. Mungo Park, the explorer, was one of the first Europeans to trace the river's course to the sea.

Nigeria The area of this independent Republic and Federation, 375,000 square miles, is four times that of Great Britain; its population is about 55.6 million. Except for the Nile Valley in Egypt, it is the most densely settled territory in Africa. Nigeria is rainy and tropical along the Gulf of Guinea, dry and hot along the Sahara. Palm oil and cacao are main products of the coastal areas; peanuts and cotton, of the north. Nigeria's once-rich tin deposits are nearly exhausted. Low-quality coal is mined at Enugu, east of the Niger River. There are also valuable deposits of manganese and monazite, which contains radioactive thorium, and oil has been found in the delta area. Most trade is with Britain. Railways deliver products of the interior to the two seaports: Lagos (population over 600,000), the federal capital; and Port Harcourt, near the Niger delta.

The chief African tribes of Nigeria are the Hausa and the Fulani, who inhabit the north and are Moslems, and the Yoruba and Ibo, in the south. Africans in the Yoruba country live in huge, clustered villages. Ibadan (population 800,000) is a sprawling settlement of native huts, though the country's largest university is there. Many settlements consist of villages-within-a-city, established by native farmers, craftsmen and traders as a

Okapi

defence against the warlike roving tribes of the north. Now independent, Nigeria adopted a federal form of government in 1954, and this includes part of the former British Cameroons. In 1967 the Eastern States broke away from the Federal republic and renamed themselves Biafra. Federal troops only succeeded in reconquering the province in 1970, after three years of fierce fighting and severe suffering in Biafra.

Nile River Longest river in Africa, and the longest in the world if measured from its first source — the Kagera River, in central Africa. The Kagera enters Lake Victoria from the west. From Lake Victoria, the Nile flows north-west through marshy Lake Kyoga, and then into Lake Albert, from which it flows out as the Albert Nile. Continuing north, the river enters the Sudan as the Bahr el Jebel. In the Sudd marshes, it loses half its water by evaporation, but soon receives water from the Ethiopian highlands, via the Sobat River.

At Khartoum, the river, now called the White Nile, is joined by the Blue Nile, which has travelled 1,000 miles from Lake Tana, in Ethiopia. The combined Nile, now crossing the desert, receives its last tributary, the Atbara, while still 1,700 miles from the Mediterranean. It forms a large S-shaped curve across the Nubian Desert, and reaches the great Aswan Dam, which regulates the river's floodwaters in order to provide an all-the-year-round water supply for the farm lands in Egypt. Between Khartoum and Aswan, the Nile drops 1,000 feet in a series of six rapids, called

cataracts. For most of this stretch, the river is not navigable. Elsewhere, there is a steamer service for most of the year — between Alexandria and Wadi Halfa, on the Sudanese border, and between Khartoum and Juba, near to the Uganda border. The floods on the lower Nile reach their peak in August and September, when the river carries 16 times more water than in April.

nomads People who raise livestock, and wander from place to place in search of food for their animals. Nomads live largely on milk and dairy products. They rarely eat meat, for they cannot afford to kill their livestock. Usually, they move between summer pastures on high mountain meadows and winter pastures in the lowlands, a movement termed *transhumance*, meaning movement from one piece of land (humus) to another.

Nuba A Negro people living in the Kordofan area of the Sudan. Their characteristic round mud huts have pointed grass roofs.

oasis A fertile area in a desert, which may be little more than a cluster of palm trees, or a green island of several hundred square miles. Some oases have springs; in others, the water is brought to the surface by artesian wells or underground channels; still others draw water from rivers that rise in more humid regions and cross the desert on their way to the sea. Oases along the Nile in Egypt, and the Euphrates in Mesopotamia (Iraq), support millions of farmers, who direct floodwaters on to their land. Characteristic of the oasis is the date palm.

okapi A relative of the giraffe, discovered in 1901 in the heart of the Congo. The long, slender limbs and hair-covered horn bosses are like those of the giraffe, but the neck is much shorter. The okapi is the size of a mule, with a reddish-brown coat, and is striped black and white on hindquarters and upper legs. Like the giraffe, the okapi can thrust out its long tongue and grasping lips to pick foliage off trees.

Oran The second-largest city (325,000 people) of Algeria. It has a fine natural harbour on the Mediterranean, and exports wine and grain. The town has a southern European air, having a Spanish castle, Santa Cruz, and it was formerly the chief centre of French settlement.

Orange River A 1,300-mile-long stream of southern Africa, rising in Lesotho and flowing west across the Republic of South Africa to the Atlantic Ocean. Near its mouth are several important diamond deposits. The river has a very low flow in the hot season and is of little use for navigation.

South African ostriches

ostrich The largest of living birds, reaching a height of 8 feet and a weight of 300 pounds. Its wings, though too short for flying, help this heavy bird to speed across the desert at 40 miles an hour. The demand for ostrich plumes as ornaments was so great in the 19th century that the birds were threatened with extinction. Ostrich farming then began, but the demand for the feathers soon faded away. The hen lays 15 to 20 eggs in a shallow hole scraped by the cock. The eggs, which weigh 3 pounds each, are relished by African natives. Contrary to popular opinion, ostriches do not hide their heads in the sand when in danger. Their chief defence is a mighty kick with their two-toed feet. North and South African ostriches vary only in colour.

Date palms

palm, date A highly useful plant grown in oases of North Africa, and also widely cultivated in South-West Asia. Date palms, sometimes reaching 100 feet, bear their first fruit when 8 years old. At 30, they yield up to 400 pounds of fruit a year. The date, 1 to 3 inches long, reddish-brown and oblong, is very nutritious, containing 50 per cent sugar. In many dry areas, the date is the main food and chief source of income of the population. Outside tropical deserts, this palm is planted as an ornament. In North Africa, the wood and leaves are used in building and thatching desert dwellings, and the dried fruit is shipped from North Africa and the Middle East to Europe.

palm, dwarf fan A palm of Africa and southern Europe. Its leaves, cut into strips, are used for mattress and pillow stuffing. A fibre obtained from the dwarf fan palm's leaves, known as African hair, is used for cordage.

Oil palms

palm, oil A palm tree native to the Guinea coast of West Africa, it is now grown in other tropical areas, and yields palm oil and palm-kernel oil. Palm oil is obtained from the husk or pulp of the fruit, by boiling or more modern methods. It is used in soap and candles, for coating metal to be tin-plated, and for lubricants. It also yields carotene, used to counteract Vitamin A deficiency. Palm-kernel oil is taken from the kernels that remain after palm oil has been squeezed out of the fruit. The kernels yield an edible oil used in margarine. Whereas palm oil is extracted in the oil-palm countries (Nigeria, Congo, Guinea), the palm kernels are processed in industrialised countries of Europe and America. The oil palm is replacing the coconut palm because, for every ton of copra yielded by the coconut palm, the oil palm yields one ton of palm oil and also one ton of kernels.

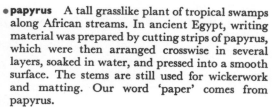
Papyrus swamp

papyrus A tall grasslike plant of tropical swamps along African streams. In ancient Egypt, writing material was prepared by cutting strips of papyrus, which were then arranged crosswise in several layers, soaked in water, and pressed into a smooth surface. The stems are still used for wickerwork and matting. Our word 'paper' comes from papyrus.

parrot, grey A West African parrot famous as a talking bird. Its colouring is rather subdued for parrots — ashy-grey, with red tail-feathers. It has been shipped abroad in countless numbers. Some grey parrots have survived 80 years in captivity.

parrot, vasa An African parrot of unusual colouration — almost uniformly blackish-brown. It is found in Madagascar and nearby islands.

peacock, Congo A peacock of the Congo, smaller than the common peacock and with a smaller fan. Its discovery in 1936 was an important event, because experts had long believed that native peacocks could be found only in South-East Asia.

penguin, jackass The only penguin common on the coasts of South Africa. It has a striking black-and-white pattern and its cry suggests the braying of an ass.

pig, bush A West African wild pig, also known as red river hog because of its colour. Wary but fierce, with long tufted ears, it is active at night.

pigeon, Cape A medium-sized petrel, and one of the commonest of the southern hemisphere. Its chequered mantle makes the identity of this ship-follower quite unmistakable.

plantain eater — see **touraco**

Crested porcupine

porcupine, crested The largest living porcupine (3 feet long) and native to Africa. It is heavily armed with needle-sharp quills — some a foot long. When disturbed, the animal rattles the quills on its short tail. To attack, the porcupine erects its quills and charges backward; few animals dare to bother it. Unlike its tree-dwelling American cousins, the crested porcupine makes its nest in a burrow.

Port Elizabeth A seaport (over 381,000 inhabitants) in the Republic of South Africa on the Indian Ocean. Its largest industry is the assembly of motor-cars, and it has machinery, leather, glass and chemical industries, as well as fruit-canning. Port Elizabeth exports wool, hides, diamonds, gold and other products from the interior. The city was established in 1820, following the building of a fort in 1799.

Port Said A seaport of Egypt at the Mediterranean entrance to the Suez Canal. It was established in 1859 by the French builders of the canal. Since the closure of the Canal and the war with Israel, Port Said has been almost completely evacuated. Previously it had a population of about 250,000.

Port Sudan The only seaport (60,000 people) of the Republic of the Sudan, on the Red Sea. Railways lead inland to the Nile Valley, to Atbara, and to Sermar on the Blue Nile. Cotton and gum arabic are the main exports.

Portuguese West Africa — see **Angola**.

Pretoria The seat of government of the Republic of South Africa. This city of 500,000 inhabitants, founded by the Boers in 1855 as the capital of Transvaal province, lies 30 miles north of Johannesburg at an elevation of 4,500 feet. It has gardens, parks, and wide, flower-trimmed boulevards. A cluster of government buildings lies at the centre of the city. Steel mills have risen in the western suburbs, and about 20 miles east is the Premier Mine, one of the world's largest diamond mines, where 'Cullinan' — the largest known white diamond — was found in 1906.

pygmies A dwarf Negroid people of central Africa. They are found in a narrow zone along the equator, among the true Negroes. Their average stature is less than 5 feet. Pygmies, numbering about 100,000, are hunters and food-gatherers on a low cultural level. They live in primitive huts of plaited twigs, or under simple shelters of twigs and leaves. Pygmies exchange the wild game they hunt for crops.

The Great Sphinx at Giza, Egypt, sculptured out of natural rock – at least 4,500 years ago

● **pyramids** Great stone structures in Egypt, raised over the tombs of ancient kings. They were built of huge limestone blocks, averaging over 2 tons, with a surface layer of polished stones which have now disappeared. These enormous tombs were raised by thousands of slaves using ramps, rollers and levers; the pulley was unknown at that time. The earliest, largest and best-known of the pyramids were erected about 2900 B.C. Largest is the Pyramid of Cheops, at Giza, near Cairo. Its height was originally 482 feet, but about 30 feet have weathered away; the base covers 13 acres.

Beneath each pyramid is the tomb chamber, where the mummified Pharaoh was laid, with his jewels, clothing, food and other articles that he was believed to need in his future life. Although most of the pyramid tombs have been looted in the course of the centuries, a few remained intact until modern times. In them, archaeologists have found great treasures, as well as objects and records that tell much about the culture of the ancient Egyptians.

● **Rabat** The capital of Morocco. This attractive residential city of 261,450 on the Atlantic Ocean,

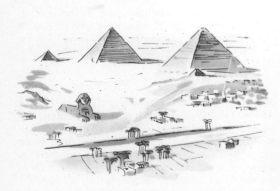

The Great Pyramids and Sphinx

50 miles north-east of busy Casablanca, is known for its beautifully handwoven Moroccan rugs. The King of Morocco makes this city his place of residence. Most of the buildings in the old part of Rabat date from the 12th—14th centuries. The former seat of French administration, it also has a modern European district.

● **Red Sea** The arm of the Indian Ocean which separates Africa from the Arabian Peninsula. One of the warmest seas of the world, and very saline (4 per cent), it is 1,400 miles long, up to 200 miles wide, and as much as 8,000 feet deep. It is connected to the Mediterranean by the Suez Canal, and to the Gulf of Aden (Indian Ocean) by the narrow strait of Bab el Mandeb. During the time the Suez Canal was operating, from 1869 to 1967, the Red Sea was one of the World's busiest shipping lanes. It has no large port cities, because most of the coastline is desert and the shore is lined with coral reefs. The water is sometimes tinted by the presence of billions of tiny red organisms — hence the name.

● **reedbuck** A small, water-loving antelope of Africa, about 3 feet high. When frightened, it flees into the dry bush. Relatively unsociable, the reedbuck travels alone or in pairs.

● **Republic of South Africa** occupies the greater part of southern Africa — 472,500 square miles (five times the size of Great Britain) — and is divided into four provinces: Cape Province, Natal, Orange Free State and Transvaal. Even though it is the main region of white settlement in Africa, Europeans are outnumbered by Africans. The total population of 21.2 million includes over 14.8 million Bantu Africans, 3.7 million inhabitants of European stock, 1.9 million Cape Coloured (people of mixed blood), and 614,000 Asians, mostly of Indian descent.

Race differences in recent years have provided the country's gravest problems. *Apartheid*, the attempt to separate white and African communities completely, has not yet been carried into full effect. The population of European origin consists of the English-speaking group (less than 40 per cent of the total), the Afrikaans-speaking group, of Dutch and Huguenot origin (the Afrikaners, or Boers), and a number of immigrants from Germany, Greece, Italy and so on.

South Africa was originally peopled by Bushmen and Hottentots. These tribes have been greatly reduced, but their descendants form part of the Cape Coloured population. The Bantu Africans in the Republic include the Kaffir, Zulu, Basuto and Matabele, all of whom fiercely resisted European expansion in the 19th century.

The southern tip of Africa was rounded by a Portuguese navigator, Bartholomew Diaz, in 1486. Table Bay, on which Cape Town is now situated, became a supply station on the route to India. In 1652, the Dutch leader Jan van Riebeck established the first permanent settlement there. Britain occupied the Cape region about 1800. Resenting British interference, the Dutch-speaking settlers began their great trek (migration) into the interior. There they founded the South African Republic, also called Transvaal, and the Orange Free State.

The discovery of gold in the Witwatersrand (the 'Rand') led to a gold rush into Afrikaner territory. A British-led raid into the Transvaal started the war for Boer independence, 1899—1902. The Boers were defeated, but promised self-government under the British flag. In 1910, the English and Boer territories (Cape Province, Natal, Transvaal and the Orange Free State) were federated into the Union of South Africa. Pretoria, the former capital of Transvaal, became the administrative capital of the new dominion, and Cape Town the seat of the Union legislature. The mandated territory of South-West Africa (a former German colony) is now administered as part of the Republic.

The vast interior plateau of South Africa rises gently towards the north; it is dry, but has grass for

stock-raising. Its local name, *veld*, means a rolling, treeless grassland with scrub in the lower areas. Large herds of sheep are found everywhere in the veld; there are three sheep for every inhabitant, and wool ranks first among the exports of the Republic. The country also exports citrus fruit, grown with the help of irrigation, hides and skins.

Above all, South Africa is a mining country, and has the many and varied enterprises of a highly industrialised nation. Johannesburg and its surrounding towns on the Rand grew up on the gold mines, which employ 455,000 people. The Republic also exports diamonds (especially from the Kimberley area), copper, manganese, chrome, asbestos and, in recent years, radioactive materials recovered from the gold tailings in the Rand. The Republic is, moreover, the only African country with a major iron and steel industry. Most of the big plants are in the Rand, exporting via Durban.

Durban, a city on the Indian Ocean, is the main port for the Rand. Cape Town, on the Atlantic coast, is at the end of a railway that runs north across the Rand and into Rhodesia. This line forms the first section of a railway which, it was once hoped, would link Cape Town with Cairo across a string of then British-controlled territories.

● **Réunion** An overseas Department of France and an island of 970 square miles in the Indian Ocean, south-west of Mauritius. Its capital is Saint-Denis (85,992 people). Two volcanoes rise steeply from the coast. The island produces rum, sugar, oils for perfumes, and vanilla. The population of 445,000 is of mixed French and African descent. A French possession since 1643, Réunion was formerly named Bourbon. Réunion has several dependencies, including Adelieland in the Antarctic.

● **rhinoceros** A huge, ungainly mammal which rivals the hippopotamus for second place among the land animals (the elephant is the biggest). It is a left-over from prehistoric times; one of its ancestors, the baluchitherium, stood 17 feet high. Though generally not aggressive, the rhinoceros has a short temper and is apt to charge without provocation — perhaps because of its poor eyesight, low intelligence, or desire to protect its young. The one or two horns on the head are actually an outgrowth of the thick hide. For its size, the rhinoceros is surprisingly light on its feet; it can wheel and start off in another direction almost as easily as a polo pony.

The rhinoceros is found in Africa and southern Asia. The most common African species is the black, or hook-lipped, rhinoceros. This animal (actually a dark slate-grey) uses its grasping upper lip to browse on shoots and twigs of trees. The white, or square-lipped, rhinoceros, larger and rarer, is actually a smoky-grey; its square lips are used to pluck grasses.

● **Rhodesia** A region in southern Africa named after Cecil Rhodes, who took possession of it for Britain in 1888. The British South Africa Company, created by Rhodes to develop the country, governed Rhodesia from 1890 until 1923. Then it was turned over to the British government, and divided into Northern and Southern Rhodesia. In 1953, the two Rhodesias and neighbouring Nyasaland were united in the Federation of Rhodesia and Nyasaland (Central African Federation), with the capital at Salisbury. Most of the Europeans lived in Southern Rhodesia, because the climate was more to their liking. When the Federation was disbanded in 1963, Nyasaland became independent as Malawi (q.v.), Northern Rhodesia achieved independence as Zambia, and Southern Rhodesia reverted to internal self-government, final and complete independence remaining in abeyance until Britain felt satisfied that the country's inhabitants were all content with the terms of Rhodesia's 'independence' constitution. Rhodesia's white minority government declared itself unilaterally independent on 11 November, 1965, and went to break all ties with Britain and the Commonwealth on 13 February, 1970. The government remains unrecognised by Britain and most of the world. A settlement was proposed in 1972 by Britain, but failed to be accepted by the African majority.

● **Zambia** (290,000 square miles; population 3.8 million), formerly called **Northern Rhodesia** and now independent, is noted for the extensive copper deposits across the northern region to the border of the Congo. Huge quantities of ore are mined, smelted and refined, and the metal is exported via Beira, on the Indian Ocean. Zinc, lead and cobalt are also mined there. The seat of government, now at Lusaka, was formerly at Livingstone, near Victoria Falls. David Livingstone first reached the region in 1851, discovered the Falls in 1855, and died in 1873 in a native village near marshy Lake Bangweulu.

● **(Southern) Rhodesia** (150,000 square miles; population 5,090,000), was a self-governing colony from 1923 until 1953, and reverted to internal self-government after the dismemberment of the Central African Federation. Rhodesia seized full independence from Britain, unilaterally and illegally on 11th November, 1965. Maize is widely grown, but tobacco is the chief product of European-operated farms. Cattle-raising is extensive in the highlands, but the lowlands, infested by the tsetse fly, are avoided by all. Rhodesia exports asbestos, gold and chromite, and has one of the few high-quality coal deposits of tropical Africa. Industrial development will be speeded up by the huge hydro-electric power project in the Kariba Gorge of the Zambezi River. Salisbury is the seat of government (q.v.).

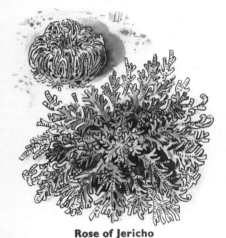

Rose of Jericho

● **rose of Jericho** A desert plant, noted for the way it contracts when the weather is dry and expands when water is again available. To medieval pilgrims who visited the Holy Land, this behaviour seemed to symbolise the Resurrection.

● **Rwanda** A republic of east-central Africa, north of Burundi, and likewise a part of the former United Nations trust territory of Ruanda-Urundi, administered by Belgium as part of the former Belgian Congo. Before 1917, and from 1899, it was a part of German East Africa. Rwanda has an area of over 10,000 square miles, with a population of nearly 3.3 million, largely Bantu Negroes. The Republic became independent in 1962, and its capital is Kigali, with several thousand inhabitants. It exports some cotton, coffee, tobacco and tin. There are large deposits of methane gas under Lake Kivu.

● **Sahara** A desert extending across northern Africa from the Atlantic to the Red Sea. The Sahara is bordered to the north by the Atlas Mountains and the Mediterranean Sea, but to the south it gradually merges with the drier savanna. The largest of all deserts, the Sahara is an empty land, except for scattered· oases supporting a total population estimated at 2,500,000. Most of the Sahara is 900 to 1,600 feet above sea level, with an irregular surface. A few mountain ranges, such as the Tibesti and Ahaggar, rise thousands of feet above the plateaux.

Only a fraction of the Sahara is sandy. In some areas, crescent-shaped sand-dunes follow each other like waves on a sea; elsewhere, *hammadas* (rock surfaces) have been swept clean of sand. Hot, dry, dust-laden winds, or *khamsins*, blow from the desert to the Mediterranean. (*Khamsin* is the Arabic word for fifty, and the Arabs say the wind blows for 50 days, April to June.)

The most dependable means of transport is still the camel, but nowadays buses and motor-cars cross the desert from Algeria to West Africa. The trip, which formerly took two months by caravan, now takes five or six days. Many projects to develop the Sahara have come to nothing, but the recent discovery of oil and natural gas in the south Algerian area have prompted a rapid development there.

● **St Helena** A British islet of 47 square miles and 4,829 people in the middle of the South Atlantic Ocean, 1,700 miles north-west of Cape Town. In the 17th and 18th centuries, sailing ships bound for the Orient stopped there, and Napoleon was confined on St Helena from 1815 until his death, in 1821. The island of Ascension, 760 miles northwest, is a dependency of St Helena; it has an area of 34 square miles and a population of just over 739. About 1,500 miles south of St Helena, and some 1,700 miles westward from Cape Town, lies the tiny British group of islands called Tristan da Cunha. The chief island of the group, Tristan, has 270 inhabitants who were evacuated to England in 1961, when the volcano it consists of erupted. However, most of them returned in 1963, and are still there.

● **Salisbury** The capital of (Southern) Rhodesia, Salisbury is linked by railway with the Republic of South Africa, Zambia, and the port of Beira, on the Indian Ocean. Founded in 1890, Salisbury has a population of over 384,500 including 96,400 Europeans. Head offices of the mining companies in the Copper Belt are located in this rapidly-developing modern city, situated 4,800 feet above has 270 inhabitants, who were evacuated to England in 1961, when the volcano it consists of erupted. However, most of them returned in 1963, and are still there.

Savanna

● **savanna** Any of the tropical grasslands between the equatorial rain forests and the deserts, particularly in Africa. In the park savanna, tall grasses alternate with wooded areas; in the savanna proper, grasses predominate with a scattering of trees, especially the flat-canopied acacia. Along the edge of the desert are dry short-grass savannas, with trees along river courses only. The tall grass of the humid savanna favours such grass-eating animals as the elephant, rhinoceros and antelope, but is not suitable for grazing by domestic livestock. Natives often burn the dry grass to make room for young shoots, on which their herds can graze. In South America, savannas are known as *llanos* (Venezuela) or *campos* (Brazil).

● **secretary bird** A bird of prey with long plumes sticking out from the back of its head as quill pens once did from behind the ear of a secretary. The bird eats venomous snakes, which it kills with blows of its strong feet. African ranchers often tame the bird as a snake-killer. It is a bird of the savanna lands and rarely flies.

● **Semites** A group of peoples of the Middle East, speaking related languages. The Semitic languages are now represented chiefly by Arabic and Hebrew, but in ancient times included also Babylonian, Assyrian and Phoenician. Semites and Hamites have become intermixed in North Africa to such an extent that they are often grouped together as Semito-Hamites.

● **Senegal** The oldest of the former French colonies in West Africa and an independent republic since 1960. It was settled in the 15th century, and its former capital, St Louis (47,900 people), had an active slave trade with the West Indies. The Senegal River, weaving its way for 1,000 miles, was once important as a waterway to the interior. A railway now links St Louis with the present capital of Dakar (q.v.) and runs 700 miles inland to Bamako, on the Niger River in Mali. The population is largely Fulani and Sudan Negroes, numbering about 3.5 million. Senegal exports groundnuts, vegetable oils and phosphates.

● **Senusi** A Moslem sect, founded in 1837 to propagate Islam and combat Western influence. Its members are found in oases of North Africa, notably the Kufra oasis in Libya. The ruling family of Libya is a branch of the Senusi.

● **shoebill** A wading bird known in Arabic as Abu Markub ('father of the shoe'). It has a huge, shoe-like bill, hooked at the tip. About 3 feet high and light grey, the bird resembles the marabou in habits.

● **Sierra Leone** An independent state within the Commonwealth since 1961, Sierra Leone has an area of 28,000 square miles in West Africa, bordering on Liberia. It grew from a settlement of freed slaves which provided a refuge for destitute Negroes from England in 1787. This community was sited at Freetown, now the chief city of Sierra Leone and one of the finest natural harbours on the West African coast, with a population of 150,000. The inland region has three provinces, where 2.5 million Africans maintain their tribal ways. Principal exports are coffee, palm oil, palm kernels and ginger — all from the humid coastal districts, which have 150 inches of rain in the wet season. Sizable deposits of iron, gold, diamonds and chromite are mined in the interior and exported.

● **sisal** A hard fibre taken from an agave plant which is native to the African tropics. Sisal furnishes a strong, durable, white fibre (3 to 5 feet long) used largely for cordage — principally binding twine for automatic grain-binders and harvesters. Sisal is used also in furniture coverings. Half of the world's production comes from East Africa (Tanzania, Kenya and Uganda). Henequen, a similar fibre, comes mainly from an agave of Yucatán, Mexico, which is grown in Brazil, Florida, Java and Mexico.

● **Somalia** A republic of East Africa bordering the Indian Ocean and the Gulf of Aden in the east, and Ethiopia in the west. The Somalis who live in the area are Moslems. About 2.7 million people roam the 246,000 square miles of dry, rocky land in search of grazing areas for their livestock. The Republic was created from former British and Italian Somaliland in 1960. It has a dry tropical climate. Between the two world wars, the Italians established plantations in the valleys of the few permanent streams to the south; there are grown cotton, sugar cane, tobacco, bananas and maize. Off-shore fisheries yield tunny and mother-of-pearl. Mogadishu, the main port and capital city, has a population of 100,000. Once owned by the Sultan of Zanzibar, his palace and mosques still stand in the city.

● **Somaliland (French)** see **French Territory of the Afars and Issas**

Sorghum

● **sorghum** A cereal grass that grows in the tropics. It does well, even in dry areas. The kind called grain sorghum is grown for human food in Africa and Asia, and for poultry and livestock feed in the United States. The main grain varieties are durra, grown in southern Asia and northern Africa, and kaoliang, in China. Syrup sorghums, or sorgos, have sweet stalks, and are raised either for forage or for their sweet juice, from which syrup and sugar are made. Kaffir, which is a syrup sorghum, is widely grown in southern Africa. Broom sorghum, a bristly plant, is used to make whisk brooms. Grass sorghums are cultivated for pasture and hay.

● **sorghum, Kaffir** A cereal grass (sugar sorghum) containing a sweet juice in its stem and leaf stalks.

Africans get the juice by squeezing the grass. In the south-western United States and other dry areas, this sorghum is grown for grain or forage.

● **South-West Africa** A former German colony, administered as a mandate under the Treaty of Versailles by the Republic of South Africa (which does not recognise the United Nations trusteeship of the territory). It is a dry country (318,000 square miles), with a coastal desert, the Namib, and an interior upland on which stream beds are dry, except after occasional heavy rains. In the east, the upland merges with the Kalahari Desert. The capital city, Windhoek (36,000 people), lies in the central upland, which is reserved for European settlers. The native Ovambo, Herero, Hottentots and Bushmen raise sheep and cattle. After World War I, karakul sheep were brought to South-West Africa, and today karakul pelts are a growing export product. Mining, however, is still the chief activity. Diamonds are washed near Lüderitz and close to the mouth of the Orange River. Lead and zinc are mined near Tsumeb and sent by rail to Walvis Bay, the chief seaport. Gold, iron, copper and salt are also mined. The population of 749,000 includes 90,000 inhabitants of European stock.

● **Spanish Sahara** A Spanish desert province (about 100,000 square miles) on the north-west coast of Africa. It is a barren region, peopled by about 60,000, mostly roaming Berber herdsmen. Off-shore trawl-fisheries are the main source of income. The territory is divided into two provinces: Rio Rojo, in the north, and Rio de Oro, in the south. Separate and to the north is the former Spanish enclave of Ifni, with an area approaching 1,000 square miles and a population of 54,000. Its capital is Sidi Ifni, a town on the south Moroccan coast. It was Spanish, but was added to Morocco in 1969.

● **Sphinx of Giza** A giant stone figure of a recumbent lion with the head of a man, at Giza, Egypt. It is 172 feet long and 66 feet high, and was supposed to represent the Egyptian god of the morning sun. The notion that it typifies mysterious wisdom comes from the Greeks. In Grecian

mythology, the Sphinx was a female monster who proposed riddles and destroyed those who failed to solve them.

● **springbok** A gazelle-like antelope with the habit of making sudden soaring leaps. It stands about 30 inches high, and has a hair-lined fold of skin along the rear of its back. When alarmed, the springbok turns the fold inside out, displaying the white hair as a warning signal. It is mainly to be found in the Kalahari desert.

● **spurge** A large family of plants found throughout the world, especially in the tropics. Spurges grow as shrubs, trees or lianas in humid areas, and as thorny and cactus-like plants in arid regions. The cactus-like leafless forms are common in the African savanna. In the United States, spurges are a common field and garden weed, also found along the roads and in woodlands and marshy areas.

● **Stanleyville** (now **Kisangani**) A town of 70,000 in the Congo, on the Congo River below Stanley Falls. There goods are transferred from river boats to a railway, which then by-passes a section of the river that is too rough for boats. Below this obstacle, the Congo is navigable as far as Kinshasi The town was named after H.M. Stanley, who discovered this stretch of the Congo in 1877. Kisangani at the centre of an insurrection against the Kinshasi government, was the scene of considerable bloodshed in 1964.

● **sting ray** A flattened, disc-shaped fish of tropical seas and rivers. It hides in sand or silt on the bottom. Halfway down its long, flexible tail there is a spine with saw-teeth, and this is driven into the leg of anyone who steps on it; poison injected into the wound causes intense pain.

Abdim's stork

● **stork, Abdim's** A migratory bird of Africa that builds its nest in trees. As many as 30 nests have been found in a single tree.

● **stork, saddle-billed** A rare bird of tropical Africa; the largest and tallest of the stork group. A triangle of bright yellow skin at the base of the bill gives the head the shape of a saddle.

● **Sudan** A broad belt of north-central Africa between the Sahara and the tropical rain forest, extending from the Atlantic to the upper Nile Valley and to the Ethiopian highlands. Its 4 million square miles cover parts of several countries. The western Sudan, drained by the Niger River, makes up part of former French West Africa (Niger, Volta and Mali). Central Sudan extends over most of the Chad Republic and takes in the drainage basin of Lake Chad. The eastern Sudan reaches the valley of the upper Nile. The Republic of the Sudan (*see next page*) does not include all these regions.

A busy road bridge, over the River Nile, in Cairo

In the Sudan, the Arabs first met Negroes in their southward advance across Africa. (In Arabic, *Sudan* means 'black'.) High temperatures are typical; in Timbuktu, for example, every month has an average over 70° F. Annual rainfall varies from 80 inches nearest to the equator, to 10 inches along the edge of the Sahara, but nowhere in the Sudan does it rain at all times of the year.

● **The Republic of the Sudan** (968,000 square miles; population 14.77 million), founded in 1956, lies between Uganda and Egypt. It has an outlet to the Red Sea at Port Sudan. At Khartoum, the capital, the Blue Nile (coming from the Ethiopian highlands) meets the White Nile (coming from Lake Victoria). From there, the combined waters flow across the desert towards Egypt. Cotton is the leading export crop; it is produced in the Gezira, an area between the two arms of the Nile above Khartoum. This country is also the world's chief source of gum arabic; other products include senna leaves, groundnuts, dates, hides and skins. The chief grain crop, durra (millet), is used locally. The northern region is inhabited by Arabic-speaking Moslem whites, and the more backward south, by various Negroid tribes. What is now the Sudan Republic was ruled jointly by Britain and Egypt from 1899 until 1956, and was known as the Anglo-Egyptian Sudan.

● **Suez** An Egyptian city of 203,000 people at the southern end of the Suez Canal, on the Red Sea. Before the Arab-Israeli War it owed its importance to its position at the entrance of the canal. Its industries included a fertiliser plant and oil refineries. However, by 1969, Suez had been almost totally evacuated.

● **Suez Canal** A man-made waterway across the desert, connecting the Mediterranean with the Red Sea. It is one of the most important waterways in the world, because the only other route for ships between Europe and the Orient is the long one around the southern tip of Africa. Seen from the air, the Suez Canal looks like a big ditch cutting across the desert sands. It is 101 miles long and has a minimum width of 200 feet. The canal has no locks; it thus crosses the narrow isthmus linking Asia with Africa at sea level. The canal is deep enough for large passenger and merchant ships (up to 37 foot draught) to pass through; the journey takes about 13 hours from Port Said, at the northern entrance, to Suez, on the Red Sea. Special pilots guide the ships through the canal.

The Suez Canal was built between 1859 and 1869 under the direction of a Frenchman, Ferdinand de Lesseps. It was owned by an international company, in which Britain held a controlling interest. The canal, which cuts across Egyptian soil, was to be handed over to Egypt in 1968, 99 years after it was opened. In 1956, however, the Egyptian government seized control of the canal. An attempt by France and Great Britain, in the November of that year, to reoccupy the canal zone, after the outbreak of fighting between Egypt and Israel, ended in the withdrawal of Anglo-French forces, following action by the United Nations. It has been blocked since the Arab-Israeli War of 1967 and is no longer in use.

● **Swahili** A Bantu Negro people of East Africa, living in scattered groups along the coast of Kenya and Tanzania, and also on Zanzibar Island. Because the Swahili are important traders, their language has become the common tongue of East Africa. Although classed as a Bantu language, Swahili has borrowed heavily from Arabic, Hindu, Persian, Portuguese and English.

● **Swaziland** A British dependency with internal self-government, Swaziland achieved full independence in 1968. Enclosed on three sides by the Republic of South Africa, and sharing

Arched gateways and medieval battlements guard entrances to the Moslem quarter in Tunis

its eastern frontier with the Portuguese territory of Mozambique, Swaziland lies to the east of the Drakensburg Mountains. The total area of Swaziland is 6,705 square miles, with a population of 374,571 administered from the town of Mbabane (14,000 inhabitants). The principcal agricultural products are cotton, tobacco, citrus fruits, sugar and rice, and there are rich deposits of asbestos and iron in the western part of Swaziland.

● **Tangier** A seaport of Morocco, on the North African side of the Strait of Gibraltar. With its surrounding territory, it once formed the International Zone of Tangier (147 square miles; population 166,290), controlled by eight European countries and the United States. In 1960, Tangier became part of Morocco. The city has long been a trading and banking centre. Its modern European quarter contrasts with the walled Moorish district, an area of crowded white buildings and painted minarets.

● **Tanzania** The United Republic (360,000 square miles) is in eastern Africa, and consists of Tanganyika, independent since 1961, and Zanzibar, independent since 1963. Most of it is too dry for many settlers; large areas are covered by grasslands and scrub forest. Where there is enough rain, the land is cultivated. Such areas are the slopes of the volcanoes Mt Meru and Kilimanjaro (Africa's highest peak), the south shore of Lake Victoria, the highlands near Lake Malawi, and the coast near Tanga and Dar es Salaam.

Largely agricultural, Tanganyika produces sisal (a third of the world's supply), coffee, cotton and beans — also gold and diamonds. After World War II, the British tried growing groundnuts on a large scale in the south, but neither the soil nor rainfall was satisfactory. A railway crosses the country from Dar es Salaam (the capital — q.v.) on the Indian Ocean to Lake Tanganyika in the west; a spur runs north to Lake Victoria. Less than 1 per cent of the land is set aside for European plantations, and Europeans number only about 17,000. There are some 116,000 Asians and Arabs, mostly merchants. The African population of Tanganyika numbers over 10 million, and is made up of Bantu-speaking tribes.

The territory was explored in the 1850s by Burton, Livingstone and Stanley. The last two met at Ujiji, on Lake Tanganyika, in 1871. Claimed by the Germans in 1885, the territory was called

German East Africa until 1916, when it was taken by Britain during World War I. Together with the 354,000 inhabitants of Zanzibar (with Pemba), Tanzania's present population is approximately 12,231,000.

● **Zanzibar** An island of 640 square miles in the Indian Ocean, off the east coast of Africa. Navigators approaching Zanzibar can truly 'smell' their way to it, because the aroma of the clove trees carries far and wide. The cultivation and shipping of this spice support the 190,117 Africans, Arabs and Indians of Zanzibar. Together with its sister island of Pemba (380 square miles; 164,243 people), Zanzibar was a British protectorate, also including the minor islands of Lamu, Manda, Patta and Siu. The sultan, the former ruler, was deposed in 1964, shortly after independence, and the islands are now part of the United Republic of Tanganyika and Zanzibar (Tanzania).

● **Lake Tanganyika** is the largest of the great lakes that occupy the bottom of Africa's rift valleys. It is 400 miles long, separating the Congo and Tanzania. The lake's greatest depth is 4,700 feet — over 2,000 feet below sea level.

● **Timbuktu** A former caravan and slave-trading centre of the Sahara, on the great bend of the Niger River in Mali. The town lost much of its importance when motor-cars began crossing the

The waterbuck is a species of antelope

desert along a shorter route, and has a population of only about 9,000 people. Upstream from Timbuktu, the French have built dams and reservoirs to supply water to an extensive cotton- and rice-growing district.

- **Togoland** A former German colony in West Africa. After World War I, it was mandated to Britain and France, and later became a trust territory of the United Nations under British and French administration. British Togoland (13,000 square miles) has been part of independent Ghana, the former Gold Coast, since 1957. French Togoland (21,000 square miles, with a population of over 1,955,000) has been independent, as the Republic of Togo, since 1960, the capital being Lome (135,000). Humid, tropical Togo produces coffee, hardwoods, cotton, groundnuts, cacao, and oil and copra from the palm tree; it also possesses rich deposits of phosphates and bauxite.

- **touraco (or plantain eater)** One of the most beautiful birds of Africa, living south of the Sahara. Most touracos are brilliantly coloured — notably green, blue and purple. The grey touraco is a plainer form. As it runs along tree branches, with the agility of a squirrel, the touraco calls with loud, resonant notes. It feeds mostly on small soft fruits.

Traveller's tree

- **traveller's tree** A plant related to the banana, with a trunk 10 to 20 feet high. Grown in the tropics as an ornamental plant, it has hollow leaf-stalks which collect water that can be tapped by thirsty travellers. The plant originated from Madagascar.

- **Tripoli** A seaport of 245,000 people on the Mediterranean, and one of the two capitals of the Republic of Libya (Benghazi being the other). Its port facilities were built by the Italians when Libya was an Italian colony. Founded in the 7th century B.C., Tripoli was occupied in turn by Romans, Arabs and Turks. Under the Turks, it became a stronghold of pirates, who were dislodged at the beginning of the 19th century by United States Marines. The official name of the town is now Tarabulus.

- **Tuareg** A Moslem nomad people of the western Sahara. They speak a language related to that of the Berbers. A strong military organisation, ability to travel quickly (by means of camels), and a central location in the Ahaggar Mountains of the Algerian Sahara, once gave the Tuareg almost complete command of desert trade routes. The French took control of the area, however, after 1900. Tuareg men go veiled, while the women, unusually, go unveiled.

- **Tunis** The capital (789,000 people) of Tunisia. It lies on a mountain-fringed bay of the Mediterranean, less than 150 miles from the western tip of Sicily. It ships out phosphates, iron ore, citrus fruits, wine, dates, olive oil, and esparto grass for European paper mills, from its harbour of La Goulette. Modern Tunis was built while the French controlled the area, from 1881—1956. There is also the old walled Moslem quarter, with very narrow lanes.

- **Tunisia** An independent republic of North Africa on the Mediterranean Sea. It occupies 45,000 square miles between Algeria and Libya. Two thousand years ago, as a Roman province, it supplied Rome with wheat and olive oil. After the Arab conquests in the 7th century, Tunisia fell into neglect. Under its Turkish governors, or beys, it became a pirate stronghold — one of the Barbary States.

  The French occupied Tunisia in 1881 and established a protectorate that lasted for 75 years. French and Italian farmers settled there and restored the country's agriculture, producing citrus fruit, wine, tobacco, flowers for perfume, and cereals. Closely planted olive groves line the eastern coast-line, and some of the world's best dates are grown in the inland oases of Bled-el-Jerid. Phosphate rock is Tunisia's leading export product; railways link the mines with the ports of Tunis and Sfax. Bizerte, on the north coast, is a naval base. Kairouan, one of the principal inland towns, is a Moslem holy city. The Arab population numbers 4.7 million; there is a European colony of 200,000.

  During World War II, the Allied invasion of North Africa led to fierce battles for control of Tunisia. The remains of Germany's African armies surrendered in the Cape Bon Peninsula.

- **Uganda** The most prosperous of the East African countries, independent since 1962, and occupying a savanna-covered tableland (4,000 to 6,000 feet above sea level) between Kenya and the Congo. Its area of 94,000 square miles is larger than Great Britain and has a population approaching 9.54 million, including 88,000 Asians and 9,000 Europeans. The Africans include 1 million Baganda, the Bantu tribe from which the country takes its name. The Baganda were the most advanced natives when the first European explorers came in the 1860s. Uganda became a British protectorate in 1894.

  The soil is fertile and there is plenty of rain — 40 to 55 inches per year. The main commercial crops are cotton, sugar, coffee, groundnuts, sisal and tobacco. Cotton, the chief export, is grown by Africans on their small farms; their work explains Uganda's relative prosperity. Uganda has acquired new industries as a result of the completion of the Owen Falls hydro-electric project at Jinja on the Nile.

  Kampala, with about 170,000 inhabitants, is the capital and chief commercial centre, and the end of the railway from Mombasa, Kenya's port on the Indian Ocean.

- **Upper Volta** A republic of West Africa with an area of 100,000 square miles and a population of over 5.3 million. Formerly part of the French colony of the Ivory Coast, it gained full independence in 1960. The principal occupations are cattle and sheep rearing. The largest tribe is the Mossi, whose king still exerts some influence over the country.

- **uranium** Since the splitting of the uranium atom has opened up the vast field of atomic energy, uranium ore has been the object of world-wide search. Many deposits are being discovered, not only by trained geologists, but by amateurs equipped with Geiger counters. Because of the military applications of uranium in nuclear weapons, all producing countries keep their output figures secret. The Katanga area of the Congo was the principal producer before the boom started, and is presumably still in first place. Other important mines are found in the United States, Canada, the Soviet Union, Czechoslovakia and East Germany.

- **Victoria, Lake** The largest of the African lakes and the second-largest of the world's bodies of fresh water. (Lake Superior covers a larger area than the 26,000 square miles of Lake Victoria. The Caspian Sea is the world's largest lake, but has saline water.) It lies 3,700 feet above sea level on the East African tableland, and is so large that one can travel on it for hours without seeing the shore. Its greatest depth is 250 feet. The lake is divided between Uganda, Tanzania and Kenya.

In South Africa, a herd of wary zebras, always on the lookout for prowling lions, pauses long enough to drink at a waterhole

Tutsi, or Watusi, warriors – arrayed here in traditional war-dress – are often seven feet tall and are Burundi people

From the west it is fed by the Kagera River (main source of the Nile), and in the north it is drained by the Nile (here known as the Victoria Nile). A dam at Owen Falls, just below the outflow of the Nile, provides hydro-electric power for Uganda. The main towns on the lake are Jinja and Entebbe in Uganda, Kisumu in Kenya, and Mwanza in Tanzania. The lake shore is densely populated in several areas where coffee and cotton are grown. Lake Victoria was discovered by John Speke in 1858.

- **viper, rhinoceros** A poisonous snake related to the puff adder and found in West Africa. It has olive-reddish markings topped off with large blue blotches along the back. It is named from the horn-like scales protruding from the snout.

- **vulture, eared** A large African vulture deriving its name from two small ear-like flaps on the sides of the head. It lives in highlands up to an altitude of 12,500 feet.

- **vultures** The most common birds in Africa, and in many areas of southern Asia and tropical America. They feed on carrion — some even on dung and other refuse. Wherever there is a dead animal, vultures rapidly gather; they devour not only the flesh, but the entrails and small bones, leaving the bare skeleton. Some vultures stay near towns, where they search for food around slaughter-houses and refuse dumps. Since the birds make good garbage collectors, the inhabitants look upon them favourably. On most vultures the head is naked, or has only a few feathers. Old World vultures, related to the hawks and eagles, include the griffon vulture of southern Europe, the Egyptian white vulture of the Middle East, the hooded vulture, and the eared vulture. Typical New World vultures are the condor, the black vulture, and the king vulture.

- **wadi** A desert stream bed that is usually dry and contains water only at times of heavy rain. Wadis (the word is Arabic) generally lose themselves in the desert. After a downpour, sometimes only once in ten years, wadis become raging torrents, and sweep rocks and vegetation downstream at great speed.

- **waterbuck** A water-loving antelope of the African plains that feeds and rests on dry land. When alarmed, it seeks refuge in the nearest water. The common waterbuck has a conspicuous white line encircling the rump.

- **Watusi** A Bantu Negro people of Rwanda and Burundi. They have been described as the tallest people in Africa, and are cattle-herders.

Welwitschia mirabilis

- **Welwitschia** A curious African plant with a short stem, 3 to 5 feet thick. From the stem emerge a single pair of long, leathery leaves, up to 6 feet long. The leaves keep on growing at the base and die at the tips. Discovered in the desert regions of South-West Africa in 1860, they may reach an age of more than a hundred years.

- **Yoruba** The most numerous group of Negro people in western Nigeria. At the time of the slave trade, they founded city states in the back country of Lagos, the present capital of Nigeria. They are largely a farming people, well-known for their wood-carving.

- **Zambezi River** Largest in southern Africa — it flows 1,600 miles across Rhodesia and Mozambique to the Indian Ocean, north-east of the port of Beira. Near the town of Livingstone, it forms the famous Victoria Falls. Beyond the falls, the Zambezi flows swiftly through a series of gorges. At the Kariba Gorge, 200 miles below the falls, the river has been dammed for hydro-electric power. The main tributary of the lower Zambezi is the Shire, the outlet of Lake Malawi.

- **Zaire —** see **Congo**

- **Zambia** — see **Rhodesia**.

- **Zanzibar** — see **Tanzania**.

- **zebra** The wild horse of the grassy plains of Africa. Zebras have the well-known black-and-white striped coat, a short, stiff mane, and a tufted tail. The true zebra of South Africa, or mountain zebra, was the first known to Europeans. It has extremely broad, widely spaced stripes on its hind flanks. The Hartmann zebra is a variety of the mountain zebra. The Grevy zebra, of north-east Africa — largest of the zebras — has a pattern of very narrow stripes all over its body.

- **Zimbabwe** A group of ruins of a human settlement in (Southern) Rhodesia, estimated to be perhaps 1,000 years old. The structures include a massive wall, a temple, and a citadel. They are possibly of Arab origin.

- **Zulu** An important Bantu Negro people of South Africa, belonging to the Kaffir group. They number about 2 million. In the 19th century, the Zulus formed a great tribal confederation and waged wars against the European settlers. The main economy of the people is cattle-rearing, while the women work the fields.

North America

Shaped like a huge triangle and fringed by three oceans, North America (population 250 million; area 8,400,000 square miles) reaches north to a point less than 500 miles from the North Pole — Cape Morris Jesup, in Greenland. (This is the world's most northerly tip of land, and Greenland is geologically and geographically part of North America, though part of Denmark politically.) It stretches south to a point just over 500 miles from the equator (where the Isthmus of Panama joins the land mass of South America). This tremendous latitudinal spread is equalled by only one other continent — Asia, which also spans 75° of latitude from Singapore, close to the equator, to the Arctic shores of Siberia.

North America's east-west extent is almost as impressive as that of Asia, for, from Alaska to Newfoundland, the continent embraces eight time zones, so that, when it is noon at Gander, Newfoundland — the easternmost airport on the North American mainland — it is only 5 a.m. at Nome, Alaska, a mere 150 miles from Soviet Siberia. (In actual practice, Newfoundland time is half-an-hour later than the time zone — Atlantic Time — in which it is located.) The continent narrows southwards, however, for below the latitude of Mexico (where a single time zone prevails from coast to coast) it is little more than a land bridge to South America; and it is at its narrowest at the Panama Canal, where only 40 miles of rugged land had to be cut to connect the Atlantic and Pacific Oceans, for the use of world shipping.

Prior to construction of the Canal (which was opened to traffic in 1914), the continuous land mass of the Western Hemisphere provided an obstacle to east-west navigation for over 8,000 miles, or one-third the circumference of the globe.

The history of the discovery of America does not begin with Christopher Columbus in 1492. About five hundred years earlier, the coast of North America was visited by Leif Ericsson, a Viking sailor who reputedly had lost his way to Greenland, where his father (Eric the Red of Iceland) had just established a settlement. Ericsson landed on the coast of Labrador (Vinland). In any case, Columbus did not even reach the North American mainland. On the day he finally sighted land, after five weeks at sea, his discovery was a small island in the Bahamas, the gateway to the West Indies, the very name of which serves as a permanent reminder that Columbus had hoped to reach far-off India when he set out from Spain in 1492. Others followed him in search of the true Indies. Thus it happened that the coast of North America was explored by frustrated seamen whose westward progress to the Orient was barred by the New World.

The name 'America' appeared for the first time on a map in 1507, drawn by the German cartographer Waldseemüller (1470 — 1518). This map-maker wished to honour Amerigo Vespucci, who in 1500 — 02 explored thousands of miles of South American

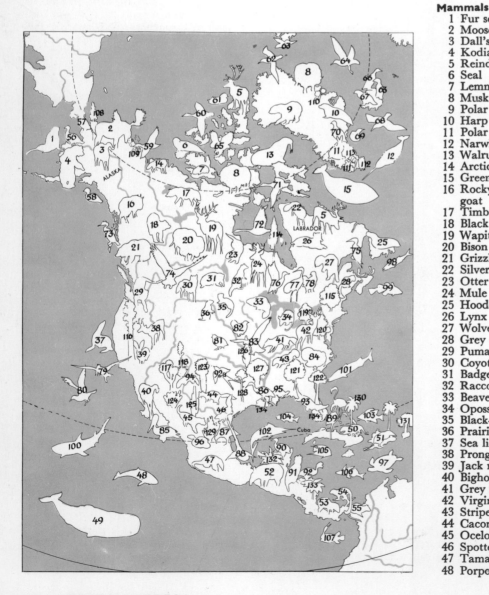

Wild Animals and Plants

Mammals
1 Fur seal
2 Moose
3 Dall's sheep
4 Kodiak bear
5 Reindeer
6 Seal
7 Lemming
8 Musk ox
9 Polar bear
10 Harp seal
11 Polar hare
12 Narwhal
13 Walrus
14 Arctic fox
15 Greenland whale
16 Rocky Mountain goat
17 Timber wolf
18 Black bear
19 Wapiti
20 Bison
21 Grizzly bear
22 Silver fox
23 Otter
24 Mule deer
25 Hooded seal
26 Lynx
27 Wolverine
28 Grey squirrel
29 Puma
30 Coyote
31 Badger
32 Raccoon
33 Beaver
34 Opossum
35 Black-footed ferret
36 Prairie dog
37 Sea lion
38 Pronghorn
39 Jack rabbit
40 Bighorn sheep
41 Grey fox
42 Virginia deer
43 Striped skunk
44 Cacomistle
45 Ocelot
46 Spotted skunk
47 Tamandua
48 Porpoise

49 Sperm whale
50 Hutia
51 Solenodon
52 Baird's tapir
53 Paca
54 Geoffroy's tamarin
55 Yapok (Water opossum)

Birds
56 Emperor goose
57 Tufted puffin
58 Harlequin duck
59 Surf scoter
60 Snow goose
61 King eider
62 Parasitic jaeger
63 Atlantic puffin
64 Glaucous gull
65 Snowy owl
66 Guillemot
67 Gyrfalcon
68 Black-backed gull
69 Red-throated loon
70 Ptarmigan
71 Blue goose
72 Whistling swan
73 Cormorant
74 Bald eagle
75 Gannet
76 Mallard duck
77 Sandhill crane
78 Spruce goose
79 Royal tern
80 Heermann's gull
81 Bobwhite
82 Prairie chicken
83 Osprey
84 Turkey
85 Brown pelican
86 Blue heron
87 Black vulture
88 Quetzal
89 Flamingo
90 Black-bellied tree duck
91 Harpy eagle
92 Great curassow
92a Scissor-tailed flycatcher

Reptiles and Amphibians
93 Alligator
94 Gila monster
95 Painted turtle
96 Rattlesnake
97 Hawk's-bill turtle

Fishes
98 Mackerel
99 Cod
100 Tiger shark
101 Barracuda
102 Blue marlin
103 Pigfish
104 Yellow grunt
105 Blue angelfish
106 Flying fish
107 Black sea-devil

Plants
108 Douglas fir
109 Birch
110 Iceland poppy
111 Arctic willow
112 Cotton grass
113 Bellflower
114 White fir
115 Red oak
116 Giant sequoia
117 Joshua tree
118 Agave
119 Tulip tree
120 Hickory
121 Magnolia
122 Bald cypress
123 California fan palm
124 Opuntia (prickly pear)
125 Cereus cactus
126 Poplar
127 Oak
128 Pine
129 Cereus cactus
130 Royal palm
131 Cabbage palmetto
132 Pisang
133 Tree horn
134 Mangrove forest

coastline in search of a southern passage to the Orient.

Following these voyages of discovery, the New World was settled by those European nations that had shown the greatest interest in exploration. The French and the British penetrated North America, while the Spanish took possession of Mexico and Central America.

Thirsty for gold, Spanish *conquistadores* quickly destroyed the civilisation of the Mayas and the Aztecs, two highly cultured Indian nations whose architectural wonders are still in evidence near Mexico City and in the Yucatán Peninsula. The present capital of Mexico has been built over the ruins of Tenochtitlán, the Aztec metropolis which Hernán Cortés captured in 1521. Although the Spanish conquerors pushed northward to Colorado, in search of precious metals, and westward to California, in search of Indians to Christianise, they failed to gain effective control over the territory north of the Rio Grande.

Following the trail blazed by Cartier, the French settled Canada from Quebec. They established their roots so firmly that Quebec, the largest province in modern Canada, still has a predominantly French-speaking population, with French one of the country's two official languages. In the second half of the 17th century, the French drove deeper into the continent following the Mississippi south to the Gulf of Mexico. La Salle promptly claimed the whole Mississippi Valley for France, and called it Louisiana in honour of his king, Louis XIV.

In the meantime, Britain had colonised the east coast with two settlements, one in Massachusetts and one in Virginia, that formed the nucleus of what was to grow into the 13 States. Friction between the British westward advance across the Appalachians and the French drive to the south led to the French and Indian War (1754—63), and to France's eventual surrender of her Canadian territories to Britain in 1763.

Thus North America came to be divided into political units that do not fit within homogeneous physical regions. On the contrary, the longest boundary on the continent, that between Canada and the United States (long known as the longest undefended border in the world), cuts across all but one of the major physiographic divisions of North America. The United States-Mexico line follows a river — the Rio Grande; but this river is vastly more important as a cultural divide (between 190 million Anglo-Americans and 180 million Latin Americans) than as a physical barrier.

One of the major physiographic regions of the continent is the eastern coastal lowlands, fringed on the west by the long chains of the Appalachians, extending from Nova Scotia and the Gaspé Peninsula of Quebec southward to Florida. Spanning half the width of the United States from the Appalachians to the Rocky Mountains, the interior lowlands — the major food-producing area — are drained southward to the Gulf of Mexico by the Missouri-Mississippi system. In Canada, the central lowlands

Discovery and Settlement

Native Peoples
1 Alaskan Eskimo with reindeer sledge
2 Ingalik Indian
3 Arctic Eskimo
4 Greenland Eskimo woman
5 Greenland woman
6 Arctic Eskimo woman
7 Copper River Eskimo
8 Reindeer Eskimo with Eskimo dog
9 Labrador Eskimo
10 Tlingit Indian
11 Kwakiutl Indian
12 Chipewyan Indian
13 Nascapi Indian hunting the caribou
14 Ottawa Indian
15 Iroquois
16 Mandan Indian

(Sioux)
17 Blackfoot Indian
18 Crow Indian hunting buffalo
19 Indian squaw
20 Shoshone
21 Apache
22 Chinook
23 Seminoles
24 Tarahumara Indian
25 Aztec
26 Maya
27 Quiche woman
28 Choco Indian
29 Cuban woman

History
30 Bering passing through Bering Strait in 1728
31 Panning for gold in the Klondike in 1900
32 The Northwest Passage (1851-53)
33 Amundsen in the Northwest Passage (1903-06)
34 Eric the Red landing in Greenland (981 A.D.)
35 Gold prospector in mid-19th century
36 Beaver trapper about 1850
37 Woodsman in the Indian wars
38 Norsemen land in America (about 1000 A.D.)
39 The Mayflower reaches America in 1620
40 La Salle explores the Mississippi valley in the 17th century
41 William Penn, who obtained the Pennsylvania charter in 1681
42 Cornwallis surrenders to Washington at Yorktown in 1781
43 Prairie schooners moving west

44 19th century mail coach
45 Mormons
46 Completion of first continental railway at Promontory Point, Utah, in 1869
47 Texas Ranger, late 19th century
48 Battle of San Jacinto (1836) leading to independence of Texas
49 Cortes lands in Mexico in 1519
50 Tonatiuc, the Aztec sun god
51 Columbus lands in West Indies in 1492
52 Dessalines, leader of Haitian independence and first president (1804-06)

Landmarks and Characteristic Dwellings
53 Igloo
54 Eskimo summer tent
55 Totem pole
56 Wigwam
57 Fort dating from about 1850
58 Birch-bark hut of the Algonquin Indians
59 Tepee
60 Statue of Liberty, New York Harbour
61 White House, Washington, D.C.
62 Pueblo Indian village
63 Pyramid of the Sun at Teotihuacán near Mexico City
64 Mayan temple at Chichen-Itza
65 Mayan stele (pilar-like stone monument)

Early Transportation
66 Boat of the seafaring Haida Indians
67 Eskimo kayak (men's boat)

68 Eskimo umiak (women's boat)
69 Eskimo dog sledge
70 Indian canoe
71 Travois
72 Mississippi paddle-wheel steamer
73 Mexican ox-cart
74 Costa Rican ox-cart
75 Cuban ox-cart

Useful Plants
76 Wild rice
77 Sugar maple
78 Tobacco
79 Maize
80 Cotton
81 Sugar cane
82 Cacao

Miscellaneous
83 Aleut salmon-drying rack
84 Rocky Mountain goat in Glacier National Park
85 Black bear in Yellowstone National Park
86 Giant sequoia in Sequoia National Park
87 Giant saguaro cactus in Saguaro National Park, Arizona
88 Bald cypress in Everglades National Park
89 Kentucky Derby
90 Chinese in San Francisco
91 Shooting films in Hollywood
92 Rodeo in Arizona
93 Cowboy herding cattle
94 Cotton picker
95 Mexican bullfight
96 Turkeys
97 Chorotega Indian pottery
98 Panama Canal
99 Francis Drake enters San Francisco Bay in 1579

are not quite so wide, for they are squeezed between the Canadian Shield and the Rocky Mountains. The third major region forms the mountainous west of the continent. Basically, it consists of two great chains — the Rockies and the Sierra Nevada-Cascades — which enclose the rugged and spectacular tablelands dissected by the Columbia and Colorado rivers. The Great Basin, an arid expanse of broad valleys and parallel ranges, also lies between the Rocky Mountains and the Sierra Nevada. It is so large that the entire State of Nevada is contained within this dry and sparsely populated region. In Canada, the Rockies approach the Coast Ranges, and a single chain, the Alaska Range (towered over by Mt McKinley, 20,320 feet), continues westward across the 49th State (Alaska) to the Aleutian Islands.

South of the United States, the mountains are known as the Sierra Madre. They consist of two ranges which enclose the high tableland on which Mexico City is located. Farther south, in Central America, the mountains are surmounted by impressive volcanoes.

The Canadian Shield, formed during the Archaeozoic Era, is the remnant of a very old rock mass that fringes Hudson Bay in a horseshoe from Labrador to the mouth of the Mackenzie River. Only in two places, south of Lake Superior (in Minnesota and Wisconsin) and in northern New York, does the Shield enter the United States.

The climate of North America is shaped by the interaction of three atmospheric factors: (1) the cold-air masses that descend from the Arctic Ocean or from the winter-frozen interior of northern Canada; (2) humid tropical air from the Gulf of Mexico, moving northward into the Great Plains and along the east coast, mainly in summer; and (3) the westerly winds of the temperate latitudes, which mix the air masses from north and

south, and bring about a more or less regular succession of high and low pressure systems moving eastward across the continent. West of the 100th meridian, the moist air from the Gulf rarely penetrates; hence, the western portion of the Great Plains, also sheltered from the moist Pacific air masses by the Rocky Mountains, is dry. Completely cut off from humid air-flows, the southwestern United States has a desert climate, especially southern Arizona, Nevada and the Death Valley of southern California, where the lowest point of the continent — 280 feet below sea level — also boasts the highest temperatures ever recorded in North America, 134°F.

From Iowa's record-yielding, rolling, maize fields to the impoverished, eroded hillsides of Mexico, from the vast and empty northland of Canada to the overcrowded islands of the Caribbean, and from the 'oil, cattle and cotton' wealth of Texas to the abject poverty of a Central American republic, North America is a continent of extremes, of changes, and — as its short history has proved — of virtually unlimited opportunity.

THE UNITED STATES

With a population now above 200 million (204,765,770 in 1970), the United States is not only one of the world's largest countries but one whose numbers are currently growing faster than those of India. But while India is overcrowded and its people poor, the United States is able to provide a more-than-adequate livelihood for most of its people. Furthermore, there is every indication that, by the early 1980s, 50 million additional Americans are going to be equally well off.

This position of great economic strength is due to a most fortunate combination: land, location, and people.

THE LAND: Within its 3,600,000 square miles of territory

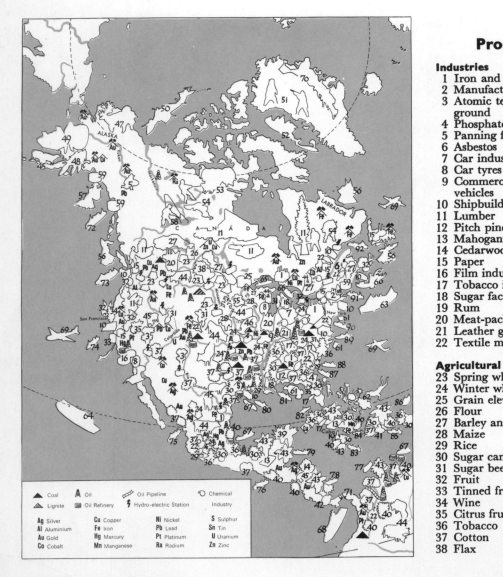

Production, Mineral Resources and Trade

Industries
1 Iron and steel plant
2 Manufacturing
3 Atomic testing-ground
4 Phosphate mining
5 Panning for gold
6 Asbestos
7 Car industry
8 Car tyres
9 Commercial vehicles
10 Shipbuilding
11 Lumber
12 Pitch pine
13 Mahogany
14 Cedarwood
15 Paper
16 Film industry
17 Tobacco industry
18 Sugar factory
19 Rum
20 Meat-packing
21 Leather goods
22 Textile mills

Agricultural Products
23 Spring wheat
24 Winter wheat
25 Grain elevator
26 Flour
27 Barley and oats
28 Maize
29 Rice
30 Sugar cane
31 Sugar beets
32 Fruit
33 Tinned fruit
34 Wine
35 Citrus fruit
36 Tobacco
37 Cotton
38 Flax

39 Sisal
40 Coffee
41 Cacao
42 Coconut
43 Bananas

Livestock and Animal Products
44 Cattle
44a Milk
45 Sheep
46 Pigs
47 Reindeer
48 Fox farming
49 Fur seals
50 Eskimos on a sealing expedition
51 Polar-bear hunting
52 Whaling
53 Musk-ox hunting
54 Fur-trapping
55 Furs
56 Fishing
57 Salmon-fishing
58 Trout-fishing
59 Fish canneries
60 Lobster
61 Oysters
62 Pearl and sponge fishing

Transportation and Trade
63 Passenger liner
64 Freighter
65 Ore vessel
66 Coal barge
67 Tanker
68 Aircraft-carrier
69 Passenger aircraft
70 Dog-sledge expedition
71 Panama Canal

Exports
72 Tinned fish (Juneau)
73 Lumber (Seattle)
74 Fruit, wine (San Francisco)
75 Coffee (Mexico)
76 Coffee (El Salvador)
77 Coffee, gold, hides (Barranquilla)
78 Cacao, coffee (Costa Rica)
79 Lumber (British Honduras)
80 Petroleum, sulphur, cotton (Houston)
81 Cotton, petroleum, lumber (New Orleans)
82 Sugar, tobacco (Havana)
83 Sugar, rum, bananas (Jamaica)
84 Ores, sugar (Santiago)
85 Sugar, coffee (Santo Domingo)
86 Sugar, tobacco, coffee, pineapples (Puerto Rico)
87 Naval stores (Savannah)
88 Lumber, cotton, (Charleston)
89 Coal (Norfolk)
90 Coal, tinned goods (Baltimore)
91 Manufactured goods, textiles (Boston)
92 Wheat, paper, metals (Canada)

(including Alaska), the United States is unusually well endowed with natural resources. These resources include a favourable climate, excellent soils, and a wealth of minerals and fuels.

Between the Rockies and the Appalachians lies some of the finest farmland in the whole world. There one is almost always in sight of neatly cultivated fields, fine pastures, and prosperous-looking farm buildings. Farm machinery can be put to its best use on its broad plains. Grain grown there is fed to pigs raised on the farm, or to cattle brought from the western ranges for fattening. The area embracing the Great Lakes is the chief supplier of the nation's dairy products. The flat wheat lands of the Great Plains, paradoxically in difficulties because of grain surpluses, could feed a great many more people than live in the United States today.

Where rainfall is too scarce for crops, in some of the western inter-mountain and plains regions, cattle and sheep are grazed on the grasslands — where there is enough land to provide 20 to 40 acres of pasture per animal. There is wealth enough to build dams for flood control and hydro-electric power, and to provide water to irrigate the desert.

The United States is abundantly provided with minerals and fuels, so necessary to an industrial society. Iron, copper, lead, zinc, molybdenum, and many other ores, have up to now been in adequate supply; so, also, has been the storehouse of fuels. The United States is the world's largest producer of coal. Ranking first in the world as a producer of petroleum, the United States has oil-wells all along the Gulf coast of Texas and Louisiana, in West Texas and New Mexico, Oklahoma and Kansas, North Dakota, and in California near Los Angeles. Uranium, the fuel of the future as atomic power is developed, is taken from the Colorado Plateau area.

Incredible as it may seem, each American uses up about 18 tons of materials each year. He needs 7 tons of fuel to keep warm, and to run the machines that have been perfected to replace human energy; 5 tons of building materials; 800 pounds of metals; and 2½ tons of agricultural products for food and clothing. The United States (unlike Great Britain and Germany) has hitherto been able to draw the bulk of its material needs from domestic sources, and there has been enough to spare for export. But as domestic raw materials are exhausted, the United States will have to depend to an increasing degree upon the natural resources of other countries. Even now the American economy imports tin from the Far East, manganese from India, bauxite (the ore from which aluminium is extracted) from the West Indies and Surinam, and iron ore from Canada and Venezuela. With only five per cent of the world's land area and less than seven per cent of its population, the United States consumes almost half of what the world produces.

THE LOCATION: The United States has the advantage of a frontage on two oceans, allowing for easy commerce with both Europe and Asia. The two oceans have, until now, offered protection in time of war. Unlike the nations of Europe, United States territory has felt no devastation from war since 1865. For almost a century it has been able to develop its manpower and resources to their greatest usefulness, with only minor interruptions. In the future, this two-ocean shield may be less secure than in the past. With aircraft now able to fly the great circle route across the North Pole, United States industrial centres are only a few short hours from bases in northern Asia. Also, with truly inter-continental ballistic missiles in existence, the United States will have to rely on something other than the oceans for its protection from any enemy attack of the future.

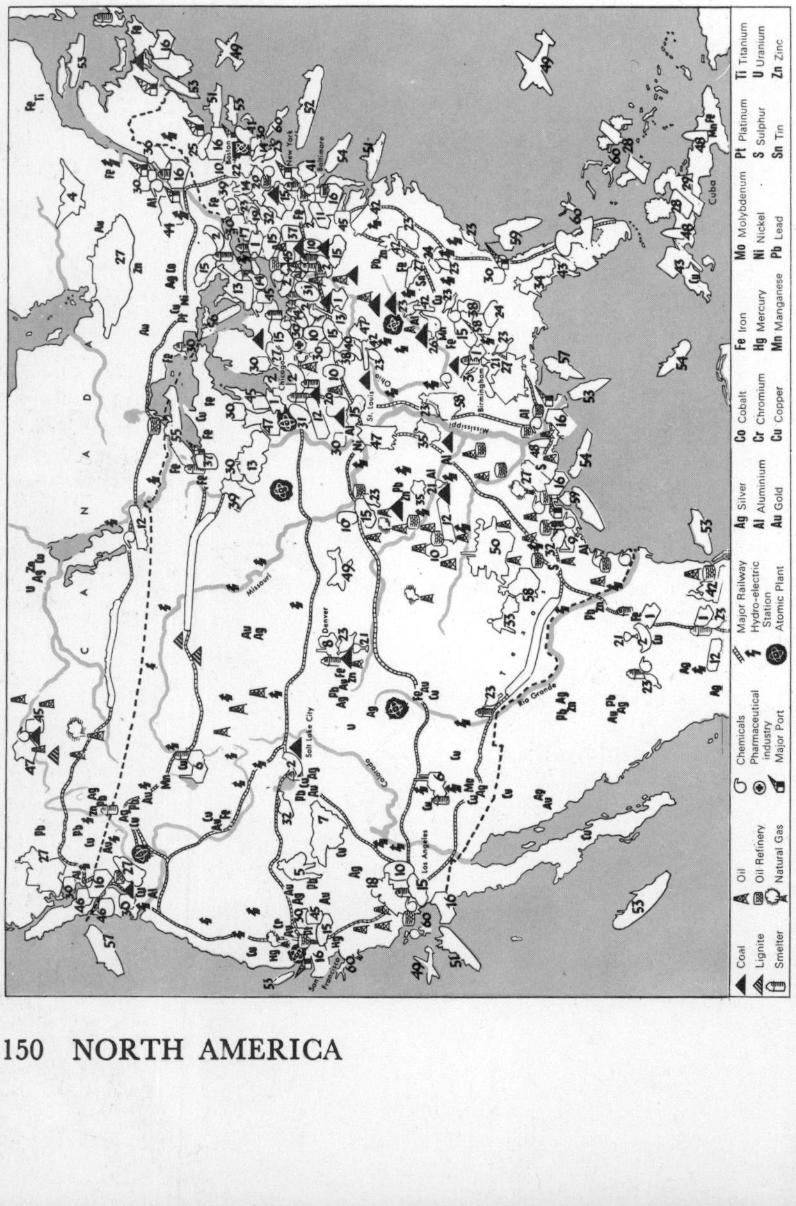

Coal ▲ Oil ⚙ Chemicals ⚓ Major Railway ⚓ Hydro-electric Ti Titanium
Lignite ▲ Oil Refinery ⚙ Pharmaceutical Station
Smelter Natural Gas Industry ⚛ Atomic Plant Major Port

Ag Silver Co Cobalt Fe Iron Mo Molybdenum Pt Platinum Ti Titanium
Al Aluminium Cr Chromium Hg Mercury Ni Nickel S Sulphur U Uranium
Au Gold Cu Copper Mn Manganese Pb Lead Sn Tin Zn Zinc

Production, Mineral Resources and Trade

Minerals and Industries
1 Iron
2 Steel
3 Steel pipe
4 Gold dredge
5 Panning for gold
6 Copper smelter
7 Copper mine
8 Lead smelter
9 Tin smelter
10 Machinery
11 Locomotives
12 Railway rolling-stock
13 Farm machinery
14 Electrical equipment
15 Car industry
16 Shipyard
17 Photographic equipment
18 Films
19 Optical goods
20 Watches
21 Glass
22 Typewriters
23 Textiles
24 Cotton
25 Wool
26 Nylon
27 Lumber
28 Mahogany
29 Cedarwood
30 Paper
31 Rubber
32 Salt
33 Potash
34 Phosphate
35 Bauxite
36 Asbestos
37 Cement
38 Pottery
39 Leather
40 Shoes
41 Leather goods
42 Tobacco
43 Cigars
44 Grain elevator
45 Tinned goods
46 Tinned fish
47 Meat packing
48 Sugar factory

Transportation and Trade
49 Airliner
50 Aircraft production
51 Warship at naval base
52 Passenger liner
53 Freighter
54 Tanker
55 Iron-ore shipping
56 Coal-carrier
57 Timber exports
58 Cotton market
59 Cotton exports
60 Seaside resort

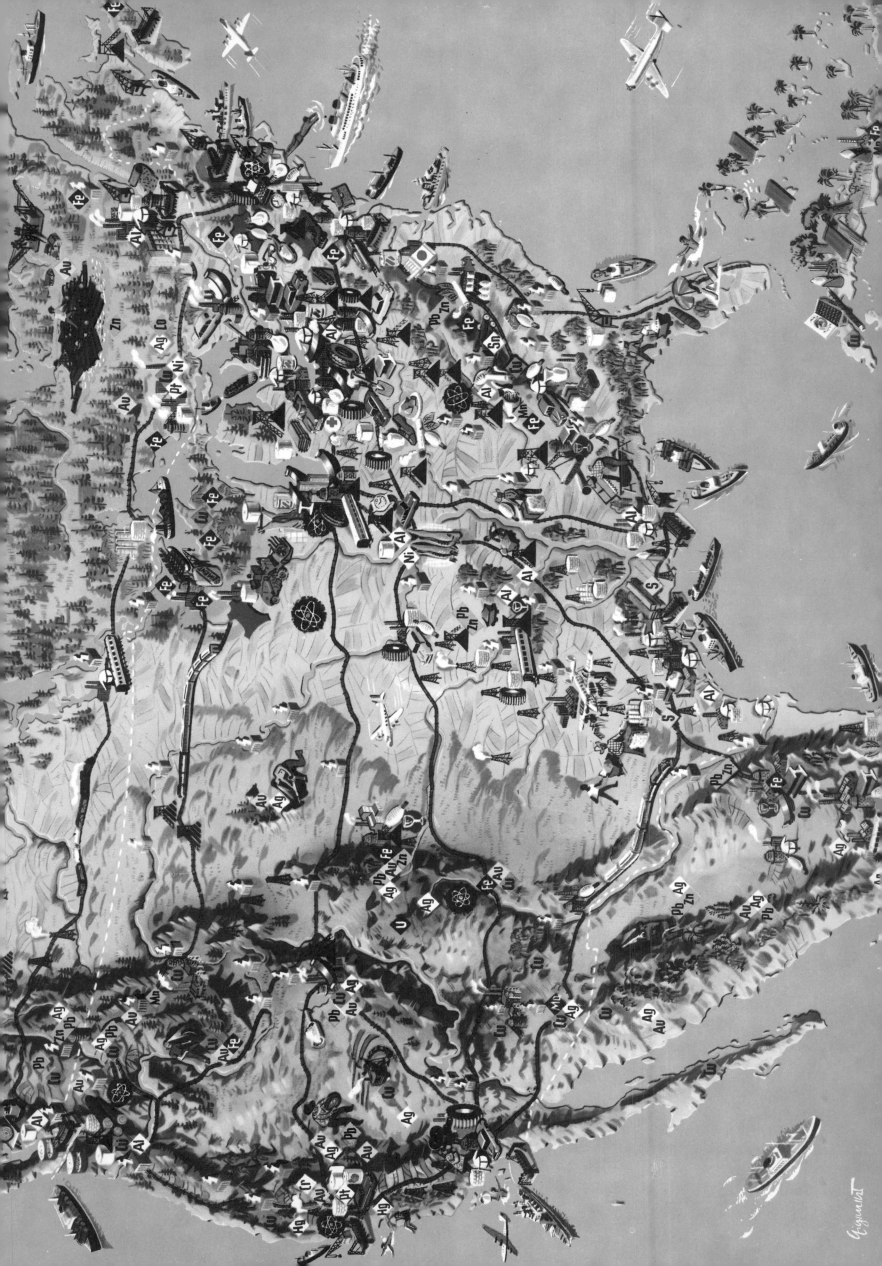

THE PEOPLE: The United States has traditionally been a country of immigration. Between 1820 and 1956, the doors of this new and growing nation opened to 10 million British and Irish, 6,600,000 Germans, 4,900,000 Italians, 7 million eastern and central Europeans, and 1 million Orientals. They brought with them invaluable skills and an extraordinary degree of human enterprise. This influx of peoples did not occur evenly, but rather in waves, reaching a peak before World War I, and declining after the passage of restrictive immigration laws in 1924.

Since World War II, there have been important changes in the pattern of migration and settlement within the nation. For nearly 250 years, the Negroes, held in bondage, were the mainstay of the South's cotton economy; and for many years after their emancipation, in 1863, they remained overwhelmingly rural. Today, however, more than two-thirds of the nation's 19 million Negroes live in cities, with a steady flow to the larger urban centres of the North. There they are engaged in many of the same activities as the white population, even though their opportunities for advancement and better housing are still limited. Additionally, in the last ten years, several large cities, especially New York, have felt the influx of more than half a million Puerto Ricans.

The American Indians make up one of the smallest minority groups in the United States today. They number about half a million, and only 15 per cent of them live in towns. Most of the Indian population is found on some 200 reservations, almost all of which are west of the Mississippi. Towards the end of the 19th century, their number had greatly diminished; but, although poverty is still widespread among this remnant of North America's proud Indian tribes, the last quarter-century has brought marked improvement in the living conditions of many of them. A number of products which we take for granted today were entirely unknown to Europeans before they made contact with the North American Indians. How would we get along today without potatoes, maize, beans, tomatoes, pumpkins, cacao and tobacco? Today, many important discoveries of oil, uranium, and other metallic ore deposits, have been made on their reservations, and exploitation of these has, in some cases, become a source of great wealth to the fortunate Indian communities.

In less than 200 years, the United States has emerged from being an underdeveloped, underpopulated, strictly agricultural nation, with little industry and no interest in the world at large, into a global power which supplies economic assistance to many less-favoured lands. Its cities have expanded from small communities at crossroads, where only farm produce was traded, into large machine-run manufacturing centres, able to supply the nation and the world with a great variety of products. The U.S.A. is also a country that has very recently discovered its proximity to a 'shrinking' world, and which is having to learn to exercise astute diplomacy far beyond its own shores.

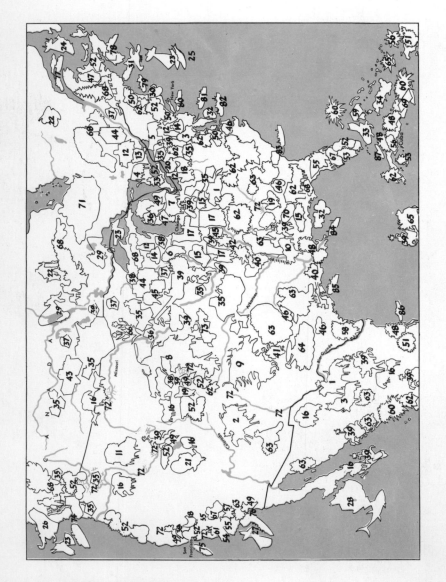

Fishing, Agriculture and Forestry

Livestock and Animal Products
1 Horse-breeding
2 Mustangs
3 Cattle-raising
4 Holstein-Friesian cattle
5 Jersey cattle
6 Guernsey cattle
7 Santa Gertrudis cattle
8 Hereford cattle
9 Texas longhorn cattle
10 Brahman zebu cattle
11 Bison
12 Milk
13 Butter
14 Cheese
15 Pigs
16 Sheep
17 Meat-packing
18 New Hampshire poultry
19 Plymouth Rock poultry
20 Eggs
21 Turkey-farming
22 Fur-trapping

Fishing
23 Herring
24 Cod
25 Mackerel
26 Salmon
27 Sardine
28 Tuna
29 Trout
30 Rosefish
31 Lobster
32 Oysters
33 Turtle
34 Sponge

Agricultural Products
35 Wheat
36 Rye
37 Oats
38 Barley
39 Maize
40 Rice
41 Sorghum
42 Soya beans
43 Grain elevator
44 Flour mills
45 Flour
46 Peanuts
47 Potatoes
48 Sugar cane

49 Sugar beets
50 Vegetables
51 Coffee
52 Fruit
53 Wine
54 Raisins
55 Oranges
56 Bananas
57 Dates
58 Peaches
59 Tomatoes
60 Pineapples
61 Olives
62 Tobacco
63 Cotton
64 Helicopter spraying cotton field with insecticide
65 Sisal
66 Flax
67 Flowers
68 Lumber
69 Mahogany
70 Pitch pine
71 Forest fire
72 Irrigated land
73 Dust-bowl

Exports
74 Tinned fish, lumber (Seattle)
75 Fruit (San Francisco)
76 Tinned fish, petroleum (Los Angeles)
77 Wheat, paper, metals (Canada)
78 Apples (Halifax)
79 Manufactured goods, textiles (Boston)
80 Manufactured goods, wheat (New York)
81 Machinery (Philadelphia)
82 Coal, tinned goods (Baltimore)
83 Naval stores (Savannah)
84 Cotton, petroleum, lumber (New Orleans)
85 Petroleum, sulphur, cotton (Houston)
86 Coffee, vanilla, hides (Veracruz)
87 Sugar, tobacco (Havana)

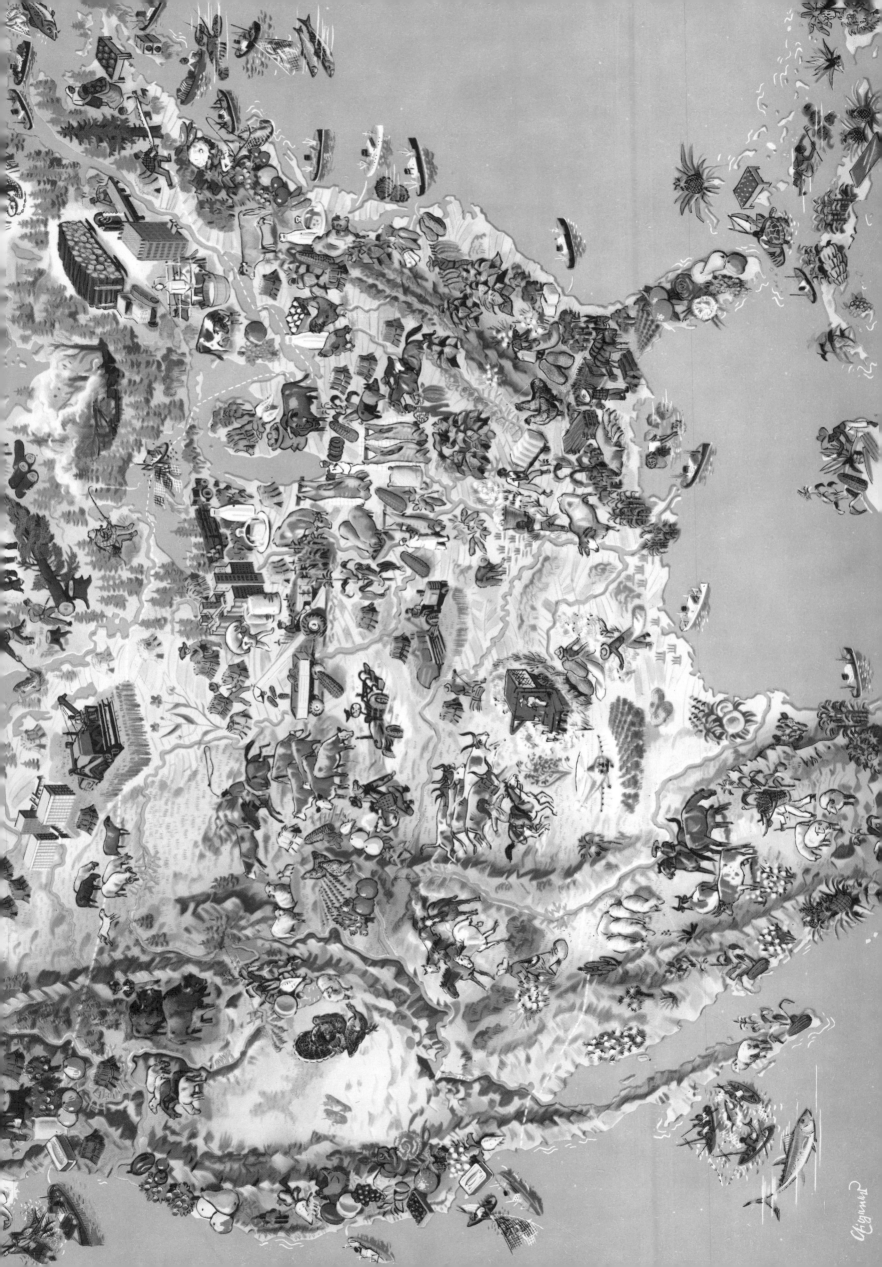

A brown bear by Lake Louise, in Alberta, Canada

A Saturn I rocket on the launching pad at Cape Kennedy, in Florida, U.S.A.

● **Akron** The greatest rubber-manufacturing centre of the world, in north-eastern Ohio, about 30 miles south of Cleveland. The city's growth dates from 1910, when the mass production of motor-car tyres began. Its present population is 299,341.

● **Alabama** The 'Cotton State' (51,609 square miles; population 3,444,000), in the Deep South of the U.S.A. between the southern Appalachians and the Gulf of Mexico. Montgomery is the State capital; Mobile its only port, and Birmingham the largest city. Birmingham manufactures so much iron and steel that it is called 'the Pittsburgh of the South'. Alabama's main product, however, is still cotton, grown in the Black Belt and in the Tennessee Valley. Maize is also grown on many thousands of acres. Other crops include hay, peanuts, sweet potatoes, sugar cane, peaches and melons. Alabama is becoming an important cattle-raising State. Almost two-thirds of Alabama is covered with forests, chiefly pine, which is logged for lumber and pulp and paper-milling; turpentine is also a forest product.

First settled by the French around 1700, Alabama was admitted to the Union in 1819 as the 22nd State. Large numbers of Negroes (now almost one-third of the population) were used to work the prosperous cotton plantations. During the Civil War, Alabama was a Confederate State.

● **Alaska** Largest and 49th State (586,400 square miles; population 297,000) of the United States, in the far north-west of North America. It reaches from the Arctic Ocean (Point Barrow is 5° north of the Arctic Circle) to within 600 miles of the State of Washington. It also extends to within 55 miles of Soviet Asia at Bering Strait. The Pacific coast of Alaska has a generally mild climate, heavy rainfall, and a dense forest cover. High, snow-covered mountains and several glaciers come down

abruptly to the sea. A maze of wooded islands lies off-shore. Near the base of the Alaska Peninsula, Mt Katmai stands guard over the Valley of Ten Thousand Smokes — a strange region where smoke rises from numerous openings in the ground. North of the coastal mountains lies the Alaska Range, rising to the highest peak in the United States, Mt McKinley (20,320 feet), in Mt McKinley National Park. Most of the centres of population are in southern Alaska and in the Peninsula. Anchorage, the largest city, is linked by railway with Fairbanks, the chief town of the interior. Juneau, on the island-studded 'Inside Passage' between Seattle and Anchorage, is the capital of the State. Sitka was the capital before 1900, and Ketchikan is the centre of salmon fisheries. One of the most intense earthquakes of all time severely damaged many Alaskan towns in 1964.

The northern part of Alaska is barren and cold, has a short summer, and is inhabited chiefly by Eskimos, whose main occupations are fishing, fur-trapping, and reindeer-herding. Overland communication is difficult because of the terrain, climate, and the great distances involved. The aeroplane has become the principal means of transport; there is hardly a village where a 'bush pilot' cannot land. Communication with the 'outside' is primarily by ship, but since World War II, it has become possible to motor from the western United States across the Canadian provinces of Alberta and British Columbia, through Yukon Territory, to Fairbanks via the Alaska Highway.

The three principal products of Alaska are fish, furs, gold, and oil. In 1969, large areas were leased at high prices to oil companies all over the world. A pipeline connecting the oil fields of the North to the South is planned.

Alaska was discovered by a Dane, Vitus Bering, in 1741. Russian fur-traders came to Alaska after the middle of the 18th century. In 1867, Russia sold the territory to the U.S.A. for $7,200,000, a sum considered extravagant at the time. However, it has been repaid many times over by the rich resources the Territory has yielded to the U.S.A., besides which Alaska is now one of the nation's most valuable defence outposts. Economically, Alaska is far from fully developed. Beginning with the gold rush of the 1890s (in the Klondike, at Fairbanks, and near Nome in the far north-west), mining, fur-trapping, fishing and fish-canning, and military needs, brought more and more people to the Territory. Congress, asked repeatedly to grant Statehood to Alaska, admitted the Territory to the Union in 1959.

● **Alberta** A western province (255,000 square miles; population 1,600,000) of Canada, in the Great Plains, east of the Rocky Mountains. Canada's most scenic mountain region is included in Banff and Jasper National Parks, along the Alberta-British Columbia border. Despite inadequate rainfall, Alberta is an important agricultural region with extensive cattle ranches and wheat farms. Sugar beets are grown in irrigated districts

NORTH AMERICA

Scale 1:30,000,000

| | 100 | 200 | 300 | 400 | 500 | Miles |

■ NEW YORK — Cities over 1,000,000 population
● Milwaukee — Cities of 250,000 — 1,000,000 population
○ Galveston — Cities under 250,000 population
⊛ Capitals of Countries

Depths in feet:

over 650 | 0-650

Heights in feet:

Below sea level | 0-650 | 650-1650 | 1650-4900 | over 4900

Arid Regions · · ·   Tundra · ·   Swamp, marsh

Railroads ┤┤┤   Canals ═══   ⊥ Head of navigation   ✕ Falls

The red-hot slag, or residue, is poured off at a copper-smelting plant near Morenci, Arizona, U.S.A.

near Calgary. Edmonton, the provincial capital, lies at the centre of an oil-field that has been in production since 1947. Alberta produces 70 per cent of Canada's oil output. Petroleum and natural gas are piped, both east and west, to Canada's largest cities and to some parts of the United States. Alberta also contains Canada's largest coal deposits, mined near Lethbridge.

Alberta was first reached by French traders from Quebec about 1750. The Hudson's Bay Company, which had taken over the fur trade from the French, ceded the territory to Canada in 1870. It attained provincial status in 1905.

● **Aleutian Islands** A chain of volcanic islands off south-western Alaska, extending over 1,000 miles towards Siberia and belonging to the U.S.A. The islands are rugged, treeless, and often shrouded in fog. They are inhabited by a few thousand Aleuts, an Eskimo race. Fishing and fur-trapping are the main occupations. The islands have a population of about 15,000, the main town being Dutch Harbour on Unalaska Island.

● **alligator** Once common in southern swamps, particularly in Florida, alligators have been greatly reduced in number by hunters. In Florida alone, 2 million were killed in the 19th century for their hides. Nowadays, they are maintained in wild-life refuges, such as the Okeefenokee Swamp in Georgia. Large specimens reach a length of 12 feet, and may be 20 or 25 years old. The alligator is agile in water and clumsy on land. It feeds mainly on fish, turtles, birds and other water-life. Eggs are hatched by the heat of the sun, in nests made of decaying plants and mud. The mother alligator is one of the few reptiles that guards its nest.

Alligator

● **Antilles** — see **West Indies**.

● **Apaches** An Indian tribe of the south-western United States, and among the last to resist the advance of the European settlers, surrendering in 1886.

●**Appalachian Mountains** The longest mountain chain of eastern North America, extending more than 1,500 miles south-west from the St Lawrence River in Quebec, Canada, to the Gulf coastal plain in Alabama. Several differing types of land forms are included in the Appalachians — long, narrow folded ranges, separated from each other by equally narrow valleys; a sharp-crested ridge, called the Blue Ridge, that extends uninterrupted from Pennsylvania to Georgia, along the eastern margin of the Appalachians; extensive, gently sloping tablelands, such as the Allegheny Plateau and the Cumberland Plateau, that merge in the west with the great interior lowlands of the central United States; and the high, forest-covered Green and White Mountains of New England. Mt Mitchell, in North Carolina, is the highest point (6,708 feet) east of the Mississippi River. The mountains of Vermont and New Hampshire, and parts of the Blue Ridge, are favourite tourist areas. The Appalachians long formed the barrier to westward movement of colonisers.

● **Arizona** The 'Apache State' (113,909 square miles; population 1,750,000), Arizona lies in the dry and scenic south-west U.S.A.; it borders on Mexico. Phoenix is the State capital and largest city, with a population of 552,043. Winter tourists gather there and in Tucson (227,433), attracted by the healthful climate; summer travellers flock to the colourful northern part of the State, to see the Grand Canyon of the Colorado, the Painted Desert, the Petrified Forest, and such man-made marvels as the 725-foot-high Hoover Dam on the Colorado River. Mining is the chief industry; more copper is mined there than in any other State, and the crude ore is smelted and refined as well. There are immense cattle ranches, and more than a million sheep are raised, largely on grazing lands owned by the Federal government. Water for agriculture comes from the Salt and Gila Rivers, and from numerous deep wells. Chief crops are cotton (picked by machine), cereals, vegetables (especially lettuce), citrus fruit and dates; without water and irrigation ditches, these could not be grown. Farming is highly mechanised.

Arizona has an Indian population (Navajos, Hopis, Apaches) of 83,000, who live on reservations and weave blankets, rugs and baskets for sale to tourists. Spanish explorers first visited the area in 1540. Together with New Mexico, Arizona was ceded to the United States by Mexico in 1853 (the Gadsden Purchase); it became a separate territory in 1863, and the 48th State of the Union in 1912.

● **Arkansas** The 'Wonder State', or the 'Bear State' (53,104 square miles; population 1,923,000), Arkansas lies partly in the broad plain of the Mississippi River and partly in the Ozark and Ouachita Mountains, U.S.A. It is crossed by the 1,500-mile-long Arkansas River and several other tributaries of the Mississippi. 'Bow of Smoky Waters' is the Indian name for the Arkansas. Little Rock is the capital and the largest city. Arkansas is primarily an agricultural state, and cotton is still 'king'. Other crops are rice (grown in low-lying areas near the Mississippi), soya beans, maize and fruit. Many parts of the State are densely forested with pine, oak, red gum, cypress and hickory. Lumbering, paper-milling and furniture-making are therefore the chief industries. Southern Arkansas has petroleum and natural-gas fields, and the country's only important bauxite deposits (the ore of aluminium) are located near Little Rock. The state also has large coal fields. The Boston Mountains, which form part of the Ozarks, are full of wild-life, and attract a great many tourists, who seek out the mountain resorts.

The old Spanish mission, San Xavier del bac ('The White Dove of the Desert'), at Tucson, Arizona

UNITED STATES
AND
SOUTHERN CANADA

Scale 1:15,000,000

0 50 100 150 200 250 Miles

Desert Swamp, marsh Railroads Canals

Heights in Feet:

Depths in Feet:

The Athabaska River flows past the pine-covered slopes of Mt Fryatt, in the Canadian Rockies

bear, grizzly This bear has almost disappeared from the United States, only about 500 surviving in national parks. Extremely strong, it can break the neck of an ox with one stroke of its paw. The grizzly owes its name to the grizzled appearance of its silver-tipped fur.

bear, Kodiak This huge brown bear, named after an island off Alaska, exceeds 1,000 pounds in weight and eight feet in height, though it is not aggressive. The Kodiak bear feasts on salmon, when the fish ascend the rivers to spawn.

bear, polar The polar bear's scientific name (Thalarctos) means 'sea bear', though in Greenland it is known as 'ice bear'. The bear is in fact very much at home in the sea, swimming and diving in the icy waters of the Far North, and stalking seals and walrus cubs. The polar bear is one of the largest meat-eating animals. Its slender body may reach a length of nine feet and weigh 1,500 pounds. The bear's dense white fur overlies a thick insulating layer of fat. The female cares for her young in a hole dug into the snow. Eskimos hunt the bear for its flesh, bones and hide.

Explored by De Soto in the 1540s and by La Salle in 1682, Arkansas came to the United States as part of the Louisiana Purchase (1803). It became a State in 1836, the 25th in the Union.

Athabaska River A southern tributary of the Mackenzie River in north-western Canada, it rises in the Rocky Mountains, crosses Jasper National Park, and flows more than 700 miles north to Lake Athabaska (3,000 square miles). Throughout the 19th century, fur-traders followed the route of the Athabaska to the Mackenzie valley. In recent years, large deposits of uranium have been discovered on the shore of Lake Athabaska, and a new mining centre, Uranium City, is in full operation.

Atlanta The capital of Georgia and one of the fastest-growing cities (population 1,295,757) of the South. It is a major rail hub, and serves as the principal commercial and distribution centre for the south-eastern States. Many large nation-wide corporations have branch plants in Atlanta. They produce textiles, furniture, machinery, fertiliser, paint, paper, electrical appliances, etc. Meat-packing and the assembly of cars are especially important, and there is a large aircraft plant.

Bahama Islands British island colony (land area, 4,400 square miles; population 166,200), with internal self-government, in the West Indies. Over 80 per cent of the population are Negroes or Mulattos, descendants of slaves. The 700-odd islands, reefs and cays extend 750 miles south-eastward from Florida in the direction of Haiti. Only 20 islands are inhabited; they include Andros (the largest one), New Providence (on which Nassau, the capital and leading tourist resort, is located), and San Salvador, or Watling Island, where Columbus is said to have made his first landfall on October 12, 1492. The Bahamas have a sub-tropical climate with mild winters. They export pineapples, oranges, melons and vegetables.

Baltimore Largest city (population 2,070,670) of Maryland, and a leading seaport on the East Coast of the United States. It lies on an inlet of Chesapeake Bay formed by the mouth of the Patapsco River. Harbour installations occupy 40 miles of waterfront; they include coal and ore piers, grain elevators, and extensive shipyards. One of the nation's largest steel mills is located at nearby

Sparrows Point. Baltimore imports iron ore from Venezuela, Canada and Liberia, as well as sugar, rubber, coffee, tea and spices from the tropics. Its leading exports are flour, coal from the Appalachian coal-fields, steel, cement, and machinery. Baltimore's industries include canneries and freezing plants, aircraft and car-assembly plants, railway workshops, a copper smelter, sugar and petroleum refineries, and factories producing clothing, tin cans and straw hats. Baltimore is noted for its blocks of row houses, each with clean, white door-steps. The city was established in 1729, and became a shipping centre for grain and tobacco to Great Britain.

Banana plants and fruit

banana A native of the Old World, the banana is now grown in almost all tropical countries. Although not strictly a tree, the banana plant reaches a height of 10 to 20 feet. Its leaves, which tear easily, look much like palm fronds. Each stem bears a single bunch of bananas. A banana ship loads up to 20,000 bunches, cut while the fruit is still green. The plantain is a variety of the banana, with a larger fruit that is more starchy and less sweet. The plantain is eaten where it is grown, while the banana is one of the leading tropical products in international commerce. The world's leading banana exporters — Honduras, Costa Rica, Panama and Guatemala — account for almost half of the world's supply. The U.S.A. imports 60 per cent of all bananas in international trade.

bear, black Despite its name, this bear varies from black to brown (Cinnamon bear) in colour. Although the black bear is afraid of people, it loves to investigate their belongings, quite often robbing campers in the western United States and Canada.

Bering Strait separates Siberia from Alaska and forms a 55-mile-wide link between the Bering Sea (a northern arm of the Pacific) and the Arctic Ocean. The International Date Line passes through the middle of the Strait. The Danish explorer Bering (1681—1741) sailed through it in 1728.

Bermuda An internally self-governing colony possessed by Britain since 1684, situated in the western Atlantic and consisting of about 300 small coral islands (the Bermudas, or Somers), of which only about 20 are inhabited. It is a favourite resort for Americans, for Bermuda lies only 750 miles — a little over two hours by air — from New York City. The population of 50,927 (almost two-thirds Negro) lives on the tourist trade or raises vegetables for New York. Britain and the United States have air and naval bases on the islands. Bermuda was discovered in 1515 by a Spaniard, Juan de Bermúdez; British seamen first landed there in 1609, when the islands were still unpopulated.

Birmingham Largest city (population 780,000) of Alabama, and the leading steel-manufacturing centre of the South. All the raw materials for the iron and steel industry — coal, iron ore, and dolomite — are mined in the immediate vicinity. The city was founded in 1871, and named after the great British manufacturing centre.

bison The American bison, or buffalo, is the largest mammal of North America. Weighing about 2,000 pounds and standing almost six feet at the shoulder, bison once roamed the plains in vast herds. The gradual settlement of the country led inevitably to their virtual extermination. Bison survive today only in government reservations. The strong and dignified bison, with its massive head and black beard, has become a symbol of the early days of the American West. Not only the Indians, but the European settlers, depended on the buffalo for their food, clothing, shelter and heat. Major rail and highway routes still follow the trails once trod by the bison, for they are the best routes across the continent.

Boston The capital of Massachusetts and the largest city (population 2,753,700) of New England, on Boston Bay (an arm of the Atlantic), at the mouth of the Charles River. It is the cultural and financial centre of the State and is surrounded by a host of residential and industrial communities.

Boston produces textiles, leather goods, machinery, and a variety of foods. Printing and publishing are important activities. Boston has an active trade in wool and fish. Though overshadowed by New York, its port enjoys the advantage of nearness to Europe. Rich in historical shrines, Boston played an important part in the American struggle for independence. It was the scene of the Boston Tea Party (1773) and of the decisive battle of Bunker Hill. The city has many universities and colleges, including Harvard and MIT, and the city is surrounded by many research laboratories along its Western Boulevard.

●**British Columbia** Westernmost province (366,255 square miles; population 2.07 million) of Canada, on the Pacific Ocean. It includes Vancouver and Queen Charlotte Islands, offshore. The capital, Victoria, is on Vancouver Island, opposite Vancouver, the largest city of western Canada with a population of 955,000. The province is almost wholly mountainous; it is crossed by the Rockies, the Selkirk Mountains and the Coast Mountains, which drop steeply on to the rocky coast. Extensive evergreen forests cover this well-watered province. Next to lumbering, aluminium-refining (at Kitimat) is the largest industry. Salmon and herring fisheries are important along the coast. Several national parks in the Rocky Mountains attract tourists to this scenic region.

British Columbia was visited by Captain James Cook in 1778. It became a British crown colony after 1850, when gold was found in the Fraser River valley in 1858. The colony joined the new Dominion of Canada in 1871, and in 1886 the Canadian Pacific Railway reached Vancouver, its western terminus, from Montreal, the journey taking 136 hours.

●**British Honduras** A British colony (8,900 square miles; population 119,645) in Central America, facing the Caribbean Sea. This humid, tropical lowland is almost entirely dependent on the products of its dense forests — mahogany, cedar, pine and rosewood. Citrus fruits and bananas are grown in clearings in the jungle. Chicle, the raw material for chewing-gum, is collected by the descendants of Mayan Indians, whose civilisation flourished in the area before the Spanish conquests of the 16th century. Belize is the colony's only city; it had a population of 33,000 before being destroyed by a hurricane in 1961. Its population in 1970 was 39,257 after reconstruction. The capital, Belmopan, since 1970, is being constructed 50 miles inland, it is hoped, away from hurricane paths.

Buffalo, New York, maintains splendid port facilities on Lake Erie for grain barges and lake steamers

English is the official language of British Honduras, though Spanish is widely used. The territory was first colonised from Jamaica in 1638, and now has a large measure of internal self-government. Neighbouring Guatemala has laid claims to the country.

●**Buffalo** The second-largest city (population 1,349,211) of New York State, situated at the eastern end of Lake Erie, where the Niagara River forms the U.S.-Canadian border. The Niagara Falls are 15 miles to the north. Buffalo is a major Great Lakes port, where wheat from the Great Plains is unloaded and milled into flour. The products of its many factories (steel, rubber, plastics, machinery, textiles, electrical equipment) are shipped by rail or the New York highway to the coastal cities. Buffalo also handles traffic bound for New York City on the Barge Canal. This waterway, generally known as the Erie Canal, gave Buffalo its start as a commercial centre in 1825.

●**Calgary** A commercial city (population 384,436) of western Canada, in the province of Alberta, near the foothills of the Rocky Mountains. It is a livestock market and oil-refining centre in the midst of an irrigated agricultural district. Banff National Park lies to the west.

●**California** The 'Golden State' (158,693 square miles; population 19,953,000 in 1970) is third in area and first in population in the United States, and is also the fastest-growing State in the Union. California is full of contrasts: it contains Mt Whitney (14,495 feet), the nation's second highest point, and Death Valley, the lowest (282 feet below sea level). The desert areas near the Mexican border are almost rainless, while the northern Coast Ranges receive more than 100 inches of rain every year. The Sierra Nevada forms the State's mountain rampart in the east; between it and the Coast Ranges lies the Central Valley with but one outlet to the sea, where the Sacramento River enters San Francisco Bay. There is wonderful scenery in California: along the coast, where the giant redwood trees grow; in Yosemite National Park and in the High Sierra; and in the north, where Mt Shasta and Lassen Peak (the only active volcano on the mainland of the United States) tower over the Central Valley. California also boasts a wealth of natural resources, among them soil and climate ideal for specialised agriculture. Over 6 million acres are irrigated; they comprise the most valuable farmland in the country. Southern California specialises in citrus fruit and sub-tropical products such as avocados, dates, figs and nuts; table grapes, raisins and wine come chiefly from the Central Valley; the coastal valleys grow lettuce, artichokes and flower seeds; and many regions grow cotton, flax, alfalfa, sugar beet and a variety of fruit and vegetables. For a long time, the most valuable industry has been the milling, canning and packing of farm products. Fishing fleets land about 40 per cent of the nation's deep-sea catch. Underground, California has vast mineral wealth; petroleum and natural gas, produced mainly in the Los Angeles basin, are most valuable; gold, silver, copper, lead, zinc and borax are also produced. The aircraft and the motion-picture industries have contributed to the phenomenal growth of Los Angeles, now the second largest city in the United States, with a population of over 7 million. San Francisco, with its fine harbour and the Golden Gate and Bay Bridges, remains the leading Pacific seaport and has a population approaching 3.1 million people. Sacramento is the State capital.

First explored in the 16th century, the California coast was not settled until the end of the 18th century, when the Spaniards established a

California's rocky coastline stretches for more than 1,000 miles along the eastern rim of the Pacific Ocean, from Oregon to the Mexican frontier

Cypress Gardens, near Charleston, South Carolina, U.S.A.

chain of missions. The territory was ceded to the United States after the Mexican War (1848), and immediately, the great gold-rush of the 'Forty-niners' began. San Francisco became a boom town, and California was admitted to the Union as the 31st state in 1850. With the completion of the first trans-continental railway in 1869, the immigrant rush got under way. It has continued to this day, with almost 300,000 Americans every year choosing to work or to retire in California.

● **Canada** An independent country of North America, a member of the British Commonwealth of Nations, and northern neighbour of the United States with which Canada shares an undefended 4,000-mile-long boundary spanning the width of the continent. Ottawa is the national capital. Sprawling from the Atlantic to the Pacific, and from the Great Lakes and the 49th Parallel to the Arctic Ocean, Canada ranks third in size (3,852,000 square miles) among the nations of the world, after the U.S.S.R. and China. Much of Canada,

however, is empty or sparsely settled, as 90 per cent of its 21.5 million people live in a 150-mile-wide belt in the south-east, along the United States border. In the great northland — the area of the Canadian Shield — settlement is limited to mining camps, fur-trading posts, and weather stations. Joint U.S.-Canadian early-warning radar bases have been installed in recent years for the defence of North America against trans-polar attack.

In eastern Canada, the Maritime Provinces, with their forests, their deep-cut bays and river estuaries, offer scenery and fishing which attract tourists. Fishing has long been the mainstay of the region. There are many stories to the effect that Europeans were coming to the Grand Banks off Newfoundland long before Columbus came to America. Today, much lumbering is engaged in, for Canada's great pulp and paper mills. Farming is productive in limited areas, especially in the apple-growing Annapolis Valley of Nova Scotia and on the red soils of Prince Edward Island. The heart of Canada is reached via the St Lawrence River, the fertile shores of which have been cultivated by French-Canadian farmers for 300 years. The river flows past the two great cities of Quebec Province, quaint old Quebec itself and the bustling seaport of Montreal, until recently the head of ocean navigation on the St Lawrence. The completion of the St Lawrence Seaway in 1959 (one of the world's great engineering projects, to circumvent the rapids of the river above Montreal) brought the Great Lakes in direct contact with overseas markets, to the great benefit of Canada's foreign trade.

Like southern Quebec, south-eastern Ontario (bordered by Lakes Ontario, Erie and Huron) has much diversified agriculture, including orchards, tobacco-fields and dairy farms. Industries in the cities of Toronto, Hamilton and Windsor range from food-processing to the manufacture of heavy machinery, motor-cars, chemicals and textiles. Ontario is linked to the west by road and rail through some empty country, north of the Great Lakes, where mining, especially for iron, is making new headway. To the west of the Great Lakes lie the Prairie Provinces — Manitoba, Saskatchewan and Alberta. They are one of the great wheat-growing regions of the world. Winnipeg, along the eastern edge of this farm belt, is the centre from which grain is dispatched to the twin lake-ports of Port Arthur-Fort William, and thence to Montreal and abroad.

Alberta has booming oil-fields and vast, low-grade coal reserves. In the north, new mines are being opened where aerial surveys have located valuable deposits of nickel, copper and uranium, and tracks have been built to link them to the existing rail network. Pipelines have been laid across the prairies and mountains to bring oil to eastern Canada and to the Pacific Coast. The cities of the Prairie Provinces, notably Edmonton and Calgary, have in recent years seen a tremendous

increase in industries based on the region's natural resources. The Rocky Mountains, which rise sheer from the western plains, are majestic in their beauty.

In Banff and Jasper National Parks, Canada has tourist attractions which match the finest that the United States has to offer in alpine grandeur. British Columbia, Canada's westernmost province, is a land of peaks, tumbling mountain streams, narrow valleys, and elongated glacial lakes. Though much of the province is wooded wilderness, more than a million Canadians have found a home there, especially in the south-west, around the Pacific Coast port of Vancouver and on Vancouver Island, just offshore. The Pacific salmon fisheries, lumbering and fruit-growing have contributed to the wealth of this region, once almost wholly dependent on mining. The aluminium industry, fed by abundant hydro-electric power, is the most recent addition to British Columbia's booming economy and rapidly growing population.

Although industry — based on the country's rich endowment in mineral resources, timber and ample waterpower — is expanding rapidly, Canada still depends heavily on its exports in order to pay for the manufactured goods that must be imported, chiefly from the United States. Newsprint, wheat, wood pulp and aluminium rank highest among the country's exports, while shipments of iron ore are growing annually, as the newly discovered deposits of northern Quebec and Labrador enter full exploitation.

The Norse explorer Leif Ericsson probably reached the shores of Canada in A.D. 1000, but recorded history dates from 1497, when John Cabot, then in the service of England, set foot on Newfoundland or Nova Scotia. The land was claimed for France in 1534 by Jacques Cartier, but actual settlement of New France, as it was then called, began in 1604, when Port Royal was founded on the coast of Nova Scotia. A little later (1608), Champlain founded the city of Quebec. France was not very successful in colonising Canada but, by the end of the 17th century, its explorers had penetrated beyond the Great Lakes to the western prairies and southward to the Mississippi. Meanwhile, the English Hudson's Bay Company had been established in 1670, to pursue the fur trade. The conflict between England and France in Europe was paralleled by the French and Indian Wars in North America, and by 1763 the English were the sole rulers of Canada. By the British North America Act of 1867, the self-governing Dominion of Canada was created through the union of Upper (British) and Lower (French-speaking) Canada, Nova Scotia and New Brunswick. In 1869, Canada purchased from the Hudson's Bay Company the vast mid-western territories from which the Prairie Provinces were later formed. British Columbia joined the Dominion in 1871, largely on the promise of a trans-continental railway, which was not completed until 1886. Canada reached its present size in 1949, when Newfoundland (with Labrador) became the 10th Province. Also included in Canada are the Yukon and the Northwest Territories. Both English and French are official languages, though most of the French Canadians live in Quebec.

● **Canadian**, or **Laurentian, Shield** A vast region of ancient rock formations, covering about half of Canada centred on Hudson Bay. The monotonous forested landscape is dotted with thousands of lakes and marshes, remnants of continental ice-sheets that covered the region during the Ice Age. The southern boundary of the Shield runs roughly along the north shore of the St Lawrence River, across central Quebec and Ontario, and through Lakes Winnipeg, Great Slave and Great Bear to the Arctic Ocean, near the mouth of the Mackenzie River. Two extensions reach southward into the United States: one into New York State, embracing the Adirondack Mountains; the other into northern Michigan, and adjacent parts of Minnesota and Wisconsin. The Canadian Shield is sparsely

The harbour at Sanford, a tiny fishing village in Nova Scotia, on Canada's rocky Atlantic coast

populated, despite the wealth of its mineral and forest resources. Many swiftly-flowing streams have been harnessed, as they drop off the Shield, to provide power for Canada's growing industries.

Cape Kennedy Named in memory of the late President Kennedy, and a renaming of Cape Canaveral, it is the chief missile and space-capsule launching and testing station in the United States. Brevard County has seen the rapid development of avionic and electronic industries which serve the Cape Kennedy experimental operations. It was from this base that the first men landed on the moon in 1969.

Caribbean Sea A large sea (750,000 square miles), marginal to the Atlantic Ocean and between the north coast of South America, the West Indies, and Central America. It is connected by the Yucatán Strait to the Gulf of Mexico, and by the Panama Canal to the Pacific Ocean. Sugar, bananas and petroleum are the chief export products from the lands bordering the Caribbean. The sea takes its name from the Carib Indians, who inhabited parts of the area before its discovery by Columbus. During colonial days, the Caribbean was a favourite hunting ground for pirates and buccaneers. Nowadays, it is a winter resort for American tourists.

Cascade Range The Cascade mountains stretch for 700 miles across Oregon and Washington into British Columbia. The range parallels the Pacific coast at a distance of about 100 miles inland. Its highest peaks — Mt Rainier (14,408 feet), Mt Adams, Mt Hood and Mt Shasta — are snow-covered volcanoes. The well-watered western slopes are covered by magnificent fir, cedar and pine forests. The drier eastern valleys are noted for their apple orchards. The Columbia River gorge cuts squarely across the Cascades at the Oregon-Washington line.

Central America The narrow, winding strip of land connecting the continental land masses of North and South America. Politically, this mountainous, volcano-studded isthmus includes the southern part of Mexico (including the Yucatán Peninsula), the Republics of Guatemala, Honduras, El Salvador, Nicaragua, Costa Rica and Panama, as well as British Honduras. The region's chief crops are bananas, grown in the coastal lowlands, and coffee in the uplands. Indians (descendants of the Mayans) form the majority of the population in southern Mexico and Guatemala. Elsewhere, *mestizos* (people of mixed European and Indian blood) predominate, except along the Caribbean coast, where Negroes from the West Indies have settled. Spanish is the official language of the entire area. About 16 million people live within its 230,000 square miles.

cereus This common type of cactus of the southwestern United States and Latin America occurs mainly in columnar, or long-stemmed, forms. It includes the night-blooming cereus, whose large white flowers open for only one night, and the giant saguaro cactus, up to 50 feet high.

Charleston A seaport of South Carolina with a busy trade in timber, cotton and maize. Founded in 1672, many of its stately old homes date from Colonial days. Fine gardens and remains of pre-Civil War plantations surround the city. The azalea festival is an annual event that brings tourists to Charleston. Its industries include timber, metal and fertilisers. It has a population of 313,000. fishing grounds have been seriously depleted.

Chesapeake Bay The largest inlet of the Atlantic

This pleasant farm, in Maryland, U.S.A., is on the western shore of Chesapeake Bay

along the east coast of the United States. It penetrates almost 200 miles inland and thus separates the Delmarva Peninsula (also called the Eastern Shore) from the mainland of Maryland and Virginia. The Susquehanna, the Potomac and the James are but three of the many rivers forming wide estuaries on Chesapeake Bay. Baltimore, and Hampton Roads (which is the anchorage for Norfolk, Newport News and Portsmouth), are the major seaports. The bay has long been famous for its oysters and crabs; in recent years, however, the fishing grounds have been seriously depleted.

Chicago The third-largest city (population 6,978,947) of the United States and the metropolis of the Middle West, near the southern end of Lake Michigan and 700 miles west of New York. It is the country's busiest transportation centre, served by 25 trunk railway lines, numerous highways, 21 airlines using two major commercial airports (Midway and O'Hare), and Great Lakes shipping. As part of the Illinois Waterway, the Chicago River links the Great Lakes with the Mississippi River. Chicago owes its fame as the world's largest grain and livestock market and meat-packing centre to the fertility and wealth of the farmlands that extend southward and westward for hundreds of miles. Sprawling industrial and residential communities surround the city, except on the eastside, where Michigan Avenue — Chicago's most attractive park-fringed thoroughfare — fronts on Lake Michigan. Steel-milling, the area's most important industry, occupies the lake shore south of the city proper in the Calumet district along the Illinois-Indiana line, adjoining Gary in neighbouring Indiana State. Favourably located as a supplier of the Middle West, Chicago produces agricultural machinery, railway equipment, electrical appliances, fertiliser and chemicals, and hundreds of food products and consumer goods for the national market. The Loop (so named because it was surrounded by elevated transit lines) is the hub of the city's commercial and financial activity. Nicknamed the 'Windy City', because of the stiff breezes it receives from the lake, Chicago has a typically 'continental' climate, noted for its cold winters and hot summers. Originating as a French trading post, and reinforced in 1804 by a fort (Fort Dearborn), Chicago grew slowly until the development of lake steamer traffic and the coming of the railway, shortly before the outbreak of the Civil War. A city of ramshackle wooden houses, Chicago was almost wiped out by the great fire of 1871. Then began the steady inflow of immigrants which has made Chicago almost as cosmopolitan a centre as New York. Hundreds of thousands of Negroes have come there from the South, to find industrial employment. Over 6½ million people now live within the Chicago metropolitan area.

chicle This chief ingredient of chewing-gum is the juice of the rubber-yielding tree known as

A green belt of parkland lies between the skyscrapers of Chicago and the shores of Lake Michigan

A peak in the Colorado Rockies, the mountains which form part of North America's Continental Divide and provide wonderful scenery in the Rocky Mountain National Park

sapodilla. Chicle is collected chiefly in Yucatán and Guatemala.

Cincinnati A large city (population 1,384,851) and river port on the Ohio River in southern Ohio, facing Kentucky. Its leading industry is soap-making. In addition, there are plants producing steel products, machinery, alcoholic drinks, plastics, watches, shoes and clothing. Cincinnati was founded in 1789, and many settlers bound for the mid-western plains came through the town. The city has suffered repeatedly from disastrous river floods.

Citlaltépetl Highest mountain (18,696 feet) in Mexico, east of the city of Puebla. An inactive volcano, its perfectly shaped, snow-covered summit is visible from Mexico City, 120 miles away.

Cleveland The largest city (population 2,064,194) of Ohio, on Lake Erie at the mouth of the Cuyahoga River. Iron ore from the Lake Superior mines is unloaded there for the city's steel mills (on the banks of the winding Cuyahoga), and for shipment by rail to other steel centres in Ohio and nearby Pennsylvania. Seven major railways serve Cleveland, and the Ohio Turnpike (a link in the New York-Chicago toll highway system) passes just south of the city. Cleveland's industries include meat-packing, oil-refining, manufacturing of cement, motor-car parts, machine tools, paints and textiles.

Coast Ranges Narrow belts of mountains along the Pacific coast of North America, extending from Alaska southward to southern California. They receive up to 150 inches of rainfall annually and support a dense growth of evergreen forests. A wilderness area has been preserved in the Olympic National Park in the State of Washington. The islands off British Columbia and southern Alaska form part of the Coast Ranges; they are separated from the mainland by the Inside Passage.

Colorado A Rocky Mountain State (104,247 square miles; population 2,207,259) of the U.S.A., crossed through its centre by the Continental Divides. Fifty-five of the State's towering peaks are more than 14,000 feet high; among them is Pikes Peak (14,110 feet), which overlooks the Great Plains to the east and is Colorado's favourite tourist attraction. The highest is Mt Elbert, 14,431 feet. Some of the grandest scenery is in Rocky Mountain National Park (north-west of Denver) where snow-covered summits, glaciers, sheer granite cliffs, and blue-and-green mountain lakes, can be seen from a highway that reaches 11,992 feet in the Loveland Pass. Mesa Verde National Park is noted for the cliff-dwellings of early Indian peoples who built their homes in the high canyon walls. Wild animals abound in the Rockies; there are brown and grizzly bears, deer and elk, mountain sheep and antelopes. Colorado has been a mining state since gold was first discovered in 1858 and caused a rush similar to California's days of the 'Fortyniners', despite the presence of hostile Indians along the route. The State joined the Union in 1876. Today, Colorado is a leading producer of uranium, molybdenum and vanadium; it has soft coal-mines, oil-fields, and enormous deposits of oil shale as yet unexploited; gold, silver, copper, zinc and lead are also mined, and there are many 'ghost' towns. More than two-thirds of the population is found in a 30-mile-wide belt at the foot of the Front Range of the Rockies. There are situated: Denver, Colorado's capital and largest city of all the mountain States, with a population of 1,125,000: Colorado Springs, the health resort at the foot of Pikes Peak; and Pueblo, a steel-milling centre with 104,000 inhabitants. Crops are even more important than mining or stock-raising. In eastern Colorado, dry farming is the rule and wheat is grown extensively; however, because rainfall is insufficient and unreliable, the land would be better off if it were not ploughed; the eastern region was, in fact, part of the 'dust bowl' of the 1930s. At the foot of the Rockies, and in the valleys of the South Platte and Arkansas Rivers, lie most of Colorado's 3 million irrigated acres; much of the water is piped through tunnels from the wetter areas lying west of the Front Range. There alfalfa is the main crop; others are hay, sugar beets (Colorado raises more of these than any other State), vegetables and fruits. It is also becoming popular as a winter sports area.

Colorado River The chief river of the south-western United States, known chiefly for the Grand Canyon, a deep gorge which the river has cut through the Colorado Plateau on its way to the Gulf of California, an arm of the Pacific Ocean.

It rises at an elevation of 10,000 feet in the Rocky Mountains of north-western Colorado, and flows 1,400 miles through some of the most scenic, wild stretches of the South-West. Its waters are vital for irrigation in Colorado, in the desert areas of Arizona and southern California, and for water supply in the Los Angeles basin. Hoover Dam, one of the world's great engineering feats, straddles the Colorado River on the Nevada-Arizona line, near Las Vegas, Nevada; it controls floods, provides power, and has formed a 115-mile-long lake (Lake Mead) of the backed-up waters of the Colorado River.

Columbia River The largest river of the Pacific North-West. It rises in the Rocky Mountains of British Columbia and reaches the Pacific Ocean at the Washington-Oregon line, after a winding course of 1,200 miles. The river carries a tremendous volume of water from the snow-fields of the Rockies, across falls and rapids, and through several gorges — notably the great gorge through the Cascade Range east of Portland, Oregon. It has been dammed for hydro-electric power at Grand Coulee and Bonneville Dams, and at several points in between. The power produced at these sites supplies homes and industries throughout the Columbia Basin, a vast region of over 250,000 square miles. At Grand Coulee, the river's waters are being used to irrigate the once barren lands. At Richland, a huge atomic-energy plant has been built on the river's banks. Salmon-fishing is an important activity on the lower Columbia. Fish ladders have been built at the dam sites, to enable the salmon to reach their up-river spawning grounds. The Columbia is navigable for sea-going ships as far as the river ports of Vancouver, Washington and Portland (Oregon), the latter on the Willamette River near its junction with the Columbia. The Snake River, Columbia's chief tributary, drains southern Idaho.

Columbus The capital of Ohio and the trade centre (population 548,119) for a prosperous farm area along the eastern margin of the Corn Belt. Its industries include meat-packing, paper-milling, and the manufacturing of machinery. Columbus was laid out in 1812 on a site chosen for the State capital.

Connecticut A New England State (5,009 square miles; population 3,032,000) of the U.S.A. on Long Island Sound. Rolling uplands in the east and west are separated by the Connecticut River lowland. Here tobacco is grown on thousands of acres that are shaded from the sun by cheesecloth awnings held up on poles. Connecticut tobacco goes into the making of high-priced cigars. Most of the State's soils are too rocky and shallow to grow crops; but poultry-raising and dairying are important, because there are many large cities within easy reach of the farms. Hartford (651,000 inhabitants), the State capital and largest city, lies on the Connecticut River and contains the head offices of many of the nation's insurance companies. Bridgeport (385,746 people) and New Haven (348,424 people) are important industrial centres on the Connecticut shore, for this is first and foremost a manufacturing State that specialises in high-value products requiring much skill. Connecticut makes more clocks and more silver-plated ware than any other State; it makes firearms and ammunition, typewriters and sewing machines, hardware of all kinds, precision tools, pins and needles, hats (especially at Danbury) and textile goods. There are many delightful beach resorts along Connecticut's long shoreline on Long Island Sound. Yachting is becoming a favourite pastime of city-dwellers. In the hills, there are many quaint villages and pretty lakes to attract the summer tourists.

The first permanent white settlement was founded (1633–35) by English colonists from Massachusetts in the Connecticut valley. The 'Nutmeg State' was one of the original 13; it was the fifth to ratify the Constitution of the United States in 1788.

corn A native American plant, called corn in the United States, Canada and Australia, and maize elsewhere. Cultivated on the American continent long before the coming of the Europeans, it has become one of the world's leading fodder crops. The United States, which offers ideal growing conditions in its Corn Belt, accounts for 60 per cent of the world's production. Almost all the corn produced in the United States is fed to livestock, about half of it to pigs. High yields are obtained from hybrid corn, which has almost entirely replaced ordinary seed since the 1930s. The Soviet Union has been engaged in a major drive to imitate the 'corn-hog' economy of the United States since 1954.

Costa Rica An independent republic (19,650 square miles; population 1,680,000) of Central America. Several mountain ranges, topped by volcanic cones, run the length of the country. Most of the volcanoes are inactive, but severe earthquakes have occurred in recent times. Most of the people of Costa Rica live on the central plateau (average elevation 4,000 feet above sea level), which is covered with fertile volcanic ash. There lies the capital, San José, a prosperous and progressive city of 203,100 inhabitants. Coffee and bananas are the country's leading export crop. Bananas are grown in large plantations along the Pacific coast, and shipped via the ports of Golfito and Quepos. Older plantations along the Caribbean shore, ravaged by banana disease, have had to be abandoned. West Indian Negroes who came here at the turn of the century have shifted to cacao, which is exported via the Caribbean port of Limón. Coffee is the chief crop of the highlands. Unusual for Central America is the fact that most Costa Ricans are white and of Spanish descent; *mestizos* (people of mixed Spanish and Indian blood) are in the minority, and the Indian population is dwindling. The country also has the highest literacy rate in Central America, and trades chiefly with the United States.

Columbus landed on the Caribbean shore of Costa Rica (Spanish for 'the rich coast') in 1502. The region then became part of the captaincy-general of Guatemala in 1539. It proclaimed its independence from Spain in 1821. Costa Rica has a stable, democratic form of government.

cotton At the beginning of the 19th century, only 4 per cent of all fabric was made of cotton thread. Nowadays, cotton supplies 80 per cent of the world's textiles. Although cotton had been grown in the Pacific-Asian region since antiquity, it was only with the invention of ginning, spinning and weaving machinery that the plant became the chief textile fibre of modern civilisation. The principal type of cotton is the medium-length upland cotton of the United States. Other types are the Egyptian long staple and the Indian short, coarse type. The boll, or fruit, of the cotton plant is a capsule that bursts open when ripe, and allows the seeds and attached lint (fibres) to be easily picked. Although most of the world's cotton is still

Coyotes

picked by hand, machinery is being increasingly used in the United States and the Soviet Union. After being harvested, the fibre is separated from the seeds by ginning. The seeds furnish an oil used in cooking, margarine and soap-making, while the residue is fed to livestock in the form of oil-cake or cottonseed meal. After ginning, the cotton lint is graded, baled and shipped to milling centres. There, spindles spin the lint into yarn, and looms weave the cotton yarn — often in combination with wool and synthetic fibres — into cloth. In general, the cotton textile industry has tended to concentrate in industrialised countries, far removed from cotton-growing areas. This has brought about a general movement of raw cotton from surplus producers, such as the United States, Egypt and Brazil, to raw cotton consumers, such as

Salmon fishing in Oregon, on the Columbia River

Britain, Japan, France and West Germany. The United States is the world's leading producer of raw cotton and cotton textiles, followed by the Soviet Union, China and India.

coyote This prairie wolf is still common in the western plains, despite efforts to exterminate it. The coyote is best known for its long, sustained howling after sundown.

Cuba An island republic (44,000 square miles; population 8,100,000) of the West Indies, strategically situated at the entrance to the Gulf of Mexico, opposite the tip of Florida. The largest of the Greater Antilles (and larger than all the other West Indian islands combined), Cuba extends over 700 miles from east to west; it averages 50 miles in width. Havana, on the north coast, is the capital, with a population of 1,500,000 people. Most of the country is level or gently rolling; it is, therefore, ideally suited to the large-scale cultivation of sugar cane, which also requires a sub-tropical climate. Cuba is one of the largest sugar producers in the world; sugar accounts for 75% of the country's exports in value, and employs two-thirds of the labour force. There are more than 150 sugar mills, called *centrales*. World-famous Cuban tobacco is grown in Piñar del Rio province, in the far west of the island; Havana cigars are a prime export product. Coffee and cordage fibre are also grown for export. Cuba's mineral resources are found in the Sierra Maestra, the only mountainous section of the country, in Oriente province. They include iron ore, copper, nickel and chromite. The coastal waters yield shellfish and sponges, and extensive deep-sea fisheries are based at several south-coast ports and on the Isle of Pines. Cuba's mild winter climate, its beaches, and bustling Spanish-style cities, formerly attracted tourists from the nearby mainland of North America.

Cuba was discovered by Columbus in 1492, and it soon became an important base for the fleet of ships carrying precious metals from the mainland of New Spain (Mexico, Central America) to the Old World. Known as the 'Pearl of the Antilles', the island flourished as a haven for pirates preying on shipping. Sugar was introduced in the 18th century, and so were Negro slaves to work on the plantations. Cuba remained a Spanish possession until 1898, when the United States defeated Spain and occupied the island. A republic was established in 1902, but U.S. troops returned for another three years in 1906. Guantanamo Bay naval base was leased to the United States in 1903. Spanish is the official language of the country, and until 1934 it was a protectorate of the United States, which

Cars are manufactured in vast numbers at these works in Detroit, U.S. industrial centre in Michigan

Coffee is grown in rich soil on the lower slopes of El Salvador's volcanoes. This is Mt San Vicente

supplied industrial capital and was the recipient of far more Cuban exports than any other country. From then until 1959, Cuba was closely related to the United States economically, after which the left-wing government of Fidel Castro took over control, and all relations with the U.S.A. were broken off. Assistance was then sought from Russia, and later from other Communist countries, which resulted in the US Navy blockading Cuba for one month in 1962. Today most of Cuba's trade is with the Communist bloc.

● **Curaçao** is the main island of the Netherlands Antilles (a domestically self-governing Dutch Colony embracing several islands), off the coast of Venezuela. Curaçao has a population of 141,393, and the capital and port is Willemstad (45,000). Curaçao has many oil refineries. Nearby Aruba also has refineries. The language, *Papiamento*, is a mixture of Spanish, Dutch, French and English.

● **cypress, bald** This conifer, which sheds its leaves in the autumn, is a typical tree of the swamps of the south-eastern United States. Its hard, red wood, very resistant to rotting, is used for posts, sleepers and construction.

● **Dallas** A city (population 1,555,950) in northern Texas with a large cotton market. It is considered to be the leading industrial and financial centre of the entire South-West. Dallas produces aircraft equipment, cotton gins, leather goods, and oil-field machinery. It is also known as a regional fashion centre for the women's clothing industry, especially hats and cotton dresses. The growth of the oil industry in eastern Texas has contributed to the city's prosperity.

● **Dayton** An industrial city (population 501,644) in western Ohio, about 50 miles from Cincinnati. It is a leading aviation centre, with an air-force station and several commercial airfields. Cash registers, precision tools and air-conditioning appliances are the chief products of the city's factories. The Wright brothers built their early aeroplanes in Dayton.

● **Death Valley** A desert area in California, east of the Sierra Nevada. The lowest point in the Western Hemisphere, at 282 feet below sea level, is located there. It hardly ever rains in Death Valley, and summer temperatures reach 56.6 °C., one of the highest air temperatures in the world.

● **Delaware** A small East Coast State (2,057 square miles; population **542,979**) of the United States, on the shore of Delaware Bay. Only one State, Rhode Island, is smaller. Dover is the capital (17,165 people), but Wilmington is by far the largest city, with a population of **79,977**. There are shipbuilding yards, and factories where chemicals, firearms, railway-wagons, synthetic fibres, textiles, and glazed kid leather (a local speciality), are produced. Despite its small size, Delaware is perhaps the most important fruit-growing and market-gardening region along the East Coast. Its orchards are famed for their delicious peaches; and plums, pears, cherries and apples are also grown. Poultry (especially broilers) is a major source of income. Lewes, a little sea-coast town, was settled in 1631 by the Dutch, who came to raise wheat and tobacco and to catch whales. Today it is the chief fishing port, where oysters and other shellfish are landed in large quantities; these are brought up from beds in Delaware Bay by boats equipped with great derrick-like dredges.

The 'Diamond State' is one of the original 13 States, and was the first to ratify the Federal Constitution in 1787. During the Civil War, it remained in the Union, even though slavery was legal there.

● **Delaware River** Rising in the Catskill Mountains of New York, this river flows generally south-east to Delaware Bay at Wilmington. Its headwaters are tapped for New York City's water supply. Below Trenton, the river is navigable for ocean-going ships. Philadelphia is the main seaport on this 300-mile-long river.

● **Denver** Capital and largest city of Colorado, located at the eastern foot of the Rocky Mountains. With its 1,125,000 people, Denver calls itself the 'metropolis of the Rockies'. It serves as a market centre for the ranching and irrigation-farming region of the High Plains (to the east), and the mining towns and resorts of the Rockies. Settled in 1858, Denver mushroomed in the 1870s and '80s, when gold and silver were found in the vicinity. The city lies 5,300 feet above sea level. Its bracing climate and the proximity of Rocky Mountain recreation areas bring tourists to Denver during the summer season.

● **Detroit** The largest city (population 4,199,931) of Michigan, and the fifth-largest in the United States, Detroit is a port on the Detroit River, linking Lake Huron and Lake Erie opposite Windsor, Canada. The world's leading motor-car manufacturing centre, Detroit owes its growth and its fame to Henry Ford who, at the beginning of the 20th century, developed the technique of assembly-line mass production, with which he gained leadership in the industry. Today, the manufacturing of motor-cars has spread to a ring of cities around Detroit, especially Dearborn, and extends into nearby Ohio and Indiana. Detroit also produces chemicals (based on extensive salt deposits in the area), aircraft parts and electrical equipment. The opening of the St Lawrence Seaway has enhanced the city's importance as a great inland port.

Detroit traces its origin to a fort established in 1701 by the French explorer and fur-trader, Cadillac. The settlement passed to Britain in 1760 and to the United States in 1796, when its population barely exceeded 1,000.

● **District of Columbia** A Federal district (69 square miles; population 820,000) on the Potomac River, equal in area to the city of Washington, the capital of the United States. It was established by Acts of Congress in 1791, on land ceded to the United States Government by the State of Maryland. It is governed by Congress, and residents cannot vote in Federal elections.

● **Dominican Republic** A Spanish-speaking republic (18,811 square miles; population 4,174,490) of the West Indies, occupying the eastern two-thirds of the island of Hispaniola. Santo Domingo is the capital. Most of the country is mountainous, but several interior lowlands are well-suited to agriculture. Sugar is the main crop; coffee, cacao, tobacco, cotton, rice and bananas are also grown. Mineral deposits, including iron ore and bauxite (the raw material for aluminium), are still being assessed, though gold has been washed in the streams since early colonial days.

Columbus discovered the island in 1492 and named it La Espanola. The native Indians were soon exterminated, and Negro slaves were brought from Africa to work in the sugar plantations. In 1822, the Spanish colony of Santo Domingo was invaded and held by Haitians, from the western

Today, remnants of the Seminoles live on an Indian reservation in the Florida Everglades, U.S.A.

part of the island. The country gained its independence in 1844, but was occupied by U.S. Marines between 1916 and 1924. U.S., and other American forces, landed in the Dominican Republic in 1965, to restore stable government, following a large-scale insurrection. The capital is Santo Domingo (822,862).

The beach at Fort Lauderdale, on Florida's Atlantic coast, is warmed by the waters of the Gulf Stream

Bald eagle

- **eagle, bald** This white-headed sea eagle was made the national emblem of the United States because of its proud bearing and independent spirit. It rarely catches fish, which provide the bald eagle's food, by its own efforts; instead, the bird either searches the beach for dead fish, or pursues other fish-catching birds until they drop their prey.

- **Edmonton** A rapidly growing industrial city (1941 population 94,000); 1971 population 50,000)) of western Canada, capital of the province of Alberta, and on a trans-continental railway near the eastern foothills of the Rocky Mountains. Large oil and gas deposits, discovered in this area in 1947, have brought refineries and chemical plants to Edmonton. The city lies near the southern terminus of the Alaska Highway, and serves as an outfitting point for expeditions to the Yukon and the North-West Territories. Trans-polar airlines call at Edmonton's international airport. Jasper National Park lies to the west. Fort Edmonton was established in 1794 as a fur-trading post of the Hudson's Bay Company. Only 2,500 people lived there in 1900. The city is surrounded by fertile farming land and is close to rich coal-mines.

- **elk** The largest of the deer family, reaching 8 feet at the shoulders. The elk lives largely in the coniferous and mixed forests of Alaska and northern Canada, as well as in Scandinavia, Finland and Siberia.

- **El Salvador** The smallest and most densely populated (8,300 square miles; population 3,150,000) of the Central American republics, and the only one without an Atlantic coastline. San Salvador (population 253,000) is the capital city. The country is crossed by two volcanic ranges that rise to 7,800 feet in the volcano Santa Ana, also the name of a city with 130,000 inhabitants. Lava and volcanic dust from past eruptions of the volcano have settled on the adjacent plateau, the soils of which are therefore very fertile. A mild, high-grade variety of coffee is grown on these slopes, and the remainder of the cultivable land raises sugar, cotton, tobacco, and local food crops. Coffee provides almost 80 per cent of the country's exports in value, the United States being its main customer. The country's prosperity fluctuates with the size of the annual crop and the price it fetches on the world market. A sizeable hydro-electric dam on the Lempa River supplies power for El Salvador's industries, which produce textiles, sisal bags, straw hats, shoes and flour. The country has good roads and is also linked by railway with

Guatemala's Caribbean seaport of Puerto Barrios. El Salvador's own ports are nothing but road-steads, where ships anchor offshore. Most of the people are of mixed white and Indian descent; more than half the population is illiterate. Spanish is the official language.

Conquered by Spanish conquistadores in 1524-1526, the country formed part of the captaincy of Guatemala until 1821, when it proclaimed its independence from Spain, becoming fully independent in 1839. The Republic has had a turbulent history of revolutions and dictatorships. Its population is growing so rapidly that there is continuous emigration to neighbouring countries.

- **Erie, Lake** The fourth-largest of the Great Lakes, situated in both the United States and Canada. It covers an area of almost 10,000 square miles and lies 572 feet above sea level. The St Clair and Detroit Rivers provide a navigable link with Lake Huron to the west. The lake empties into Lake Ontario to the east, via the Niagara River, whose Niagara Falls are by-passed for shipping by the Welland Canal. Lake Erie is connected with the Atlantic Ocean via the New York State Barge Canal (the old Erie Canal) and the Hudson River. Iron ore and grain from Lake Superior ports are unloaded on the shores of Lake Erie, at Toledo and Cleveland, Ohio; at Erie, Pennsylvania; and at Buffalo, New York. French forts and trading posts

were established on the lake near the beginning of the 17th century.

- **Everglades** Swampy region of southern Florida, south of Lake Okeechobee. A national park since 1947, it contains mangrove forests, canals and meadowlands where many unusual varieties of birds and water-loving animals make their home. There, too, is a Seminole Indian reservation.

- **fir, Douglas** This tall coniferous tree of great size is an important timber tree of the American West. Formerly much in use for ships' masts, it was introduced into Europe in 1827.

- **Florida** The 'Peninsula State' (58,560 square miles; population 6,789,000) of the United States; with its 700 miles of shoreline on the Atlantic and the Gulf of Mexico, its endless sandy beaches, and mild winters, it is first and foremost a holiday land. Many tourists like it so much that they settle or retire there. Between 1940 and 1956, the population of Florida has doubled and continues to increase. Miami, Miami Beach, Palm Beach, Fort Lauderdale, Daytona Beach and other resorts along the straight Atlantic coast are centres of tremendous growth; Tampa (301,789), St Petersburg (324,842) and Sarasota on the Gulf coast are

Mile after mile of citrus groves thrive in the sub-tropical climate of Florida's east coast

Granite is quarried at Elberton, Georgia

increasingly popular. Next to tourism, the State's principal activity is market-gardening and the growing of citrus fruit (oranges, grapefruit, tangerines, limes), mostly in the central part of the peninsula. Sugar cane is grown on the shores of Lake Okeechobee. Florida has also become a leading cattle-raising State with Brahman hybrid cattle. Its pine forests, palmettos and cypress trees furnish the raw material for an important woodprocessing and paper industry. The State also leads the U.S. in the manufacture of cigars.

Off the Florida Keys and the Atlantic coastline, the warm Florida Current, a branch of the Gulf Stream, attracts sport fishermen who catch tarpon, shark or swordfish. At Tarpon Springs, sponges are brought up from the ocean floor. From its huge deposits of phosphate, Florida supplies the American fertiliser industry. Not many years ago, the southern end of the state was a huge swamp; much of which has now been drained and turned into farmland, but a million acres of swampland have been preserved in Everglades National Park. South of the Everglades, the Straits of Florida are dotted with a chain of coral islets, called 'keys', that are now linked to the mainland by a long causeway ending at Key West, the southernmost city in the United States. In the north-west, Florida's peninsula reaches along the Gulf; in that region, there are corn, cotton and tobacco fields, and also the State capital, Tallahassee (52,000). The busy commercial centre of Jacksonville (372,569) is Florida's northern gateway.

Because of its early discovery, in 1513, by the Spaniard Ponce de Leon, Florida boasts the oldest city in the United States — St Augustine, founded in 1565. The territory was purchased from Spain in 1821, and became the 27th State of the Union in 1845. Defeated by European settlers, the Seminole Indians were either removed to Oklahoma or forced to flee into the Everglades and Big Cypress Swamp, where they now live in several reservations especially set aside for them.

- **flying fish** The commonest flying fish of the tropical oceans has greatly enlarged pectoral fins, which constitute its wings. With them the fish can glide (not fly) short distances through the air, after having driven its body out of the water by means of its tail motion. In some flying fish, both the pectoral and pelvic fins are enlarged, giving the fish two pairs of wings.

- **Fort William-Port Arthur** Twin cities on Lake Superior, in Ontario province, Canada, with a joint population of 84,195. Wheat from the western provinces is stored there in huge elevators and shipped, via the Great Lakes, to the cities of eastern Canada.

- **Fort Worth** A rapidly growing city (population 638,000) of northern Texas, 30 miles west of Dallas. An important grain and livestock market, Fort Worth has stock yards, flour mills, and meatpacking plants. Oil-refining and aircraft manufacturing are among the more recent industries.

- **fox, Arctic** This is one of the few animals that spends the winter in the frozen reaches of the Arctic. Its thick fur is grey-brown in summer and snow-white in winter. The fox provides for the lean winter days by storing the bodies of its victims (lemmings, mice and other rodents) in rock crevices.

- **fox, grey** This common North American fox is especially plentiful in the East and South. It prefers open forest and is the only fox that can climb trees.

- **Galveston** A port on the Gulf of Mexico, built on a sand-bar off the Texas coast. It ships sulphur, cotton and flour. A deep-water channel leads from the port to Houston, 40 miles inland. Buccaneers made Galveston their headquarters for pirate raids on Spanish shipping early in the 19th century. The city was levelled by a hurricane in 1900; it is still threatened from time to time by tropical storms, most seriously in 1964. Galveston has a population of 61,809.

- **Gander** Airport in Newfoundland, Canada, formerly used as a fuel stop by transatlantic planes. It was an important air-communications centre during World War II.

- **Georgia** The largest State (58,876 square miles; population 4,672,593) east of the Mississippi River, chartered by George II in 1732, and one of the original 13 States, Georgia was first among the southern States to ratify the Constitution of the United States in 1788. Atlanta, the capital, founded in 1836, is a busy railway centre and one of the largest cities of the South, with over 770,000 inhabitants (1970). Savannah, Georgia's oldest

Colorado Plateau

town (1733), is located on the Savannah River, so near the Atlantic Ocean that it is a bustling seaport with 149,000 people. More than 200 miles upstream from Savannah lies Augusta, a cotton market and a textile-manufacturing centre, which can be reached from the coast by river boats. Warm Springs is the State's most famous health resort, noted for its mineral springs. Georgia no longer grows cotton only, although it still produces the fine, long-staple Sea Island variety. King George II hoped that his colony would produce silk, but this soon proved to be no more than a dream. The largest area of land is used for growing maize, but peanuts and tobacco are more important cash crops. Georgia leads the United States in peanut and pecan production, and ranks high in peaches (it is sometimes called the 'Peach State'), water-melons, peppers and sweet potatoes. The State's extensive forests supply a thriving woodprocessing and paper industry. The yellow pine is found everywhere in the coastal plain; it is sought out by lumbermen and its sap is made into turpentine, rosin (resin) and pine-tar — products known as 'naval stores'. Georgia, in fact, produces threequarters of the country's naval stores. It is also the nation's leading supplier of china clay, and an important source of granite and marble. Numerous textile mills are found along the 'fall line', the seaward edge of the piedmont or Appalachian foot-hills, where falling water used to spin waterwheels, and it was there that Eli Whitney invented the cotton gin in 1793. Today, there are hydroelectric power plants to run Georgia's factories, and their dams have formed large reservoirs in the southern Appalachian Mountains. Georgia's coastline has lovely stretches of white sandy beaches, islands and inlets, and the ever-present palmetto trees and hedges of wild Cherokee roses. In the south-east, the Okeefenokee Swamp, a jungle of cypress and vines and high reeds, is a haven for birds, alligators and other wild animals.

In 1754, Georgia became a royal colony; it is named after King George II. Negro slaves were greatly used on the vast cotton plantations in the early 19th century, though the plantation system broke down after the Civil War; even today, however, almost half of the farmland is cultivated by tenants.

- **Gettysburg** A town in southern Pennsylvania, near the battlefield which marked the turning point of the Civil War (1863) when General Lee was defeated by the northern armies of General Meade. Lincoln delivered his famous address at the dedication of the Gettysburg National Cemetery.

- **Gila monster** This lizard, found in Arizona and New Mexico, is the only poisonous lizard in the United States. European settlers first came to know this two-foot-long reptile in the valley of the Gila River.

- **goose, snow** This pure-white Arctic goose nests in Greenland and winters on the Gulf Coast, in California and Mexico.

- **Grand Banks** A major fishing ground in the North Atlantic Ocean, off the south-east coast of Newfoundland. Fleets of fishing boats from the United States, Canada, western Europe and Scandinavia meet there to fish for cod and herring. In the shallow waters of the Grand Banks, the cold Labrador Current meets the warm Gulf Stream, producing dense fog-banks. Icebergs carried south from Greenland threaten transatlantic shipping in this area.

- **Grand Canyon** Deep gorge of the Colorado River in north-western Arizona. It is 280 miles long, up to 15 miles wide from rim to rim, and up to one mile deep. The surrounding Colorado Plateau lies at an elevation of 9,000 feet above sea level. One of the great natural wonders of the world, the canyon reveals in its successive rock layers the geological history of millions of years. Tourists view the multicoloured rock formations, the rock towers and mesas along the side of the gorge, and the swirling waters of the Colorado far below, from observation points on both the north and south rims. Scenic trails lead to the bottom of the canyon. John Wesley Powell, the great explorer and surveyor of the West, led the first boat trip through the gorge in 1869. In 1919, the area was made into a National Park.

● **Great Basin** A vast desert and semi-desert region of the western United States, between the Sierra Nevada (west), the Wasatch Range of the Rocky Mountains (east), the Columbia Plateau (north), and the deserts of Arizona and Mexico (south). Rugged, parallel mountain ranges separate arid basins whose bottoms contain salt flats or temporary salt lakes. River channels are usually dry, and vegetation is scanty. The most arid portions of the Great Basin (Mojave Desert, Death Valley, Carson Sink) were formerly named the Great American Desert. Most of Nevada and western Utah lie within the Great Basin.

● **Great Bear Lake** In the North-West Territories of Canada, on the Arctic Circle. The lake covers an area of 12,000 square miles and drains into the Mackenzie River. Port Radium is an important mining centre of radio-active minerals, as well as copper, silver, lead, zinc and nickel.

Freighter

● **Great Lakes** The largest chain of fresh-water lakes in the world, on the U.S.-Canadian border. They occupy 95,000 square miles, an area larger than Great Britain. The lakes are inter-connected and drain eastward to the Atlantic, via the St Lawrence River. They include Lakes Superior, Huron, Michigan (the only one entirely in the United States), Erie and Ontario. With the completion of a 27-foot-deep water route along the St Lawrence Seaway, ocean-going ships are now able to reach such inland centres as Cleveland, Detroit, Chicago and Duluth, the last-named being 2,340 miles from the Atlantic coast. The lakes are

also linked to the Gulf of Mexico by the Illinois Waterway (extending southward from Chicago) and the Mississippi River. The Great Lakes provide a shipping lane of tremendous importance to American commerce and industry. Chief cargoes are iron ore, carried from the Lake Superior region to steel mills in Indiana, Ohio and Pennsylvania; grain from the United States and Canadian wheat belts; coal; and limestone. Ice closes the lakes for at least four months every year.

● **Great Plains** The western portion of the interior lowland of North America. Wheat is the main crop, but in the western areas (near the foot of the Rockies) extensive cattle-grazing is the principal form of land use. Rainfall decreases from east to west. The areas that receive less than a yearly average of 20 inches of rain are frequently threatened by droughts. During the 1930s, parts of Kansas, Colorado, Oklahoma and northern Texas were turned into a 'dust bowl' when winds whipped up the dry soils that had been ploughed or grazed in previous years.

● **Great Slave Lake** In north-western Canada, and one of a chain of lakes at the western edge of the Canadian Shield. It covers an area of over 11,000 square miles and is drained by the Mackenzie River. Fur-trapping is carried on along the wooded west shore. Yellowknife, on the lake's northern arm, is the chief gold-mining centre of Canada's North-West Territories. Supplies are brought in and gold is shipped out by air.

● **Guadalajara** Second-largest city (population 1,196,200) in Mexico, in an attractive setting 5,000 feet above sea level, about 300 miles north-west of Mexico City. Wheat, maize and beans are the chief products of the surrounding farmlands. The city is famous for its fine glassware and pottery. Its central plaza is bordered by colonial buildings dating from the 16th and 17th centuries. Its university was founded in 1792.

● **Guatemala** The northernmost, and the most populous (42,031 square miles; population 5,400,000), of the Central American Republics, with a predominantly Indian and mestizo population. Two-thirds of the country is mountainous, with a string of high volcanoes (Tajumulco: 13,816 feet) towering over the narrow Pacific coastal plain. The wider lowland on the Atlantic slope includes the almost uninhabited forest region of Petén, where the collection of chicle is the principal activity of the Mayan population. An excellent grade of coffee is grown at elevations ranging from 3,000 to 6,000 feet; coffee accounts for three-quarters of the country's exports. Bananas, the third ranking export crop, are grown on the

The Colorado River flows through the natural wonder of the Grand Canyon

Pacific slope and inland from the Caribbean port of Puerto Barrios. Sugar is the second most important export, and Guatemala is one of the world's largest sources of essential oils (citronella and lemon grass). A 'transcontinental' railway, 275 miles long, links Puerto Barrios with San Jose, on the Pacific coast, via Guatemala City, the nation's capital and largest town (population 768,987). The native Indians live in their own villages, wear distinctive and colourful clothes, and cultivate their own fields in the highlands, though they also work on plantations owned by people of European origin or *ladinos* (people of mixed white and Indian blood who have adopted modern ways of life). Guatemala offers the tourist a wide selection of scenery: magnificent volcanoes, wild gorges, rolling uplands, and mountain-fringed lakes — notably Lake Atitlán; the picturesque Indian market town of Chichicastenango; and the impressive ruins of Antigua, the old colonial capital, which was destroyed by an earthquake in 1773.

Guatemala was the home of the Mayas, a highly civilised Indian nation, long before the Spanish conquest. Their cities, of which only ruins remain in Guatemala and in neighbouring Yucatán, were marvels of architecture and social organisation. In 1524, the Mayas were defeated by the conquistador Pedro de Alvarado, who claimed all of Central America for Spain. Independence from Spain was proclaimed in 1821, and 18 years later the Republic of Guatemala was born. Spanish is the official language, but the Indians communicate in their own languages. At least two-thirds of the people are illiterate. A five-year development plan 1971-5 is aimed at increasing exports.

● **Gulf Stream** A warm ocean current, flowing from the Gulf of Mexico generally north-eastward across the North Atlantic Ocean to the shores of Portugal, France and Britain. From the Straits of Florida, the Gulf Stream follows the U.S. coast, then veers eastward near the latitude of New York. It moves at about 4 miles per hour, has a deep-blue colour, and is rich in marine life, especially off the Florida coast. The waters of the Gulf Stream have a marked influence in warming the air masses which reach Western Europe.

● **gull, glaucous** This large Arctic gull, also known as the 'burgomaster', is white with a bluish mantle. It is the lightest-coloured of all the large gulls.

Chichicastenango, Guatemala, is a market town for present-day descendants of the Mayan Indians

Islands can be easily reached by ship and air from California. Honolulu offers fine hotels, famous Waikiki Beach, and the traditional flower-wreath (*lei*) welcome to the tourist from the mainland. Tourism plays an extremely large part in the state's economy. The islands were discovered by Captain James Cook in 1778. He named them Sandwich Islands. During the 19th century, they formed an independent kingdom. They became part of the United States in 1898, and were organised into a Territory in 1900. Congress granted Statehood to Hawaii in 1959, and it became the 50th State of the Union. The islands have a vastly important strategic role in American and Pacific affairs, and over a quarter of the population are employed in the various defence installations.

Pineapples

On Oahu Island, in Hawaii, lies Diamond Head – an extinct volcano near Honolulu's Waikiki Beach

● **Haiti** An island republic (10,710 square miles; population 4,700,000) of the West Indies, occupying the western third of the island of Hispaniola. Port-au-Prince, at the head of the Gulf of Gonaïves, is the capital. The overwhelming majority of the population are Negroes who speak Creole (a French dialect mixed with African words). French is the official language, though Europeans number only a few thousands. Most of the country is mountainous, with jumbled scrub and forest-covered ranges extending the length of the two peninsulas that enclose the Gulf of Gonaïves. Haiti is one of the most densely populated areas of the Western Hemisphere; most of the people eke out a poor living on small plots of steeply sloping, eroded land. Coffee is grown for export; sugar and rice are the chief crops of the irrigated lowlands; sisal does well in the drier areas. A new irrigation project in the Artibonite Valley should make the country self-sufficient in rice production. Most of Haiti's mineral resources are undeveloped; however, bauxite (the ore of aluminium) is now mined and shipped to the United States, Haiti's major foreign trade partner.

In 1804, the French colony of Saint-Domingue proclaimed its independence, and Dessalines (a former slave) became president, and later emperor, of the 'black republic' of Haiti. Internal strife continued throughout the 19th century. Between 1915 and 1934, the country was occupied by U.S. marines. Poverty, illiteracy and over-population are Haiti's most pressing problems.

● **Halifax** The principal Canadian seaport on the Atlantic coast, founded in 1749, Halifax is the capital and largest city (population 198,193) of the province of Nova Scotia. It is the main port of call for transatlantic shipping during the months when the St Lawrence River is frozen. There, too, is the eastern terminus of Canada's two trans-continental railways. Lobsters are shipped to the United States.

● **Hamilton** Industrial city (population 449,116) of Ontario province, Canada, at the western end of Lake Ontario. The lake port is surrounded by steel and textile mills, and railway workshops. The town is an important distribution centre for fruit and vegetables, and has a university.

● **hare, polar** Two feet in length and weighing as much as nine pounds, this large hare makes its home in the Arctic regions. Its fur is almost pure white in the winter.

● **Havana** Capital and major seaport (population 1,217,700) of Cuba, with a fine deep-water harbour on the Gulf of Mexico. Havana is the largest city of the West Indies and the cultural hub of this Spanish-speaking island. Sugar, tobacco (Havana cigars especially) and tropical fruits (pineapples, pimentos, tomatoes) are exported. Tourists come to this picturesque Spanish-colonial city, especially in winter, when the climate is at its best and beach-and night-life at their most active. Morro Castle, built in 1590, guards the entrance to the harbour. The old section has many fine examples of Spanish architecture. Founded in 1519, Havana has served as a gateway to the Spanish part of the New World since the middle of the 16th century. In 1898, the American battleship *Maine* was blown up in Havana harbour, an event which led to the Spanish-American War.

● **Hawaii** or **Hawaiian (Sandwich) Islands** A group of islands in the mid-Pacific, more than 2,000 miles south-west of San Francisco, that form a State of the United States. Of 28 islands (land area, 6,423 square miles), only 7 are inhabited. The island of Hawaii is the largest. Honolulu, the capital and largest city (324,871), lies on Oahu, where Pearl Harbour, of World War II fame, is also situated. The total population of Hawaii was 769,000 in 1963; it includes people of Japanese, Filipino and Chinese origin, as well as native Hawaiians, and Americans from the mainland who have made this Pacific paradise their home. The islands are volcanic, with fertile soils and a balmy climate. They are surrounded by coral reefs. They contain some of the world's largest volcanoes: on Hawaii, Mauna Kea (13,820 feet) and Mauna Loa (13,675 feet); on the island of Maui, Haleakala (10,032 feet). Cane sugar and pineapples are the chief crops; they are grown on large, carefully tended plantations and are shipped to the West Coast. Coffee, bananas and fresh flowers (orchids especially) are also exported. The Hawaiian

● **hickory** This tall shade tree, the American walnut, yields a sweet edible nut, and a valuable elastic hardwood used in skis and furniture.

● **Honduras** An independent republic (43,260 square miles; population 2,490,000) of Central America, fronting on both the Caribbean and the Pacific Ocean. It is almost entirely mountainous, except for narrow coastal strips and the undeveloped Mosquito Coast (on the Caribbean), which is still inhabited by Indian tribes. Tegucigalpa (population 218,000) the country's capital and largest city, lies in a narrow inter-mountain basin at 3,000 feet above sea level. Bananas, the chief export crop, are grown in large American-operated plantations along the Caribbean coast. Other products are coffee (grown in the hills by small farmers), coconuts (from the islands in the Gulf of Honduras), rice and livestock. Gold and silver rank among the leading exports. The luxuriant forests of Honduras yield mahogany, rosewood and pine. The country's development is hampered by poor communications; though the country has over 1,000 miles of railway, much of which is American-owned, the aeroplane provides the only efficient means of transport. Most of the population is of mixed Spanish and Indian blood (*mestizos*). Illiteracy is widespread. Spanish is the official language, but English is spoken by Jamaican Negroes who came to work in the banana plantations. During colonial days, Honduras formed part of the Spanish-ruled captaincy of Guatemala. Independence from Spain was proclaimed in 1821, and it has been a republic since 1838.

● **Houston** Largest and fastest-growing city (1971 population 1,985,031) of Texas and one of the major bulk-cargo seaports of the United States. Its man-made harbour (reclaimed from a swamp) is connected by a 60-mile-long deep-water channel with the Gulf of Mexico. It exports petroleum, sulphur, cotton and cottonseed products, chemicals and lumber. Located in the midst of the highly-productive Gulf Coast oil-field, Houston has several oil refineries and growing chemical industries, based on the vast resources of petroleum, natural gas, sulphur and salt found in the area. The city was founded in 1836 and served for two years as the capital of the Texas Republic. It owes its amazing growth to the development of the oil-fields and the dredging of the ship channel in 1914. The city has two universities.

Hudson Bay Inland sea (almost 500,000 square miles) of north-central Canada, connected with the Atlantic Ocean by Hudson Strait and with the Arctic Ocean by Foxe Strait. Baffin Island lies to the north. Churchill, the chief port on the bay, is linked by rail with Canada's Prairie Provinces. It provides a shorter and more direct route for wheat shipments to Europe than the Great Lakes and the St Lawrence River, but Hudson Bay is frozen for at least half of the year. The bay was discovered by Henry Hudson in 1610. Chartered in 1760, the Hudson's Bay Company held exclusive rights to the fur trade throughout this vast area, until the territory became part of Canada in 1868.

Hudson River An important waterway in the north-eastern United States which enters the Atlantic Ocean at New York City. It rises in the Adirondacks of northern New York State, flows 315 miles south, and separates Manhattan Island from New Jersey before emptying into New York Bay. Its lower course forms part of the Port of New York; piers jut out into the stream on the Jersey City, Hoboken and Manhattan shore. The river is tidal to Albany 150 miles upstream, at the head of deep-water navigation. A deep submarine canyon extends 200 miles into the Atlantic from the mouth of the Hudson River. The river forms part of an important inland water route to the Great Lakes (via the New York State Barge Canal, formerly the Erie Canal) and the St Lawrence River (via Lake Champlain). A high cliff (known as the Palisades) lines the west shore of the Hudson for 30 miles above Jersey City.

The lovely Hudson Valley was first explored by Henry Hudson in 1609 and was settled by the Dutch, who purchased Manhattan Island from the Indians in 1626.

Huron, Lake The second-largest (23,000 square miles) of the Great Lakes, divided between the United States and Canada. It lies 580 feet above sea level and is up to 750 feet deep. It receives the waters of Lake Superior via St Mary's River and the Sault Step Marie Canals (better known as the 'Soo'), and is connected with Lake Michigan via the Straits of Mackinac, recently bridged; it empties into Lake Erie through the St Clair and Detroit Rivers. Georgian Bay, on the Canadian side, is a popular resort and fishing area. French fur-traders discovered Lake Huron early in the 17th century.

hutia This rare tree-rat is restricted to the West Indies. It is a large species, two feet in length with a grasping tail, found in Cuba. A smaller, short-tailed hutia occurs in Jamaica and the Bahamas.

Idaho The 'Gem State' (83,557 square miles; population 713,008); it has this nickname because Idahoans think it is the loveliest of the U.S. mountain States. The rugged ranges of the Rockies run along the Montana border. Wild and almost uninhabited mountain masses in central Idaho separate the Snake River Valley in the south from the scenic lake country in the narrow northern strip, touching on Canada. In northern Idaho are the lead and silver mines of the Coeur d'Alene district; there, too, are most of the lumber mills, surrounded by western and lodgepole pine, Douglas fir and spruce forests. Many of these valuable stands are in national forests; they are protected against fire and careless cutting by forest rangers of the U.S. government. The land along the Snake River, in the south-west, was once a dry area covered with sagebrush. Now, watered by irrigation ditches, it blooms with apple and pear orchards and grows a variety of vegetables. Wheat and sugar beets are the chief field crops, but Idaho is best known for its baking potatoes, grown along the upper Snake River, a crop worth over £15,000,000 annually. Dairying and sheep-raising are also important. Strange volcanic formations attract the tourist to the lava-covered Snake Valley. Farther west, the river flows through a narrow gorge, 7,000 feet deep from rim to bottom, where huge dams have harnessed the river for hydro-electric power. In the mountains, hunting and fishing are a favourite pastime, and famous Sun Valley attracts skiers from all over the country. There are no large cities in Idaho; Boise, the capital, Pocatello and Idaho Falls process the crops of the Snake River Valley. The isolation of the State has rendered it an important area for the establishment of atomic reactors, and Arco was the first town to be lit by atomic power.

Explored by Lewis and Clark in 1805, Idaho was not settled until 1860, when gold was discovered. Mormons from the Salt Lake area were among the earliest farmers in southern Idaho. Organised as a Territory in 1863, Idaho was admitted to the Union in 1890 as the 43rd State. The Shoshone and Blackfeet Indians still herd their sheep in the mountains.

Illinois A Midwestern State (56,400 square miles; population 11,113,976) of the U.S.A., extending southward from Lake Michigan to where the Mississippi and the Ohio Rivers meet. The 'Prairie State' is a level, agricultural land, covered with cornfields from east to west; only Iowa grows more maize. Other crops are oats, hay, winter wheat and soya beans. Some of the maize is grown for eating, but most of it is fed to pigs and cattle, of which there are millions in Illinois. Many of the cattle are dairy cows, but most of them, along with the pigs, are shipped to the Chicago stockyards, where they are turned into meat and hides. Slaughtering and meat-packing therefore constitute the State's leading industry. Illinois is also known for its farm

Houston, a fast-growing U.S. seaport in Texas

machinery, its watches and electrical equipment; printing and publishing are important. Most of these industries are found in the Chicago area. Southern Illinois mines coal and produces some petroleum. Railway lines from all directions converge on Chicago, the great transportation centre on Lake Michigan; and the St Lawrence Seaway now brings ocean-going ships to its bustling lake port. Though Illinois is a farming State, less than 7 per cent of the population are farmers.

The region was first explored by Fathers Marquette and Joliet, who travelled up the Illinois River in 1673. It thus became part of the French province of Louisiana, but was ceded to Britain in 1763. It was organised as a Territory in 1809, and became the 21st State of the Union in 1818. Illinois is best known as the home of Lincoln, who lived in Springfield, the State capital, before his election to the Presidency in 1860.

Imperial Valley Irrigated region of southern California in the middle of the desert. It lies below sea level and is watered by the All-American Canal from the Colorado River. Excellent crops of fruit, cotton, dates and lucerne are grown in this valley, where rain hardly ever falls.

Maize-picker

The Corn Belt in Illinois supplies huge quantities of grain to feed the U.S.A.'s pigs and cattle

Montego Bay, in the Caribbean, is a famous resort which is situated on the brilliant white sands of Jamaica's northern shore

●**Indiana** A Midwestern State (36,291 square miles; population 5,193,669) of the U.S.A., between the southern tip of Lake Michigan and the Ohio River. Its capital, Indianapolis, lies near the exact centre of the State, at the crossroads of several national highways. The beautiful Wabash River winds across Indiana's rich farmlands. Maize is the leading crop — Indiana lies in the maize belt — and millions of pigs are fattened on it. In the south, there are tobacco and wheat fields; in the north, cabbages, onions, melons and peppermint are grown. Tomatoes are so plentiful that they are canned for the national market. Indiana's mineral wealth includes coal and limestone: coal-seams underlie a considerable part of eastern and western Indiana; almost all of the limestone used for building purposes comes from quarries near Bloomington and Bedford. The 'Hoosier State' has a wide variety of industries, the most important being the steel works of Gary, Hammond and East Chicago along the southern shore of Lake Michigan. Motor-cars and parts, agricultural and electrical machinery and chemicals are produced by Indiana's many factories at Fort Wayne, South Bend, Evansville and Terre Haute.

When the French fur-trader La Salle explored the region in 1679, the Miami Indians were the most powerful tribe. They attacked the early settlers as they cleared the land. Indiana Territory was established in 1800; it included the area of several of the present Midwestern States. The Indian threat was removed with the defeat of Tecumseh at the Battle of Tippecanoe (1811). In 1816, Indiana was admitted to the Union as the 19th State, and many new settlers came after the railroads in the 1840s.

●**Indianapolis** The capital and largest city (population 742,613) of Indiana is a hub of Midwestern highways and railways. Stockyards, railway workshops, and hosiery mills are the main industries. Annual car races are held at the Indianapolis speedway.

●**Indians** The original inhabitants of the Americas retained this name even after it became known that Columbus had erred in his belief that he had discovered India. Racially, the American Indians are now regarded as Mongoloid. They are believed to have penetrated into America from Asia by way of the Bering Strait about 10,000 years ago at the end of the Ice Age, when sea levels were at least 200 feet lower than now. In North America and many parts of South America, the Indians retained a primitive way of life until the arrival of Europeans. In Central America and the highlands of South America, however, Spanish conquistadores of the early 16th century found highly civilised Indian communities (such as those of the Aztecs, Mayas and Incas). The total Indian population at that time was probably 45 million. Their number was sharply reduced by European penetration and colonisation. Only 500,000 are now left in North America, mostly on reservations. South America, where European settlement is concentrated in the coastal regions, still has 18 million pure Indians, inhabiting the Andean uplands and the remote rain forests of the Amazon Basin. They have widely intermarried with the European settlers in many Latin American countries.

●**Iowa** A Midwestern State (45,280 square miles; population 2,790,000) in the heart of the U.S. maize belt. It is washed by the Mississippi on the east and by the Missouri on the west. Near the centre lies the capital and largest city, Des Moines (241,115). More than 95 per cent of this fertile, rolling prairie is prosperous farmland, and Iowa has one-fourth of all the top-grade farmland of the United States. Maize fields extend from one end of the State to the other; and, where maize is not grown, there are oats, soya beans, hay, barley, wheat, flax-seed and rye. Iowa leads the nation in the number of pigs and poultry it raises. There, too, cattle herds from the western range are fattened before being sent to the slaughterhouse. Dairying is the speciality of north-eastern Iowa, where the land is not quite level enough for the growing of crops. The State's principal industry is the processing of farm products — meat-packing, canning, grain-milling (for corn syrup, starch, feed, breakfast cereals). Iowa also produces farm machinery — the first tractor was built in Charles City, Iowa, in 1906 — fountain pens, washing machines, and drainage tile for its farmlands. Coal is mined south of Des Moines; lead is still mined where it was discovered in the 18th century (now the city of Dubuque) by a Frenchman who came there to trade with the Iowa Indians, a Sioux tribe.

Iowa was visited by Marquette and Joliet in 1673, as they paddled down the Mississippi River in a canoe. It became United States territory as part of the Louisiana Purchase, in 1803. Settlers from New England displaced the Indians; they were later joined by immigrants from central and northern Europe. In 1846, Iowa became the 29th State of the Union.

●**Iroquois** A family of Indian tribes originally settled in the St Lawrence valley, around lakes Ontario and Erie, and along the Hudson River. They were agricultural and lived in communal dwellings (long houses). In 1570, Iroquois tribes formed the Five Nations — composed of the Mohawks, Oneidas, Onondagas, Cayugas, and Senecas — a warlike confederacy that offered stubborn resistance to European settlers, but was disbanded in 1783. Iroquois tribes still live in New York State and adjoining parts of Canada, in Ontario and Quebec.

●**Jamaica** Formerly a British colonial island (4,400 square miles; population 1,972,130) in the West Indies. Kingston, with a spacious land-locked harbour on the Caribbean, is the island's chief city and capital (population 123,000). Sugar cane has been Jamaica's principal crop for over 250 years; it is grown on large estates in the coastal lowlands and by small farmers in the hills. Bananas have also been an important export crop for over 80 years; most of them are grown in the mountainous interior and shipped from the north coast. Bauxite, the ore of aluminium, was discovered in Jamaica in 1942, and the island has become one of the leading raw-material suppliers of the United States and Canadian aluminium industry. Extensive processing plants and shipping facilities have been built in recent years. Jamaica's scenic north shore, between Port Antonio and Montego Bay, has become almost as popular a winter holiday land for American tourists as Florida's east coast.

The island was discovered by Columbus in 1494. Britain took it from Spain in 1655, and African slaves were introduced to work on the sugar estates. Slavery was abolished in 1833. Port Royal, one-time stronghold of buccaneers, was destroyed by an earthquake in 1692. Many severe hurricanes, including a disastrous one in 1951, have wrought havoc on the island. The English-speaking population is about 95 per cent coloured. Jamaica was the first of the British West Indian islands to achieve self-rule (1957); complete independence, within the British Commonwealth, followed in 1962.

●**Jamestown** An island in the James River, Virginia, where John Smith and his followers established the first permanent English settlement in America (1607). Jamestown was then a peninsula, but the river had made it into an island by the mid-19th century. The colonists suffered great hardships during their first winters in the New World. With the beginning of tobacco cultivation in 1612, however, the settlement grew and in 1619 it became the seat of the government of Virginia. Jamestown declined in importance after nearby Williamsburg became the capital of

In Kentucky, this tenant farmer's family sorts the crop of thin-bodied, yellow 'burley' tobacco

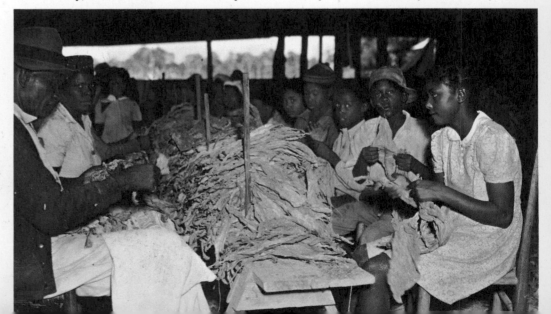

the colony in 1699. The few remains of the Jamestown buildings now form part of the Colonial National Historical Park.

Jersey City A city (population 260,545) on the New Jersey shore of the Hudson River, opposite Manhattan Island. Its railway terminals, warehouses and docks form part of the port of New York city.

Joshua tree A branched, tree-like yucca of the south-western United States. Its clustered flowers bloom spectacularly in March.

Kansas The 'Sunflower State' (82,264 square miles; population 2,249,071) lies almost in the exact centre of the United States, midway between the Mississippi River and the Rocky Mountains. Its rich, black prairie lands are drained by the Kansas and Arkansas Rivers, both flowing eastward to the Missouri or Mississippi Rivers. Water means everything to an agricultural area like Kansas, and the western part of the State receives barely enough rainfall to grow good crops, year after year; sometimes the rains fail to come, as they did in the 1930s, and then the winds blow the dry, ploughed soils high into the air. This is what caused the 'Dust Bowl'. Today, some of the driest land is not ploughed; it remains under grass. Kansas leads all States in growing wheat. Maize and oats are also major crops that are grown in the more humid north-east. Cattle are raised wherever the land is not cultivated, and Kansas City, Kansas, has the next largest stockyard and meat-packing plants to those in Chicago. Oil-wells dot southeastern Kansas, near the Ozark Mountains; petroleum-refining is as important an industry as flour-milling. Aeroplanes are built in Wichita, the largest city (282,989 inhabitants). Topeka (136,407) is the State capital. Kansas City (169,978) is smaller than its namesake across the State line in Missouri, but its factories, stockyard and railway shops occupy every square foot of the Kaw (Kansas River) Valley where it joins the Mississippi.

When the first Spaniards ventured into this part of the country, Kansas was inhabited by various Indian tribes. It became one of the United States as part of the Louisiana Purchase (1803). In 1861, in the midst of the Civil War, Kansas was admitted to the Union as the 34th State. More people arrived after 1862, when land was given away under the Homestead Act; and then again in the 1870s, when the cattle boom brought the cowboy and the dusty cow-town to the Kansas plains.

Kansas City Separated only by a State line, both Kansas City (Missouri) and Kansas City (Kansas) lie on the right bank of the Missouri River. Both are the second-largest cities of their respective States, and they had a joint population of over 1 million in 1970. Kansas City, Mo., is a leading marketing centre for agricultural products (grain, hay, seeds, livestock, poultry). It is an important railway and airline centre and has a number of industrial plants. The stockyards and meat-packing plants are on the Kansas side of the line. There, too, are oil refineries and railway workshops. The 1951 flood of the Kansas River (which enters the Missouri there) caused considerable damage to the low-lying sections of the twin cities. Kansas City is located near the geographical centre of the United States, hence its importance as a traffic hub.

Kentucky The 'Bluegrass State' (40,395 square miles; population 3,219,311) of the U.S.A. owes its nickname to the Bluegrass Region, the richest farming and livestock area in the State, famous for its thoroughbred racehorses. The grass on which the horses and cattle thrive is not actually blue, but its seeds turn blue as they ripen. The lime in the

The Hollywood Freeway – a typically up-to-date U.S. highway at Los Angeles

soils and in the grass gives the stock strong bones and tendons. The region is also noted for its distilleries, which are located there because of the special quality of the water. There also are Frankfort, the capital (20,054), and three of the State's largest cities — Louisville, where the Kentucky Derby is run every year; Lexington, a horse and tobacco market; and Covington. Kentucky has a large rural population. Tobacco, especially burley tobacco, is the chief crop, although maize, hay and pasture grasses occupy a larger area. Next to the Bluegrass Region, the Penny-royal plateau rates as a fertile farming region. There, too, is Mammoth Cave, a major attraction for those who like to explore miles of caverns and see fish without eyes in underground streams. Eastern Kentucky, where the Cumberland Plateau (the western part of the Appalachian Mountains) runs across the State, contains densely forested countryside, with hemlock, chestnut and oak. There are lumber camps throughout this region, and the mountain streams are often choked with logs on their way to the big sawmills. Kentucky is also an important mining State; it produces much coal near the West Virginia line and also in the west, between the Ohio and the Tennessee. Oil and gas wells are visible on many a hillside, and iron is mined near the city of Ashland. The Ohio River, which runs along Kentucky's northern border for hundreds of miles, is a busy waterway for barges carrying coal, lumber and other products needed by the State's industries.

The first European settlers entered Kentucky from the east through Cumberland Gap, following the Wilderness Road. Daniel Boone first explored the land in 1767, and founded Boonesboro in 1775. In 1792, Kentucky became the 15th State of the Union. Both Abraham Lincoln and Jefferson Davis were born there. In recent years, Kentucky's farms and industries (including an atomic plant near Paducah) have benefited from the cheap power made available by the Tennessee Valley Authority.

Key West The southernmost city of the United States, on the last of the Florida Keys — a chain of coral islets curving around the tip of the Florida peninsula. Key West is less than 100 miles from Havana, Cuba, across the Straits of Florida. It is linked to the mainland by a 120-mile-long causeway. Sponges and giant turtles are caught there. A naval station is situated at Key West. Sports fishing in the nearby Gulf Stream is a popular pastime. The city has a population of 27,563.

Labrador A large peninsula of north-eastern Canada, on the Atlantic Ocean. Its eastern half forms part of the province of Newfoundland. Its rocky, barren coast is almost uninhabited, except

for a few cod-fishing and lumbering settlements. Huge iron ore deposits along the Quebec border are worked in the Knob Lake area (Burnt Creek) and shipped by rail to Seven Islands, a seaport on the Gulf of St Lawrence.

The Labrador Current is a cold ocean current that sweeps southward from Greenland along the coast of Labrador, meeting the Gulf Stream off the Grand Banks. The Labrador Current carries icebergs into the shipping lanes between Europe and North America.

Long Island A 120-mile-long island extending generally eastward from the mouth of the Hudson River, parallel to the New York and Connecticut shore, from which it is separated by Long Island Sound. It forms part of New York State; two of New York City's boroughs — Brooklyn and Queens — occupy the western end of Long Island,

In August, the plains of Kansas, central U.S.A., are golden with ripe wheat

Mossy cypresses in a Louisiana Gulf Coast creek

facing Manhattan and Upper New York Bay. Its south shore, facing the ocean, is fronted by a long, narrow barrier beach on which a string of sea-side resorts has been developed: Coney Island, the Rockaways and Jones Beach are among the beaches catering for millions of New Yorkers. Much of central Long Island has become a residential extension of New York City in recent years. Eastern Long Island still raises potatoes, vegetables and poultry for the city market. New York City's two major airports — La Guardia and Kennedy (New York International) — have been reclaimed from tidewater along the shores of Long Island.

● **loon, red-throated** This skilful swimming and diving bird is not uncommon on the larger lakes and sea coasts of the United States. Its eerie call resembles wild, almost maniacal laughter.

● **Los Angeles** This booming metropolis of southern California is now the second-largest city (1940 population 1,500,000; 1920 population 577,000) in the United States, with a thriving man-made harbour on the Pacific Ocean. The 1969 population, including Long Beach was 7,032,000. Founded by Spanish missionaries in 1781, Los Angeles owes its meteoric rise to the discovery of oil in the 1890s, the growth of the film industry at Hollywood in the 20th century, and the growing importance of the aircraft industry since 1940, which came to the region because of its all-the-year-round sunny and mild weather. Additional industries drawn to this sprawling urban centre are: steel-milling, oil-refining, manufacturing of rubber goods, and food processing, especially citrus fruits, grown in the Los Angeles basin. Los Angeles is the world's most car-dominated city; limited-access highways lead to the outlying communities, which extend 30 miles inland from the shore and 50 miles in a north-south direction. There is one car, on the average, per three inhabitants. With a rainfall of only 15 inches per year (mostly in the winter months), Los Angeles has had to look for its water supply to the distant Sierra Nevada mountains and the Colorado River, and hundreds of miles of aqueducts have been built to meet the growing needs of the 7 million people in the metropolitan area.

● **Louisiana** A Gulf Coast State (48,523 square miles; population 3,643,180) of the U.S.A., straddling the delta of the Mississippi River. For 600 miles the Mississippi winds its way along Louisiana's border and then through the State, carrying

alluvium which is deposited especially where the river meets the sea; in consequence, the marshy mouth, with its many channels, reaches far into the Gulf of Mexico and extends the land area by 200 feet each year. The Bird's-Foot delta and the low coastal swampland are a jungle of reeds and clumps of cypress and cedar trees, interlaced with vines; muskrats, alligators, bullfrogs, and long-legged birds (this is the 'Pelican State') inhabit the creeks and bayous (arms of the river where the water scarcely flows). Parts of southern Louisiana and the Mississippi flood plain lie below sea level. In order to protect the fields and towns, hundreds of miles of high banks, or levees, have been built to contain the streams within their banks. The warm, subtropical climate, with its long growing season, renders Louisiana almost all the sugar cane grown in the United States, and it ranks second (after Texas) for rice. Cotton, the chief crop for the past 150 years, grows mostly in the northern, higher part of the State. The chief industries are lumbering and paper-milling, sugar-refining, and the milling of rice and cotton. Oil is found along the Gulf coast and in north-western Louisiana, bordering on Texas; also, more recently, in the shallow waters of the Gulf of Mexico. Natural gas from Louisiana is piped to homes and factories all over the eastern half of the United States, and salt and sulphur are the raw materials for the growing chemical industry. Baton Rouge (173,560) is the State capital, and New Orleans is the largest city, with an old French charm all its own. Both are on the Mississippi and can be reached by ocean-going ships. New Orleans is perhaps the busiest seaport on the Gulf Coast (even though it is more than 100 miles from the sea); it trades with the countries of South America and the Caribbean, importing bananas; Shreveport and Lake Charles thrive on the petroleum industry.

Louisiana was first settled by the French; hence its French name (after King Louis XIV), the French names given to many of its streams, towns and lagoons, and the Creole (or 'Cajun') language of the descendants of the French Acadian (and Spanish) settlers. It was sold to the United States by Napoleon in 1803 (Louisiana Purchase), and became the 18th State in 1812.

● **Louisville** Largest city (population 819,057) of Kentucky, on the left bank of the Ohio River. It is the centre of the State's tobacco industry, and its large distilleries produce most of the whisky (bourbon) made in the United States. The surrounding Bluegrass country is a prosperous farming area, noted for its tobacco, grain and horses. The Kentucky Derby, the most famous horse race in the U.S.A., is run every year at Churchill Downs race-track. Louisville was founded in 1773 and was named in honour of Louis XVI, King of France.

● **Lower California** (in Spanish, *Baja California*). An 800-mile-long peninsula of north-western Mexico, jutting south from the United States border and separating the Gulf of California from the Pacific Ocean. It is about 60—120 miles wide and the land is mountainous, dry and almost deserted, except for several mining camps (silver, lead, gold, copper) and fishing villages (shark, seal and pearl fisheries). Mexicali, situated in an irrigated fruit and cotton-growing district adjoining the United States border, is the largest city (population 390,400).

● **Mackenzie** In north-western Canada, this river flows more than 1,100 miles from Great Slave Lake to the Arctic Ocean, east of the Alaska border. Mackenzie is also the name of a large district in Canada's North-West Territories. The river is navigable from June to October, and a steamer service is maintained by the Hudson's Bay Company. The Mackenzie valley is rich in valuable oil and radioactive mineral deposits that are just beginning to be exploited. The river is named after Sir Alexander Mackenzie, who, in 1789, found its

wide delta on the Arctic Ocean while looking for the North-West Passage. The Mackenzie actually rises in the Rocky Mountains as the Athabaska, flows into Lake Athabaska, leaves as Slave River and continues to the Great Slave Lake, after which it becomes the Mackenzie (which has a total length of 2,350 miles).

● **mackerel** This important foodfish of the Northern Hemisphere travels in huge schools, and is therefore easily caught in large numbers. It is approximately one foot long and weighs about one pound. A peculiar fact about the adult Atlantic mackerel is that it must be constantly on the move to keep enough water passing over its gills. Related fish providing food include the tunny and the bonito.

● **magnolia** A handsome tree, native to the southeastern United States and eastern Asia, and now used extensively for ornament. Its large, showy flowers are pink or white.

● **mahogany** A tropical American tree, largely confined to the West Indies and the Amazon Basin. Its valuable reddish-brown hardwood is capable of taking a high polish, and is therefore used for furniture and cabinet-work.

● **Maine** The largest of the New England States (33,215 square miles; population 993,663), in the extreme north-eastern corner of the United States. It has a long and rocky sea coast, with many bays and inlets and a fringe of wooded islands. Many people go to Maine for their holidays. Most of the State is still covered by dense forests of white pine, spruce, balsam fir, hemlock, birch and maple; and scattered over the rugged land are hundreds of lakes, where fishing and canoeing are favourite pastimes. There are no very high mountains, but Mount Katahdin (5,268 feet) is well worth the climb; it lies at the northern end of the Appalachian Trail, which extends across all of the eastern States from as far south as Georgia. Lumbering is the big industry of the 'Pine Tree State'. Logs are floated down its many rivers to the factories where they are made into pulp and paper, and also into a variety of wood products. Aroostook County in the north (along the Canadian border) is famous for its potatoes; more of them are raised there than in any other State, except Idaho. Apples, vegetables, and great quantities of blueberries, are also grown in southern Maine; but, in general, farming is difficult, because the soils are thin and the growing season short. Fishing, on the other hand, is a favourite occupation along the entire coast. Portland, the largest city (92,593 people), is a fishing port. So is Eastport, where the huge catch of herring is canned, and Rockport, where lobster is put on ice and shipped out. Cod, mackerel, haddock, and many other fishes, are also hauled in. Maine's inland towns are small; their paper and textile mills were located to take advantage of water power from the State's swift streams. Augusta (59,864 people) is the capital city.

Maine was settled in 1623 by English colonists and French missionaries. From 1652 to 1820, it was part of Massachusetts, but was then admitted to the Union as the 23rd State.

● **Manitoba** A province (251,000 square miles; population 912,000) of west-central Canada, and numbered among the Prairie Provinces. In southern Manitoba, wheat, barley, oats and potatoes are the principal crops. In the north and east, there are forests and numerous glacial lakes, including large Lake Winnipeg. There, too, are important copper, gold, zinc and nickel deposits. Fur-trapping and lumbering are carried on in the sparsely populated northern part of the province. Winnipeg, the capital and one of Canada's larger cities, is the leading grain market of the Prairie

Provinces and an important route centre. A railway runs to Churchill, a grain port on Hudson Bay.

British explorers visited the area in the 17th century. For two centuries, the Hudson's Bay Company, a fur-trapping and trading organisation, held title to all the land draining into Hudson Bay, though Scottish settlers arrived in the area in 1812. In 1870, Manitoba became a province of the new Dominion of Canada. The Nelson River project doubled Manitoba's electric power capacity by 1971, and has greatly helped industrial development.

● **Maritime Provinces** Name given to Canada's three eastern provinces (New Brunswick, Nova Scotia, Prince Edward Island) bordering on the Atlantic Ocean.

● **Maryland** An East Coast State (10,577 square miles; population 3,922,399) of the U.S.A., cut in two by Chesapeake Bay. Since 1952, Maryland's Eastern Shore (Kent Island), by the Delmarva Peninsula, has been linked with the Western Shore, near Annapolis, by an impressive highway bridge. This makes it easier to ship the eastern region's fruit and vegetable crop to Baltimore's canneries. The southern border of Maryland is formed by the Potomac. Between the Mason-Dixon line (the Pennsylvania border) and the Potomac, Western Maryland is a narrow strip, less than 10 miles wide near the city of Cumberland. There, coal-mining is the main activity. Southern Maryland is primarily a tobacco-growing region, as it has been for some 300 years. Poultry-raising (especially broilers) is a speciality on the Eastern Shore, and dairying is important because two large cities, Baltimore and Washington, D.C., must be supplied with milk. Chesapeake Bay, the largest ocean inlet in the United States, is famous for its oysters, crabs and clams. Oysters dredged from its muddy bottom are eaten all over the country. Ocean steamers sail up the bay to Baltimore, the nation's 11th-largest city (with a population of 2,070,670) where piers and docks, flour mills and coal-storage dumps line the shores of the Patapsco River. At Sparrows Point, on tidewater just below Baltimore, lies one of the world's largest steel plants.

The manufacturing of men's clothing, the refining of sugar and of petroleum, and the building of aeroplanes, are among the many industries of the Baltimore area. Cumberland produces rayon, and Hagerstown (in the Great Valley) is known for its pipe-organs and aeroplane engines. Annapolis (32,000), the home of the U.S. Naval Academy, is the capital of Maryland. Ocean City is a seaside resort on the Atlantic shore of the Delmarva Peninsula. Tourism is one of the state's largest industries.

Maryland was inhabited by Algonquin Indians when the Europeans arrived after 1600. It became a royal province in 1688, and was among the 13 original States, being the 7th to ratify the Constitution (in 1788).

● **Massachusetts** A New England State (8,257 square miles; population 5,689,170) of the U.S.A., on whose shores the Pilgrim Fathers landed from the *Mayflower* in 1620. Plymouth Rock, where they stepped off the *Mayflower* and founded the first settlement, lies on a bay sheltered by the Cape Cod Peninsula. Eastern Massachusetts is dominated by Boston, the State capital and largest city in New England, with a population of 2,753,700 in 1970, and by the ring of manufacturing cities surrounding that metropolis. The richest farmland lies in the valley of the Connecticut River, which crosses the centre of the State from north to south. Hay, the feed for dairy cows, is the leading crop; maize, potatoes and onions are raised; and many fields are planted with tobacco, the mature leaf being used for cigar wrappers. Cape Cod is noted for its extensive cranberry bogs. Boston is the leading fishing port in the country, and Gloucester is also an important centre; the catch includes cod, haddock, halibut, mackerel, shad, lobsters and other shellfish. Massachusetts is a leading manufacturing State; it has a long tradition of skilled workmanship. The principal goods produced in the State are woollens and worsteds, cotton textiles shoes and boots, watches and electrical equipment, and fine paper. Worcester is the second-largest city, Springfield (in the Connecticut valley) produces machinery and books, and Cambridge is a university town (Harvard) across the Charles River from Boston.

The early Puritans settled along the shore of Massachusetts Bay; Boston was founded in 1630. In the 18th century, the colony became the centre of resistance to British rule; much of the War of Independence was fought on Massachusetts soil (battles of Bunker Hill, Concord, Lexington).

● **Maya** The most civilised of the Indian nations which existed before the arrival of Columbus. Its empire, which covered south-east Mexico, Guatemala and El Salvador, flourished from the 10th to the 12th century. Mayan priests developed a system of hieroglyphics, and a complicated calendar, based on astronomical observations, which was in advance of the European calendar in use at that time. Their ruined cities contain pyramids and palaces displaying artistic designs and elaborate ornamentation. Some of the most famous Mayan sites are Chichén Itzá, Uxmal, Uaxactun and Tikal in the Yucatán Peninsula, between the Caribbean Sea and the Gulf of Mexico.

● **Mayflower** The ship used by the Pilgrim Fathers in 1620 to cross the Atlantic and establish the first settlement in New England. The Mayflower Com-

The French West Indian island of Martinique

pact, signed before their landing, was the first written American constitution. A replica of the *Mayflower* crossed the Atlantic in 1957.

● **Memphis** The largest city (population 767,050) of Tennessee, on the high bluffs overlooking the Mississippi River. An important market for cotton, lumber and livestock (notably mules), Memphis is served by several railways and by river barges. The city has two universities, one founded in 1794.

● **Mérida** A Mexican city (population 253,800) on the Yucatán Peninsula, with a port named Progreso on the Gulf of Mexico. It exports sisal and chicle, chiefly to the United States. Tourists come to Mérida to visit the impressive Mayan ruins of Chichén Itzá and Uxmal. The city was founded in 1542 on the site of a Mayan town.

● **Mexico** A Latin American republic (760,000 square miles; population 48,313,438) occupying the southern part of North America, between the Pacific Ocean and the Gulf of Mexico. The Rio Grande (known in Mexico as *Rio Bravo del Norte*) forms the eastern part of the U.S.-Mexican border, and thus divides the English-speaking part of the Western Hemisphere from the Spanish- (and Portuguese-) speaking part. Most of Mexico is mountainous; two ranges run the length of the country, leaving but little room for coastal lowlands except in the south, where the flat limestone platform of the Yucatán Peninsula juts out into the sea. At the heart of the country, between the two ranges of the Sierra Madre, lies the semi-arid central plateau (3,000 to 7,500 feet above sea level), broken up by basins, short mountain chains, and several deeply entrenched valleys. Mexico City, the nation's capital; Puebla, the centre of the cotton textile industry; and many other densely populated districts lie in the central upland. Mexico's highest summits (Citlaltépetl, 18,701 feet; Popocatépetl, 17,887 feet) are snow-covered volcanoes which have been active in historic times.

Only about 5 per cent of the land is under cultivation because of scanty rainfall. More irrigation is needed to feed the country's population, which keeps growing at a rate of 800,000 per year. Maize is the principal crop, but yields are low; the output of wheat and other grains is rising, but the nation is still obliged to import much of its food. Cotton, a leading crop in the irrigated districts, is grown for export as well as for the country's own textile industry. Coffee, sugar cane and rice are the chief products of the tropical lowlands and Piedmont areas. Sisal, the fibre from which rope is made, is exported from Mérida, the chief centre of Yucatán, as is chicle, the raw material for chewing-gum, the sap from the sapotil tree (*Acturus sapota*)

Mexico's chief source of wealth lies underground.

This Atlantic Coast lighthouse in Maine, U.S.A., warns shipping to steer clear of the rocky shore

The country has yielded precious metals since the days before Columbus. Today, Mexico ranks high among the producers of silver, lead, zinc, copper, antimony and sulphur. It produces enough iron for a domestic steel industry, located at Monterrey. The Gulf Coast is studded with oil and natural gas wells, whose output is refined at Tampico. Mining is Mexico's main industry, yet 97 per cent of the invested capital is from abroad.

Tourism is the chief earner of foreign currency. Millions of tourists visit Mexico from 'north of the border', attracted by its mild highland climate, its volcanoes and its deserts, but above all by the strange blend of Spanish and Indian civilisations reflecting a long history of conquest and colonisation. Three great cultures thrived in Mexico before Columbus discovered America. The Toltecs, and later the Aztecs, occupied the central uplands, while the Mayas, coming from Guatemala, had established themselves in Yucatán. The first Spaniards landed on Mexican soil in 1517; in 1519, Hernando Cortez was sent from Cuba to explore the interior. Within two years, he occupied the Aztec capital, Tenochtitlán, subdued the Indians and proclaimed Spanish rule over the so-called New Spain. Interested only in the country's precious metals, the Spanish viceroys neglected the Indian population and the growing number of landless *mestizos* (of Spanish and Indian blood). Finally, after eleven years of rebellion, Mexico achieved its independence in 1821. Texas was lost to the United States in 1836, and claims to California, New Mexico and Arizona were surrendered after the disastrous Mexican War of 1846—48. For three years, 1864—67, Maximilian, a brother of the Emperor of Austria, ruled Mexico with the help of French troops sent by Napoleon III. The dictatorship of General Porfirio Díaz (1876—1911) was terminated by a revolution (1911—1921), during which a liberal constitution was put into effect in 1917. Great strides have been made in recent years towards raising the level of living of the Mexican peasants, many of whom

Opuntia (prickly pear)

are still illiterate. Spanish is the official language, but 33 Indian languages are still in use. Because of the country's poverty, thousands of Mexicans have crossed the U.S. border, legally or illegally, in search of work. Mexico is divided into 29 States, 2 territories, and the Federal District in which Mexico City is located.

● **Mexico City** is the capital and largest city (population 7,006,000) of Mexico, built on the drained Lake Texcoco at an elevation of 7,800 feet, amidst the barren mountain ranges of the Sierra Madre. It is the political, cultural and economic hub of the country. Major railways and highways radiate from Mexico City, modern industrial plants have risen in the suburbs, and a newly-completed university 'city' stands at the head of many educational institutions. Tourists admire the city's attractive wide avenues, its old churches (the cathedral was begun in the 1570s and finished in 1667) and impressive public buildings, including the National Palace. It is probably the oldest city on the continent. Before the arrival of the Spaniards in 1519, it was the capital of the Aztecs, who may

The library of the University of Mexico, in Mexico City, is covered with mosaics in Aztec design

have numbered 300,000. Its name then was Tenochtitlán. Cortez, the Spanish conqueror, levelled the Aztec city, built the first Christian church on American soil (1525), and laid out the new town in accordance with Spanish custom — a compact grid of streets focused on a spacious central square. Alongside the very old, Mexico City boasts skyscrapers, offices, apartment buildings of ultra-modern design, and public buildings decorated with murals by contemporary artists. The 1968 Olympic Games were held here.

● **Mexico, Gulf of** An arm of the Atlantic Ocean, off the southern United States and eastern Mexico. It connects with the Atlantic through the Straits of Florida, and with the Caribbean Sea via the Yucatán Channel, between Cuba and the Yucatán Peninsula of Mexico. It covers an area of about 700,000 square miles and reaches a depth of 12,500 feet. The Mississippi and the Rio Grande empty into the Gulf of Mexico. The shallow floor of the sea, off Louisiana and Texas, harbours extensive deposits of petroleum.

● **Miami** A leading winter resort on the east coast of Florida. It is connected by several causeways across Biscayne Bay with Miami Beach (1,267,792 people), where a row of luxury hotels fronts the Atlantic Ocean. Miami is one of the most rapidly-growing cities in the U.S.A., the city owing its prosperity to a long holiday season, and to its location at the point of departure for air travel to the Caribbean and Latin America.

● **Michigan** This Midwestern State (58,216 square miles; population 8,875,083) of the U.S.A. is almost completely surrounded by water. Four of the Great Lakes wash its shores, and two of them, Lake Michigan and Lake Huron, cut the State in two by linking arms at the Straits of Mackinac. The Upper Peninsula, in the north, is wild and rugged and thickly forested. It has many attractions for tourists and was the scene for Longfellow's 'Song of Hiawatha'. Iron ore is mined here, and is shipped to the steel mills from ports on Lake Superior through the 'Soo' canal. More freight moves through the 'Soo' than through any other canal in the world. The Upper Peninsula also has high-grade copper deposits on the Keweenaw Peninsula.

The main part of Michigan, called the Lower Peninsula, is connected with the Upper Peninsula by a 5-mile-long highway bridge across the Straits of Mackinac. This bridge will bring new industries

to the less developed north country. Lower Michigan has many farm and industrial activities. First, there is general farming (hay, maize, oats, sugar beets), horticulture (potatoes, cucumbers, onions, peppermint), and, along the southern shore of Lake Michigan, fruit-growing (apples, grapes, cherries, pears, peaches, strawberries). Dairying is an important occupation because the State's many cities need a lot of milk, butter and cheese. Mining is also important. Salt is pumped up from deep pools of brine, as it is the raw material for a large chemical industry. Both limestone and gypsum are quarried, and transported cheaply by water to the factories. By far the leading activity in Michigan, however, is the production of motor-cars and trucks in some 400 factories located in Detroit, the nation's 5th city, and in the ring of manufacturing centres (Dearborn, Highland Park, Flint, Pontiac, Lansing, etc.) around it. Grand Rapids is known for its fine furniture, Kalamazoo for paper, Battle Creek for cereal foods, and Fremont is the world's largest producer of baby foods. Lansing is the State capital, with 373,474 inhabitants.

The Sault Sainte Marie and Mackinac areas were explored by Frenchmen as early as 1618. Trading posts were established after 1668, including Fort Pontchartrain (1701) where Detroit now stands. Ceded to Britain at the end of the French and Indian War, the Lower Peninsula was organised as a separate United States Territory in 1805. Enlarged to include the Upper Peninsula, Michigan became the 26th State of the Union in 1837.

● **Michigan, Lake** The third-largest (22,400 square miles) of the Great Lakes and the only one entirely within the United States. It is 300 miles long, more than 900 feet deep, and lies at an elevation of 572 feet above sea level. The north end of the lake is linked with Lake Huron by the Straits of Mackinac, crossed by a long highway bridge. From Chicago, near the lake's southern end, the Illinois Waterway connects the Great Lakes with the Mississippi River and the Gulf of Mexico. Iron ore from the Lake Superior district is unloaded at Gary (south-east of Chicago), where huge steel mills line the lakeshore. Lake Michigan was discovered by the French in 1634.

● **Milwaukee** The largest city (population 1,403,688) of Wisconsin, on the west shore of Lake Michigan. It is best known for its breweries, but also has meat-packing plants, heavy metalworks, and factories making Diesel engines, outboard motors, motor-car parts and leather goods. Despite the city's proximity to Chicago, Milwaukee has preserved its individual character and commercial importance. The forefathers of its large German population came to the United States after 1848.

● **Minneapolis** The largest city (population 1,813,647) of Minnesota, on the upper Mississippi River, forming — with neighbouring St Paul — an urban area known as the Twin Cities. Flour-milling and processing of dairy products are the chief industries. The city was settled about 1847 at a point below the 20-foot-high Falls of St Anthony, where the Mississippi becomes navigable. From there, river boats can travel without obstacle to New Orleans and the Gulf of Mexico. Many people of Scandinavian origin live in Minneapolis.

● **Minnesota** An upper Midwestern State (84,068 square miles; population 3,805,069) of the U.S.A., bordering on Canada and on Lake Superior. It is a land of more than 10,000 lakes. In the north, the lakes are almost hidden by evergreen forests. Lake of the Woods reaches up into Canada, and in its vicinity lies a region which is a fishing and canoeing paradise. One of Minnesota's lakes is the source of the Mississippi. At Minneapolis, the Falls of St Anthony mark the point where boats begin their trip down the Mississippi to the Gulf of Mexico; there, too, are the falls of the Minnehaha, the 'laughing water' of the Sioux Indians.

Minnesota is a prosperous farm State. It grows maize, oats, barley, rye, flax, hay, potatoes and sugar beets. It produces more butter than any other State and almost as much cheese as Wisconsin. It raises cattle and pigs that find their way to the slaughterhouses and packing plants of St Paul. Minnesota's iron mines — the biggest and deepest ones are in the Mesabi Range — have kept America's steel mills in production for over 70 years. Now that these valuable deposits are nearing exhaustion, the State's large resources of low-grade ore, called taconite, are becoming increasingly important. The ore is shipped from Duluth, a busy port at the western end of Lake Superior, to the steel centres of Indiana, Ohio and Pennsylvania. On their return trip, the ore-carriers bring coal for Duluth's own steel industry. There western wheat is stored during the winter, and shipped east during the 'open season' on the Great Lakes. Minneapolis is the State's major flour-milling centre and grain market; St Paul, its twin city, is the State capital.

Explored by French fur-traders and missionaries in the 17th century, the area was settled about 1820, when steamboats reached Fort Snelling (on the site of present-day Minneapolis). It became a Territory in 1849, and the 32nd State of the Union in 1858. Lumbering, the main activity of those early days, is described in the stories of the legendary Paul Bunyan.

● **Mississippi** A Southern State (47,716 square miles; population 2,216,912) of the U.S.A. on the lower Mississippi River and on the Gulf of Mexico. Cotton is the chief crop. It is grown in the wide, fertile lowland of the Yazoo basin, between the Mississippi and its tributary, the Tallahatchie. The annual crop is third only to that of Texas and California, and much of the cotton is of the valuable long-staple variety. Other crops are maize, sweet potatoes, rice, pecans, tung-nuts and sugar cane. Livestock is raised on some of the eroded cotton and maize lands. Lumbering is the chief industry; more than half of the State is covered with yellow pine and hardwood forests. These provide the raw material for a rapidly growing pulp and paper industry. The state's mineral production consists almost entirely of oil and natural gas. Jackson, the largest city and State capital, with 154,000 inhabitants, lies on the Pearl River. Vicksburg, of Civil War fame, lies on a bluff overlooking the winding Mississippi; the

nearby farmlands are protected by levees from the river's frequent floods. The people of the 'Magnolia State' are poor; many of them are illiterate share-croppers, who do not possess any land of their own, but pay the rent as tenant farmers with part of their crop. Negroes make up almost one-half of the total population of Mississippi; but, since World War II, many of them have moved to the North. Industrialisation is growing apace, including paper, food and textiles.

Mississippi was settled in 1699 by the French. It was organised as a Territory in 1798, and was admitted to the Union in 1817 as the 20th State.

● **Mississippi River** The greatest river of the United States, draining all of the country's interior lowlands between the Appalachians and the Rocky Mountains. Together with the Missouri, its principal tributary, it ranks as the world's third-longest river (3,892 miles), exceeded in length only by the Nile and the Amazon. Its drainage basin extends across two-fifths of the United States, and covers all or part of 31 States. The Mississippi rises in Minnesota, not far from the Canadian border; it flows generally south to the Gulf of Mexico, 100 miles below New Orleans. The length of the Mississippi proper is 2,350 miles. It is navigable below Minneapolis for flat-bottomed river boats, and ocean-going ships can reach Baton Rouge, La., almost 200 miles upstream from its mouth. The 'Father of Waters' carries tremendous quantities of silt downstream, and dumps these sediments where it reaches the sea, constantly building up its delta. Below Cairo, Ill. (where it receives the Ohio), the Mississippi flows in a wide flood plain, forming numerous loops and bends, splitting up into arms, and shifting its channel from time to time. In the lower course, the river has built up its banks above the surrounding countryside. Floods are frequent, and when the river bursts its banks vast areas of fertile cropland are inundated. In recent decades, the Corps of Engineers of the U.S. Army has been responsible for the control of floods in the Mississippi river system. Hundreds of miles of levees have been built to contain the river within its channel; flood-ways and reservoirs also regulate the course of the stream. Although the days of the paddle-driven steamboat and booming river ports are gone, and the railways have claimed much of the traffic formerly carried by the Mississippi, bulky raw materials — such as coal, steel, sand, cement and aluminium ores — are still shipped from New Orleans to Pittsburgh, and from the Great Lakes (via the Illinois Waterway) to the Gulf.

De Soto discovered the Mississippi in 1541—42. La Salle claimed the whole drainage area for France in 1682. With the Louisiana Purchase

(1803), the Mississippi became an all-American river and subsequently played an important part in the opening up of the West.

● **Missouri** A Midwestern State (69,686 square miles; population 4,677,399) where the 'Big Muddy' (Missouri River) meets the 'Father of Waters' (Mississippi). The northern part of the State lies in the vast interior lowland of the United States. This is a rich farmland where maize dominates. The lesser crops include winter wheat, oats, hay, soya beans and tobacco. Cotton is grown in the extreme south-east, along the bottom lands of the Mississippi River. The southern third of the State is hilly and forested; it forms part of the Ozarks, an isolated and backward region. Missouri is the leading United States producer of lead; this mineral occurs in the St Francis Mountains (the highest section of the Ozarks), where zinc, iron and barite are also mined. Joplin, in south-western Missouri, is an important lead and zinc-processing centre. Cattle, pigs and poultry are raised throughout the State, but the best-known animal is the Missouri mule, in demand all over the country. Missouri's geographical location, near the centre of the United States and on two major navigable rivers, makes it an important focus of transportation and trade. St Louis, with over 2.3 million inhabitants, and Kansas City, with more than 1 million people, at opposite ends of the State, have large railway yards, major airports and many factories. Meat-packing, flour-milling and food-processing, the manufacturing of shoes, chemicals, textiles and farm machinery, are the chief industries. One-third of the State's population lives in the two main centres; St Joseph, Springfield and Independence are smaller cities. Jefferson City (28,000), on the Missouri, is the capital.

The region was first settled by fur-traders in 1735, and they, in 1764, established St Louis as a strategic trading post, near the junction of the two great rivers. Missouri came to the United States in 1803, as part of the Louisiana Purchase. The town of Independence became the outfitting point for pioneers going westward along the Santa Fé and California trails. Missouri was admitted to the Union in 1821 as the 24th State. Mark Twain, whose world-famous stories describe life along the Mississippi in the 19th century, was born in Hannibal, Missouri.

● **Missouri River** The chief tributary of the Mississippi, the Missouri rises in the Rocky Mountains of Montana, and flows 2,700 miles across the high plains and midwestern prairies before joining the 'Father of Waters' a few miles above St Louis. In its course across Montana and the Dakotas, the

Opencast mine in Minnesota's Mesabi Range. From here, iron ore is shipped to U.S. steel-producing centres in Indiana, Ohio and Pennsylvania

Sioux Indians lived and hunted buffalo on the Great Plains that are drained by the Missouri River

'Big Muddy' has been dammed to provide water for irrigation of the dry plains and to control spring floods farther downstream. Several additional dams have been projected as part of a basin-wide (500,000 square miles) development programme. The principal cities on the Missouri are Sioux City (Iowa), Omaha (Nebraska), and Kansas City (Kansas and Missouri). Lewis and Clark were the first American explorers to follow the Missouri upstream, in their search for a passage to the Pacific North-west during 1804—06.

● **Montana** The 'Mountain State' (147,138 square miles; population 694,409) of the U.S.A. is not actually mountainous throughout, for more than half of it lies in the High Plains. Except for isolated buttes and ridges, the traveller from the east sees nothing but level land until, suddenly, he stands face-to-face with the sheer wall of the Rocky Mountains. The Bitterroot Range forms the rugged boundary between Montana and Idaho. In the Lewis Range — 9,000 to 11,000 feet high — lies Glacier National Park, with some of the finest scenery in the United States. Snow-capped peaks rise high above the forested slopes; majestic glaciers move slowly down the U-shaped valleys they have carved out and emerald-green lakes fill the valley bottoms. These impressive mountains extend northward across the border into Canada. In central Montana, where the buffalo once roamed, are extensive ranches where cattle and sheep graze.

In the east, wheat is the main crop; barley and hay are also grown. In the irrigated districts along the upper Missouri (which rises in Montana) and Yellowstone Rivers, there are sugar beet, bean and potato fields. Cherries and apples are grown in the mountain valleys, notably by beautiful Flathead Lake. Montana's underground wealth is great; in the Butte area, copper, gold, silver, zinc and lead are found. The copper ore from deep mines under the city of Butte is smelted at Anaconda and refined at Great Falls, where hydro-electric power is generated on the Missouri River. Manganese, sapphires and phosphate are mined in the southwest. Extensive lignite deposits have been found in many places, and eastern Montana has a developing petroleum and natural gas industry. Lumbering is an important activity in the north-western ranges, where Douglas fir, lodgepole pine and spruce trees are logged. A new aluminium smelter uses the abundant water power in this part of the State. Helena (22,730) is the State capital; Billings and Missoula are food-processing centres. The largest town in Montana is Great Falls (60,091 inhabitants).

● **Monterrey** Mexico's third-largest city (population 830,300) and the country's leading steel-making centre. It lies on the main highway and railway from the U.S.A. (Texas) to Mexico City. Large silver, lead, gold and antimony mines are located in the area. Monterrey was founded in 1546.

● **Montreal** Largest city (metropolitan population 2,436,817) of Canada, in Quebec province, on an island in the St Lawrence River. One of the busiest seaports of North America and trans-shipment point for traffic on the Great Lakes, Montreal has miles of docks, warehouses and grain elevators. The Lachine Rapids, on the St Lawrence River immediately above the city, have been by-passed by the St Lawrence Seaway, which makes the Great Lakes accessible to ocean-going vessels. Montreal is the banking and insurance centre of Canada, and also its most rapidly growing industrial city. More than half the population is of French descent, and both English and French are the city's official languages. A magnificent view of Montreal Island and the St Lawrence is afforded from the top of Mount Royal, 900 feet above the city. This rocky hill was first sighted by the French navigator Jacques Cartier in 1535. A French fur-trading station was established in 1611, and Maisonneuve founded a mission in 1642. Britain occupied the settlement in 1760. The town is a great cultural centre, with several universities and colleges.

● **moose** The largest member of the deer family, standing six feet at the shoulder. A clumsy-looking animal, it has huge antlers and an odd mouth with an overhanging upper lip, well suited for feeding on foliage. The moose is found in the moist lowlands of Alaska and northern Canada.

● **motor-cars** The production of motor-cars plays an enormous part in American industry. In no other country does the car play quite so decisive a role in everyday life and in the national economy. The United States produces about 70 per cent of the world's motor-cars, and sells 95 per cent of its output in the domestic market. A major development since the Second World War has been the rapid development of the European motor-car industry in Britain, West Germany, France and Italy. These countries generally produce smaller cars, a large number of which are exported, even to the United States. The Soviet Union produces only a small percentage of the world's road vehicles, with trucks and buses outnumbering cars by four to one.

● **musk ox** This native of the American Arctic is not in reality an ox at all, but a relative of the chamois of Europe and the takin of Asia. Although this shaggy, robust beast appears clumsy, it is as agile as an antelope. The heavy chocolate-brown coat protects the musk ox against the Arctic cold. It is one of the few animals that will join forces against a common foe; by uniting in a circle, with the calves safely inside, musk oxen present an impregnable front to the enemy, such as wolf packs. The musk ox has no special musk glands, but there is a musky odour about the animal at mating time.

● **natural gas** This increasingly important fuel is found alone or in combination with petroleum. The United States accounts for 80 per cent of the world's output of natural gas, which is generally carried by pipeline to consuming centres. Other producers are the Soviet Union, Canada and Venezuela.

● **Nebraska** (77,227 square miles; population 1,483,791) is a State of the U.S.A. which extends across the Great Plains west of the Missouri River. The treeless prairie has a rich black soil, well suited to the growing of crops. Only the Sand Hills area has escaped the plough and here livestock is raised extensively. Few States grow more maize and wheat than Nebraska. Oats and barley, buckwheat and sorghum, all grow tall and golden in the hot summers of the plains. Sugar beets and

Today, the Mississippi River carries more freight than it did in the era of the steamboats

vegetables are raised in the irrigated districts along the Platte River, which crosses the State from west to east on its way to the Missouri. Meat-packing and flour-milling are the chief industries. Omaha is the largest city; its stockyards and grain elevators extend for miles along the railway tracks. The State capital is at Lincoln (145,092), and there are no other large cities.

The Pawnees, the Omahas and the Winnebago Indians hunted buffalo and antelope on the Nebraska plains before the Europeans came. Then pioneers in covered wagons followed Lewis and Clark westward along the Oregon Trail. In 1867, Nebraska became a State (the 37th), having given Negroes the right to vote. A tremendous land boom took place after 1867, when the Union Pacific Railroad was completed across the State.

Grain elevator

● **Nevada** The 'Silver State' (110,540 square miles; population 488,738) of the U.S.A. owes its nickname to the precious minerals it stores underground. When silver and gold were discovered at the Comstock Lodge, Virginia City, in 1859, a stampede of prospectors invaded this empty, arid land. Nevada lies wholly within the Great Basin; it has a very dry climate because the high Sierra Nevada range (along the California border) robs the clouds of their moisture. There are few rivers in Nevada, and most run dry after the short rainy season. They do not flow to the sea, but empty into shallow lakes from which the water quickly evaporates. The wide, desert-like valleys are covered with sage-brush, creosote brush and bunchgrass. Parallel mountain ranges, either bare or covered with dwarf trees, piñon or juniper, separate the valleys. The only way to use this arid land is to graze cattle and sheep. Hay, alfalfa, oats and sugar beets are grown in irrigated districts, chiefly as cattle-fodder.

Hundreds of mining camps are scattered over the State. In addition to silver and gold, there are copper, zinc, lead, tungsten, mercury, vanadium and many other mines. Reno, with 72,863 people, and Carson City (15,468), the capital, are not far from Lake Tahoe, which Nevada shares with California. The shores of this beautiful lake are lined with resorts. In southern Nevada, Las Vegas (125,787) with its gambling establishments provides a different kind of tourist attraction.

The Washoe and Shoshone Indians had the free run of this area until, almost overnight, small mining camps grew into boom towns. Many of these soon turned into ghost towns, but new gold-strikes brought on new booms. Nevada became the 36th State of the Union in 1864. Although its population has grown very rapidly since World War II, Nevada still has fewer people than any other State.

● **Newark** The largest city (population 1,856,556) in New Jersey, 9 miles west of New York's Manhattan Island. It is the centre of heavy industry for New York's metropolitan area. Harbour installations on Newark Bay form part of the Port of New York. Main highways and railways from New York City lead through Newark on their way west and south. Several insurance companies have their headquarters there. Newark Airport is one of three major air traffic centres in the metropolitan area.

● **New Brunswick** A province (28,354 square miles; population 616,788) of eastern Canada. New Brunswick is one of the Maritime Provinces on the Atlantic Ocean, and bordered, too, by the Bay of Fundy. Extensive forests cover most of New Brunswick, and much of the lumber can be floated down-river to the sawmills and paper mills. Sea fisheries are next in importance, and there are several canneries and fish-curing plants, especially at St John, the chief seaport. Fredericton (38,521), the provincial capital, is located in the agricultural valley of the St John River. There are substantial copper, lead, zinc, iron and manganese deposits in the province, as well as oil and natural gas near Moncton.

The coast of New Brunswick was visited by John Cabot in 1497. In the 17th century, the French established forts and trading posts in the region which, together with present-day Nova Scotia, they called Acadia. The area passed to Britain in 1713, and was settled by Scots, and by Americans from New York and New Jersey who remained loyal to the crown after the Revolutionary War. In 1867, the province became part of the new Dominion of Canada.

● **Newfoundland** Canada's easternmost province (156,185 square miles, including Labrador; population 517,000) on the Atlantic Ocean. It comprises the island of Newfoundland (43,000 square miles) off the Gulf of St Lawrence, and the barren mainland territory of Labrador. The island is hilly, densely forested, and drained by numerous fast-flowing streams. Fishing, paper milling and mining are the chief industries. Cod, salmon and herring are fished along the coast and on the Grand Banks, where fishing fleets of many nations meet during the cod season. Cod-liver oil is an important product of Newfoundland. Seals are taken mainly for their skins. Iron ore, mined at Bell Island, near the seaport and provincial capital of St John's, is shipped to steel mills at Sydney, Nova Scotia. Copper, lead and zinc are also mined. Gander (in Newfoundland) and Goose Bay (in Labrador) are both important calling points on transatlantic air routes.

Claimed in 1583 by Great Britain, after its discovery (1497) by John Cabot, Newfoundland is considered to be the oldest-founded colony in the Empire and enjoyed Dominion status for many years. In 1949, it voted for union with Canada, becoming its tenth province. It was in 1901 that Marconi heard the distant radio signals from England on Telegraph Hill.

● **New Hampshire** A New England State (9,304 square miles; population 737,681) of the U.S.A., with a narrow coastline and a short common boundary with Quebec; the Connecticut River

A lumberjack frees a log-jam on the Flathead River, in north-western Montana, U.S.A.

separates it from Vermont. The picturesque, tree-covered White Mountains dominate the State's scenery, the highest summits being named after the country's first Presidents; Mt Washington, 6,288 feet above sea level, is one of the highest points east of the Mississippi. Today, New Hampshire has become a favourite holiday land and skiing is popular in the White Mountains. The rough surface of the land, poor soil and short growing season have restricted agriculture to the valleys of the Connecticut and Merrimack Rivers. Hay is the chief crop, and it is used to feed dairy cows during the long winter months. Manufacturing is concentrated along the Merrimack River, where water power has been used for a long time. Chief products are boots and shoes, cottons, woollens and worsteds, paper, and wooden products. They are made in Manchester, the largest city (87,754 inhabitants), Nashua, Concord — the State capital — and Berlin. Portsmouth is a naval base.

The first English settlement dates from 1623. New Hampshire became a separate royal province in 1679, and was one of the 13 original States of the Union; it ratified the Constitution in 1788.

● **New Jersey** (7,836 square miles; population 7,168,164) has so many industries and so many people living in a small area that little room seems to be left for farming. Its north-eastern portion lies within the New York-New Jersey metropolitan

Virginia City, Nevada, is the mining town where the Comstock silver lode was discovered in 1859

Preparing to make maple sugar on a farm in New Hampshire

area, the largest gathering of people in the country. It also lies astride the main highway and railway routes along the East Coast. The New Jersey Turnpike leads from the Hudson River, opposite New York City, across the State to Delaware Bay. New Jersey's ocean front is fringed by long, narrow, sandy islands extending all the way from New York Bay to Cape May, at the State's southern tip. There are situated numerous beach resorts, the largest being Atlantic City. New Jersey's farms are so near New York and Philadelphia that many of their products go directly to the city markets; they include a variety of vegetables, apples, peaches and berries, and hay for New Jersey's fine dairy cows. Poultry-raising is important. The southern farming areas near Camden deliver their fruit and vegetables to canneries and freezing plants. Cranberries are grown in the State's extensive marshlands. Oysters and clams are caught in Delaware Bay. New Jersey was once an important iron and zinc-mining State. Nowadays, glass sand, clay for pottery and tiles, and basalt for road building, are the chief industrial minerals. New Jersey is a leading State in the refining of copper and petroleum. It also produces a large variety of chemicals (in the Newark-Elizabeth area), wire, machinery, rubber and leather goods, textiles,

furniture, and the many other articles used by city-dwellers. Newark is the largest city; and New York's skyscrapers can be seen from there. Jersey City, with piers on the Hudson River, forms part of the Port of New York; so does Hoboken. Paterson is a silk-weaving centre. Trenton, near the spot where Washington crossed the Delaware, is the State capital.

The region was first settled by the Dutch, along the Hudson, in 1620, and the Swedes, along the Delaware, in 1640. New Jersey was one of the 13 original States, the 3rd to ratify the Constitution, in 1787.

● **New Mexico** (121,666 square miles; population 1,016,000) is a State of the U.S.A. which displays a variety of landscapes. The Rocky Mountains are represented by the Sangre de Cristo range, which rises to 13,160 feet in the northern part of the State. The high plains reach westward from Texas to the Pecos River. The Colorado Plateau, with its mesas and canyons, and the U.S.A's largest uranium deposits, occupies the north-west. Desert flats and dry, jumbled mountain blocks are found in the south-west and along the Mexican border. The native vegetation consists of creosote bush, yuccas, cottonwood and short grass in the south, piñon and juniper woodlands above 5,000 feet, and evergreen forests in the northern mountains. Cattle and sheep are raised on grazing lands that are often too dry. Alfalfa, hay and sorghums are grown for fodder, and cotton is a very profitable crop in the irrigated district along the Rio Grande and Pecos Rivers. New Mexico is rich in minerals: copper, silver and gold are mined in the south-west; the country's richest potash deposits occur near Carlsbad; and oil, natural gas and coal are valuable energy resources. Albuquerque is the largest city, with 297,445 inhabitants; Santa Fé (41,167), a quaint Spanish town, is the capital. Over 40,000 Indians (Navajos, Apaches, Zuñis and Hopis) live on reservations; Indian pueblos — villages with houses of sun-baked clay — in the Rio Grande valley attract tourists and artists. Other areas of interest are Carlsbad Caverns National Park (with immense limestone caves), White Sands National Monument (150,000 acres of drifting snow-white sand-dunes), and Los Alamos, the research centre where the first atomic bomb was made.

The Spanish explorer Coronado discovered the home of the Pueblo Indians in 1540, and Santa Fé was founded in 1609. The region was first a

possession of the Spanish king and later a province of Mexico. It was ceded to the United States after the Mexican War of 1846—48. Indian resistance came to an end in 1886, when Geronimo, the Apache chief, surrendered to government forces. New Mexico became the 47th State of the Union in 1912. About one-third of the population is of Spanish or Mexican origin, and Spanish is still widely spoken.

Cotton

● **New Orleans** A major river-harbour and sea-port of the United States, on the lower Mississippi River, about 110 miles above the Gulf of Mexico. It is the largest city (population 690,521) of Louisiana and the commercial metropolis of the Deep South. Among the products New Orleans exports are cotton, petroleum (refined there) and lumber. There are sugar and textile mills, chemical plants and shipyards. New Orleans became the capital of the French colony of Louisiana in 1722. It passed under Spanish rule in 1763. The United States acquired the city as part of the Louisiana Purchase (1803). Until the Civil War, New Orleans flourished with an important trade in slaves and cotton. Nowadays, the city's business activities are increasingly directed toward Latin America; it has become the leading importer of such products of the tropics as coffee, sugar and bananas. It is also gaining in importance as a trans-shipment centre from ocean-going freighters to river barges that serve factories as far north as Ohio and Pennsylvania. The city's famous restaurants serve excellent dishes of shellfish, and the annual Mardi Gras pre-Lenten celebration overshadows all other tourist attractions.

● **New York** (49,576 square miles; population 18,190,740) ranks second as a State in population, and first in the value of goods produced in its factories. It owes this leadership to New York City, the U.S.A.'s largest city and principal seaport. In the north, New York State has a long water boundary with Canada, running through Lake Erie, along the Niagara River, across Lake Ontario, and along the upper St Lawrence River. The forested mountain wilderness of the Adirondacks also lies in the northern part of the State; there rises the Hudson, which flows majestically southward past Albany (115,000), the capital, to New York City and the Atlantic Ocean.

West of Albany, the Mohawk Valley gives access to the Great Lakes. In 1825, the Erie Canal was completed through this valley, and a 'water-level route' was thus established between New York City and Buffalo, a Great Lakes port and the State's second-largest city. The Finger Lakes in western New York, Lake George, and the smaller lakes found in the Adirondacks, are among the State's playgrounds, which also include world-famous Niagara Falls, the wooded Catskill Mountains, the Thousand Islands area on the St Lawrence, and the sandy beaches on Long Island.

Because millions of urban New Yorkers leave the big city at week-ends and on holidays, there is a fine system of State parks that can be reached over a network of parkways. New York's farms are busy supplying city-dwellers with milk, butter and cheese. Hay, oats, maize and other fodder crops are grown, but the State is chiefly known for its

The Vieux Carré – French quarter – of New Orleans is famous for its profusion of delicate wrought-iron grille-work

fruit; excellent wine grapes are grown on the shores of Lake Erie and the Finger Lakes and the Hudson Valley is lined with apple, peach, pear and cherry orchards.

Almost two-thirds of New York State's manufacturing is done in the New York metropolitan area, which receives many of its raw materials through the bustling Port of New York. The manufacturing of clothing is easily the largest industry; it is followed by printing and publishing, food-processing, and metalworking. Buffalo is the country's main flour-milling centre; it also has meat-packing plants and steelworks. Rochester specialises in photographic equipment, Syracuse in typewriters and chinaware, Schenectady in electrical and railway equipment, Corning in glass products, and the St Lawrence district (where the river's rapids have been by-passed by the canals and locks of the St Lawrence Seaway) in aluminium.

In the 17th century, the region was inhabited by the Five Iroquois Nations. In 1609, Champlain, coming from the north, explored Lake Champlain, and Henry Hudson sailed up the Hudson River. The Dutch began to settle there in 1623; they purchased Manhattan Island from the Indians and established a fort, called Nieuw Amsterdam. In 1664, the Dutch had to surrender their colony to the English, who renamed it New York. The scene of several battles during the Revolutionary War, New York was one of the original 13 States to sign the Constitution of the United States.

The Statue of Liberty

New York City The largest city (population 11,528,649 in 1970) of the United States (and possibly of the world, if all its Metropolitan area is included). It is the leading financial, commercial and cultural centre of the U.S.A., and the home (since 1952) of the United Nations. Situated on New York Bay, at the mouth of the Hudson River, the city is composed of 5 boroughs, each with its own waterfront: Manhattan, the heart of a sprawling urban area of 364 square miles, on an elongated island; the Bronx, on the mainland to the north-east, separated from Manhattan by the Harlem River and Spuyten Duyvil Creek; Queens, at the north-western end of Long Island, facing Manhattan and the Bronx across the East River; Brooklyn, on Long Island, adjacent to Queens and fronting on the Upper Bay; and Richmond, which is on Staten Island, just across the Bay from the southern tip of Manhattan.

Beyond the city, the metropolitan area of residential and industrial suburbs, and of satellite towns, extends eastwards on Long Island, northward into Westchester County, and westward across the Hudson into northern New Jersey, embracing at least 15 million people within a 40-mile radius of the Statue of Liberty. This mammoth urban region, with its intricate network of highways, railways, tunnels and bridges is focused on Manhattan — the business heart of the nation — and on the Port of New York, with its magnificent natural harbour. Along its 750 miles of waterfront, the Port of New York (which also

embraces part of the New Jersey shore) handles more than 40 per cent (in value) of U.S. foreign trade; shipping routes link it with all the great ports of the world; and the Erie Canal (now known as the New York State Barge Canal) gives direct access to the St Lawrence and the Great Lakes.

Pre-eminent as a world hub of trade and banking, New York City also leads the nation as an industrial centre, producing about 10 per cent of all manufactured products, chiefly consumer goods. The clothing industry, for which the city is famous, is crowded into the most congested portion of Manhattan, as is the making of furs, hats, leather goods, jewellery and many clothing accessories. Most of the nation's publishers have their headquarters in Manhattan, and the advertising industry is closely identified with Madison Avenue. In recent years, 'midtown' Manhattan has experienced a new wave of skyscraper construction, to house the head offices of an ever-growing list of leading corporations which have made this the management centre of the United States. The 'downtown' district, with its impressive skyline overlooking Battery Park, still houses the stock and commodity exchanges, banks, insurance companies and shipping firms. Despite the grand scale of recent construction, the Empire State Building, with its 102 storeys, still towers over the city.

New York has great museums and art galleries; varied educational centres; Central Park, beaches, zoos, and botanical gardens; opera and musical institutions; lavish places of entertainment on Times Square and along Broadway — including the best in theatre and musical comedy; fine shops along Fifth Avenue, and bustling department stores. It has striking contrasts in architecture and in wealth; colourful nationality neighbourhoods, that are beginning to lose their identity under the impact of slum clearance and the mass exodus to the suburbs; the fabulous new Kennedy International Airport, and equally busy La Guardia and Newark domestic air traffic centres; public housing projects, and forward-looking arterial highway construction programmes.

The site of New York may have been visited by Verrazano in 1524; it was certainly walked upon by Henry Hudson in 1609. Settlement dates from 1626, when Peter Minuit of the Dutch West India Company, having purchased Manhattan from the Indians for an alleged $24 in trinkets, chose the island's southern tip as his headquarters, naming it Nieuw Amsterdam. The English seized the growing Dutch colony in 1664, expanding it and renaming it after the Duke of York.

New York's strategic location for trade with the interior soon gave it a decided advantage over other coastal settlements. By 1789 (when for a few months it was the first capital of the United States, George Washington having been inaugurated at Federal Hall), it had become the largest city in the

Navajos live in Arizona and New Mexico

United States, with a population of more than 30,000. The opening of the Erie Canal in 1825 soon made New York the nation's leading port, a position it has maintained despite the competition of Boston, Philadelphia and Baltimore. Greater New York, with a new charter consolidating the 5 boroughs into one city, came into being in 1898. The Flatiron Building, erected in 1902, was the first of New York's sky-scrapers, a form of building necessitated by the scarcity, and hence the fabulous cost, of land in Manhattan. New York's reputation as a cosmopolitan city is due in part to its primacy in international trade and finance, to its experience in absorbing successive waves of immigrants, and to its more recent role as host to the United Nations.

Niagara Falls One of the great natural wonders of North America, on the Niagara River, which forms the boundary between the United States and Canada. The spectacular falls are more than 160 feet high; they consist of the American Falls (1,000 feet wide) and the Canadian, or Horse-shoe Falls (2,500 feet wide), separated by Goat Island. A narrow gorge, with the raging Whirlpool Rapids, lies below the foaming cataract. The falls have been harnessed for hydro-electric power, used

South-western U.S. Indians live in adobe dwellings ('pueblos'), like this one at Taos, New Mexico

The headquarters of the United Nations stands on the East River, in the heart of midtown Manhattan, New York City

in the factories of Niagara Falls, N.Y., and Niagara Falls, Ontario.

The Niagara River, 34 miles long, carries the outflow of Lake Erie to Lake Ontario. The Welland Canal, a part of the St Lawrence Seaway, provides a by-pass for Great Lakes shipping.

●**Nicaragua** The largest but the most thinly populated (57,128 square miles; population 1,780,000) of the Central American Republics. The eastern part of the country, between the two fresh-water lakes (Nicaragua and Managua) and the Caribbean shore, is undeveloped, except for several American and Canadian-owned gold mines. The rich forest resources of this eastern lowland remain almost untouched. Most of the people live in western Nicaragua, where the soil has been formed from lava flows and ash deposits from a chain of intermittently active volcanoes. There, coffee is by far the leading commercial crop.

Cotton is another rapidly expanding export product. There are banana plantations on the west coast, near the port of Corinto, terminal of a railway from Managua (the country's capital, population 300,000) and the smaller cities of León and Granada. Nicaragua has few industries and poor communications, although the Inter-American Highway runs from the Honduran to the Costa Rican border. Most of the people are of mixed Spanish and Indian descent (*mestizos*), and their language is Spanish. Along the Caribbean coast, however, English is spoken by West Indian Negroes who went there early in the century, to work on the banana plantations.

The first Spanish settlements in Nicaragua date from 1524. The region was then part of the captaincy-general of Guatemala. Independence from Spain was proclaimed in 1821. Between 1912 and 1933, the country was occupied by U.S. marines. For over 40 years, the United States has been considering the construction of a canal across

Nicaragua to supplement the Panama Canal. The projected waterway would cross 100-mile-long Lake Nicaragua, which extends to within 12 miles of the Pacific Ocean.

●**Norfolk** A major seaport on the east coast of the United States, situated on Hampton Roads, near the entrance to Chesapeake Bay and opposite the ports of Newport News and Portsmouth. It is the largest city in Virginia, with more than (681,521) inhabitants. Norfolk has large shipyards, a naval base, and miles of docks where freighters take on coal, farm products (especially tobacco) and lumber. Oil, woodpulp and tropical staples are unloaded there. Eight trunk freight railway lines lead inland from Norfolk.

●**North Carolina** (52,712 square miles; population 5,082,059) reaches from stormy Cape Hatteras on the Atlantic Ocean to the Blue Ridge and Unaka Mountains along the eastern wall of the Appalachians. The coastal plain, with the exception of the Dismal Swamp and other marshy stretches along the shore, is the main agricultural area. North Carolina leads all the States of the U.S.A. in tobacco-growing; cotton and peanuts are important cash crops; maize is grown in every county, and pigs are raised on almost every farm. Two-thirds of the State is forested; there are sawmills in the coastal region, where pine, cypress and sweet gum grow, and also in the mountains of the west, where the natural vegetation is oak, poplar, hickory and spruce. Swift streams have been dammed on their way down from the mountains, to provide hydro-electric power for factories and farms. North Carolina has the U.S.A's largest supplies of mica and feldspar, and is second in the production of olivine and crushed granite. North Carolina has become the leading industrial State of the South. Some of the nation's largest and most modern textile mills dot the North Carolina landscape; many of them moved there from New England, to take advantage of cheaper raw materials and power, pure water and ample space. Charlotte, a textile centre, is the largest city (202,000 inhabitants). Raleigh (94,000), named after Sir Walter Raleigh, who landed on the Carolina coast in 1585, is the State capital. Asheville, in western North Carolina, is the gateway to the Great Smoky Mountains (which include a national park), the Blue Ridge Parkway (a scenic ridge-top highway), and the dams and reservoirs built by the Tennessee Valley Authority. Also nearby is Mt Mitchell, which rises to the highest point (6,684 feet) east of the Mississippi.

A view of the Manhattan skyline from across the Hudson River in New Jersey, showing New York's docks and several transatlantic liners

The earliest colonists settled about 1650 along Albermarle Sound. The Indians were pushed back into the Appalachians, and Negro slaves were brought in to work the large cotton plantations. North Carolina was made a royal colony in 1729. It was one of the original 13 States to sign the Constitution, in 1789.

● **North Dakota** A wheat-growing State (70,665 square miles; population 617,761) in the northern Great Plains, on the U.S.-Canadian border. The greater part of the State is rolling prairie, with few trees except along water courses. The Missouri flows through the western part of North Dakota, and the Red River of the North forms the eastern boundary. During the Ice Age, the Red River Valley was occupied by a large lake. The old lake-bed is covered with rich black soil, on which some of the finest spring wheat in the world is grown. Barley, rye, maize and flax are also raised, often in rotation with wheat. Rainfall and harvests can vary enormously. In the west, the climate is too dry for crops; in that area, there are ranches on which cattle, horses and sheep are raised. The Missouri marks the approximate boundary between the wheat country (to the east) and the range lands (to the west). Oil was discovered along the Montana border in 1951, in what were previously called 'Badlands', and numerous wells are now in operation. Brown coal deposits underlie much of the State. There are few cities and few industries. Bismarck (34,703 inhabitants), on the Missouri River, is the capital; Fargo, on the Red River, is the largest urban centre, with 53,363 people. Grand Forks and Minot are grain-milling towns.

North Dakota was crossed by Lewis and Clark on their way to and from the Pacific North-West. Fur-trading was the main activity until about 1850. The first permanent settlers had to fight the Sioux Indians (1863—66). North Dakota was admitted into the Union in 1889, as the 39th State. Some 10,000 Indians now live on reservations. Under the Missouri Basin project, it is planned to irrigate another million acres of land.

● **North-West Territories** Vast region (1,300,000 square miles; population 26,000) of north-western Canada, comprising all the land north of 60° N. and west of Hudson Bay, as well as the multitude of islands in the Arctic Ocean to the north of the continent. It is a cold wasteland, covered with scrub vegetation or muskeg and dotted with numerous lakes (Great Slave Lake, Great Bear Lake). It is drained by the Mackenzie River, the region's chief artery of communication. Aircraft serve the fur-trading posts and mining centres (Yellowknife, Port Radium), where gold and radio-active minerals are recovered. In the far north, United States and Canadian forces are manning a net of radar aircraft-detecting posts, known as the DEW (Distant Early Warning) line. A new railway was opened in 1965 connecting major base metal deposits at Pine Point to Great Slave Lake and the southern networks.

● **Nova Scotia** A province (21,425 square miles; population 730,000) of eastern Canada; one of the Maritime Provinces. It consists of a peninsula, linked to the mainland by the isthmus of Chignecto, and of Cape Breton Island (to the north-east), separated from the peninsula by 2-mile-wide Canso Strait (crossed by a causeway). Halifax, Canada's principal winter seaport, is the provincial capital, for it is virtually ice-free. Nova Scotia is hilly and forested, with many lakes and short streams. The Annapolis valley, along the Bay of Fundy, is noted for its extensive apple orchards. Deep-sea fishing and lumbering are important industries, with a rapidly growing pulp and paper industry. Coal is mined in several places, including Sydney, on Cape Breton Island, where a large steel mill uses iron from nearby Newfoundland-Labrador. The peninsula was discovered by John Cabot in 1497; it was settled around 1600 by the French, who called it Acadia. In the 18th century, Britain and France fought over the territory, which became

Aerial view of Niagara Falls, between Lake Erie and Lake Ontario, on the U.S.-Canadian frontier

British in 1713. Nova Scotia became a province of the new Dominion of Canada in 1867.

● **oak, red** This common North American tree (*Quercus palustris*) is one of the largest oaks, occasionally 125 feet high. It is an important timber tree, but is also grown for ornamental planting, because of its rich red leaf colouring in the autumn.

● **Oakland** An industrial and port city (population 361,561) in California, on the eastern shore of San Francisco Bay, which is spanned there by the nearly 8-mile-long Bay Bridge. Two trans-continental railways have their western terminus in Oakland. Industries include canneries, motor-car assembly plants, oil refineries, shipyards and lumber mills.

● **ocelot** This long, lithe American jungle cat loves darkness. It spends the daytime in a rocky cave or hollow tree, and hunts for food at night. Its bright fur is used to decorate women's coats.

● **Ohio** A leading manufacturing State (41,222 square miles; population 10,652,000) of the U.S. Middle West, between Lake Erie and the Ohio River. Columbus, near the centre, is the State

Maize

A typical upland farm in the Great Smoky Mountains of North Carolina – former homeland of the Cherokee Indians

A herd of dairy cattle grazing on the broad, rolling pastureland of Logan County, Ohio, U.S.A.

capital. Eastern Ohio is a region of hills and valleys; it forms part of the Appalachian Plateau. There coal-seams are found near the surface, and mining is therefore an important activity. Large clay deposits have made Ohio particularly important in the production of fire bricks, tiles and pottery. Western Ohio is a level farmland; it forms part of the Corn Belt. A variety of crops is grown there, but maize occupies the greatest acreage; and where there is maize there are also pigs and cattle. Wheat and oats add to the State's agricultural wealth, as do potatoes, tobacco and soyabeans. More sheep are sheared for their wool in Ohio than in any other State east of the Mississippi.

Ohio's leadership as an industrial State is based on its coal, oil and natural gas resources, and also on its excellent transportation facilities. Iron ore from Minnesota is received via the Great Lakes at Cleveland, Toledo, and smaller ports on Lake Erie. Limestone is brought from Michigan to Cleveland's steel mills, along the navigable Cuyahoga River, making this the largest city and leading manufacturing centre in Ohio.

Canton is a steel town, as is Youngstown, in the Mahoning Valley, near the Pennsylvania line. Akron is known as 'the rubber city', its main product being rubber tyres; Dayton makes cash registers; and Cincinnati, the State's second city, is a centre of the soap industry. Cincinnati's importance is enhanced by its location on the Ohio, a navigable waterway that reaches into the heart of the coal-mining and steel-making country; barges ply the river from the Mississippi Valley to Pittsburgh and beyond.

A prehistoric people called the Mound Dwellers once inhabited the Ohio Valley. Remains of their culture (snake-shaped Serpent Mound, for example) are found in several places. The first permanent European settlers came on flatboats via the Ohio River. Cincinnati was founded in 1789, and various Indian tribes were defeated in 1794. With an increased flow of settlers, Ohio was admitted to the Union in 1803, as the 17th State. Seven U.S. presidents were native sons of Ohio.

● **Ohio River** The chief eastern tributary of the Mississippi, and a major navigable waterway through the industrial areas of the eastern Middle West. At Pittsburgh is the junction of the Allegheny and Monongahela Rivers, which then flow — as the Ohio — 1,000 miles south-west to the Mississippi at Cairo, Ill. Its chief tributaries are the Tennessee and the Cumberland. Barges on the Ohio carry coal, coke, steel, cement and other bulky materials to the numerous manufacturing plants that line the river in Ohio, West Virginia, Kentucky, Indiana and Illinois. Cincinnati is the largest river port below Pittsburgh. Spring floods have caused considerable damage, and extensive flood control works (dams, levees, floodways) have been built to contain the water within its channel.

Oilfields such as this are found in many areas of California, Louisiana, Texas and Oklahoma

● **Oklahoma** When Oklahoma (69,919 square miles; population 2,559,253) became the 46th State of the U.S.A. in 1907, the full extent of its natural resources was not yet known. Within a few years, wheat, cattle and oil brought people and wealth to Oklahoma. Wheat is grown on the rich soil of the endless, level prairie. In the west, where the climate is too dry for crops, livestock is raised on ranches; some of these ranches are larger than counties in other parts of the country. Cotton is grown in the more humid sections of the State, and maize is also an important crop. Oklahoma is the 4th-ranking oil-producing State in the Union. Pipelines lead north, west and east from the oil and gas-fields that underlie the central part of the State; Tulsa calls itself proudly 'the oil capital of the world'. Oklahoma City, the capital, has oil refineries and manufactures the equipment needed by the petroleum industry; oil is pumped to the surface from wells located within the city limits. Zinc and lead are mined in the north-east, where the Ozarks reach into the State from Missouri.

In the 1930s, Oklahoma, along with other States in the Dust Bowl area, suffered from severe droughts and wind-storms. Many farmers were ruined and left the State; a large number of them went to California, and they were known as the 'okies'. Today, over 70,000 Indians live in Oklahoma — more than in any other State.

● **Oklahoma City** The capital and largest city (population 363,225) of Oklahoma, located in the midst of an oil-producing region. Many wells are within the city limits, and petroleum-refining is the chief industry. The city was founded in 1889, the year in which the Territory was opened up to homesteaders.

● **Omaha** Largest city (population 327,789) of Nebraska, on the right bank of the Missouri. It is an important transportation centre, from which the products of the surrounding farming areas are shipped to Chicago and other eastern markets. Stockyards and grain-elevators line the railway sidings. Founded in 1854, Omaha's growth dates from 1865, when the first railway bridge was built across the Missouri. Omaha has also attained a new importance as the world headquarters of the U.S. Air Force's Strategic Air Command.

● **Ontario** Largest English-speaking province (412,582 square miles; population 7,345,000) of Canada, bordering on all the Great Lakes and upon Hudson Bay. Toronto is the provincial capital. Ottawa, the national capital, lies in eastern Ontario on the Quebec border. One-third of Canada's population lives in Ontario, mostly in the Upper Ontario Peninsula, between Lakes Huron, Erie and Ontario, and especially in the 'Golden Horseshoe', on the western shore of Lake Ontario around Toronto. The northern part of the province is densely wooded and studded with lakes. Central Ontario is one of the world's richest mining areas (nickel, gold, copper, silver, platinum, iron ore). Timber-stands supply pulp and paper mills. Ontario leads all the other provinces in manufacturing; it has many branch plants of U.S. industries and vast resources of hydro-electric power. Hamilton produces steel, Windsor (opposite Detroit) makes motor-cars, and Sarnia refines petroleum brought in by pipeline from the Prairie Provinces. Port Arthur and Fort William, close together on Lake Superior, are important grain and iron ore ports. The southernmost part of the province, the Lakes peninsula, is a rich farming, dairying and fruit-growing country.

Champlain visited the interior of Ontario in 1615; French missionaries and fur-traders followed. Ceded to Great Britain in 1763, and separated from Quebec in 1791, the region was known as Upper Canada until 1867, when it became a province of the newly formed Dominion of Canada.

- **Ontario, Lake** The smallest (7,500 square miles) and easternmost of the Great Lakes, in the United States and Canada. It lies only 246 feet above sea level, but is almost 800 feet deep. Lake Ontario receives the outflow of the four upper lakes through the Niagara River, and empties into the St Lawrence River at its north-eastern end. Toronto and Hamilton are the largest cities on the Canadian shore; Rochester, N.Y., is the main U.S. city on the south shore. The lake was discovered by French fur-traders in 1615.

- **opossum** America's only marsupial is found in all parts of the continent. The most common is the Virginia opossum, which is the size of a house cat and has a naked 10-inch tail. Like other marsupials, it carries its young in a pouch. The expression 'playing 'possum' comes from the animal's habit of playing dead when exposed to danger. Other opossums include the yapok, or water opossum, a water-loving animal of the South American jungle, and the mouse opossum, found throughout Latin America.

- **opuntia** This common type of cactus, also known as prickly pear, is made up of flat joints studded with spines or prickly hairs. It bears yellow or red flowers. Its sweet, fig-like fruit is edible and is used as fodder in arid regions.

- **Oregon** A State of the United States (96,981 square miles; population 1,768,687) in the Pacific North-West. The mighty Columbia River forms its northern boundary, and flows into the Pacific Ocean at the salmon-fishing centre of Astoria. Part of the eastern boundary is formed by the Snake River, which has cut a gorge a mile deep on its way to the Columbia.

The Cascade Range forms a mountain wall across the State, about 100 miles inland from the Pacific coast. Its highest peaks are inactive volcanoes, whose slopes are scarred by congealed lava flows; snow covers the summit area. Mount Hood (11,245 feet high), one of the most perfectly-shaped volcanoes in the range, is visible from Portland, almost 50 miles to the west. Its lower slopes are covered with apple orchards. The Cascades divide Oregon into two distinct climatic zones. West of the mountains there is ample rainfall throughout the year, so the countryside is green; between the Cascades and the Coast Ranges, lies the Willamette Valley, a region of intensive fruit and vegetable growing. Pears, prunes, cherries, strawberries, walnuts, poultry and dairy products make this one of the most prosperous farming areas in the country. East of the Cascades, rainfall is scanty, so the land is dry. A million acres of near-desert have been turned into cropland by means of irrigation ditches. Wheat is the chief crop, and hay is grown to provide feed for the livestock grazing on the range.

Oregon's extensive forests supply the raw material for its leading industry — sawmilling. Most of the State's industrial plants are found in the Willamette Valley and especially at Portland, the largest city, where the Willamette flows into the Columbia. Portland contains fruit and vegetable canneries, meat-packing plants, shipbuilding yards and paper mills. The Bonneville Dam, on the Columbia River, supplies electric power. Oregon is the only U.S. producer of nickel.

The coast of Oregon was visited by Spanish explorers in the 16th century. The mouth of the Columbia was discovered by an American in 1792. Lewis and Clark reached the lower Columbia from the east, by crossing the Rocky Mountains and the lava-covered Columbia Plateau. The Oregon country was owned jointly by the United States and Britain until 1846, when the 49th parallel was made the international boundary, the present boundary with Canada. In 1859, Oregon was admitted to Statehood. Its capital is Salem (49,000), a small town in the Willamette Valley. The largest city is Portland, with a population of 375,162 inhabitants.

The town of Balboa, in the Canal Zone, marks the place where the Panama Canal enters the Pacific

- **Ottawa** Capital (population 384,397) of Canada, on the Ottawa River (largest tributary of the St Lawrence), about 100 miles west of Montreal. It lies on the border of Canada's two largest provinces, Ontario and Quebec. Paper-milling and woodworking are the city's chief industries. Canada's Parliament buildings are on a bluff overlooking the river; nearby are Rideau Hall (official residence of the governor-general), museums, archives, and other government buildings. Founded in 1826 as Bytown, the city (renamed Ottawa in 1854) became the capital of the new Dominion of Canada in 1867. Ottawa has had a university since 1848.

- **Ozark Plateau** In southern Missouri and northern Arkansas, this region has remained isolated and backward because of ruggedness and unproductive soils. The highest summits — no higher than 2,800 feet — are found in the Ouachita Mountains, Arkansas.

- **paca** This rabbit-like rodent of the American tropics has large, expressive eyes and an attractively-spotted coat. It hides in underground burrows by day, and comes out to feed at night. Paca meat is considered a great delicacy in Latin America.

- **palm, royal** A tall graceful palm of southern Florida and Cuba, about 80 feet high. Because of its stately appearance, it is grown for ornamental purposes and forms perfect avenues.

Royal palms

Some 'Pennsylvania Dutch' farmers still paint their barns with hex signs, which were formerly believed to ward off evil

From Philadelphia's Independence Hall, the Liberty Bell 'proclaimed liberty throughout the land' in the year 1776

50 miles long from its channel entrance on the Caribbean (at the ports of Colon and Cristobal) to the breakwaters on the Pacific at Balboa, a suburb of Panama City. By means of three sets of double locks (Gatun Locks) — on the Atlantic slope, and the Pedro Miguel and Miraflores Locks on the Pacific side — ships are raised, and then lowered 85 feet, as they cross the Continental Divide. For almost 25 miles, the Canal crosses artificial Gatun Lake, the water level of which is regulated by Madden Dam. The average time of passage through the Canal is 7 to 8 hours; ships travel simultaneously in both directions. In 1970, the Panama Canal was used by as many as 13,658 vessels, with a total cargo of 114 million long tons. About one-quarter of these were American-flag ships, linking the Atlantic, Gulf and Pacific coasts of the United States, and the east and west coasts of South America. A railway and a first-class highway parallel the Canal from shore to shore. By a curious accident of geography, the Pacific entrance lies some 25 miles to the east of the Atlantic entrance to the Canal. There is also a considerable difference in tidal range, averaging 13 feet on the Pacific side and less than 1 foot on the Atlantic (Caribbean Sea). The Canal, first opened in 1914, has been in continuous operation since 1917, when a landslide at Gaillard Cut temporarily blocked the waterway.

● **Panama** An independent republic (28,745 square miles; population 1,414,737) of Central America, occupying the narrowest section of the Americas (Isthmus of Panama) between the Caribbean Sea and the Pacific Ocean. It is cut in two by the 10-mile-wide Canal Zone, which is gradually being integrated with the Republic of Panama, although the U.S.A. retains certain rights, including military bases. Most of the country is undeveloped, and its rich forest resources (especially mahogany) remain virtually untapped. Bananas, cacao and abacá fibre are the principal exports, and rice is grown for local use. The Panama Canal is the chief source of income and employment for the people of Panama. The two main cities — Panama City, the capital, on the Pacific coast (with 412,000 inhabitants), and Colón, on the Caribbean (with 134,500 people) — lie next to the entrances of the Canal. Two-thirds of the population are *mestizos* (of mixed Spanish and Indian blood), and 15 per cent are Negroes from the West Indies.

Columbus dropped anchor off the Panamanian coast in 1502. In 1513, Balboa made his famous crossing of the 30-mile-wide isthmus and sighted the Pacific Ocean. Panama then became the route by which the treasures of the Inca empire of South America were shipped to Spain. With the fall of the Spanish colonial empire in the 1820s, Panama became part of Colombia. A railway was built across the isthmus in the 1850s, and the development of the American West increased the need for a waterway to link the two oceans. In 1903,

Panama, supported by the United States, declared its independence from Colombia.

The Panama Canal

● **Panama Canal** A man-made waterway across the narrowest portion of the Americas (Isthmus of Panama), linking the Atlantic Ocean (its Caribbean part) with the Pacific. The Canal is operated for the benefit of the shipping of all nations, and the Canal Zone, over which the Panama Republic is gradually assuming sovereignty, is subject to a certain degree of U.S. control, including military bases. The Canal was built (1906—14) across the lowest section of the mountain range that constitutes the backbone of Central America. It is

● **pelican, brown** This bird, common in Florida, on the Gulf Coast and in California, is remarkable for its long bill and large pouch. The brown pelican has been known to engulf in its pouch a large fish that the bird could neither swallow nor disgorge, thus causing its own death.

● **Pennsylvania** An Eastern State (45,333 square miles; population 11,755,000) of the U.S.A. that lies almost entirely within the Appalachian mountain system. In the east, it borders on the Delaware and, in the north-west, it touches on Lake Erie. Between these two bodies of water there is but little level land. In the north and west, tributaries of the Ohio River have cut narrow, winding valleys across the Allegheny Plateau. East of the Allegheny Front (the steep edge of the tableland), parallel ridges and valleys follow one another in a broad belt (known as the Folded Appalachians, or Ridge and Vale area) that curves across the State in a north-east to south-west direction. Then comes the Blue Ridge and Great Valley, while in the more gently rolling portions of eastern Pennsylvania one finds the State's most fertile and prosperous farmlands — the 'Pennsylvania Dutch' (meaning Deutsch = German) country around York and Lancaster. Lancaster county is noted for the cigar leaf-tobacco grown on its carefully groomed acres. It is also a major fruit producing state. Dairying is the State's leading agricultural industry, for there are many large urban centres to be supplied with milk. Philadelphia, the 4th-largest city in the United States, is one of the country's leading seaports and a diversified industrial centre. Harrisburg, on the Susquehanna River and the Pennsylvania Turnpike, is the State capital. In the west, Pittsburgh is the largest of a cluster of steel-milling centres. Pennsylvania is fifth in the U.S.A. in the value of its mineral production, over three-quarters of which is coal. Vast horizontal deposits of bituminous, or soft, coal are mined in the Allegheny Plateau, largely with mechanised equipment. Almost all of the nation's anthracite, or hard and smokeless coal, comes from the Scranton and Wilkes-Barre districts.

Most of Pennsylvania's soft coal supply is used by industries, especially the mills that produce almost one-third of the country's steel in the Pittsburgh-Johnstown region. Anthracite is used to heat homes, but it is currently in low demand because of competition from oil and natural gas. The first successful oil-well in the United States was sunk at Titusville, Pa., in 1859. After a century of production, many of Pennsylvania's oil basins are depleted, but heavy lubricating oil is still in great

Pittsburgh, steel-producing centre of the United States, stands on the Ohio River in Pennsylvania

demand. Extensive limestone deposits are used to make cement, an industry that is concentrated in the Lehigh Valley. Next to its large output of steel, Pennsylvania is an important producer of textiles (in the Philadelphia area), petroleum products (refineries along the Delaware), ships, chemicals and electrical equipment. It ranks second only to New York State in the total value of its manufactures.

Pennsylvania was settled after 1681, when William Penn, an English Quaker, received a grant of land that included most of the State's present area. Religious freedom attracted thousands of Quakers, Germans (the Pennsylvania Dutch) and French Protestants to the colony. The 'Keystone State' played an important role in the American Revolution. Both of the Continental Congresses were held in Philadelphia, and the Declaration of Independence was signed there. Pennsylvania was among the original 13 States to ratify the Constitution, in 1787.

● **Philadelphia** The largest city (population 4,817,914) of Pennsylvania, the fourth-largest in the country, and a leading seaport on the Delaware, 100 miles from the Atlantic. Philadelphia's main industries include oil-refining, shipbuilding, manufacturing of chemicals, textiles, railway-wagons and Diesel engines. One of the nation's largest steel mills lies on the Delaware, north-east of the city. Philadelphia imports oil, iron ore, sugar and sulphur; it ships out building materials, railway equipment, petroleum products, and heavy machinery.

Founded by William Penn as a Quaker colony, the 'City of Brotherly Love', Philadelphia has been a centre of American culture for almost 300 years. The Declaration of Independence was signed in 1776 at Independence Hall, where the Liberty Bell is kept as a symbol of freedom. Philadelphia was the capital of the Thirteen Colonies during the Revolutionary War and, until 1800, the capital of the newly formed United States.

Prairie chickens

● **pine, pitch** The name of several trees of the south-eastern United States that furnish turpentine, resin and other naval stores.

● **Pittsburgh** One of the leading industrial centres of the U.S.A., and the second-largest city (population 2,401,245) of Pennsylvania, where the Allegheny and Monongahela Rivers meet to form the Ohio. The 'Steel City' lies near the centre of a major coal-mining region. Together with its surrounding industrial towns, Pittsburgh produces almost one-third of U.S. iron and steel. It is an important transportation centre, served by major railways and the Pennsylvania Turnpike. The Ohio River is navigable from Pittsburgh to the Mississippi, and the Monongahela is navigable above the city as far as West Virginia's northern coal-mining district. In Pittsburgh's business district — the 'Golden Triangle', at the confluence of the Ohio's two headstreams — are the head offices of the largest steel and aluminium-producing corporations. In 1754, this strategic site was occupied by Fort Duquesne, a French fur-trading post, later renamed Fort Pitt by the British.

● **poplar** A fast-growing, moisture-loving tree of the United States, northern Europe and eastern Asia, usually planted for shade near farm homes, along streets, and also used in windbreaks. The flower is a drooping catkin. The poplar's soft, light wood is used for pulp, boxes, shavings and matches.

● **Popocatépetl** Mexico's second-highest mountain (17,887 feet), a snow-covered volcano with a huge crater, situated 45 miles from Mexico City. Although it has not erupted for 300 years, clouds of smoke still rise occasionally from the sulphur-filled crater.

● **Portland** The largest city (population 375,161) of Oregon, near the Columbia River, 110 miles from the Pacific Ocean. Its port, on the Willamette River, can be reached by ocean-going ships. Portland has shipyards, paper mills, canneries and meat-packing plants. Lumber, wool, frozen and canned foods (especially Columbia River salmon) are among the chief exports. The city was laid out in 1845 and was named after Portland, Maine. The California gold rush and its expanding salmon fisheries contributed to its growth. Cheap hydro-electric power from Bonneville Dam (completed 1937) has attracted numerous industries.

● **prairie** The name given to the almost flat, treeless, grassy plains of North America, sloping from the Rocky Mountains east to the Mississippi River. It is one of the world's great wheat-growing areas, corresponding to the pampas of Argentina and the steppes of the Soviet Union.

● **prairie chicken** This grouse of the Great Plains is noted for its weird booming sounds. The male produces the noise by distending bright-coloured air sacs on the side of the neck and then expelling the air.

● **prairie dog** This rodent, closely related to the ground squirrel, is social, living in underground colonies. At any sign of danger, it utters a shrill whistle of warning and disappears underground.

● **Prairie Provinces** Name given to three Canadian provinces — Manitoba, Saskatchewan and Alberta — in the Great Plains, east of the Rocky Mountains. Wheat is their chief crop.

● **Prince Edward Island** The smallest province (2,184 square miles; population 110,000) of Canada, an island in the Gulf of St Lawrence, separated from the mainland of Nova Scotia and New Brunswick by Northumberland Strait, over which a causeway is planned. Seed potatoes, grain and fruit are grown on the island's fertile red soils. Lobster, cod and oysters are caught offshore and exported. Charlottetown (19,427) is the provincial capital.

The island was discovered in 1497 by John Cabot. Claimed for France by Champlain (who visited the island in 1603), it was known as Isle St John until the middle of the 18th century. Held by the British after 1758, it was settled chiefly by Scots. It joined Canada in 1873.

● **pronghorn** This swift, graceful, antelope-like animal has distinctive pronged horns that shed their outer coverings each year. Pronghorns once roamed the Far West in millions. Because their great curiosity made them easy victims for hunters, they have been greatly reduced in numbers.

Popocatépetl, a dormant volcano in Mexico

● **Providence** The capital of Rhode Island and a diversified manufacturing centre with a population of 208,000. Silverware, jewellery, textiles, textile machinery and tools are among its many products. The city lies at the head of Narragansett Bay and has a deep-water port. It was founded in 1636 as a centre of religious freedom.

● **Puebla** One of Mexico's oldest and most colourful cities (population 321,900), with cotton textile and pottery manufactures; articles made of onyx are also produced there. It lies more than 7,000 feet above sea level on the Inter-American Highway. Known as the city of churches (with more than 60), Puebla has a 400-year-old cathedral in pure Spanish style.

● **Pueblo** The Pueblo Indian civilisation flourished in the south-western United States from A.D. 1000 to 1200. It was characterised by the use of pueblos (large, terraced communal village dwellings, several storeys high), advanced farming techniques, and great skill in arts and crafts, especially pottery. The Pueblo Indians, which include the Hopi and Zuñi, are found in Arizona and New Mexico. Modern pueblos can still be seen in the upper Rio Grande valley of New Mexico.

● **Puerto Rico** A West Indian island (3,435 square miles; population 2,689,932) in the Caribbean Sea, associated with the United States as a locally self-governing commonwealth. The smallest and easternmost of the Greater Antilles, the Commonwealth of Puerto Rico is a densely settled mountainous island (650 people to the square mile), with a pleasant tropical climate cooled by year-round trade winds. Sugar is still the main crop, but tobacco, coffee, pineapples and citrus fruit diversify the agricultural exports. Since the end of

Vegetation-clad mountain slopes of tropical Puerto Rico

World War II, Puerto Rico has acquired a variety of new industries, because of the accessibility of the American market and sources of capital. More than 500 factories have been built, and thousands of poverty-stricken peasants have learned new skills and found employment in the thriving cities. At the same time, some 500,000 Puerto Ricans, taking advantage of their American citizenship, have come to the mainland — especially to New York City — where jobs are more plentiful and better paying than on their crowded island. San Juan (population 444,952), with its modern international airport and luxury hotels, is becoming increasingly popular as a winter resort for American tourists.

When Columbus landed there on his second voyage (1493), the island was inhabited by Arawak Indians. San Juan was founded in 1521, and it soon became one of the leading Spanish strongholds in the New World. Wiping out the native population, the Spaniards then brought in Negro slaves to work on the sugar plantations. In 1898, Puerto Rico was ceded to the United States by the treaty ending the Spanish-American War. Self-rule in all but foreign affairs dates from 1952. Both Spanish and English are official languages, but only a minority of the population actually speak English. The United States maintains several naval bases in Puerto Rico.

● **Puget Sound** A deep fjord inlet of the U.S. Pacific coast which penetrates 100 miles into the State of Washington. It is accessible for ocean-going ships, through Juan de Fuca Strait, using the ports of Seattle and Tacoma, and is flanked on the north by Vancouver Island (British Columbia) and on the south by the towering Olympic Mountains, rising to 7,954 feet in Mt Olympus. Puget Sound was explored and named by Captain George Vancouver in 1792.

● **Quebec** Canada's largest province (594,860 square miles; population 6,004,000), inhabited largely by French Canadians. Canadians of French descent now number over 5 million, a third of the country's population. Quebec city, the provincial capital and cultural centre of the French-speaking population, and Montreal, Canada's largest city, lie on the St Lawrence River. This important waterway is navigable for ocean-going ships, except during the winter months. Most of the people live in the St Lawrence lowland, between Montreal and the Gaspé Peninsula. Northern Quebec borders on Hudson Bay, Hudson Strait and Labrador. It is a vast, rocky wasteland, studded with lakes and marshes. Huge iron deposits have been discovered in this remote part of the province. From Knob Lake (on the Labrador line), the ore is shipped 350 miles by railway to Seven Islands, a port on the lower St Lawrence. Quebec also mines gold, asbestos (75% of world output), copper, chrome, zinc, molybdenum and titanium ore. Its enormous output of hydro-electric power is used in pulp and paper mills, and in aluminium smelters (in the upper Saguenay River district). Intensively cultivated southern Quebec specialises in dairy and maple products.

New France, founded by Champlain in 1608, was settled by immigrants from France in the 17th century. Captured by the British in 1760, it bore the name of Lower Canada until 1867, when it joined the newly formed Dominion of Canada as the province of Quebec.

● **Quebec** A French-Canadian city (population 174,782; with suburbs, 450,000) of eastern Canada and the capital of Quebec province, on a high cliff overlooking the wide St Lawrence River. Transatlantic liners and cargo ships dock there, except in winter, when the river is frozen. Grain, pulpwood and furs are exported. Tourists flock to Quebec to see its quaint 17th-century buildings and the well-preserved ramparts of the old city. The French navigator Jacques Cartier visited an Indian village on the site of Quebec in 1535. Champlain founded a colony there in 1608, and the city became the capital of New France in 1663. It was captured by Britain in 1759. The Canadian Confederation, making Canada a Dominion within the British Empire, was established there in 1867.

● **rabbit, jack** This long-eared hare of the West owes its name to its jackass-like ears. It is well adapted to life in semi-arid areas and can get along with little water. It eludes pursuers with leaps of up to 20 feet. Because the jack rabbit multiplies rapidly, an over-abundance of animals often threatens crops; big rabbit drives are then organised, and the animals are destroyed in thousands.

● **raccoon** This well-known relative of the bear has the odd habit of washing its food, no matter how clean it may be. Catlike in size, the raccoon is identified by its black face-mask and banded, bushy tail. Early American settlers hunted the raccoon for its meat, and also for its fur, which was used for coonskin caps.

● **rattlesnake** This well-known American poisonous snake is distinguished by the horny rattle at the end of its tail. The rattle gains a segment each time the snake sheds its skin. The largest rattlesnake is the eastern diamondback, which grows to eight feet in length.

● **Regina** The capital (population 143,000) of Saskatchewan, in western Canada; founded in 1882, the city is 350 miles west of Winnipeg. Regina is the centre of an extensive wheat-growing region, with grain elevators and a meat-packing plant.

● **Rhode Island** A New England State (1,214 square miles; population 949,723) and the smallest in the Union. It is not, in fact, an island, but there are many islands in Narragansett Bay, a deep inlet of the Atlantic Ocean which reaches inland as far as Providence, the State's largest city and also its capital. The biggest island in the Bay is called Rhode Island; on it is the fashionable resort of Newport. The State is so small, so densely settled, with 800 people to the square mile, and most of it is so hilly that there is little room for agriculture, except for dairying, poultry-raising, and market-gardening. Rhode Island Red chickens are bred there. There are several busy fishing centres on Narragansett Bay; the catch includes oysters, lobsters, clams, flounder, bluefish and swordfish. Block Island, 10 miles off-shore, is a well-known holiday spot; it was discovered by an Italian, Verraganao, but a Dutchman later named it after himself, in 1614. Rhode Island is first and foremost a manufacturing State. It has a large force of skilled workers and produces a variety of specialities, including precision-made metal products, jewellery and silverware. Providence is a major centre of the textile industry; so are the nearby towns of Woonsocket and Pawtucket, the site of the first cotton mill in the United States, built in 1790 by Slater.

The first permanent white settlement was made at Providence in 1636, on land bought from the Narragansett Indians. In 1663, a royal charter was granted to what later became the colony of 'Rhode Island and Providence Plantations'. This is still the official name of the State, but the last part is always dropped to make it less cumbersome. Religious freedom attracted many settlers from other colonies. Newport flourished as a commercial

The mighty Rocky Mountains separate the Great Basin from the Great Plains and the prairies

centre and as a haven for privateers during the 18th century. In 1790, Rhode Island accepted the federal Constitution and entered the Union as the last of the 13 original States.

●**Richmond** The capital (population 540,856) of Virginia, on the James River, navigable from there to the ocean. Richmond is a great tobacco market and cigarette-manufacturing centre. A trading post was established there in 1637. It became the capital of Virginia in 1779. As the capital of the Confederacy (1861—65), Richmond was the target of several Federal campaigns during the Civil War. It was captured by General Grant in 1865. The city has two universities, one founded in 1832 and the other in 1865.

●**Rio Grande** The border river between the United States and Mexico, known in Latin America as *Rio Bravo del Norte*. It rises in the south-ern Rocky Mountains, flows south across New Mexico, and reaches the Mexican border at El Paso, Texas. It enters the Gulf of Mexico near Brownsville, after forming the international line for 1,300 miles. Its main tributary is the Pecos. The river's waters have been used for irrigation since the time of the Indian villages (*pueblos*) which Coronado discovered in the 1540s. In recent times, dams (Elephant Butte in New Mexico) and canals (in southern Texas) have been built to spread the water over the dry lands next to the river.

●**Rochester** A manufacturing city in western New York, specialising in photographic and optical equipment. Rochester has a port on Lake Erie and also lies on the New York Barge Canal, better known as the Erie Canal. The State's third-largest city (population 828,000) owes much of its in-dustrial importance to George Eastman, inventor of the roll photographic film, and founder of an enormous international film and camera-manu-facturing company.

●**Rocky Mountains** Mountain ranges of North America, extending at least 3,000 miles from the south-western United States, across western Canada, and into Alaska. The Rockies rise sharply from the Great Plains to the east, while, in the west, they merge gradually with the Great Basin and the Colorado and Columbia Plateau. The Pacific border mountains, such as the Sierra Nevada and the Coast Ranges, are not considered a part of the Rocky Mountains. The highest peaks in the United States section are found in Colorado; within a rather small area, 45 snow-covered peaks top 14,000 feet (e.g., Mt Elbert, 14,431 ft.; Longs Peak, 14,252 ft.; Pikes Peak, 14,110 ft.). In Canada, Mt Robson rises to 12,972 feet.

A formidable barrier to east-west communica-tions, the Rocky Mountains form the Continental Divide, which separates the headwaters of rivers flowing to the Pacific Ocean (Colorado, Columbia) from those draining eastward to the Gulf of Mexico (Missouri, and other tributaries of the Mississippi and the Rio Grande). The spectacular scenery and natural grandeur of the Rockies have been pre-served in national parks that are visited by millions of city-dwellers and people of the lowlands; best-known of these in the United States are Yellow-stone, Grand Teton and Rocky Mountain National Parks. The currently forested ranges were formed during the Alpine earth movements of Tertiary times, and contain varied mineral deposits.

●**rum** An alcoholic liquor distilled from molasses (syrup) or other sugar-cane product. It is made chiefly in the West Indies.

●**Sacramento** The capital of California, 75 miles north-east of San Francisco, in the middle of the Central Valley, with a population of 257,413. It contains canneries and freezing plants that process the vegetables, fruit and meat from the surround-ing farming areas, and was founded in 1840. Prospectors, setting out from Sacramento, found gold at nearby Coloma, and this touched off the stampede of the 'Forty-Niners' for the Mother Lode country to the east.

●**Sacramento River** gives its name to the north-ern half of the Central Valley. Shasta Dam, near its headwaters in northern California, regulates the stream for navigation and flood control. It also provides hydro-electric power and water for irrigation in the drier parts of the Central Valley.

●**St Augustine** The oldest city in the United States, on the Atlantic coast of northern Florida, about 40 miles from Jacksonville. It was founded by the Spaniards in 1565, but was soon burned down by Sir Francis Drake. Many of St Augustine's historic buildings have been restored and are open to visitors.

●**St John** Canadian seaport (population 100,192) on the Bay of Fundy (a deep inlet of the Atlantic Ocean), founded in 1783 and in the province of New Brunswick. It has an ice-free harbour with a large dry-dock for ship repair and several grain elevators. Lumber is exported. At the rising tide, the St John River reverses its flow at the Reversing Falls Rapids in mid-city, the tidal range being the greatest in the world, reaching 70 feet.

●**St John's** A Canadian seaport (population 101,161) and the capital of the province of New-foundland, with a fine natural harbour. It is the centre for the Newfoundland cod and herring fishing fleet. St John's is the easternmost city in North America and nearest to Europe on trans-atlantic shipping lanes. The town has various metal, food-processing and ship-repair industries.

●**St Lawrence River** One of North America's largest and most important rivers and the chief outlet of the Great Lakes. It provides a navigable waterway over 2,000 miles long from the head of Lake Superior to the Atlantic Ocean. The St Lawrence flows 750 miles from the eastern end of Lake Ontario to the Gulf of St Lawrence. Below Lake Ontario, the river forms the U.S.-Canadian border for about 100 miles. There lie the scenic Thousand Islands and the International Rapids section. Another stretch of rapids occurs just above Montreal, where the St Lawrence becomes navi-gable for ocean-going vessels. Below the city of

Quebec, the river is tidal; it widens gradually to a width of 90 miles at its mouth, north of the Gaspé Peninsula. Its chief tributaries are the Richelieu (which forms a navigable link with Lake Champlain and the Hudson River) and the Saguenay, which joins the lower St Lawrence from the north in a deep canyon. The river and its tributaries are an important source of hydro-electric power for eastern Canada's cities, paper mills and aluminium smelters.

The first European to ascend the St Lawrence was the French navigator Jacques Cartier in 1535. Quebec was established by Champlain in 1608. The French occupied the valley until 1763, when Canada was surrendered to the British. The St Lawrence Seaway, a project to improve naviga-tion on the waterway, was officially opened in June, 1959. It provides for deep-water by-passes of the rapids — a series of locks, dams and large hydro-electric plants. It has been built jointly by the United States and Canada. Ocean-going ships are now able to reach such inland cities as Buffalo, Cleveland, Detroit, and even Chicago, without transferring their cargo to smaller riverboats. The St Lawrence has thus become one of the world's busiest shipping lanes.

●**St Louis** A major focus of communications in the Middle West and the largest city (population 2,363,017) of Missouri, on the Mississippi River, 10 miles below its junction with the Missouri. It is an important market for livestock, grain, wool, fur and lumber. Meat-packing, brewing, and manu-facturing of drugs, motor-cars, railway-wagons and machinery, are among its diversified indus-tries. The busy river-port handles bulky cargoes of oil, coal, cement and farm products. Founded as a French fur-trading post in 1764, and named after King Louis IX, who became a saint for his participation in the Crusades, St Louis passed to the United States as a result of the Louisiana Purchase. During the 19th century, it became a gateway to the West and a booming river-port. It has two universities, founded in 1815 and 1857.

●**St Paul** The capital of Minnesota, on high bluffs overlooking the upper Mississippi River. Across the river lies Minneapolis, the other of the Twin Cities. Meat-packing is the chief industry, and butter is an important product of St Paul. 309,980 people live there.

●**St Pierre and Miquelon** Small French island group in the Atlantic, just south of Newfoundland; the last remnant of France's 17th and 18th century colonial empire in North America. The frequently fog-bound islands — eight in all — are inhabited by about 5,235 fishermen of Norman French

St Louis lies on the west bank of the Mississippi River, ten miles below its junction with the Missouri

The historic Alamo, in San Antonio, Texas

descent. The town of St Pierre is a base for the nearby Grand Banks fisheries.

● **salmon** One of the most important food-fish of the United States, chiefly in Oregon, Washington, Alaska and off Nova Scotia. Each year, millions of salmon leave the sea and enter the streams in which they were hatched, to lay their eggs and then die. On their way upstream great numbers are caught in traps and nets, principally for canning. The construction of dams and hydro-electric projects has greatly reduced the salmon in many rivers.

● **Salt Lake City** The capital and largest city (population 175,888) of Utah, at the foot of the Wasatch Range. Nearby is Great Salt Lake, a shallow body of salt water covering from 1,500 to 2,500 square miles, according to rainfall. The lake is several times more saline than the ocean; it is the remnant of an enormous prehistoric body of water which geologists have called Lake Bonneville. The old shoreline of the larger lake is still visible along the mountain slopes above Salt Lake City. The city was founded in 1847 by Brigham Young, who had led the Mormons across the Great Plains and the Rocky Mountains to this 'promised land'. Industries are largely concerned with the mineral and agricultural produce of the region.

● **San Antonio** A commercial centre (population 832,000) of southern Texas, with an active trade in cattle, cotton, wool, fruit and pecans from a wide agricultural area. It has oil refineries and meat-packing plants. Tourists go there to enjoy the mild climate, and to visit old Spanish missions. The Alamo, whose heroic defenders were killed during Texas's struggle for independence from Mexico, is one of the best-known U.S. historic shrines. The city was founded in 1718, and became an important settlement under Spanish and Mexican rule. It still has a large Mexican population.

● **San Diego** A seaport and a thriving resort city on the coast of southern California, near the Mexican border. Its population (696,769 in 1970)

has doubled since 1940, with increased naval activity during World War II and the phenomenal growth of the aircraft industry in this area. People go there to retire, attracted by the mild climate and handsome residential districts overlooking the ocean. At least one-half of the nation's catch of tunny is brought ashore in San Diego's excellent natural harbour. The first Spanish mission in California was established there in 1769.

● **San Francisco** A cosmopolitan seaport and commercial centre on the Pacific Ocean. It is the second-largest city (population 3,111,509) of California, famous for its Golden Gate Bridge, a 4,200-foot suspension span across the entrance to San Francisco Bay. The bay is one of the best natural harbours in the world; 50 miles long and 3 to 12 miles wide, it is fringed by industrial and residential cities contained within the San Francisco-Oakland metropolitan area. The port of San Francisco serves the Orient, the Hawaiian Islands, and Oceania. It is the outlet for the Central Valley of California, one of the richest grain, fruit and vegetable-growing districts in the country. Surrounded on three sides by the sea, and frequently shrouded by a blanket of fog, San Francisco is one of the most interesting cities in the United States.

The city was founded in 1776, when a Spanish mission was established there. Two hundred years earlier, Sir Francis Drake had visited the bay. San Francisco's growth dates from 1848, when gold was discovered in the Sacramento Valley. The city was almost levelled by the 1906 earthquake and the resulting fire, but it was quickly rebuilt. Completion of its two major bridges (1936—37) brought the city closer to the surrounding communities. In 1945, the United Nations Charter was signed in San Francisco.

● **Santo Domingo** The capital (population 822,862) of the Dominican Republic, with a man-made harbour on the Caribbean Sea. It exports sugar, molasses, cacao and coffee. A clean, attractive city, with a pleasant winter climate and good hotels, Santo Domingo appeals to American tourists. Founded in 1496 by Bartholomew Columbus, the brother of Christopher, the city is the oldest European settlement in the New World. Santo Domingo also has the oldest university in America, founded in 1538.

● **Sargasso Sea** A portion of the North Atlantic Ocean between the West Indies and Bermuda.

Relatively free from ocean currents, its warm, salty waters carry large quantities of sargasso sea-weed in suspension. Eels spawn there.

● **Saskatchewan** A province (251,700 square miles; population 942,000) of west-central Canada; one of the Prairie Provinces. Wheat-farms occupy the southern half of the province; forests and lakes predominate in the north. The Saskatchewan and Churchill Rivers flow eastward towards Hudson Bay. Sparsely settled northern Saskatchewan has copper, zinc and gold deposits, and a uranium mine at Beaverlodge Lake, near Lake Athabaska. Petroleum, natural gas and low-grade coal deposits are found in the south, near the U.S. border. Regina is the provincial capital, with a population of 143,000.

French fur-trappers and, later, representatives of the Hudson's Bay Company established trading-posts along the Saskatchewan River in the 18th and 19th centuries. The territory became part of Canada in 1870, and was organised as a separate province in 1905. The huge wheat crop of the south, more than a half of the national total, is shipped east to Winnipeg and the Great Lakes. The South Saskatchewan River irrigation project was completed in 1967, and has 40,000 acres under development.

● **Savannah** A port on the Savannah River in Georgia, not far from the Atlantic Ocean. Naval stores (turpentine, resin, recovered from nearby pine forests,) are sold there, and Savannah has large pulp and paper mills. The first steamboat to cross the Atlantic sailed from there to Liverpool in 1819. Founded in 1733, the town has a population of 150,000.

● **sea lion** The California (or southern) sea lion is easily trained, intelligent and equipped with a good sense of balance. The Steller's (or northern) sea lion of the Aleutians is the largest of the sea lions, weighing up to a ton.

● **seal, fur** The northern fur seal, also known as sea bear, is found in the northern part of the Pacific Ocean. It is about six feet long and weighs 500 to 700 pounds. Its thick, soft fur is the commercially valuable sealskin. Every spring the animals converge on the bleak Pribilof Islands to mate. There they used to be slaughtered indiscriminately for their fur, but legal restrictions now limit the number that may be killed each year. The cape seal is a South African relative of the northern fur seal.

The Golden Gate Bridge spans the straits leading into San Francisco's beautiful 50-mile-long bay

Sea lions

seals The true seals, or earless seals, are the most common marine mammals, found mostly in the Arctic regions, but also in inland lakes. Seals leave the water to breed, and the young remain on land for several weeks before they are taught to swim. The hind limbs serve as flippers for swimming, and the forelimbs for balancing and turning in the water. Seal meat and blubber are the Eskimos' chief sources of food during the winter. Seals are intelligent and can be easily trained. They include the common harbour seal, which remains close to land; the ringed seal, marked by a number of rings and found far to the north; the harp seal, or saddle-backed seal, whose markings resemble a saddle or harp; the hooded seal, named for a hood, or bag, on its head, which it inflates when excited; and the crab-eating seal of the Antarctic.

Seattle The largest city (population 516,909) of the State of Washington, in the Pacific North-West, on Puget Sound. From there ships travel to the Orient and to Alaska, via the Inside Passage — between the Canadian mainland and the off-shore islands. The halibut fishing fleet is fitted out in Seattle, and fish-canning is among the city's leading industries. Shipbuilding, lumber-milling and aircraft-manufacturing add to Seattle's importance as a growing industrial centre. The city was built on a narrow strip of land between the Sound and Lake Washington, a fresh-water lake crossed by a floating bridge. Bursting at its seams, Seattle is expanding in all directions. The snow-capped giants of the Cascade Range — Mt Rainier and Mt Baker — can be seen on the eastern horizon. To the west, across island-studded Puget Sound, lies the mountain wilderness of Olympic National Park. Seattle was settled in 1852 as a lumber camp. The Alaska gold rush of 1897 made it a boom town overnight. Its importance as a seaport dates from 1914, when the opening of the Panama Canal shortened the sea route between the eastern United States and the Pacific North-West.

Seminole An Indian tribe of Florida which is an

Giant sequoia

The town of Taxco, Mexico, was founded by the Spanish in 1529, on the slopes of Mt Atachi

offshoot of the Creeks. Most of the Seminoles were removed to Oklahoma in 1843, after a seven years' war.

sequoia These gigantic California trees are probably the oldest and largest conifers in the world. The giant sequoia, or big tree, is found in Sequoia National Park, on the west slope of the Sierra Nevada. The closely-related redwood is still felled for timber in the Coast Range. Sequoias range from 200 to 300 feet in height, and attain an age of 4,000 years.

sheep, bighorn This mountain sheep, noted for its great, curling horns, ranges through the Rocky Mountains from Alaska to Mexico. An excellent climber, it negotiates the sheerest cliffs at a break-neck gallop.

Shoshone An Indian tribe of the southern Rocky Mountains. Like the Apaches, they once were foes of the sedentary Pueblo Indians. Some were originally bison hunters, others root-gatherers.

Sierra Madre Mountain ranges of Mexico which, together with the high central plateau enclosed by them, cover about three-quarters of the country. They extend from the U.S. border as far as Guatemala, where they are continued by the volcanic chains of Central America. Both the western and eastern Sierra Madre decline steeply towards the coast, leaving but little room for the Atlantic and Pacific lowlands. There, silver, lead, zinc and copper are mined. The highest summits — Ciltaltépetl, Popocatépetl — are snow-covered, inactive volcanoes.

Sierra Nevada Mountain range of eastern California which separates the Central Valley from the Great Basin country to the east. Mt Whitney (14,495 feet) is the highest peak in the United States, outside Alaska. The mountains rise gradually from the west and decline steeply to the east. The highest portion, known as the High Sierras, lies south of Lake Tahoe. It contains some of the finest mountain scenery in the United States, including Yosemite and Sequoia National Parks, with giant redwood groves, canyons and waterfalls. The heavy snowfall on the western slope of

the Sierra feeds California's principal rivers and the pipelines leading to the Los Angeles basin. Highways and railroads cross the Sierra at passes ranging in elevation from 5,000 to 10,000 feet.

Striped skunk

skunk This black-and-white member of the weasel family is famous for its ability, when threatened, to discharge its scent, stored in two glands under its tail, for a distance of up to ten feet.

solenodon This rare West Indian animal, found only in Cuba and on Hispaniola, looks like a long-snouted rat. It is close to extinction, because it produces only one young per litter and is preyed upon by cats and dogs.

South Carolina A Southern State (31,055 square miles; population 2,590,516) of the U.S.A., with a long coastline on the Atlantic Ocean and a fringe of sandy and marshy islands, called Sea Islands, once famous for the fine, long-staple cotton grown there. After the Civil War, the large plantations disappeared, and nowadays cotton is grown throughout the State by small farmers and tenants who pay their rent in cash, or as a share of the harvest. Tobacco is the principal crop of the coastal plain; maize is grown widely as a feed for pigs and cattle, and peanuts are planted in order to enrich the soil for growing other crops.

Many parts of the State have become severely eroded, because the farmers do not yet know how to stop water washing the soil off their sloping fields. Many rivers flow across the State from the Blue Ridge (in the western corner) to the ocean. On the Santee River, there are several dams and man-made lakes; they supply the electricity needed by farms and cities, and by the growing number of cotton mills.

Columbia (310,700), the capital, lies on the Santee River, near the centre of the State. Charleston, with its sheltered harbour, ships cotton all over the world. It also has some paper mills; the pulp is made out of pine trees that grow in the coastal plain. In the hillier sections, there are fine stands of oak, poplar, laurel and hickory that are used to make furniture.

The State was first settled in 1670, Charleston being founded in 1680. Negro slaves were brought from West Africa to work on rice and indigo plantations. South Carolina was one of the 13 original colonies to sign the Constitution of the United States. However, in 1860 it was the first of the Southern States to secede from the Union. Four months later, Fort Sumter, in Charleston Harbour, was fired on, and the American Civil War broke out.

On this Texas plantation on the Gulf Coast, cotton is cultivated and picked by machine

● **South Dakota** A Great Plains State (77,047 square miles; population 666,257) of the U.S.A., bisected by the Missouri River. Pierre (10,000) is the capital; Sioux Falls is the largest city. Most towns are small, because the people live on farms and ranches. The best farmland lies east of the Missouri; there, wheat, rye, barley, oats and maize are grown on deep, fertile soils. To the west lies the ranch country, where immense herds of cattle and sheep are raised. Dairying, meat-packing and flour-milling are the principal industries. In southwestern South Dakota, the treeless prairie gives way to the Badlands, a region of strange rock formations, cut by rain and wind into ragged peaks and deep, narrow ravines. To the west of the Badlands lie the Black Hills, the State's only mountains reaching to over 7,000 feet. They get their name from the forests of dark-green pine trees that cover them; but their wealth is stored underground, in the form of gold, silver, lead and precious stones.

The Dakotas were explored by French fur-traders in 1743. The first permanent trading post was founded in 1817. Agricultural settlement was hampered by periodic droughts and by danger of Indian raids. The gold rush of the 1870s brought thousands to the Black Hills. South Dakota was

Sugar-cane

admitted to the Union in 1889 as the 40th State. Most of its 20,000 Indians live on reservations that are located in every part of South Dakota.

● **squirrel, grey** This is a familiar animal in the eastern half of the United States. Following its introduction to Great Britain, the grey squirrel has multiplied alarmingly and frequently ousted the native red species.

● **sugar cane** This tropical plant is one of the world's two sources of sugar, the other being sugar beets. Sugar cane needs frequent heavy rainfall, high temperatures, and much sunshine. After planting, it takes 12 to 24 months to mature. The ripe stalk is then cut to the ground, and a new growth starts from the stubble. In Cuba, where climate and soil are ideal for sugar cane, four to eight crops can be obtained from one planting. The raw sugar is extracted in mills, but must then be further refined to yield commercial white sugar. About half the world's sugar cane grows in India, Brazil and Cuba, but of these three countries only Cuba produces for export. Cane sugar that enters into trade is usually in the form of raw sugar, which is then refined in the consuming countries. Most of Cuba's exported sugar goes to communist countries.

● **sulphur** The most important raw material in the chemical industry, sulphur is obtained in natural form (mainly in the United States) or from sulphur-bearing metal ores, especially iron pyrites and copper ores. In addition to the production of sulphuric acid, sulphur is used in the fertiliser, rubber and woodpulp industries.

● **Superior, Lake** The most westerly of the Great Lakes, in the United States and Canada, and the largest fresh-water lake in the world (31,800 square miles). It lies 602 feet above sea level and reaches a depth of 1,300 feet. Superior connects with Lake Huron via the St Marys River, whose rapids are by-passed by the Sault Ste. Marie canals and locks (usually called the 'Soo'). Important iron and copper deposits are found near the lake's shores in Minnesota and Michigan. Huge tonnages of iron ore are shipped from Duluth, Minnesota, and Superior, Wisconsin, to steel-mining centres on the lower lakes in Indiana, Ohio and Pennsylvania. Grain from Canada's wheat belt is shipped eastward from the twin ports of Fort William and Port Arthur, Ontario. The French established missions and fur-trading posts on Lake Superior in the middle of the 17th century.

● **Tampico** An important Mexican seaport and oil-producing centre (population 196,100) on the Gulf of Mexico.

● **Taxco** A small town in central Mexico where colonial buildings and atmosphere have been preserved by the government. It attracts thousands of tourists from north of the border who buy the silverware, jewellery and other handicrafts for

In Trinidad, West Indies, machetes and sickles are used in harvesting the sugar-cane crop

which the town is famous. A silver mine has been in operation there for over 400 years.

Tennessee (42,246 square miles; population 3,924,164) is a long, narrow State of the U.S.A., extending from the highest summits of the Appalachian Mountains to the winding course of the Mississippi River. The Tennessee River flows in a great bend, first through the Great Appalachian Valley in eastern Tennessee, then across northern Alabama, and back into Tennessee; it is joined by the Cumberland River before meeting the Ohio River, almost within reach of the Mississippi. The Tennessee Valley Authority (T.V.A.) is a public agency formed in 1933 to build power and flood-control dams (of which there are 32) on the river and its tributaries, to improve navigation, and to develop the resources of the region. Before the Authority was created, Tennessee had been a backward agricultural State, with cotton, maize and tobacco as the principal crops.

Its hilly eastern and central areas were severely eroded; the 'mountaineers' lived in drab cabins without electricity or water supply Today, the region is prosperous. The Tennessee River has been changed into a chain of lakes. There is plenty of cheap power to light the homes and to run new factories, including the atomic plants in the once-secret atom town of Oak Ridge. Tennessee produces textiles (synthetic fibres, cotton and woollen goods), plastics and fertiliser, wood and metal products, and cement. The State is rich in minerals that can be shipped long distances on navigable waterways. Coal, marble, limestone, copper and phosphates are mined. Aluminium smelters have taken advantage of the region's abundant supply of electric power. T.V.A. headquarters are located in Knoxville, the chief city of eastern Tennessee. Nashville (250,887), near the centre of the State, is the capital. Memphis, on a bluff overlooking the Mississippi, is the largest city.

When De Soto discovered the Mississippi in 1541, he found a Cnickasaw village where Memphis now stands. The first permanent settlers came from Virginia in 1757. Tennessee was admitted to the Union in 1796 as the 16th State.

Texas Second in area only to Alaska, Texas (267,339 square miles; population 11,196,730) extends almost 800 miles from east to west and also from north to south; it occupies nearly 9 per cent of the area of the United States. The Rio Grande forms the long boundary with Mexico. Much of the land is level or gently rolling, except in the south-west, where several ranges over 8,000 feet high form a link between the Rocky Mountains and the Sierra Madre of the Mexican highlands. The Gulf coast, with its many lagoons, bays and marshes, has a warm and humid climate and a long growing season. Rainfall decreases towards the interior; the treeless Staked Plains of western Texas are near-desert. With its wide open spaces, Texas leads all the States in the number of livestock it raises; this includes cattle, sheep, horses and goats. The latter supply most of the mohair used in the nation. More cotton is grown in Texas than in any other State, even though yields per acre are not as high as in areas where it is grown under irrigation. Wheat is the leading crop in the north of Texas; maize occupies over 5 million acres, and grain sorghum some 3 million acres. Rice and sugar cane are grown along the Gulf, near the Louisiana line. Most of the State's 2½ million irrigated acres are devoted to vegetables and fruit chiefly potatoes, tomatoes, onions, spinach, carrots, beets and watermelons. The lower Rio Grande Valley is one of the nation's three major citrus-growing areas. Texas ranks first in pecans, and produces a fine harvest of peaches, apples, pears and figs. Most of the State's farms are large and highly mechanised. Pigs are raised in the maize-growing eastern half of Texas; so are turkeys and chickens, in huge quantities.

Texas is the State with the highest value of mineral production. Thousands of oil-wells are

Tobacco

found in the High Plains area, the central plains, the north-east (near Tyler), the Gulf coast, and the offshore water overlying the continental shelf, giving 45% of U.S.A. oil reserves. Natural gas is associated with oil in most of the producing areas, including helium in the north; gas is piped to the western, north-central and eastern States. About three-quarters of the nation's sulphur comes from the Gulf Coast of Texas; it is dissolved underground and piped to the surface. Salt is also recovered there.

The greatest concentration of petroleum refineries is found along the coast near Beaumont, Houston and Corpus Christi. Chemical plants, producing synthetic rubber or magnesium from sea water, are increasingly important. Texas is the birthplace of the 'petrochemical' industry, which uses oil as a raw material for a variety of chemical processes. Meat-packing, centred at Fort Worth, ranks immediately after petroleum in the value of its product. Other plants produce cottonseed oil, canned fruits and vegetables. Modern paper mills are at Lufkin and Houston. Houston, linked by a deep-water ship channel to Galveston Bay, is the largest city (1,985,031 inhabitants with suburbs in 1970) of Texas and the chief cotton-export centre of the United States. Large inland cities are Dallas and Fort Worth (only 40 miles apart), San Antonio, Austin (251,808), the State capital, and El Paso on the Rio Grande.

Spanish explorers visited the coast of Texas as early as 1520. In 1836, Texas declared itself independent of Mexico. It remained an independent republic for nine years, and then, in 1845, joined the Union as the 28th State. The discovery of oil at Spindletop, near Beaumont, in 1901,

marked the beginning of the State's spectacular growth, a process which is still under way.

● **tobacco** Long known to the Indians, and discovered by Europeans when they first came to America, tobacco spread rapidly through the world in the 17th century. A tall, annual plant of rapid growth, it blooms with pink tubular flowers. The leaves are dried and fermented to develop aroma and flavour; they contain up to 8 per cent nicotine. The main tobacco products are cigars, cigarettes, pipe tobacco and snuff. The United States is the chief supplier of so-called Virginia tobacco (for cigarettes), and Turkey of Oriental tobacco, but there are many other kinds. Britain and West Germany are the chief tobacco importers.

● **Toledo** A port city (population 383,818) of Ohio, near the western end of Lake Erie. Lake vessels load coal, oil and farm products. Iron ore comes to Toledo from Minnesota, via the Great Lakes. Industries include steel mills, motor-car plants, glass works and ship building yards. It is also an important railway centre.

● **Toronto** Capital of the province of Ontario and second-largest city (population 2,158,496) of Canada, on the north shore of Lake Ontario. Toronto is an important commercial and financial centre, with headquarters of mining companies, a stock exchange, and textile and metal industries. With completion of the St Lawrence Seaway, sea-going ships are now able to reach Toronto's spacious lake port. A French fur-trading centre was established there in 1749. The site was occupied by the British in 1759, and the settlement which was founded in 1793 (then called York) became the capital of Upper Canada in 1796, and the whole of Canada from 1849 to 1859. The city received the name Toronto in 1834, and its large university was founded in 1827.

● **totem pole** A totem is an object or animal with which a tribe or family group considers itself closely related. The totem pole, on which this 'emblem' is usually carved, is believed to protect the home in front of which it stands. Totemism is especially common among the Indians of the north-west coast of North America.

Texas, famous for cattle ranches, still raises more livestock than any other State in the U.S.A.

The U.S.A.'s national memorial to Thomas Jefferson, on the Potomac River, in Washington, D.C.

● **tulip tree** This North American timber tree grows to 120 feet. Common in the eastern United States, the tree is named after the greenish-yellow, tulip-like flowers it bears. The soft, creamy yellow wood of the tulip tree is much used in cabinet-making, for which it is eminently suitable.

Tulip tree

● **turkey** The wild turkey formerly roamed over vast stretches of North America. Today, this magnificent bird — three feet tall, with a dazzling, fan-like display of feathers — occurs in limited numbers. The Pilgrim Fathers celebrated the first Thanksgiving Day with a wild-turkey dinner. Today, modern turkey-farms raise the birds on a scientific basis, breeding them for smaller frames and meatier breasts so that they take up less oven space. The turkey was domesticated by the Aztecs

long before the coming of the European. The Spaniards brought the bird to Europe, and it was only later that the domestic bird was reintroduced into North America. The bird owes its name to the fact that it was long confused with the guinea-fowl, which was brought to Europe from Africa via Turkey.

● **turtle, hawksbill** Apart from its pronounced beak, this marine turtle is distinguished by the overlapping shingle-like pattern of its shell. The hawksbill is an important source of commercial tortoise-shell.

● **turtle, painted** These small turtles of North America, five to six inches long, are very attractively marked with red and yellow.

● **Ungava** A district of northern Quebec, Canada, along Hudson Bay and Hudson Strait. A barren and empty land of lakes, marshes and tundra, Ungava contains enormous iron deposits that are now being exploited.

● **United Nations** This international Organisation to preserve peace and promote co-operation among countries was set up after the Second World War as successor to the League of Nations. The principal bodies of the U.N. are the Security Council, the General Assembly, the International

Court of Justice, and a number of specialised economic and cultural agencies. The headquarters of the U.N. is in New York. By the end of March, 1972, membership of the Organisation has risen to 132 countries.

● **Utah** A Western mountain State (84,916 square miles; population 1,059,273) of the U.S.A. which is noted for the variety of its surface features and its Great Salt Lake. The landscape is dominated by two mountain ranges: the Wasatch, which crosses the State from the north; and the Uinta, which runs from east to west, and rises almost to 13,500 feet above sea level. South of the Uinta Mountains lies the vast expanse of the Colorado Plateau, carved by wind and water into spectacular cliffs, natural bridges, isolated buttes and mesas, and the splendid gorges of the Colorado and Green Rivers. Western Utah is a land of desert salt flats and dry mountain ranges; it is almost empty, except for mining camps. Most of the people live in the irrigated valleys just west of the Wasatch Range. Here the land is cultivated intensively and with great care. Wheat, hay, alfalfa, oats, potatoes, sugar beets, vegetables, apples and peaches are the principal crops. Sheep are raised extensively in the drier areas. The chief source of income in Utah is mining. The State is a leading producer of copper (at Bingham Canyon), lead, silver, zinc and gold. There are also large reserves of coal, iron ore, salt, phosphate and vanadium. Salt Lake City (the capital and largest city) and Logan have oil

Vanilla

refineries; a large steel plant is in operation near Provo; and uranium is processed in several mills scattered over south-eastern Utah. Travellers are always eager to see the Mormon temple and other monuments in beautiful Salt Lake City, founded by Brigham Young in 1847. Colourful south-western Utah is frequently used as a location for 'Western' films. There, too, are the natural wonders of Bryce Canyon and Zion National Parks.

The Mormons came to Utah from Illinois in 1847. When they sighted the valley at the foot of the Wasatch ("This is the place!" cried Brigham Young), they called it Deseret. They made it productive by using the water from mountain streams to irrigate their arid fields. Grasshopper plagues and Indian raids made life difficult for the first settlers. In 1869, the trans-continental railway became a reality when the tracks from east and west were linked at Promontory Point.

● **Vancouver** Canada's largest seaport on the Pacific and its third-largest city (population 955,000), situated on the coast of British Columbia near the U.S. border, and facing 300-mile-long Vancouver Island. Ice-free all the year round, the port has shipping services to Alaska, the west coast of the United States, and the Far East. Salmon-canning, lumbering and shipbuilding are the city's chief industries. Founded only a century ago, Vancouver has grown into a modern metropolis with skyscrapers and sprawling suburbs. Fishing and lumbering are the chief activities on densely wooded, mountainous Vancouver Island. Its largest city, Victoria (population 173,455), is the capital of the province of British Columbia. Coal and iron ore are present.

George Washington's plantation, Mount Vernon, is situated in north-eastern Virginia

vanilla This tropical American climbing orchid furnishes the familiar flavouring extract. Vanilla, obtained by curing the long, podlike capsules, is widely used in confectionery and perfumes. Vanillin, the active agent of vanilla, is now also prepared artificially.

Veracruz A Mexican seaport (population 242,300) on the Gulf of Mexico. It exports coffee, vanilla and hides, and is Mexico City's nearest outlet to the sea. Cortés landed there in 1519, to begin his conquest of the Aztec empire.

Vermont A New England State (9,609 square miles; population 444,732) crossed lengthwise by the spruce and fir-covered Green Mountains. The Connecticut River forms the eastern border with New Hampshire. Lake Champlain, of which Vermont owns about two-thirds, separates it from New York in the west. Mountain lakes, swift streams, scenic trails and quaint villages attract holidaymakers from Boston and New York City. In the wintertime, the State is invaded by skiers bound for Stowe, Woodstock or Middlebury. Except for dairying, farming is on the decline. The land is rocky and rugged, the winters are long and cold, and the young people are leaving the farms for the cities. The major dairying area is the lowland adjoining Lake Champlain; the milk is sent by lorry to metropolitan centres 300 miles away. Like the Iroquois before them, Vermonters draw the sap from the sugar-maple and boil it into syrup and sugar. Vermont has large deposits of high-quality marble (near Rutland) and granite (near Barre), used in monuments and for construction work. Woodworking and textile-milling are traditional Vermont industries. Burlington (38,633), on Lake Champlain, is the largest city; Montpelier (8,609) is the State capital.

In 1609, Champlain discovered the lake now named after him, yet the region was not settled until 1724, when a fort was established. Having declared its independence from Britain in 1777, Vermont was the first State to be admitted to the Union (1791) after the original 13.

Virgin Islands A group of 100 small islands in the West Indies, east of Puerto Rico. Discovered by Columbus on his second voyage (1493), the islands are now partly British and partly U.S. owned. St Thomas, St John and St Croix are the three principal islands under the U.S. flag. They have a population of 63,200, and the capital is at Charlotte Amalie on St Thomas. A national park was established on St John in 1957. They were owned by Denmark from 1671, 1684 and 1733 respectively, and sold to the United States in 1917. The British Virgin Islands (67 square miles; population 7,300) trade mainly with Puerto Rico and St Thomas. They have been in British hands since 1666, and the largest island is Tortola. Most of the population is Negro. The Virgin Islands produced sugar cane and rum, but these have been phased out and replaced by food crops.

Virginia A State (40,815 square miles; population 4,648,500) of the U.S.A., situated between Chesapeake Bay and the Appalachian Mountains. Its capital and largest city is Richmond. Hampton Roads, consisting of the ports of Norfolk, Newport News and Portsmouth at the mouth of the James River, command the entrance to Chesapeake Bay. There there are important shipbuilding yards, a naval station, and miles of docks where coal is transferred from railway-wagons to cargo ships.

Eastern Virginia is flat, though cut up by the wide estuaries of the Potomac, Rappahannock, York and James Rivers. Across Chesapeake Bay, the southern tip of the Delmarva Peninsula also belongs to Virginia. The central portion of the State is hilly; it is called the 'piedmont'. The impressive, 5,000-foot-high barrier of the Blue Ridge runs the full length of Virginia from northeast to south west.

West of the Blue Ridge is the valley and ridge country of the folded Appalachian Mountains; there lies the historic Shenandoah Valley, known for its apple orchards, turkeys and lush farms. Numerous caves are found in the limestone rock which underlies the valley. Almost everything is grown in the 'Old Dominion', Virginia tobacco being the principal cash crop; it has been famous ever since Sir Walter Raleigh learned to smoke it, more than three centuries ago. Over 16 million acres are used as farm or pasture land. Most of the crops (hay, maize, oats, peanuts) are fed to livestock — cattle, pigs, poultry, and some sheep. Horses are reared in the piedmont and peaches are grown there. Potatoes (white and sweet), peas, beans, cabbage and other vegetables are the products of eastern Virginia's market-gardens. Chesapeake Bay is a great fishing area, especially for oysters, clams and crabs. Coal is mined in the Cumberland Plateau, in the extreme south-western corner of the State. Tobacco products — especially cigarettes made in Richmond — are the State's leading industry. Lumber, wood products and paper are made from the oak and pine that are native to the coastal plain and the piedmont. Virginia also has a number of modern cotton and rayon mills, and chemical plants.

The first permanent English settlement in America was at Jamestown, founded in 1607 by Captain John Smith and a band of hardy pioneers. Soon, Negro slaves were brought from Africa to work the cotton and tobacco plantations. Virginia was one of the original 13 colonies to sign the Constitution of the United States. In 1861, it seceded from the Union, and Richmond became the capital of the Confederacy. The counties west of the Appalachians opposed secession, and in 1863 they returned to the Union as the State of West Virginia. Virginia was the chief battleground of the Civil War, and returned to the Union in 1870.

walrus This droll-looking relative of the seal is at home on Arctic ice-packs off the coasts of North America and northern Asia. Generally peaceful, this ten-foot-long animal, weighing 2,000 pounds, uses its fierce tusks for fighting the polar bear and killer whale, and for digging clams.

Washington A State (68,192 square miles; population 3,409,169) in the Pacific North-West of the U.S.A., bounded by Canada on the north and the Pacific Ocean in the west. The rugged Cascade Range, with its row of volcanic peaks, divides the State in two: to the west lies Puget Sound, an island-studded, 100-mile-deep inlet of the Pacific, bordered by a narrow coastal lowland; to the east lies the vast expanse of the Columbia Plateau, a level tableland underlain by lava beds, and crossed by low ridges and dried-up river channels. East of the Cascades, the climate is dry and the natural vegetation scanty. Vast cattle and sheep ranches occupy the sparsely populated land. West of the Cascades, the Puget Sound lowland enjoys a temperate, humid climate with cool summers and mild winters. It is the State's dairying, poultry-raising, and specialised market-gardening centre. Washington is the nation's leading apple-growing State. The fruit districts (where pears, plums, peaches and grapes are grown) are in the irrigated sections of the Yakima, Wenatchee and Okanogan Valleys, at the eastern foot of the Cascades.

The Columbia River crosses Washington in two great bends; its lower course, after receiving the Snake River, forms the Oregon line. Salmon are caught, and Washington leads the nation in the total catch of fish for food. Puget Sound is the centre for North Pacific fishing fleets, and canneries

Dome of the U.S. Capitol, Washington, D.C.

The white spire of the village church is a familiar sight in the green valleys of Vermont, U.S.A.

Virginia's fertile Shenandoah Valley lies between the Blue Ridge Mountains and the Appalachians

in the towns along its shore produce tinned halibut, tuna, cod, and many other species. With more than half of its area forested, Washington is third only to Oregon and California in lumber production. Hundreds of sawmills dot the Puget Sound shore and the Pacific coast; pulp, paper and plywood mills use up the splendid stands of Ponderosa pine, Douglas fir, and spruce. Seattle, a major seaport for the Alsakan and Oriental trade, is the largest city; it has fish-processing plants, aircraft and aerospace industries and railway shops. Farther south, on Puget Sound, lies Tacoma, a seaport and lumber-milling centre. Spokane is the only major city in eastern Washington. Olympia is the State capital (23,111 inhabitants). The construction of power dams on the Columbia River (notably Grand Coulee and Bonneville dams) and the sale of cheap electricity have brought new industries to the State. Six modern aluminium reduction plants, and a major atomic energy installation, have been built since 1945. Washington's fine natural setting offers many opportunities for the tourist industry. In the Cascades, snow-covered Mt Rainier (14,410 feet) offers the most spectacular scenery. The region formed part of Oregon Territory until 1853. It entered the Union in 1889 as the 42nd State.

● **Washington, D.C.** The capital city (population 2,861,133) of the United States, in the District of Columbia, on the left bank of the Potomac River. The site for the Federal capital was selected by George Washington, and the land, 10 miles square, was granted to the United States by Maryland in 1790. The gridiron pattern of streets, overlaid by avenues radiating from the Capitol and the White House, was designed by the French architect Pierre L'Enfant. Jefferson was the first President to be inaugurated in Washington, and the Congress first convened there in 1800. Most of the city's public buildings were burned down, after it fell to British troops in the War of 1812. Washington was repeatedly threatened by Confederate forces during the Civil War, but it was not captured. The city grew slowly during the 19th century; not until World War I did it begin to look like a dignified centre of government.

Outstanding among its impressive public buildings are the Capitol, the seat of the law-making branch of the government, with the Senate and House chambers; the White House, official home

of the President, on broad Pennsylvania Avenue the 555-foot column of the Washington Monument; the Lincoln Memorial; the Jefferson Memorial; 'embassy row', along Massachusetts Avenue; the Library of Congress, and the white marble Supreme Court building. The huge Pentagon building (which houses the Department of Defense) and Arlington National Cemetery, with the Tomb of the Unknown Soldier, are just across the Potomac in Arlington County, Virginia. Mount Vernon, the home of George Washington and now a national shrine, is linked to the city by a parkway along the south shore of the Potomac. As the federal government has grown, government buildings and the homes of thousands of civil servants have spilled over into adjacent areas, in Maryland and Virginia.

● **West Indies** or **Antilles** A chain of islands off Central America, extending in a 2,500-mile-long arc from Mexico to the northern coast of South America. The West Indies enclose the Caribbean

Sea; to the north lies the Gulf of Mexico, and to the east the Atlantic Ocean. The islands are usually divided into three groups: the Bahamas, off the coast of Florida; the Greater Antilles, which include the large islands of Cuba, Jamaica, Hispaniola and Puerto Rico; and the Lesser Antilles, between Puerto Rico and the coast of Venezuela. The islands lie in the sub-tropical belt of the trade winds, which blow from an easterly direction all the year around. Local temperatures and rainfall vary with altitude, and the windward or leeward location, but mild winters make the West Indies one of the world's favourite resort areas. The Dominican Republic, Cuba, Haiti, Barbados, Jamaica, and Trinidad and Tobago, are independent countries, the last three being members of the British Commonwealth. Britain still possesses a number of colonies in the West Indies, many of them in the process of achieving independence. Islands such as Grenada, St Lucia, St Kitts, St Vincent, Antigua and Dominica were given self-government in 1967, with aid from Britain and retention of control over their finance, defence and foreign relations by the British government, through a local commissioner appointed by London. The French possessions (Martinique, Guadeloupe, and a few smaller islands) are governed as part of metropolitan France. The Netherlands Antilles (Curaçao, Aruba, and others) have local rule, but are joined to the Netherlands by the Crown. Puerto Rico is a commonwealth, with local self-government freely associated with the United States. Sugar is traditionally the main crop of the West Indies. Beginning in the 17th century, European planters brought thousands of African slaves to the islands for work in the cane fields. In the 19th century, labourers from India replaced the liberated slaves on the sugar estates. Most of the islands are poor in natural resources, short on cultivable land, and over-populated. The total population of the West Indies is about 20 million.

● **West Virginia** The 'Mountain State' (24,181 square miles; population 1,744,237) of the U.S.A. is mostly hilly, and level land is therefore at a premium; it is found only along the rivers which flow either to the Ohio, in the west, or to the Potomac, in the north-east. The Ohio and its main tributaries have been made navigable (by means of locks) for barges that carry coal, lumber, sand and other raw materials to the factories along the banks.

The chief industrial centres are located on these waterways: Huntington, Wheeling (a steel centre), Parkersburg (with chemical and aluminium plants) are on the Ohio: Charleston (246,900), the capital, lies on the Kanawha; Clarksburg and Fairmont

Ruin of an ancient Mayan temple at Chichén Itzá, on Mexico's isolated Yucatán Peninsula

on the Monongahela. West Virginia is, above all, a mining State; it has the nation's largest coal reserves (50%), a dwindling supply of oil and natural gas, silica sand for the glass industry, and abundant salt occurring at great depth in the Ohio basin. High-grade clay deposits have given rise to numerous potteries in the north. The State is a leading supplier of hardwoods for walnut, chestnut, oak, yellow poplar and ash forests cover almost two-thirds of its area. Much of the remaining land is used for grazing, rather than for crops, because cultivated hillsides are subject to severe erosion. Most of the farms are small, and few are prosperous. Maize and hay are stored as feed for the livestock. Apples are an important cash crop in the east, and tobacco is raised near Huntington.

The area that is now West Virginia formed part of Virginia until the Civil War. When Virginia seceded, the western counties remained loyal to the North, and were organised into a separate State in 1863, the 35th to be admitted to the Union.

whale, Greenland This Arctic giant, also known as bowhead, is 50 to 60 feet long. The Greenland whale has been hunted so extensively for its whalebone and oil that it is almost extinct.

Williamsburg A historic city in Virginia, near Chesapeake Bay. Thousands of visitors go to see its restored colonial buildings every year. It was settled in 1632, and was the capital of Virginia during most of the 18th century.

Windsor An industrial city (population 211,697) of Ontario, Canada, on the Detroit River, opposite Detroit, Michigan. It has motor-car and steel-product plants. A bridge, tunnel and ferries link the two cities; the international border between Canada and the U.S.A. runs through the middle of the river.

Winnipeg Largest city (population 524,000) of central Canada and capital of Manitoba, situated on the Red River and on trans-continental railways, about 60 miles north of the U.S. border. One of North America's leading wheat markets, Winnipeg is the distributing centre for Canada's Prairie Provinces. Lake Winnipeg, 40 miles to the north, drains into Hudson Bay by the Nelson River. There are timber and paper industries based on local water power. The lake (9,400 square miles) is a remnant of a much larger body of water (known to geologists as Lake Agassiz) which covered parts of Minnesota and the Dakotas during the Ice Age.

Wisconsin A Midwestern State (56,154 square miles; population 4,417,933) of the U.S.A. known as 'America's Dairyland'. It produces more milk and cheese than any other State, and almost as much butter as Minnesota. It borders on Lake Michigan and Lake Superior. Lake-studded northern Wisconsin is a holiday centre. Its valuable forests were cut down many years ago, but some have been replanted, and once again supply sawmills and paper mills. Wisconsin's main crops — hay, maize, oats — are grown for the dairy industry. Its prosperous farms also raise sugar beets, potatoes, vegetables, strawberries, and even tobacco. Cherry orchards line the Door Peninsula on Lake Michigan. Only one person in six, however, lives on a farm, and the chief industrial centres are in south-eastern Wisconsin, not far from Chicago. They make parts for motor-cars and farm machinery, household appliances, leather goods and furniture. Milwaukee, by far the largest city, is famous for its beer. Racine and Kenosha are smaller manufacturing cities. In the far north, Superior ships the iron ore from Wisconsin's mines to ports on the lower Great Lakes. Madison (287,501) is the State capital. Tourism is third in economic importance in Wisconsin.

French fur-traders, explorers and missionaries visited the region in the 17th century. They called it New France. The British took over in 1763, at the end of the French and Indian War. They in turn ceded the area to the United States as part of the North-West Territory. Called the 'Badger State', Wisconsin was admitted to the Union in 1848, and was settled by newly-arrived German and Scandinavian immigrants.

wolf, timber A grey wolf of North America, especially common in Canada and Alaska. It grows up to six feet long, and is almost 30 inches high at the shoulder. Wolves howl in loud, mournful tones that sound very sinister. Actually, their howls indicate lively interest and vigour, rather than sadness or despair. Timber wolves sometimes hunt in packs, tracking their prey for a distance up to 100 miles, until it becomes exhausted and can be easily killed.

Wyoming A Western state (97,914 square miles; population 332,416) of the U.S.A. where the Great Plains meet the Rocky Mountains. It consists of vast tablelands that lie 5,000 to 7,000 feet above sea level, such as the Big Horn, Shoshone and Great Divide Basins. Several mountain ranges curve across the State; the highest are the Wind River Range and the lovely, snow-covered Tetons (13,766 feet); others are the well-known Laramie and Big Horn Mountains. Dry, treeless and barren, Wyoming is a leading sheep-raising State; it ranks next to Texas in the amount of wool and mutton it produces. There are large cattle ranches as well. All the crops, except wheat, are grown under irrigation; they include sugar beets, hay, beans and fruit. Wyoming has many high-grade coal-fields, some of which have yet to be mined. Petroleum and natural gas are piped to homes and factories throughout the Rocky Mountain area. Iron is mined for Colorado's steel mills, and there are important phosphate and uranium deposits. Wyoming has few industrial plants, apart from oil refineries and beet-sugar mills. The main business of its cities is the sale of livestock. Cheyenne (40,914), the capital and largest city, is famed for its annual rodeo.

Tourists come to Wyoming to climb mountains, hunt, catch trout, and see the geysers and boiling springs of Yellowstone, the nation's oldest and largest national park.

The first permanent fur-trading post was established at Fort Laramie in 1834. Despite raids by the Cheyenne Indians, settlement proceeded rapidly as the Pony Express, and later the railway, provided access from the East. Wyoming was admitted to the Union in 1890, as the 44th State. It is nicknamed the 'Equality State', because it was the first to grant women the right to vote, in the year 1869.

Yellowstone National Park Largest and oldest of the U.S. national parks, it was established in 1872, occupying 3,500 square miles in the northwest corner of Wyoming. Yellowstone is famed for its hot springs that throw jets of steam or hot water high into the air. The best-known is Old Faithful, which spouts hot water to a height of 140 feet at hourly intervals. The region is a volcanic upland bordered by ranges of the Rocky Mountains; it lies at an elevation of 7—8,000 feet. Deer, elk, moose, mountain sheep and bison roam freely in the park, and bears are often met along roads and near camp grounds.

The Yellowstone River, a major tributary of the Missouri, crosses the park, forming three spectacular falls and Yellowstone Lake. It has also cut a 1,500-feet-deep canyon below the surface of the plateau.

Yorktown An historic town in Virginia, not far from Williamsburg. It was settled in 1631 and became an important seaport. The surrender of

Ribbon Falls, a scenic attraction in the Yosemite National Park, California

Cornwallis to Washington at Yorktown, in 1781, marked the end of the Revolutionary War.

Yosemite A spectacular mountain region in the Sierra Nevada of central California, about 150 miles east of San Francisco. Deep canyons, towering cliffs, high waterfalls, lakes and magnificent old trees compete for the visitor's attention in the National Park. U-shaped Yosemite Valley, carved out by a glacier and flanked by near-vertical cliffs, is one of the most prominent features.

Yucatán A peninsula (70,000 square miles) in Central America, separating the Gulf of Mexico from the Caribbean Sea, except for a 130-mile-wide channel (the Yucatán Channel) between the mainland and the western tip of Cuba. Most of the peninsula lies in Mexico, and the southern part in British Honduras and Guatemala. It consists of an almost level limestone tableland, with scanty vegetation in the north (where the rain seeps into the porous rock where it falls), and dense tropical forest in the south. Its main products are sisal — 50% of the world's output — (a fibre for rope-making), chicle (the raw material for chewing-gum), and mahogany and dyewoods. Centuries before the Spanish invasion, Yucatán was the centre of the Mayan civilisation, the fascinating ruins of which are well preserved near Mérida, the largest modern city of the peninsula. Mayas still form the majority of the rural population. Yucatán teems with exotic tropical animals — among them the armadillo, iguana, and unique ocellated turkey.

Yukon A Territory (207,000 square miles; population 20,000 — following a mining boom) of north-western Canada, bordering on Alaska. Crossed by the northern ranges of the Rocky Mountains, it contains Mt Logan (19,850 feet), Canada's highest summit. It is drained by the Yukon River (2,000 miles long), which empties into the Bering Sea after crossing Alaska. Gold was discovered in the Klondike district in 1896, and by 1901 more than 25,000 prospectors had joined the gold rush. Whitehorse (7,500), the region's chief town, is linked by railway with the Pacific coast at Skagway. The Yukon is navigable below Whitehorse during the summer months. The Alaska Highway, built during World War II, has made the Territory more easily accessible from the south. Fur-trapping has been carried on by the Hudson's Bay Company for more than a century. The country abounds with big game, such as moose, caribou, mountain sheep and bears. Mining, however, is the main concern, as there are large deposits of silver, gold, zinc and lead. Yukon was separated from the Northern Territories in 1898.

South America

The southern of the two continents of the Western Hemisphere (7 million square miles in area; population 165 million) extends farther south than any other continent: at Cape Horn, its southernmost point, it is separated only by the 650 miles of Drake Strait from Graham Land, on the Antarctic continent.

From the isthmus of Panama to the barren uplands of Tierra del Fuego, South America is traversed by a continuous chain of mountains known as the Andes. The Andean backbone of South America is rather slender and, throughout its length, it hugs the continent's Pacific coast. Second in height only to the Himalayas, the Andes constitute a formidable barrier to communications from the Pacific to the Atlantic shore. The Andes contain the highest peak in the Western Hemisphere (Aconcagua, 22,834 feet) and, unlike the Rocky Mountains of North America, they do not offer any low passes for highway or railway crossings. Thus, Uspallata Pass, between Argentina and Chile, lies more than 12,464 feet above sea level, and the rail line that crosses it is frequently interrupted by snow and rock avalanches.

As a result of this mountain range, and because there are no other physiographic obstacles (the Brazilian plateau and the Guiana highlands are lower and much more dissected), South America boasts a lowland that occupies nearly the full width of the continent, roughly parallel with the equator.

This lowland is drained by the Amazon, which carries more water than any other river in the world and is as long as the combined courses of the Missouri and Mississippi Rivers. From its source, high in the Andes and less than 100 miles from the Pacific coast, the Amazon flows majestically across 3,500 miles of tropical rain-forest to its huge delta on the Atlantic Ocean. With its innumerable tributaries, it drains an area that is almost as large as the United States, but which remains almost uninhabited and unexploited to this day.

The second-largest river system in South America is that of the Rio de la Plata, which empties the combined water of the Paraguay, Paraná and Uruguay Rivers into an enormous estuary, on which the busy seaports of Montevideo (Uruguay) and Buenos Aires (Argentina) are located. Though smaller in size than the Amazon, the Río de la Plata has played a much more important part in the economic development of its drainage basin. The fertility of the Argentine Pampa is chiefly responsible for the intensive utilisation of the plains bordering on the Río de la Plata. There is situated South America's corn belt, potentially as productive as the maize and wheat belts of the central United States and the black-earth districts of the Soviet Ukraine. There, too, is an area of warm, temperate climate comparable to that of the south-eastern United States, the only such area between the tropical and sub-tropical coastal regions of Brazil to the north, and the cold and windy near-desert expanse of Patagonia to the south.

It would be misleading simply to state that three-quarters of South America lies within the Tropics, for it is necessary to realise that there is just as great a variety of climate in the Tropics as there is in the Temperate Zone, in which Great Britain lies. We must distinguish, for instance, between the

M Mangrove Forest
R Rain Forest
S Savanna
Sc Scrub

Wild Animals and Plants

Mammals

1 Solenodon
2 Baird's tapir
3 Mountain tapir
4 South American tapir, northern type*
5 South American tapir, southern type*
6 Yapok (Water opossum)
7 Azara's opossum*
8 Spectacled bear*
9 Coati*
10 Unau (two-toed sloth)
11 Ai (three-toed sloth)
12 Squirrel monkey
13 Uakari monkey
14 Red howling monkey
15 Grey woolly monkey
16 Marmoset
17 Guemul
18 Marsh deer
19 Pampas deer*
20 Pudu deer
21 Vicuña*
22 Guanaco*
23 Manatee*
24 Jaguar*
25 Puma*
26 Patagonian puma
27 Water hog*
28 Nutria*
29 Woolly tree porcupine
30 Patagonian cavy
31 White-lipped peccary*
32 Collared peccary*
33 Round-eared dog
34 Azara's dog*
35 Maned wolf
36 Giant ant-eater*
37 Nine-banded armadillo*
38 Three-banded armadillo
39 South American sea lion*
40 Sea leopard*
41 Bottle-nosed dolphin*
42 Pygmy sperm whale*
43 Humpback whale*

Reptiles and Amphibians

44 Black caiman
45 Iguana*
46 Marine iguana
47 Giant tortoise
48 Boa constrictor*
49 Bushmaster

Birds

50 Common flamingo*
51 Andean flamingo*
52 Quetzal
53 Great curassow
54 Smooth-billed curassow
55 Red-tailed tropic bird*
56 Yellow-billed tropic bird*
57 Cock of the Rock*
58 Ararauna*
59 Hyacinthine macaw
60 Blue-fronted amazon
61 Jendaya conure
62 Toco
63 Frilled coquette (humming-bird)
64 Jabiru*
65 King vulture*
66 Condor*
67 Rhea*
68 Darwin's rhea
69 Flightless cormorant
70 White-breasted Peruvian cormorant*
71 Galapagos penguin*
72 Humboldt penguin*
73 King penguin*
74 Magellan penguin*
75 Macaroni penguin*
76 Jackass penguin*
77 Sooty shearwater*
78 Sooty tern*
79 Wilson's storm petrel*

Fishes

80 Sting-ray*
81 Swordfish
82 Shark*

Plants

83 Coconut palm*
84 Royal palm*
85 Cabbage palmetto*
86 Assai palm*
87 Wax palm*
88 Carnauba palm
89 Agave*
90 Philodendron*
91 Tree fern*
92 Brazil nut
93 Hevea rubber tree*
94 Odontoglossum orchid
95 Cattleya orchid
96 Cacao tree*
97 Calabash tree*
98 Giant bromelia
99 Opuntia (prickly pear)*
100 Cereus cactus*
101 Araucaria pine*

Plants and animals designated with an asterisk (*) have a wide distribution. Others are found only where pictured.

cool and frequently overcast desert weather of the Peruvian coast, the rainy and monotonously hot, humid climate of the Amazon Basin, and the striking climatic diversity in the inter-tropical Andes, where temperatures decrease with altitude and where each valley has its own climate. At 9,000 feet above sea level in Quito, Ecuador, which is sited on the Equator, the population enjoys what has been called 'an eternal spring', with cool nights and pleasantly warm days. At elevations of 14,500 feet in Colombia, not very far to the north, one encounters the perpetual snow-line, even though a few miles away, at sea level, bananas are grown under humid tropical conditions.

Climate is only one of the factors responsible for the pattern of settlement in South America. It is true that Amazonia remains virtually empty because its tropical red soils, leached of their nutrients and minerals by daily downpours all the year round, do not lend themselves to continuous crop cultivation; yet there are other parts of the continent which could be more intensively utilised for the production of food and fibre crops, but for their remoteness from large markets and the widespread dislike on the part of the population to live on the land, rather than in the cities. As can be readily seen on a map of South America, almost all the major cities are located either on the coast or at higher elevations within easy reach of a seaport. The interior of the continent, on the other hand, cannot boast of a single important urban centre.

The people of South America are derived from three utterly different racial and cultural origins. First there were the Indians; then came the white *conquistadores* from Spain and Portugal; and soon after that the Europeans brought Negro slaves from West Africa to work on their plantations. In the course of more than 300 years of living together on the same continent, the three racial groups have intermixed freely and almost without restriction, so that today there is no longer a clear-cut distinction between red, white and black. The *mestizo* (of mixed Indian and European parentage), the *mulatto* (mixed Negro and European), and people of various gradations in between, now make up the majority of South America's population of approximately 165 million. Yet most of the wealth is still in the hands of people of European origin, who dominate life in the major cities and control the sources and production of the principal export commodities. Most of the Negro population is found on the Caribbean coast of Colombia and Venezuela, in the Guianas,

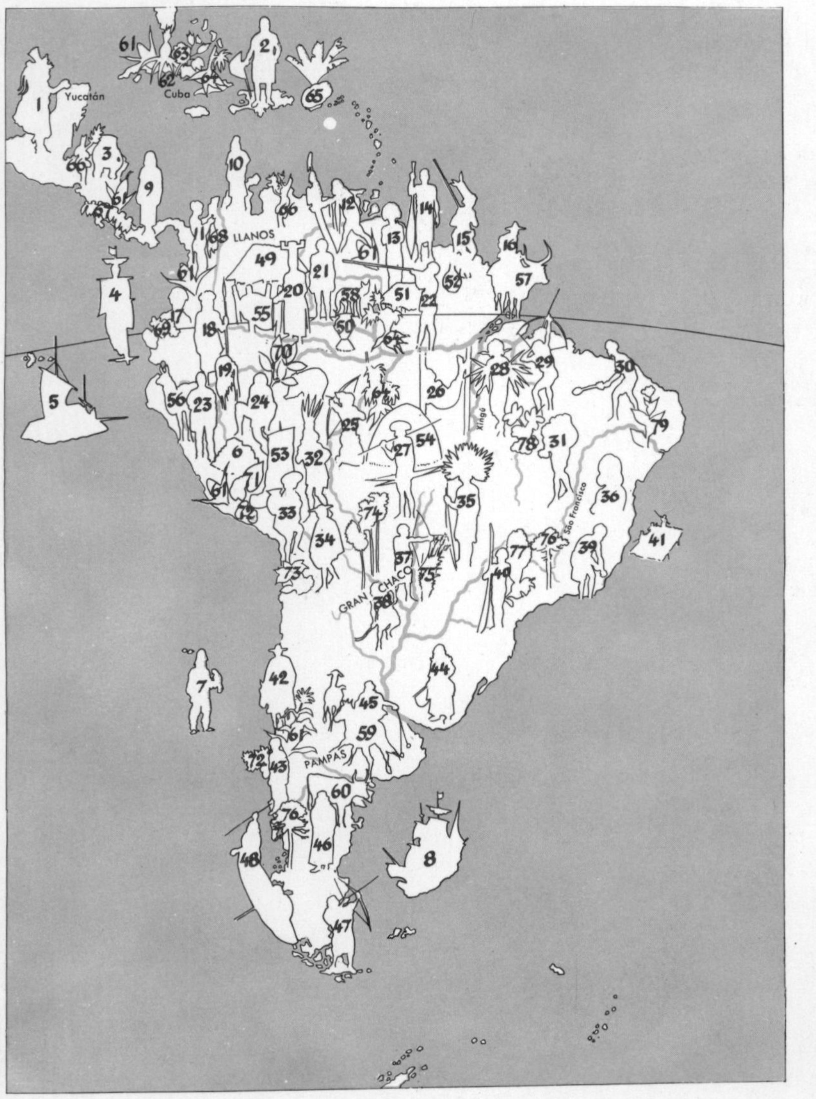

Peoples, Domestic Animals and Useful Plants

Ethnic grups

Ay Aymara
Ac Araucanian
Ar Arawak
C Caraib
Ch Chibcha
G Ges
Gu Guaycuru
P Pano
Pt Patagonian
T Tupi

History

1 Ancient Mayan priest
2 Dessalines, leader of Haitian independence and first president (1804-06)
3 Chorotega Indian pottery
4 Francisco Pizarro conquering Peru and Ecuador (1531-33)
5 Balsa raft of Inca design, used by the Kon-Tiki expedition in 1947
6 Incan Temple of the Sun at Machupicchu, ancient Incan capital
7 Alexander Selkirk, reputed prototype of Robinson Crusoe, on Juan Fernandez Islands
8 Magellan on the first voyage around the world (1519-22)

Peoples

9 Guaymi girl (Ch)
10 Aruac Indian (Ch)
11 Choco Indian
12 Guarauno Indian in a shield game
13 Taulipang Indian (C)
14 Bush Negro
15 Rukuyenne (C)

16 Gaucho on Marajo Island
17 Colorado Indian (Ch), hair and body dyed red with annatto seed
18 Jivaro Indian
19 Shrunken head
20 Opaina masked dancer
21 Umaua Indian (C)
22 Ticuna Indian with blowpipe
23 Chanca Indian (Ay)
24 Chipibo (P) bast weaver
25 Caripuna (P) on peccary hunt
26 Bakairi (C) woman
27 Tucari Indian
28 Cayapo (G) in bird-feather costume
29 Chavantes Indian (G)
30 Guajajara Indian (T) with club
31 Acroa woman (G) carrying basket on back
32 Dancing Aymara Indian with panpipe
33 Quechua Indian
34 Aymara Indian
35 Bororo Indian
36 Botocudo woman (G)
37 Toba Indian (Gu)
38 Mocovi Indian (Gu), playing a kind of hockey
39 Guarani Indian (T)
40 Bugre Indian (G) with 7-foot-long bow
41 Seafaring Goyataca Indians
42 Chilean gaucho
43 Huilliche Indian (Ac)
44 Gaucho in 19th-century dress
45 Puelche Indian using the bola on guanaco hunt

46 Tehuelche Indian (Pt)
47 Ona Indian (Pt)
48 Chono Indians in boat made of bark

Characteristic Dwellings and Implements

49 Native lean-to, 100 feet by 50 feet
50 Catapolitani Indian pottery
51 Open-walled family dwelling of the Ticuna Indians
52 Caraib Indian pottery
53 Balsa boat on Lake Titicaca
54 Beehive hut of the Tucari Indians
55 Signal drum

Domestic Animals

56 Llama
57 Zebu cattle of Marajó Island
58 Indian dog
59 Cimarrones (half-wild horses)
60 Creole cattle

Useful Plants

61 Maize
62 Pineapple
63 Cotton
64 Cassava
65 Bananas
66 Cacao tree
67 Coffee
68 Lima beans
69 Annatto seed
70 Coca leaves
71 Tree tomato
72 Potatoes
73 Peruvian cotton
74 Acuri palm
75 Wild rice
76 Araucaria pine
77 Mate
78 Peanuts
79 Tobacco

and along the coast of Brazil. The Andean Republics of Ecuador, Peru, Bolivia and Chile embrace the largest elements of pure Indians who tend to live apart from the *mestizo* and white population in self-contained highland villages. In the course of the past century, the original white population of Spanish and Portuguese origin has been enlarged and strengthened by several waves of European immigrants, chiefly Italians, Germans and Poles. These immigrants settled some of the finest coffee lands of south-eastern Brazil, established rural communities in southern Brazil, where they proceeded to grow typically European crops, and spread into Uruguay and Argentina, where they bolstered the grain-and-livestock economy of the Pampa.

When Pizarro invaded Peru in 1531, he found that the Andean region, extending from Ecuador to Chile, formed part of a powerful empire with an agricultural economy based on the cultivation of maize, a native South American plant. The empire was ruled by the Inca (the Emperor), who had conquered a number of tribes and had welded them into a single well-knit State. Control was sometimes maintained by moving conquered tribes to other regions and resettling the area with those most loyal to the emperor. The Inca was an absolute monarch, demanded slave-like obedience, and collected his taxes by making the people work for him for a stated number of days. Religion was in the hands of a priestly class which led the people in the worship of the god Viracocha and his servants — the sun, thunder, moon, stars, earth and sea. Inca engineers had developed extraordinary skills in order to overcome the difficulties of terrain and climate. They were the only American Indians to use beasts of burden. Although they were not familiar with the principle of the wheel, with the aid of llamas as draft animals,

they yet managed to construct elaborate palaces and temples, intricate suspension bridges, and a network of roads that survive to this day. Some of the stone blocks used in building were as much as 20 feet high and many tons in weight. Having no written language, they kept records by means of a complicated system of knotting coloured strings, known as *quipu*. The Incas also excelled in metalwork, in the manufacture of cotton and woollen textiles, and in the art of ceramics. Their empire was torn by civil strife at the time of Pizarro's conquest, and it fell apart overnight after the Spanish had captured and executed the emperor.

Pizarro and the *conquistadores* who followed him into South America were driven by three motivating forces — 'Greed, Gold, and God'; but they were reluctant to settle down and engage in the kind of hard labour needed to establish a permanent basis for agriculture in the New World. They preferred to exploit the Indians, and to force them to work in the mines so that more gold and silver could be shipped from the Spanish Main. The policy of the distant Spanish government led to a revolt in her colonies in 1810. By 1824, Venezuela, Argentina, Chile and Peru, under the dedicated leadership of Simon Bolivar, had forced Spain to recognise them as independent republics. Brazil freed herself from Portuguese rule in the same period.

'Exploitation of resources' has been the recurrent motive throughout the colonial and modern history of the South American continent — starting with gold, and then changing to diamonds, to sugar, to coffee, and to whatever product would bring a quick return at the expense of destroying or impoverishing the land. Yet urban luxury and speculation in real estate still predominate over the systematic development of the continent's inherent wealth in land and mineral resources.

Production, Mineral Resources and Trade

Industries
1 Smelting works
2 Chemical plant
3 Chilean nitrate mine
4 Bauxite mine
5 Asphalt
6 Diamond field
7 Paper mill
8 Textile mill
9 Panama hats
10 Meat-packing
11 Meat extract
12 Tobacco factory
13 Rum

Agricultural Products
14 Wheat
15 Maize
16 Rice
17 Wine
18 Mangoes
19 Bananas
20 Pineapple
21 Coconuts
22 Brazil nuts
23 Sugar cane
24 Coffee
25 Cacao
26 Mate
27 Tobacco
28 Linseed
29 Cotton
30 Sisal
31 Jute
32 Natural rubber
33 Rosewood
34 Quebracho
35 Mahogany
36 Cedarwood
37 Cinchona bark

Livestock and Animal Products
38 Cattle

39 Milk
40 Hides
41 Sheep
42 Wool
43 Skins
44 Pigs
45 Deep-sea fishing
46 Whaling
47 Whaling station
48 Guano
49 Sponge-fishing
50 Pearl-fishing

Transportation and Trade
51 Panama Canal
52 Airliner
53 Passenger ship
54 Freighter
55 Sailing ship

Exports
56 Sugar, tobacco (Havana)
57 Ores, sugar (Santiago)
58 Coffee, sugar (Port-au-Prince)
59 Sugar, coffee (Santo Domingo)
60 Sugar, rum, bananas (Jamaica)
61 Sugar, tobacco, coffee, pineapples (Puerto Rico)
62 Lumber (British Honduras)
63 Coffee (El Salvador)
64 Coffee, bananas, cotton (Nicaragua, Costa Rica)
65 Coffee, gold, hides (Barranquilla)

66 Coffee, cacao (La Guaira, Venezuela)
67 Bauxite
68 Bauxite, sugar
69 Gold (Guiana)
70 Rubber, Brazil nuts, hardwoods (Belém)
71 Sugar, cotton (Recife)
72 Sugar, tobacco, cacao (Salvador)
73 Coffee (Rio de Janeiro)
74 Coffee (Santos)
75 Meat, mate, hides (Rio Grande)
76 Meat, wheat, corn, linseed oil (Buenos Aires)
77 Wheat, wool (Bahia Blanca)
77a Petroleum (Comodoro Rivadavia)
78 Whale oil (Falkland Islands)
79 Whale oil (South Georgia)
80 Wine, farm products (Valparaiso)
81 Nitrates, copper (Antofagasta)
82 Nitrates, iodine, salt (Iquique)
83 Copper, borax, tin (Arica)
84 Cotton, sugar (Lima-Callao)
85 Bananas, balsa wood, cacao (Guayaquil)
86 Gold, platinum, coffee (Buenaventura)

Symbol		
Oil		Refinery
Oil Pipeline		Power Station
Coal		
Ag Silver	Ni Nickel	
Al Aluminium	Pb Lead	
Au Gold	Pt Platinum	
Bi Bismuth	Sb Antimony	
Co Cobalt	Sn Tin	
Cr Chromium	V Vanadium	
Cu Copper	W Tungsten	
Fe Iron	Zn Zinc	
Mn Manganese	I Iodine	

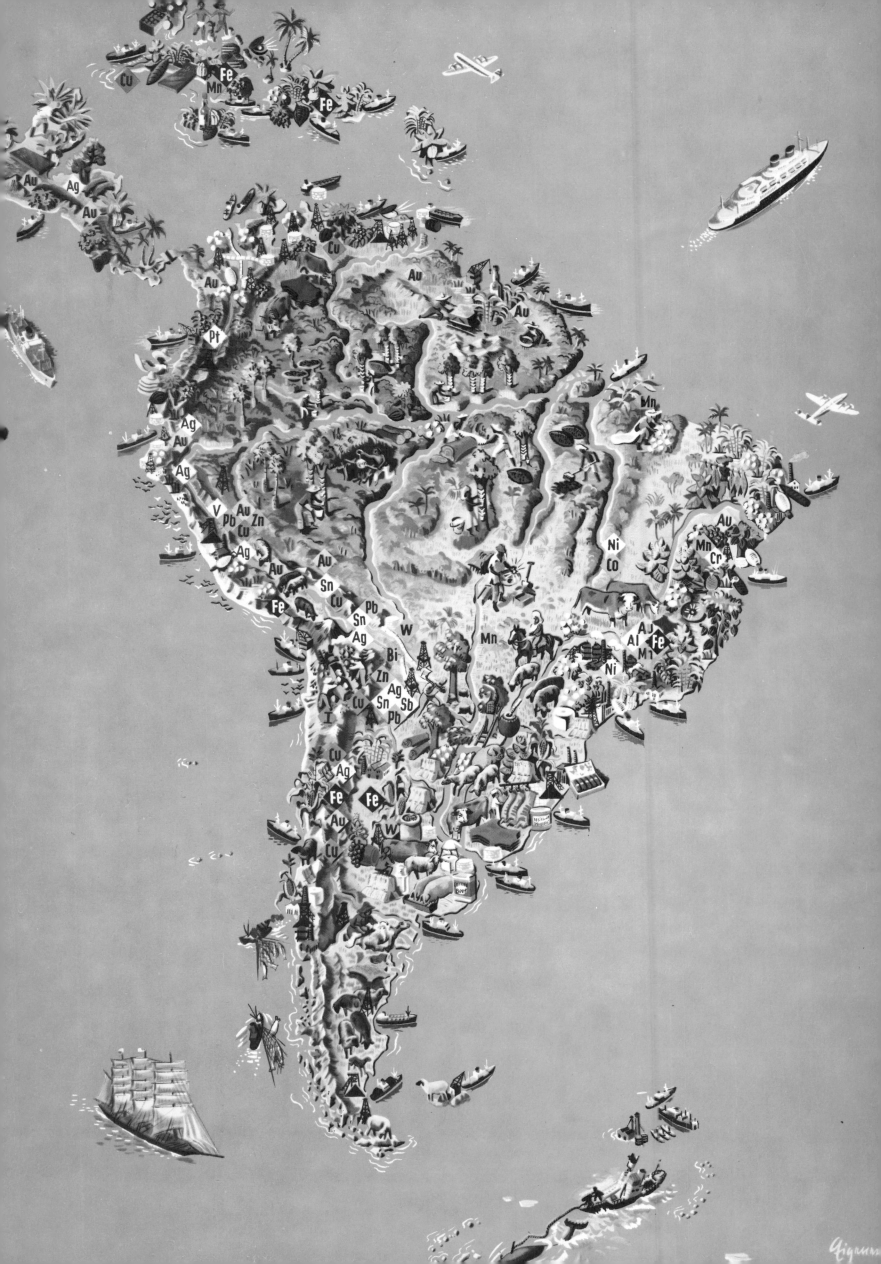

Goahira Indians at a street market in Ziruma, Venezuela

of activity to the upper Amazon Basin; a short railway was built around the rapids of the Madeira River, to ease the shipment of latex (gathered from wild rubber trees) to Manaus, the metropolis of Amazonia. With the collapse of the boom (due to Brazil's inability to compete with the efficient rubber plantations of South-East Asia), the region went into a decline. In 1927, an American company established an experimental rubber plantation on a tributary of the Amazon, but this experiment has not led to the large-scale production of rubber in Brazil.

Ocean-going vessels ascend the Amazon to Manaus (1,000 miles from the Atlantic), and smaller ships reach Iquitos (Peru), 2,300 miles from the sea. Belém, on the main arm of the delta, is the largest city and the chief outlet for the forest products of the Amazon Basin. These include cabinet woods, Brazil nuts, and gums. An airline serves the main towns on the Amazon and its largest tributaries.

● **Andes** A massive mountain chain, known in Spanish as *Cordillera de los Andes*. It extends over 4,000 miles along the west coast of South America, forming the continent's 'backbone' from the Isthmus of Panama to Tierra del Fuego. In the north, the Andes link up with the ranges of Central America, and in the south they are continued (after submergence in Drake Passage, south of Cape Horn) by the mountainous Palmer Peninsula (Graham Land) jutting out from Antarctica. The Andes boast the highest summit (Aconcagua, 22,834 feet) in the Western Hemisphere, and a chain of active or dormant volcanoes (Chimborazo, Illampu, Illimani, Huascarán, and others), their snow-capped cones rising more than 20,000 feet above sea level. The Andes are narrow (less than 200 miles wide on the average), except in Bolivia where the ranges enclose a barren, high plateau known as the *altiplano*. In Peru, Ecuador and Colombia, the Andes consists of two or three

● **Aconcagua** Highest mountain (22,834 feet) of the Andes of South America and the highest summit in the Western Hemisphere. It lies in Argentina, near the Chilean border. The trans-Andean railway passes close to Aconcagua's southern foot, over the Uspallata Pass.

● **alpaca** Like the llama, to which it is related, the alpaca is a domesticated descendant of the guanaco. The alpaca's unusually long, soft wool is woven into a strong, durable cloth known the world over. Alpacas are raised by the Indians of Bolivia and southern Peru.

● **Amazon River** Great river of South America which drains a basin only slightly smaller than the area of the continental United States. It is considered the world's largest river, if measured by the volume of water carried to the sea. The Amazon rises in the Andes of Peru, less than 100 miles air distance from the Pacific coast; it flows almost 4,000 miles eastward across the widest part of Brazil, just south of the Equator, and reaches the Atlantic Ocean in a delta 200 miles wide. The swirling, silt-laden waters of the Amazon can be distinguished far out to sea, and sediments have been deposited for hundreds of miles along the Guiana coast. With its 500-odd tributaries, many of which are major streams in their own right, the Amazon drains not only the northern half of Brazil, but also those parts of Bolivia, Peru, Ecuador and Colombia that lie east of the Andes. The Amazon Basin — a vast lowland covered by dense rain forest — is, perhaps, the largest remaining undeveloped region of the world (except for Antarctica); its total population is less than 2 million. Uncivilised Indian tribes still inhabit parts of the basin, and settlement by white men has been limited to a few places on the banks of the major navigable streams. Exploration began in the 16th century with the downstream voyage of Francisco de Orellana; his account of an encounter

with female warriors (Amazons) gave the river its name. Regular navigation dates from 1850, when small clusters of settlers established short-lived clearings in the jungle. At the turn of the present century, the natural-rubber boom brought a flurry

The busy fishing harbour at Puerto Montt, in southern Chile

parallel ranges separated by inter-mountain basins or deep river valleys (for example, the Magdalena River valley in Colombia). The rugged terrain hinders east-west communications across the Andes; the only trans-Andean railways are in the south, where two lines connect Pacific coast ports in Chile with Argentina. The mineral wealth of the Andes attracted the Spanish *conquistadores* to this mountain fastness early in the 16th century. Today, shipments of copper, lead, tin, platinum and silver make up the bulk of the region's exports. The Andean Republics are noted for some of the highest mines (Cerro de Pasco, Potosí, Chuquicamata), highest cities (La Paz — 12,000 feet; Quito — 9,400 feet), and the highest navigable lake (Lake Titicaca — 12,500 feet), in the world. Tourists flock to the impressive remains of the Inca civilisation in the Peruvian Andes, as well as to the scenic lake districts of southern Argentina and Chile.

Alpacas

● **ant-eater, giant** This odd-looking animal, also known as ant-bear, measures eight feet from the tip of its long snout to the end of its hairy tail. After it has torn down a termite nest with its claws, the ant-eater sweeps up the insects with its long, sticky tongue.

● **Antofagasta** The largest (population 120,000) and most important city of northern Chile, with a sheltered harbour on the Pacific Ocean. As the principal outlet for Chile's and Bolivia's mining areas, Antofagasta exports copper, nitrates, sulphur and borax. A new railway leads across the Andes to Salta, in northern Argentina; another line runs into Bolivia. It hardly ever rains in Antofagasta, but the cool Peru (or Humboldt) Current offshore makes the desert heat bearable. The city was founded in 1870, when the exploitation of nitrates began on a large scale. It passed from Bolivia to Chile in 1884, after the War of the Pacific (the Nitrate war) of 1879—84.

● **Araucanian** An Indian tribe of southern Chile and the adjacent Andean regions. Intermediate in culture between the advanced Incas and the primitive Patagonians, the Araucanians were among the last Indians to resist the penetration of Europeans in South America.

● **araucaria** A tall pine of the Southern Hemisphere, with scalelike leaves, large cones and edible seeds. It yields a valuable timber. The araucaria pine is found in southern Chile, Australia and New Guinea. It is related to the monkey-puzzles which grow in some European gardens.

● **Arequipa** One of the most colourful cities of Peru, on the Pacific slope of the Andes, 8,000 feet above sea level. It is the country's leading wool market and a growing textile-manufacturing centre. Its population of 167,080 includes many

Indians, who gather in the city squares on market days to sell their hand-made products. The perfectly shaped cone of El Misti volcano towers over Arequipa. The city was founded by the Spanish in 1540.

● **Argentina** An independent republic and the second-largest country (1,085,000 square miles; population 23,319,000) of South America, with its capital at Buenos Aires, the largest city in the Southern Hemisphere, with nearly 7 million people living in the greater Buenos Aires area. One-third the size of the United States, Argentina forms an elongated triangle, contained between the Andes in the west and the Atlantic Ocean in the east, tapering off towards the southern tip of the continent on the island of Tierra del Fuego. Argentina lies wholly within the temperate zone, and its agriculture — especially in the fertile Pampa — corresponds to that of the prairies in the American Middle West. A vast, treeless plain, reaching more than 300 miles inland from the Atlantic Ocean and from the deep inlet of the Río de la Plata, the Pampa is the most productive and densely inhabited region of Argentina. Rich crops of wheat, maize, flax and lucerne are grown on its deep, black soils. There, too, is the home of the *gaucho* (the South American cowboy) and his herds of cattle, which have made Argentina the world's leading exporter of frozen and canned meat. The country's main agricultural-processing and meat-packing centres are found on navigable waterways along the edge of the Pampa: Buenos Aires, a major seaport at the hub of all overland transportation routes; La Plata, on the Río de la Plata; Rosario and Santa Fé, on the Paraná River; and Bahía Blanca, on the Atlantic Ocean at the southern rim of the Pampa. Farther south, between the Pampa and the Strait of Magellan, lies the barren, windswept plateau of Patagonia, where sheep are raised. The sparse population is scattered over far-reaching ranches. The wool clip is exported from small seaports, such as Rawson, on the inhospitable Patagonian coast. West of the Pampa, the country is arid in the rain-shadow of the towering Andes. Córdoba, Argentina's third city, lies in this transition belt surrounded by fruit orchards irrigated by water from the Sierra de Córdoba. Other oases in the Andean foothills are those of Mendoza, San Juan, Tucumán and Salta, which produce wine, sugar, olives and citrus fruit. The Chaco of northern Argentina, another 'empty' area, yields some cotton, maté (a South American tea leaf), and a tanning extract from quebracho bark. The Andes of Argentina contain the highest summit of the entire mountain range — Aconcagua, 22,834 feet — as well as a number of snow-capped volcanic peaks. They form an effective barrier between Argentina and Chile, and only three railways have been built across them, one from Mendoza to Valparaiso, in Chile; another from Salta, in the north, to Antofagasta; and a third, in the south, from Zapala. Argentina exports livestock, meat and grains in exchange for fuel and manufactured goods from abroad. The lack of adequate coal and petroleum resources has hampered the development of a heavy industry. Mining is of only minor importance with small amounts of gold, coal, silver, iron and oil. Yet despite this handicap, Argentina is the only South American country with more people working in factories than in agriculture.

Amerigo Vespucci was probably the first European to explore the Argentine coast, in 1502. He was followed by Juan Diaz de Solís (killed by Indians while exploring the Río de la Plata in 1516), by Magellan (1520), and by Sebastian Cabot, who ventured up the Paraná River. In 1536, Pedro de Mendoza founded Buenos Aires but was forced to abandon the site under Indian attack. Next to be founded were towns in the Andean foothills, reached by Spanish explorers venturing southward from Peru. Finally, in 1580, Buenos Aires became a permanent settlement. The city grew slowly, but in 1776 it became the seat of a Spanish viceroy who, for about three decades,

The Kuarup natives, of Brazil's great Amazon Basin, trap fish in dams built of bamboo poles

ruled all of the lands tributary to the Paraná and Paraguay Rivers. The viceroy was deposed in 1810, and in 1816 Argentina proclaimed its independence under the leadership of José de San Martín. With the beginning of large-scale Italian immigration after 1850, the Argentine Pampa developed into the nation's corn-belt. The present population of Argentina is overwhelmingly European in origin (chiefly Italian and Spanish), while the dwindling Indian population is estimated at less than 30,000. Spanish is the official language.

● **Arica** A small town of northern Chile, on the Pacific Ocean, at the edge of the Atacama Desert. It is the seaport for much of Bolivia's trade, having a free harbour for that country, and a railway leading from Arica to La Paz. Exports include tin from Bolivia, copper nitrates, and borax from the arid hinterland. The town belonged to Peru until 1880.

● **armadillo** This 'little armoured thing', as the Spaniards named it, is a descendant of ancient armadillos of considerable size. The modern animals reach a length of about three feet. Their armoured plating consists of large bony shields in front and behind, separated by a number (3 to 20) of movable bands. The common nine-banded armadillo ranges from Argentina to the southern United States. It digs for ants and has a long, sticky tongue to eat them. Armadillos have many teeth (from 25 to 100). The three-banded armadillo rolls itself into a ball, hedgehog-like, when menaced. The flesh of the armadillo is eaten by many Indians.

● **Asunción** Capital and largest city (population over 437,136) of Paraguay, Asunción is a port on the Paraguay River (principal artery of communications in the country), 600 miles north of Buenos Aires. There are the country's major industrial plants, producing cotton textiles, alcohol, vegetable oil and flour. Tropical hardwoods, hides and maté are shipped downstream on river boats to Argentina. Asunción was founded in 1537 as a Spanish trading post on the route from the Río de la Plata to Peru. Its importance diminished in the 17th century with the growth of Buenos Aires.

● **Atacama Desert** A hot, arid region of northern Chile, between the Andes and the coastal mountains. For almost 600 miles south of the Peruvian border, there is virtually no vegetation and hardly any rainfall. The Atacama is noted chiefly for its enormous nitrate deposits, which have been mined for about a century. Until World War I, Chilean nitrates were the only available source of nitrogen

for explosives and fertilisers. When the Germans invented a process 'fixing' nitrogen from the air, Chile's nitrate industry went into a decline. Almost two-thirds of the world's iodine production is recovered as a by-product of the nitrate industry.

● **Aymara** An Indian tribal group of the Andean high plateaux of Bolivia and southern Peru. The Aymaras developed an advanced culture before the Incas, who conquered them in the 13th and 14th centuries. The great ruins of Tiahuanaco, near Lake Titicaca, are generally thought to be of Aymara origin.

● **Bahia** A coastal State of north-eastern Brazil, (population 7.4 million) traversed by the Sao Francisco River. Its capital is Salvador. Cacao and sugar are grown in quantity in irrigated coastal plantations. Castor beans and carnauba wax are products of the drier interior. Bahia yields black diamonds used in industry, gold, and semi-precious stones. Industries will be attracted by cheap hydro-electric power developed on the Paulo Afonso Falls of the São Francisco River. Negroes make up a large part of the population; they were brought there from West Africa in the 17th and 18th centuries, to work on Portuguese-owned sugar plantations. The coast of Bahia was discovered by the Portuguese navigator Cabral in 1500.

● **Bahía Blanca** A seaport (population about 160,000) of Argentina, on the Atlantic Ocean. It is the chief outlet for the products of the southern Pampa—grain, wool, meat and hides. The port has excellent rail connections with Buenos Aires, 350 miles to the north-east. It was settled in the 19th century, largely by Italian immigrants.

● **balsa** A tree of tropical America. Its strong wood is lighter than cork and is used in the manufacture of floats, canoes and aeroplanes.

● **Barbados** A West Indian island (166 square miles; population 238,000) in the Atlantic Ocean. It has full independence within the British Commonwealth. The island is composed largely of coral limestone and is surrounded by a coral reef. Sugar is the only major crop, efficiently cultivated on plantations and by small farmers. Rum and molasses are also exported. Flying fish, caught off-shore, are an important part of the diet of the rapidly-growing population. Barbados is one of the most densely-populated places on earth — almost 1,400 inhabitants to the square mile. Descendants of African slaves make up the bulk of the population. Originally inhabited by Arawak Indians, Barbados was occupied by the English in 1627 and

has never changed hands — an unusual history for an island in the West Indies. English is spoken universally. The island's fine beaches, balmy trade-wind climate and modern airport have made it a tourist resort of growing popularity. The main town is Bridgetown, with 12,400 inhabitants.

● **Barranquilla** Colombia's largest seaport (population 640,800), on the Caribbean, near the mouth of the Magdalena River. Most of Colombia's exports (coffee, tobacco, gold, hides) pass through this city. Its modern industries include textile mills, cement works and chemical plants. A large international airport is near by. Founded over 300 years ago, Barranquilla was a sleepy coastal town until the 1930s, when the swampy mouth of the Magdalena was dredged for river traffic.

● **bear, spectacled** This Andean black bear is the only bear of South America. It owes its name to whitish rings around the eyes. A small bear, it weighs less than 200 pounds.

● **Belém** A city (population 642,514) of northern Brazil, on the Rio Para, an arm of the Amazon River situated 90 miles from its mouth on the Atlantic Ocean. With its deep-water port, Belém serves as the commercial outlet for the entire Amazon Basin. It exports natural rubber, Brazil nuts, jute, cacao, rice, tropical hardwoods, and a variety of other forest products. Its international airport is used by airlines linking the two Americas, as well as Africa and Europe. Despite its humid tropical climate, Belém is gaining in importance and population as the resources of the Amazon Basin are gradually developed. The city was founded in 1615, and has long been known under the name of Pará (also the name of the Brazilian State of which it is the capital).

● **Belo Horizonte** A modern city (population 1,232,708) of Brazil and the capital of the mineral-rich State of Minas Gerais, Belo Horizonte was laid out on the pattern of Washington, D.C., in 1895. It owes its rapid growth to the exploitation of iron, gold and manganese in the surrounding highlands. The city has several large textile mills and serves as the chief commercial centre for the cattle-raising country to the south and west. A modern highway links Belo Horizonte, at an elevation of 3,000 feet, to Rio de Janeiro, 200 miles away on the Atlantic coast.

● **black caiman** This large South American crocodile differs from the alligator in having overlapping bony plates both on its back and on its abdomen. The black caiman reaches a length of 20 feet and lives in the Amazon Basin.

● **blue-fronted amazon parrot** This blunt-tailed South American parrot, with a blue forehead, excels in repeating words and in imitating sounds.

● **boa constrictor** This non-poisonous snake of South America is about ten feet long. Because of its attractive colours, a combination of tan and dark brown, and its tameness when captive, this snake is a favourite with snake-charmers in circuses. It is named after its practice of killing prey by squeezing, or constriction.

● **Bogotá** The capital and largest city (population 2,512,000) of Colombia, situated high in the Andes on a plateau 8,700 feet above sea level. Because of its elevation, the city has a pleasantly mild climate all the year around, despite its location near the Equator. Bogotá is more important as a cultural centre than as an industrial city, for its institutions of learning include a university founded in 1572.

The dense, humid jungle of the Amazon Basin crowds the river's banks with lush vegetation

SOUTH AMERICA

Scale 1:30,000,000

0 100 200 300 400 500 Miles

SÃO PAULO   *Cities over*   1,000,000 *population*
Barranquilla *Cities of 250,000 —* 1,000,000 *population*
Puerto Montt *Cities under*   250,000 *population*
⊙ *Capitals of Countries*

Depths in feet: Heights in feet:

| Below sea level | 0-650 | 650-1650 | 1650-4900 | over 4900 |

◦ Salt lake

Railroads ---- Canals ↓ Head of navigation ↘ Falls
⌇ Swamp, marsh

The snow-crowned Cordillera Blanca of the towering Peruvian Andes

Excellent examples of Spanish colonial architecture, including many fine churches, may be found side by side with modern office buildings and apartment houses. Established in 1538, Bogotá served as the capital of the Spanish vice-royalty of New Granada from 1598 until the beginning of the 19th century, when Bolívar took the city (in 1815, and again in 1819) during the country's war of independence.

● **bola** A missile weapon consisting of stone or iron balls, attached to the ends of cords. The gauchos of Argentina use it to entangle animals. The bola thus serves the same purpose as a lasso, and is also known among the Eskimos, who use it for bird-catching purposes.

● **Bolivia** An independent republic (400,000 square miles; population 5,062,500) of South America; one of two landlocked States in South America (the other being Paraguay). Most of the people (including the Indian peasants) and the rich tin-mines (at Oruro and Potosí) are found high in the Andes on a barren and windswept inter-mountain tableland (10,000 to 15,000 feet above sea level) known as the *altiplano*. There the Indians still speak their own languages and eke out a meagre living from the rocky soil; they grow maize, barley and potatoes, and raise wool-bearing llamas. Several thousand work in tin-mines owned by the government. Bolivia is fifth among the world's leading tin producers, and the country's welfare depends on its ability to sell this and other minerals (silver, lead, tungsten) abroad at favourable prices. Tin is shipped by railway to ports on the Peruvian and Chilean coasts, for Bolivia lost her seaports during the Pacific War of 1879—82. Although the country's largest cities are linked by rail, the aeroplane has done much to ease communications in this rugged country near the 'roof of the Andes'. La Paz, with a population of 562,000, is the seat of the Bolivian government; it lies in a steep-sided canyon, 12,000 feet above sea level, and is the highest metropolis in the world. Sucre, the legal capital — which contains the St Francisco Xavier University, founded in 1624 — has a population of about 84,900 and is, like Cochabamba (a resort of 149,900 inhabitants in a fertile agricultural basin), a small highland city. Three-quarters of the nation's territory lies east of the Andes, in the tropical lowlands drained by the headwaters of the Amazon and Paraguay Rivers. This scantily populated forest zone is only now being developed. Its

only important town, Santa Cruz, has railway connections with Brazil and Argentina, but is separated by jungles and Andean ranges from the highland centres of Bolivia. The region produces some oil, and very large petroleum reserves are suspected. Pipelines lead to a refinery in Cochabamba, which satisfies Bolivia's oil needs and provides an export surplus as well as to the ports of Arica and Rosario. Industry in Bolivia is small because of the lack of capital and skilled workers. About 80 per cent of the population is still illiterate.

Inca civilisation spread into Bolivia long before the Spanish conquest. The discovery of silver brought the Spaniards to the forbidding *altiplano* in the 1540s, and Indians were put to work in the mines at Potosí. The country formed part of the Spanish vice-royalty of Peru until 1776, when it came under the rule of the Spanish viceroy at Buenos Aires. Bolivia gained its independence in 1825, after the two heroes of Latin America — Bolívar and San Martín — had defeated the Spaniards at Ayacucho (Peru) in 1824. In the War of the Pacific (1879—84) Bolivia lost its Pacific coast to Chile, and in 1903 it ceded much of its eastern territory to Brazil. Finally, in the Chaco War of 1932—35 with Paraguay, Bolivia was stripped of her claims in the Gran Chaco, so that the country now embraces less than one-half the territory it held a hundred years ago. In recent years, the United States has helped Bolivia to grow a larger proportion of its food supply in areas that had never been farmed before.

● **Brasilia** The capital of Brazil since 1960, and still under construction in an isolated part of the central plateau in the State of Goiás. The area has a healthy upland climate and the city has many fine ultra-modern buildings. It had a population of 544,862 by 1970.

● **Brazil** (officially: United States of Brazil) The largest country (3,290,000 square miles; population 92,237,570 in 1971) of South America, with almost one-half the continent's area and population. It borders on all but two (Chile and Ecuador) of the nations of South America, and has a 4,600-mile-long coastline on the Atlantic Ocean. Brazil is larger than the continental United States, but its vast interior remains virtually unpopulated. Most of the cities, industries and productive farmlands are clustered along the coast, and on the fringe of the Brazilian plateau nearest the coastal escarpment. Northern Brazil, drained by the mighty Amazon River, and western Brazil, watered by the Paraná-Paraguay River system, are the most sparsely populated parts of the country and their resources are untapped, except for gold and diamond washings and a few scattered attempts to grow rubber on a commercial basis. The two main

cities of Amazonia — Belém, near the river's mouth, and Manaus, more than 1,000 miles upstream — grew up almost overnight during the short-lived natural rubber boom of the 1890s. By 1910, Brazil had lost trade to the efficient rubber plantations of South-East Asia, and the Amazon Basin again was left to the Indians (a few savage tribes still survive in the tropical rain forest) and to a handful of lumbermen, but the recent discovery of petroleum has renewed interest in the development of Amazonia. Although Brazil has many large cities, it is primarily an agricultural country. It supplies about one-half of the world's coffee, grown on the fertile red soils of São Paulo and Paraná. The city of São Paulo owes its spectacular growth to the coffee trade, and Santos, its nearby port, is the world's premier coffee-shipping centre. Cacao is grown in the State of Bahia, sugar in north-eastern Brazil (around the city of Recife) and in the State of Rio de Janeiro, cotton in São Paulo, and wheat and rice in Rio Grande do Sul, and is second only to the U.S. in production of oranges. Although livestock is raised extensively throughout the Brazilian highlands (which stretch westward from the coast as far as the State of Matto Grosso), the finest beef and hogs come from the temperate grasslands of the far south, where the landscape resembles the pampa of Uruguay and Argentina. Brazil is also a store-house of mineral resources. The interior State of Minas Gerais contains high-quality deposits of iron ore, which are used in nearby steel mills and are also shipped by rail to the modern steel-making centre of Volta Redonda, not far from Rio de Janeiro. Important manganese deposits have been found along the Paraguay River in Matto Grosso and in the territory of Amapá, north of the Amazon delta. Bauxite, quartz, gold, semi-precious stones, industrial diamonds and rare minerals have been discovered in various parts of the country, and the full extent of Brazil's petroleum reserves is still unknown. Because it is short of coal, Brazil is developing huge hydro-electric power plants on the São Francisco River at the Paulo Afonso Falls. Still untamed are the rapids and falls on the rivers of the Amazon Basin, and the famous Iguaçu Falls of southern Brazil. The country's largest hydro-electric plant lies at the foot of the coastal escarpment, near Santos, and supplies energy to the diversified industries of the São Paulo area. One reason for the slowness of the country's development is the lack of road and rail communications to the interior, and from one section of the coast to another. However, aeroplane services to remote towns and villages have been greatly expanded since World War II, and ambitious plans have been laid for a highway network to link up the densely settled south-east with northern and western Brazil. As a symbol of the 'advancing frontier', a magnificent new capital city, Brasilia, has been established near Brazil's geographical centre in an uninhabited part of the State of Goiás.

West of Argentina's pampas rise the foothills of the Andes Mountains; beyond them lies Chile

Brazil is the only Portuguese-speaking country in Latin America. It was discovered in 1500 by the Portuguese navigator Pedro Alvares Cabral and was first settled (along the coast of São Paulo) in 1532. After defeating several French and Dutch landing attempts, the Portuguese built up a prosperous sugar economy in north-eastern Brazil, using Negro slaves imported from Africa. Then came the rush to the interior, when gold and diamonds were found in the rivers of the Brazilian highlands. Intrepid adventurers (called *bandeirantes*) reached the headwaters of the Paraná and the Paraguay about 1720, but few of them settled down on the land. They preferred the pleasures of Rio de Janeiro (the centre for gold shipments to Portugal), which in 1763 replaced the north-eastern city of Bahia (now called Salvador) as the colonial capital. When Napoleon invaded Portugal in 1807, its king fled to Brazil, and Rio thereupon became the capital of the Portuguese Empire. Brazil declared its independence in 1822, but was governed by emperors until 1889, when a republic was proclaimed. Italian and German immigrants, who came in increasing numbers after 1850, contributed to the rapid expansion of coffee cultivation in São Paulo and to mixed farming in the southern States. About 60 per cent of the present population is white, and 35 per cent Negro or mulatto. There is no racial discrimination in Brazil. The country is divided administratively into 22 States, 4 territories, and the federal district surrounding Brasilia.

Brazil nuts

● **Brazil nut** The Brazil nut tree reaches a height of 150 feet and a trunk diameter of nearly 15 feet. Its large, globular fruit contains 18 to 24 of the familiar three-cornered Brazil (or Pará) nuts.

● **Buenaventura** The chief port (population 98,000) on the Pacific coast of Colombia, with a railway to the interior city of Cali. It exports coffee, platinum and gold. The town has an unhealthy, wet, tropical climate.

● **Buenos Aires** The capital and chief seaport of Argentina, on the south shore of the wide Río de la Plata. It is the largest city in the Southern Hemisphere, as well as of all the Spanish-speaking countries. From its vast modern harbour, Argentina ships frozen and processed meat, hides, dairy products, cereals, linseed oil and quebracho extract (a dye for tanning) to Europe, Brazil and the United States. The approaches to the Atlantic Ocean (over sandbanks and mud-flats) are kept open by constant dredging. A city of culture and considerable wealth, Buenos Aires was attractively and spaciously laid out; its architecture bears more than a casual resemblance to that of central Paris. At the head of Avenida de Mayo, the broad central thoroughfare, stands the Presidential Palace,

On the Atlantic coast, at Belém, Brazil, the mouth of the Amazon River is nearly three miles wide

called Rosada (the 'Pink House'), and there are many parks and squares.

Most of the country's large industries (food-processing plants, textile mills, sugar and oil refineries, motor-car assembly plants, etc.) are concentrated in Buenos Aires, whose suburbs have sprawled many miles into the surrounding Pampa to provide a greater metropolitan population in the region of 9 million.

Buenos Aires was founded in 1536, but it was soon abandoned when Indians attacked the small band of Spanish colonists. Its growth dates from the 18th century, when it became the capital of the Spanish vice-royalty of Río de la Plata. The city played an important part in Argentina's struggle for independence after 1810. It was raised to the status of federal district in 1880. The population of Buenos Aires is chiefly Italian and Spanish in origin.

● **bushmaster** The largest venomous snake of tropical America, the aggressive bushmaster grows to a length of more than 10 feet. It is handsomely marked, being yellowish-brown with a series of black saddles.

● **Cali** A commercial city (population 917,600) of western Colombia in the fertile Cauca Valley, where sugar, rice and coffee are grown. It lies on the Bolívar highway, which links Venezuela with Ecuador, and on a railway to the nearby Pacific Ocean port of Buenaventura. Founded in 1536, the city has preserved several attractive Spanish colonial buildings. A large proportion of its population is Negro or mulatto.

● **Campos** A Brazilian coastal city in the delta of the Paraíba River, about 150 miles north-east of Rio de Janeiro. Surrounded by large plantations, the city has sugar mills, alcohol distilleries, and factories for coffee and tobacco.

The name *campos* is also given to the grasslands that cover much of the upland in the interior of Brazil, south of the Amazonian rain forest. In some areas, the *campos* consist of grasslands mixed with stunted trees and, in the north-east, with cactus and other drought-resistant vegetation. A large part of the Brazilian *campos* is undeveloped and scantily populated.

● **Cape Horn** (or **Cabo de Hornos**) is a rocky, wave- and weather-beaten headland, the southernmost point of South America, at the southern tip of Tierra del Fuego. Its latitude is 56°S. It was discovered by Dutch navigators in 1616. Because of shoals and prevailingly stormy weather, the voyage around Cape Horn has long been considered a hazardous undertaking.

● **Caracas** The capital of Venezuela and one of the most modern cities of Latin America. Its rapidly growing population now tops 2,000,000. Situated in the coastal mountains 3,000 feet above sea level, Caracas is linked with its nearby seaport of La Guaira by a marvellously engineered four-lane highway. The centre of the city has been completely rebuilt in recent years; entire blocks of modern office and apartment buildings have replaced old colonial structures, and wide avenues have been substituted for the narrow, winding streets of a less motorised age. An assortment of impressive new buildings — the University City, the Military Academy and the Simón Bolívar Centre — has been added to the city's mushrooming skyline, and attractive workers' residences have made their appearance in the outskirts. The face-lifting of the Venezuelan capital was made possible by the country's oil boom and the income derived from taxes paid by American, British and Dutch petroleum companies. New industries are also being attracted to Caracas and the city's standard of living continues to rise.

Founded in 1567, Caracas played a leading part in the country's struggle for independence from Spain early in the 19th century. Simón Bolívar, the Liberator of Venezuela and of several other countries of South America, was born in Caracas and is also buried there. The central plaza is named in his honour. Caracas has been the capital of independent Venezuela since 1830.

Belém, capital of Pará State, Brazil, lies close to the equator

Carib An Indian tribal group of northern South America and the West Indies. They originated in the Guianas and migrated into the West Indies before the coming of the Spaniards. Remnants of the group are found in the Guianas, Venezuela, the Lesser Antilles and on the coast of Central America.

carnauba The most important of the wax palms of tropical America. Its young leaves are covered with a 1 to 2 inch-thick waxy secretion. The brittle, yellowish carnauba wax is used in the making of candles, shoe polish and varnish. Carnauba wax has a fairly high melting-point (180°F.).

Cartagena A picturesque, old seaport (population 318,800) of Colombia on the Caribbean Sea. It is linked by canal and railway with the Magdalena River (the country's principal traffic artery) and by pipeline with the oilfields of central Colombia. Gold, petroleum and agricultural products are exported. Founded in 1533, Cartagena soon became a shipping centre for precious stones and metals brought down by river from the interior. Cartagena was burnt by Drake in 1585. The harbour was once guarded by 30 forts; remnants of the wall that surrounded the city can still be seen. During the war for independence, it was the first city to proclaim its freedom from Spain (1811). A 16th-century cathedral and several fine colonial palaces are witness to the city's past importance.

cavy The Patagonian cavy, a large relative of the guinea-pig, looks rather like a hare. It has big eyes, large ears and long legs. When threatened, it takes off at a peculiar galloping, hopping run, stopping at intervals to look back.

Cerro de Pasco The leading copper-mining centre (population 31,000) of Peru, and one of the highest cities (14,000 feet) in the world. It dates back to 1630, when silver was discovered in the area. Only Indians accustomed to the thin air of the high Andean plateau are able to work in the mines. A copper-smelter has been built nearby.

Chaco or **Gran Chaco** A lowland region of central South America, divided among Paraguay, Bolivia and Argentina. Covered by scrub forests and tropical grasslands, the Chaco supports a sparse population engaged in extensive stock-raising and in stripping the bark of the quebracho tree (which yields an extract for the tanning industry). Cotton is raised in irrigated districts of the Argentine Chaco. Bolivia and Paraguay fought (1932—35) over possession of the northern Chaco; in 1938, most of the territory in dispute was awarded to Paraguay.

Chibcha A group of Indian tribes of Colombia and Panama. They are well known from accounts of the Spanish *conquistadores*, who found huge treasures of gold among them. The Chibchas were early cotton cultivators, and the technique of irrigation was known to them. Stone temples still survive to show their highly developed cultural level.

Chile An independent republic (286,000 square miles; population 9,670,000) of South America, between the Andes and the Pacific Ocean; it reaches some 2,600 miles from the Peruvian border, at 18°S., to the southern tip of Tierra del Fuego, facing Antarctica, at 56°S. latitude; its width averages only 110 miles. Several island groups in the Pacific belong to Chile, including mysterious Easter Island, 2,350 miles to the west. The watershed of the Andes forms the long border between Chile and Argentina; it is studded with dormant or extinct volcanoes, whose snow-covered cones reach elevations of 20,000 feet. This formidable mountain barrier is crossed by three railways, one in the north from Antofagasta (Chile) to Salta (Argentina); another from Valparaiso (Chile's leading seaport) to the Argentine city of Mendoza; and the third from Lebu (Chile) to Bahia Blanca (Argentina). Northern Chile is so dry that several years may go by without any recorded rainfall. There lies the Atacama Desert, whose salt flats have yielded large quantities of nitrates, iodine, potash and salt. Northern Chile also contains some very rich copper mines, and their output constitutes over 80 per cent of the value of the country's exports. High grade deposits of iron ore in the province of Atacama and Coquimbo have overtaken nitrates as Chile's second mineral. Cent-

Coati

ral Chile consists of several inter-connected lowlands known as the Central Valley. This fertile region grows olives, wine grapes, citrus and other fruit, and a variety of grains. It enjoys a Mediterranean-type climate which resembles that of central California. Santiago, the capital, is among the healthiest cities on the continent. It is also the country's industrial centre, with textile mills, leather and chemical factories. Chile's new steel industry is centred at Concepción; its coal is mined nearby, and high-grade iron ore is shipped coastwise from El Tofo mine, some 500 miles to the north. More than 90 per cent of the people live in central Chile.

The southern portion of the country is densely forested, rainy, and undeveloped. It has a spectacular coastline of deep fjords and rocky islands, and a scenic lake district visited by tourists from many countries. Except for the remnants of the Araucanian Indians (whose forefathers had fought both Inca and Spanish invaders), southern Chile is scantily populated. In the far south, the town of Punta Arenas was once an important coaling station on the Strait of Magellan. Today, it is a wool market and the centre of a growing oil industry.

Pedro de Valdivia conquered Chile for the Spanish crown in 1540. He founded Santiago and other cities, many of which were promptly sacked by the Araucanians. Chile was made a dependency of the vice-royalty of Peru. Not finding any precious metals, the Spaniards established large plantations worked by Indians in the Central Valley. With the help of San Martín, the liberator of Argentina, Chile attained its independence in 1818, and Bernardo O'Higgins guided the new republic during the first years of its freedom. Chile enlarged its territory during the War of the Pacific (1879—84) when it took possession of the nitrate fields of the Atacama Desert, formerly held by Peru and Bolivia. By establishing new industries and increasing the efficiency of its agriculture, Chile is trying to reduce its dependence on the export of minerals. The great majority of the population is of mixed Spanish and Indian stock. In the 19th century, several thousand German immigrants settled in the southern districts, around the town of Valdivia. Spanish is the official language.

Chimborazo A snow-covered, inactive volcano of the Ecuadorean Andes, just south of the Equator. It rises to 20,600 feet and is visible from the Pacific coast of Ecuador as well as from Quito, the country's capital. The famous German scientist Alexander von Humboldt climbed Chimborazo in 1802; he believed it to be the highest peak in the Andes, and yet the summit was not conquered until 1880.

chinchilla This small South American rodent bears the most valuable fur in the world. The fur, pale blue-grey or silver-grey, is so fine that single hairs are hardly visible to the naked eye. It takes 100 of these small pelts to make a coat. The chinchilla was once common in the high Andes,

Buenos Aires, the capital of Argentina, is a city of beautiful parks and broad avenues

but is now nearly extinct. Since 1923, it has been bred on farms in the United States.

● **Chuquicamata** One of the world's largest copper-mining centres, in the Andes of northern Chile, Chuquicamata lies 10,000 feet above sea level. The town was built by an American mining company.

● **coati** This South American member of the raccoon family resembles the raccoon in having a light-coloured facial mask and a ringed tail. Unlike the raccoon, however, the coati has a long, flexible snout, which it uses to poke into burrows and holes of trees, when looking for birds and insects.

● **coca** The leaves of this South American shrub are chewed by Indians for their stimulant properties. Native to the Andes, the coca plant is cultivated in Indonesia for its cocaine content.

● **Cochabamba** A city (population 149,900) of Bolivia, at the centre of a rich agricultural basin surrounded by Andean ranges. It is Bolivia's chief resort city, amidst gardens and orchards. A railway leads to the tin-mining centre of Oruro, and a new highway has been completed to the city of Santa Cruz, on the eastern slope of the Andes. It is also a centre of international air traffic. Elevation: 8,400 feet above sea level.

Caracas, Venezuela, is 3,000 ft above sea level, at the foot of a spur of the Andes Mountains

Coffee

● **coffee** The coffee plant, native to Ethiopia, is now grown in most tropical countries. The coffee tree grows to a height of four feet and may live for as long as 60 years. It has shining evergreen leaves and fragrant white flowers. The green fruit matures into a reddish, cherry-like coffee berry. This berry contains two seeds — the coffee beans — which contain up to 2.5 per cent caffeine, the stimulant in coffee, and up to 13 per cent fat. The green coffee of commerce is the seed, freed from the pulp and dried in the sun. Among the coffee varieties are Mocha coffee (from Yemen), Java and Sumatra (from Indonesia), and Brazil coffee. The 'mild' coffees are grown in Colombia and Central America. The coffee sold in the retail trade is usually a blend of several varieties. Three-fourths of the world's supply originates in Latin America — Brazil accounting for 50 per cent and Colombia for 15 per cent of the total output. Coffee cultivation was first introduced into Brazil in 1774; it began to expand there rapidly after 1860, and production now reaches 2 million tons each year in Brazil, half of the world's crop. The United States, the greatest coffee-drinking nation, imports 65 per cent of the world's coffee. Since the demand for coffee is constant, prices fluctuate with the supply. In years of over-production, millions of bags have been burned and dumped, because the coffee could not be sold even at low prices.

● **Colombia** The only South American State (440,000 square miles; population 21,160,000) with a coastline on two oceans — the Pacific in the west, and the Caribbean Sea in the north. The isthmus of Panama (which belonged to Colombia until 1903) separates the two oceans. Colombia is a land of great physical contrasts. In the east, vast, empty lowlands reach out towards the savannas of the Venezuelan *llanos* and the tropical rain forests of the Amazon Basin. In the west, there is a hot, swampy and unhealthy coastal lowland, where gold and platinum mining are the principal economic activity. In the north, facing the Caribbean, lie Colombia's chief seaports, Barranquilla and Cartagena; there, too, lies the snow-covered Sierra Nevada de Santa Marta range, flanked by banana plantations. Except for the coastal cities, the northern lowlands are sparsely settled; however, they yield gold and petroleum. Next to Venezuela, Colombia is the continent's leading oil producer. The great majority of the people live in the highlands that occupy about a quarter of the country in a central location. There the massive Andes are split up into three fan-shaped ranges, and the country's two main rivers — the Magdalena and its tributary the Cauca — flow northward through mountain-fringed valleys. The Magdalena is the country's principal traffic artery; railway spurs link the river with Colombia's principal cities, including the capital, Bogotá, which lies at an elevation of 8,700 feet in an Andean basin. Coffee is the leading crop of the highlands; because of its mildness, it commands a premium price on world markets, and is commonly blended with lower-grade Brazilian coffees. Medellín, also situated in an intermountain basin, is a thriving textile-manufacturing centre. A modern steel mill is in operation not far from Bogotá. Because of the country's mountainous terrain and the isolation of its highland communities, Colombia has been a pioneer in commercial aviation; many of its towns would still be very much out-of-touch with the world but for the aeroplane. Roads are generally poor, but the recently completed Simón Bolívar highway crosses Colombia on its way from Venezuela to Ecuador.

The first Spanish settlements on the north coast date from the early 16th century. They formed the nucleus of an important Spanish colony, known after 1718 as the vice-royalty of New Granada. The struggle for independence began at Bogotá in 1810 and was led to a successful conclusion by Bolívar, one of the heroes of Latin American freedom. His victories over Spain resulted in the creation of Greater Colombia, an independent country of which Venezuela, Panama and Ecuador originally formed part. Venezuela and Ecuador, however, became separate States in 1830, and the remaining territory assumed the name of New Granada until 1863, when it adopted the present name. Spanish is the official language. Because of its exceedingly rapid population growth, the country's greatest task is to develop its rich natural resources.

● **Comodoro Rivadavia** The principal oil-producing centre of Argentina, with a small seaport on the inhospitable coast of Patagonia. Oil was discovered there in 1907.

● **Concepción** Chile's third-largest city (population 178,000), Concepción serves a grain- and wine-growing district. The government-owned Huachipato steel mill is nearby, on the Pacific coast, coal being mined in the vicinity. Founded in 1550 by the Spanish *conquistadores* of Chile, Concepción has been repeatedly destroyed by earthquakes — the most recent being in 1939 and 1960. It is, therefore, a city of modern, low buildings.

● **condor** This South American vulture, with a wingspread of ten feet, is found in the Andes; it soars as high as 25,000 feet. Unlike other vultures, the condor lives not only on carrion but also attacks calves and lambs. The condor has a red head and neck, black body plumage and a white ruff around the neck.

● **Córdoba** The third-largest city (population 610,000) of Argentina, at the western margin of the Pampa, amidst irrigated grain fields and fruit orchards. It is an important railway hub and a centre of the leather, textile and glass industries. Founded in 1573, Córdoba has the country's oldest university, dating from 1613. Many old churches and fine homes have been preserved from colonial days.

cormorant, Galápagos This large member of the cormorant family, with very small wings, is a flightless bird.

Cotopaxi An active volcano in the Andes of Ecuador. Its majestic, snow-covered cone rises to 19,344 feet, constantly emitting smoke. It lies almost astride the Equator. Eruptions have caused severe damage in the surrounding valleys and in Quito, the country's capital, 30 miles away.

coypu A large water-loving rodent of South America, also known as nutria, the Spanish word for 'otter'. The coypu has been introduced into the United States and Europe, where it is raised for its soft pelt.

Curaçao The chief island (174 square miles; population 141,393) of the Netherlands Antilles, in the Caribbean Sea, off the shore of Venezuela. Willemstad is the main port. Curaçao owes its economic importance to huge oil refineries which process crude petroleum from the highly productive Maracaibo Basin oilfields of Venezuela. Calcium phosphate is mined on the island. Most of the island's food has to be imported, due to the rocky, barren soil cover. The nearby island of Aruba (68 square miles; population 59,231) is also a major oil-refining centre. Although Dutch is the official language, most of the people (Negroes and mulattos) speak *Papiamento*, a mixture of

Spanish, Dutch, English and French — living proof of the islands' checkered history. In recent years, Curacao has become a favourite visiting-place for Caribbean cruise ships.

curare An arrow poison used by the Indians of the Amazon and Orinoco Basins. It is obtained from a tropical woody vine, belonging to the strychnine-yielding plants, and is used in modern medicine.

curassow This fowl-like bird of the American tropics spends most of its time in the treetops and descends only to feed. The globose curassow, with a yellow wattle at the base of its bill, is found in Mexico. The crested curassow lives in northern South America.

Curitiba A Brazilian city (population 510,000), capital of the southern State of Paraná. It is a rapidly growing industrial centre with an active trade in livestock and maté. It produces paper, furniture, cement and chemicals. There is a rail link to the coffee-growing zone of northern Paraná. Its port on the Atlantic is Paranagua. Founded in the 17th century as a gold-mining camp, Curitiba has grown in recent years with the arrival of German, Polish and Italian immigrants.

Cuzco An ancient city (population 78,289) of Peru, in an Andean valley 11,000 feet above sea level. It was the capital of the Inca Empire until its capture by Spanish *Conquistadores* in 1533. In Cuzco are lavishly decorated Indian temples and other remnants of Inca culture, as well as a number of fine churches of the Spanish colonial period, including the Baroque cathedral. Several earthquakes have inflicted severe damage on the city and its archaeological treasures.

deer, marsh The largest and handsomest of the South American deer, this swamp-loving animal ranges from Brazil to Argentina.

dolphin The dolphins, which are ocean mammals and small-toothed whales, are generally harmless

and friendly to man. The common dolphin is distinguished by a sharp-pointed snout, rather like a beak and six inches long. This playful, intelligent animal, six to eight feet long, often cruises for lengthy periods at about 15 knots, producing bursts of speed reaching 20 knots.

Easter Island A volcanic island (45 square miles; population about 500) in the South Pacific Ocean, 2,300 miles west of Chile, to which it belongs. It is peopled by Polynesians, who grow tobacco, sugar cane and root crops on its fertile soils. The island was first visited in 1687 by British buccaneers. It has long been known for its remarkable carved stone heads, 30 to 40 feet tall and weighing up to 8 tons, whose origin remains a mystery to this day.

Ecuador A small country (106,000 square miles; population 5,585,400) on the Pacific coast of South America, astride the Equator. It consists of three regions: the coastal lowland (called *Costa*), the Andean uplands (*Sierra*), and the upper reaches of the Amazon Basin, to the east of the Andes (*Oriente*). Principal export fruit crops are grown in the humid tropical lowlands along the coast. Ecuador is the world's largest exporter of bananas. There, too, is the country's chief seaport and its largest city, Guayaquil. From Guayaquil, a magnificently engineered railway climbs more than 9,000 feet to Quito, the capital city, which lies in a mountain valley surrounded by a host of snow-capped volcanoes. Ecuador boasts more than 20 active volcanoes, among them Cotopaxi (19,344 feet) and Cayambe (19,170 feet). Chimborazo, though inactive, is even higher (20,577 feet). Almost two-thirds of the population lives in the cool highlands, where the average temperature scarcely varies from season to season. About 40 per cent of the people are pure Indians, who speak the Quechua language; another 40 per cent are *mestizos*, of mixed Spanish and Indian blood; the white population is in the minority. Food crops are grown in the highland valleys, and cattle, sheep and llamas are grazed at elevations exceeding 10,000 feet. Coffee is grown on the lower slopes; it is an increasingly important export crop. Textiles and 'Panama' hats are the main industrial products. The eastern lowlands of Ecuador are a vast, almost uninhabited jungle from which the light balsa wood (used in the raft *Kon-Tiki*), natural rubber, tagua nuts, and other forest products, are recovered. An Indian tribe, the Jibaros, have the region almost to themselves. Ecuador's boundary with Peru, in the upper Amazon Basin, has long been in dispute and has yet to be accurately traced. The country's mineral resources include a fairly productive oilfield on the Pacific coast, though some crude oil still has to be imported, and some gold, silver and copper deposits. The Galapagos Islands, some 650 miles west of the mainland, have belonged to Ecuador since 1832.

The territory of Ecuador had been a centre of several Indian civilisations when, in the 15th century, it was conquered by the Incas. The Spaniards defeated the Inca nation in 1533, and made Ecuador part of the vice-royalty of Peru, later attaching it to New Granada. It remained under Spanish control until 1822, when Simón Bolívar liberated the north-western portion of South America and founded Greater Colombia, which included Ecuador, Colombia and Venezuela. In 1830, however, Ecuador declared itself an independent republic.

Falkland Islands A group of treeless, windswept islands in the South Atlantic Ocean, about 250 miles off the coast of southern Argentina, found in 1592 by John Davis (Davys). Sheep-farming and seal-fishing are the only occupations of the small population of 2,098, chiefly British; there are over 630,000 sheep. South Georgia — once an island depot for whaling ships, now occupied by the British Antarctic Survey — the South Shetlands, South Orkneys, and other small islands along the approaches to Antarctica, are depen-

Dolphins

Indians gather at an open-air market in Cuzco, Peru. the ancient capital of the Inca Empire

dencies of the Falkland Islands. Although the Falkland Islands have been (and remain) a British colony since 1771 (though not continuously occupied), Argentina claims sovereignty over them, and has renamed the Falkland Islands 'Islas Malvinas'. Both Argentina and Chile have laid claim to their Antarctic dependencies. Stanley is the colony's capital, with a population of 1,100.

These 'llaneros' of the Chilean plains are herders of cattle, and correspond to cowboys of the U.S.A

● **Galápagos Islands** A group of volcanic islands in the Pacific Ocean, about 650 miles west of Ecuador to which they belong. Most of the islands are roughly circular, with craters rising in their centre. The climate is dry and tempered by the cool Peru (or Humboldt) Current. With a total area of 3,000 square miles, the Galápagos are inhabited by fewer than 2,000 people, mostly fishermen. The islands owe their fame to the peculiar animals (among them iguanas and flightless cormorants) and plants that are found there. The giant tortoises, after which the Galápagos are named, are thought to be the oldest living animals on earth. Charles Darwin landed on the Galápagos in 1833, during the famous voyage of the *Beagle*. His observations of the islands' wildlife provided the first substantial scientific evidence for his theory of evolution.

● **gaucho** This term was originally applied to herdsmen of the pampas of mixed Spanish and Indian descent; it was later extended to all Argentine cowboys.

● **Guadeloupe** A French-owned island (583 square miles; population 312,724) in the chain of the Lesser Antilles, between the Caribbean Sea and the Atlantic Ocean. It consists of two parts (low-lying Basse-Terre and volcanic Grande-Terre) separated by a narrow channel. Chief products are bananas, sugar, rum, coffee and cacao — all of which are exported to France. Sugar mills and distilleries are centred at Pointe-à-Pitre (chief town of Grande-Terre); the island capital is at Basse-Terre. All-the-year-round trade winds temper the tropical climate of Guadeloupe. This West Indian island was discovered by Columbus in 1493, and settled by the French in 1635. Negro slaves were imported to work on the sugar plantations. The present population is largely mulatto — i.e., of mixed European and Negro stock. Several islets, including nearby Marie Galante, are dependencies of Guadeloupe; they are inhabited by Normans and Bretons whose forebears came to the West Indies 300 years ago.

● **guanaco** This New World relative of the camel is the wild form from which the domesticated llama, and possibly the alpaca, descended. The guanaco ranges in herds of about 100 through the Andean highlands and the cooler lowlands of Argentina. It is also raised on farms for its wool and pelt, used in the fur trade.

● **guano** An accumulation of sea-bird droppings, many feet thick, found on the arid coasts of Chile and Peru and the offshore islands. Guano is rich in phosphates and nitrates, and is consequently used as fertiliser.

● **Guaraní** The principal Indian tribal group of Paraguay. The Guaraní were Christianised by the Jesuits in the 17th century, and their language became an important commercial tongue in that part of South America.

● **Guayaquil** Largest city (population 680,209) of Ecuador and its chief seaport, on the Guayas River, near the Pacific Ocean. The equatorial lowland surrounding the city grows Ecuador's principal export crops, cacao and bananas. Balsa wood and natural rubber from the Amazon Basin of eastern Ecuador are also shipped from Guayaquil. The city's industrial output includes Panama hats, shoes, textiles, cement and soap. Founded in 1536, the city suffered from pirate attacks in the 17th century, and from yellow fever plagues until the early part of the 20th century.

● **guemel** This small Andean deer, which lives at elevations of 15,000 feet, has short, massive antlers with a simple forked structure.

● **Guiana** A humid tropical region in north-eastern South America, between the deltas of the Amazon and the Orinoco Rivers. Most of the people live along the low, marshy coastal belt within 30 miles of the Atlantic Ocean. There, a few hundred square miles have been dyked against salt-water intrusion, and are devoted to the cultivation of sugar cane, rice and tropical fruits. The higher inland areas are almost undeveloped, except for mining. Extensive deposits of bauxite (the ore of aluminium) are worked along the Demerara, Berbice, Cottica and Suriname Rivers. The shipment of minerals (bauxite, gold and diamonds) ranks first among the exports, which also include rice, and tropical hardwoods from the huge virgin forests of the interior. The region is divided into three territories (*see below*), each linked to a European power. French Guiana and Surinam (Dutch possession) represent the only two dependent areas on the South American continental mainland. About 50 per cent of the population is made up of the descendants of former Negro slaves, and the other half of East Indians (both Hindu and Moslem) who, because of their higher birth rate, will soon be in the majority. There are also an unknown number of native Indians in the interior.

● **French Guiana** (35,000 square miles; population 44,392) has Cayenne (24,581) as its territorial capital. It is governed as an overseas department of France.

● **Guyana** (83,000 square miles; population 740,196), formerly the crown colony of British Guiana, has Georgetown (195,250) as its capital. Internal disorders brought about the suspension of the country's first constitution as an independent State, but a second grant of full independence, within the British Commonwealth, was made with effect from May, 1966. Guyana, as it is now called, has a mixed population of Indians and Negroes, and each of the two racial groups supports bitterly—opposed political parties. It is now hoped that the new constitution will help to bring about growing co-operation and national unity between the two groups. Guyana became a Republic in 1970.

● **Surinam, (or Dutch Guiana)** (54,000 square miles; population 400,000), is an internally self-governing territory, united with the kingdom of the Netherlands; its capital is Paramaribo (150,000). Surinam is the world's second-largest exporter of bauxite.

● **Guiana Highlands** A thickly forested tableland in South America, occupying the southern half of Venezuela, and extending into neighbouring Brazil and the territories of French Guiana, Guyana and Surinam. Mount Roraima is the highest point at 9,200 feet. The Highlands contain important deposits of gold and precious stones, but development has been hampered by their remoteness and inaccessibility. Parts of the plateau are still unexplored, and Venezuela's Angel Falls (3,212 feet), the world's highest waterfall, was only discovered from the air in recent years.

Mt Osorno, a volcano in the Chilean Andes

humming-birds These incredibly small and beautiful birds of the New World derive their name from the distinct sound made by their wings in flight, moving at about 60 beats a second. They range in size from two inches (the bee hummingbird of Cuba) to eight inches (the giant hummingbird of the Andes). The frilled coquette is, perhaps, the most highly adorned representative of the small humming-birds.

Iguaçu or **Iguassú Falls** A spectacular cataract on the Iguaçu River, along the border of Brazil and Argentina. The river drops 210 feet into a narrow gorge along a 'lip' that is more than 2½ miles wide. Higher and broader than Niagara, the falls have a tremendous potential for the development of electric energy, but at the present time the surrounding country is almost uninhabited.

iguana This large tropical American lizard attains a length of six feet, of which two-thirds is tail. A pure vegetarian, the iguana is equipped with high standing spines along its back and a dewlap suspended from its throat. The iguana's white, tender meat is regarded as a delicacy, not unlike frog's legs.

iguana, marine This coal-black lizard of the Galápagos Islands lives on sea rocks, from which

Jaguar

Inca Indians used to make fine cloaks of the brilliantly-coloured plumage of the parrots which inhabit South America

it plunges into the ocean to feed on seaweed. The marine iguana is about a yard long.

Inca Properly speaking, the name Inca is applied to the ruling group of Indians who established a great empire in the Peruvian highlands before the Spanish conquest. The empire, founded about 1200, was at its height about 1500, when it extended from Ecuador to northern Chile. It was destroyed by the Spaniards in 1533. The culture of the Incas in many ways resembled that of the ancient Babylonians and Egyptians. The Incas used huge stone blocks in their buildings; they had roads and a swift mail service. Their social organisation consisted of nobles, freemen and slaves, with priests occupying a special position. The Incas worshipped the sun, from which the ruling group was said to have descended. The economic life of the country was regulated along the lines of modern State socialism. The land was collectively owned and worked; crops, notably maize, were stored in State reserves and then distributed to the population. Mining, handicrafts, and the raising of llamas and alpacas for wool, were also carried on.

Iquique A seaport (population 63,600) of northern Chile, at the edge of the Atacama Desert. Nitrates, iodine and salt are exported. Fish-canning and oil-refining are the chief industries. Iquique is virtually rainless and draws its water supply from an oasis 60 miles away. It was taken from Peru in 1879, during the War of the Pacific.

Iquitos A city (population 69,000) of northeastern Peru, on the upper Amazon River. It is an important river port, for it can be reached by ocean-going ships, even though it lies more than 2,000 miles from the mouth of the Amazon on the Atlantic Ocean. Rubber and other forest products from the tropical jungle are shipped downstream.

jabiru This largest of the American storks has a white body plumage. Its bare head and neck are black, turning to red in the lower parts. The bird is found from Mexico to Argentina.

jaguar The largest of the cat family in the New World, the jaguar looks like a leopard at first glance. However, its head is larger, its body is longer, and the rosettes on its coat are wider. Also, some of the rosettes on the animal's flanks contain a central black spot, which the leopard lacks. The jaguar attains its greatest size in tropical regions. It is found from the southern U.S.A. southward as far as northern Argentina.

jungle The hot, wet, evergreen forest of equatorial regions, where it rains almost daily throughout the year. Owing to persistent heat and humidity, the tropical rain forest (a more accurate term than the popular word 'jungle') distinguishes itself by its dense and luxuriant growth. In the struggle to reach the sunlight, many trees grow to tremendous heights, while lianas twist themselves around the trunks and branches of trees to reach the dense canopy of leaves. Many different species of tree are to be found in the rain forest, but trees of any one species are so scattered that logging is difficult and often uneconomic. Such valuable tropical hardwoods as mahogany, rosewood and ebony are in great demand, however, and constitute the main export from the Amazon and the Congo Basins, the world's largest regions of tropical rain forest. The wild rubber tree, whose bark is tapped for latex (natural rubber), is also a native of the equatorial forest, notably in Amazonia. The dense jungles of central Africa and the Amazon Basin are sparsely settled, except along stream banks. Neither man nor wild animal finds the dark and almost impenetrable rain forest an attractive place in which to live.

Kon-Tiki Name of the balsa-wood raft used in 1947 by Thor Heyerdahl, a Norwegian scientist, to show that Polynesia could have been settled from South America, rather than from Asia. Using ocean currents and winds, the raft floated in 101 days from the port of Callao, in Peru, to Polynesia.

La Guaira Venezuela's leading seaport, at the foot of a steep coastal range, 7 miles north of Caracas, with which it is connected by a modern four-lane highway. Coffee, cacao and hides are the chief exports. Four ocean liners can berth simultaneously in the fine artificial harbour.

Incan Temple of the Sun at Machu Picchu

La Paz Largest city (population 562,000) of Bolivia, and highest (12,000 feet) of the large cities of the world, La Paz is the seat of the country's government, even though Sucre (a smaller town, 250 miles away) is the legal capital of Bolivia. Two railway lines from the Pacific coast, and one from Argentina, reach La Paz, perched on a cold and barren high plateau called the *altiplano*. The volcano Illimani towers over the canyon in which the city is located; Lake Titicaca lies 30 miles to the north-west. Spanish *conquistadores* founded La Paz in 1548. To this day, a large part of the population remains native Indian.

La Plata A modern industrial city (population 450,100) of Argentina, on the Río de la Plata, 35 miles below Buenos Aires. It has meat-packing and cold-storage plants, flour mills and cement works. The agricultural products of the Pampa (grains, meat, wool) are exported.

Lima The capital city (population 1,883,700) of Peru, 7 miles inland from Callao (population 135,000), its seaport on the Pacific Ocean. Lima is the country's cultural centre, with a university dating from 1551, which is said to be the oldest in the Americas, and the seat of an archbishopric which dates from 1545. Several of its 50 or more churches are fine examples of Spanish colonial architecture. Francisco Pizarro, who conquered Peru and defeated the Incas in 1533, lies buried in one of the cathedrals. For almost three centuries (1535—1821) Lima, the seat of the Spanish viceroys, was the wealthiest and most influential city of Spanish America. Independence was proclaimed in 1821, when José de San Martín, the liberator of Argentina, occupied the city. Lima has a dry, tropical climate with almost no rainfall, but suffers from frequent fogs which are not unlike those of the San Francisco area. Cotton, sugar and grains are grown in the irrigated valley of the Rímac River. The city's growing industries include textile mills, tanneries, and food-processing plants. A railway leads to the mining centres of the Peruvian Andes.

llama The largest and strongest member of the llama group, which includes the domesticated llama and alpaca, and the wild guanaco and vicuña. The llama is covered with a thick mass of hair of fine texture, which may be brown, white or black. From early times, this animal has been used as a beast of burden and as a source of wool and meat. It has played an important part in Andean mining, as the carrier of ores from pit to crusher or railway. The llama has an unpleasant habit of spitting when overloaded or mishandled.

llanos Spanish term for the prairies of northern South America, especially the grasslands of the Orinoco Basin of Venezuela. Despite their hot climate and insect plagues, the llanos have long been known as an extensive cattle-raising region. This is the home of the *llanero*, the South American cowboy who drives his herds over the vast range.

macaw The macaw of tropical America is one of the most brilliantly coloured of all the parrots. With its huge hooked bill, the bird can easily crack a Brazil nut, and extract the meat with its bill and tongue. Among these gaudy birds are the ararauna, a blue-and-yellow macaw, and the hyacinthine macaw, deep blue in colour, both living in the Amazon Basin.

Machu Picchu A ruined Indian city of pre-Inca times in the Andes of Peru, about 50 miles north-west of Cuzco. The fortified town was built on a steep mountain side, nearly 7,000 feet above sea level. Almost inaccessible until recent times, it was rediscovered in 1911.

Madeira River A 2,000-mile-long tributary of the Amazon River in north-western Brazil. During the rubber boom of the early 1900s, a railway was built around falls and rapids on the headwaters of the Madeira. From Pôrto Velho, at the northern end of the line, the river is navigable all the way to Manaus.

Magdalena River Longest river (1,000 miles) and chief traffic artery of Colombia, linking the country's mountainous interior with the Caribbean Sea at the port of Barranquilla. Coffee, sugar and gold are shipped downstream, and most of Colombia's imports travel up the Magdalena to a number of railheads serving the cities of Bogotá, Medellín and Cali. Navigation is slow and cumbersome during the dry season, because of shallows in the river. A railway now runs parallel to the Magdalena.

Magellan Ferdinand Magellan (1480—1521) was a Portuguese navigator who sailed westward across the Atlantic Ocean in 1519, rounded the southern tip of South America, and reached the Philippines, where he was killed in 1521. His ships then went on to complete the first trip around the world in the year 1522.

The island of Tierra del Fuego

Magellan, Strait of A passage, 2 to 20 miles wide, connecting the South Atlantic with the southern Pacific Ocean, and separating the mainland of South America from Tierra del Fuego. Magellan discovered the passage in 1520, in the course of his ill-fated voyage around the world. Punta Arenas, a Chilean town, is the principal settlement on this fjord-like, mountain-fringed strait. The strait's importance as a shipping route declined after the opening of the Panama Canal, in 1914.

Manaus A Brazilian city (population 249,797), more than 1,000 miles above the mouth of the Amazon on the Atlantic Ocean. Rubber, Brazil nuts and hardwoods are shipped from floating wharves that are not affected by fluctuations of up to 35 feet in the river level. The city's most prominent landmark is a sumptuous opera house that was built during the short-lived natural rubber boom of the early 1900s. Manaus declined somewhat in importance with the growth of rubber plantations in the Far East.

manioc A plant native to Brazil and now cultivated throughout the tropics, manioc is also known as cassava. Its fleshy tubers, which grow to 18 inches and a weight of 20 pounds, are (except for potatoes) man's principal source of starch. The bitter cassava, the most common type, contains poisonous hydrocyanic acid, which is removed by cooking. Its starch is marketed under the name of Brazilian arrowroot and is used to make tapioca.

Maracaibo A city (population 510,100) of Venezuela on shallow Lake Maracaibo, in the midst of one of the world's most productive oil-fields. Some of the petroleum is refined on the

Cassava

Inca ruins dot the mountains of Bolivia and Peru

Venezuelan shore, but most of it is shipped by shallow-draft tankers through the narrows connecting Lake Maracaibo with the Caribbean Sea to the off-shore Dutch islands of Curaçao and Aruba. The lowlands of Maracaibo are one of the hottest areas of South America; they are surrounded by the northernmost spurs of the Andes, a region still inhabited by hostile Indian tribes. Lake Maracaibo was discovered by the Spaniards in 1499. The natives' thatched huts, built on stilts in the shallow water, reminded the explorers of Venice, hence the country's name: Venezuela — in Spanish, 'Little Venice'. The city's growth, from a disease-ridden settlement to a modern metropolis, dates from 1917, when oil was discovered in the area. The vast petroleum resources are being exploited by 19 companies among which are American, British and Dutch companies.

Marañón River One of the principal head-streams of the Amazon. It rises high in the Andes of Peru, flows through deep mountain gorges, and finally breaks into the tropical lowlands of eastern Peru, where it joins the Ucayali to form the Amazon River. Its length is estimated at 1,000 miles.

Twigs are removed from coffee beans on a coffee plantation ('estancia') in the cool uplands of Ecuador

marmoset This near-monkey of eastern Brazil is smaller than the average squirrel. It has soft, silky fur, a banded tail, and tufts of long, white fur behind the ears.

Martinique A volcanic island (427 square miles; population 320,030) belonging to France and in the chain of the Lesser Antilles. It has a dense tropical vegetation and receives up to 90 inches of rainfall on the Atlantic slopes. Martinique is dominated by Mt Pelée (4,500 feet), a volcano which erupted in 1902 and destroyed St Pierre, then the island's chief city. The main port and trading centre is now Fort-de-France (99,051 inhabitants), the capital of this French West Indian Department. The chief export products of Martinique are sugar, rum and bananas; coffee, cacao and pineapples are grown on a smaller scale. The predominantly Negro population — descendants of African slaves — is poor, because of the scarcity of cultivable land. Martinique was discovered by Columbus in 1493.

maté A type of holly, native to Paraguay and southern Brazil, whose leaves yield a tea-like beverage which is popular in South America as a stimulant. The leaves are dried over low fires, ground to a coarse powder, and fermented. Mate is traditionally drunk from a small bottle gourd.

Matto Grosso An inland State of Brazil in the sparsely populated far-western part of the country, south of the Amazon River. Stock-raising is the chief activity on the central plateau and along the flood plain of the Paraguay River. More than 300 years ago, Portuguese adventurers found gold and diamonds in the beds of several rivers, but today manganese is a more important mineral resource. Early in the 20th century, the gathering of natural rubber ('the rubber-fever') brought temporary prosperity to northern Matto Grosso, along the headwaters of the Madeira River. A new railway across the State connects Brazil with Bolivia, near the river port of Corumbá. Cuiabá is the State capital. Several hundred thousand Indians live in the remote parts of Matto Grosso. The population numbers 1,475,117.

Medellin The principal industrial centre (population 1,089,000) of Colombia, in a narrow valley enclosed by Andean ranges, Medellin was founded in 1675. It is linked by railway with the Pacific port of Buenaventura, and by rail and river with the Caribbean port of Barranquilla. It lies in the midst of a fertile coffee-growing district. The country's leading gold-mines are also nearby. The city's prosperity results from its modern textile mills.

Mendoza A city of Argentina, on the eastern slopes of the Andes, and on the main railway linking Argentina with Chile. Primarily a wine-growing centre, Mendoza is surrounded by irrigated vineyards and orchards. Founded in 1561, the city belonged to Chile for more than two centuries, before its transfer to the vice-royalty of Rio de la Plata in 1776, later to become the Republic of Argentina. The town was severely damaged by an earthquake in 1861, but Italian immigrants soon brought new prosperity to the region.

Minas Gerais An inland State of Brazil, with a population of 11 million and known for its rich mineral deposits. These include high-grade iron ore, manganese, gold (mined there for almost 300 years), diamonds, bauxite and semi-precious stones. Ranchers raise cattle on the rolling grasslands of the central plateau, and farmers grow coffee in the south, along the border of São Paulo. Belo Horizonte is the modern State capital.

monkey, howling Like most New World monkeys, the large howler has a long, grasping tail. A 'sound box' in the windpipe enables this monkey to utter a loud roar that can be heard at a distance of three miles.

monkey, night This American monkey differs from other monkeys because of its preference for nocturnal activity. It has large eyes and utters an eerie cry, but makes a gentle pet when tamed. Unlike most New World monkeys, the creature cannot use its tail for grasping.

Red howler monkey

monkeys This name is given to a group of mammals which, together with Man, the apes and certain other creatures, are classified as Primates (one of the orders of mammals). The monkeys fall into two major families: New World and Old World. New World monkeys live in the tropical forests of Central and South America. They are small and light in build and have a grasping tail. The Old World monkeys are more highly developed than their American cousins and include the baboons. All monkeys are agile climbers, and subsist on leaves and fruit. They are sociable creatures and live in family groups.

Montevideo Capital and largest city (population 1,290,900 in 1970) of Uruguay, with a seaport at the northern outer part of the Rio de la Plata. As the country's only industrial centre, Montevideo has meat-packing houses, tanneries, flour mills and textile mills. The port accommodates South Atlantic fishing fleets; through it, Uruguay ships the products of its ranches and farms, largely brought to Montevideo by British-built railways. With its beautifully laid-out streets and residential districts, its nearby sandy beaches (notably fashionable Punta del Este), and mild climate, Montevideo is a pleasant place in which to live. It is visited by tourists from Argentina and Brazil. Founded in 1726, the city became the capital of independent Uruguay in 1828.

Natal A city and port (population 270,124) of north-eastern Brazil, less than 2,000 miles from the coast of West Africa across the narrowest part of the Atlantic Ocean. Its airport is used by intercontinental airlines, and was a strategic base for U.S. military planes during World War II. Natal handles hides, sugar and bananas, and was founded in 1597.

nitrates They occur in vast natural beds in the Atacama Desert of northern Chile. Until the First World War, Chilean nitrate or saltpetre was almost the only source of nitrogen for fertiliser. Since then, most of the world's nitrogen has been produced synthetically from air or from by-product coal-gas.

orchid The large family contains about 20,000 species, found mostly in the humid tropics and subtropics of South-East Asia and South America. Many tropical orchids are epiphytes, growing on trees without the benefit of soil. Most orchids have large, showy flowers. Among the most familiar orchids are the Odontoglossum and the Cattleya. About 40 orchids are known in Britain.

Orinoco River One of the great rivers of South America; it flow across Venezuela to the Atlantic Ocean, south of the island of Trinidad. The length

The ancient Inca fort at Machu Picchu lies 7,000 ft above sea level in the cloud-swept Peruvian Andes

The cathedral looks down on Pizarro's statue, and a 17th-century fountain, in Lima's Plaza de Armas

widely spoken. Despite its inland location, Paraguay was among the first areas in South America to be explored by Europeans. Sebastian Cabot sailed up the Paraguay in 1527, in search of an overland route to Peru. Asunción was founded in 1537, and it was from there that Spanish expeditions were sent out to establish Buenos Aires and other downstream settlements. The Jesuits were active in colonising the interior until 1767, when they were banned from the continent. After 1776, the region came under the rule of the Spanish viceroy in Buenos Aires, but in 1811 Paraguay gained its independence without a struggle. Between 1865 and 1870, the country's dictatorial rulers fought a disastrous war against Brazil, Argentina and Uruguay, losing over 400,000 of their able-bodied men. The Gran Chaco War against Bolivia (1932–35) once again left the country exhausted, even though Paraguay added to its western territory and increased the chance of possessing oil reserves.

● **Paraguay River,** some 1,300 miles long, is the principal tributary of the Paraná. It rises in the Matto Grosso plateau of Brazil, and is navigable below the Brazilian city of Corumbá.

● **Paraná** A State in southern Brazil, south of São Paulo. Some of the country's finest coffee is grown on the red soils of northern Paraná, where land has been only recently cleared for settlement. Curitiba is the State capital and largest city. The population of the whole state is 6,741,520.

● **Paraná River** A river of South America, which rises in central Brazil and flows 2,400 miles southwards, across Paraguay and northern Argentina, to the Atlantic Ocean, where — together with the Uruguay — it forms a wide estuary known as the Río de la Plata. Together with its main tributary, the Paraguay River, the Paraná drains the continent's interior, south of the Amazon Basin. The river is navigable all the year round to Corrientes (Argentina), and from that point the Paraguay can be ascended, by ships drawing 17 feet, to Asunción, the capital of Paraguay. It is used to ship maté and quebracho (a tanning extract) from Paraguay, and the products of the Argentine pampa (maize, livestock, wheat, flax), to Buenos Aires and abroad.

of the main river exceeds 1,500 miles; its exact source, on the Brazilian border, was not located until 1951. It has long been known, however, that, at certain times of the year, some of the Orinoco's headwaters are diverted southward to the Amazon Basin, via the natural waterway of the Casiquiare. This phenomenon was established around 1800 by a famous German explorer and geographer, Alexander von Humboldt. For most of its length, the Orinoco crosses the low grasslands of central Venezuela, known as the *llanos*. Ciudad Bolívar, at the narrows of the Orinoco, is the only important town in this sparsely settled region. When huge deposits of iron ore were discovered south of the Orinoco in the early 1950s, the river and its delta were dredged, so that today the ore is loaded on to freighters at the river's edge, and then shipped direct to the steel mills along the Atlantic seaboard of the United States.

● **Oruro** A major tin-mining and smelting centre of Bolivia in the Andes, 12,150 feet above sea level. First settled in 1595, it was a thriving silver-mining centre during Spanish colonial times. Its present population is about 119,700, and other ores — notably copper, wolfram and antimony — are also mined.

● **palmetto** A tropical American dwarf fan-palm, found in Central America and the West Indies. Its leaves are used in weaving baskets, hats and mats.

● **pampa** (or **pampas**) The fertile grasslands of Argentina extending some 300 miles inland from Buenos Aires and the shores of the Río de la Plata. This level, treeless plain is the 'bread-basket' of Argentina; it may be compared to the Prairies and Great Plains of the American Middle West. The humid eastern Pampas yield wheat, maize, alfalfa, and flax for linseed. Cattle and sheep are raised along the drier western and southern fringes. The Pampa is served by a dense railway network converging on Buenos Aires.

● **Paraguay** A small independent country (157,006 square miles; population 2,395,614) of South America, without a seacoast, but with access to the Atlantic Ocean via the navigable Paraguay and Paraná Rivers; the Paraguay actually cuts the country in two. The western region, better known as the Gran Chaco, is a 'green-hell', containing a hot, rather dry area of scrub and grass and

swamps, where cotton is grown on a small scale, chiefly by Mennonite immigrants. In the Oriental section there are huge reserves of hardwoods and cedars awaiting exploitation. The Japanese are experimenting with mulberries for silk growing. Eastern Paraguay is a fertile lowland, where cotton, maize, tobacco, oranges, sugar cane, and subtropical fruits and rice, are cultivated, mainly in the vicinity of Asunción, the country's capital and its largest city (population 437,136). The chief exports (shipped on river boats to Buenos Aires) include cotton, quebracho (a tanning extract), maté, timber, vanilla and processed meats. A railway also links the capital with Argentina, crossing the upper Paraná River (via ferry) at Encarnación. There are few industries, and the majority of the population (which is predominantly *mestizo*; i.e., of mixed European and Indian stock) is poor and illiterate. Most of the peasants are tenants of sharecroppers on large estates, or else gatherers of forest products. Spanish is the official language but Guarani, the language of the native Indians, is

The offshore area of Venezuela's shallow Lake Maracaibo is dotted with row after row of oil-derricks

Herds of llamas and sheep graze near Pisacoma, Peru. Crops are grown on terraced mountain slopes

Patagonia A windswept and desolate tableland of southern Argentina, between the Andes and the Atlantic Ocean. Its 300,000 square miles of dry grassland are devoted almost entirely to sheep-raising. Many of the ranchers originally came from Scotland. There are few cities and almost no sheltered harbours in Patagonia, and the inhospitable climate has kept the population to a scanty 1 per square mile. The region was first settled by Europeans in the 1880s.

peccary The only piglike animal native to America. The more common collared-peccary, so-named because of the light-coloured stripe round its shoulders, ranges from Texas to Patagonia. The larger, white-lipped peccary, with a white area around the chin, is found from Central America to Paraguay.

Peru An independent republic (area about 500,000 square miles; population approximately 13,586,000) of South America, with a 1,400-mile-long coastline on the Pacific Ocean. It is the third-largest country of the continent, but more than half of it lies in the rainy, tropical Amazon Basin, where the population is sparse and the natural resources remain virtually undeveloped. The centre of the country is traversed by three parallel ranges of the Andes, and these form an almost insurmountable barrier between the Amazon Basin to the east and the narrow coastal plain to the west. The Andes reach an elevation of 22,205 feet in the snow-capped volcano Huascarán. The mineral wealth of the Peruvian Andes was one of the main reasons why Lima, the capital, became the leading city of Spanish America, soon after its founding in 1535. Today, Peru mines and exports copper, lead and zinc. It is also the world's principal supplier of vanadium, and it provides the new steel plant at Chimbote with domestic iron ore. It supplies its neighbours with petroleum from two oilfields, one on the northern coast and another in the Amazon Basin. Peru also exports cotton and sugar, both grown in irrigated coastal valleys. The coast is almost rainless, because the sea air over the cool Peru Current (also known as the Humboldt Current) has only a very low humidity. Peru is the world's largest exporter of fish meal.

High in the Andes, the Indians raise sheep, llamas, alpacas and vicuñas, and their wool, sold in the market of Arequipa, is either exported or used in local textile factories. Lima, with its seaport of Callao, is the cultural centre of Peru and the ocean terminus of a skilfully engineered railway to the Andean mining centres (notably Cerro de Pasco) located at elevations from 12,000 to 15,000 feet. A recently completed highway leads eastward from the mining towns into the thick rain-forest of the Amazon Basin. It ends at Pucallpa, a small rubber-gathering centre, from which point boats sail downstream, past the Peruvian river port of Iquitos, to the Atlantic Ocean, 3,000 miles away.

Cuzco was the capital of the flourishing Inca Empire when, in 1533, Francisco Pizarro and his small band of Spanish *conquistadores* undertook the conquest of Peru. The Inca civilisation was destroyed almost overnight, and Peru soon became the wealthiest possession of Spain in the New World. From there, Spanish expeditions set out to conquer other parts of western South America. In 1821, Peru proclaimed its independence from Spain with the aid of José de San Martín, the liberator of Argentina. Since then, it has had border disputes with most of its neighbours, some of them still unresolved. Peru lies alongside one of the world's earthquake prone belts and suffered a devastating series of earthquakes in 1970.

Peru Current or **Humboldt Current** A cold ocean current, off western South America, which moves northward along the coast of northern Chile and Peru. By cooling off the moisture-laden air from the Pacific Ocean, the Peru Current is the cause of the extreme dryness of the coastal climate west of the Andes. The waters of the Peru Current abound in fish, and many sea birds live on offshore islands.

piranha This South American fresh-water fish, only 10 inches long, is more dangerous than the shark. Its powerful, broad jaws are equipped with razor-sharp teeth. The piranha is also known as *caribe*, which means 'cannibal' in Spanish, for they can rapidly remove all the flesh from the bones of large animals, even horses and men.

Pizarro Francisco Pizarro (1475—1541) left Panama with a small army in 1531 and captured Cuzco, the capital of the Inca Empire, two years later. He founded Lima in 1535.

Pôrto Alegre Brazil's southernmost large city (population 885,567) and the capital of the State of Rio Grande do Sul. Its port, on an almost land-locked lagoon (Lagoa dos Patos) of the Atlantic Ocean, can be reached by medium-sized ocean-going ships; larger vessels dock at the outport of Rio Grande, 150 miles to the south. Pôrto Alegre ships meat and animal by-products, wool, cereals, wine, fruit and rice — all products of the fertile agricultural region around the city. Although Pôrto Alegre was founded in 1742 by Portuguese immigrants from the Azores, it has the appearance of a thoroughly modern city, with skyscrapers and broad avenues. Thousands of German and Italian settlers who went there during the 19th and early part of the 20th century have contributed to the city's importance as a trade centre.

Potosí One of the highest cities (13,200 feet) of the world, in the Andes of Bolivia, 60 miles south-west of Sucre, the legal capital of the country. It is a major tin-mining centre. The city was founded by the Spaniards in 1546, after rich silver deposits had been located in the region. In 1610, it had over 160,000 inhabitants, and was then the largest city of the Western Hemisphere; Potosí's present-day population is about 96,800.

pudu This reddish-brown deer, 13 inches high at the shoulder, is the smallest deer of the Americas. It is found in southern Chile, in the temperate rain forests of that region.

puma Unlike the spotted jaguar, this large American cat is of uniform hue: grey, tan or reddish-brown. The six-foot-long puma is found from the U.S.A. to Patagonia under a variety of local names, such as cougar, mountain lion and panther. It sleeps by day and stalks big game by night, but does not normally attack man. The puma discloses its presence by a screaming cry, persistent and weird. Unlike the jaguar, the puma attains its greatest size in colder regions, such as Patagonia.

Punta Arenas A Chilean city (population 67,600) on the Strait of Magellan which is considered to be the southernmost town of the world (except for the nearby Argentine settlement of Ushuaia, on Tierra del Fuego). It has active fish-canning, tanning and sawmilling industries, and is the major shipping centre for wool from the ranches of Patagonia and Tierra del Fuego. Punta Arenas was founded in 1847 as a coaling station for ships sailing around the tip of South America. It declined with the opening of the Panama Canal, in 1914, but now has a growing oil industry.

Quechua An Indian tribal group that constituted the principal element of the Inca Empire. Its language was the official tongue of the Incas, and is still spoken by 6 million people in Ecuador, Peru and northern Bolivia.

quetzal This green, scarlet, black-and-white bird is one of the outstandingly beautiful birds of the world. Its brilliant green train is two feet long. The quetzal was the sacred bird of the Aztecs and is now the national bird of Guatemala. It lives in the forested mountains of Central and South America.

Quito The capital (population 520,000) of Ecuador, in a high mountain valley surrounded by snow-covered peaks of the Andes. At 9,402 feet above sea level, Quito is one of the highest cities in the world. It can be reached by air, by Pan-American Highway from Colombia, and by rail from Guayaquil, the country's chief seaport on the Pacific Ocean. With its 50 or more ornate churches, its spacious squares, and cobble-stone streets, Quito has preserved all the charm and quaintness of a Spanish colonial town. Indian markets enhance the local colour. It is believed that the city dates back to prehistoric times. In the 15th century, it was captured by the Incas, who made it their stronghold in the Andes of Ecuador. The Spaniards occupied the town in 1534, but they had to rebuild

Puma

it from ruins. Quito was freed from Spanish rule in 1822, and in 1830 it became the capital of the newly formed Republic of Ecuador. A large part of its population is of mixed Spanish and Indian blood (*mestizos*).

● **Recife** A seaport (population 1,078,819) on the eastern coast of Brazil, Recife is the country's third-largest city and the capital of the State of Pernambuco, named after the coral reef which shelters its spacious harbour. Recife exports sugar, cotton, tobacco, castor oil and hides. The city's hinterland is dry and sparsely populated. Many farmers have migrated to southern Brazil, and Recife has thus lost some of the commercial importance it enjoyed in the heyday of the sugar boom. Today, cotton mills provide employment for a population that prefers city life to the hardships of the *sertão* (the arid frontier). The suburb of Olinda was founded by the Portuguese in 1530. The Dutch occupied the city (1630 — 1654), and their fort still overlooks the harbour. Recife (sometimes called Pernambuco) has a tropical climate, tempered at times by ocean breezes.

● **rhea** This South American cousin of the African ostrich is several feet shorter and has three toes instead of two. The plumes of the rhea, less valuable than those of the ostrich, are collected to make feather dusters. The common rhea is found in northern Argentina, and the rare Darwin rhea in Patagonia.

● **Rio de Janeiro** The former capital (population 4,296,782) of Brazil, on Guanabara Bay (a deep inlet of the Atlantic Ocean), the mile-wide entrance to which is overlooked by the cone-shaped peak of Sugar Loaf Mountain (1,300 feet; reached by aerial cable-car), the city's distinguishing landmark. Surrounded by steep-sided hills (including Corcovado Peak, surmounted by a giant statue of Christ) and stretched out along semicircular bays, Rio justly lays claim to be the most beautifully sited of any large city in the world. It is the country's cultural and tourist centre, famed for its broad, sandy beaches (notably Copacabana, fronting on the Atlantic Ocean); its 19th-century palaces (now occupied by government offices) and modern office buildings; the tree-lined main thoroughfare, Avenida Rio Branco, with its coloured mosaic pavements; and the annual pre-Lenten carnival, marked by several days of wild street celebrations. While Rio is the nation's largest passenger port, it is exceeded by Santos, the great coffee port, as an outlet for exports. Nor can it compete as a manufacturing centre with São Paulo, the hub of Brazilian industrial and commercial activity. Rio has a tropical climate marked by humid summers, when the well-to-do *cariocas* (citizens of Rio) prefer to live in the nearby hill towns of Petrópolis and Teresópolis.

The Portuguese discovered Guanabara Bay in January, 1502; believing it to be an estuary, they named it 'River of January'. The city was founded in 1567. It became the seat of the Portuguese

viceroy in 1763, and in 1822 the capital of the Brazilian empire, which became a republic in 1889. In 1960, the seat of government was theoretically transferred to Brasilia, a new city being built from the ground up in the Brazilian highlands, near the country's geographical centre.

● **Río de la Plata** (in English often called River Plate) A 200-mile-long inlet of the South Atlantic Ocean between Argentina and Uruguay, formed by the combined estuaries of the Paraguay and Uruguay Rivers. It is relatively shallow and obstructed by mud and sand-banks, so that constant dredging is necessary to provide free access to the great ports of Buenos Aires and Montevideo. The estuary was explored by Magellan in 1520. Its Spanish name — 'river of silver' — probably reflects the interest of European explorers in the silver trinkets worn by the native Indians along its shores.

● **Rio Grande do Sul** The southernmost State of Brazil, on the border of Uruguay. It is a prosperous agricultural region, where the country's finest cattle, sheep and horses are raised — usually on large ranches run by *gauchos* (South American cowboys). Because of its temperate climate, the State (which lies outside of the tropics) produces most of Brazil's wheat, fruits and wine. Meat-packing, the leading industry, is concentrated at Pôrto Alegre, the modern capital of Rio Grande do Sul. German and Italian immigrants have made a significant contribution to the State's progressive land use, and stock-rearing. Its population exceeds 6.6 million.

● **Río Negro** The name of several rivers in South America: (1) A left-bank tributary of the Amazon, in northern Brazil, whose headwaters rise near the Venezuelan border. A natural channel links the source of the Río Negro with the Orinoco River, thus connecting the two major river basins of northern South America. At the city of Manaus, below which it enters the Amazon, the Río Negro is up to 20 miles wide. It is more than 1,500 miles long; (2) A tributary of the Uruguay River which has been dammed for hydro-electric power in the

midst of the rolling pampa of central Uruguay. Its length is 500 miles; (3) Two rivers in Argentina, one an affluent of the Paraná River in the Chaco, the other a stream in Patagonia.

● **Rosario** The second-largest city (population 761,000) of Argentina, on the navigable Paraná River. Grain, meat, hides, wool and quebracho extracts for the tanning industry are shipped downstream to Buenos Aires for export. Large meat-packing plants, flour mills, breweries and sugar refineries line the waterfront. Rosario has an important railway junction.

Rio de Janeiro and Sugar Loaf Mountain

● **Salvador** A seaport (population (1,000,647) of north-eastern Brazil, on the Bay of All Saints and at the hub of a fertile agricultural district known as the Recôncavo. It is the fifth largest city of Brazil and the capital of the State of Bahia. From its docks, sugar, tobacco, cacao, hides and carnauba wax are exported to Europe and the United States. Sugar refineries, distilleries and cotton mills are the chief industries of this busy commercial and cultural centre. Brazil's principal oil-wells and refineries are located nearby. Salvador was founded in 1549, and was the capital of all Portuguese settlements on Brazilian soil until 1763, when the seat of government was transferred to Rio de

Although **Quito** is very near the equator, its climate is cool, as the city stands 9,400 ft up in the Andes

Janeiro. Government buildings and many baroque churches of the 17th and 18th centuries remind the visitor of the city's early prosperity and importance. Thousands of Negroes, whose forefathers were brought from Africa as slaves to work on the sugar plantations of Bahia, form part of the colourful multi-racial population of the city. The business and harbour districts are connected by elevators and inclined-plane railways with the residential quarters on the hills overlooking the port. The city was formerly known by the names of Bahia and São Salvador. It official name is São Salvador da Bahia de Todos es Santos.

● **Santa Cruz** A Bolivian city (population 124,900) situated in the tropical lowlands, just east of the Andes. From Santa Cruz, railways lead to Brazil and to Argentina, and a highway link has been completed to the highland cities of Bolivia. There are important oil deposits in the area and there is a pipeline for oil from the Santa Cruz field to Arica (Chile). There is also a natural gas pipeline to the Argentine border.

● **Santa Fé** A city (population 220,000) of Argentina, and an inland port on a tributary of the Paraná River. It is a commercial centre for the wheat-growing and stock-raising districts of the north-eastern Pampa. Frozen meat, quebracho extracts (used in the tanning industry), flax and grains are shipped to Buenos Aires for export. Founded in 1573, Santa Fé soon became a centre for Jesuit missionaries sent out to civilise the Indian tribes.

● **Santiago de Chile** The capital and largest city (population 2,566,000) of Chile, located in the fertile Central Valley and fringed by the snow-capped peaks of the Andes. A manufacturing centre, it produces textiles, leather goods, chemicals, paper, and a variety of processed foods. Lying at an elevation of almost 2,000 feet, Santiago enjoys warm days and cool nights — a healthful climate all the year round. The principal cultural and government buildings are clustered around historic Plaza de Armas, the huge central square. The city has a modern appearance, most of the early colonial buildings having been wiped out by earthquakes and floods. Pedro de Valdivia,

the Spanish conqueror of Chile, founded Santiago in 1541. In the same year, however, this settlement was completely wiped out by the Araucanian Indians. It became the capital of the independent Republic of Chile in 1818, and its greater metropolitan area has a population of more than 3.2 million.

● **Santos** Brazil's leading seaport (population 350,000), serving São Paulo — the country's largest and most industrialised city, 35 miles inland and situated on a tableland 2,700 feet above sea level. Through Santos passes most of Brazil's huge coffee crop, on its way to Europe and North America. Coffee plays so dominant a role in the city's activities that its fragrance can be detected everywhere. The railway between São Paulo and Santos across the coastal escarpment is one of the busiest in the world. Built by British engineers in 1867, it was hailed as a marvel of engineering; its completion marked the beginning of São Paulo's spectacular growth as a city and manufacturing centre. Nowadays, a four-lane highway has reduced the trip to less than an hour's drive. As many as 50 ships can be loaded at one time along Santos's three miles of well-equipped docks. There, too, raw materials and machinery are unloaded for São Paulo's factories. A few miles from the port is the huge hydro-electric plant which produces power for both cities. Santos was settled in 1543, but remained an insignificant fishing port until the beginning of the coffee boom, which occurred over 100 years ago.

● **São Francisco** A river of eastern Brazil which flows 1,800 miles from the central highlands to the Atlantic Ocean, just south of the great north-eastern bulge. Hydro-electric power is generated at the Paulo Afonso Falls, not far from the river's mouth. Flat-bottomed river-barges provide access to the interior of the States of Bahia and Minas Gerais.

● **São Paulo** Brazil's largest and most rapidly growing city (population 5,901,533), its leading manufacturing centre, and the thriving metropolis of an upland region that produces more than half of the world's coffee. A busy railway and a modern four-lane highway lead to Santos, São Paulo's

seaport, 35 miles away at the foot of the coastal escarpment. Rio de Janeiro lies about 220 miles to the north-east. Due to its elevation (2,700 feet), São Paulo enjoys a healthful, invigorating climate, despite its location astride the Tropic of Capricorn. Its industrial activity exceeds that of any other Latin American city, and the end of its explosive growth (from 40,000 people in the 1880s, and less than 600,000 in 1920) is nowhere in sight. The city produces specialised machinery, steel products, textiles from natural and synthetic fibres, shoes, cement, and a variety of food items. It has branch plants of many American corporations, and the central business district resembles that of the larger U.S. cities, except that the skyscrapers are more modern and bolder in design. A huge hydro-electric plant at Cubatão (at the foot of the tableland, near Santos) supplies the city with cheap and abundant power.

São Paulo was founded in 1554 by Jesuits, who had come to civilise the Indians. From there, Portuguese adventurers (known as *bandeirantes*, or 'flag bearers') drove into the unknown interior, in search of gold and diamonds, during the 17th and 18th centuries. The extension of coffee cultivation throughout the State of São Paulo (95,000 square miles; 1970 population 17.7 million) gave the city its commercial start, and the large-scale immigration of Europeans (especially Italians) provided the skills needed for industrial development. The citizens of São Paulo (called *paulistas*) are well known as enterprising, hardworking, business-minded people.

● **Sierra Nevada de Santa Marta** An outlying mountain range of the northern Andes in Colombia. Snow-covered peaks, up to 19,000 feet in height, rise sheer from the Caribbean coast, east of the port of Barranquilla. Banana plantations surround the mountain range. Primitive Indian tribes still inhabit the region.

● **sloth** No other warm-blooded animal is as slow and lethargic as the tree sloth. It usually hangs upside down from tree branches, holding on with its long, hooked claws. There are two main kinds of sloth. The two-toed sloth, or unau, has two toes on its front limbs. The three-toed sloth, or ai, has nine neck vertebrae (two more than the ordinary mammal), enabling the creature to turn its head upside down.

● **sooty shearwater** This relative of the petrel owes its name to the habit of 'shearing the water' by skimming low over the waves. Except when nesting, the sooty shearwater spends its life at sea.

● **Sucre** The legal (but not the governmental) capital (population 84,900) of Bolivia, in the eastern Andes, 9,400 feet above sea level. It has a 16th-century cathedral, an early 17th-century university, and several old government palaces. It is the seat of an archbishop and of the supreme court of Bolivia. Since 1900, however, the actual seat of the government has been the larger city of La Paz, 250 miles to the north-west.

● **swordfish** This giant relative of the mackerel grows to 500 pounds or more. Its sword, a bony prolongation of the upper jaw, makes up one-third of the fish's total length. The swordfish uses its beak to slash left and right through a school of fish, and then consumes its victims. The swordfish is prized as a game fish because of its tasty meat.

● **tagua nut** (or **ivory nut**) A nutlike seed of a South American palm, the size of a hen's egg. It contains a very hard tissue, known as vegetable ivory, which can be carved into buttons and a variety of ornamental objects.

Rio de Janeiro, Brazil, on Guanabara Bay, is one of the most beautiful ports in the world

tapir This strange, primitive animal with its elongated snout and upper lip is quite timid and inoffensive. The tapirs of today are the last of a great family that ranged throughout the world in prehistoric times. Outside tropical America, the tapir is found only in Malaysia. The American types include the giant tapir of Central America, weighing up to 600 pounds; the mountain tapir of the Andes, which has a heavy coat of coarse hair; and the common South American tapir of the lowland forests.

Tierra del Fuego A group of islands (27,000 square miles; population about 10,000) at the southern tip of South America, separated from the mainland by the Strait of Magellan. It is a barren and desolate region, with much rainfall, high winds and dense fog adding to its forbidding character. Sheep-raising is the principal activity. The islands were discovered by Magellan in 1520. He gave them their present name (in English, 'land of fire') because he was astonished by the number of fires kindled by the natives, seeking protection from the inclement weather. Tierra del Fuego is now divided between Chile and Argentina. The Argentine town of Ushuaia is the southernmost permanent settlement in the world. Rocky Cape Horn forms the southern tip of Tierra del Fuego.

Titicaca, Lake The highest lake (12,500 feet) in the world, and the largest lake (3,200 square miles) of South America, Titicaca is situated on a high Andean plateau along the Peru-Bolivia border. A steamship service across the lake connects the highway networks of the two countries. Nearby is the ruined city of Tiahuanaco, the seat of a pre-Inca Indian civilisation, and one of the most important archeological sites in South America.

toucan This queer bird, which inhabits the South American tropics, has a bill so large that one wonders how it can maintain its balance. Actually, the huge bill is not as heavy as it looks, because of its spongy structure. In order to sleep, the toucan must turn its head backwards and rest it on top of its back. Then the bird spreads its tail like a fan, folding it over the bill. The largest of the 37 species of big-billed toucans is the toco.

Trinidad and **Tobago** Two West Indian Islands which, together, form a fully independent country (1,980 square miles; population 1,010,000) of the British Commonwealth, situated off the coast of Venezuela, just north of the delta of the Orinoco River. It is the southern 'anchor' of the island chain of the Antilles. Port-of-Spain (130,000), on Trinidad, is the national capital and chief port. Tobago's capital is Scarborough, and the island's population 33,200. The two tropical islands have fertile soil in which sugar cane, cacao, coconuts, coffee and citrus fruit are grown. Rum is an important export, but Trinidad's main source of income is oil, which is refined on the island; natural asphalt is recovered from a pitch lake.

Trinidad was discovered by Columbus in 1498; it was settled by Spaniards in 1532 and, later, by French refugees from Haiti. The British occupied the island in 1797, and it became a British colony in 1802. Negroes, who were brought there as slaves, now make up almost two-thirds of the population; next in number are East Indians, who first came to Trinidad in 1845, to replace the freed slaves as workers in the cane-fields. The European population forms a small minority. English is spoken generally. The territory was a part of the short-lived West Indies Federation (1957–62). Trinidad is well known for its colourful annual pre-Lenten carnival and for its steel-drum bands, the originators of calypso music.

Tucumán A city (population 251,000) of northwestern Argentina, in a sugar-growing district at the foot of the Andes. Citrus fruit, rice, tobacco and grains are grown in the irrigated fields and orchards surrounding the city. Sugar-milling is the main industry. Tucumán was founded in 1565.

uakari This monkey differs from all other American types in having a very short tail. The size of a house cat, the uakari makes its home in the Amazon Basin and looks remarkably like the orang-utan.

Ucayali River One of the main headstreams of the Amazon. It rises in the Andes and crosses the tropical lowlands of eastern Peru, where the Ucayali joins the Marañón to form the Amazon River. The Ucayali is navigable to Pucallpa, a rubber-gathering centre at the end of a highway leading across the Andes to the Pacific coast at Lima, Peru. The river is about 1,000 miles long.

Uruguay The smallest (72,150 square miles) republic of South America, on the Río de la Plata and the Atlantic Ocean, between Argentina and Brazil. Montevideo, with about one-third of the country's population of 2,800,000, is the capital city. Stock-raising is the principal activity on Uruguay's rolling grasslands — an extension of Argentina's humid pampa. Wool is the leading export, followed by salted, frozen and tinned meat, leather, hides and animal fats. Two-thirds of the land is devoted to natural pasture, which is lush in this well-watered sub-tropical country. Wheat, corn, linseed, barley, tobacco and rice are grown near the southern coast. The predominantly European population is chiefly of Italian and Spanish descent. Spanish is the official language, even though the Portuguese ruled the country in the 17th century. The Spaniards, who came in 1724, established ranching as the mainstay of the economy. Uruguay gained its independence in 1828, and since 1900 has had a democratic and progressive form of government. For a while, Uruguay was run by a Swiss-style National Council, but today it is governed by a president and his appointed cabinet.

Uruguay River Rising in southern Brazil, this river forms Uruguay's western frontier, and is almost 1,000 miles long. Above Buenos Aires, the Uruguay joins the Paraná River to form the Río de la Plata estuary.

Valdivia An industrial town (population 89,500) of southern Chile, in a densely forested coastal region. It is the gateway to the country's lake district, a mountain-fringed resort area of great beauty. Valdivia was named after the Spanish conqueror of Chile, who established a settlement there in 1552. In the mid-19th century, Valdivia was enlarged by an influx of thousands of German immigrants, who have given the town a noticeably European character. Ship-building is an important industry. The town was largely destroyed by an earthquake in 1960.

Valparaiso Chile's principal seaport (on the Pacific) and second-largest city (population 296,000), about 60 miles from Santiago, the country's capital. Through its port pass most of the exports from Chile's fertile Central Valley. A railway leads across the Andes to Mendoza, in Argentina. Valparaiso's mild climate and fine beaches attract tourists. The nearby resort of Viña del Mar (population 168,800) enjoys an international reputation. Levelled by a severe earthquake in 1906, Valparaiso has been rebuilt along modern lines. The bay on which it is located was discovered by Spanish navigators in 1536.

Venezuela An independent republic (352,050 square miles; population 9,600,000) of northern South America, extending southward from the Caribbean shore to within 1° of the Equator. Its vast interior lowlands, known as the *llanos* (tropical grasslands), are drained by the Orinoco, one of the continent's great rivers. Extensive herds of cattle, many of Indian zebu stock, are grazed there. To the south of the Orinoco lie the Guiana Highlands. They occupy fully one-half of the country's area but, except for the recovery of gold and precious stones, the highlands have remained undeveloped and almost uninhabited. The discovery of high-grade iron deposits in the early 1950s has awakened new interest in the region south of the Orinoco. American companies are mining the ore and shipping it downriver, and then directly to steel mills on the Atlantic seaboard of the United States. Venezuela has profited from these mining ventures, but its prosperity (greater than that of any other South American country, with a per capita income of over $1,000 per head) rests above all on its wealth of 'black gold'. Venezuela is one of the world's leading oil producers, and the largest single exporter of crude and refined petroleum. One of the oil-fields lies in north-eastern Venezuela, not far from the island of Trinidad, but at least two-thirds of the nation's petroleum comes from the Maracaibo Basin, near the Colombian border, where thousands of wells dot the shores and the shallow-water reaches of Lake Maracaibo. Although this is the most productive region of Venezuela (for coffee is grown in the highlands enclosing the Maracaibo Basin), most of the population is found in the cooler coastal highlands, where the larger cities are situated. Caracas, the thriving modern capital, lies in a mountain valley less than 10 miles from its Caribbean seaport of La Guaira. Valencia (204,273 inhabitants) is the centre of a prosperous agricultural district in an upland basin where coffee, sugar, tobacco and cotton are grown. Cacao is the chief crop of the warmer coastal lowlands. Textile milling is the country's chief industry, but the development of hydro-electric power in the Orinoco Valley foreshadows the establishment of a steel industry based on the country's abundant iron reserves. A large petro-chemical complex is being developed at Morón.

Cumaná, a fishing port on the Caribbean, is considered the oldest permanent Spanish settlement (1521) on the South American continent. In 1718, the territory became part of the vice-royalty of New Granada. During the 18th century, the Venezuelan coastline was frequently attacked by British buccaneers. Venezuela won its independence through Simón Bolívar, a native son, who also liberated Colombia and Ecuador from Spanish domination. He united the three countries into the Republic of Greater Colombia (1819), but Venezuela seceded from that federation in 1830. The discovery and development of the country's immense petroleum resources after 1917, mark the beginning of Venezuela's rapid rise to prosperity.

vicuna A wild member of the llama family, of the South American Andes. Standing less than three feet at the shoulder, it is smaller than the guanaco. Its silky hair is woven into a soft, woolly fabric, used for coats, felt hats and carpets.

Volta Redonda Brazil's main steel-milling centre, on the road between Rio de Janeiro and São Paulo. It was built after World War II and uses Brazil's high-grade iron ore, brought there from the State of Minas Gerais.

vulture, king This is the most colourful of the New World vultures. White, satiny body feathers, black wings and tail, and a bare head and neck brightly coloured in red and yellow, produce a gaudy and repulsive appearance.

Australia and Oceania

Australia, often referred to in Europe as the 'down under' continent, has always been hampered by its location. The nickname 'down under' reminds us that Australia, as far as the countries bordering on the North Atlantic Ocean are concerned, lies on the opposite side of the globe, for it is at least a four weeks' voyage from Europe to Australia, and the voyage from London to Sydney via Suez is almost the same length as half of the world's circumference.

Remoteness from the mother country — Great Britain — and the lack of readily exploitable resources largely account for Australia's slow rate of growth in the three centuries since its discovery by the Dutch, who landed on the west coast of the Cape York Peninsula in 1605. New Holland, as it was called by Dutch navigators, at first appeared to be only a barren land inhabited by several thousand savages. In 1770, Captain Cook explored the eastern coast and raised the British flag over picturesque Botany Bay, not far from present-day Sydney Harbour. In 1801—2 Matthew Flinders succeeded in sailing completely round Australia, so revealing it to be a vast island. The Australians, by and large, are nearly as British as the British themselves. Roughly 55 per cent of the population of approximately 13 million are of English origin, and a further 15 per cent of Scottish and 25 per cent of Irish origin. Other immigrants are Italians, Greeks and Central Europeans. Only about 80,000 inhabitants are aborigines or of aboriginal origin.

Although the first settlements — penal colonies for convicts from the United Kingdom — were established in the part of Australia most suitable for agriculture, the going was even more difficult than for the early colonists of North America. The land had never before been cultivated. Native plants were strange and not suitable for food, so that European crops and livestock had to be adapted slowly, by trial and error, to the local environment. Fortunately, the new settlers soon discovered that much of Australia was ideal 'sheep country'. The prospect of raising sheep attracted more people to Australia, until, by the middle of the 19th century, the white population numbered about 650,000. The gold rush (1851—59) almost doubled the population in a decade. In the past 100 years, the population has grown more slowly and steadily, but a wave of immigrants after World War II helped to push the total to the 10 million mark by about 1957. Even so, Australia is far from densely settled, for it is nearly as large as the continental United States.

The lack of water in over four-fifths of the continent has

Wild Animals and Plants

M Mangrove Forest
R Rain Forest
S Savanna
Sc Scrub
B Bluebush
A Alang grass
G Grassland
SD Semi-Desert
D Desert
Sm Salt marsh
C Coral reef
V Active volcanoes

Mammals
1 Papua wild pig
2 Dingo
3 Wild rabbit*
4 Sea leopard*
5 Sea lion*
6 Flying fox*
7 Fold-lipped bat*
8 Cachalot*
9 Risso's dolphin*
10 Bottle-nose dolphin*
11 Porpoise*
12 Dugong
13 Great grey kangaroo
14 Red kangaroo
15 Black wallaroo
16 Wallaroo
17 Tree kangaroo

18 Tasmanian wolf
19 Tasmanian devil
20 Dasyure
21 Bandicoot
22 Wombat
23 Koala
24 Great flying phalanger
25 Squirrel flying phalanger
26 Honey mouse
27 Echidna
28 Platypus

Birds
29 Emu
30 Papuan cassowary
31 One-wattled cassowary
32 Two-wattled cassowary
33 Bennett's cassowary
34 Australian cassowary
35 Mantell's kiwi
36 South kiwi
37 Macaroni penguin*
38 Little penguin
39 Arctic tern*
40 Sooty tern*
41 Ash-grey tern*

42 Noddy tern
43 Fairy tern
44 Grey-headed albatross*
45 Frigate bird*
46 Booby*
47 Red-tailed tropic bird*
48 Wilson's storm petrel*
49 Thin-billed prion*
50 Australian crane
51 Kagu
52 Notornis
53 Straw-necked ibis
54 Purple gallinule
55 Megapode
56 Brush turkey
57 Black swan
58 Cape Barren goose
59 Crowned pigeon
60 Fruit pigeon
61 Tooth-billed pigeon
62 Australian sea eagle*
63 Masked owl
64 Honey-eater
65 Mamo
66 White-eye
67 Blue wren
68 Piping crow
69 Laughing kingfisher

70 Lyrebird
71 Wreath-billed hornbill*
72 Greater bird-of-paradise
73 Blue bird-of-paradise
74 King-of-Saxony bird-of-paradise
75 Satin bowerbird
76 Kakapo owl parrot
77 Kea
78 Eclectus parrot
79 Cherry-brown lory
80 Black-rumped lory
81 Margaret's lory
82 Ruby-coloured lory
83 Sapphire lory
84 Crested parakeet
85 Zebra parakeet
86 Hooded parakeet
87 Rosella parakeet

Reptiles and Amphibians
88 Green turtle
89 Leatherback turtle
90 Salt-water crocodile
91 Perentie monitor

92 Frilled lizard
93 Shingle-backed skink
94 Thorny devil
95 Tuatara

Fishes
96 Smooth dogfish
97 Thresher shark

Shellfish
98 Pearl Oyster

Plants
99 Coconut palm*
100 Sago palm*
101 Fan palm*
102 Nipa palm*
103 Banana*
104 Pandanus*
105 Eucalyptus*
106 Acacia
107 Grass tree
108 Spinifex
109 Tree fern*
110 Conifer
111 Araucaria pine*
112 Kauri
113 Bottle tree

Plants and animals designated with an asterisk (*) have a wide distribution. Others are found only where pictured.

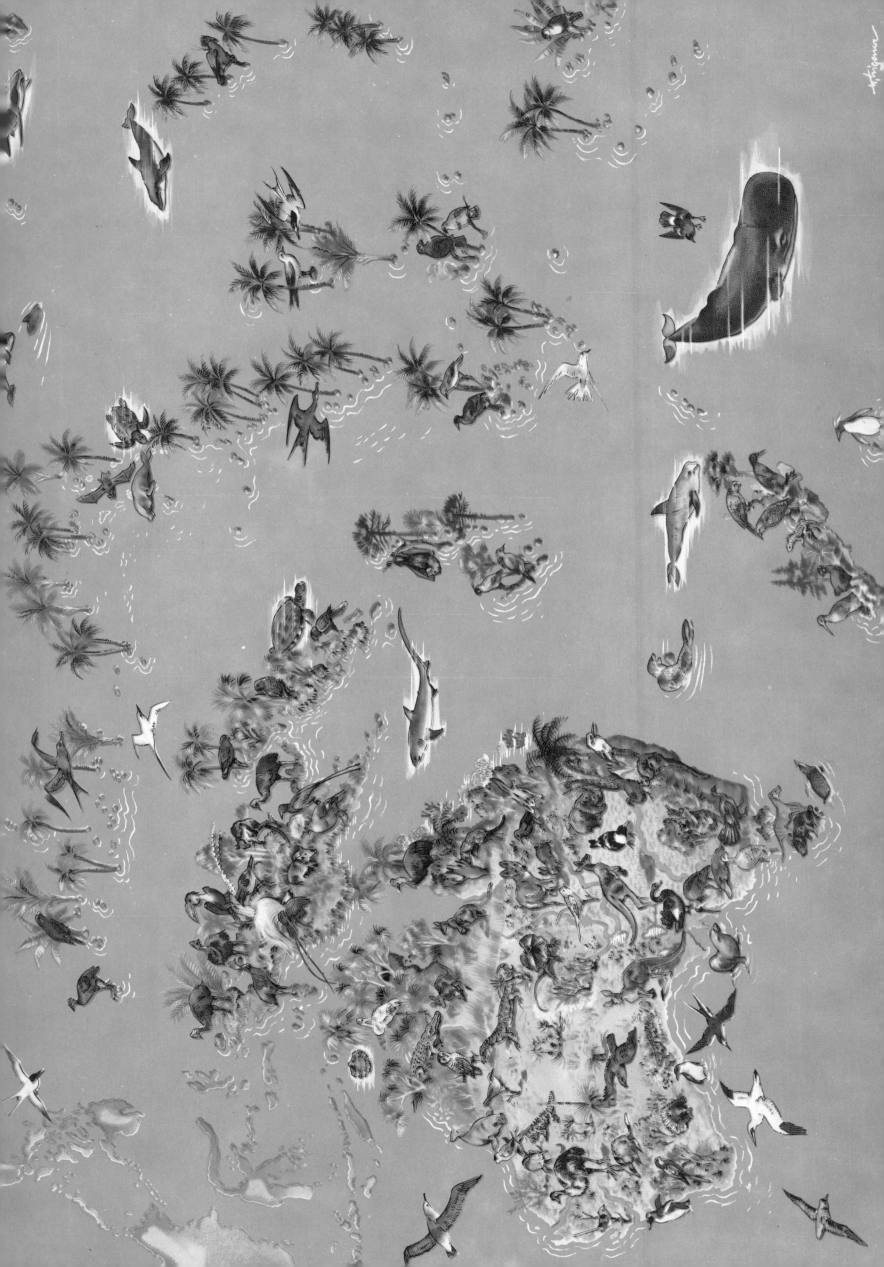

been the crucial factor in hindering the island up to now from becoming a powerful nation. Forty per cent is desert, another forty per cent is as dry as the high plains of the western United States, and much of the remainder is afflicted either by too long a dry season or (as in the jungles of the far north) by a super-abundance of tropical rainfall. Only the south-eastern part, between the Great Dividing Range and the sea, enjoys a reasonably dependable rainfall throughout the year. However, there are artesian basins in the central areas. To the south, across a narrow stretch of ocean, lies the mountainous and densely wooded island of Tasmania, blessed with adequate moisture, which forms part of the Australian Commonwealth. The Great Dividing Range runs from Melbourne on the south coast up into the Cape York Peninsula, and between and around the two are high plateaux, on one of which stands the capital, Canberra.

Stock raising is central to the country's economy. It is carried on chiefly along the dry margin of the eastern highland where as much as 15 acres is needed to support a sheep, and where cattle must be herded overland for hundreds of miles to the slaughterhouses of the coastal cities. Even with the radio and the aeroplane, the flying veterinary and the travelling library, life along the Australian 'frontier' remains lonesome, hard, and,

in times of drought, precarious, with bush fires an added danger, even in the long-settled zones.

However, there are areas in the interior and in the north and west where water, and hence life, are more abundant. These places are fed by artesian wells whose supply seeps underground through layers of permeable rock from distant outcrops where rainfall is more plentiful. Where forage can be grown, stock-raising is as scientific and as efficient an enterprise as it is in the American corn belt. For Australia must sell its animal products — its wool, meat, hides and dairy products — as well as its minerals, in order to be able to pay for its imports.

Settlement in Australia is largely confined to the south-east, where the trade winds are rain-bearing. Here there are the large cities of Sydney, Melbourne, and on the outer parts, Brisbane to the north-east and Adelaide in the western part of this area. Here there is intense farming, many industries, wine production, bathing and holiday resorts, a sharp contrast to the under-populated centre and north. There is only one large urban area outside the south-east — Perth, located on the south-western coast.

The six original states — New South Wales, Victoria, Queensland, South Australia, Western Australia and Tasmania — set up a Federal Commonwealth in 1901, without diminishing

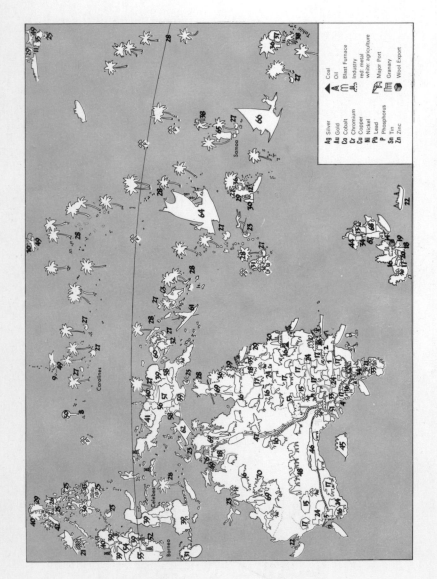

Peoples, Production, Mineral Resources and Trade

Centres of Trade
1 Canberra
2 Sydney
3 Melbourne
4 Adelaide
5 Perth
6 Darwin
7 Manila
8 Yap Island
9 Guam
10 Wake Island
11 Honolulu
12 Suwa, capital of Fiji Islands
13 Auckland
14 Wellington

Livestock and Animal Products
15 Sheep Ranch
16 Cattle
17 Sheep
18 Meat

19 Butter
20 Cheese
21 Fishing
22 Whaling station
23 Pearl-fishing

Agricultural Products
24 Wheat
25 Rice
26 Corn
27 Copra
28 Coconut palm
29 Sugar cane
30 Sugar mill
31 Coffee
32 Cacao
33 Fruit
34 Tinned goods
35 Pineapples
36 Bananas
37 Oranges
38 Vanilla
39 Natural rubber

40 Tobacco
41 Cotton
42 Hemp
43 Sisal
44 Lumber

Communications, Transportation and Trade
45 19th- century sailing ship
46 Perth-Melbourne railway
47 North-south high-way and telegraph line
48 Desert caravan
49 Airport
50 Radio station
51 Shipyard
52 Oil pipeline
53 Windmill

Peoples and Characteristic Dwellings
54 Dyak
55 Tree house
56 Papuan native
57 Meeting house
58 Papuan domestic animals
59 Pottery
60 Melanesian pile dwellings
61 Dugout
62 Outrigger
63 Melanesian woman
64 Double canoe with mat sail
65 Polynesian
66 Outrigger with sail
67 Maori
68 Maori house
69 Australian aborigines
70 Primitive lean-to

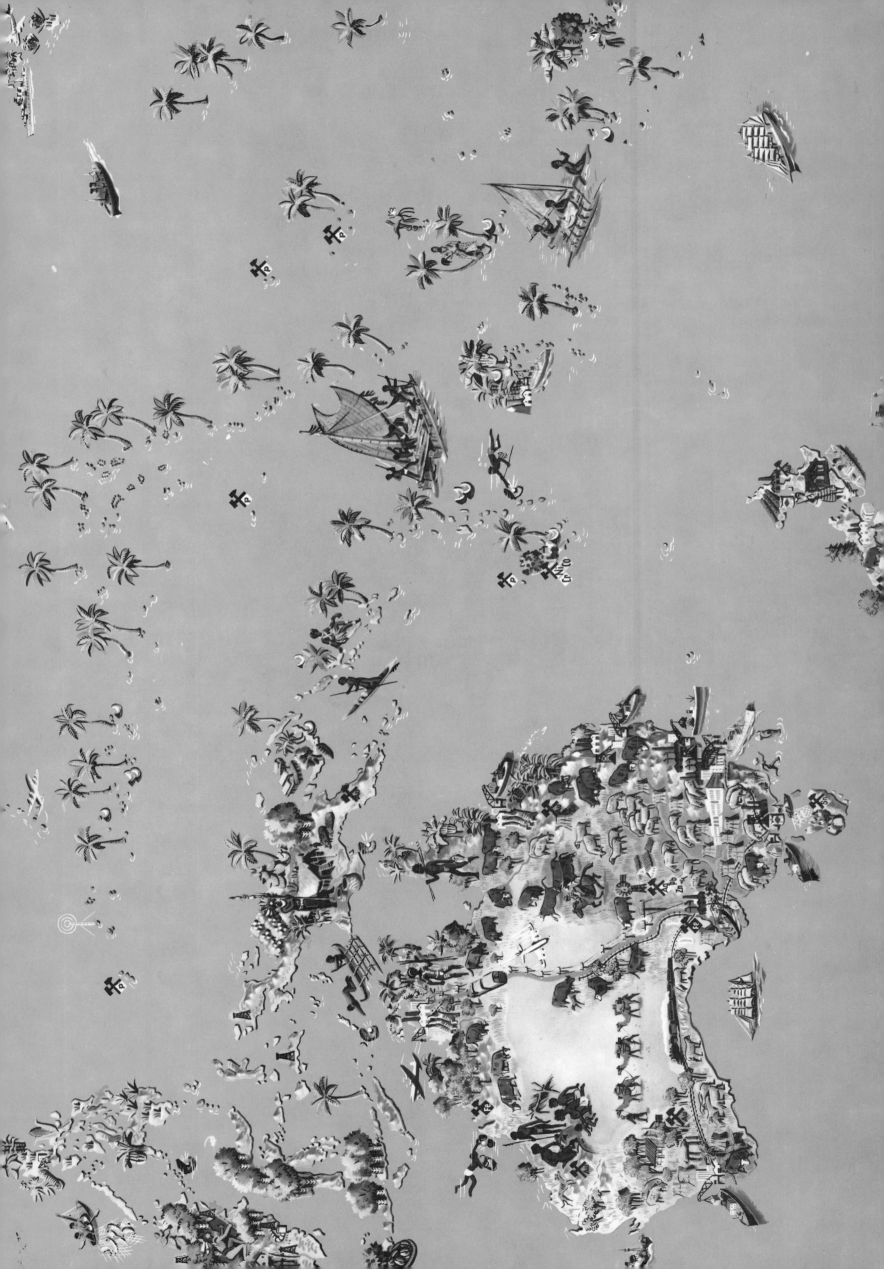

their individual independence. In addition, there are the Northern Territory and the Australian Capital Territory.

Australia was once a part of Asia, but became separated from it in the geologically distant past, so that many distinctive plants and animals are found only in Australia, and are very different in composition and form from those of other parts of the world. There are very few higher mammals in Australia, apart from those introduced by man.

New Zealand, even more remote from the world's main population clusters than its larger neighbour, is a greener and more scenic land. It, too, was settled chiefly by emigrants from Britain, and, like Australia, it has remained a faithful member of the British Commonwealth of Nations. The people of New Zealand — there are now more than 2 million, including the 160,000 Maoris of Polynesian stock — have built up a way of life that will remain prosperous as long as they can sell their livestock and their butter to markets half-way round the globe.

To the north and east of New Zealand lies the island world of the Pacific. It is spread over a huge expanse of water, which extends northward to the Hawaiian Islands and eastward to the mysterious Easter Island, whose giant stone faces were carved by an as yet unknown civilisation. The palm-fringed coral atolls and volcanic islands of the South Seas have been inhabited by seafaring peoples for many centuries. In their hand-made outrigger canoes they sailed from island to island, and some of them — the Maoris — even reached New Zealand. But when the white men reached the 'down under' lands in the 18th and 19th centuries, they treated the brown-skinned Maoris as natives.

The needs of the Pacific islands are simple and few, and the coconut palm gives them food, materials to build their shelters, and an export product (copra, or dried coconut meat) that ships from the outside world pick up every once in a while. In recent years, some of these tiny specks in the Pacific Ocean have been selected as refuelling stops on intercontinental airline routes. Their importance as firmly anchored aircraft carriers is, in fact, many times greater than all the coconuts they can ever hope to harvest.

Visitors to Mundaring Weir, near Perth, in Western Australia, watch the cascading waters of the Helena River

This Australian faller is cutting a 'scarfe' in a karri tree, as this helps to ensure that it will fall in the required direction

AUSTRALIA
AND OCEANIA

Scale 1:30,000,000

SYDNEY   Cities   over   1,000,000 population
Brisbane   Cities   of   250,000   1,000,000 population
Davao   Cities   under   250,000 population
⊚ Capitals of Countries

Heights in feet:

Below Sea level | 0-650 | 650-1,650 | 1,650-4,900 | over 4,900

Depths in feet:

over 650 | 0-650

Intermittent streams   ···· Wadi

Salt Lake   Desert   Swamp, marsh   Railroad

Inside the coral reef, surrounding this South Pacific atoll, are several islands and a lagoon

A steaming pool near Rotorua, the centre of New Zealand's extensive thermal area in North Island

●**Adelaide** An Australian city (population 825,000), capital of the State of South Australia. Surrounded by parks and playing fields, it is one of the most attractive places in which to live on the continent. Wheat and wool are exported from Port Adelaide, 7 miles to the north-west on the Gulf of St Vincent. There are vineyards on the slopes of the nearby Mt Lofty ranges, founded by German immigrants. Adelaide was settled in 1836 and the first university was opened in 1882.

●**Alice Springs** An Australian town (population 8,000) in the sparsely populated range lands of the country's Northern Territory. A narrow-gauge railway built in 1929 leads south to Adelaide, and a modern highway, built in 1941—2, runs north to Darwin. There are no other towns for hundreds of

miles in any direction, and much of today's transport is by aircraft.

●**artesian well** A type of water well in which the water is forced upward by hydrostatic pressure. Artesian wells can be dug where a gently dipping, permeable layer of rock, such as sandstone, is sandwiched between two impermeable layers, such as shale. If the source of the water is sufficiently high, the well will gush out as a fountain without any pumping. Such wells are valuable for irrigation in dry regions, such as the Great Plains of the United States and parts of Australia. The name derives from the discovery of the principle in Artois, in France, in 1126. The Australian artesian basin is the largest in the world, with an area of over ½ million square miles, and they are especially important for agriculture in western Queensland.

Artesian well

New Zealand's giant Benmore Dam, South Island

This wallaby has a baby in its pouch

atoll A coral reef in the shape of a ring or horseshoe, enclosing a lagoon, typical of many islands of the Pacific Ocean. Coral is built up by coral polyps, which are small marine creatures constructed like the sea anemone. Coral polyps have a hard skeleton made of calcium carbonate extracted from the sea water. When the polyp dies, the skeleton is left behind. Masses of coral thus gradually grow to enormous size, forming coral reefs and islands.

Auckland The largest city (population 448,000) of New Zealand and the country's leading seaport, on North Island about 1,300 miles from Sydney, Australia. Butter, frozen meat, and wool are the chief exports. Auckland has meat-packing plants and clothing factories. The spacious harbour contains shipyards and a naval base and an international airport. The first permanent European settlement in New Zealand was established here in 1840 on Hauracki Bay, after the Maori chiefs had ceded the territory to Britain. About 100,000 Maoris now live in the Auckland district.

Melbourne, capital city of Victoria, Australia, is a seaport at the mouth of the Yarra River

Australia An island continent in the southern hemisphere off South-East Asia, and a member nation of the British Commonwealth. Its area, including the island of Tasmania, is 2,967,909 square miles — nearly as large as the United States. Nevertheless, Australia is the smallest continent (or the largest island) of the world, the only one lying wholly south of the equator, and, except for Antarctica, the least densely settled one. Despite its vast open spaces, Australia has a population of only 13 million, over half of whom live in the five largest cities. The people are of European stock — predominantly British — and immigration, though encouraged, is limited almost exclusively to whites. The interior is a vast desert region, and except for mining and livestock-raising (in the semi-arid portions), is empty and useless. No other region on earth is similarly affected by the unreliability of rainfall; only one-fifth of Australia (the eastern seaboard, the south-east, and the south-western corner) receives enough rain to support a permanent population, and even here irrigation from surface streams (especially the Murray River and its tributaries) and wells (chiefly in the Great Artesian Basin of Queensland) is necessary to grow the nation's grain and fruit crops. Only the coastal areas of Queensland are blessed with abundant year-round rain; here one finds sugar cane plantations and grazing for cattle and dairy herds. South-western Australia, separated by more than a thousand miles of desert and scrub from the settled portions of South Australia, grows wheat and raises sheep, but not as intensively as the well-watered plains of Victoria and New South Wales. The rugged island of Tasmania, off the south-east coast, has plenty of rain but little fertile land; it is largely covered by dense forests.

Though sheep-raising is still the mainstay of the Australian economy (there are about 13 sheep for every inhabitant), mining and manufacturing have added significantly to the country's prosperity since World War II. Gold, discovered in Victoria more than a century ago, is still mined, but coal has become much more important, for it is needed in the steel mills of New South Wales and for the generation of electric power. Broken Hill is one of the world's leading silver and lead-mining centres. Moreover, extensive iron, nickel, zinc, bauxite and uranium deposits have been located in the far north and west, and oil was discovered in Western Australia in 1953.

Australia cannot live without exporting, and wool and meat (chiefly mutton) account for at least half the value of all shipments. Japan is the best customer. Exports are channelled through Sydney and Melbourne, the country's largest cities, as well as through Adelaide (wool, wheat, lead) and Brisbane (wool, preserved meat, sugar). A railway crosses the continent from east to west (Sydney to Perth), but a projected line from north

to south (Darwin to Adelaide) has never been finished; however, a connecting highway was built during World War II. The aeroplane has become an essential means of transportation in this

Aboriginal native of Australia

sparsely settled country; thus, a flying medical and veterinary service has been established in the interior of Queensland and in the Northern Territory.

Australia was the last continent but one to be discovered (Antarctica was the last). The Dutch explored the north coast of Australia in 1605 and named the continent New Holland. In 1642, Tasman (also a Dutchman) sailed around the southern shore, discovering Tasmania. In 1770, Captain James Cook reached Botany Bay (near Sydney), sailed north to Cape York, and claimed the territory for Great Britain. The first settlement (1788) was founded as a penal colony for convicts from England. Few white settlers followed until gold was discovered in Victoria in 1851, after which immigrants poured in. In 1901, the six separate colonies (now called States) united to form the Commonwealth of Australia, a British dominion. A small area of New South Wales was selected as the Australian Capital Territory in 1908, and the seat of government was moved in 1927 from Melbourne to the new capital city of Canberra. Australia has several island dependencies in the South Pacific, and governs north-eastern New Guinea (together with outlying islands) as a United Nations trust territory. A large section of Antarctica has also been claimed by Australia.

Remote from any other continent, Australia has preserved many distinctive forms of plant life — notably the giant eucalyptus, the bottle tree and the dry grasses of the arid scrubland — and an even more diversified animal life, including the kangaroo, the wombat, the platypus, the spiny anteater, the koala, and such unusual birds as the lyrebird and the emu. Animals introduced by man from

other continents have adjusted only too well in Australia; thus rabbits, brought there in 1788, multiplied so fast that a 1,000-mile-long fence had to be built in 1907 to protect the sheep pastures of Western Australia.

AUSTRALIAN CAPITAL TERRITORY (939 square miles; population 146,000) surrounds Canberra, the seat of government for the Commonwealth of Australia.

NEW SOUTH WALES (309,400 square miles; population 4,617,000). A state of the Commonwealth of Australia with its capital at Sydney. Its main products are wool, meat, wheat, coal, silver, lead and steel.

NORTHERN TERRITORY (520,300 square miles; population 86,000). This sparsely settled territory of Australia is noted for its cattle production and minerals. Darwin is the capital city.

A Melanesian builds a grass hut on Viti Levu, Fiji

QUEENSLAND (667,000 square miles; population 1,836,000) An Australian State whose chief products are livestock, wool, sugar and tobacco. Its capital city and major seaport is Brisbane.

SOUTH AUSTRALIA (380,070 square miles; population 1,179,000) A State of the Commonwealth of Australia noted for its wheat, iron, wine and wool products, with Adelaide as its chief city.

TASMANIA (26,383 square miles; population 391,000) An island State off south-eastern Australia, with Hobart as its administrative centre. Timber, zinc, wool and also fruits are the main products.

VICTORIA (87,884 square miles; population 3,515,000) Melbourne is the capital city of this densely populated Australian State noted for its wool, mutton, wheat, wine and dairy products.

WESTERN AUSTRALIA (975,900 square miles; population 1,036,000). Known for its wheat, wool and gold products, Western Australia is a State of the Commonwealth of Australia, with its capital at Perth.

●**Australian Alps** A mountain range of south-eastern Australia which contains the continent's highest peak, Mt Kosciusko (7,316 feet). These mountains have neither the height nor the rugged, glaciated features of the European Alps or the Rocky Mountains. They are densely forested and,

Bandicoot

in winter, provide excellent ski slopes. The Australian Alps form a section of the Great Dividing Range which separates the well-watered south-eastern coastal belt from the extensive, dry interior plains of the continent.

●**Ballarat** and **Bendigo** in Victoria, became famous in 1851, when the first gold rush in Australia began. The two towns are now known more for machinery and wheat-marketing.

●**bandicoot** This pouched animal is distinguished by rabbit-like ears and a long, pointed face. Its hind legs are enlarged and enable it to hop around like a kangaroo. Several varieties of bandicoots in Australia and nearby islands range in length from nine to twenty-two inches.

●**Bass Strait** The shallow, narrow strait between Australia and Tasmania, discovered in 1798.

●**bird-of-paradise** This bird of New Guinea and nearby islands is famed for the magnificence of the male's plumage. Bird-of-paradise plumes were once prized by the millinery trade. In 1910 alone, 100,000 birds were killed for their feathers. Conservation laws and a change in fashion have saved the birds from extinction. The greater bird-of-paradise is the best-known member of the family, with flame-coloured plumes ending in smoky tips. The rare blue bird-of-paradise is found only in the Owen Stanley Mountains of south-eastern New Guinea.

●**Blue Mountains** Consist of grey sandstones, but, like many other ranges, they appear blue from a distance. They provided a barrier to westward exploration and settlement until a road was first built in 1814—15, reaching to Bathurst.

●**Botany Bay** A small inlet on the south-east coast of Australia, just south of Sydney. Captain James Cook landed here in 1770 and proclaimed British sovereignty over the territory stretching from Botany Bay to Cape York. Botany Bay derives its name from the many new plants found by the early explorers.

●**bottle tree** An Australian tree characteristic of Queensland, so called for its swollen trunk. It may reach a height of 60 feet.

Greater bird-of-paradise

●**Brisbane** Australia's third-largest city (population 853,000), the capital of Queensland, and a thriving seaport on the Pacific Ocean. Palm trees line the streets of this sub-tropical city which serves as an outlet for a rich stock-raising and sugar cane-growing district. In less than 50 years, Brisbane has grown from a small trading centre (1901 population 31,000) to a diversified industrial metropolis. Only a little more than a century ago, in 1824, the area was founded as a British penal colony.

●**Broken Hill** Australia's leading silver, lead and zinc-mining centre, in New South Wales, with a population of 31,000. The ores are shipped by rail to smelters at Port Pirie on the coast of South Australia. First used in 1875, the mines have been in continuous operation since 1884, and are among the world's richest. Uranium deposits are being worked at nearby Radium Hill.

●**Cairns** A seaport (population 28,000) of Queensland, north-eastern Australia, along the palm-lined tropical coast of Cape York and sheltered by the Great Barrier Reef. It ships sugar, hardwoods and tropical fruit. A railway leads 1,000 miles south to Brisbane.

●**Canberra** Capital (population 146,000) of the Commonwealth of Australia, in the foothills of the Australian Alps between the cities of Sydney (190 miles north-east) and Melbourne (400 miles south-west). The site for this well-planned garden city was chosen in 1908 by the Australian parliament, founded in 1913, while the seat of government was transferred from Melbourne to Canberra in 1927. A quarter of the residents are government employees. The Australian Capital Territory (939 square miles) embraces Canberra, the surrounding watershed and grazing lands, and the harbour of Jervis Bay (on the Pacific, 85 miles away), which has been developed as the capital's seaport. With the exception of a half-dozen departments in Melbourne, all central Government offices are in Canberra, as well as the Australian National University, founded in 1946 largely for post-graduate research work in science and sociological subjects.

●**Caroline Islands** Island group of Micronesia scattered over 1,500 miles of the western Pacific Ocean. Some of the islands are volcanic, but the majority consists of tiny coral atolls. The total land area is less than 500 square miles, inhabited by 35,000 Micronesians and some Polynesians. The islands have been ruled by Spain, Germany and Japan. The latter established formidable sea and air bases at Palau, Truk and Yap prior to World War II. In 1947, the group was included in the U.S. Territory of the Pacific under United Nations trusteeship.

●**Carpentaria, Gulf of** A shallow bay of the Arafura Sea in northern Australia, between the Cape York Peninsula and Arnhem Land. Its

Australia exports huge quantities of mutton and wool. This sheep station is in New South Wales

marshy, mangrove-lined shores are unproductive and almost uninhabited.

●**cassowary** This flightless bird, related to the emu, is found in New Guinea, on nearby islands and at the northern tip of Australia. It wears a large, bony helmet and its head and neck are brilliantly coloured. Unlike other ostrich-like birds, the cassowary prefers deep forests to open grasslands. It is an aggressive bird and kicks with lightning speed when cornered or wounded. Cassowaries are classified depending on whether they have two, one or no wattles hanging from their lower neck.

●**Christchurch** The largest city (population 220,000) of New Zealand's South Island and the principal trade centre of the Canterbury Plain, the nation's most fertile agricultural region. Christchurch has meat-freezing plants, butter and cheese factories, tanneries, and fertiliser plants. Exports are shipped via Lyttleton, the nearby seaport. Christchurch was laid out on a regular street pattern in 1850; it is a clean and attractive city, with a cathedral and university.

●**Christmas Island** The largest atoll (222 square miles) in the Pacific Ocean, just north of the equator. It was discovered in 1777 by Captain James Cook. Coconuts are the island's only product. It is administered by Britain as part of the Gilbert and Ellice Islands Colony.

●**Christmas Island** An isolated island (52 square miles) in the Indian Ocean, 300 miles south of Java. Extensive deposits of phosphate of lime are worked and exported. The population consists of 3,361 Chinese, Malays, and Europeans. The island is an Australian territory.

●**Cocos** (or **Keeling**), **Islands** An isolated group of coral islands in the Indian Ocean, more than 1,100 miles south-west of Singapore. They are thickly covered with coconut palms. The population of 611 is chiefly Malayan. Charles Darwin visited the islands in 1836 and based his theory of the formation of coral reefs on observations made here. Administered by Australia since 1955, the Cocos serve as a re-fuelling stop for aeroplanes flying across the Indian Ocean from Australia to South Africa.

●**Cook Islands** A densely settled (population 18,500) group of Polynesian islands in the south-western Pacific Ocean. They were discovered by Captain James Cook in 1773. Volcanic Rarotonga is the largest island; it ships copra, citrus fruit and pineapples. Most of the other islands are coral atolls. The group obtained complete internal self-government under New Zealand in 1965.

●**cuscus** The spotted cuscus is one of the few mammals in which the colour pattern of the male differs greatly from that of the female. The male is dark with white or grey spots, while the female is uniform in colour and has no markings. This pouched mammal is a tree dweller, and has a thick, woolly coat and long, grasping tail.

●**Darling River** Australia's longest river (1,700 miles), in New South Wales. It is the chief tributary of the Murray River. Despite the unreliability of its flow (it forms unconnected pools during droughts and is subject to sudden floods), it is used extensively for irrigation.

●**Darwin** Australia's northernmost town (population 33,000), administrative centre of the Northern

Large herds of beef cattle are raised on the broad, sparsely—settled, prairie-like plains of Australia's Northern Territory

Territory, on an inlet of the Timor Sea. Darwin's airport is the first stop in Australia for aircraft from Europe and Asia. Because of Darwin's strategic importance during World War II, a highway was built from the town half-way across the continent to Alice Springs, whence a railway runs to the south coast. Founded in 1869, the town was named after Charles Darwin, the famous naturalist.

●**dingo** This wolflike dog is the only wild carnivore now living in Australia. It is believed to have been a tame companion of the first men who came to the island continent about 40,000 years ago, and to have run wild. Because it preyed on sheep, the dingo was hated and feared but is now largely exterminated in populated areas.

Dingoes

●**dugong** This marine mammal was originally taken by sailors for a siren, or mermaid, and was therefore assigned to the order of the Sirenians. It is not related to the other marine mammals, such as seals, but is believed to be descended from elephant-like ancestors. A seaweed-eating animal, the dugong is hunted by the Australian aborigines for its blubber and thick hide.

●**Dunedin** A city (population 105,000) of New Zealand, on South Island. It has woollen mills, clothing and shoe factories. It was settled in 1848 by Scottish immigrants who had found gold in the vicinity. Dunedin is the Gaelic name for Edinburgh. It is linked by rail to Christchurch and to

Invercargill in the extreme south of the island.

●**echidna** This primitive egg-laying mammal is native to Australia, where it is also known as the porcupine ant-eater because of its prickly spines. One of the last remaining mammals to lay eggs, the echidna hatches and carries them in a pouch on its abdomen True to its name, this ant-eater feeds on ants and termites, digging for them with its strong claws and snatching them up with its long, snake-like tongue.

●**emu** This flightless bird is today found only in Australia and is the national bird of that country. The emu differs from its near-relative, the cassowary, by being dull-coloured, having a feathered head (instead of a bony helmet), and living in grasslands (instead of forest). Adults average five feet in height and are second only to the ostrich in size, and, like the ostrich, can run at great speed. The hen lays 7—12 eggs in a simple nest, which the male takes care of.

●**eucalyptus** This tall tree of Australia may grow to a height of 300 feet or more. It yields a valuable timber and bears leaves that contain an oil used in medicine. Some species of eucalyptus (of which there are many) have been introduced into warm, dry areas of the world, and provide useful timber.

●**Fiji** An island group of Melanesia, in the south-western Pacific Ocean, comprising over 300 islands (80 inhabited). Fiji is the most important British possession (population 401,000) in the Pacific, now with internal self-government. The larger islands are volcanic, with a mountainous centre and distinctly different types of vegetation on the humid windward slope, which has a rainfall of over 200 inches, and the dry leeward side with 40 inches of rain. Suva, the capital (population 38,000), is on Viti Levu, the largest island. Sugar and coconuts are the main exports. There are gold mines and two dozen sawmills. Rice is grown for local consumption. The first Indian immigrants were brought to Fiji in 1879 to work on the sugar plantations after the islands became British in 1874. They have multiplied so rapidly that, by 1954, there were more Indians than native Fijians (of Melanesian stock) in the colony. The European population totals 8,500, the Indians

The fine deep-water harbour at Sydney, Australia, is one of the largest in the world

northern Australia and New Guinea. All of the kangaroos are grass eaters.

● **kauri** A tall timber tree of New Zealand, yielding a fine white wood for construction. Kauri gum is a resinous product found in the ground where the tree has grown. It is used to make varnish and as a substitute for amber.

● **kea** This parrot-like bird of New Zealand lives high in the mountains of South Island. It uses its powerful, hooked bill to grub out roots. However, when driven by hunger, it has been known to attack sheep.

● **kiwi** In many ways the kiwi of New Zealand is the oddest bird in the world. It lays an egg that is one-fourth of its own weight and over 5 inches long, by far the largest bird egg in proportion to the size of the adult. A flightless bird, the kiwi is the size of a large domestic fowl and is covered with long, straggly, hairlike feathers. It uses its long, curved bill to dig for earthworms. The kiwi is a relative of the extinct moa — a giant, flightless bird that weighed 500 pounds. The nest is built of moss and leaves under tree roots, for the bird lives in mountain forests.

● **koala** This pouched nocturnal animal of eastern Australia looks like a living teddy bear. Actually, it is not even related to the bear. Three feet long and weighing 30 pounds, the koala has large bush ears and a protruding black nose. It spends nearly its entire life on eucalyptus trees, feeding on the foliage. Only one young is born, which is carried on its mother's back when too large for her pouch.

● **laughing jackass** This Australian bird, also known as kookaburra, is a member of the kingfisher family. It utters a wild, laughlike call at daybreak and nightfall, and is strictly protected by law.

● **lizard, frilled** The most remarkable feature of this Australian lizard is its large frill, an expansion of loose skin around its neck. When the lizard is threatened, it suddenly erects the frill to frighten its assailant. This lizard is also remarkable in being able to run on its two hind legs.

● **lyrebird** This unusual bird of south-western Australia is famous for its beautiful tail feathers shaped like a lyre. A great mimic, the lyrebird is said to be able to imitate any sound it hears, including that of a motor-car horn.

Mangrove forest

● **mangrove** A small tropical maritime tree whose many long, arching, aerial roots form an almost impenetrable tangle at ground level. Mangrove trees form a dense jungle in the low coastal lands of tropical regions, especially in the vicinity

200,000 and the native Fijians only 167,000. The Indians are now so dominant in trade and agriculture that Fiji is coming to be known as the 'little India in the Pacific Ocean'.

● **frigate bird** This large tropical sea bird, also known as man-o'-war bird, never settles on water or on level land. With a six-foot wing-spread, greater than that of any other bird in proportion to its size, the frigate bird spends virtually its entire life in the air. It pursues fishing birds and forces them to drop or disgorge the prey they have caught. The male inflates its brilliant throat pouch when courting. The young are hatched and reared on cliffs or in trees, one egg being laid in a very rough nest.

● **Geelong** A town with 119,320 people near Melbourne on Port Phillip Bay, which has a lignite field nearby and hence has developed into an industrial town, concerned with cars, textiles and paper manufacture. Geelong also has an oil refinery.

● **Great Barrier Reef** A natural breakwater of coral formations along the north-east coast of Australia. The reef has a length of 1,250 miles and a width of 15—20 miles, and consists of shoals and islets built up by multi-coloured coral polyps which thrive in the warm Coral Sea. Channels between sections of the reef give access to towns and cities along the Queensland coast. With its flower-like coral banks, its slender Pandanus palm trees and multitude of exotic tropical birds, the Great Barrier Reef is one of Australia's prime tourist attractions.

Coral reefs

● **Guam** The largest (209 square miles; population 67,000) of the Marianas Islands and the westernmost U.S. outpost in the Pacific Ocean. Its chief export is copra, the dried meat of the coconut. Discovered by Magellan in 1521, Guam was taken by the United States during the Spanish-American War (1898) and now enjoys internal self-government. It was occupied by the Japanese during most of World War II. A commercial airport was completed in 1950.

● **Hobart** The capital (population 151,000) of the island of Tasmania, one of the states of the Commonwealth of Australia. Beautifully situated at the foot of Mt Wellington (4,160 feet), Hobart has a zinc smelter, woollen mills and fruit canneries. A railway leads to Launceston (population 60,450), a town on the Tamar River, facing the mainland of Australia. Hobart has both large wool and food preserving industries.

● **kagu** This flightless fowl-like bird is found only in New Caledonia, and figures on the postage stamps of that island. It is uniformly grey and has an erectile crest which it displays in courtship. It is a nocturnal bird, living on snails and worms.

● **Kalgoorlie and Boulder** The chief gold-mining centres of Western Australia, on the trans-continental railway 380 miles east of Perth. Gold was discovered here and at Coolgardie in 1893, and the town grew up after 1903. Its present population is 23,000, while Coolgardie is now only a small settlement of 600 people.

● **kangaroo** One of the families of pouched animals, with greatly elongated hind limbs used for jumping, and a thick, muscular tail, which serves as a support. There are many different kinds of kangaroo. The most familiar is the great kangaroo, which may weigh 200 pounds and stand six feet high. It can hop along at a speed of 25 miles an hour. The great kangaroo is found in open forests and grasslands. The wallaroo is a mountain kangaroo of eastern Australia. The wallaby is a small kangaroo that prefers rocky areas. The tree kangaroo has shorter and broader hind limbs adapted for life in trees. It is found in the rain forest of of river mouths. The seeds sprout on the mother tree and then send down their own roots.

● **Maori** The native people of New Zealand, the Maoris are believed to have migrated there from Polynesia about 1350. They resisted British colonisation in the 19th century, and the resulting hostilities greatly reduced the size of the Maori population. They now number only about 160,000, most of whom live on North Island. The Maoris are now full-fledged citizens of New Zealand with representation in Parliament. They have great skill in weaving and have their own rich literature.

● **Marianas Islands** A group of volcanic islands in the western Pacific Ocean, 1,500 miles east of the Philippines. Guam is the largest of the chain, whose total area is less than 400 square miles; population 30,000. Discovered in 1521 by Magellan, the Marianas were Spanish until 1898. Then Guam passed to the United States and the other islands were sold to Germany, only to be claimed by Japan after World War I. They were captured by the United States in 1944 and now form part of U.S. Territories in the Pacific under United Nations trusteeship.

● **Marshall Islands** Were it not for their fringe of coconut palms, these 30-odd coral atolls would escape the attention of the passing traveller. Spread out over hundreds of miles of the western Pacific, the Marshalls are administered by the United States under a United Nations trusteeship. Occupied by Germany until World War I, then claimed by Japan, the islands were captured by United States forces in 1944 during World War II. Bikini and Eniwetok atolls have been the scene of several atom and hydrogen-bomb tests since 1946. The native Micronesians have been resettled on other islands.

● **megapode** This fowl-like bird of Oceania differs from all other birds in its incubating habits. It uses its strong legs and claws to scrape together huge mounds of soil and decaying vegetation. There it lays its eggs and leaves them to hatch. In addition to the name of megapode, which means 'big feet', the bird is also known as a mound-builder.

Megapode

● **Melanesia** An island region of the south-western Pacific Ocean extending in a great arc around north-eastern Australia. It includes New Guinea, the Solomon Islands, the New Hebrides, Fiji and New Caledonia. The dark-skinned Melanesians are for the most part primitive. Many tribes, especially on New Guinea, have not yet been touched by Western culture. Others fought savagely against the European 'invasion'.

● **Melbourne** Australia's second-largest city (metropolitan population 2,425,000), capital of the state

A zinc-refining plant at Rosbery, in north-western Tasmania, the island-State of Australia

of Victoria, and a bustling port on Port Phillip Bay, an inlet of the Indian Ocean and the mouth of the Yarra River. With its stately, dark-hued public buildings, Melbourne reminds one of London. The Australian city, however, is neither as congested nor as foggy as its English counterpart. There is room for parks and sports fields, and most of the people live in the 40 or more suburbs which form a 30-mile ring around the inner city. Melbourne is an industrial centre with textile mills, a motor-car factory, metalworks and chemical plants. It exports wheat, wool, frozen meat and flour — all products of the agricultural hinterland. Founded in 1835 by Tasmanian colonists, and named after the British prime minister, Melbourne was the temporary capital of the Commonwealth of Australia until the transfer (1927) of the seat of government to Canberra and has been the capital of Victoria since 1851. The 1956 Olympic Games were held at Melbourne.

● **Micronesia** Island region of the western Pacific Ocean, mostly north of the equator. The chief island groups are the Marianas, Carolines, Marshall, Gilbert and Ellice Islands. Except for the Marianas, which are volcanic, most of the islands of Micronesia have the distinctive oval or horse-shoe shape of coral atolls and the typical fringe of coconut palm trees. Some 170,000 Micronesians of mixed Malay, Negro and Mongolian stock inhabit these scattered islands in the Pacific, whose land area totals a mere 1,300 square miles.

● **Mildura** with 13,000 inhabitants, and **Echuca**, with 7,000 people, are two of the principal settlements in the Murray plains where oranges, vines and other crops are reared by irrigation.

● **moloch** A very spiny, but harmless lizard of Australia's deserts. It is the counterpart of the horned lizard of the south-western United States. It is also known as the thorny devil in Australia.

● **Murray River** The principal river of Australia. It rises in the Australian Alps and flows 1,600 miles west, mostly along the border of Victoria and New South Wales, to the Indian Ocean near Adelaide. The Darling River and the Murrumbidgee River are its chief tributaries. The Murray has been dammed all along its course in order to provide hydro-electric power and water storage needed

for Australia's most ambitious irrigation projects.

● **Nauru** A coral island (8 square miles; population 4,500) in the south-western Pacific Ocean, 1,300 miles from New Guinea. The surrounding coral reef is exposed at low tide. The island has extensive phosphate deposits which are actively worked. It was administered by Australia under a United Nations trusteeship until 1968, when it was granted independence.

● **New Caledonia** A large volcanic island (7,200 square miles) in the western Pacific — an Overseas Territory of France. Its capital is the port of Nouméa (12,000). Coffee is grown for export and fine herds of cattle are raised. Of much greater importance, however, are the island's rich nickel and chrome ore deposits, a vital mineral resource for French heavy industry. Iron and manganese are also mined. One-third of the total population (68,000) is European (mostly French) and one-half native Melanesian. Nouméa has regular air and steamship services to France, Australia and the United States. The French governor of New Caledonia formerly administered the Wallis and Futuna Islands (north-east of Fiji), but these groups became, collectively, the sixth Overseas Territory of France by a referendum held in 1959. New Caledonia was discovered in 1774, and the French have been there since 1853.

● **Newcastle** A seaport (population 347,000) of New South Wales, Australia, to the north of Sydney. It lies at the centre of the country's main coal-mining district and has a large steel mill.

● **New Guinea** An irregularly shaped tropical island in the western Pacific Ocean, just north of Australia (from which it is separated by 100-mile-wide Torres Strait) and east of Indonesia. After Greenland it is the largest island (300,000 square miles) on earth, and also one of the world's least explored inhabited regions. New Guinea's population, estimated at 2 million, consists of Melanesian and Negrito tribes, many of whom have never been in regular contact with Europeans and some of whom still practise headhunting. The lowlands are hot, humid and malaria-infested, and access to the highlands, which extend over the full length of the 1,500-mile-long island, is difficult. Peaks that rise more than 16,000 feet have been seen from the air. New Guinea's fauna resembles that of Australia; it includes venomous snakes, marsupials, and a wide variety of butterflies, flightless cassowaries and the rare birds-of-paradise. Coffee, cacao, bananas and other tropical fruit grow abundantly, but the economy is not organised for export. Only copra (dried coconut meat) from non-native plantations is shipped. There are several gold mines and indications of considerable mineral wealth, including petroleum.

The western half of New Guinea was ruled by the Dutch for some 300 years as part of the Netherlands East Indies. After World War II, the Dutch-held islands off South-East Asia declared their independence and became the Republic of Indonesia, except for western New Guinea, which the Dutch continued to rule until passing over control to Indonesia in 1963 as West Irian. The north-eastern section of New Guinea, together with the Admiralty Islands and the Bismarck Archipelago, is administered by Australia under a trusteeship of the United Nations. The south-eastern section, Papua, is an Australian territory.

● **New Hebrides** A group of Melanesian islands in the south-western Pacific Ocean between Fiji and New Caledonia. The humid, mountainous islands are the home of a backward native population of 56,000. Malaria and tuberculosis are still prevalent.

Coconut meat, or copra, is spread out to dry at a native Polynesian village on Upolu, in the Samoa Islands of the South Pacific Ocean

One of the palm-fringed Marquesas Islands

New Guinea pile dwellings

Coconut palms are cultivated on plantations, and copra, the dried meat of the coconut, is the chief export product shipped from Port Vila. Cacao and coffee are also shipped in small quantities. The New Hebrides are ruled jointly by France and Great Britain — a form of government which is called a condominium.

● **New South Wales** A State (309,400 square miles; population 4,617,000) of the Commonwealth of Australia in the south-eastern part of the continent. Its capital, Sydney, and the coal-mining and steel-milling cities of Newcastle and Port Kembla, are situated along the Pacific coast in a region of adequate rainfall. The land to the west of the Great Dividing Range is dry, except where it is artificially watered from the Murray River (along the Victoria border) and its tributaries, the Darling and the Murrumbidgee. Rice, grapes and citrus fruit are grown in these irrigated stretches called the Riverina. However, most of the land is given to sheep-raising, Australia's oldest industry; the state supports some 60 million head of sheep. Dairying is important in the coastal belt, which also has banana and pineapple plantations. New South Wales is the leading coal-mining State of the island continent and also has the oldest silver-lead-zinc mines in the Broken Hill area.

Visited by Captain James Cook in 1770, New South Wales was the site of the first British settlement in Australia — a penal colony — in 1788. It is now the most populous State of the Commonwealth. In 1911 it ceded an area of 900-odd square miles to the Federal Government for the establishment of a capital, now the city of Canberra.

● **New Zealand** An independent member of the British Commonwealth of Nations consisting of two major and several small islands in the south-western Pacific Ocean, 1,200 miles south-east of Australia. Slightly larger (104,000 square miles) than the United Kingdom, New Zealand has a population of only 2½ million — 24 people to the square mile. Most of the inhabitants are descendants of English and Scottish settlers who went there after 1840. The native Maoris, who savagely resisted British colonisation until 1871, now enjoy full citizenship privileges; they number about 160,000.

New Zealand's two main islands are mountainous, but there the similarity ends. Volcanic North Island (44,300 square miles) has several active craters, numerous hot springs and beautiful geysers; it is the home of the tall kauri pine and of the majority of Maori farmers. South Island (58,000 square miles) is crossed lengthwise by an alpine range, whose jagged summits are flanked by glaciers that end near sea level at the head of deeply indented fjords. Mt Cook (12,349 feet), the country's highest peak, overlooks the rugged west coast of South Island. Cook Strait, 16 miles wide, separates the two islands. New Zealand's temperate climate, comparable to that of southern France, appealed to the first European settlers. Blessed with plentiful year-round rainfall, they built up a prosperous, intensive agricultural economy based on livestock. The country is today one of the world's leading exporters of mutton, lamb, wool, butter and cheese. Meat-freezing, canning and dairying are the chief industries. Sawmills draw their timber from virgin forests that cover one-third of the land area. New Zealand is amply supplied with hydro-electric power and additional dam sites are available for power harnessing. There are four large cities: Wellington, the capital, and Auckland, the leading seaport, both on North Island; Christchurch, an agricultural centre, and Dunedin, on South Island. More than one-third of the people live in these metropolitan areas. Several scenic and wilderness areas have been preserved in national parks. New Zealand's distinctive native fauna include the strange kiwi bird, the parrot-like kea, the owl parrot, the 'living fossil' tuatara.

The islands were discovered in 1642 by Tasman, a Dutch navigator; they were visited by Captain James Cook in 1769. In 1840, Britain negotiated a treaty with the Maoris and New Zealand became a colony. It achieved dominion status in 1907. New Zealand has several island possessions in the Pacific, and it claims sovereignty over a segment of Antarctica (Ross Dependency).

Oceania The all-inclusive name given to the islands of the southern and western Pacific Ocean. It includes the islands of Micronesia, Polynesia and Melanesia, as well as New Guinea and its adjacent islands. Australia and New Zealand are sometimes considered part of Oceania.

outrigger A canoe equipped with a projecting log or other device to keep it from upsetting. It is used by the Pacific islanders.

An outrigger of the Pacific islands

Pacific Ocean The largest (64 million square miles, not including adjacent seas) of the world's salt-water bodies, so named by Magellan because of its calmness during his voyage from the southern end of South America to the Philippines in 1520 — 21. Balboa, who had sighted the Pacific from the Isthmus of Panama in 1513, called it the South Sea. This name is still in use, especially when describing a 'South Sea island' — a mere dot of palm-fringed coral in an ocean vaster than all the land areas of the world added together. The Pacific is linked with the Arctic Ocean by the Bering Strait, with the Atlantic by the waters around the southern tip of South America and by the man-made Panama Canal, and with the Indian Ocean by passages in the Indonesian archipelago and the open sea south of Australia. The world's deepest ocean, the Pacific has an average depth of 14,000 feet; depths of around 34,500 feet have been recorded off Mindanao — one of the Philippine Islands — and in the Mariana Trough off Guam. Off the coast of South America and along the island arcs that fringe Asia, the Pacific is skirted by a series of deep trenches in the ocean floor whose origin has not been fully explained. It is known, however, that the unsettled ocean floor in these areas is the cause of earthquakes which give rise to huge sea waves (called tsunamis) that have wreaked severe damage along mainland and island shores hundreds of miles away. Another phenomenon are the isolated, flat-topped underwater summits (called guyots) that rise by the hundreds from the ocean floor between Hawaii and the Marianas. The southern and western reaches of the Pacific, known collectively as Oceania, are dotted with thousands of volcanic islands and coral atolls whose main product is copra from the coconut palm. In the northern Pacific, a chain of islands — many of them densely populated — extends from Indonesia to North America: the Philippines; Taiwan (Formosa); the Ryukyus; the island realm of Japan; the Kuriles; and in the far north the Aleutian Islands. The currents of the Pacific Ocean flow in two great ovals, one clockwise north of the equator and the other counter-clockwise south of the equator. The California and the Peru (Humboldt) Currents, which flow along the west coast of the Americas from the north and the south respectively, are cold and their waters contain abundant marine life. The most important of the warm, highly saline, currents is the Japan Current (also called the Kuroshio) which moves north-east from the Philippine Sea along a course similar to that of the Gulf Stream off the east coast of the United States. The western Pacific is also subject

to very violent hurricanes called typhoons.

Many of the Pacific islands changed hands during World War II as the Japanese extended their bases southward toward Australia and eastward in the direction of Hawaii. At present the chief American outposts in the Pacific are Hawaii, Guam, and several strategic island groups of Micronesia (east of the Philippines) administered as United Nations trust territories. The French, British, New Zealanders and Australians rule the islands of Polynesia (in the South Pacific) and Melanesia (an island arc extending from New Guinea to Fiji).

palm, coconut The tall, slender tropical palm that produces the coconut. The dried meat of coconuts, known as copra, yields coconut oil, which is used in making soap, candles, cosmetics and margarine. The coconut palm grows in all equatorial regions, particularly in southern Asia and Oceania. There it supplies the natives with food, drink, fibres and building material. The world's leading producers of copra and coconut oil are the Philippines, Indonesia, Ceylon and Malaya.

palm, nipa A multi-purpose palm of the East Indies, New Guinea and Queensland. Its leaves are widely used as thatching and matching material, and its juice yields sugar and alcohol.

Nipa palms

palm, sago A lofty palm of Malaysia and New Guinea. Its pith yields sago, a starch used in puddings, and also in stiffening textiles.

Sago palm

pandanus A tropical, slender, palmlike plant, also known as the screw pine. Its sword-shaped leaves furnish a useful fibre for baskets, mats, nets and ropes.

Papua, see **New Guinea** (south-eastern)

parrot, owl This bird is peculiar to New Zealand, where it is also known as the kakapo. It has

well-developed wings but is strictly a ground-dweller. It is called owl parrot because of its nocturnal habits and because its green plumage is marked with brown like that of the owl.

parrots A large family of tropical birds, characterised by strong, hooked beaks, an ability to imitate human speech, a long life, and an arrangement of toes (two in front and two behind) that permits them to handle food. Parrots vary in size from that of a small sparrow to the large South American macaw, about three feet long. Their plumage varies from dull to brilliant colours. The principal sub families are the kea and the owl parrot of New Zealand, the lories and lorikeets, the cockatoos, the macaws, parakeets and the parrot itself.

Perth The capital of Western Australia at the western end of the trans-continental railway. Together with Fremantle, its port on the Indian Ocean, Perth has a population of 663,000. The city enjoys 280 days of sunshine a year and has a mild sub-tropical climate. Founded in 1829, Perth remained a small settlement until gold was later discovered at Coolgardie and Kalgoorlie. It is now the first Australian port-of-call for ships inbound from Europe. Fremantle is named after its discoverer, who landed in 1829, near the mouth of the Swan River.

Pitcairn Island A volcanic islet in mid-Pacific, half-way between Australia and America. It was settled in 1790 by the mutineers of the *Bounty* and by natives from Tahiti. In 1856, part of the population was removed to Norfolk Island, north of New Zealand. Pitcairn is a British colony.

platypus This Australian egg-laying mammal is called the duck-billed platypus owing to the shape of its snout. The body of this rare animal is well suited for swimming. Among its unusual features are strong webbed feet (for digging underground dens), the duck's bill, which is soft and sensitive instead of horny, and a beaver-like tail.

Polynesia Island region of the South Pacific Ocean contained within a huge triangle based on Hawaii, Easter Island and the islands north of New Zealand. The principal island groups are Samoa, Tonga, Tokelau, Tuamotu, Cook, and Marquesas. The Polynesian islets — merely dots in the vast Pacific — were formed either by volcanoes or by coral reefs. Many of them are atolls shaped like an oval or a horseshoe. The coconut palm is the typical form of vegetation and also the main source of food. The origin of the brown-skinned Polynesians is still uncertain. One theory suggests that they came from South America, in balsa rafts swept westward by ocean currents. Because of their isolation and dependence on the sea, they have become expert boat-builders, specialising in the construction of outrigger canoes. They are known as 'the Vikings of the Pacific'. The Maoris of New Zealand are of Polynesian stock, having left the islands for their new home in the 14th century. Captain James Cook visited Polynesia in the 18th century and befriended the native population on Tahiti and in the Tonga Islands. Most of the island groups are now controlled by Great Britain and France.

Port Kembla An Australian steel-milling centre in New South Wales about 60 miles south of Sydney. There are coal mines at nearby Wollongong. Iron is obtained from Kimberley and nickel from various Pacific islands.

Port Moresby Chief town of New Guinea, on the island's south-eastern peninsula facing Australia.

New Guinea tribesmen, dressed for
a ceremonial dance

Sydney Harbour Bridge

native handicrafts. Western Samoa (population 114,000) belonged to Germany before World War I. From 1920 it was administered by New Zealand as a United Nations trust territory, and is now the first fully independent Polynesian State. American Samoa (population 20,000) has had a U.S. naval station at Pago Pago (on Tutuila Island) since 1872. Polynesians own nearly all of the land (75 square miles). The islands were discovered by the Dutch in 1722.

● **sheep** These domestic animals are bred mainly for meat or for wool, although in some parts of the world their milk is used for cheese production. In terms of numbers of sheep, the principal countries are Australia, the Soviet Union, Argentina, China and New Zealand. Wool and mutton prices affect the number of sheep on farms. A high price for wool encourages producers to expand their flocks, while a higher return for meat increases the number of slaughterings, particularly of lambs. New Zealand specialises in mutton sheep and exports a large part of its output to Britain. Australia raises sheep primarily for wool.

Sheep-shearing

It is the seat of the Australian administration of the eastern half of the island. During World War II, Port Moresby was an important Allied base from which the Japanese invasion was repulsed. Its non-indigenous population is 10,000.

● **Port Pirie** A seaport of South Australia, on Spencer Gulf of the Indian Ocean, about 135 miles north-west of Adelaide. There are smelters for silver and lead mined at Broken Hill. Port Pirie lies at the eastern end of the Commonwealth Trans-continental Railway.

● **Queensland** A State (667,000 square miles; population 1,835,000) of the Commonwealth of Australia comprising the whole north-eastern part of the continent fronting on the Pacific Ocean. Brisbane is its capital and major seaport. The major part of the coastline is sheltered by the Great Barrier Reef. The coastal belt is fertile, warm and sufficiently rainy to grow sugar cane in large plantations. The arid interior plains are watered by wells in the Great Artesian Basin where livestock is raised extensively. Queensland exports sugar (there are over 30 sugar mills in the state), wool, preserved and frozen meat, butter, minerals (gold, copper, lead, coal), and cabinet-woods from the eucalyptus, pine and cedar forests of the tropical north. The jungles of the Cape York Peninsula are being explored for bauxite and other mineral deposits. Queensland was visited by Captain James Cook in 1770. It formed part of the colony of New South Wales until 1859, when it was granted self-government. In 1901 it became a State of the Commonwealth. Over half the population of Queensland live in urban areas, with Brisbane taking in 853,000 of them.

● **Rockhampton** A town on the coast of Queensland with 48,000 inhabitants. It is a port serving a large hinterland, exporting wool, copper and gold and importing industrial goods.

● **Samoa** An island group in the South Pacific Ocean in Polynesia, east-north-east of Fiji. The main islands are volcanic, the highest peak rising to 6,000 feet. There are also several coral atolls. The chief exports are copra, cacao, bananas and

● **Society Islands** A group of volcanic and coral islands scattered over 450 miles of the South Pacific Ocean on the latitude of southern Peru. Captain James Cook named the islands in honour of the Royal Society in London (1769). At present they constitute an Overseas Territory of France. Tahiti is the principal island of the group. The population is of Polynesian stock.

● **Solomon Islands** A group of mountainous, forest-clad, malaria-infested islands in the south-western Pacific Ocean east of New Guinea. They include Bougainville (the largest and most rugged island, with mountains rising to 10,000 feet), Guadalcanal, Choiseul, Malaita, and many other volcanic and coral islands. The population, of Melanesian stock and still very primitive, totals about 150,000. Copra is the only cash crop of any importance, but gold was recently discovered near Honiara (on Guadalcanal), where the British High Commissioner of the Solomon Islands protectorate resides. Two islands (Bougainville and Buka) are governed separately by Australia under United Nations trusteeship. The population of European descent is very small.

● **South Sea** (or **South Seas**) The island-studded portion of the Pacific Ocean between Hawaii and New Zealand. A typical South Sea island is a small, coral-fringed atoll whose shores are lined with graceful coconut palms swaying in the gentle ocean breeze. Because of their geographic isolation and mild climate, the islands are often represented as a tropical paradise, despite the poverty of the native Polynesian or Melanesian population.

● **Sydney** Australia's largest city (population, including suburbs, 2,780,000), its leading seaport and capital of New South Wales, the most populous state of the Commonwealth. Sydney Harbour, a naturally sheltered bay divided into numerous coves, has the country's largest shipyards, a naval base, miles of docks, and huge grain silos and warehouses. Wool, wheat, flour, iron and steel are the leading exports; most of the trade is carried on with the island of Japan. Sydney Harbour Bridge, with an arch span of 1,650 feet and under which large ships can pass, is the city's chief landmark; it leads to the northern suburbs where most people live in detached houses. Sydney's first inhabitants were members of a prison colony established in 1788.

● **Tahiti** The largest (400 square miles; population 44,000) of the Society Islands in the South Pacific Ocean. Rising to 7,600 feet and covered by tropical vegetation, this beautiful volcanic island is often described as a South Sea paradise. It exports copra, vanilla, mother-of-pearl and phosphates. The town of Papeete (population 17,000) is the capital of all French Overseas Territories in the Pacific; it has a steamship service to New Zealand and the United States. Tahiti was visited by the *Bounty* in 1788. French and British missionaries arrived in 1800.

● **Tasman Sea** An arm of the Pacific Ocean between Australia and New Zealand. It is known for its frequent storms.

● **Tasmania** An island (26,383 square miles; population 391,000) off south-eastern Australia, from which it is separated by the 100-mile-wide Bass Strait. It lies between the Indian Ocean (west) and the Tasman Sea, an arm of the Pacific Ocean. Geologically a continuation of the continent, Tasmania constitutes a State of the Commonwealth of Australia. Its capital is Hobart. The mountainous, well-watered island has many excellent hydro-electric sites where power is generated for the refining of zinc, lead and copper, pulp and paper-milling, and the manufacture of chemicals. Tasmania exports fresh fruit, metals, wool and woollen textiles, and saw timber from its extensive virgin forest. Launceston, in the north, has a steamer service to Melbourne across Bass Strait. The island was discovered in 1642 by Tasman, a Dutchman. It was claimed by Britain in 1803, and for 50 years was used as a penal colony. The unusual fauna includes the platypus, the spiny ant-eater, the wombat, and two animals (the Tasmanian devil and Tasmanian wolf) which are peculiar to this island.

● **Tasmanian devil** This pouched mammal owes its sinister name to its deep black colour and forbidding look. About three feet long, it superficially resembles a small bear with a foot-long tail. It raids sheep ranges and chicken farms at night.

Tasmanian wolf

●**thylacine** This Tasmanian wolf is the largest of the flesh-eating pouched mammals. It is the size of a large dog and has distinctive brown stripes across the rear of its back. It preys upon wallabies and other marsupials, as well as upon sheep and poultry.

●**Tonga** or **Friendly Islands** A Polynesian island group in the South Pacific Ocean, consisting of 150 volcanic and coral islands that grow coconuts and bananas for 65,000 brown-skinned inhabitants. The climate is mild and healthy and the people are well-educated and engage in farming or fishing. Captain Cook visited the islands in 1773 and befriended the natives — hence the name Friendly Islands. They form a self-governing State under a British protectorate which dates from 1900. Tonga is a monarchy with its own royal family.

●**tuatara** This 'living fossil' is the sole survivor of an ancient group of reptiles. About two feet long, it superficially resembles some lizards. It survives only on some islands off New Zealand.

●**turtle, green** The flesh of this sea-going turtle is greatly esteemed as an ingredient of turtle soup. The shell of the green turtle is covered with large shields that do not overlap. The weight of these turtles ranges from 200 to 800 pounds.

Green turtle

●**turtle, leatherback** This gigantic sea-going turtle is eight feet long and weighs more than half a ton. As the name implies, the leatherback does not have the usual horny plate found in most turtles. It has a smooth leathery skin covering a bony shell.

●**Victoria** The most densely settled State (87,884 square miles; population 3,514,000) of the Commonwealth of Australia, in the south-eastern part of the continent. Its capital, Melbourne, has two-thirds of the state's population. A prosperous agricultural region, Victoria yields wheat, wool and, from the irrigated fields along the Murray River, vegetables, fruits and wine grapes. Gold-mining, the principal activity when Victoria first became a colony in 1851, has declined, but large workings of brown coal east of Melbourne now supply the State's growing industries and its electric power stations. Tourism thrives along the Melbourne

beaches and in the Australian Alps. The first permanent settlement, on Portland Bay, dates from 1834. Dairying is increasing in importance in the southern part, close to the large urban markets. In 1960, over 15 million tons of lignite were mined, supplemented by electric power from dams in the Goulburn valley.

●**Wellington** The capital (population 151,000) of New Zealand, a seaport on Cook Strait at the southern tip of North Island. Mutton, wool and butter are exported in large quantities to the United Kingdom. The town has grown since 1840, and has a large university and Parliament Buildings.

●**Western Australia** This State has a population of only 1,036,000 and a total area of 975,900 square miles, or less than 1 person per square mile. This total includes 10,000 full-blooded aboriginals. Yet Western Australia is the largest Australian State, taking up the western arid third of the continent. Only the south-western part is productive agriculturally, with the westerly winds bringing rain to the Swan River basin. There are wide-spreading wheat fields and eucalyptus woods. Artesian basins between Shark Bay and North West Cape render possible banana and early vegetable production around Carnarvon.

The interior has widespread sand and rock deserts and many salt lakes. Deserted towns bear witness to long-past gold rushes, and only Kalgoorlie survives. Traffic out of the Perth area is virtually confined to aircraft.

Western Australia was first settled in 1829. The main crop is wheat, and cattle and sheep are reared. There is a small vine area planted, while the forests have high quality hardwood. Gold production is worth about £10 million annually and minerals about £20 million.

●**Whyalla** An iron-mining centre of South Australia, on Spencer Gulf about 25 miles from Port Pirie. It has steel works and a shipyard.

●**wombat** This pouched animal is the Australian equivalent of the badger. It is equipped with sharp claws and sturdy legs, well suited for digging. Its burrow is usually fifteen feet long and has a nest at

the end. The wombat reaches a length of three feet. Two kinds are known, living on islands in the Bass Strait, on Tasmania and parts of Australia.

Wombat

●**wool** Raising sheep for wool is practicable only in countries where plenty of land is available for grazing. A single animal yields about 9 to 10 pounds of wool. The three chief types of wool are the fine merino and crossbred grades and the coarser carpet wool. About 80 per cent of the world's wool clip is of the finer types. The leading wool producers are Australia, Argentine, Soviet Union, New Zealand and the United States. In addition to the United States, the principal wool importers are Britain, France, West Germany, Belgium and Italy. Small quantities of wool are also obtained from the Angora goat of the Middle East (mohair wool), from the Cashmere goat of the Himalayan region, and from the alpaca of South America.

●**Woomera** A township of South Australia known, since 1948, as the site for British-Australian rocket-launching experiments. The rocket range extends 1,200 miles across the Great Australian Desert to the continent's north-western coast.

●**Yallourn** A coal-mining town in Victoria, Australia, 87 miles east of Melbourne. One of the country's largest electric power plants uses local brown coal as a fuel.

Native fishermen of Papeete, Tahiti, sail far out in the calm South Pacific in an outrigger canoe

Polar Areas

The Polar regions are generally considered to be the areas enclosed by the Arctic and Antarctic circles at 66°30′ N and 66°30′ S, respectively. The two areas contrast sharply in that the Arctic is an almost landlocked ocean, whereas the Antarctic is an ocean-surrounded land mass. These are the circumstances which cause the difference in climate between the two, the Antarctic being much more severe, and consequently more difficult of access.

If more meaningful climatic lines than the Arctic and Antarctic Circles are used to define the regions, one finds that the area of permanent freezing is much greater in the south than in the north. The extremely cold winds blowing from the centre of the Antarctic continent extend this bitter climate as far north as latitude 50° S. The weather boundary in the north varies much more with the seasons. The coldest temperatures are always over north-central Siberia and north-central Canada, but, even there, there is at least one month of above-freezing temperatures. The summer vegetation is varied and abundant, including many colourful flowers; whereas the Antarctic 'summer' can boast only mosses, lichens and algae. Emperor penguins are the only year-round residents, and these only on the continental fringes. Adélie penguins and some smaller birds, whales and seals are summer visitors.

The Arctic regions, on the other hand, have abundant animal life, including seal, whale, walrus, and many fish, as well as sea birds and water fowl. It is this animal life which supports over 100,000 human inhabitants of the Arctic regions. These include 30,000 Lapps (Samer) living in northern Norway, Sweden, Finland, and the Kola Peninsula of the U.S.S.R., and about 40,000 Eskimos in North America and Greenland. The Eskimos, who have spread throughout the Arctic and sub-Arctic regions from western Alaska eastward to Greenland, are quite homogeneous in physical appearance, language and culture, and as a group are distinct in these traits from all their neighbours. Their Mongolian features — broad face and high forehead — point to an Asiatic origin. Almost all of their food and clothing, the oil they use for lighting and cooking, their tools and their weapons come from sea mammals which they hunt with great skill. A few Eskimos keep caribou (reindeer) and roam seasonally with their herds; the great majority, however, are nomadic hunters and fishermen, and rove inland during the summer for game and fresh-water fish. Their summer tents of caribou or sealskins are reinforced in winter with turf or stones. Only the Eskimo of the far north of central Canada uses the familiar igloo. By eating raw meat, the Eskimo keeps certain nutritional elements in his diet which would otherwise be completely lacking. Dog sledges solve the problem of long-distance or heavy transport, while the manoeuvrable skin canoe or *kayak* is used extensively for fishing and hunting seals. Eskimos band together in small groups under a leader-provider and share all but the

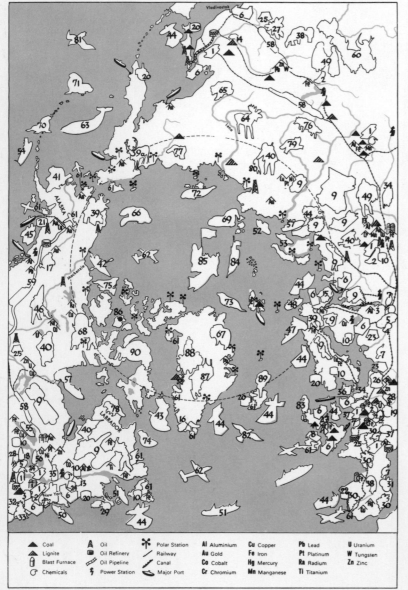

Arctic Region

Minerals and Industries

1 Iron
2 Steel
3 Machinery
4 Electrical goods
5 Car industry
6 Shipyard
7 Textile industry
8 Linen
9 Lumber mill
10 Paper
11 Rubber industry
12 Potash
13 Asbestos
14 Graphite
15 Apatite
16 Cryolite
17 Panning for gold
18 Sugar
19 Beer
20 Tinned fish
21 Salmon-fishing
22 Sardine-fishing

Agricultural and Animal Products

23 Rye
24 Oats
25 Wheat
26 Potatoes
27 Soya beans
28 Sugar beets
29 Fruit
30 Wine
31 Oranges
32 Cotton
33 Tobacco
34 Animal husbandry
35 Milk
36 Butter
37 Cheese
38 Sheep
39 Reindeer
40 Fur trapper
41 Fur seal hunter
42 Eskimo on sealing expedition
43 Whaling
44 Fishing
45 Salmon-fishing
46 Trout-fishing

Transportation and Trade

47 Ore exports
48 Lumber exports
49 Fur trade
50 Passenger ship
51 Freighter
52 Icebreaker
53 Sea-going tugboat
54 Warship
55 Ore-carrier
56 Coal-carrier
57 Lumber-carrier
58 Railway
59 Alaska Highway
60 Yak caravan
61 Airport
62 Airliner

Mammals

63 Whale
64 Elk
65 Brown bear
66 Polar bear
67 Musk-ox-reserve
68 Musk-ox-hunt
69 Walrus
70 Fur seal
71 Northern sea lion
72 Bearded seal
73 Harp seal
74 Hooded seal
75 Common seal
76 Wolf
77 Silver fox
78 Arctic fox
79 Sable
80 Ermine

Birds

81 Pomarine jaeger
82 Glaucous gull
83 Guillemot

Miscellaneous

84 The ship *Fram* of the Nansen expedition (1893-96)
85 Peary at the North Pole (1909)
86 North Magnetic Pole
87 Observation post on Greenland's ice-cap
88 Dog-sledge expedition
89 Geyser
90 Eskimos and igloo

most personal possessions. They are skilled in working bone, ivory and stone. However, their culture is generally thought to be on the decline, due perhaps to innovations introduced by Europeans.

Some of the most unusual sights in the heavens are visible in the polar regions. The aurora borealis in the north and the aurora australis in the south (the northern and southern lights) are luminous displays of varying intensity, form and colour. The lights range through all the colours of the rainbow and take the shape of streamers, rays and draperies. They range in altitude from 35 to 600 miles above the earth. It is known that the occurrence of an aurora is accompanied by a 'magnetic storm', which is a disturbance in the ionosphere interfering with long-distance radio and telegraph communications. The number of auroral displays and magnetic disturbances varies from year to year, reaching their peak of intensity about every 11 years. The number of spots on the sun varies in a similar manner. It is believed that the sun gives off electrical particles at times of sunspot activity. As these particles come into the earth's atmosphere, they enter along the lines of force of the earth's magnetic field, converging at the north and south magnetic poles, exciting the gases — especially oxygen and nitrogen — and thereby producing the colours of the aurora.

The polar regions (but especially the Arctic) are often romantically described as the 'lands of the midnight sun', for at the North Pole the sun shines continuously from March 21 to September 23, and seems to travel in a circular path above the horizon. This is due to the 23° inclination of the earth's axis to the plane of its orbit. This makes it possible for the northern half of the earth to receive the more direct rays of the sun during the summer months, while the southern half receives the more oblique rays. During that season the North Pole 'leans' towards the sun and receives light throughout the day and night. The number of days of continuous light decreases as one proceeds southward from the North Pole. At the Arctic Circle the sun is visible at midnight only once during the summer, at the solstice. While the North Pole is enjoying this abundance of sunshine, the South Pole is shrouded in continuous night because the earth's axis is here inclined away from the sun. The situation is exactly reversed during the Northern Hemisphere's winter.

The purpose of the International Geophysical Year (1957—58) was to promote exploration and scientific observations in both polar areas. The effort has been more concentrated and the results more spectacular in the Antarctic, because physical conditions in the Far South are more severe than in the Arctic and the area is much less well known. The seventh continent will undoubtedly be heard from more frequently in the future as a source of weather and climate information and of other useful scientific data. Its strategic importance as a storehouse of industrial raw materials is also being investigated.

While neither pole is isolated any longer, the importance of the north polar regions is more obvious and immediate. The centres of population are in the Northern Hemisphere; and although it has long been known that the shortest routes between the densely settled areas of North America, Europe and Asia lie along the great circle routes across the Arctic regions, it is only since the advent of reliable long-range aircraft that these short cuts can be used for commercial travel.

Consequently, Alaska, northern Canada and Greenland are growing in significance, as are the Arctic fringes on the other side of the North Pole. At the same time, the dawning age of long-range missiles has propelled the Arctic area into the forefront of potential military operations across the North Pole. It is therefore both for military and commercial reasons that we are seeking, with increasing urgency, to expand our current knowledge of the northland.

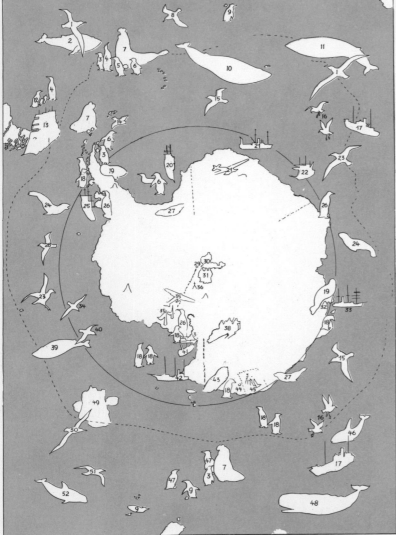

Antarctica

Mammals
2 Humpback whale*
7 Sea elephant
10 Blue whale*
11 Finback whale*
19 Weddell's seal*
24 Sea leopard*
27 Crab-eater seal
39 Pygmy sperm whale*
43 Ross seal
46 Killer whale*
48 Cachalot*
52 Risso's dolphin

Birds
1 Albatross*
3 Jackass penguin*
4 King penguin
5 Macaroni penguin
6 Bearded penguin
8 Southern black-backed gull*
9 Rock-hopper penguin*
12 Magellan penguin
14 Snow bunting
15 Skua
16 Wilson's storm petrel*
18 Adélie penguin*
23 Giant petrel*
26 Emperor penguin
28 Antarctic petrel*
34 Snow petrel*

40 Cape pigeon*
47 Royal penguin
50 Black-browed albatross
51 Sooty shearwater

Explorations and Landmarks

13 19th-century sailing ship
17 Whaling ship
20 James Weddell reaching southernmost point of his journey in 1823
21 German Schwabenland expedition (1938-39)
22 James Cook crossing the Antarctic Circle in 1773
25 Russian Admiral von Bellingshausen sights the Antarctic mainland in 1820
29 South Pole
30 Amundsen, first to reach the South Pole in 1911
31 Southernmost point

reached by Shackleton in 1909
32 Mount Gauss
33 The ship *Gauss* of the German Drygalski expedition (1902)
35 Little America, base of Admiral Bird's Antarctic expeditions
36 Robert Scott perished here in 1911 on his return from the South Pole, which he reached shortly after Amundsen
37 The active volcano, Erebus
38 Scott's first Antarctic expedition (1901-04)
41 James Ross discovering the Ross Sea in 1841
42 Norwegian Antarctic expedition (1894-95) lands on Cape Adare in first landing on the mainland
44 South Magnetic Pole
45 French observation post in Adélie Land, founded 1950
49 Floating icebergs

Plants and animals designated with an asterisk (*) have a wide distribution. Others are found only where pictured.

Rawin Dome – part of the installations maintained by the U.S.A. at Little America Station, on the Ross Shelf Ice in Antarctica

Adélie Coast A section of Antarctic coast land fronting on the Indian Ocean. It forms part of Wilkes Land. Discovered in 1840 by Dumont d'Urville, a French explorer, it has long been claimed by France, which maintains a weather station there. Adélie Coast is one of the windiest places in the world; gales, sometimes reaching speeds of 200 miles an hour, sweep off the Antarctic ice plateau on to the coast. Breeding grounds of the emperor and Adélie penguins are located there. In 1957, the French set up two weather stations, one on the coast and the other almost 200 miles inland, to participate in the scientific work of the International Geophysical Year.

Aklavik A fur-trading post and weather station of northern Canada on the lower Mackenzie River near its delta on the Arctic Ocean. The average daily temperature in January, when daylight is very short, is – 28.9 °C. The town has been replaced by the more modern Inuvik, which was begun in 1961. It has schools, a hospital, churches, a power station supplying heat to all the buildings, shops and hotels. It will be a trading post for Indians and Eskimos and a centre for Arctic research.

albatross This large sea-bird, with stout body, rather large head and elongated neck, reaches a wing span of almost 15 feet. It is found in the southern oceans, where it spends a great part of its life in the air, gliding over the waves with its narrow pointed wings held almost motionless. It feeds on fish and other marine animals, which it kills with its stout, hooked bill. The best-known type of albatross is the wandering albatross. Others are the sooty, the black-browed and the grey-headed albatrosses.

Albatross

Alexander I Island A large island lying off the west coast of Graham Land, Antarctica. It

was discovered in 1821 by the Russian navigator Bellingshausen. Almost surrounded by shelf ice, it was considered part of the mainland until proved an island by the U.S. expedition of 1941.

Antarctic Circle The astronomical line of latitude drawn around the globe at 66½° S. Enclosed within it lies all of Antarctica except the extreme tip of protruding Graham Land. Because of the inclination of the earth's axis, the sun does not set at the Antarctic Circle on one day of the year — the summer solstice in the Southern Hemisphere (about December 21). The number of such days increases inside the Antarctic circle with respect to proximity to the South Pole.

Antarctica The world's seventh continent, the last to be discovered (after 1819) and explored, surrounding the South Pole. The waters which separate it from all the other land masses are sometimes called the Antarctic Ocean, but actually they are only the southernmost parts of the Atlantic, Pacific and Indian Oceans. Whipped by violent, frigid winds and choked by pack ice and icebergs, the sea approaches to Antarctica are notoriously dangerous to shipping. This explains why the continent defied exploration until relatively recent times. With an area of 5½ million square miles, Antarctica is larger than Europe or Australia. Its roughly circular shape is broken by two deep inlets, the Ross and Weddell Seas, and by the peninsula of Graham Land which reaches out to within 650 miles of the southern tip of South America. The surface of Antarctica appears as a featureless waste of snow that arches up gently towards the centre and splits up into crevasse-ridden glacial tongues along the edges. Under the mantle of ice (found to be 10,000 feet thick in at least one sounding on Marie Byrd Land), Antarctica may consist of two parts separated, perhaps, by a trough of below-sea-level elevations running roughly from the Weddell Sea to the Ross Sea. West of this trough, the land is formed by an extension of the folded Andes of South America with isolated peaks and ranges rising above the ice cap to 10,000 feet in Graham Land and to 20,000 feet in the little-known ranges of Marie Byrd Land. Eastern Antarctica is a relatively undisturbed plateau that rises gradually toward the 'pole of inaccessibility', the area farthest from any coast, at 14,000 feet above sea level.

Unquestionably, Antarctica has the severest climate on earth. In 1957, a winter temperature of –74.4 °C below zero was recorded at the South Pole, and even summer temperatures average some 6 °C lower than in the Arctic Regions. In winter, the sea surrounding the continent freezes over for several hundred miles beyond the coast, while in summer the ice breaks up and moves northward, sometimes leaving belts of open water or loose pack ice along the land's edge. The limit of drift ice may be traced to within 400 miles of South Africa, 500 miles of Australia, 150 miles of New Zealand, and to within 100—200 miles of the east coast of South America as far north as Uruguay.

The resources of Antarctica are far from completely known. Deposits of low-grade coal provide evidence that the continent must have supported vegetation during a warmer climatic cycle. Copper, nickel and other industrial minerals have been spotted, and oil is almost certain to be found under the heavy mantle of ice. Currently exploited resources, however, are limited to the whales and seals which abound in the surrounding ocean. Whaling has been an important industry since 1908, and several of the sub-Antarctic islands (notably South Georgia) serve as bases for the world's largest whaling fleets. While the Arctic Regions boast a diversity of summer plants and animal life (as well as year-round human inhabitants), the Antarctic is much less hospitable to living things. The emperor penguin and the skua gull are the only permanent residents. The Adélie penguin breeds on land but feeds offshore, and smaller birds are regular summer visitors.

Aurora and Airglow Tower at Little America Station, Antarctica; here 'southern lights', the aurora australis, are photographed

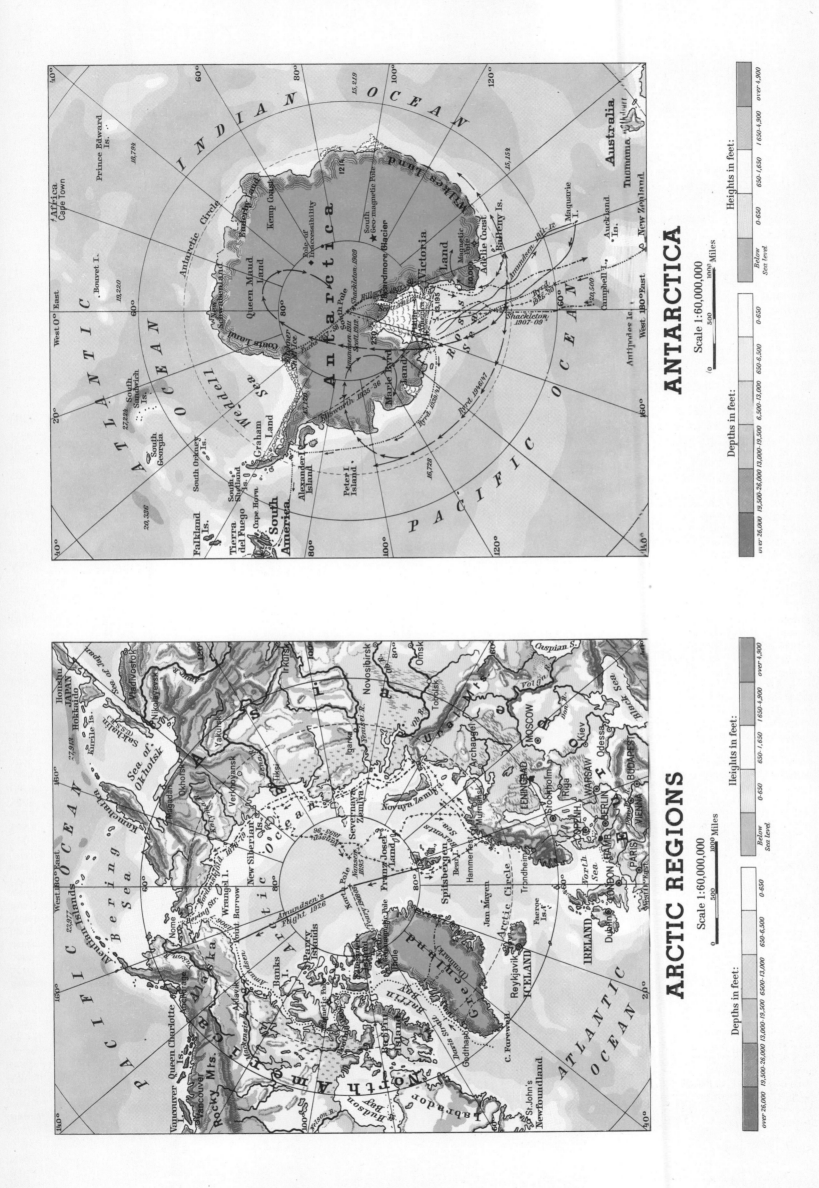

ARCTIC REGIONS

Scale 1:60,000,000

0   500   1000 Miles

Depths in feet:

over 26,000 | 19,500-26,000 | 13,000-19,500 | 6,500-13,000 | 650-6,500 | 0-650

Heights in feet:

0-650 | 650-1,650 | 1,650-4,900 | over 4,900

Below
Sea level

ANTARCTICA

Scale 1:60,000,000

0   500   1000 Miles

Depths in feet:

over 26,000 | 19,500-26,000 | 13,000-19,500 | 6,500-13,000 | 650-6,500 | 0-650

Heights in feet:

0-650 | 650-1,650 | 1,650-4,900 | over 4,900

Below
Sea level

Polar hares

Some kinds of seal, including the leopard seal, inhabit the ice pack off the Antarctic shore. A few mosses and lichens are the only plants that brave the Antarctic climate.

Except to satisfy his curiosity, man has avoided Antarctica as a place to live. Its very discovery came as a by-product of the search for new whaling grounds. Whalers of several nations have claimed the honour of discovery, but it is difficult to say just who was there first. It seems that in 1819—21 both English and American navigators sighted several islands off Graham Land, while at the same time a Russian explorer called Bellingshausen was sailing around the still unknown continent. Progress lagged until the 20th century when, in the first decade, several expeditions converged on Antarctica, aiming for the South Pole. Roald Amundsen of Norway was first to reach this goal in 1911. He was followed within a month by Robert Scott (English), who perished while returning to his base on the Ross Shelf Ice. After World War I, the aeroplane provided an easier means of exploring the white continent. Between 1929 and 1956, Admiral Richard E. Byrd (American) led a series of American expeditions that culminated in Operation Deep Freeze, the most extensive assault on Antarctica yet attempted (1955—56). Finally, in 1957—58, the efforts of 12 nations were coordinated in an ambitious research programme under the auspices of the International Geophysical Year. A network of some 60 stations on the continent and the surrounding islands was established to study the Antarctic weather, the thickness of the icecap, the nature of the underlying rock, the offshore ocean currents, and other facts that will give us a better understanding of natural phenomena. IGY findings indicate, for example, that most of the coastal 'mountains' of Antarctica are actually islands and that the continent itself is probably much smaller than the extent of the ice cap. During the IGY, scientific groups moved freely across Antarctica (a British team crossed the continent by way of the South Pole) without regard to the territorial claims advanced by a number of countries. These claims cut the continent and its surrounding waters like pieces of a pie, with the circumference along latitude 60° S. Those of Great Britain, Argentina and Chile overlap in the area of Graham Land and the Weddell Sea; the claims of Australia and New Zealand embrace sectors of Antarctica facing these two countries; the French claim is centred on the Adélie Coast; and Norway has declared her sovereignty over a sector of the continent facing Africa. In 1959, all of these countries, and others, signed the Antarctic Treaty, which reserves the areas south of latitude 60°S for peaceful purposes, and for international research, while preserving present boundaries.

● **Arctic Circle** The imaginary line of latitude drawn around the globe at 66½°N. Because of the inclination of the earth's axis, the sun does not set here on one day of the year (June 21), the summer solstice in the Northern Hemisphere. The number of such days increases inside the Arctic Circle with respect to proximity to the North Pole. Exactly

opposite conditions prevail at the Antarctic Circle, at the line of latitude 66½°S.

● **Arctic Ocean** An ice-covered sea (5½ million square miles) at the top of the world, surrounded by the Arctic shores of North America, Greenland, Europe and Asia. The North Pole is near its centre. The Arctic Ocean connects with the Atlantic Ocean on both sides of Greenland, and with the Pacific Ocean via Bering Strait. The cold East Greenland and Labrador currents carry the waters of the Arctic as well as icebergs 'calved' off the Greenland ice cap into the North Atlantic Ocean. The greatest sea depth, recorded by Sir Hubert Wilkins (1927), is 17,850 feet; in 1948 the Russians discovered a submarine ridge (Lomonosov Range) extending from Siberia to Greenland and dividing the Arctic Ocean into two major basins. Further soundings have been made as part of the International Geophysical Year observations. Most of the Arctic Ocean is covered by broken-up pack ice less than 10 feet thick; open passages exist along the continental coasts for at least several weeks each year. Several scientific teams of both the U.S. and the U.S.S.R. have established research stations on drifting ice floes in the Arctic Ocean. A four-man team under Wally Herbert successfully made a surface crossing of the Arctic Ocean using dog sledges.

● **Arctic Regions** Since there is no single land mass in the Arctic, the region has never been accurately defined. It consists of the Arctic Ocean

Antarctic meteorological station

and of the land areas bordering on it — northern Alaska and Canada, the island clusters off the North American continent, Greenland, the islands of Spitsbergen and Franz Josef Land, and the Arctic shores of Norway, of the European U.S.S.R. and of Siberia. The Arctic Circle is sometimes

given as the southern limit of the Arctic Regions. The northernmost point of land is Cape Morris Jesup at the northern tip of Greenland, less than 450 miles from the North Pole. In summer, the coldest points are on the ice pack near the Pole and on the Greenland ice cap; in winter, temperatures of −51 °C are recorded in northern Siberia. Animal life is abundant: seals, walruses, whales, fur-bearing animals and water fowl. The Eskimos are well adapted to the Arctic climate and its food resources; explorers have learned from them how to keep warm and how to survive under adverse climatic conditions.

The first explorers in the Arctic area were the Vikings. The search for the North-east and the North-west passages brought intrepid adventurers like Frobisher, Davis, Hudson, Baffin (English) and Barents (Dutch) to the north-lands in the 16th and 17th centuries. Not until the end of the 19th century, however, could the voyage through these ice-barred passages be completed. Robert E. Peary (American) reached the North Pole in 1909; Richard E. Byrd and Floyd Bennett (Americans) flew over the Pole in 1926. The use of the 'great circle' route by military and commercial aircraft greatly increased the strategic and economic importance of the Arctic Regions. The Russians in particular have shown considerable interest in developing their northern areas by establishing permanent settlements along the Arctic fringe. Numerous weather and other scientific observations were recorded in the Arctic as part of the International Geophysical Year, 1957—58.

● **Baffin Bay** An inlet of the North Atlantic Ocean between Greenland and the islands off the northern coast of Canada. It is linked by three passages (called 'sounds') with the Arctic Ocean to the north and west. The cold Labrador Current passes southward through Baffin Bay, carrying many icebergs into the North Atlantic shipping lanes. The bay is navigable during the summer months, but is closed to shipping during the long winter season. It was named after William Baffin, who explored it in 1616.

● **Baffin Land** Largest (200,000 square miles) of the islands in the Canadian Arctic, and fifth-largest in the world, separating Hudson from Baffin Bay and Davis Strait. The 1,000-mile-long island is partly mountainous and has a rugged coastline cut up by deep fjords. It is peopled by about 1,000 Eskimos who engage in hunting, trapping and whaling (in Davis Strait). There are several weather and radar-warning stations as well as two air bases on Baffin Land. It was first visited by William Frobisher (English) in the 1570s, but is named after William Baffin.

Summer tent of an Eskimo family living on Kotzebue Sound, Alaska – just north of the Arctic Circle

Kane Basin, Greenland, is only 10° south of the North Pole. Icebergs are 'calved' in Baffin Bay, and then drift southward into Atlantic shipping lanes

Balleny Islands A group of volcanic islands 150 miles off the Victoria Land coast of Antarctica, in the Pacific Ocean. The icy tongues of glaciers project into the sea. Discovered in 1839 by John Balleny, a British sealer, the islands are claimed by New Zealand. They lie astride the Antarctic Circle.

Banks Island The westernmost of Canada's northern islands in the Arctic Ocean. Less than 20 miles of ice and water separate it from the Canadian mainland. Tundra and meadows cover this lake-studded island, which is visited by Eskimos on sealing expeditions. The interior was explored by Vilhjalmur Stefansson, a Canadian of Icelandic origin, in 1914—17.

Barents Sea A part of the Arctic Ocean off the northern coast of Norway and the European portion of the U.S.S.R. It is bounded by Spitsbergen (NW) and Novaya Zemlya (E). A shallow body of water, the Barents Sea is warmed by the North Atlantic Drift, which reaches this latitude at the North Cape. Murmansk is Russia's principal ice-free port on the Barents Sea and is ice-free all the year round. The sea is named after the Dutchman Willem Barents (1550—97).

Bay of Whales An inlet of the Ross Sea off the mainland of Antarctica. Admiral Byrd established his first base, Little America, on this indentation of the ice shelf in 1929. Other explorers used this 'port of entry' to the Antarctic between 1900 and about 1950, after which time the bay disappeared with the advance of the ice front. The Norwegian explorer Amundsen began his successful dash to the South Pole in 1911 at the Bay of Whales.

Bellingshausen Sea A section of the South Pacific Ocean off Antarctica, west of the base of Graham Land. It is named after a Russian explorer who travelled around Antarctica in 1819 — 21, discovering Peter I Island and Alexander I Island (which he believed to be part of the mainland). Future Russian claims on a sector of Antarctica may be based on Bellingshausen's discoveries, made at a time when British and American explorers were also beginning to explore the new continent.

Boothia Peninsula The northernmost headland of the North American continent is Cape Murchison (72° N) at the northern extremity of the 200-mile-long Boothia Peninsula. It was discovered around 1830 by the Englishman, Sir James Ross, who established the location of the North Magnetic Pole in this area in 1831. The Arctic ice pack is especially thick and impenetrable along the Boothia

Peninsula. The area forms part of Canada's Northwest Territories, extending into the Arctic Circle.

Cape Chelyuskin Northernmost point of Asia and of the U.S.S.R., on the Arctic Ocean about 900 miles from the North Pole. It lies at the northern tip of the Taimyr Peninsula in Siberia. It is named after an 18th-century Russian navigator.

Cape Morris Jesup The northern extremity of Greenland and also the northernmost point of land in the Arctic Ocean, about 450 miles from the North Pole. It was explored by Peary (American) in 1892.

cryolite A sodium-aluminium fluoride $Na_3 AlF_6$ found in the natural state almost solely at Ivigtut in Greenland. It is used in the manufacture of aluminium, glass, soda and soap. Most of the world's cryolite is now produced synthetically, and the Greenland deposit is almost worked out.

Davis Strait An arm of the North Atlantic Ocean between Greenland and Baffin Island. It forms the shallow entrance to Baffin Bay. Whaling is carried on during the late summer months when the strait is navigable, especially along the Greenland coast. Several weather stations in the area are participating in scientific observations connected with the International Geophysical Year. The strait is named after the explorer John Davis (1550—1605).

Edith Ronne Land A section of the coast of Antarctica, on the Weddell Sea and behind the Filchner Shelf Ice. The British expedition across Antarctica, led by Dr Vivian Fuchs, left Shackleton Station on Filchner Shelf Ice off Edith Ronne Land in November, 1957, and established an advance depot at South Ice, 400 miles inland.

Ellesmere Island Northernmost island of North America, in the Arctic Ocean just west of Greenland. The coast of this 500-mile-long island is indented by many fjords. Its surface is largely covered by ice and reaches altitudes of 10,000 feet, but several ice-free 'islands' support herds of musk ox. Although the island forms part of Canada, it is the site of a number of U.S.-Canadian weather stations and defence posts. The area was first explored in the 1850s by such men as Grinnell, Peary and Sverdrup. Cape Columbia, the northernmost point of Ellesmere Island and of Canada, lies less than 500 miles from the North Pole.

Enderby Land Part of the coast of Antarctica,

on the Indian Ocean. It was discovered in 1831 by a British sealer named John Biscoe, the first man to give a name (Cape Ann) to any feature of the Antarctic continent.

Eskimo About 40,000 Eskimos inhabit the Arctic coasts of North America and Greenland. The name Eskimo, meaning 'eater of raw meat', was given them by Algonquin Indians who lived farther south and were fish- rather than meateaters. The Eskimos call themselves Inuits, which means 'people'. Eskimos are still mainly hunters and fishermen, living in small family or tribal groups. In the winter they dwell in snow huts called igloos, and in the summer in tents. Eskimos use dog sledges as their chief means of transport, and dogs are their most valuable possession. The animals killed by the Eskimos — seals, walruses, polar bears, birds and fish — supply them not only with food, but with clothing, skins for their tents and oil for light and fuel. Since the end of the 19th century, governments and missionaries have sought to improve the lot of the Eskimos by supplying them with food, clothing, tools and permanent dwellings. Scientists are not agreed as to the racial origin of the Eskimos. Their language, like those of the American Indians, is distinguished by the practice of combining word elements into a single long word, which would be equivalent to a sentence in other languages.

Filchner Ice Shelf A thick, level-surfaced mass of ice attached to the mainland of Antarctica and extending for 100 miles into the Weddell Sea. It is named after a German officer who discovered it in 1912. More than 1,000 miles of ice front were mapped in 1957, and three International Geophysical Year stations were established on the shelf — Ellsworth Station (United States), General Belgrano Station (Argentina), and Shackleton Station (United Kingdom).

Franz Josef Land (or Fridtjof Nansen Land) A group of 85 islands in the Arctic Ocean, less than 600 miles from the North Pole. They constitute the northernmost outpost of the Soviet Union and are used for weather and other scientific observations. Most of the land (8,000 square miles) is covered by ice. The archipelago was discovered in 1873 by an Austrian expedition which gave it the name of their emperor. Nansen overwintered there in 1895—96.

glacier A mass of ice that moves slowly down a valley from above the snowline toward the sea. It is formed in vast snowfields where the pressure of the overlying snow solidifies the lower layers first into granular ice, or névé, and then into clear compact ice which is plastic. Glaciers flow far below the

When a glacier reaches the coast, huge chunks break off its ice-face, and icebergs float out to sea

and Vesterbygd in Godthåbsfjord. His son, Leif Ericsson, sailed to North America in the year 1000. The settlements in Greenland died out in the 15th century and the island was re-discovered by explorers in search of the North-west Passage in 1585. In 1721, a Danish missionary, Hans Egede, landed at Godthaab and began the modern period of settlement. Whaling was important during the 17th and 18th centuries. Later, Greenland served as a base for Arctic expeditions which reached a climax early in the 20th century with Peary's dash to the North Pole in 1909. Weather stations and air bases were established in Greenland during World War II. In recent years, the United States has built a radar network, supply depots, and a major base at Thule with the permission of the Danish government. In the trans-polar air age, Greenland has acquired strategic importance in the defence of North America, and is crossed by modern airliners flying from Copenhagen to the Pacific seaboard of North America and to Tokyo. Many expeditions are set up in Greenland to study glaciation.

snowline, where they gradually decrease in size and finally melt altogether. Glaciers may originate at very high elevations (20,000 feet in tropical regions) or at sea level (in polar regions). Their speed depends on the volume and slope, and may vary from 100 feet a year to 70 feet a day — the speed attained by the Jakobshaun Glacier in Greenland. The longest valley glacier in the world is the Fedchenko Glacier (45 miles long) in the Pamir mountains of the Soviet Union. The gradual retreat of glacier tongues in many parts of the world today is taken as a sign that the climate is becoming warmer. Glaciers accomplish intensive erosion and moulding of rocks, which, when the ice melts, reveals many crushed or smoothed rocks, deep U-shaped valleys and layers of glacial till.

● **Godthaab** The administrative centre of Greenland, on the island's south-west coast. Godthaab Fjord extends 60 miles inland to the edge of the Greenland ice cap where there are traces of earlier Viking settlement. A small fishing fleet operates out of Godthaab harbour; Eskimos raise sheep and go on hunting expeditions. The region was first settled by Norsemen 1000 years ago. The modern era of colonisation began in 1721, when Hans Egede landed at Godthaab to establish a whaling base. The town's population is 7,963 (1972). Industries include a fish-canning plant.

● **Graham Land** see **Palmer Peninsula**

● **Greenland** The world's largest island (840,000 square miles — more than 3 times the size of

Texas) in the North Atlantic Ocean off the north-eastern coast of North America. Its northernmost point, Cape Morris Jesup, is but 440 miles from the North Pole. Its southern point is Cape Farewell, on the same latitude as Oslo. Almost nine-tenths of the land area (geologically related to Canada) is covered by an ice cap that reaches a thickness of 2 miles. The south-western coastal fringe is the only large ice-free area. Numerous glaciers flow from the ice cap to the deeply indented fjords; where they reach the water, they 'calve' huge icebergs that are carried southward by ocean currents into North Atlantic shipping lanes. Greenland became an integral part of Denmark — it used to be a colony — in 1953 and functions as a county. Most of its 46,331 people are of mixed Eskimo and Scandinavian origins; they live in some 180 settlements, which are usually single-storeyed houses, brightly painted and dotted at random on the rocky, soil-free coastal fringe. Most are along the south-west coast, where Godthaab, the administrative centre, is situated. Eskimos of pure stock live in the Thule area and along the Arctic fringe. Seal-hunting and whaling used to be the principal activities of the population. Today, cod and halibut fisheries are growing in importance, and sheep are raised on the limited patches of grazing land. There are a few herds of musk oxen in the far north of Peary Land and in East Greenland. Cryolite, used in the manufacture of aluminium, is mined at Ivigtut and exported, though the mines are now exhausted. Lead and zinc deposits, at Mestersvig, East Greenland, will soon be exhausted.

The island was discovered and settled by Norsemen in the 10th century (Erik the Red, A.D. 985). He founded Østerbygd near present Julianehåb,

● **iceberg** A floating mass of land ice that has been broken off or 'calved' from the end of a glacier or from an ice shelf or barrier. A berg calved from a glacier is irregular in shape, while a berg from an

Iceberg

ice shelf is flat-topped or tabular. The main sources of icebergs are the glaciers of western Greenland and the ice shelves of the Antarctic. The rectangular icebergs of the Antarctic are 10 to 40 miles long. Only about one-ninth of an iceberg is visible above water, so that a berg which rises to 150 feet above the surface must also reach 1,200 feet below the surface. Greenland icebergs, carried south by the Labrador Current toward the Grand Banks off Newfoundland, may pose a danger to North Atlantic shipping lanes. Since the *Titanic* disaster in April, 1912, when 1,517 lives were lost, a regular iceberg warning service has been organised.

● **Jan Mayen** A small Norwegian island (144 square miles) in the Arctic Ocean between Greenland and northern Norway. It is formed by an extinct volcano which rises to 8,350 feet. Visited by sealers, fox hunters and fishermen, the bleak island does not have a permanent population except for the crew of a weather station. Discovered in 1607 by Hudson, Jan Mayen has been under Norwegian sovereignty since 1929. Foggy and stormy weather prevails in this area, where the warm North Atlantic Drift and the cold Greenland Current meet.

● **kayak** An Eskimo hunting canoe made of seal-skin stretched over a light framework of bone or wood. About 15 feet long and 1½ feet wide, the kayak is completely decked and is made water-tight by a closure around the waist of the paddler. The kayak is highly manoeuvrable, and is used in sport. Its oar is called a pagaj.

Umanak, on the west coast of Greenland, a vast Danish-ruled island largely within the Arctic Circle

Narwhal, an Arctic delphinoid cetacean

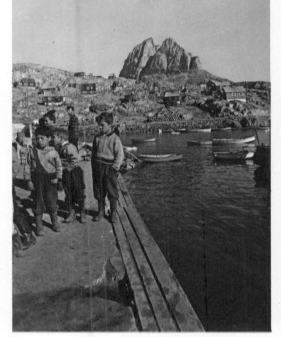

Young inhabitants of Umanak, Greenland

●**Kerguelen Islands**   A group of over 300 islands in the far southern Indian Ocean, 1,400 miles off the Antarctic mainland. They have belonged to France since 1893 and are a dependency of the French island of Madagascar. They serve as a base for whaling and seal-hunting. Settlement and sheep-raising has been attempted, but the main use of these isolated dots of land is for weather observation. The islands were discovered in 1772 by the Frenchman Yves de Kerguelen.

●**Little America**   The name given to five successive American bases established by Admiral Byrd on the Ross Shelf Ice of Antarctica. The first base dates back to 1929; the last, built in 1956 during Operation Deep Freeze, was designated as the centre for the collection of weather data during the International Geophysical Year.

●**Mac-Robertson Coast**   A section of the coast of Antarctica, on the Indian Ocean, east of Enderby Land. A permanent Australian weather base (Mawson Station) was established there in 1954. Another Australian base (Davis Station) was built in 1957 on Ingrid Christensen Coast, 400 miles to the east.

●**Marie Byrd Land**   A coastal section of Antarctica between the Ross Shelf Ice and Graham Land. It was discovered by Admiral Byrd, U.S. Navy, in 1929. Byrd Station, established at 80° S. (about 400 miles inland) as one of the American outposts in the International Geophysical Year (1957—58), appears to rest on almost 2 miles of ice extending from about 5,000 feet above sea level to 5,000 feet below. Studies of the thickness of the Antarctic ice cap will supply more accurate estimates of the earth's total water supply.

●**narwhal**   This whale, with a long, twisting tusk of ivory, is at home in the Arctic and the North Atlantic. The animal itself may reach a length of 20 feet, and the tusk, which is actually a tooth, may be as long as nine feet. Narwhal tusks washed ashore in early days are believed to have given rise to the legend of the mythical unicorn.

●**New Siberian Islands**   A group of Russian-owned islands in the Arctic Ocean off the north coast of Siberia. Heavily glaciated, the islands are sparsely settled. They are important, however, for their weather stations, which assist navigation along the north coast of the U.S.S.R. from Archangel to Bering Strait. Well-preserved mammoth fossils have been found there. The island group was discovered in the 18th century by the Russian merchant, Lyakhov.

●**Nome**   The chief trading centre (population about 2,000) of western Alaska, on Bering Strait. In 1900, Nome was the scene of a gold rush which brought thousands of prospectors to this cold and bleak tundra country. Fur-farming, trapping and

the tourist trade are more important today than gold dredging. Nome can be reached by ship between May and November, but most of the traffic is by air.

●**North Cape**   A headland of northern Norway rising 1,000 feet above the turbulent waters of the Arctic Ocean. Although another headland along the coast is actually nearer the North Pole, North Cape is usually considered Europe's northernmost point at latitude 71° 10′ N. Many tourists come to visit North Cape by ferry.

●**North Pole**   The northern extremity of the earth's axis at latitude 90° N. Unlike the South Pole, which is located on an ice-covered land-mass (Antarctica), the North Pole lies near the centre of a body of water, the Arctic Ocean, here about 12,000 feet deep. Pack ice covers most of the surface. The North Pole was first reached in 1909 by the American explorer Robert E. Peary. Aeroplanes now regularly fly over it and atomic submarines have sailed under the ice.

The North Magnetic Pole, to which all compass needles point, was located (in 1831) on Boothia Peninsula in the far north of Canada by Sir James Ross. Its exact position varies a few miles each year, but recent investigations indicate an approximate position of 76° N., 100° W. for the North Magnetic Pole.

●**North-east Passage**   The sea route along the northern coast of Europe and Asia from the North Atlantic to the Pacific Ocean at Bering Strait. The voyage of 3,500 miles was first accomplished in 1878—79 by the Swedish explorer, Nordenskjöld. In recent years, the passage has become a regular shipping route serving Siberian ports on the Arctic Ocean. The route is kept open between June and September by a fleet of Russian icebreakers assisted by aircraft reconnaissance and a chain of weather stations.

●**North-west Passage**   The sea route along the Arctic coast of North America from the Atlantic to the Pacific Ocean. From Davis Strait (between Labrador and Greenland) the passage winds through the straits that separate the northern Canadian islands, follows the shore of the Yukon and of northern Alaska, and enters the Pacific via Bering Strait. Explorers began looking for the North-west Passage in the 16th century. Martin Frobisher reached Baffin Island in 1576; Henry Hudson discovered Hudson Bay while searching for the passage in 1610; in 1616, William Baffin declared that no east-west passage existed in the Arctic; Robert McClure penetrated the passage from the west in 1851—53, reaching Viscount Melville Sound overland. The first successful voyage through the North-west Passage was made by Roald Amundsen aboard the *Gjøa* in 1903—06. Because the various straits are only rarely ice-free, navigation is hazardous, even though alternate passages through the maze of islands are theoretically available. The North-west Passage is therefore of insignificant economic importance for commercial shipping, although it has been suggested that super-tankers with large ice breakers use it as an oil shipping route after the recent success of an icebreaker in penetrating this passage.

●**Novaya Zemlya** (Russian for 'new land')   Two islands (35,000 square miles) in the Arctic Ocean, forming the northern extension of the Soviet Union's Ural Mountains. The Barents Sea lies to the west, the Kara Sea to the east. The southern

On Greenland's mountainous coast, glaciers meet the sea. They may move as much as 100 ft per day

A spectacular iceberg towers above the surface of the ocean – but eight times as much is hidden underwater

penguin, about 25 inches long, with yellow lines on each side of the crest. On land it hops with both feet placed together.

● **penguins** Flightless sea-birds of the Southern Hemisphere who are the most completely marine of all birds. Their wings, or flippers, covered with small scale-like feathers, are used only for swimming. Penguins live in large colonies both at sea and when breeding. They walk upright on land, either hopping or waddling. When congregated in rookeries on land they are generally very noisy. Although their speed in the water rivals seals and porpoises, penguins are awkward on land. The birds feed on fish and shellfish obtained by diving. Most penguins build a shallow nest of grass or weeds; others use a hollow in the ground and line it with stones. Young penguins, when hatched, are densely covered with down, which is replaced by adult feathers before the birds venture into the sea. The largest penguins are the emperor and king penguins, with yellow markings on the sides of the neck. Most of the penguin varieties are found in the Antarctic; some range as far north as Australia, the Galápagos Islands and South-West Africa.

● **Peter I Island** A small, mountainous islet (4,000 feet high) in the South Pacific Ocean, less than 400 miles from the Antarctic mainland at longitude 90° W. It was discovered by the Russian explorer Bellingshausen during his voyage round Antarctica in 1819—21. The island is claimed by Norway, for it was a Norwegian expedition which first landed there in 1929.

● **petrel, giant** A close relative of the albatross, this marine bird reaches a wing span of 20 feet. It is a scavenger, and also kills penguins and smaller petrels.

● **Point Barrow** Northernmost point of Alaska on the Arctic Ocean at 71° N. An important scientific station engaged in weather and geological research is at the nearby village of Barrow. Barrow is the main hunting and trapping centre of northern Alaska and a trading point for Eskimos. It is the centre of an oilfield which has been maintained as an underground fuel reserve. Barrow has played an important part in Arctic exploration; it was the starting point of Australian Sir Hubert Wilkins's flight across the North Pole in 1928, and earlier flights of 1926—27.

● **Queen Mary Coast** A sector of the coast of Antarctica, on the Indian Ocean, west of Wilkes Land. Huge glaciers flow off the Antarctic plateau (average elevation 5,000 feet) and thrust massive ice tongues far out to sea. The region was explored in 1911—14 by Douglas Mawson, leader of an Australasian expedition. In 1957, the Soviet Union established two bases called 'Mirny' and 'Oasis' on this coast in order to participate in International Geophysical Year research activities. 'Mirny' base was then utilised as the point of

island has a monotonous tundra landscape; the rugged northern island rises to 3,500 feet in a glaciated mountain range. About 400 fishermen and hunters inhabit the somewhat sheltered west coast. Weather stations guide Soviet ships along the North-east Passage. Discovered in the 16th century, Novaya Zemlya has been a Russian outpost in the Arctic since 1877. The islands are now the site for atomic-weapon testing in the Soviet Union.

● **Palmer Peninsula (or Graham Land)** A mountainous prong of Antarctica extending 800 miles toward the southernmost tip of South America. Because of its location and topography, it is assumed that the peaks of Palmer Peninsula (reaching an elevation of 13,750 feet at Mt Andrew Jackson) form a southern continuation of the Andes of South America. The land is covered by glaciers which merge with the ice shelf of the Weddell Sea to the east. Discovered in 1820 by an American sealer, Palmer Peninsula was long thought to be a group of islands separated by ice-covered channels; however, intensive exploration in 1948 proved it to be a peninsula of Antarctica, surrounded by numerous islands. Britain claims

ownership on the basis of early explorations, calling it Graham Land. Chile and Argentina have also advanced claims to the area. All three nations have established scientific stations on the peninsula, a total of 21 having been listed as participating in the International Geophysical Year.

● **penguin, Adélie** A medium-sized penguin, about 30 inches long, distinguished by a black throat and head. It breeds on the Antarctic mainland.

● **penguin, emperor** This largest of all penguins reaches a length of 48 inches. It has vivid colouring, a black head and shoulders, white belly and yellow patches on the sides of the neck.

● **penguin, king** This close relative of the emperor penguin is smaller and has a more northerly range in the Antarctic. It is up to 38 inches long and is distinguished by orange-yellow bands bordering its black throat.

● **penguin, rockhopper** A medium-sized crested

King penguins

departure for a Russian expedition to the South Geomagnetic Pole and the 'pole of inaccessibility' on the Antarctic continent.

● **Queen Maud Land** Part of Antarctica east of the Weddell Sea. It lies due south of Africa. Discovered by a Norwegian explorer in 1930, the region was claimed by Norway in 1939, but some nations do not recognise any national claims in Antarctica. A Norwegian research station, established on the coast at longitude 2° W., participated in the International Geophysical Year.

● **Ross Island** A mountainous island in the Ross Sea off the mainland of Antarctica. It lies at the edge of the Ross Shelf Ice. Mt Erebus, the only active volcano in Antarctica, rises to 13,200 feet at the island's centre; steam issues from its crater. Scott Station (New Zealand) and adjacent McMurdo Sound airstrip (U.S.) were established on Ross Island as part of the International Geophysical Year operations, and since then New Zealand has sponsored occupation and exploration continously. In 1958, Sir Edmund Hillary and four other New Zealanders reached the South Pole via this route.

● **Ross Sea** A large inlet of the Pacific Ocean in Antarctica, between Marie Byrd Land and Victoria Land. The Ross Shelf Ice — a level-surfaced ice formation up to 1,000 feet thick — constitutes the frozen southern portion of the Ross Sea pointing directly at the South Pole. The seaward edge of the ice shelf is a wall of ice about 400 miles long from which huge, flat-topped icebergs break off at all times. Discovered in 1841 by the British explorer, Sir James Ross, the ice shelf has served as the point of departure for several expeditions to the interior of Antarctica. Robert Scott (British) died here on his return from the South Pole in 1912. Admiral Byrd (American) wintered at an advanced weather station near Roosevelt Island in 1934; his successive bases at Little America (1929—56) were located at the edge of the Ross Shelf Ice. Several International Geophysical Year research stations have been established along the shores of the Ross Sea. The sea and adjacent land areas form part of New Zealand's claims in Antarctica.

● **seal, elephant** This largest of all seals, which can weigh 5,000 pounds, owes its name to its long nose. This projection hangs down loosely over the animal's mouth when it is quiet. When the seal roars, the snout swells up with air. The elephant seal has been killed for its oil and fat for many generations, and is almost extinct.

● **South Georgia** A mountainous island (1,600 square miles) in the South Atlantic Ocean about 800 miles east of the Falkland Islands (of which it is a dependency). It has an average population of 11 who are members of the British Antarctic Survey stationed at King Edward Point. It is noted for its outstanding wildlife, including penguins and seals. Captain Cook claimed South Georgia for Britain in 1775. However, Argentina has maintained a weather station there (since 1903) and claims ownership of the island.

● **South Orkney Islands** A group of islands in the far South Atlantic Ocean between Cape Horn (the southern tip of South America) and Graham Land. Barren and mountainous, the islands are ringed by sheer cliffs and are ice-locked during the winter. They were discovered in 1821 jointly by the British and the Americans. Britain claims ownership, as does Argentina, which has maintained a weather station there since 1904.

● **South Pole** The southern extremity of the earth's axis at latitude 90° S and longitude 0°, in Antarctica. The North and South Poles are the only two points on the earth's surface to remain stationary as the globe rotates about its axis. The South Pole is located on a featureless, snow-covered plateau, 9,200 feet above sea level and 400 miles inland from the Ross Shelf Ice. The Norwegian explorer, Roald Amundsen, was the first to reach it (by dog sledge) in December, 1911. The British explorer, Robert Scott, reached the Pole a month later but perished on the Ross Shelf Ice on the way back to his base. In 1929, Admiral Richard E. Byrd, the American explorer, became the first man to fly over the Pole. No one set foot there until 1956, when the U.S. Navy established the Amundsen—Scott Station at the South Pole to conduct research for the International Geophysical Year, 1957—58. A temperature of 74.4° below zero (Centigrade) was recorded here in 1957 by 17 men wintering at the Pole. The South Magnetic Pole, to which compass needles point, is about 1,500 miles from the geographic South Pole; its exact position varies constantly, but recent Antarctic survey results suggest that 66°S., 139°E. is approximately the position of the South Magnetic Pole. The South Geomagnetic Pole marks the southern axis of the earth's magnetic field; it lies almost 800 miles from the geographic Pole and does not migrate. In 1958, the Soviet Union established a research station called 'Vostok' at this point.

The 'pole of inaccessibility' marks the area farthest inland from any coast in Antarctica. In 1958, the Soviet Union built a research base called 'Sovietskaya' at this point, 14,000 feet above the polar plateau.

● **South Shetland Islands** A group of islands in Antarctica off the west coast of Graham Land. Barren and snow-covered, the islands once served as bases for whaling ships. Discovered and charted by the British in 1820, the South Shetlands are claimed by Britain. Chile and Argentina have also laid claim to the islands. All three nations have recently established weather and scientific stations on the South Shetlands. Admiralty Bay was the chief British station participating in the International Geophysical Year. These islands are now uninhabited.

● **Spitsbergen (or Svalbard)** A group of islands in the Arctic Ocean, 400 miles north of Norway, to which they belong. Together with Bear Island (200 miles south), the archipelago bears the Norwegian name of Svalbard (24,000 square miles; permanent population 950 Norwegians and 2,739 Russians). The raw, windy climate of Spitsbergen is somewhat tempered by the North Atlantic Drift, whose warming influence is felt up to this latitude (80° N). The west coast is open to shipping for six months. The inland plateau is covered by tundra, and water fowl (especially the eider duck) abound along the glacier-fed fjords. The island's wildlife, almost exterminated by hunters in the 19th century, is now protected. Sealing and whaling are still carried on, but coal-mining has been by far the chief occupation since the beginning of the 20th century; Norwegian and Russian mines ship a total of 843,149 tons to their respective homelands. Several countries have been prospecting for oil, but so far they have only made one deep drill. In 1968, a permanent research station was established at Ny-Alesund, to deal with data received from satellites.

Discovered by the Vikings in the 12th century and re-discovered by the Dutchman, Barents, in 1596, the islands were claimed by many nations in the 17th century as bases for whaling. Russian and Scandinavian fur-traders came in the 18th century. They were followed by explorers and scientists who used Spitsbergen as a base for Arctic expeditions. Norwegian sovereignty was proclaimed in 1925. A German garrison was expelled from the islands during World War II.

● **Thule** An Eskimo settlement on the north-west coast of Greenland facing Baffin Bay. It is a centre for walrus and polar-bear hunting. In the 19th century, Eskimos came here from northern Canada. The Danish explorer, Knud Rasmussen, established his base here in 1910, and the northern parts of Greenland became Danish in 1921. In recent years, Thule has become a major American airbase and radar station with a runway used by trans-polar commercial airlines and a radar tower higher than the Eiffel Tower. The Eskimos have moved their hunting operations to a quieter spot farther north. Thule is also the name given by ancient geographers to the northernmost lands of Europe. The term 'Ultima Thule' describes any imaginary region that is too remote to be reached.

● **tundra** The cold, treeless plains of northern North America along the Arctic Circle and on the Canadian islands in the Arctic Ocean. In summertime, mosses, lichens and some flowering plants appear on the ground, but the subsoil remains permanently frozen. In winter, the thawed surface refreezes. Extensive areas are swampy. This is the home of many migrant marsh birds and also of the hardy reindeer. Herds of reindeer have been

A large herd of walruses sun themselves and dive for shellfish in a rocky cove on the Alaskan coast

domesticated and supply the needs of the sparse Eskimo and Indian population.

● **Victoria Island** A large island (80,000 square miles) in the Arctic Ocean off the northern coast of Canada. A joint U.S.-Canadian weather station is on its south-east shore. It is visited by herds of reindeer and by Eskimo hunting expeditions.

● **Victoria Land** A section of the coast of Antarctica along the west side of the Ross Sea. It lies due south of New Zealand. Mt Sabine in the Admiralty Range rises to 11,880 feet; at its foot a joint U.S.-New Zealand base (Hallett Station) was established to participate in International Geophysical Year observations. Numerous glaciers flow off the edge of Victoria Land and break up into icebergs where they reach the sea. The region was discovered in 1841 by Sir James Ross, a British explorer.

● **Weddell Sea** An arm of the South Atlantic Ocean in Antarctica, east of Graham Land. Ice-floes 'calve' off the ice shelves lodged along the Antarctic coast and float generally westward in the direction of Cape Horn at the southern tip of South America. The sea is named after James Weddell, a British navigator, who discovered it in 1823 and reached as far south as 74° 15′. In 1915, a treacherous ice pack in the Weddell Sea crushed the ship of the British explorer Shackleton. In 1957, the United States, Britain and Argentina established International Geophysical Year stations on the Filchner Shelf Ice, which extends up to 100 miles into the Weddell Sea.

● **Wilkes Land** A section of Antarctica bordering on the Indian Ocean south of Australia. It is named after Charles Wilkes, U.S. Navy, who led an expedition to this part of the coast in 1840 and was the first to establish the existence of an Antarctic continent. Two French stations and one American station (named after Wilkes) were established in Wilkes Land for the International Geophysical Year.

● **whale, blue** This is not only the largest whale, but it is thought to be the biggest animal that ever lived. The biggest blue whale ever weighed on shipboard registered more than 300,000 pounds and measured 90 feet. At home in both the Atlantic and the Pacific, the blue whale supplies about three-fourths of the world's whale oil.

● **whale, finback** The common finback, or rorqual, is the fastest swimmer of all the whales, reaching a speed of 30 miles an hour. It grows to a length of 60 feet. Finbacks are distinguished by a series of lengthwise furrows on the throat and by a dorsal fin, to which they owe their name. Other members of the finback group are the Humpback, the blue whale and the sei whale.

● **whale, sperm** Perhaps the most famous of all whales, this powerful creature may grow to a length of 65 feet. It has a square, blunt head that can shatter the sides of a whaleboat. The head contains a huge reservoir filled with a yellowish oil substance known as spermaceti. The sperm whale is widely hunted for its oil, which has a variety of industrial uses in the making of cosmetics and lubricants. Ambergris, a waxy secretion of the whale's intestine, is a highly valued ingredient of perfumes.

● **whales** Fishlike mammals that spend their entire life in the water. Their round body is streamlined, tapering to a broad flat tail, which is not vertical,

The wide, marshy expanses of the Labrador tundra support lichens, grasses and even low-growing trees

like a fish tail, but horizontal. The whale uses its front limbs, known as flippers, for balancing and steering. There are no visible hind limbs. For all its resemblance to a fish, the whale is warm-blooded, breathes air, and brings forth its young alive. Below its skin is a thick layer of fatty tissue, known as blubber, which protects the whale against extreme temperatures. Large, elastic lungs enable it to stay under water for long periods of time. When rising to the surface, the whale expels its water-saturated air in a tall spout through its blowhole. There are two kinds of whales: the toothed whales, which include porpoises, dolphins, killer whales and sperm whales; and whalebone whales, which include the finbacks. Toothed whales usually eat only large fishes and swallow their food whole. Whalebone whales have hundreds of thin whalebone blades hanging from the roof of the mouth which act as a comb to strain their food — plankton and small jellyfish.

● **whaling** Whales are hunted for their oil, meat, ambergris and whalebone. Whale oil is used in soap, cosmetics, edible fats, glycerin and special lubricants. Whale meat is eaten, particularly in Japan. Ambergris, a waxy substance formed in the intestine of the sperm whale, is valuable in making perfumes. Whalebone was once used as a stiffener in collars and corsets. In early days, whaling was carried on in coastal waters and in the Arctic, and

a whaling ship would catch about 50 whales during a three-year cruise. Today, whaling is carried on by flotillas which include a factory ship to process the whale immediately upon its capture by the hunting ships. Whaling has now shifted largely to the Antarctic and is strictly regulated to prevent extermination of these valuable mammals. The most important whaling nations are Norway, Japan, Britain and the Soviet Union.

● **Wrangel's Island** A tundra-covered island (1,750 square miles) in the Arctic Ocean off the north-east coast of the U.S.S.R. It is separated from the Siberian mainland by the 80-mile-wide Long Strait. The island commands the northern entrance to Bering Strait. It was sought in 1823 by the Russian navigator after whom it is named, and was long believed to be the extremity of an Arctic continent. An American whaler, Long, really discovered it in 1867. A Russian weather station guides ships into the North-east Passage.

● **Wrangell Island** (U.S.), also named after the Russian navigator, Wrangel, lies off the southern peninsula of Alaska. In 1834, it was occupied by Russian fur-traders who built a fort, now the town of Wrangell (population 1,300). Lumbering and fishing are the main activities.

In Alaska, at the foot of Mendenhall Glacier, melting ice forms a beautiful glacial lake

Index

249